INSIDE
VISUAL C++™

INSIDE
VISUAL C++™

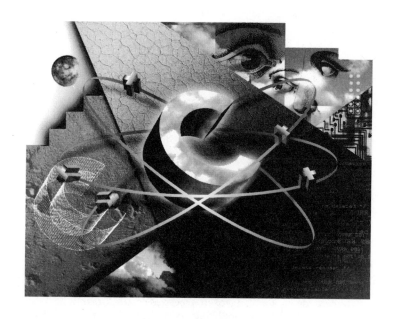

Microsoft
PRESS

DAVID J. KRUGLINSKI

PUBLISHED BY
Microsoft Press
A Division of Microsoft Corporation
One Microsoft Way
Redmond, Washington 98052-6399

Library of Congress Cataloging-in-Publication Data
Kruglinski, David J.
    Inside Visual C++ : the new way to program for Windows / David J.
Kruglinski.
        p.   cm.
    Includes index.
    ISBN 1-55615-511-5
    1. C++ (Computer program language)   2. Microsoft Visual C++.
3. Windows (Computer programs)   I. Title.
QA76.73.C153K78   1993
005.26'2--dc20   93-20773
                                                            CIP

Printed and bound in the United States of America.

    456789 MLML 876543

Distributed to the book trade in Canada by Macmillan of Canada, a division of Canada Publishing Corporation.

Distributed to the book trade outside the United States and Canada by Penguin Books Ltd.

Penguin Books Ltd., Harmondsworth, Middlesex, England
Penguin Books Australia Ltd., Ringwood, Victoria, Australia
Penguin Books N.Z. Ltd., 182-190 Wairau Road, Auckland 10, New Zealand

British Cataloging-in-Publication Data available.

Acquisitions Editor: Dean Holmes
Project Editor: Jack Litewka
Technical Editor: Jim Fuchs
Manuscript Editor: Pat Coleman

Contents Summary

INSIDE VISUAL C++

PART 4: ADVANCED TOPICS

PART 5: APPENDIXES

Table of Contents

PART 2: THE CLASS LIBRARY VIEW CLASS

PART 3: THE DOCUMENT–VIEW ARCHITECTURE

PART 4: ADVANCED TOPICS

PART 5: APPENDIXES

Acknowledgments

When I first compiled the list of people who helped me with this book, I was surprised at its size. How could I have guessed, when I started this project, that so much of my time and so much of other people's time would be absorbed to produce the 600-plus pages you have in your hands?

At the top of the list must go Jim Fuchs, the Microsoft Press technical editor who logged extra-long days for many weeks, checking every example and expunging hidden Bart Simpson icons. Next is the project editor, Jack Litewka, who had an amazing ability to focus on both the entire project and all the details. Special thanks to acquisitions editor Dean Holmes, who lent support during the crucial but prolonged developmental stage. Other contributors were manuscript editor Pat Coleman and developmental editor Erin O'Connor, indexer Lynn Armstrong, and a legion of behind-the-scenes players, including Judith Bloch, Wallis Bolz, Carolyn Magruder Davids, Kim Eggleston, Patrick Forgette, Jennifer Harris, Peggy Herman, Carol Luke, Jeannie McGivern, Steve Murray, Nikki Naiser, Shawn Peck, Ruth Pettis, Barb Runyan, Lisa Sandburg, Alice Copp Smith, Lisa Theobald, Jean Trenary, and Cheryl Whiteside.

How could I have sifted through the intricacies of the Microsoft Foundation Class Library and App Studio without help from the Microsoft AFX group? These patient souls had to put up with my endless questions, most of which were stupid ones. At the top of the list here is Mark Walsen, my official liaison. Many times, however, I needed information directly from the source, and for this I thank Scott Randell, the chief architect of the class library. Other helpful developers were Dean McCrory and John Seghers, followed by Bob Anderson, Brad Christian, Lon Fisher, Rich Guion, Brian Meyers, Chris Shaffer, Steve Sinofsky, and Clif Swiggett.

Special thanks go to Kathleen Thompson, who helped with network access, the AFX printers, and space to set up my computer. Thanks go also to Jeff Beehler, a Visual C++ project manager, and his group, who put up with my intrusive "input" on the design of certain Visual Workbench project option features.

My old colleagues at Languages User Education—particularly Robert Keller, Rita Margolies, Phil Nelson, and Chuck Sphar—were most helpful in providing information and support. Also helpful were outside reviewers Ed Hiskes and Karen Cunningham, together with Mike Larosa from Microsoft University, Walter Wittel from Microsoft Product Support Services, and Dale Rogerson from the Microsoft Software Developer Network.

Not to be left out are my training-class students at Wal-Mart and Intel, who endured early copies of the manuscript and were so willing to point out errors.

Finally, my fellow members of the Northwest Paragliding Club provided me with ample opportunity to get my mind off the project.

David Kruglinski
July 1993

Introduction

It isn't often that a truly new software product category comes along. The "application framework" is such a category, and Visual C++ contains what is arguably the most powerful Windows-based application framework to date. The product has substantial credibility because it comes from Microsoft, the author of Windows itself. Even though the Microsoft Visual C++ application framework is quite different from anything else you might have used, it builds on elements you might be familiar with already, including the C++ language, the Windows Software Development Kit (SDK) for the C language, and the original Microsoft Foundation Class Library version 1.0 that was delivered with Microsoft C/C++ version 7.0.

Microsoft Foundation Class Library version 2.0—which I'll often refer to as "the class library," for short—is an important part of Visual C++ and the core of the application framework. The class library consists of a library of C++ classes and global functions with source code included. Other Visual C++ components—including AppWizard, ClassWizard, App Studio, Visual Workbench, the compiler, and the linker—are the tools you'll use to construct your applications.

This book explains the class library classes, and it shows you how to use the classes and the tools to build Windows-based applications. If you already own Visual C++, INSIDE VISUAL C++ provides useful techniques, points of view, examples, and theory that are not included in the product documentation. If you're contemplating buying Visual C++, this book gives you an overall picture of the product's capabilities.

Who Can Use This Book

When I started working with version 1.0 of the class library, after a not-so-successful attempt to learn Windows SDK programming, I realized that C++ and Windows were a natural fit and that it was actually easier to learn Windows-based programming the C++ way. Why not try to teach it that way? Why not assume that the reader has a programming background and then bypass all the "ugly stuff" that beginning SDK programmers have to learn?

My editors agreed, but they also said, "Don't forget the experienced Windows programmers, the ones who have been buying all the Petzold books." "OK," I said, and set my sights on an approach that would serve those with and without prior Windows experience.

Next there was the question of C++ knowledge. Surely, with so many C++ books out there, everyone would know the language by now. "Everyone has bought at least one C++ book" would be a truer statement, however. Perhaps you began to read a book, did a few of the examples, and then lost interest and dropped back to C. Version 2.0 of the class library is a good excuse to become really proficient at C++, and this book will help.

As a writer, it was easier to assume that my readers didn't know Windows than it was to assume that they didn't know C++. Given the prototype for an ellipse function, for example, it's pretty easy for any programmer to write code that draws an ellipse on the screen, with either an ordinary C function or a C++ member function. But if the programmer doesn't understand C++ classes and objects, he or she is in trouble. For this reason, I've included a review of C++ in Appendix A. Because it wasn't possible to cram all of C++ into 32 pages, the editors made me label it a "personal view" of the language. If you're new to C++, read through Appendix A, but keep those other C++ books handy. You might finally be motivated to read them!

Notice that I've been talking about programmers. Yes, you do have to be one, or at least a student of programming. Compilers, tools, and operating systems have become so complex in recent years that it's impossible to go from zero to expert Windows programmer within one book. A background in C is the absolute minimum because even the "personal view" in Appendix A assumes that you can read C code.

Oh, I almost forgot. You should know how to run Windows-based applications. If you don't know what a program for Windows is supposed to do, how can you design and write one? If you're looking for an application to start with, try Microsoft Word for Windows. It's a good example of a modern Windows-based program. Besides that, it's a darn good word processor, and you can write help files with it. I used it to write this book.

How to Use This Book

When you're starting off with Visual C++, you can use this book as a tutorial by going through it sequentially. Later you can use it as a reference by looking up topics in the table of contents or the index. Because of the tight interrelationships among many application framework elements, it wasn't possible to cleanly isolate each concept in its own chapter, so the book really isn't an encyclopedia. When you use this book, you'll definitely want the *Class Library Reference* by your side.

The Organization of this Book

As the table of contents shows, there are four main parts to this book:

Part 1: Windows, Visual C++, and Application Framework Fundamentals

In this part, I try to strike a balance between abstract theory and practical application. After a quick review of modern Windows and of Visual C++ components, you'll be introduced, in a gentle way, to the application framework and the document–view architecture. You'll see a simple "Hello world!" program, built with the class library classes, that requires only 30 lines of code.

Part 2: The Class Library View Class

The class library documentation presents all the application framework elements in quick succession, with the assumption that you already know Windows SDK programming. Here you're confined to one major application framework component—the "view," which is really a window. It's here that you'll learn what SDK programmers know already, but in the context of C++ and the class library classes. There's something for Windows gurus too, because the class library view environment supports extras such as dialog data exchange, graphical buttons, and Visual Basic controls. You'll use the Visual C++ tools a lot, and that in itself eliminates much of the coding drudgery in the life of SDK programmers.

Part 3: The Document–View Architecture

Now the real core of application framework programming is introduced—the document–view architecture. You'll learn what a document is (think of it as something much more general than a word processing document), and you'll see how to connect it to the view that you learned about in Part 2. You'll be amazed, once you have written a document class, at how the class library simplifies file I/O and printing.

Along the way, you'll learn about command message processing, toolbars and status bars, splitter frames, and context-sensitive help. You'll also be introduced to the Windows Multiple Document Interface (MDI) that's featured so prominently in class library applications.

Pay special attention to the section "Speeding Up the Build Process" on page 39 because the speed-up hints will help you save time as you work through the book's examples.

Part 4: Advanced Topics

This part is a catchall for many useful Windows programming techniques directly supported by the class library. You'll start with several bare-bones Windows-based applications that bypass the document–view architecture, and then you'll see a useful class for device-independent bitmaps. You'll see an example that uses the Microsoft Open Database Connectivity (ODBC) programming interface. The final two chapters cover Object Linking and Embedding (OLE) and class library–style dynamic link libraries (DLLs).

Going Further with Windows: The Purpose of the "For SDK Programmers" Sidebars

This book can't offer the kind of detail—the tricks and hidden features—found in the newer, specialized books about Windows. Most of these books are written from the point of view of a C-language SDK programmer. In order to use these books, you'll have to understand the underlying SDK application programming interface (API) and its relationship to the class library.

This book's "For SDK Programmers" sidebars, scattered throughout the text, help you make the connection to the Windows SDK. These specially formatted boxes help experienced Windows C programmers relate new class library concepts to SDK principles they already know. If you're unfamiliar with SDK programming, you should skip these notes the first time through, but you should read them on your second pass through the book because they'll help you understand the mainstream literature about Windows after you get up to speed with the class library.

If You've Worked with Other Application Frameworks

You're probably already aware of other application framework products. (The best known is *MacApp*, for the Apple Macintosh.) The class library is similar to and different from these other products; therefore, please don't make any assumptions about terminology or the function of any similarly named class.

Hardware Requirements

If you haven't discovered this already, your Windows development machine needs more horsepower than a standard target machine. Because your time is valuable, go for a fast 80486 computer with 8 megabytes (MB) or more of random access memory (RAM). The extra RAM will be used for a disk cache and a RAM disk that will work together to speed compiles and links. Chapter 3 shows you how to configure your extra RAM.

As far as disk space is concerned, plan on 30 MB for the Visual C++ programs alone. Each project can require as much as 4 MB (including precompiled headers, map files, and a browser database), and you'll have lots of projects. A 100-MB hard disk drive is the minimum; a 200-MB hard disk drive is more realistic.

Also consider a large-screen monitor with a super VGA board. With the large monitor, you can simultaneously display Visual Workbench, the Help window, and a Windows-based program that's being debugged.

Using the Companion Disk

The companion disk that's bound into the inside back cover of this book contains the source code files and make files for all the sample programs. The executable program files are not included, so you'll have to use Visual C++ to build the samples that you're interested in. To install the companion disk's files, insert the disk in drive A (or B), change to that drive, and type *INSTALL* at the command prompt. Follow the on-screen instructions.

With a conventional C-language Windows SDK program, the source code files tell the whole story. With the class library application framework, things are not so simple. Much of the C++ code is generated by AppWizard, and the resources originate in App Studio. The examples in the early chapters include step-by-step instructions for using the tools to generate and customize the source code files. You'd be well advised to walk through those instructions for the first few examples. There's very little code to type. For the middle chapters, use the code from the companion disk, but read through the steps anyway in order to appreciate the role of App Studio and the Wizards. For the final chapters, not all the source code is listed. You'll need to examine the companion disk's files for those later examples.

Technical Notes and Sample Programs

You can access a Visual C++ help file that contains 35 useful technical notes. These notes cover advanced class library features not discussed in the documentation. This book contains references to technical notes that are identified by numbers. To read a technical note in the help file, you have two options: You can run WINHELP and then select \MSVC\HELP\MFCNOTES.HLP, or you can double-click the MFC Tech Notes icon in the Visual C++ Program Manager group.

You can find 23 useful class library sample programs in the \MSVC\MFC\SAMPLES subdirectory. These programs, documented in the \MSVC\HELP\MFCSAMP help file (accessible from the MFC Samples Help icon in the Visual C++ Program Manager group), illustrate more advanced class library features. This book contains occasional references to these sample programs.

WINDOWS, VISUAL C++, AND APPLICATION FRAMEWORK FUNDAMENTALS

1

Microsoft Windows and Visual C++

Enough has already been written about the acceptance of Microsoft Windows and the benefits of the graphical user interface (GUI). This chapter summarizes the Windows programming model and shows you how the Visual C++ components work together to help you write applications for Windows. Along the way, you'll learn some new things about Windows. We'll be looking toward the future rather than dwelling on the past.

The Windows Programming Model

No matter which development tools you use, programming for Windows is different from old-style batch or transaction-oriented programming. To get started, you need to know some Windows fundamentals. As a frame of reference, we'll use the well-known MS-DOS programming model. Even if you don't currently program for plain MS-DOS, you're probably familiar with it.

Message Processing

When you write an MS-DOS application in C, the only absolute requirement is a function called *main*. The operating system calls *main* when the user runs the program, and from that point on, you can use any programming structure you want. If your program needs to get user keystrokes or otherwise use operating system services, it calls an appropriate function such as *getchar* or perhaps uses a character-based windowing library.

When the Windows operating system launches a program, it calls the program's *WinMain* function. Somewhere your application must have *WinMain*, which performs some specific tasks. The most important task is creating the application's "main window," which must have its own code to process messages that Windows sends it. An essential difference between a program written for Windows and a program written for MS-DOS is that an MS-DOS program calls the operating system to get user input, but a Windows program processes user input via messages from the operating system.

> **Note:** *Many development environments for Windows, including Microsoft Visual C++ with the Microsoft Foundation Class Library version 2.0, simplify programming by hiding the* WinMain *function and structuring the message-handling process. When you use the class library, you need not write a* WinMain *function, but understanding the link between the operating system and your programs is helpful.*

Many messages in Windows are strictly defined and apply to all applications. For example, a WM_CREATE message is sent as a window is being created, a WM_LBUTTONDOWN message is sent when the user presses the left mouse button, a WM_CHAR message is sent when the user types a character, and a WM_CLOSE message is sent when the user closes the window. Other messages ("command" messages) are sent to an application window in response to user menu choices. These messages depend on the application's menu layout. The programmer can define still other messages, known as "user messages."

Don't worry about how your code processes these messages yet. That's the job of the application framework. Be aware, though, that the Windows message processing requirement imposes a lot of structure on your program. Don't try to force your Windows programs to look like your old MS-DOS programs. Study the examples in this book, and then be prepared to start fresh.

The Windows Graphics Device Interface (GDI)

Many MS-DOS programs wrote directly to the video memory and the printer port. The disadvantage of this technique was the need to supply driver software for every display card and every printer model. Windows introduced a layer of abstraction called the Graphics Device Interface (GDI). Windows provides the display and printer drivers, so your program doesn't need to know the type of display card and printer attached to the system. Instead of addressing the hardware, your program calls GDI functions that reference a data structure called a device context. Windows maps the device context structure to a physical device and issues the appropriate input/output instructions. The GDI is almost as fast as direct video access, and it allows different applications written for Windows to share the display.

Resource-Based Programming

To do data-driven programming in MS-DOS, you have to code the data as initialization constants, or you have to provide separate data files for your program to read. When you program for Windows, you store data in a resource file using a number of formats. Windows merges a resource file into a linked program through a process called "binding." Resource files can include bitmaps, icons, menu definitions, dialog box layouts, and strings. They can even include custom resource formats that you define.

You use a text editor to edit a program, but you generally use "what you see is what you get" (wysiwyg) tools to edit resources. If you're laying out a dialog box, for example, you select elements from an array of icons called a control palette, and you position and size the buttons, list boxes, and so forth with the mouse. With the Visual C++ App Studio resource editor program, you can effectively edit most resource formats. (Note: In Microsoft Visual Basic and in Microsoft Access, the control palette is called a toolbox.)

Memory Management

In the old days, the MS-DOS conventional memory limit of 640 kilobytes (KB) restricted the size of your programs. You could use various overlay management techniques and extended/expanded memory managers to allow larger programs, but all had shortcomings. An 80386SX-based (or better) computer usually has 4 megabytes (MB) or more of memory, and its CPU has built-in memory management hardware. Windows, together with the Visual C++ compiler, offers additional memory management features. The net result is that memory usually isn't a problem anymore.

Chapter 9 describes current memory management techniques for Windows. If you've heard horror stories about locking memory handles, thunks, and burgermasters, don't worry. That's all in the past. Today you simply allocate the memory you need, and Windows takes care of the details. Parts of your program, including resources, can be automatically swapped to and from disk and then shuffled in physical memory, but chances are your computer has so much memory that your entire program will fit into physical memory.

Dynamic Link Libraries (DLLs)

In the MS-DOS environment, all a program's object modules were statically linked during the build process. Windows allows dynamic linking, which means that specially constructed libraries can be loaded and linked at runtime. Multiple applications can share dynamic link libraries (DLLs), which saves memory and disk space. Dynamic linking increases program modularity because you can compile and test DLLs separately.

Designers originally created DLLs for use with the C language, and C++ has added some complications. After considerable effort, the Microsoft Foundation Class Library developers succeeded in combining all the application framework classes into a single DLL. Thus, you can statically or dynamically link the application framework classes into your application. In addition, you can create your own DLLs that build on the Microsoft Foundation Class Library. Chapter 26 includes information on creating DLLs.

New Windows Features—OLE and TrueType

The Windows operating system has been evolving over the years. Two recent additions are Object Linking and Embedding (OLE) and TrueType fonts. With OLE, you can enhance your programs by combining objects created in different applications. You can, for example, include charts, sounds, drawings, and so forth in a single document. When the user activates an OLE object, the Windows program that created the object executes, allowing the user to manipulate the object. OLE programming with the Windows SDK tools was extremely difficult, but as you'll see in Chapter 25, the Microsoft Foundation Class Library greatly simplifies the job.

TrueType fonts radically improve the appearance of Windows text display on both the screen and the printer. Because you can scale these fonts to any size and because they work with practically any printer, you the programmer are relieved of the burden of matching a screen font to a printer font.

Windows NT

When Microsoft shipped Visual C++, Windows NT was in the late stages of beta testing. This new operating system has an advanced file system with security features, multithreading, true preemptive multitasking, enhanced network access, and portability to selected RISC computers. Windows NT can run both existing Windows-based 16-bit applications and new high-performance Windows-based 32-bit applications.

How do you develop Windows 32-bit applications? Early beta testers had to use the Win32 SDK, which includes a new C-language application programming interface (API). Because of the need for 32-bit parameters, most Win32 function prototypes are different from their 16-bit equivalents. In addition, many functions are new, particularly in the area of disk I/O. Windows 32-bit applications access files through the Win32 API rather than through the MS-DOS API.

The Win32 SDK contains an extension, called Win32s, that allows the creation of 32-bit applications that can run both under Windows version 3.1 and under Windows NT. These applications cannot yet take advantage of some advanced NT features and thus are restricted to a subset of the Win32 API.

Existing C-language 16-bit applications for Windows will need extensive conversion to become true 32-bit applications. A Microsoft Foundation Class Library application, on the other hand, will require only recompilation because the Microsoft Foundation Class Library was designed with the Win32 API in mind. When Windows NT is released, a Win32 version of Visual C++ will be released along with it. You can use the 32-bit version of Visual C++ to produce applications targeted for Windows NT and Win32s. See Appendix D for information on Visual C++ for Windows NT.

The Visual C++ Components

Visual C++ is two complete Windows application development systems in one product. If you so choose, you can develop C-language Windows programs using the API first introduced in the Windows SDK. Windows SDK programming techniques are well known and have been documented in many books, including Charles Petzold's *Programming Windows 3.1* (Microsoft Press, 1992). You can use many tools newly introduced in Visual C++ to make Windows SDK–style programming easier.

This book is not about Windows SDK–style programming, however. It's about C++ programming within the Microsoft Foundation Class Library application framework that's part of Visual C++. You'll be using the C++ classes that are documented in the *Class Library Reference,* and you'll be using application framework–specific Visual C++ tools such as AppWizard and ClassWizard.

> **Note:** *Use of the Microsoft Foundation Class Library programming interface doesn't cut you off from the Windows SDK functions. In fact, you'll almost always need some direct Windows SDK calls in your class library programs.*

A quick run-through of the Visual C++ components will help you get your bearings before you zero in on the application framework. Figure 1-1 on the following page shows an overview of the Visual C++ application build process.

Visual Workbench and the Build Process

The Visual Workbench is a Windows-hosted interactive development environment that's a direct descendant of Microsoft QuickC for Windows. If you're accustomed to running a compiler from the command line, please try Visual Workbench. Trust me. It's really good. I avoided the old character-mode Programmer's Workbench, but I use Visual Workbench now for all my projects. All examples in this book are built with Visual Workbench.

Two Visual C++ Versions: Standard Edition and Professional Edition

Visual C++ is available in two versions: the Standard Edition and the Professional Edition. The Standard Edition provides all the components necessary to produce both Windows SDK applications and application framework–based applications for Windows. The Professional Edition includes additional printed documentation, an optimizing version of the compiler, some additional tools, and the capability of producing MS-DOS applications and p-code Windows applications. Yes, you read that right. If you want to write MS-DOS applications, you must buy the more expensive Professional Edition.

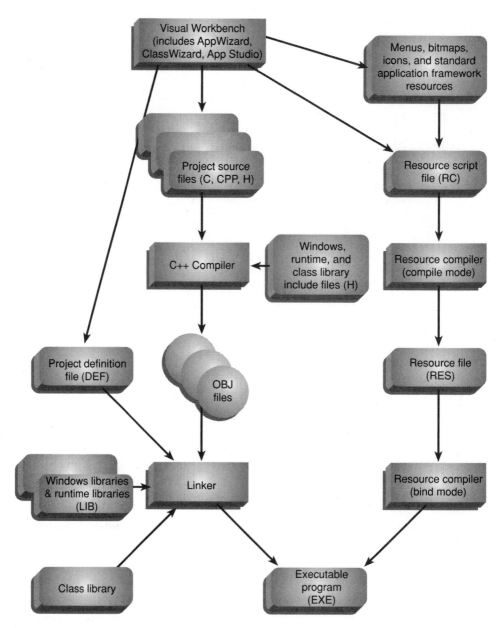

Figure 1-1.
The Visual C++ application build process.

If you've used QuickC for Windows, Programmer's Workbench, or the Borland IDE, you already understand how Visual Workbench operates, but if you're new to integrated development environments, you'll need to know what a project is. A project is a collection of interrelated source files that are compiled, linked, and bound to make up a working Windows program. Project source files are generally stored in a separate subdirectory. A project depends on many files outside the project subdirectory too, such as include files and library files.

Experienced programmers are familiar with make files. A make file expresses all the interrelationships among source files. (A source code file needs specific include files, an executable file requires certain object modules and libraries, and so forth.) A make program reads the make file and then invokes the compiler, assembler, linker, and resource compiler to produce the final output, which is generally an executable file. The make program uses built-in "inference rules" that tell it, for example, to invoke the compiler to generate an OBJ file from a specified CPP file.

In a command-line environment, you need to code the make file by hand. Visual Workbench automatically generates the make file, known as a "project file." In most cases, you want your project to include all the source files in the project subdirectory, but you can exclude files in the project subdirectory and use files from other subdirectories. After you create a project, you can edit source code files in individual child windows. Visual Workbench "remembers" which source code files you were working with and maintains a list of most recently used projects. As part of the project, you can save compiler and linker switch settings as specified through a series of dialog boxes. To generate the executable program, you simply choose the Build command from the Visual Workbench Project menu.

Visual Workbench contains a useful text editor that follows Windows interface standards and uses color to highlight C++ syntax. Unfortunately, you can't fully customize this editor or install your own editor. If you do decide to use your own editor, you'll forfeit the smooth integration that the integrated development environment provides. For example, Visual Workbench highlights lines containing errors in your source code files when you build a project and allows you to set debugging breakpoints.

The App Studio Resource Editor

The original Windows SDK included separate tools for editing dialog boxes, bitmaps, and fonts. With Visual C++, you use App Studio to edit most resources. Chapter 3 shows some App Studio windows. (See pages 35 and 36.) App Studio includes both a wysiwyg menu editor and a powerful dialog box editor that is far superior to the old Windows SDK DIALOG program. You can use App Studio as your resource editor for Windows SDK–style programming, but when you use App Studio for class library programming, you can interactively insert Microsoft Visual Basic controls in your dialog boxes for later connection to your C++ code.

App Studio's native file format is the ASCII Windows resource (RC) file format, and each project usually has one RC file with *#include* statements to bring in resources from other subdirectories. Editing the RC file outside App Studio is not recommended. App Studio can also process EXE and DLL files, so you can use the clipboard to "steal" resources, such as bitmaps and icons, from other Windows applications.

App Studio compares favorably to the best applications written for Windows, so it's significant that App Studio was written using the Visual C++ tools and the class library. App Studio can even edit its own resources! Try it. (You'll need to copy App Studio to another file and load the copy.)

The C/C++ Compiler

The Visual C++ compiler can process both C source code and C++ source code. It determines the language by looking at the source code filename extension. A C extension indicates C source code, and CPP or CXX indicates C++ source code. The compiler is compliant with ANSI version 2.1 and has additional Microsoft extensions. Template and exception syntax are not supported in Visual C++ version 1.0. The Visual Workbench's Use Microsoft Foundation Classes option (in the Project Options dialog box) determines whether the compiler uses the Microsoft Foundation Class Library include files.

The Linker

To generate an EXE file, the Visual C++ linker processes the OBJ files that the compiler produces. If you specify the Visual Workbench option Use Microsoft Foundation Classes, the linker uses the Microsoft Foundation Class Library file for the appropriate memory model.

The Resource Compiler

The Visual C++ resource compiler operates in either compile mode or bind mode. In compile mode, an ASCII resource (RC) file from App Studio is compiled into a binary RES file. In bind mode, the RES file is merged with an executable (EXE) file. If you update a RES file, you can rebind it to its EXE file without relinking.

The Debugger

If your program works the first time, you don't need the debugger. The rest of us might need one from time to time. The Visual C++ debugger is the first-ever Windows-hosted C++ debugging environment. The debugger works closely with Visual Workbench to ensure that breakpoints are saved on disk. Toolbar buttons toggle breakpoints and control single-step execution. Figure 1-2 illustrates the Visual C++ debugger in action. Note how the Locals window can expand an object

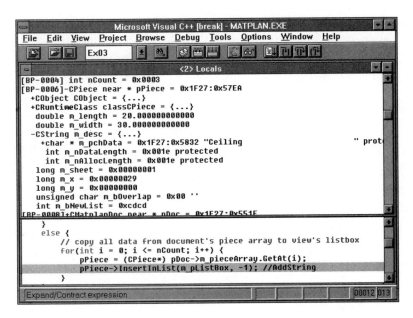

Figure 1-2.
The Visual C++ debugger window.

pointer to show all data members of the derived class and base classes. To debug a program, you must build the program with the compiler and linker options set to generate debugging information.

With the Professional Edition of Visual C++, you get the character-mode CodeView debugger in addition to the Windows-hosted debugger. CodeView for Windows debugs p-code, and it has several other useful features.

AppWizard

AppWizard is a code generator that creates a working skeleton of a Windows application with features, class names, and source code filenames that you specify through dialog boxes. You'll use AppWizard extensively as you work through the examples in this book. Don't confuse AppWizard with conventional code generators such as Caseworks CASE:W and Blue Sky WindowsMAKER. AppWizard code is minimalist code; the functionality is inside the application framework base classes. Its purpose is to get you started quickly with a new application.

ClassWizard

ClassWizard is a program (implemented as a DLL) that operates both inside the Visual Workbench and inside App Studio. ClassWizard takes the drudgery out of maintaining Visual C++ class code. Need a new class or a new function to handle a

Windows message? ClassWizard writes the prototypes, function bodies, and code to connect the messages to the application framework. ClassWizard can update class code that you write, so you avoid maintenance problems common to ordinary code generators.

The Source Browser

If you write an application from scratch, you probably have a good mental picture of your source code files, classes, and member functions. If you take over someone else's application, you'll need some assistance. The Visual C++ Source Browser (the "browser," for short) lets you examine (and edit) an application from the class or function viewpoint instead of from the file viewpoint. It's a little like the "inspector" tools available with other object-oriented libraries such as Smalltalk. The browser has the following viewing modes:

- Definitions and References—You select any function, variable, type, macro, or class and then see where it's defined and used in your project.

- Call Graph / Caller Graph—For a selected function, you get a graphic representation of the functions it calls or the functions that call it.

- Derived Class Graph / Base Class Graph—These are graphic class hierarchy diagrams. For a selected class, you see the derived classes or the base classes. You can control the hierarchy expansion with the mouse.

A typical browser window is shown on page 31 in Chapter 3.

> **Note:** If you rearrange the lines in any source code file, you must rebuild the browser database.

Online Help

The entire contents of the Windows SDK reference manuals and the class library reference manuals are included in the Visual C++ online Help. Help is also available for App Studio, AppWizard, and ClassWizard. Don't underestimate the value of Help. Many programmers at Microsoft use it exclusively. If you want help on a function, simply click on (or move the cursor to) the function in the Visual Workbench editor and press F1; you'll see a Help window, as shown in Figure 1-3.

Visual C++ Help resolves conflicts between Windows SDK function names and identical Microsoft Foundation Class Library names. If you select a function name that corresponds to member functions in several classes, you can choose the class from a list box. If you ask for help on a class, you'll see a member function and data member list in functional order.

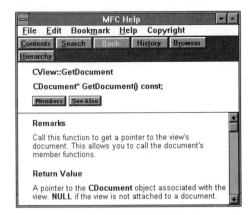

Figure 1-3.
The Visual C++ Help window.

Windows Diagnostic Tools

The Professional Edition of Visual C++ contains the same set of diagnostic tools that were included with the Windows SDK when it was a separate product: SPY for observing Windows messages, HEAPWALK for examining memory, HC31 for compiling Help files, STRESS for artificially limiting available memory, and a profiler program that alerts you to bottlenecks in code.

Both the Visual C++ Standard Edition and the Professional Edition include the DBWIN utility, which displays diagnostic output, and the NMAKE program, which processes hand-coded make files. NMAKE is used to build nonstandard versions of the Microsoft Foundation Class Library.

The Microsoft Foundation Class Library Version 2.0

The Microsoft Foundation Class Library version 2.0 (aka the class library) is really the subject of this book. It defines the application framework that you'll be getting to know intimately. Chapter 2 gets you started with actual code and some important concepts.

2

The Microsoft Foundation Class Library Application Framework

This chapter introduces the Microsoft Foundation Class Library version 2.0 (aka the class library) application framework by explaining its benefits. Early on, you'll see a stripped-down but fully operational class library program for Windows that should help you understand what application framework programming is all about. Theory is kept to a minimum here, but the message mapping and document–view sections contain important information that will help you with the examples that follow in later chapters.

Why Use the Application Framework?

If you're going to develop applications for Windows, you've got to choose a development environment. Assuming you've already rejected the interactive options such as Microsoft Visual Basic, you must choose among the following options:

- The tried-and-true Windows SDK (Software Development Kit)

- The new Microsoft Foundation Class Library application framework

- Other Windows-based application frameworks such as Borland's Object Windows Library (OWL)

If you're starting from scratch, any option involves a big learning curve. If you're already a Windows SDK programmer, you'll still have a learning curve with the class library. So what benefits can justify this effort?

The Microsoft Press editors told me not to make this section sound like a marketing brochure, but I couldn't help it. I'm really enthusiastic about the product. It's the application development environment I've been waiting on for 10 years.

Here are the class library benefits as I see them.

Class library version 2.0 is the C++ Microsoft Windows API. Your acceptance of this premise depends on your acceptance of the C++ language. If C++ takes over from C—and many people expect it to—then it's natural for Windows to have a C++ programming interface. It's highly unlikely that the Windows–C++ interface standard will come from any company other than Microsoft, the producer of Windows itself.

I believe C++ will take over because it's the only universally accepted object-oriented language, and object-oriented programming is necessary for large software projects that require reusable, modular components. As users demand more sophisticated software, we can't keep writing bigger C programs!

Application framework applications use a standard structure. Any programmer starting on a large project develops some kind of structure for the code. The problem is that each programmer's structure is different, and for a new team member to learn the structure and conform to it is difficult. The class library application framework includes its own application structure—one that's been proven in many software environments and in many projects. If you write a program for Windows that uses the class library, you can safely retire to a Caribbean island, knowing that your minions can easily maintain and enhance your code back home.

Don't think that the class library's structure makes your programs inflexible. With the class library, your program can do anything that a Windows SDK program can do, and that means you can take maximum advantage of Windows.

Application framework applications are small and fast. Function for function, class library programs are almost as small as Windows SDK programs. A class library "Hello, world!" program is only 80 KB with the class library functions statically linked. The same program is 23 KB with the class library dynamic link library (DLL). As for speed, in some circumstances a class library application is actually faster than its Windows SDK equivalent.

The class library application framework is feature-rich. The class library version 1.0 classes, supplied with Microsoft C/C++ version 7.0, were essentially a C++ programming interface for Windows. Some significant features were added, however:

☐ General-purpose classes (non-Windows-specific), including

  ☐ Collection classes for lists, arrays, and maps

  ☐ A useful and efficient string class

  ☐ Time, time span, and date classes

  ☐ File access classes for operating system independence

  ☐ Support for systematic object storage and retrieval to and from disk

- [ ] A "common root object" class hierarchy

- [ ] Streamlined Multiple Document Interface (MDI) application support

- [ ] Effective support for OLE (Object Linking and Embedding)

The class library version 2.0 classes pick up where the version 1.0 classes left off by supporting many user interface features that are found in current Windows-based applications. Application framework architecture aside, here's a summary of the important new features:

- [ ] Full support for File Open, Save, and Save As menu items with the most recently used file list

- [ ] Print preview and printer support

- [ ] Scrolling windows and splitter windows

- [ ] Toolbars and status bars

- [ ] Access to Microsoft Visual Basic controls

- [ ] Context-sensitive help

- [ ] Automatic processing of data entered in a dialog box

- [ ] An easy-to-program interface to OLE

- [ ] DLL support

You'll see examples that exploit all these features, but to appreciate what the class library offers, consider print preview and printer support. The Windows SDK offers no support for print preview. Charles Petzold devotes 60 pages to printer support in *Programming Windows 3.1;* other books about Windows ignore the subject completely. The class library contains several thousand lines of "invisible" code that makes print preview and printing "automatic." The Print Preview and Printer support features alone might justify the use of the class library.

The Visual C++ tools reduce coding drudgery. App Studio, AppWizard, and ClassWizard significantly reduce the time needed to write code that is specific to your application. For example, App Studio creates a header file that contains assigned values for *#define* constants. AppWizard generates skeleton code for your entire application, and ClassWizard generates prototypes and function bodies for message handlers.

The Learning Curve

All the benefits listed above sound great, don't they? You're probably thinking that "you don't get something for nothing." Yes, that's true. To use the application framework effectively you have to learn it thoroughly, and that takes time. If you have to learn C++, Windows, and the class library all at the same time, it will be at least six months before you're really productive. Interestingly, that's close to the learning time for the Windows SDK alone.

How can that be if the class library offers so much more? For one thing, you can avoid many programming details that Windows SDK programmers are forced to learn. From my own experience, I can say that an object-oriented application framework makes programming for Windows easier to learn—that is, once you understand object-oriented programming.

The class library won't bring real Windows programming down to the masses. Windows programmers have usually commanded higher salaries than other programmers, and that situation will continue. The class library learning curve, together with the application framework's power, should ensure that class library programmers will be in strong demand.

What's an Application Framework?

One definition of an application framework is "an integrated collection of object-oriented software components that offers all that's needed for a generic application." That isn't a very useful definition, is it? If you really want to know what an application framework is, you'll have to read the rest of this book. The application framework example that you'll familiarize yourself with later in this chapter is a good starting point.

The Application Framework vs. the Class Library

One reason that C++ is a popular language is that it can be "extended" with class libraries. Some class libraries are delivered with C++ compilers, others are sold by third-party software firms, and still others are developed in-house. A class library is a set of related C++ classes that can be used in an application. A matrix class library, for example, might perform common mathematical operations involving matrices, and a communications class library might support the transfer of data over a serial link. Sometimes you construct objects of the supplied classes; sometimes you derive your own classes—it all depends on the design of the particular class library.

An application framework is a superset of a class library. An ordinary class library is an isolated set of classes designed to be incorporated into any program, but an application framework defines the structure of the program itself. This sounds like a fine distinction, and it is. Most Windows development class libraries, including Microsoft Foundation Class Library version 1.0, Borland OWL, and Microsoft Foundation Class Library version 2.0, are considered application frameworks. Microsoft Foundation Class Library version 2.0, however, provides significantly more features than the others.

An Application Framework Example

Enough generalizations. It's time to look at some code—not pseudocode but real code that actually compiles and runs with the class library. Guess what? It's the good old "Hello, world!" application with a few additions. (If you've used version 1.0 of the class library, this code will be familiar except for the frame window base class.) It's about the minimum amount of code for a working class library application for Windows. Contrast it with the equivalent Windows SDK application! You don't have to understand every line now. Don't bother to type it in and test it. Wait for the next chapter, where you'll start using the "real" application framework.

Note: *By convention, class library class names begin with the letter* C.

Following is the source code for the header and implementation files for our MYAPP application. The two classes, *CMyApp* and *CMyFrame*, are each derived from the class library base classes. First the MYAPP.H header file for the MYAPP application:

```
// application class
class CMyApp : public CWinApp
{
public:
    virtual BOOL InitInstance();
};

// frame window class
class CMyFrame : public CFrameWnd
{
public:
    CMyFrame();
protected:
    // 'afx_msg' indicates that the next two functions are part of the
    //  class library message dispatch system
    afx_msg void OnLButtonDown(UINT nFlags, CPoint point);
    afx_msg void OnPaint();
    DECLARE_MESSAGE_MAP()
};
```

And now the MYAPP.CPP implementation file for the MYAPP application:

```
#include <afxwin.h> // class library header file declares base classes
#include "myapp.h"

CMyApp NEAR theApp; // The one and only CMyApp object

BOOL CMyApp::InitInstance()
{
    m_pMainWnd = new CMyFrame();
    m_pMainWnd->ShowWindow(m_nCmdShow);
```

(continued)

19

```
        m_pMainWnd->UpdateWindow();
        return TRUE;
    }

    BEGIN_MESSAGE_MAP(CMyFrame, CFrameWnd)
        ON_WM_LBUTTONDOWN()
        ON_WM_PAINT()
    END_MESSAGE_MAP()

    CMyFrame::CMyFrame()
    {
        Create("AfxFrameOrView", "MYAPP Application");
    }

    void CMyFrame::OnLButtonDown(UINT nFlags, CPoint point)
    {
        TRACE("Entering CMyFrame::OnLButtonDown - %lx, %d, %d\n",
              (long) nFlags, point.x, point.y);
    }

    void CMyFrame::OnPaint()
    {
        CPaintDC dc(this);
        dc.TextOut(0, 0, "Hello, world!");
    }
```

Here are some of the program elements:

The *WinMain* function. Remember that Windows requires your application to have a *WinMain* function. You don't see *WinMain* here because it's hidden inside the application framework.

The *CMyApp* class. An object of class *CMyApp* represents an application. The program defines a single global *CMyApp* object, *theApp*. The *CWinApp* base class determines most of *theApp*'s behavior.

Application startup. When the user starts the application, Windows calls the application framework's built-in *WinMain* function, and *WinMain* looks for your globally constructed application object of a class derived from *CWinApp*. Don't forget that, in C++, global objects are constructed <u>before</u> the main program is executed.

The *CMyApp InitInstance* member function. When *WinMain* finds the application object, it calls the *InitInstance* member function, which makes the calls needed to construct and display the application's main frame window. You must override *InitInstance* in your derived application class because the *CWinApp* base class doesn't have the slightest idea about what kind of main frame window you want.

The *CWinApp Run* member function. The *Run* function is hidden in the base class, but it dispatches the application's messages, thus keeping the application running. *WinMain* calls *Run* after it calls *InitInstance*.

The *CMyFrame* class. An object of class *CMyFrame* represents the application's main frame window. When the constructor calls the *Create* member function of the base class *CFrameWnd*, Windows creates the actual window structure and the application framework links it to the C++ object. The *ShowWindow* and *UpdateWindow* functions, also member functions of the base class, must be called in order to display the window.

The *CMyFrame OnLButtonDown* function. This is a sneak preview of the class library's message-handling capability. We've elected to "map" the left mouse button down event to a *CMyFrame* member function. You'll learn the details of the class library's message mapping in Chapter 4. For the time being, accept that this function gets called when the user presses the left mouse button. The function invokes the class library *TRACE* macro to display a message in the debugging window.

The *CMyFrame OnPaint* function. The application framework calls this important mapped member function of class *CMyFrame* every time it's necessary to repaint the window: at the start of the program, when the user resizes the window, and when all or part of the window is newly exposed. The *CPaintDC* statement relates to the Graphics Device Interface (GDI) and is explained in later chapters. The *TextOut* function displays "Hello, world!"

Application shutdown. The user shuts down the application by closing the frame window. This action initiates a sequence of events, which ends with the destruction of the *CMyFrame* object, the exit from *Run*, the exit from *WinMain*, and the destruction of the *CMyApp* object.

Look at the example again. This time try to get the big picture. Most of the application's functionality is in the class library base classes *CWinApp* and *CFrameWnd*. In writing MYAPP, we've followed a few simple structure rules, and we've written key functions in our derived classes. C++ lets us "borrow" a lot of code without copying it. Think of it as a partnership between us and the application framework. The application framework provided the structure, and we provided the code that made the application unique.

Now you're beginning to see why the application framework is more than a class library. Not only does the application framework define the application structure but it also encompasses more than C++ base classes. You've already seen the hidden *WinMain* function at work. Other elements support message processing, diagnostics, DLLs, and so forth.

Class Library Message Mapping

Refer to the *OnLButtonDown* member function in the previous example. You might think that *OnLButtonDown* would be an ideal candidate for a virtual function. A window base class would define virtual functions for mouse event messages and other standard messages, and derived window classes could override the functions as necessary. Some Windows class libraries do work this way.

The class library application framework doesn't use virtual functions for messages used in Windows. Instead, it uses macros to "map" specified messages to derived class member functions. Why the rejection of virtual functions? Consider this situation: You have a hierarchy of five window classes in Windows, and the base class defines virtual functions for 140 messages. C++ requires a virtual function dispatch structure called a "vtable" that has a 4-byte entry for each class–virtual function combination, regardless of whether the functions are actually overridden in the base classes. Thus, for each distinct type of window or control, the application needs a 2.8-KB table to support virtual message handlers.

What about message handlers for menu command messages and messages from button clicks? You couldn't define these as virtual functions in a window base class because each application might have a different set of menu commands and buttons. The class library message map system avoids large vtables, and it accommodates application-specific command messages. It also allows selected nonwindow classes, such as document classes and the application class, to handle command messages. Unlike the "dynamic dispatch table" system that Borland supplied as part of OWL, message maps require no extensions to the C++ language.

A class library message handler requires a function prototype, a function body, and an entry in the message map. ClassWizard helps you add message handlers to your classes. You select a Windows message ID from a list box, and the Wizard generates the code with the correct function parameters and return values.

Documents and Views

The previous example used an application object and a frame window object. Most of your class library applications will be more complex. Typically, they'll contain application and frame classes plus two other classes that represent the "document" and the "view." This "document–view architecture" is not new. It originated in the early 1980s in the academic world and was then adopted by Apple Computer in 1985 for the MacApp application framework product.

In simple terms, the document–view architecture separates data from the user's view of the data. One obvious benefit is multiple views of the same data. Consider a document that consists of a month's worth of stock quotes stored on disk. Suppose there is a table view and a chart view of the data. The user updates values through the table view window, and the chart view window changes because both windows display the same information (but in different views).

In the class library, documents and views are represented by C++ classes and objects. Figure 2-1 shows three objects of class *CStockDoc* corresponding to three companies: AT&T, IBM, and GM. All three documents have a table view attached, and one document also has a chart view. As you can see, there are four view objects—three of class *CStockListView* and one of class *CStockChartView*.

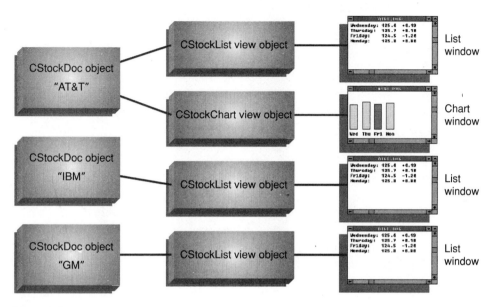

Figure 2-1.
The document–view relationship.

The document base-class code interacts with the File Open and File Save menu items; the derived document class does the actual reading and writing of the document object's data. (The application framework does most of the work of displaying the File Open and File Save dialog boxes and opening, closing, reading, and writing files.) The view base class represents a window that is contained inside a frame window; the derived view class interacts with its associated document class and does the application's display and printer I/O. The derived view class and its base classes handle messages in Windows. The class library orchestrates all interactions among documents, views, and frame windows, and the application object, mostly through virtual functions.

Don't think that a document object must be associated with a disk file that is read entirely into memory. If a "document" were really a database, for example, you could override selected document class member functions, and the File Open menu item would bring up a list of databases instead of a list of files.

THE CLASS LIBRARY VIEW CLASS

3

Getting Started with AppWizard— "Hello, world!"

Chapter 2 sketched the Microsoft Foundation Class Library version 2.0 document–view architecture. This hands-on chapter shows you how to build a functioning class library application, but it insulates you from the complexities of the class hierarchy and object interrelationships. You'll work with only one document–view program element, the "view class" that is closely associated with a window. For the time being, you can ignore elements such as the application class, the frame window, and the document. Of course, your application won't be able to save its data on disk, and it won't support multiple views, but Part 3 of this book provides plenty of opportunity to exploit those features.

Because resources are so important in Windows-based applications, you'll use the App Studio resource editor to visually explore the resources of your new program. You'll also get some hints for setting up your Windows environment for maximum build speed and optimal debugging output.

Requirements: To compile and run the examples presented in this and the following chapters, you must have successfully installed Microsoft Windows (version 3.1 or later) and all the Visual C++ components. Be sure that the Visual Workbench binary, include, and library directories are set correctly. (You can change the directories by choosing Directories from the Options menu.) If you have any problems with the following steps, please refer to your Visual C++ documentation and README files for troubleshooting instructions.

What's a View?

From the user's standpoint, a "view" is an ordinary window that he or she can size, move, and close in the same way as any other Windows-based application window. From the programmer's perspective, a view is a C++ object of a class derived from the class library *CView* class. Like any C++ object, the view object's behavior is determined by the member functions (and data members) of the class—both the application-specific functions in the derived class and the standard functions inherited from the base classes.

With Visual C++, you can produce interesting applications for Windows by simply adding code to the derived view class that the AppWizard code generator produces. When your program runs, the class library application framework constructs an object of the derived view class, and it displays a window that is tightly linked to the C++ view object. As is customary in C++ programming, the class library view class is divided into two source modules—the header file (H) and the implementation file (CPP).

Single Document Interface (SDI) vs. Multiple Document Interface (MDI)

The class library supports two distinct application types, SDI and MDI. An SDI application has, from the user's point of view, only one window. If the application depends on disk-file "documents," only one document can be loaded at a time. Windows Notepad is an example of an SDI application. An MDI application has multiple "child windows" that correspond to individual documents. The Visual Workbench is a good example of an MDI application.

When you run AppWizard, MDI is the default application type. For the early examples in this book, we'll be generating SDI applications because fewer classes and features are involved. Be sure you uncheck the AppWizard Multiple Document Interface option for these examples. Starting with Chapter 17, we'll be generating MDI applications. The class library application framework architecture ensures that most SDI examples can be upgraded easily to MDI applications.

The "Do-Nothing" Application

The AppWizard program generates the code for a functioning class library application. This working application simply brings up an empty window with a menu attached. Later you'll add code that draws inside the window. Follow these steps to build the application:

1. Run AppWizard to generate SDI application source code. Choose App-
Wizard from the Visual Workbench Project menu. When AppWizard starts,
you'll see the MFC AppWizard dialog box, as shown here:

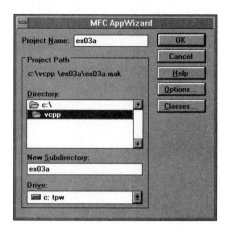

   Type the program name as shown, but do not press Enter or click the OK
button. You can enter a different name if you want, but AppWizard uses the
program name when it creates files and classes. If you enter a different name,
your files and classes will have a name different from that of the files and
classes shown in this AppWizard dialog box example.
   Next click the Options button, and specify the options in the Options dialog
box, as shown here:

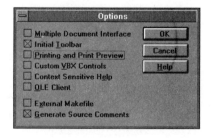

   Click the OK buttons in the Options and MFC AppWizard dialog boxes.
   AppWizard generates files based on the parameters you type in the MFC
AppWizard dialog box. Immediately before AppWizard generates your code, it
shows the New Application Information dialog box on the next page:

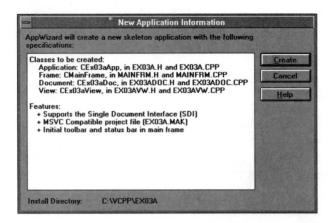

Click the Create button, and AppWizard begins to create your application's subdirectory, files, and classes. When AppWizard is finished, look in the application's subdirectory. The following files are of interest (for now):

File	Description
EX03A.DEF	Windows module definition file
EX03A.MAK	Project file that allows Visual Workbench to build your application
EX03A.RC	Resource script file
EX03AVW.CPP	View class implementation file that contains *Cex03View* class member functions
EX03AVW.H	View class header file that contains the *CEx03aView* class declaration
README.TXT	Text file that explains the purpose of all generated files
RESOURCE.H	*#define* constant definitions

Open the EX03AVW.CPP and EX03AVW.H files and look at the source code. Together these files define the *CEx03aView* class, which is central to the application. An object of class *CEx03aView* corresponds to the application's view window, where all the "action" takes place.

2. **Compile and link the generated code.** AppWizard, in addition to generating code, creates a custom project file for your application. This file, EX03A.MAK, specifies all the file dependencies together with the compile and link option flags. Because the new project becomes Visual Workbench's current project, you can now build the application by choosing Build EX03A.EXE from the Project menu.

Note: *The Compile, Build, and Execute items on the Project menu display the current project's name.*

If the build is successful, an executable program called EX03A.EXE is created in the application's subdirectory.

The EX03A.DEF file provides useful information to the linker. Most important is the name of the application, contained in the DEF file's first noncomment line:

```
NAME        EX03A
```

Tip: *If you have two or more programs with the same DEF file NAME parameter, Windows won't let you run them simultaneously. (You'll probably see two copies of the application you run first.) Be careful.*

3. **Test the resulting application.** Choose Execute EX03A.EXE from the Project menu. Experiment with the program. It really doesn't do much, does it? (What do you expect for no coding, anyway?) Actually, as you might be able to tell from the size of the EXE file, the program has a lot of features—you simply haven't activated them yet. Close the program window when you've finished experimenting.

4. **Browse the application.** You can use the Visual C++ browser only after you have successfully compiled an application. Choose Open EX03A.BSC from the Browse menu, and the browser window appears. Set the following parameters:

Type: Base Class Graph

Subset: Classes (default)

Symbol: CEx03aView

Note: *The Symbol text box is case-sensitive, so be sure to enter the information exactly as shown.*

Now click the Display Result button and expand the class hierarchy by clicking on the icons. The browser window with *CEx03aView* and base classes should eventually look similar to this:

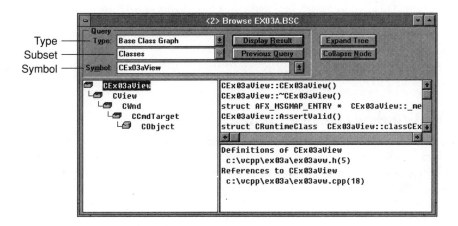

The *CEx03aView* View Class

AppWizard generated the *CEx03aView* view class, and this class is specific to the EX03A application. (AppWizard generates classes using the project name you entered in the MFC AppWizard dialog box.) *CEx03aView* is at the bottom of a long inheritance chain of class library classes, as illustrated previously in the browser window. The class picks up member functions and data members all along the chain. You can learn about these classes in the *Class Library Reference* document, but you must be sure to look at the descriptions for every base class because the descriptions of inherited member functions aren't repeated for derived classes.

The most important *CEx03aView* base classes are *CWnd* and *CView*. *CWnd* provides *CEx03aView*'s "windowness," and *CView* provides the hooks to the rest of the application framework, particularly to the document and to the frame window that you'll see in Part 3 of this book.

Drawing Inside the View Window — The Windows Graphics Device Interface

Now you're ready to write code to draw inside the view window. You'll be making a few changes directly to the EX03A source code.

The *OnDraw* Member Function

Specifically, you'll be fleshing out the *OnDraw* member function in EX03AVW.CPP. *OnDraw* is a virtual member function of the *CView* class that the application framework calls every time the view window needs to be repainted. A window needs repainting if the user resizes the window or reveals a previously hidden part of the window, or if the application changes the window's data. If the user resizes the window or reveals a hidden area, the application framework calls *OnDraw*, but if a function in your program changes the data, it must inform Windows of the change by calling the view's inherited *Invalidate* (or *InvalidateRect*) member function. This call to *Invalidate* triggers a later call to *OnDraw*.

Even though you can draw inside a window at any time, it's strongly recommended that you let window changes accumulate and then process them all together in the *OnDraw* function. (It's more efficient to handle the changes in a group than on an individual basis.)

The Windows Device Context

Remember from Chapter 1 that Windows doesn't allow direct access to the display hardware but communicates through an abstraction called a "device context" that is associated with the window. In the class library, the device context is a C++ object of class *CDC* passed (by pointer) as a parameter to *OnDraw*. After you have the device context pointer, you can call the many *CDC* member functions that do the work of drawing.

Adding Draw Code to the EX03A Program

Now let's write the code to draw some text and a circle inside the view window. Be sure that the project EX03A.MAK is open in Visual Workbench. You can use the browser to locate the code for the function (double-click on *CEx03aView::OnDraw*), or you can open the source code file EX03AVW.CPP and locate the function yourself.

1. **Edit the *OnDraw* function in EX03AVW.CPP.** Find the AppWizard-generated *OnDraw* function in EX03AVW.CPP:

```
void CEx03aView::OnDraw(CDC* pDC)
{
    CEx03aDoc* pDoc = GetDocument();

    // TODO: add draw code here
}
```

The following screened code (which you type in) replaces the previous code:

```
void CEx03aView::OnDraw(CDC* pDC)
{
    pDC->TextOut(0, 0, "Hello, world!");   // prints in default font &
                                           //   size, top left corner
    pDC->SelectStockObject(GRAY_BRUSH);    // selects a brush for the
                                           //   circle interior
    pDC->Ellipse(CRect(0, 20, 100, 120));  // draws a gray circle 100
                                           //   units in diameter
}
```

You can safely remove the call to *GetDocument* because we're not dealing with documents yet. The functions *TextOut*, *SelectStockObject*, and *Ellipse* are all member functions of the application framework's device context class *CDC*. The *Ellipse* function draws a circle if the bounding rectangle's length is equal to its width.

The class library provides a handy utility class called *CRect* for Windows rectangles. A temporary *CRect* object serves as the bounding rectangle argument for the ellipse drawing function. You'll see more use of the *CRect* class later in this book.

2. **Recompile and test EX03A.** Choose Build from the Project menu, and, if there are no compile errors, test the application again. Now you have a program that visibly does something!

For Windows SDK Programmers

Rest assured that the standard Windows *WinMain* and *WndProc* functions are hidden away inside the application framework. You'll see those functions later in this book, when the class library frame and application classes are examined. In the meantime, you're probably wondering what happened to the WM_PAINT message, aren't you? You would expect to do your window drawing in response to this Windows message, and you would expect to get your device context handle from a *PAINTSTRUCT* structure that the Windows *BeginPaint* function returns.

It so happens that the application framework has done all the dirty work for you and served up a device context (in object pointer form) in the virtual function *OnDraw*. As explained in Chapter 2, true virtual functions in window classes are a class library rarity. Class library message map functions that the application framework dispatches handle most Windows messages. Microsoft Foundation Class Library version 1.0 programmers always defined an *OnPaint* message map function for their derived window classes. In version 2.0, however, *OnPaint* is defined in the *CView* class, and it calls *OnDraw*. Why? Because *OnDraw* needs to support the printer as well. Both *OnPaint* and *OnPrint* call *OnDraw*, thus enabling the same drawing code to accommodate both the printer and the display.

A Preview of App Studio—Resources Introduced

Now that you have a complete application program, it's a good time for a quick look at the App Studio resource editor. Although the application's resource script, EX03A.RC, is an ASCII file, modifying it with a text editor is not a good idea. That's App Studio's job.

The Contents of EX03A.RC

The resource file determines much of the EX03A application's "look and feel." The file EX03A.RC contains (or points to) the following Windows resources:

Resource	Description
Icon	The AFX logo you see in the application's About dialog box
Toolbar bitmap	The row of buttons just below the menu
Menu	The application's main menu and associated pop-up menus
Accelerators	Definitions for keys that simulate menu and toolbar selections
Dialog	Layout and contents of dialog boxes—the About dialog box for EX03A
String table	Strings that are not part of the C++ source code

In addition to the resources listed above, EX03A.RC contains the statement

```
#include "afxres.h"
```

which brings in some special class library resources common to all applications. These special resources include strings, graphical buttons, and elements needed for printing and OLE.

EX03A.RC also contains the statement '

```
#include "resource.h"
```

This statement brings in the application's *#define* constants, which are *IDR_-MAINFRAME* (identifying the menu, icon, string list, and accelerator table) and *IDD_ABOUTBOX* (identifying the About dialog box). This same RESOURCE.H file is included indirectly by the application's source code files. If you use App Studio to add more constants (symbols), the definitions ultimately show up in RESOURCE.H. If you use a text editor to add your own constants to RESOURCE.H, App Studio does not disturb them.

> **Note:** *The file EX03A.RC2, located in the project's RES subdirectory, contains resources that App Studio doesn't edit. The version resource falls into this category.*

Running App Studio

Although you can run App Studio from the Windows File Manager or Program Manager, running it from within Visual Workbench is easiest.

1. Start the App Studio program. In Visual Workbench, choose App Studio from the Tools menu. You will see the following App Studio window:

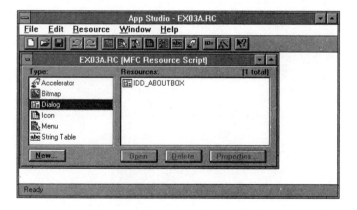

For Windows SDK Programmers

App Studio replaces the Windows SDK Dialog Editor and SDKPaint. In addition to handling dialog boxes, icons, cursors, and bitmaps, App Studio edits string tables and accelerator tables, and it has a wysiwyg menu editor. You no longer need to edit resource script files—indeed, you shouldn't because you might trip up App Studio with a syntax error.

With the SDK Dialog Editor, you must manually assign an integer and corresponding *#define* constant name to each control. App Studio assigns *#define* constants to windows, buttons, menu items, and so forth. (You can change the constants if you want.) App Studio generates and maintains a single include file, named RESOURCE.H, that contains all the definitions with sequential integer values.

Tip: *You can also activate App Studio by choosing the project's RC file in the Open File dialog box. For this to work, you must first choose Editor from Visual Workbench's Options menu and check the Open .RC Files Using App Studio check box in the Editor dialog box.*

2. **Examine the application's resources.** Now take some time to explore the individual resources. Notice that resource selection is a two-step process: First you click on the resource type on the left, and then you double-click on a specific resource on the right. When you select a resource, another window opens with tools appropriate for the selected resource. (The control palette might also open.)

3. **Modify the About dialog box.** Make some changes to the About dialog box, shown here in App Studio.

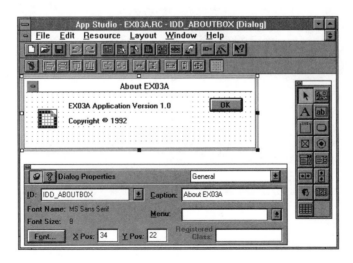

You can change the size of the window by dragging the right and bottom borders, move the OK button, change the text, and so forth. Simply click on an element to select it. When you're done, save the file and exit App Studio.

4. **Rebuild the application with the modified resource file.** In Visual Workbench, choose Build from the Project menu. Notice that no actual C++ recompilation or linking is necessary. Visual Workbench saves the edited resource file on disk, and then the Resource Compiler (RC.EXE) processes EX03A.RC to produce a compiled version, EX03A.RES. RC.EXE runs again to bind the compiled resources to the EX03A.EXE file, replacing the resources that were there before.

5. **Test the new version of the application.** Run the EX03A program again, and then choose About from the application's Help menu to confirm that your dialog box was changed as expected.

The Windows Debug Kernel and DBWIN

As a developer, you should run the Windows Debug kernel at all times. (The sidebar on the following page gives instructions for installing the kernel.) The Debug kernel (available only with the Professional Edition of Visual C++) provides important error messages that you would miss with the regular version of Windows.

To activate the Debug kernel after it is installed, run the SWITCH batch file (located in the \MSVC\BIN subdirectory) with the D parameter. This batch file copies files from the \MSVC\DEBUG subdirectory to your WINDOWS subdirectory. The message "Enhanced Mode Debug Windows 3.1" at the bottom of Windows' background screen indicates that the Debug kernel is properly installed. (This message should appear the next time you start Windows.)

If your computer is equipped with dual monitors, the error messages appear on the auxiliary monitor. If you don't have dual monitors, you should definitely run the Windows DBWIN program, located in the \MSVC\BIN subdirectory, to see the error messages in a window. DBWIN is useful not only for displaying messages from the Windows Debug Kernel, but also for displaying output from the application framework diagnostic macros *TRACE*, *ASSERT*, and *VERIFY*. The *TRACE* macro is explained in Chapter 15, on page 244. Consider inserting the line

```
load=dbwin
```

in your WIN.INI file to load DBWIN when Windows starts. You can also add a DBWIN program item in your STARTUP group.

Installing the Windows Debug Kernel

You must specifically tell the Visual C++ Setup program to install the Windows Debug kernel files. To do so, run the Visual C++ Setup program. A dialog box similar to this one appears:

(If you've previously installed Visual C++, you can uncheck all check boxes except the Tools check box.) Click the Tools button. A dialog box similar to this one appears:

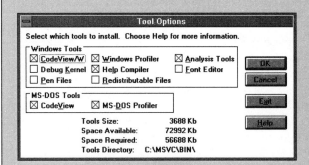

Check the Debug Kernel check box. (If you've previously installed Visual C++, you can uncheck the other check boxes.) Click the OK button in the second dialog box, and then click the Continue button in the first dialog box.

Do You Need to Use the Debugger?

Using the debugger with programs for Windows is more complicated than using the debugger with MS-DOS programs. You can't use the debugger to trace through an entire program because Windows-based programs don't execute sequentially. You must put breakpoints at the start of the message-handling functions that you need to debug.

> *Tip:* *To avoid stepping through the code in the class library, use the Step Into button, shown here,*

> *to step to the next statement in the function that you are debugging.*

You might find that you can do most of your debugging without the Visual C++ debugger. If you find that you're using the debugger infrequently, you can save considerable compile, link, and load time by eliminating debugging information from your program. The last "speedup" hint (#6 on page 43) shows you how.

Enabling the Diagnostic Macros

The application framework *TRACE* macros are particularly useful for monitoring program status. These macros, together with the *ASSERT* and *VERIFY* macros, require the Debug build option (but do not require debugging information). In addition, the *TRACE* macros require that tracing be enabled. You can enable tracing by inserting the statement

```
afxtrace = TRUE;
```

in your program. Alternatively, you can insert the statement

```
TraceEnabled = 1
```

in the [Diagnostics] section of the AFX.INI file in your WINDOWS subdirectory. You can control this trace option, together with other trace options, with the TRACER utility that is included with Visual C++. If you're using the Visual Workbench debugger, TRACE output appears in the Debug Output window. Otherwise, you need an auxiliary monitor or the DBWIN program.

Speeding Up the Build Process

As you saw with the application you created earlier in this chapter, Visual C++ can be slow when building an application. This section's information will help you speed up the process of compiling and linking applications. The speedup hints are presented here instead of in an appendix because you can begin saving time right away as you build the sample applications.

The procedures described here are optional, but their combined effect is to cut build time by more than half. Most procedures depend on your computer having sufficient installed memory.

1. **Be sure that SMARTDRV is installed.** SMARTDRV is the disk caching utility that is normally installed during MS-DOS or Windows setup. The line SMARTDRV in your AUTOEXEC.BAT file starts the utility when your computer boots. The default cache size is usually sufficient. (The default cache size is based on the amount of memory in your computer.)

   SMARTDRV generally improves the performance of all Windows-based programs. SMARTDRV comes with both MS-DOS and Windows; you should use whichever version is newer. Be sure to use SMARTDRV's double-buffering option if your hard disk requires double buffering. (See your MS-DOS or Windows manual for more information.)

2. **Set up a RAM drive.** If your computer has 12 MB or more of memory available, set up a RAM drive. The following line in your CONFIG.SYS file sets up a 4-MB RAM drive:

```
devicehigh=c:\windows\ramdrive.sys 4096 512 1024 /e
```

   Note: The RAMDRIVE.SYS device driver comes with both MS-DOS and Windows. You should use whichever version is newer. Also note that this example assumes you're using MS-DOS or a third-party memory manager to create upper memory blocks. If you're not using memory-management software to create upper memory blocks, change devicehigh *to* device *in the line above. (For more information on MS-DOS's memory management capabilities, see* The Microsoft Guide to Managing Memory with MS-DOS 6, *by Dan Gookin, Microsoft Press, 1993.)*

   If C is your only hard disk drive, the RAM drive will be drive D. Exit all applications and reboot the computer to be sure that the RAM drive is installed.

3. **Set the TMP and TEMP environment variables to D:\.** If you have successfully installed a RAM drive, these environment variables instruct the compiler and linker (and possibly other programs) to store temporary files in the RAM drive. Set these environment variables in your AUTOEXEC.BAT file:

```
set tmp=D:\
set temp=D:\
```

   (Note: Change the drive letter if your RAM drive is not drive D.)

4. Modify your class library project files to use the RAM drive for precompiled headers. This procedure must be performed for each generated class library project file, but the results are worth the effort. First, though, you need to know about precompiled headers and the way the class library uses them.

Note: Visual C++ has two precompiled header "systems": automatic and manual. Automatic precompiled headers, activated with the /Yx compiler switch, are new, but manual precompiled headers, first introduced with C/C++ version 7.0, are still available. The make files in this book use the manual precompiled headers.

Precompiled headers represent compiler "snapshots" taken at a particular source code line. In all class library programs, the snapshot is taken immediately after the statement

```
#include "stdafx.h"
```

The file STDAFX.H contains *#include* statements for the class library header files. The file's contents depend on the options you select when you run AppWizard, but the file <u>always</u> contains the following statements:

```
#include <afxwin.h>
#include <afxext.h>
```

If you are using OLE, STDAFX.H contains the statement

```
#include <afxole.h>
```

Occasionally you'll need the "private" header file that is accessed by the statement

```
#include <afxpriv.h>
```

The source file STDAFX.CPP contains only the statement

```
#include "stdafx.h"
```

and is used to generate the precompiled header file in the project directory. The class library headers included by STDAFX.H never change, but they take a long time to compile. The compiler switch /Yc, used only with STDAFX.CPP, causes <u>creation</u> of the precompiled header (PCH) file. The switch /Yu, used with all the other source code files, causes <u>use</u> of an existing PCH file. The switch /Fp specifies the PCH filename that would otherwise default to STDAFX.PCH in the project subdirectory.

AppWizard sets the /Yc and /Yu switches for you. To change these switches, choose Project from Visual Workbench's Options menu, and click the Compiler button; then click on the Precompiled Headers category, and check or uncheck the Automatic Use Of Precompiled Headers check box as necessary.

Note: *You need to choose Rebuild All from the Project menu to create the precompiled header in the RAM drive.*

You must manually set the /Fp switch to force the PCH file to reside in the RAM drive. To do so, choose Project from Visual Workbench's Options menu, and click the Compiler button; then click on the Custom Options category, and add the expression

```
/Fp"D:\STDAFX.PCH"
```

in the Other Options text box, as shown here:

Note: *Most of the projects on the book's companion disk use the /Fp switch to store the PCH file in the \VCPP subdirectory. This reduces the disk space required when all the projects are compiled, but it doesn't require a RAM drive. You can convert these projects to use a RAM drive by replacing the expression*

```
/Fp"..\STDAFX.PCH"
```

in the Other Options text box in the Custom Options category of the C/C++ Compiler Options dialog box with the expression

```
/Fp"D:\STDAFX.PCH"
```

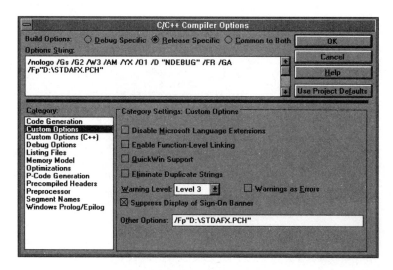

If you're working on several projects simultaneously, those projects can share the same STDAFX.PCH file because that file isn't application-dependent. Not only will you save time, but you'll save disk space because you'll eliminate duplicate copies of the very large PCH file.

Note: *You can share the precompiled header file among projects only if the contents of STDAFX.H are the same. A project that uses OLE, for example, can't use the PCH file from a project that doesn't use OLE. See the Visual C++ documentation for more information.*

Note: *Obviously, the PCH file won't stay in the RAM drive when the computer is rebooted or turned off. You can set up batch files to save and restore this file from disk, or you can force Visual Workbench to regenerate the PCH file by choosing Rebuild All from the Project menu.*

5. **Store the library files in the RAM drive.** You'll reduce link time by about 25 percent if you keep the library files in the RAM drive. Use a batch file to copy the appropriate LIB files to the RAM drive when your computer boots. (If you're using the medium model debug library, you'll want to copy MLIBCEW.LIB and MAFXCWD.LIB to the RAM drive.) Finally, tell Visual C++ to look for the library files in the RAM drive. To do so, choose Directories from the Options menu. In the Directories dialog box that appears, set the Library Files Path text box to point to the RAM drive. (Unless you have a very large RAM drive, you'll probably want to leave the class library files on your hard disk. Be sure the Library Files Path text box in the Directories dialog box still points to the class library subdirectory on your hard disk.)

6. **If you're not using the debugger, eliminate the debugging information.** You might want to get the benefits of the *TRACE, VERIFY,* and *ASSERT* macros without using the debugger. AppWizard generates project files with the compiler and linker switches for debugging information. You can save build time by turning off these switches as follows:

   ☐ Choose Project from the Options menu. The Project Options dialog box appears. Click the Compiler button. The C/C++ Compiler Options dialog box appears. Click on the Debug Options category, and then click the None radio button. Your screen now looks like this:

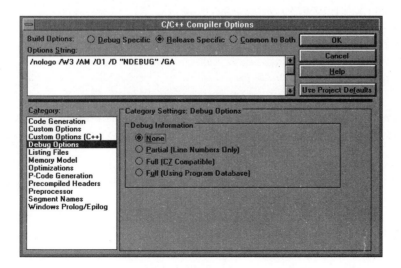

☐ Click OK to close the C/C++ Compiler Options dialog box.

☐ Click the Linker button in the Project Options dialog box. The Linker Options dialog box appears. Click on the Output category, and then uncheck the Generate Debugging Information check box. Your screen now looks like this:

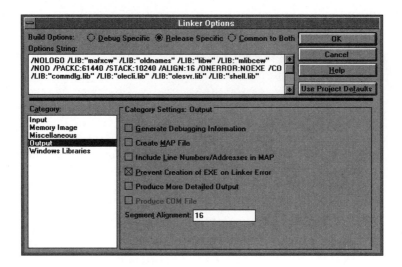

☐ Close the Linker Options and Project Options dialog boxes.

Note: The Debug radio button in the Build Mode section of the Project Options dialog box enables a set of compiler and linker options that relate to debugging. These options include the generation of debugging information for Visual Workbench and CodeView for Windows debuggers, the definition of the _DEBUG preprocessor constant (which activates certain diagnostic features in the class library), and the selection of the debug version of the class library (MAFXCWD.LIB for medium memory model applications).

It's possible to separately enable and disable each of these debugging options through the Compiler Options and Linker Options dialog boxes. If, for example, you want the class library diagnostic features, such as the TRACE macro, but you don't want to use the debugger, then you must individually adjust the compiler and linker options.

7. If you aren't using the browser, don't build the browser database. The project's browser database (BSC file) must be rebuilt every time you change any source code. If you don't need the browser, you can save build time by turning off browser information. To do so, choose Project from the Options menu. The Project Options dialog box appears. Click the Compiler button. The

C/C++ Compiler Options dialog box appears. Click on the Debug Options category, and then click the None radio button. Your screen now looks like this:

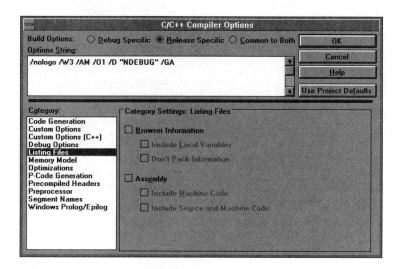

Close the C/C++ Compiler Options and Project Options dialog boxes.

Creating a New MAK File

Sooner or later you'll need to create your own MAK file for an existing project. Perhaps the MAK file from AppWizard was lost, or perhaps you prefer not to use AppWizard. Simply do the following:

1. Choose Close All from Visual Workbench's Project menu. When you start a new project, Visual Workbench leaves your old windows open, which is probably not what you want.

2. Choose New from Visual Workbench's Project menu. A subdirectory must exist for the project. If you're starting from scratch, use File Manager to create a new subdirectory. Select the subdirectory using the New Project dialog box, and then type the makefile name. You'll see a list of any CPP and C files that already exist in the selected subdirectory.

3. Add the necessary source files. Click the Add All button (or double-click on individual files). Doing so adds the files to the project. Also add the DEF file (you might have to write one) and the RC file.

4. Set up manual precompiled headers. Assuming your project has STDAFX.CPP and STDAFX.H files, fill in the Precompiled Headers category of the C/C++ Compiler Options dialog box, as shown on the next page:

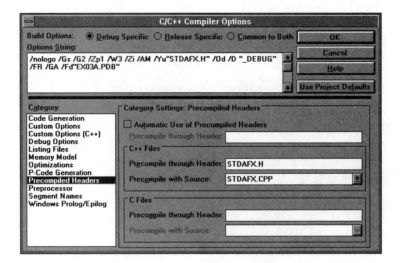

4

Basic Event Handling— Using ClassWizard

In Chapter 3, you saw how the Microsoft Foundation Class Library application framework called the view class's virtual *OnDraw* function. Take a look at the *Class Library Reference* now. If you look at the documentation for the *CView* class and its base class, *CWnd*, you'll see several hundred member functions. Functions with names beginning with *On—OnKeyDown, OnLButtonUp,* and so forth—are member functions that the application framework calls in response to various Windows "events" such as keystrokes and mouse clicks.

Most of these application framework–called functions aren't virtual functions such as *OnDraw* and thus require more effort to program. This chapter explains how to use the Visual C++ ClassWizard to set up the "message map" structure necessary for connecting the application framework to your functions' code. You'll see the practical application of message map functions.

The first two examples use an ordinary *CView* class. More often than not, you'll want a "scrolling" view. The last example uses *CScrollView* in place of the *CView* base class. Now the class library application framework inserts scroll bars and "hooks them up" to the view.

Getting User Input—Message Map Functions

Your EX03A application from Chapter 3 did not accept user input (other than the standard Microsoft Windows resizing and window close commands). The window contained menus and a toolbar, but these were not "connected" to the view code. The menus and the toolbar must wait until Part 3 of this book because they depend on the frame class, but plenty of other Windows input sources will keep you busy until then. Before you can process any Windows event, even a mouse click, however, you must learn how to use the class library message map system.

The Message Map

When the user clicks the left mouse button in a view window, Windows sends a message—specifically WM_LBUTTONDOWN—to that window. If your program needs to take action in response to WM_LBUTTONDOWN, your view class must have a member function that looks like this:

```
void CMyView::OnLButtonDown(UINT nFlags, CPoint point)
{
    // event processing code here
}
```

In addition, your class header file must have the corresponding prototype:

```
afx_msg void OnLButtonDown(UINT nFlags, CPoint point);
```

The *afx_msg* notation is a "no-op" that alerts you that this is a prototype for a message map function. Finally, your code file needs a message map macro that connects your *OnLButtonDown* function to the application framework:

```
BEGIN_MESSAGE_MAP(CMyView, CView)
    ON_WM_LBUTTONDOWN() // entry specifically for OnLButtonDown
    // other message map entries
END_MESSAGE_MAP()
```

and your class header file needs the statement

```
DECLARE_MESSAGE_MAP()
```

How do you know which function goes with which Windows message? Appendix B (and the class library online Help file) includes a table that lists all standard Windows messages and corresponding member function prototypes. You can manually code the message-handling functions—indeed, that was the only option for Microsoft Foundation Class Library version 1.0 programmers. Fortunately, Visual C++ provides a tool, ClassWizard, that automates the coding of message map functions.

Saving the View's State–Class Data Members

If your program accepts user input, you'll want the user to have some visual feedback. The view's *OnDraw* function draws an image based on the view's current "state," and user actions can alter that state. In a full-blown class library application, the document object holds the state of the application, but you're not to that point yet. For now, you'll use a view class "data member," *m_ellipseRect*, an object of class *CRect*, to hold the current bounding rectangle of an ellipse. Then you'll make the member function toggle that rectangle (the view's state) between small and large. (The toggle is activated by pressing the mouse's left button.) The initial value of *m_ellipseRect* is set in the *CMyView* constructor, and it is changed in the *OnLButtonDown* member function.

Note: By convention, class library nonstatic class data member names begin with m_.

Tip: Why not use a global variable for the view's state? Because if you did, you'd be in trouble if your application had multiple views. Besides, encapsulating data in objects is a big part of what object-oriented programming is all about.

Initializing a View Class Data Member

As Appendix A points out, the most efficient place to initialize a class data member is in the constructor, like this:

```
CMyView::CMyView() : m_ellipseRect(0, 0, 200, 200) { }
```

Invalidating the Rectangle

The *OnLButtonDown* function could toggle the value of *m_ellipseRect* all day, but the *OnDraw* function won't get called unless the user resizes the view window. The *OnLButtonDown* function must call the *InvalidateRect* function (a member function that the *CMyView* class inherits from *CWnd*). *InvalidateRect* triggers a call to *OnDraw*, and *OnDraw* can access the "invalid rectangle" parameter that was passed to *InvalidateRect*.

The smaller the invalid rectangle, the faster Windows draws the window, even if your *OnDraw* function issues drawing instructions for all elements in the window. If your *OnDraw* function is smart enough to draw only the items that are inside the invalid rectangle, the display update will be even faster.

The Window's Client Area

A window has a rectangular "client area" that excludes the border, caption bar, and menu. The *CWnd* member function *GetClientRect* gives you the client area dimensions. Normally, you're not allowed to draw outside the client area, and most mouse messages are received only when the mouse cursor is in the client area.

For Windows SDK Programmers

The class library makes it easy to attach your own "state variables" to a window through C++ class data members. In Windows SDK programming, the *WNDCLASS* members *cbClsExtra* and *cbWndExtra* are available for this purpose, but the code for using this mechanism is so complex that few developers bother with it.

The EX04A Example Program

In the EX04A example, a circle changes size when the user clicks the left mouse button while the mouse cursor is inside the view window. You'll see the use of a view class data member to hold the view's state, and you'll use the *InvalidateRect* function.

In the Chapter 3 example, drawing in the window depended on only one function, *OnDraw*. The EX04A example requires three customized functions (including the constructor) and one data member. The complete *CEx04aView* header and source code files are listed in Figure 4-1. (The steps for creating the program are shown after the program listings.) All changes to the original AppWizard output are screened in gray.

```
EX04AVW.H
class CEx04aView : public CView
{
private:
    CRect m_ellipseRect;
protected: // create from serialization only
    CEx04aView();
    DECLARE_DYNCREATE(CEx04aView)

// Attributes
public:
    CEx04aDoc* GetDocument();

// Operations
public:

// Implementation
public:
    virtual ~CEx04aView();
    virtual void OnDraw(CDC* pDC); // overridden to draw this view
#ifdef _DEBUG
    virtual void AssertValid() const;
    virtual void Dump(CDumpContext& dc) const;
#endif

// Generated message map functions
protected:
    //{{AFX_MSG(CEx04aView)
    afx_msg void OnLButtonDown(UINT nFlags, CPoint point);
    //}}AFX_MSG
    DECLARE_MESSAGE_MAP()
};
```

Figure 4-1. *(continued)*

The CEx04aView *header and source code files.*

Figure 4-1. *continued*

```
#ifndef _DEBUG  // debug version in ex04avw.cpp
inline CEx04aDoc* CEx04aView::GetDocument()
    { return (CEx04aDoc*) m_pDocument; }
#endif
```

EX04AVW.CPP

```
#include "stdafx.h"
#include "ex04a.h"

#include "ex04adoc.h"
#include "ex04avw.h"

#ifdef _DEBUG
#undef THIS_FILE
static char BASED_CODE THIS_FILE[] = __FILE__;
#endif

/////////////////////////////////////////////////////////////////////
// CEx04aView

IMPLEMENT_DYNCREATE(CEx04aView, CView)

BEGIN_MESSAGE_MAP(CEx04aView, CView)
    //{{AFX_MSG_MAP(CEx04aView)
    ON_WM_LBUTTONDOWN()
    //}}AFX_MSG_MAP
END_MESSAGE_MAP()

/////////////////////////////////////////////////////////////////////
// CEx04aView construction/destruction

CEx04aView::CEx04aView() : m_ellipseRect(0, 0, 200, 200)
{
}

CEx04aView::~CEx04aView()
{
}

/////////////////////////////////////////////////////////////////////
// CEx04aView drawing

void CEx04aView::OnDraw(CDC* pDC)
```

(continued)

Figure 4-1. *continued*

```
{
    pDC->SelectStockObject(GRAY_BRUSH);
    pDC->Ellipse(m_ellipseRect);
}

/////////////////////////////////////////////////////////////////////
// CEx04aView diagnostics

#ifdef _DEBUG
void CEx04aView::AssertValid() const
{
    CView::AssertValid();
}

void CEx04aView::Dump(CDumpContext& dc) const
{
    CView::Dump(dc);
}

CEx04aDoc* CEx04aView::GetDocument() // non-debug version is inline
{
    ASSERT(m_pDocument->IsKindOf(RUNTIME_CLASS(CEx04aDoc)));
    return (CEx04aDoc*) m_pDocument;
}

#endif //_DEBUG

/////////////////////////////////////////////////////////////////////
// CEx04aView message handlers

void CEx04aView::OnLButtonDown(UINT nFlags, CPoint point)
{
    if (m_ellipseRect == CRect(0, 0, 200, 200)) {
      m_ellipseRect = CRect(0, 0, 100, 100); // little circle
    }
    else {
      m_ellipseRect = CRect(0, 0, 200, 200); // big circle
    }
    InvalidateRect(CRect(0, 0, 200, 200));
}
```

Using ClassWizard with EX04A

Look at the following EX04AVW.H source code:

```
//{{AFX_MSG(CEx04aView)
afx_msg void OnLButtonDown(UINT nFlags, CPoint point);
//}}AFX_MSG
```

Now look at the following EX04AVW.CPP source code:

```
//{{AFX_MSG_MAP(CEx04aView)
ON_WM_LBUTTONDOWN()
//}}AFX_MSG_MAP
```

AppWizard generated the funny-looking comment lines for the benefit of Class-Wizard. ClassWizard adds message handler prototypes between the *AFX_MSG* "brackets" and adds message map entries between the *AFX_MSG_MAP* brackets. ClassWizard also generates a skeleton *OnLButtonDown* member function in EX04AVW.CPP, complete with the correct parameter declarations and return type.

Notice how the AppWizard-ClassWizard combination is different from a conventional code generator. You run a conventional code generator only once and then edit the resulting code. You run AppWizard to generate the application only once, but you can run ClassWizard as many times as necessary, and you can edit the code at any time. You're safe as long as you don't alter what's inside the *AFX_MSG* and *AFX_MSG_MAP* brackets.

Using AppWizard and ClassWizard Together

The following steps illustrate how you use AppWizard and ClassWizard together to create this application:

1. **Run AppWizard to create EX04A.** Choose AppWizard from the Visual Work-bench Project menu. Use AppWizard to generate a program named EX04A in the \VCPP\EX04A subdirectory. The options and the default class names are shown here:

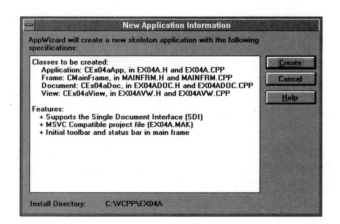

Click on the Options and the Classes buttons in the MFC AppWizard dialog box to set these options.

2. Use ClassWizard to add a *CEx04aView* class message handler. Be sure you have opened the EX04A project, and choose ClassWizard from the Browse menu of the Visual Workbench. The ClassWizard dialog box appears. Now click on *CEx04aView* at the top of the Object IDs list box, and then double-click on WM_LBUTTONDOWN in ClassWizard's Messages list box. The *OnLButtonDown* function name should appear in the Member Functions list box, and a hand symbol should appear next to the message name in the Messages list box. Here is the ClassWizard dialog box:

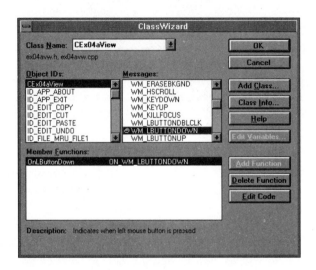

3. Edit the *OnLButtonDown* code in EX04AVW.CPP. Click on the Edit Code button. ClassWizard opens an edit window for EX04AVW.CPP in the Visual Workbench and positions the cursor on the newly generated *OnLButtonDown* member function. The following screened code (which you type in) replaces the previous code:

```
void CEx04aView::OnLButtonDown(UINT nFlags, CPoint point)
{
    if (m_ellipseRect == CRect(0, 0, 200, 200)) {
        m_ellipseRect = CRect(0, 0, 100, 100); // little circle
    }
    else {
        m_ellipseRect = CRect(0, 0, 200, 200); // big circle
    }
    InvalidateRect(CRect(0, 0, 200, 200));
}
```

4. Edit the constructor and the *OnDraw* function in EX04AVW.CPP. The following screened code (which you type in) replaces the previous code:

```
CEx04aView::CEx04aView() : m_ellipseRect(0, 0, 200, 200)
{
}
void CEx04aView::OnDraw(CDC* pDC)
{
    pDC->SelectStockObject(GRAY_BRUSH);
    pDC->Ellipse(m_ellipseRect);
}
```

5. **Add the *m_ellipseRect* data member in EX04AVW.H.** Insert the following code at the start of the *CEx04aView* class declaration:

```
private:
    CRect m_ellipseRect;
```

6. **Build and run the EX04A program.** In the Visual Workbench, choose Build from the Project menu and then choose Execute. The resulting program responds to left-button mouse clicks by shrinking and expanding a circle in the view window. (Don't press the mouse's left button quickly in succession; Windows interprets this as a double-click rather than two single clicks.)

For Windows SDK Programmers

A standard Windows SDK application registers a "window class" and, in the process, assigns a *WndProc* function to all windows of that class. The *WndProc* function is called each time Windows sends a message, and it usually has a *switch* statement for processing the incoming messages.

Microsoft Foundation Class Library version 2 takes care of window class registration by assigning a window class (not to be confused with a C++ class) to each type of window. All view windows, for example, share the same window class. The class library contains only one "hidden" *WndProc* function for all view windows. This function works with the message map system to call the appropriate class member function in response to a Windows message.

EX04B—Dragging a Circle with the Mouse

Let's do something a little more sophisticated with the mouse. The object of the next example is to draw a circle in the window and then allow the user to drag the circle with the mouse. As you study the program, you'll learn a few more things about Windows.

Mouse message handlers are necessary for the following three mouse messages:

- The WM_LBUTTONDOWN message begins the tracking process if the left mouse button is pressed when the mouse cursor is positioned over the circle.

■ The WM_MOUSEMOVE message, received periodically while the mouse moves, causes the circle to follow the mouse cursor position. This message is processed only when the left mouse button is held down and the tracking process was successfully started. (See WM_LBUTTONDOWN on the previous page.)

■ The WM_LBUTTONUP message, received when the left mouse button is released, ends the tracking processes if it was successfully started.

Now perform the following steps to produce the working EX04B example.

1. **Run AppWizard to create EX04B.** Close the EX04A project, and use App-Wizard to generate a program named EX04B in the \VCPP\EX04B subdirectory. The options and the default class names are shown here:

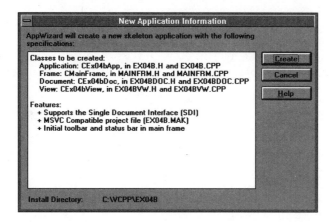

2. **Edit the *CEx04bView* class header in EX04BVW.H.** In the file EX04BVW.H, add the following lines in the class *CEx04bView* declaration:

```
private:
    CRect  m_ellipseRect;
    CPoint m_mousePos;
    BOOL   m_bCaptured;
```

3. **Use ClassWizard to add three message handlers.** Add message-handling functions for the three mouse messages previously described. Here is a list of Windows messages and their associated member functions:

Message	Member Function Name
WM_LBUTTONDOWN	*OnLButtonDown*
WM_LBUTTONUP	*OnLButtonUp*
WM_MOUSEMOVE	*OnMouseMove*

4. **Edit the *CEx04bView* mouse message-handling functions in EX04B-VW.CPP.** ClassWizard generated the skeletons for the functions previously listed. Find them in the file EX04BVW.CPP, and then type in the screened code (replacing the existing code) as follows:

```
void CEx04bView::OnLButtonDown(UINT nFlags, CPoint point)
{
    CRect rect;
    CRgn  circle;

    TRACE("entering CEx04bView::OnLButtonDown - point = %d, %d\n",
        point.x, point.y);
    circle.CreateEllipticRgnIndirect(m_ellipseRect);
    if (circle.PtInRegion(point)) {
      // capturing mouse ensures subsequent LButtonUp message
      SetCapture();
      m_bCaptured = TRUE;
      m_mousePos = point;
      // "cross" mouse cursor is active while mouse is captured
      ::SetCursor(::LoadCursor(NULL, IDC_CROSS));
    }
}


void CEx04bView::OnLButtonUp(UINT nFlags, CPoint point)
{
    if (m_bCaptured) {
      ReleaseCapture();
      m_bCaptured = FALSE;
    }
}


void CEx04bView::OnMouseMove(UINT nFlags, CPoint point)
{
    CSize offset;
    CRect tempRect, newRect, invalidRect, clientRect;

    if (m_bCaptured) {
      GetClientRect(clientRect);
      // don't move the circle outside the client window
      if (clientRect.PtInRect(point)) {
        offset = point - m_mousePos;
        newRect = m_ellipseRect + (CPoint(0, 0) + offset);
        tempRect.UnionRect(m_ellipseRect, newRect);
        invalidRect.IntersectRect(tempRect, clientRect);
        InvalidateRect(invalidRect, TRUE);
        m_mousePos = point;
        m_ellipseRect = newRect;
      }
    }
}
```

5. **Edit the constructor and the *OnDraw* function in file EX04BVW.CPP.**
AppWizard generated these skeleton functions. Find them and type in the following code:

```
CEx04bView::CEx04bView() : m_ellipseRect(0, 0, 100, 100) // constructor
{
    m_bCaptured = FALSE;
}

void CEx04bView::OnDraw(CDC* pDC)
{
    pDC->SelectStockObject(GRAY_BRUSH);
    pDC->Ellipse(m_ellipseRect);
}
```

6. **Build and run the EX04B program.** In Visual Workbench, choose Build from the Project menu and then choose Execute. The resulting program allows a circle to be dragged with the mouse.

The EX04B Program Elements

Following is a discussion of the major elements in the EX04B program.

The *m_ellipseRect* data member
This object of class *CRect* holds the current (as of the last mouse move) bounding rectangle of the moving circle. The *OnDraw* member function uses it.

The *m_mousePos* data member
The *OnMouseMove* member function must compare the current mouse position with the previous mouse position to know how far to move the circle. This object of class *CPoint* stores the previous mouse position.

The *m_bCaptured* data member
This Boolean variable is set to TRUE when mouse tracking is in progress.

The *SetCapture* and *ReleaseCapture* member functions
SetCapture is the *CWnd* member function that "captures" the mouse such that mouse movement messages are sent to this window even if the mouse cursor is outside the window. An unfortunate side effect of this function is that the circle can be moved outside the window and "lost," but I'll show you how to fix that problem on the next page. A desirable and necessary effect is that all subsequent mouse messages are sent to the window, including the WM_LBUTTONUP message, which would otherwise be lost. *ReleaseCapture* turns off mouse capture.

The *SetCursor* and *LoadCursor* Windows functions
The class library does not "wrap" some Windows functions. By convention, we use the C++ scope resolution operator (::) when directly calling Windows functions. In

this case, there is no potential of conflict with a *CView* member function, but you can deliberately choose to call a Windows function in place of a class member function with the same name and parameter types. In that case, the :: operator ensures that you call the globally scoped Windows function.

With the first parameter NULL, the *LoadCursor* function creates a "cursor resource" from the specified predefined mouse cursor that Windows uses. The *SetCursor* function activates the specified cursor resource. This cursor remains active as long as the mouse is captured.

CRect, CPoint, and CSize arithmetic

If you look in the *Class Library Reference,* you will see that the *CRect, CPoint*, and *CSize* classes have a number of overloaded operators. (Overloaded operators are explained in Appendix A.) You can, among other things, do the following:

■ Add a *CSize* object to a *CPoint* object

■ Subtract a *CSize* object from a *CPoint* object

■ Subtract one *CPoint* object from another, yielding a *CSize* object

■ Add a *CPoint* object to a *CRect* object

■ Subtract a *CPoint* object from a *CRect* object

From this list, you can begin to see that a *CSize* object is the "difference between two *CPoint* objects" and that you can "bias" a *CRect* object by a *CPoint* object. The C++ compiler enforces the rules above; it will not, for example, let you add a *CSize* object to a *CRect* object.

The *OnMouseMove* member function uses *CRect, CPoint,* and *CSize* objects to move the circle's bounding rectangle based on the last mouse move.

Is a point inside the client area?

A captured mouse can move the circle outside the client area, but that's not what we want. The *OnMouseMove* message handler first uses the *CRect PtInRect* function to see whether the mouse position is truly inside the client area. If the mouse cursor is outside the client area, the circle isn't moved.

Is a point inside a circle?

The Windows GDI provides an element called a "region" that can be used for clipping and for hit testing. Regions consist of combinations of polygons (including rectangles) and ellipses. The *OnLButtonDown* function creates a temporary *CRgn* object corresponding to the circle, and then it calls the *PtInRgn* function to find out whether the mouse cursor was inside the circle when the mouse button was pressed.

The minimum invalid rectangle

The previous example, EX04A, invalidated the entire view client area each time the circle size was changed. The EX04B example invalidates only the area known to

have changed. This rectangular area is computed by first performing a union operation on the rectangle for the circle's new position and the rectangle for the circle's
old position and then by performing an intersection operation with the window's
client area. Figure 4-2 illustrates the process.

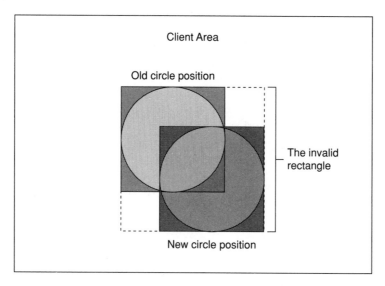

Figure 4-2.
Calculating the minimum invalid rectangle.

The *CRect LPRECT* operator

If you read the *Class Library Reference* carefully, you will notice that the *CWnd*
InvalidateRect member function takes an *LPRECT* parameter, not a *CRect* parameter.
It so happens that *LPRECT* is a pointer to a Windows *RECT* structure and that *CRect*
is derived from *RECT*. (Yes, C++ lets you derive a class from a structure.) This
derivation ensures that a *CRect∗* parameter is passed to the function, not a *CRect*
argument.

A *CRect* argument is allowed because the *CRect* class defines an overloaded operator
LPRECT() that takes the address of a *CRect* object. Thus, the compiler converts *CRect*
arguments to *LPRECT* arguments when necessary. You call functions as though they
had *CRect* reference parameters. The view member function code

```
CRect clientRect;
GetClientRect(clientRect);
```

retrieves the client rectangle coordinates and stores them in *clientRect*.

Device coordinates—necessary for this example

In the Windows default device coordinates mode, units map to display pixels with
the origin at the top left. Vertical (*y*-axis) values increase from top to bottom.

Because they call underlying Windows functions, many *CRect* operators work properly only with coordinates that have non-negative values. Also, the mouse message function *point* parameter is always in device coordinates. Chapter 5 illustrates the use of other Windows mapping modes and the appropriate conversion strategies.

A Scrolling View Window

As the lack of scroll bars in EX04A and EX04B indicates, the class library *CView* class, the base class of *CEx04bView*, doesn't directly support scrolling. The class library has another class, *CScrollView*, that does support scrolling. *CScrollView* is derived from *CView*. We'll create a new program that uses *CScrollView* in place of *CView*. The new program, EX04C, does not accept mouse input because the necessary coordinate transformation functions aren't covered until Chapter 5. The program does process keyboard messages, however, and it introduces an important Windows message, WM_CREATE.

A Window Is Larger than What You See

If you use the mouse to shrink the size of an ordinary window, the contents of the window remain anchored at the top left, and items at the bottom and/or on the right of the window disappear. When you expand the window, the items reappear. You can correctly conclude that a window is larger than the "viewport" that you see on the screen. The viewport doesn't have to be anchored at the top left of the window area. Through the use of the *CWnd* functions *ScrollWindow* and *SetViewportOrg*, the *CScrollView* class allows you to move the viewport anywhere in the window, and that includes areas above and to the left of the origin.

Scroll Bars

Microsoft Windows makes it easy to display scroll bars at the edges of a window, but Windows by itself doesn't make any attempt to connect those scroll bars to their window. That's where the *CScrollView* class fits in. *CScrollView* member functions process the WM_HSCROLL and WM_VSCROLL messages sent by the scroll bars to the view. Those functions move the viewport within the window and do all the necessary housekeeping.

Scrolling Alternatives

The *CScrollView* class supports a particular kind of scrolling—one in which there is one big window and a small viewport. Each item is assigned a unique position in this big window. What if you have 10,000 address lines to display? Instead of having a window 10,000 lines long, you probably want a smaller window with scrolling logic that selects only as many lines as the screen can display. In that case, you should write your own scrolling view class derived from *CView*.

Note: As you'll see in Chapter 24, a CScrollView-derived view can easily and efficiently accommodate as many as 2000 lines.

The EX04C Scrolling Example

The goal of EX04C is to make a window twice as wide and twice as high as the screen. The program draws a large circle at the exact center of this window such that the upper left quadrant of the circle is visible when the window is maximized. The user can scroll the window with the mouse and the direction keys.

1. **Run AppWizard to create EX04C.** Use AppWizard to generate a program named EX04C in the \VCPP\EX04C subdirectory. The options and the default class names are shown here:

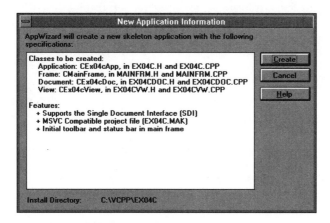

2. **Make global replacements for the *CEx04CView* Class.** Use the Visual Workbench editor on EX04CVW.H and EX04CVW.CPP to replace all occurrences of *CView* with *CScrollView*. Be sure you set the Match Case option in Visual Workbench's Replace dialog box.

   Note: The global base class replacement works in this case, but be careful otherwise. Suppose, for example, that your derived view class implemented the CView virtual member function OnUpdate:

   ```
   void CEx04CView::OnUpdate(CView* pSender, LPARAM lHint, CObject* pHint)
   ```

   If you replaced CView with CScrollView* in the function declaration, the compiler would assume you were defining a completely new nonvirtual function. When the application framework called CView::OnUpdate, the base class version would be called—not your derived class implementation.*

3. **Use ClassWizard to add message handlers for WM_CREATE and WM_KEY-DOWN messages.** ClassWizard generates the member functions *OnCreate* and *OnKeyDown* along with the necessary message map entries and prototypes.

4. Edit the *CEx04cView* message handler functions. ClassWizard generated the skeletons for the functions previously listed. Find them in file EX04CVW.CPP, and then type in the following code:

```
int CEx04CView::OnCreate(LPCREATESTRUCT lpCreateStruct)
{
    if (CScrollView::OnCreate(lpCreateStruct) == -1)
      return -1;

    // total window size is 2x screen size
    CSize totalSize = CSize(::GetSystemMetrics(SM_CXSCREEN) * 2,
                            ::GetSystemMetrics(SM_CYSCREEN) * 2);
    CSize pageSize = CSize(totalSize.cx / 2,
                           totalSize.cy / 2);      // for page scroll
    CSize lineSize = CSize(totalSize.cx / 100,
                           totalSize.cy / 100);   // line scroll
    SetScrollSizes(MM_TEXT, totalSize,
                   pageSize, lineSize);            // CScrollView function
    return 0;
}

void CEx04CView::OnKeyDown(UINT nChar, UINT nRepCnt, UINT nFlags)
{
    switch (nChar) {
    case VK_HOME:
      OnScroll(SB_VERT, SB_TOP, 0);
      OnScroll(SB_HORZ, SB_TOP, 0);
      break;
    case VK_END:
      OnScroll(SB_VERT, SB_BOTTOM, 0);
      break;
    case VK_UP:
      OnScroll(SB_VERT, SB_LINEUP, 0);
      break;
    case VK_DOWN:
      OnScroll(SB_VERT, SB_LINEDOWN, 0);
      break;
    case VK_PRIOR:
      OnScroll(SB_VERT, SB_PAGEUP, 0);
      break;
    case VK_NEXT:
      OnScroll(SB_VERT, SB_PAGEDOWN, 0);
      break;
    case VK_LEFT:
      OnScroll(SB_HORZ, SB_PAGEUP, 0);
      break;
    case VK_RIGHT:
      OnScroll(SB_HORZ, SB_PAGEDOWN, 0);
      break;
    default:
      break;
    }
}
```

5. **Edit the *CEx04cView OnDraw* function.** Change the AppWizard-generated *OnDraw* function in EX04CVW.CPP by typing in the following code:

```
void CEx04CView::OnDraw(CDC* pDC)
{
    int x = ::GetSystemMetrics(SM_CXSCREEN);
    int y = ::GetSystemMetrics(SM_CYSCREEN);

    pDC->SelectStockObject(GRAY_BRUSH); // selects a brush for
                                        //  the circle interior
    // draw a circle centered in the scrolling window
    pDC->Ellipse(CRect(x - 300, y - 300, x + 300, y + 300));
}
```

6. **Build and run the EX04C program.** In the Visual Workbench, choose Build from the Project menu and then choose Execute. The program shows a large circle in a scrolling window as shown here:

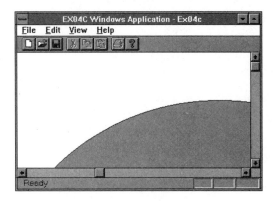

You might need to scroll to see the circle.

The EX04C Program Elements

Following is a discussion of the major elements in the EX04C program.

The Windows *GetSystemMetrics* function

The Windows *GetSystemMetrics* function returns the widths and heights of various Windows display elements, including the screen itself. *OnDraw* uses the screen size to determine the circle's center.

The *OnCreate* message-handling function

OnCreate is a message map function called in response to the WM_CREATE Windows message. This important message is sent when an application requests that a window be created. You'll learn more about the window construction/creation steps in the following chapters. For now, think of the *OnCreate* function as the logical place to initialize a window.

Calling the base class *OnCreate* function

The first statement in *OnCreate* is a call to the base class (*CScrollView*) *OnCreate* function. This statement is necessary because the *CScrollView* class and its base classes must do their own initializations.

The *SetScrollSizes* function

SetScrollSizes is a *CScrollView* member function that <u>must</u> be called during the initialization of a scrolling window. This function specifies the map mode, total window size, and page and line sizes for scrolling. The *MM_TEXT* mapping mode corresponds to device coordinates where one unit equals one pixel.

Handling keystrokes

Most of the time, you'll get keyboard input through Windows edit controls, keyboard accelerators, or the *CEditView* class, all of which will be described later. Sometimes, though, you need to process raw keystrokes. The Windows WM_KEYDOWN message gives you the exact, untranslated code for a pressed key. The message map function *OnKeyDown* handles this message with a *switch* statement that the *nChar* parameter controls.

Keystrokes that represent normal ASCII characters also generate a WM_CHAR message that delivers the translated ASCII character. We can't use WM_CHAR here because the direction keys don't generate ASCII characters.

Connecting scroll keys to *CScrollView*

In a *CScrollView* window, the scroll bars send WM_HSCROLL and WM_VSCROLL messages in response to the user's mouse actions. The handlers for these messages call the *CScrollView OnScroll* virtual member function. If you want only mouse scrolling, you don't need to write any code because the base class does the work. If you want keyboard-actuated scrolling, however, you can use the *OnKeyDown* function to simulate scroll messages. All that's necessary is a direct call to the *OnScroll* function. The Up direction key, for example, with code *VK_UP*, calls *OnScroll* with the parameters that specify "scroll up one line." The size of a line was set in the *SetScrollSizes* function called in *OnCreate*.

Coordinate transformations—not yet

EX04C is an introductory *CScrollView* example. Coordinate transformations are going on in the base class, so don't try any transformations yourself. See EX05A in the next chapter for a complete scrolling example with alternate mapping modes.

Other Windows Messages

The class library directly supports about 130 Windows message-handling functions. In addition, you can define your own messages. You will see plenty of message-handling examples in later chapters, including handlers for menu items, child window controls, and so forth. In the meantime, three special Windows messages deserve special attention. All three messages are sent during the window shutdown process, in contrast to WM_CREATE, which is sent on window initialization.

The WM_CLOSE Message

Windows sends the WM_CLOSE message when the user closes a window from the system menu and when a parent window is closed. If you implement the *OnClose* message map function in your derived view class, you can control the closing process. If, for example, you need to prompt the user to save changes to a file, you do it in *OnClose*. Only when you have determined that it is safe to close the window do you call the base class *OnClose* function, which continues the close process. The view object and the corresponding window are both still active.

> *Tip: When you're using the full application framework, you probably won't use the WM_CLOSE message handler. As Chapter 24 illustrates, you'll override the* CDocument SaveModified *virtual function instead, as part of the application framework's highly structured program exit procedure.*

The WM_QUERYENDSESSION Message

Windows sends the WM_QUERYENDSESSION message to all running applications when the user exits Windows. The *OnQueryEndSession* message map function handles it. If you write a handler for WM_CLOSE, write one for WM_QUERY-ENDSESSION too.

The WM_DESTROY Message

Windows sends this message after the WM_CLOSE message, and the *OnDestroy* message map function handles it. When your program receives this message, it should assume that the view window is no longer visible on the screen but that it is still active and its child windows are still active. Use this message handler to do cleanup that depends on the existence of the underlying window. Be sure to call the base class *OnDestroy* function. You cannot "abort" the window destruction process in your view's *OnDestroy* function. *OnClose* is the place to do that.

The WM_NCDESTROY Message

This is the last message that Windows sends when the window is being destroyed. All child windows have already been destroyed. You can do final processing in *OnNcDestroy* that doesn't depend on a window being active. Be sure to call the base class *OnNcDestroy* function.

> *Tip: Do not try to destroy a dynamically allocated window object in* OnNcDestroy. *That job is reserved for a special* CWnd *virtual function,* PostNcDestroy, *that's the base class* OnNcDestroy *calls. Technical Note 17 in the MFCNOTES.HLP Help file gives hints on when it's appropriate to destroy a window object.*

5

The Graphics Device Interface (GDI)

You've already seen some elements of the GDI. Any time your program draws directly on the display or printer, it must use the GDI functions. The GDI has functions for drawing points, lines, rectangles, polygons, ellipses, bitmaps, and text. This chapter gives you the information you need to use the GDI effectively in the Visual C++ environment. It emphasizes the use of text because graphics programming for Microsoft Windows is often intuitive. We'll cover in detail the "mapping modes" that determine the size of displayed objects.

The Device Context Classes

In Chapters 3 and 4, the *OnDraw* member function of the view class was passed a pointer to a device context. *OnDraw* selected a brush and then drew a circle. The Windows device context is the key GDI element that represents a physical device. Each C++ device context has an associated Windows device context, identified by a handle of type *HDC*.

Microsoft Foundation Class Library version 2.0 has a number of device context classes. The base class *CDC* has all the member functions (some virtual) you'll need for drawing. Except for the oddball *CMetaFileDC* class, derived classes are distinct only in their constructors and destructors. If you (or the application framework) construct an object of a derived device context class, you can pass a *CDC* pointer to a function such as *OnDraw*. For the display, the usual derived classes are *CClientDC* and *CWindowDC*. For other devices, such as a printer or a memory buffer, you construct an object of the base class *CDC*.

The "virtualness" of the *CDC* class is an important feature of the application framework. In Chapter 18, you'll see how easy it is to write code that works with both the printer and the display. A statement in *OnDraw* such as

```
pDC->TextOut(0, 0, "Hello");
```

sends text to the display, the printer, or the Print Preview window depending on the class of the object referenced by the *CView OnDraw* function's pDC parameter.

For display and printer device context objects, the application framework attaches the handle to the object. For other device contexts, such as the memory device context that you'll see in Chapter 10, you must call a member function after construction in order to attach the handle.

The Display Context Classes *CClientDC* and *CWindowDC*

Remember that a window's client area excludes the border, the caption bar, and the menu bar. If you create a *CClientDC* object, you have a device context that is mapped only to this client area—you can't draw outside it. The point (*0, 0*) usually refers to the upper left corner of the client area. As you'll see later, a class library *CView* object corresponds to a "child window" that is contained in a separate frame window, often along with a toolbar, a status bar, and scroll bars. The client area of the view, then, does <u>not</u> include these other windows. If the window contains a toolbar, for example, point (*0, 0*) refers to the point immediately <u>under</u> the left edge of the toolbar.

If you construct an object of class *CWindowDC*, point (*0, 0*) is at the upper left corner of the screen. This access to screen coordinates enables you to draw anywhere on the display—a useful but dangerous capability. You can get the bounding rectangle of an entire window (including the nonclient area) in screen coordinates by calling the *CWnd* function *GetWindowRect*.

Constructing and Destroying *CDC* Objects

After you construct a *CDC* object, it is important to destroy it promptly when you're done with it. Windows limits the number of available device contexts, and if you fail to destroy a device context object, it gives you a nasty *FatalExit* message in the debug window. Most frequently, you'll construct a device context object inside a message handler function such as *OnLButtonDown*. The easiest way to ensure that the device context object is destroyed (and the underlying Windows device context is released) is to construct the object on the stack like this:

```
void CMyView::OnLButtonDown(UINT nFlags, CPoint point)
{
    CRect rect;

    CClientDC dc(this); // constructs dc on the stack
    dc.GetClipBox(rect); // retrieves the clipping rectangle
} // dc automatically destroyed
```

Notice that the *CClientDC* constructor takes a window pointer as a parameter. The destructor for the *CClientDC* object is called upon return from the function.

You can also get a device context pointer by using the *CWnd GetDC* member function. You must be careful here to call the *ReleaseDC* function to release the device context.

```
void CMyView::OnLButtonDown(UINT nFlags, CPoint point)
{
    CRect rect;

    CDC* pDC = GetDC();     // a pointer to an internal dc
    pDC->GetClipBox(rect);  // retrieves the clipping rectangle
    ReleaseDC(pDC);         // don't forget this
}
```

Warning: *You must not destroy the* CDC *object passed by the pointer to* OnDraw. *The application framework handles the destruction for you.*

The State of the Device Context

You know already that a device context is required for drawing. When you use a *CDC* object to draw an ellipse, for example, what you see on the screen (or the printer's hard copy) depends on the current "state" of the device context. This state includes

■ Attached GDI drawing objects such as pens, brushes, and fonts.

■ The mapping mode that determines the scale of items when they are drawn.

■ Various details such as text alignment parameters and polygon filling mode. You have already seen, for example, that choosing a gray brush prior to drawing an ellipse results in the ellipse having a gray interior.

When you create a device context object, it has certain default characteristics, such as a black pen for shape boundaries. All other state characteristics are assigned through *CDC* class member functions. GDI objects are "selected into the device context" by means of the overloaded *SelectObject* functions. A device context can, for example, have one pen, one brush, or one font selected at any given time.

The *CPaintDC* Class

You'll need this class only if you override your view's *OnPaint* function. The default *OnPaint* calls *OnDraw* with a properly set up device context, but sometimes you'll

For Windows SDK Programmers

The *CPaintDC* constructor calls *BeginPaint* for you, and the destructor calls *EndPaint*. If you construct your device context on the stack, the *EndPaint* call is completely automatic.

need display-specific drawing code. The *CPaintDC* class is special because its constructor and destructor do housekeeping unique to *OnPaint*. Once you have a *CDC* pointer, however, you can use it as you would any other device context pointer.

Here is a sample *OnPaint* function that creates a *CPaintDC* object:

```
void CMyView::OnPaint()
{
    CPaintDC dc(this);
    OnPrepareDC(&dc); // explained later
    dc.TextOut(0, 0, "for the display, not the printer");
    OnDraw(&dc);      // stuff that's common to the display and printer
}
```

GDI Objects

A Windows GDI object type is represented by a class library class. *CGdiObject* is the abstract base class for the GDI object classes. A "Windows GDI object" is represented by a C++ object of a class derived from *CGdiObject*. Here is a list of the GDI derived classes:

- *CBitmap*—A bitmap is an array of bits in which one or more bits correspond to each display pixel. You can use bitmaps to represent images, including icons and cursors, and you can use them to create brushes.

- *CBrush*—A brush defines a bitmapped pattern of pixels that is used to fill areas with color.

- *CFont*—A font is a complete collection of characters of a particular typeface and a particular size. Fonts are generally stored on disk as resources, and some are device-specific.

- *CPalette*—A palette is a color mapping interface that allows an application to take full advantage of the color capability of an output device without interfering with other applications.

- *CPen*—A pen is a tool for drawing lines and shape borders. You can specify a pen's color and thickness, and whether it draws solid, dotted, or dashed lines.

- *CRgn*—A region is an area that is a combination of polygons and ellipses. You can use regions for filling, clipping, and mouse hit-testing.

Constructing and Destroying GDI Objects

You never construct an object of class *CGdiObject*, but rather you construct objects of the derived classes. Constructors for some GDI derived classes, such as *CPen* and *CBrush*, allow you to specify enough information to create the object in one step. Others, such as *CFont* and *CRgn*, require a second creation step. For these classes, you construct the C++ object with the default constructor and then call a create function such as *CreateFont* or *CreatePolygonRgn*.

The *CGdiObject* class has a virtual destructor. The derived class destructors delete the Windows GDI objects that are attached to the C++ objects. If you construct an object of a class derived from *CGdiObject*, <u>you must delete it</u> prior to exiting the program. If you don't, Windows doesn't release the memory, and you'll get another nasty message in the debug window. To delete a GDI object, you must first separate it from the device context. You'll see an example in the next section.

Tracking GDI Objects

OK, so you know that you have to delete your GDI objects and that they must first be disconnected from their device context. How do you disconnect them? Members of the *CDC SelectObject* family of functions do the work of selecting a GDI object into the device context and, in the process, return a pointer to the previously selected object (which gets deselected in the process). Trouble is, you can't deselect the old object without selecting a new object. One easy way to track the objects is to "save" the original GDI object when you select your own GDI object and "restore" the original object when you're finished. Then you'll be ready to delete your own GDI object. Here's an example:

```
void CMyView::OnDraw(CDC* pDC)
{
    CPen newPen(PS_DASHDOTDOT, 2, (COLORREF) 0); // black pen,
                                                 // 2 pixels wide
    CPen* pOldPen = pDC->SelectObject(&newPen);

    pDC->MoveTo(10, 10);
    pDC->Lineto(110, 10);
    pDC->SelectObject(pOldPen);                 // newPen is deselected
} // newPen automatically destroyed on exit
```

Stock GDI Objects

Windows contains a number of "stock GDI objects" that you can use. Because these objects are inside Windows, you don't have to worry about deleting them. (Windows ignores requests to delete stock objects.) The class library function *SelectStockObject* gives you a *CGdiObject* pointer that you can select into a device context. These stock objects are handy when you want to deselect your own nonstock GDI object prior to its destruction. You can use a stock object as an alternative to the "old" object you used in the previous example.

```
void CMyView::OnDraw(CDC* pDC)
{
    CPen newPen(PS_DASHDOTDOT, 2, (COLORREF) 0); // black pen,
                                                 // 2 pixels wide

    pDC->SelectObject(&newPen);
    pDC->MoveTo(10, 10);
    pDC->Lineto(110, 10);
    pDC->SelectStockObject(BLACK_PEN);          // newPen is deselected
} // newPen destroyed on exit
```

71

The *Class Library Reference* lists the stock objects available for pens, brushes, fonts, and palettes.

The Lifetime of a GDI Selection

For the <u>display</u> device context, you get a <u>fresh</u> device context at the beginning of each message-handling function. No GDI selections (or mapping modes or other device context settings) persist after your function exits. You must, therefore, set up your device context from scratch each time. The *CView* class virtual member function *OnPrepareDC* is useful for setting the mapping mode, but you must take care of your own GDI objects.

For other device contexts, such as those for printers and memory buffers, your assignments can last longer. For these long-life device contexts, things get a little more complicated. The complexity results from the temporary nature of GDI C++ object pointers returned by the *SelectObject* function. (The temporary C++ object will be destroyed by the application framework during the idle loop processing of the application, sometime after the handler function returns the call. See Technical Note 3 in the MFCNOTES.HLP Help file.) You can't simply store the pointer in a class data member; rather you must convert it to a Windows handle (the only permanent GDI identifier) with the *GetSafeHdc* member function. Here's an example:

```
// m_pPrintFont is a CFont pointer initialized in the CMyView constructor
// m_hOldFont is a CMyView data member of type HFONT, initialized to 0

void CMyView::SwitchToCourier(CDC* pDC)
{
    m_pPrintFont->CreateFont(30, 10, 0, 0, 400, FALSE, FALSE,
                        0, ANSI_CHARSET, OUT_DEFAULT_PRECIS,
                        CLIP_DEFAULT_PRECIS, DEFAULT_QUALITY,
                        DEFAULT_PITCH | FF_MODERN,
                        "Courier New"); // TrueType
    CFont* pOldFont = (CFont*) (pDC->SelectObject(m_pPrintFont));
    // m_hObject is the CGdiObject public data member that contains
    //  the handle
    m_hOldFont = (HFONT) pOldFont->GetSafeHdc();
}

void CMyView:SwitchToOriginalFont(CDC* pDC)
{
    // FromHandle is a static member function that returns an
    //  object pointer
    if (m_hOldFont) {
      pDC->SelectObject(CFont::FromHandle(m_hOldFont));
    }
}

// m_pPrintFont is deleted in the CMyView destructor
```

Note: Be careful when deleting an object whose pointer is returned by SelectObject. *If you've allocated the object yourself, you can delete it. If the pointer is temporary, as it will be for the object initially selected into the device context, you cannot delete the C++ object.*

A Permanent Device Context for the Display— Registering Window Classes

You've learned that you get a fresh display device context each time a Windows message handler function is called. An exception to this rule, however, is that at window creation time you can specify a permanent device context that lasts for the life of the window. The permanent device context retains its settings, including GDI object selections and mapping mode, but not its color palette.

You request a permanent Windows device context with a call to the *Afx- RegisterWndClass* function, with the *nClassStyle* parameter *CS_OWNDC* or *CS_- CLASSDC*. Even though the Windows device context is permanent, you must still ensure that it is released at the end of each message handler that uses it.

The *AfxRegisterWndClass* function is useful for assigning other special characteristics to a window. For example, you can use this function to inhibit mouse double-click messages or to prevent the user from closing the window from the system menu. To call *AfxRegisterWndClass*, override the *CWnd* virtual *PreCreate- Window* member function for the window you want to customize. Here's an example in a derived view class:

```
BOOL CMyView::PreCreateWindow(CREATESTRUCT& cs)
{
    cs.lpszClass = AfxRegisterWndClass(CS_HREDRAW | CS_VREDRAW |
                                       CS_OWNDC, NULL);
    return TRUE;
}
```

Of course, you'll need a prototype for the *PreCreateWindow* member function in your view class declaration.

Windows Color Mapping

The Windows GDI provides a "hardware-independent" color interface. Your program supplies an "absolute" color code, and the GDI maps that code to a suitable color or color combination on your computer's video display. Most Windows programmers try to optimize their applications' color display for a few common video board categories.

Standard Video Graphics Array (VGA) Display Boards

A standard VGA display board uses 18-bit color registers, and thus it has a palette of 262,144 colors. Because of video memory constraints, however, the standard VGA board accommodates 4-bit color codes, which means it can display only 16 colors at a time. Because Windows needs fixed colors for captions, borders, scroll bars, and so forth, your programs can use only 16 "standard" pure colors. You cannot conveniently access the other colors that the board can display.

Each Windows color is represented by a combination of 8-bit "red," "green," and "blue" values. The 16 standard VGA "pure" (nondithered) colors are shown in the following table:

Red	Green	Blue	Color
0	0	0	Black
0	0	255	Bright blue
0	255	0	Bright green
0	255	255	Cyan
255	0	0	Bright red
255	0	255	Magenta
255	255	0	Bright yellow
255	255	255	White
0	0	128	Dark blue
0	128	0	Dark green
0	128	128	Blue-green
128	0	0	Brown
128	0	128	Dark purple
128	128	0	Olive
128	128	128	Dark gray
192	192	192	Light gray

Color-oriented GDI functions accept 32-bit *COLORREF* parameters that contain 8-bit color codes each for red, green, and blue. The Windows *RGB* macro converts 8-bit red, green, and blue values to a *COLORREF* parameter. The following statement, when executed on a system with a standard VGA board, constructs a brush with a dithered color (one that consists of a pattern of pure-color pixels):

```
CBrush brush(RGB(128, 128, 192));
```

The following statement (in your view's *OnDraw* function) sets the text background to bright red:

```
pDC->SetBkColor(RGB(255, 0, 0));
```

The *CDC* functions *SetBkColor* and *SetTextColor* don't always display dithered colors as the brush-oriented drawing functions do. If the dithered color pattern is too complex, the closest matching pure color is displayed.

256-Color Display Boards

Many display boards can accommodate 8-bit color codes, which means they can display 256 colors simultaneously. If you have one of these "super VGA" boards, you need to install a special Windows display driver, supplied by Microsoft or your board's manufacturer, to activate the 256-color mode. Because 8-bit color images require twice as much memory as 4-bit color images, Windows display updates can be noticeably slower in 256-color mode.

If Windows is configured for a 256-color display board, your programs are limited to 20 standard colors unless you activate the Windows "color palette" system as supported by the class library *CPalette* class and the Windows API. Windows color palette programming is covered briefly in Chapter 23. In this chapter, we'll assume that the Windows default color mapping is in effect.

With a 256-color display driver installed, you get the 16 VGA colors listed in the table on the previous page, plus four more, for a total of 20. The following table lists the four additional colors:

Red	Green	Blue	Color
192	220	192	Pale green
166	202	240	Light blue
255	251	240	Off-white
160	160	164	Medium gray

The *RGB* macro works much the same as it does with the standard VGA. If you specify one of the 20 standard colors for a brush, you get a pure color; otherwise, you get a dithered color. If you use the *PALETTERGB* macro instead, you don't get dithered colors; you get the closest matching standard pure color.

24-Bit Color Display Boards

Other display boards, mostly in the high-end category (which are becoming more widely used), use 24-bit color codes. This 24-bit capability enables the display of 16.7 million pure colors. If you're using a 24-bit color board, you have full access to all the colors. The *RGB* macro allows you to specify the exact colors you want.

Mapping Modes

Up to now, our drawing units have been display pixels, also known as device coordinates. The statement

```
pDC->Rectangle(CRect(0, 0, 200, 200));
```

draws a square 200 pixels by 200 pixels, with its top left corner at the top left of the window's client area (with positive y values increasing as you move down). This square would look smaller on a high-resolution display of 1024 by 768 pixels than it would on a standard VGA display that is 640 by 480 pixels, and it would look tiny if printed on a laser printer with 300-dpi resolution.

What if you want the square to be 2 inches by 2 inches, regardless of the display device? Windows provides a number of mapping modes, or coordinate systems, that can be associated with the device context. If you assign the *MM_LOENGLISH* mapping mode, for example, a logical unit is 1/100 inch instead of 1 pixel. In the *MM_LOENGLISH* mapping mode, the y-axis runs in the opposite direction to that in the *MM_TEXT* mode: y values decrease as you move down. Thus, a 2-inch-by-2-inch square is drawn in logical coordinates this way:

```
pDC->Rectangle(CRect(0, 0, 200, -200));
```

Looks easy, doesn't it? Well, it isn't, because you can't work only in logical coordinates. Your program is always switching between device coordinates and logical coordinates, and you need to know when to convert between them. This chapter gives you a few rules that could make your programming life easier. First you need to know what mapping modes Windows gives you.

The *MM_TEXT* Mapping Mode

At first glance, *MM_TEXT* appears to be no mapping mode at all, but rather another name for device coordinates. Almost. In *MM_TEXT*, coordinates map to pixels, values of x increase as you move right, and values of y increase as you move down, but you're allowed to change the origin through calls to the *CDC* function *SetViewportOrg*. Here's some code that sets the origin to (*100, 100*) and draws a 200-pixel-by-200-pixel square. (An illustration of the output is shown in Figure 5-1.) Now the logical point (*0, 0*) maps to the device point (*100, 100*).

```
void CMyView::OnDraw(CDC* pDC)
{
    pDC->SetMapMode(MM_TEXT);
    pDC->SetViewportOrg(CPoint(100, 100));
    pDC->Rectangle(CRect(0, 0, 200, 200));
}
```

The "Fixed Scale" Mapping Modes

One important group of Windows mapping modes provides fixed scaling. With these mapping modes, you can change the viewport origin, but you cannot change the scale factor. You've already seen that, in the *MM_LOENGLISH* mapping mode, x values increase as you move right, and y values decrease as you move down. All fixed mapping modes follow this convention, and you can't change it. The only difference among the fixed mapping modes is the actual scale factor, listed in the table on the next page.

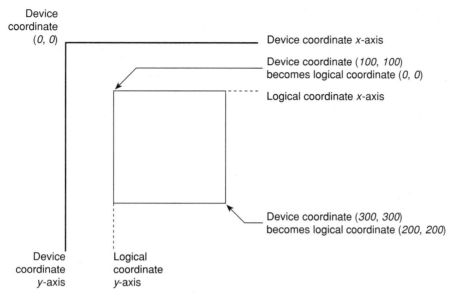

Figure 5-1.
A square drawn after the origin has been moved to (100, 100).

Mapping Mode	Logical Unit
MM_LOENGLISH	0.01 inch
MM_HIENGLISH	0.001 inch
MM_LOMETRIC	0.1 mm
MM_HIMETRIC	0.01 mm
MM_TWIPS	$\frac{1}{1440}$ inch

The last mapping mode, *MM_TWIPS*, is most often used with printers. One "twip" unit is $\frac{1}{20}$ point. (A point is a type measurement unit that is approximately $\frac{1}{72}$ inch.) If the mapping mode is *MM_TWIPS*, and you want, for example, 12-point type, set the character height to 12 × 20, or 240 twips.

The "Variable Scale" Mapping Modes

Windows provides two mapping modes, *MM_ISOTROPIC* and *MM_ANISOTROPIC*, that allow you to change the scale factor as well as the origin. With these mapping modes, your drawing can change size as the user changes the size of the window. Also, if you invert the scale of one axis, you can "flip" an image about the other axis, and you can define your own arbitrary fixed scale factors.

With the *MM_ISOTROPIC* mode, a 1:1 aspect ratio is always preserved. In other words, a circle is always a circle as the scale factor changes. With the *MM_AN-ISOTROPIC* mode, the x and y scale factors can change independently. Circles can be squished into ellipses.

Here's an *OnDraw* function that draws an ellipse that fits exactly in its window:

```
void CMyView::OnDraw(CDC* pDC)
{
    CRect clientRect;

    GetClientRect(clientRect);
    pDC->SetMapMode(MM_ANISOTROPIC);
    pDC->SetWindowExt(1000, 1000);
    pDC->SetViewportExt(clientRect.right, -clientRect.bottom);
    pDC-SetViewportOrg(clientRect.right / 2, clientRect.bottom / 2);

    pDC->Ellipse(CRect(-500, -500, 500, 500));
}
```

What's going on here? The functions *SetWindowExt* and *SetViewportExt* work together to set the scale, based on the window's current client rectangle returned by the *GetClientRect* function. The resulting window size is exactly 1000 by 1000 logical units. The *SetViewportOrg* function sets the origin to the center of the window. Thus, a centered ellipse with a radius of 500 logical units fills the window exactly as illustrated in Figure 5-2.

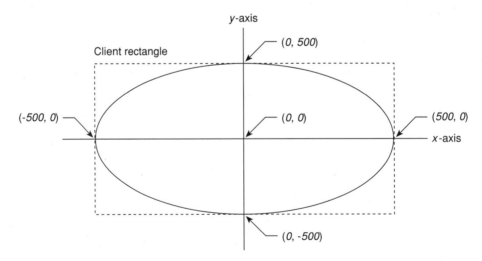

Figure 5-2.
A centered ellipse drawn in the MM_ANISOTROPIC *mapping mode.*

Here are the formulas for converting logical units to device units:

x scale factor = x viewport extent / x window extent

y scale factor = y viewport extent / y window extent

device x = logical $x \times x$ scale factor + x origin offset

device y = logical $y \times y$ scale factor + y origin offset

Suppose the window is 448 pixels wide (*clientRect.right*). The right edge of the ellipse's client rectangle is 500 logical units from the origin. The x scale factor is 448 / 1000, and the x origin offset is 448 / 2 device units. If you use the formulas above, the right edge of the ellipse's client rectangle comes out to 448 device units, the right edge of the window. The x scale factor is expressed as a ratio (viewport extent / window extent) because Windows device coordinates are integers, not floating-point values. The extent values are meaningless by themselves.

If you substitute *MM_ISOTROPIC* for *MM_ANISOTROPIC* in the example above, the "ellipse" is always a circle, as shown in Figure 5-3. It expands to fit the smallest dimension of the window rectangle.

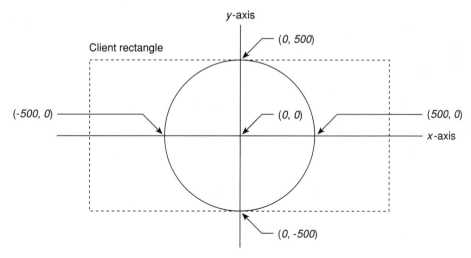

Figure 5-3.
A centered ellipse drawn in the MM_ISOTROPIC *mapping mode.*

Coordinate Conversion

Once you set the mapping mode (plus the origin and scale) of a device context, you can use logical coordinate parameters for most (but not all) *CDC* member functions. If you get the mouse cursor coordinates from a WM_MOUSEMOVE message, for example, you're dealing with device coordinates. Many other class library functions, particularly the member functions of class *CRect*, work only with device coordinates.

Furthermore, you're likely to need a third set of coordinates that we'll call "physical coordinates." Why another set? Suppose you're using the *MM_LOENGLISH* mapping mode in which a logical unit is 0.01 inch, but an inch on the screen represents a foot (12 inches) in the real world. Now suppose the user works in inches and decimal fractions. A user measurement of 26.75 inches translates into 223 logical units, which must be ultimately translated to device coordinates. You'll want to store the physical coordinates as either floating-point numbers or scaled long integers to avoid rounding-off errors.

For the physical-to-logical translation, you're on your own, but the Windows GDI takes care of the logical-to-device translation for you. The *CDC* functions *LPtoDP* and *DPtoLP* translate between the two systems, assuming the device context mapping mode and associated parameters have already been set. Your job is to decide when to use each system. Here are a few rules of thumb:

■ Assume *CDC* member functions take logical coordinate parameters. Notable exceptions are the region-related functions.

■ Assume *CWnd* member functions take device coordinate parameters.

■ Do all hit-test operations in device coordinates. Regions are always device coordinate–oriented, and functions such as the *CRect PtInRect* function work only with non-negative coordinates. Windows, not the class library, imposes this last restriction.

■ Store long-term values in logical or physical coordinates. If you store a point in device coordinates and the user scrolls a window, that point is no longer valid.

Suppose you need to know whether the mouse cursor is inside a rectangle when the user presses the left mouse button. Here is the code:

```
// m_rect is CRect data member of CMyView in MM_LOENGLISH
//   logical coordinates

void CMyView::OnLButtonDown(UINT nFlags, CPoint point)
{
    CRect rect = m_rect; // rect is a temporary copy of m_rect;

    CClientDC dc(this);
    dc.SetMapMode(MM_LOENGLISH);
    dc.LPtoDP(rect);      // rect is now in device coordinates
    if (rect.PtInRect(point)) {
        TRACE("mouse cursor is inside the rectangle\n");
    }
}
```

Notice the use of the *TRACE* macro (discussed in Chapter 3).

> **Note:** *As you get further into application framework programming, you'll see that it's better to set the mapping mode in the virtual* CView *function* OnPrepareDC *instead of in the* OnDraw *function.*

Fonts

Old-fashioned character-mode applications could display only the boring system font on the screen. Windows provides multiple, device-independent fonts in variable sizes. The effective use of these Windows fonts can significantly energize an application with minimum programming effort. The new Windows version 3.1 TrueType fonts are even more effective and easier to program than the previous device-dependent fonts. You'll see several example programs that use fonts later in this chapter.

Fonts Are GDI Objects

Fonts are an integral part of the Windows GDI. This means that fonts behave in the same way as other GDI objects. They can be scaled and clipped, and they can be selected into a device context as a pen or a brush can be selected. All GDI rules about deselection and deletion apply to fonts.

Choosing a Font

Choosing a Windows font used to be like going to a fruit stand and asking for "a piece of reddish-yellow fruit, with a stone inside, that weighs about 4 ounces." You might have gotten a peach or a plum or even a nectarine, and you could be sure that it wouldn't have weighed exactly 4 ounces. Once you took possession of the fruit, you could weigh it and check the fruit type. Now, with TrueType, you can specify the fruit type, but you still can't specify the exact weight.

Today you can choose between two font types—TrueType device-independent fonts and device-dependent fonts such as the Windows display System font and the LaserJet LinePrinter font—or you can specify a font category and size and let Windows select the font for you. If you let Windows select the font, it will choose a TrueType font if possible. The class library provides a font selection dialog box tied to the currently selected printer, so there's little need for printer font guesswork. You let the user select the exact font and size for the printer, and then you approximate the display the best you can.

Printing with Fonts

For text-intensive applications, you'll probably want to specify printer font sizes in points. (1 point = $\frac{1}{72}$ inch.) Why? Most, if not all, built-in printer fonts are defined in terms of points. The LaserJet LinePrinter font, for example, comes in one size, 8.5 points. You can specify TrueType fonts in any point size. If you work in points, you need a mapping mode that easily accommodates points. That's what *MM_TWIPS* is for. An 8.5-point font is 8.5 × 20, or 170, twips, and that's the character height you'll want to specify.

Displaying Fonts

If you're not worried about the display matching the printed output, you have a lot of flexibility. You can choose any of the scalable Windows TrueType fonts, or you can choose the fixed-size system fonts (stock objects). With the TrueType fonts, it doesn't much matter what mapping mode you use; simply choose a font height and go for it. No need to worry about points.

Matching printer fonts to make printed output match the screen presents some problems, but TrueType makes it easier than it was before. Even if you're printing with TrueType fonts, however, you'll never quite get the display to match the printer output. Why? Characters are ultimately displayed in pixels, and the width of a string of characters is equal to the sum of the pixel widths of its characters, possibly adjusted for kerning. The pixel width of the characters depends on the font, the mapping mode, and the resolution of the output device. Only if both the printer and the display were set to *MM_TEXT* mode (1 pixel or dot = 1 logic unit) would you get an exact correspondence. If you're using the *CDC GetTextExtent* function to calculate line breaks, the screen break point will occasionally be different from the printer break point.

(Note: In the class library Print Preview mode, which we'll examine closely in Chapter 18, the line breaks occur exactly as they do on the printer, but the print quality suffers in the process.)

If you're matching a printer-specific font on the screen, TrueType again makes the job easier. Windows substitutes the closest matching TrueType font. For the 8.5-point LinePrinter font, Windows comes pretty close with its Courier New font.

Points in a Window—Logical Twips

If you use twips units (1/20 point, 1/1440 inch) for printing, the obvious thing to do is set the window device context mapping mode to *MM_TWIPS*. Doing so is undesirable, however, because 10-point type that looks fine on paper is too small to read when transferred inch for inch to a VGA screen. If, instead, you use what Charles Petzold (in *Programming Windows 3.1*) calls the "logical twips" mapping mode, things work better.

The following statements set the mapping mode to logical twips.

```
pDC->SetMapMode(MM_ANISOTROPIC);
pDC->SetWindowExt(1440, 1440);
pDC->SetViewportExt(pDC->GetDeviceCaps(LOGPIXELSX),
                    -pDC->GetDeviceCaps(LOGPIXELSY));
```

Don't worry too much about the theory behind this mapping mode. Simply remember that, if you use logical twips on the display, 12-point type (with a character height of 240 twips) will look the same as it does in Visual Workbench and other Windows-based programs. The minus sign on the second *SetViewportExt* parameter ensures that *y* values decrease as you move down, as in the *MM_TWIPS* mode.

Computing Character Height

Five font height measurement parameters are available through the *CDC* function *GetTextMetrics*, but only three are significant. The *tmHeight* parameter represents the full height of the font, including descenders (for the characters g, j, p, q, and y) and any diacritics that appear over capital letters. The *tmExternalLeading* parameter is the distance between the top of the diacritic and the bottom of the descender from the line above. The sum of *tmHeight* and *tmExternalLeading* is the total character height. The value of *tmExternalLeading* is often 0.

You would think that *tmHeight* would represent the font size in points. Wrong! Another *GetTextMetrics* parameter, *tmInternalLeading*, comes into play. The point size corresponds to the difference between *tmHeight* and *tmInternalLeading*. With the *MM_TWIPS* mapping mode in effect, a selected 12-point font might have a *tmHeight* value of 295 logical units and a *tmInternalLeading* value of 55. The font's net height of 240 corresponds to the point size of 12. Figure 5-4 shows the important font measurements.

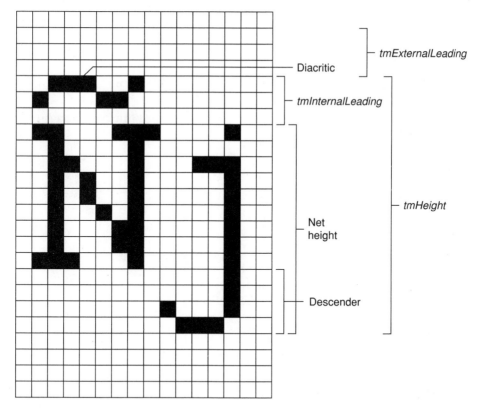

Figure 5-4.
Font height measurements.

The EX05A Program

This example sets up a view window with the logical twips mapping mode. A text string is displayed in 10 point sizes with the Arial TrueType font. Here are the steps to create the application:

1. **Run AppWizard to generate a project called EX05A.** Choose AppWizard from Visual Workbench's Project menu. The options and the default class names are shown here:

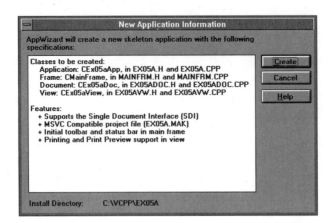

    Notice that this time we're accepting the default Printing And Print Preview option.

2. **Add function prototypes in file EX05AVW.H.** *ShowFont* is a new private member function in the *CEx05aView* class. *OnPrepareDC* is an override of a *CView* base class function. The class declaration needs prototypes for both.

```
private:
    void ShowFont(CDC* pDC, int& nPos, int nPoints);
protected:
    void OnPrepareDC(CDC* pDC, CPrintInfo* pInfo = NULL);
```

3. **Add the *OnPrepareDC* and *ShowFont* functions in file EX05AVW.CPP.** These are new functions. You've already added the prototypes in the class header.

```
void CEx05aView::OnPrepareDC(CDC* pDC, CPrintInfo* pInfo /* = NULL */)
{
    pDC->SetMapMode(MM_ANISOTROPIC);
    pDC->SetWindowExt(1440, 1440);
    pDC->SetViewportExt(pDC->GetDeviceCaps(LOGPIXELSX),
                        -pDC->GetDeviceCaps(LOGPIXELSY));
}
```

```
void CEx05aView::ShowFont(CDC* pDC, int& nPos, int nPoints)
{
    TEXTMETRIC  tm;
    CFont       testFont;
    char        text[100];
    CSize       tExtent;

    testFont.CreateFont(-nPoints * 20, 0, 0, 0, 400, FALSE, FALSE, 0,
                        ANSI_CHARSET, OUT_DEFAULT_PRECIS,
                        CLIP_DEFAULT_PRECIS, DEFAULT_QUALITY,
                        DEFAULT_PITCH | FF_SWISS, "Arial");
    CFont* pOldFont = (CFont*) pDC->SelectObject(&testFont);
    pDC->GetTextMetrics(&tm);
    TRACE("points = %d, tmHeight = %d, tmInternalLeading = %d,"
        " tmExternalLeading = %d\n", nPoints, tm.tmHeight,
        tm.tmInternalLeading, tm.tmExternalLeading);
    wsprintf(text, "This is %d-point Arial", nPoints);
    tExtent = pDC->GetTextExtent(text, strlen(text));
    TRACE("String width = %d, string height = %d\n", tExtent.cx,
        tExtent.cy);
    pDC->TextOut(0, nPos, text);
    pDC->SelectObject(pOldFont);
    nPos -= tm.tmHeight + tm.tmExternalLeading;
}
```

4. **Edit the *OnDraw* function in EX05AVW.CPP.** AppWizard always generates a
   skeleton *OnDraw* function for your view class. Find the function and edit the
   code as follows:

```
void CEx05aView::OnDraw(CDC* pDC)
{
    int nPosition = 0;

    for (int i = 6; i <= 24; i += 2) {
        ShowFont(pDC, nPosition, i);
    }
}
```

5. **Build and run the EX05A program.** In Visual Workbench, choose Build from
   the Project menu, and then choose Execute. The resulting output looks like
   this on a standard VGA card:

Notice that the output string sizes don't quite correspond to the point sizes. This discrepancy results from the font engine's conversion of logical units to pixels. The program's trace output, partially shown below, shows the display of font metrics (the numbers depending on your display driver and your video driver):

```
points = 6, tmHeight = 134, tmInternalLeading = 14, tmExternalLeading = 5
string width = 1032, string height = 134
points = 8, tmHeight = 182, tmInternalLeading = 24, tmExternalLeading = 5
string width = 1325, string height = 182
points = 10, tmHeight = 226, tmInternalLeading = 24, tmExternalLeading = 5
string width = 1829, string height = 226
points = 12, tmHeight = 274, tmInternalLeading = 34, tmExternalLeading = 10
string width = 2208, string height = 274
```

Try Print Preview. Notice, as shown below, that the printer font metrics are different from the display font metrics, particularly the value of *tmInternalLeading*:

```
points = 6, tmHeight = 150, tmInternalLeading = 30, tmExternalLeading = 0
string width = 1065, string height = 150
points = 8, tmHeight = 210, tmInternalLeading = 45, tmExternalLeading = 0
string width = 1380, string height = 210
points = 10, tmHeight = 240, tmInternalLeading = 45, tmExternalLeading = 0
string width = 1770, string height = 240
points = 12, tmHeight = 270, tmInternalLeading = 30, tmExternalLeading = 15
string width = 2130, string height = 270
```

No attempt was made here to set a print scale factor different from the display scale factor. In Chapter 18, you'll learn how to control the print scale factor separately.

The EX05A Program Elements

Mapping mode set in the *OnPrepareDC* function

The application framework calls *OnPrepareDC* prior to calling *OnDraw*, so the *OnPrepareDC* function is the logical place to prepare the device context. If you had other message handlers that needed the correct mapping mode, those functions would have contained calls to *OnPrepareDC*.

The *ShowFont* private member function

ShowFont contains code that is executed 10 times in a loop. With C, you would have made this a global function, but with C++ it's better to make it a private class member function.

This function creates the font, selects it into the device context, prints a string to the window, and then deselects and deletes the font. If you choose to include debug information in the program, *ShowFont* also displays useful font metrics information, including the actual width of the string.

The call to *CFont::CreateFont*

This call includes lots of parameters, but the important ones are the first two—the font height and width. A width value of 0 means that the aspect ratio of the selected font will be set to a value specified by the font designer. If you put a nonzero value here, as you'll see in the next example, you can change the font's aspect ratio.

> **Tip:** *If you want your font to be a specific point size, the* CreateFont *font height parameter (the first parameter) must be __negative__. If you're using the* MM_TWIPS *mapping mode, for example, a height parameter of −240 ensures a 12-point font with* tmHeight − tmInternalLeading = 240. *A +240 height parameter gives you a smaller font with* tmHeight = 240.

The last *CreateFont* parameter specifies the font name, in this case the Arial True-Type font. If you had used *NULL* for this parameter, the *FF_SWISS* specification (which indicates a proportional font without serifs) would have caused Windows to choose the "best matching" font, which, depending on the specified size, might have been the System font or the Arial TrueType font. The font name takes precedence. If you had specified *FF_ROMAN* (which indicates a proportional font with serifs) with Arial, you would have gotten Arial.

The EX05B Program

This program is similar to EX05A except that it shows multiple fonts. The mapping mode is *MM_ANISOTROPIC,* but this time the scale depends on the window size. The characters change size along with the window. This program effectively shows off some TrueType fonts and contrasts them with the old-style fonts. Here are the steps to create the application:

1. **Run AppWizard to generate a project called EX05B.** Choose AppWizard from Visual Workbench's project menu. The options and the default class names are shown here:

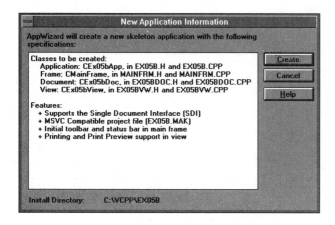

Notice that again we're accepting the default Printing And Print Preview option.

2. **Add function prototypes in file EX05BVW.H.** *TraceMetrics* is a new private member function in the *CEx05bView* class. *OnPrepareDC* is an override of a *CView* base class function. The class declaration needs prototypes for both.

```
private:
    void TraceMetrics(CDC* pDC);
protected:
    void OnPrepareDC(CDC* pDC, CPrintInfo* pInfo = NULL);
```

3. **Add the *OnPrepareDC* and *TraceMetrics* functions in EX05BVW.CPP.**

```
void CEx05bView::OnPrepareDC(CDC* pDC, CPrintInfo* pInfo /* = NULL */)
{ // called by the application framework prior to OnDraw
    CRect clientRect;

    GetClientRect(&clientRect);
    pDC->SetMapMode(MM_ANISOTROPIC);
    pDC->SetWindowExt(400, 400);
    pDC->SetViewportExt(clientRect.right, clientRect.bottom);
    // +y = down
    pDC->SetViewportOrg(0, 0);
}


void CEx05bView::TraceMetrics(CDC* pDC)
{
    TEXTMETRIC tm;
    char szFaceName[100];

    pDC->GetTextMetrics(&tm);
    pDC->GetTextFace(99, szFaceName);
    TRACE("font = %s, tmHeight = %d, tmInternalLeading = %d,"
          " tmExternalLeading = %d\n", szFaceName, tm.tmHeight,
          tm.tmInternalLeading, tm.tmExternalLeading);
}
```

4. **Edit the *OnDraw* function in EX05BVW.CPP.** AppWizard always generates a skeleton *OnDraw* function for your view class. Find the function and edit the code as follows:

```
void CEx05bView::OnDraw(CDC* pDC)
{
    CFont testFont1, testFont2, testFont3, testFont4;

    testFont1.CreateFont(50, 0, 0, 0, 400, FALSE, FALSE, 0,
                         ANSI_CHARSET, OUT_DEFAULT_PRECIS,
                         CLIP_DEFAULT_PRECIS, DEFAULT_QUALITY,
                         DEFAULT_PITCH | FF_SWISS, "Arial");
    CFont* pOldFont = (CFont*) pDC-SelectObject(&testFont1);
```

```
TraceMetrics(pDC);
pDC->TextOut(0, 0, "This is Arial, default width");

testFont2.CreateFont(50, 0, 0, 0, 400, FALSE, FALSE, 0,
                     ANSI_CHARSET, OUT_DEFAULT_PRECIS,
                     CLIP_DEFAULT_PRECIS, DEFAULT_QUALITY,
                     DEFAULT_PITCH | FF_MODERN, "Courier");
pDC->SelectObject(&testFont2);
TraceMetrics(pDC);
pDC->TextOut(0, 100, "This is Courier, default width");

testFont3.CreateFont(50, 10, 0, 0, 400, FALSE, FALSE, 0,
                     ANSI_CHARSET, OUT_DEFAULT_PRECIS,
                     CLIP_DEFAULT_PRECIS, DEFAULT_QUALITY,
                     DEFAULT_PITCH | FF_ROMAN, NULL);
pDC->SelectObject(&testFont3);
TraceMetrics(pDC);
pDC->TextOut(0, 200, "This is generic Roman, variable width");

testFont4.CreateFont(50, 0, 0, 0, 400, FALSE, FALSE, 0,
                     ANSI_CHARSET, OUT_DEFAULT_PRECIS,
                     CLIP_DEFAULT_PRECIS, DEFAULT_QUALITY,
                     DEFAULT_PITCH | FF_MODERN, "LinePrinter");
pDC->SelectObject(&testFont4);
TraceMetrics(pDC);
pDC->TextOut(0, 300, "This is LinePrinter, default width");

pDC->SelectObject(pOldFont);
}
```

The *OnDraw* function displays character strings in four fonts as follows:

☐ testFont1—The TrueType font Arial with default width selection.

☐ testFont2—The old-style font Courier with default width selection. Notice how jagged the font is in larger sizes.

☐ testFont3—The generic Roman font for which Windows supplies the TrueType font Times New Roman with programmed width selection. The width is tied to the horizontal window scale, so the font stretches to fit the window.

☐ testFont4—The LinePrinter font is specified, but because this is not a Windows font for the display, the font engine falls back on the *FF_-MODERN* specification and chooses the TrueType Courier New font.

5. **Build and run the EX05B program.** In Visual Workbench, choose Build from the Project menu, and then choose Execute. The program output is shown on the next page:

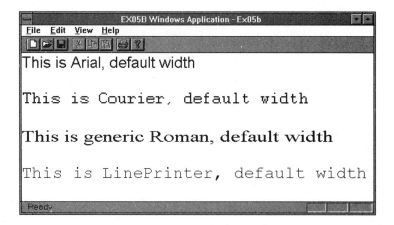

Resize the window to make it smaller, and watch the font sizes change. Compare this screen with the previous one:

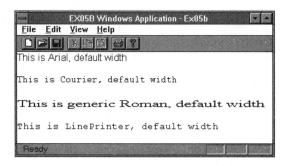

If you continue to downsize the window, notice how the Courier font stops shrinking after a certain size, and notice how the Roman font width changes.

Now choose Print Preview from the File menu. The output, as shown in Figure 5-5, is very different from the window display output because the Courier and LinePrinter

Figure 5-5.
The EX05B Print Preview output.

fonts are not TrueType fonts. The Windows Courier font maps to one of the printer's built-in fixed-size Courier fonts, and the printer's LinePrinter font is available only in 8.5 points. In Chapter 18, you'll learn more about scaling your printer output.

The EX05C Example—*CScrollView* Revisited

You saw the *CScrollView* class in Chapter 4 (in EX04C), but you couldn't do much with it because you hadn't learned about mapping modes. Even with the *MM_TEXT* mode, you could not have done mouse hit-testing because the *CScrollView* class changes the origin behind your back. Now we'll revisit the scrolling view in another example that's an amalgam of programs EX04B and EX04C. The new program allows the user to move a circle with a mouse, but it does so in a scrolling window with the *MM_LOENGLISH* mapping mode. Keyboard scrolling is left out, but you can add it by borrowing the *OnKeyDown* member function from EX04C.

As with EX04C, this example involves a view class derived from *CScrollView*. Here are the steps to create the application:

1. **Run AppWizard to generate a project called EX05C.** Choose AppWizard from Visual Workbench's Project menu. The options and the default class names are shown here:

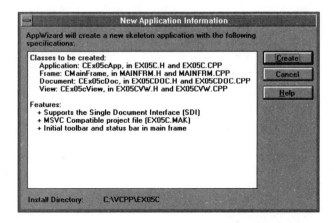

2. **Make global replacements for the *CEx05CView* Class.** Use the Visual Workbench editor in EX05CVW.H and EX05CVW.CPP to replace all occurrences of *CView* with *CScrollView*. Be sure you set the Match Case option in Visual Workbench's Replace dialog box.

3. **Edit the *CEx05cView* class header in file EX05CVW.H.** Add the following lines in the class *CEx05cView* declaration:

```
private:
    CRect  m_ellipseRect;
    CPoint m_mousePos;
    BOOL   m_bCaptured;
```

4. **Use ClassWizard to add four message handlers.** Add the message handlers as follows:

Message	Member Function Name
WM_CREATE	*OnCreate*
WM_LBUTTONDOWN	*OnLButtonDown*
WM_LBUTTONUP	*OnLButtonUp*
WM_MOUSEMOVE	*OnMouseMove*

5. **Edit the *CEx05cView* message handler functions.** ClassWizard generated the skeletons for the functions listed above. Find them in EX05CVW.CPP and code them as follows:

```
int CEx05cView::OnCreate(LPCREATESTRUCT lpCreateStruct)
{
    if (CScrollView::OnCreate(lpCreateStruct) == -1)
        return -1;

    CSize totalSize = CSize(800 * 2, 800 * 2);  // 8 inch by 8 inch
    CSize pageSize = CSize(totalSize.cx / 2, totalSize.cy / 2);
    CSize lineSize = CSize(totalSize.cx / 100, totalSize.cy / 100);
    SetScrollSizes(MM_LOENGLISH, totalSize, pageSize, lineSize);

    return 0;
}
void CEx05cView::OnLButtonDown(UINT nFlags, CPoint point)
{
    CRect ellipseRect;
    CRgn  circle;

    ellipseRect = m_ellipseRect;
    CClientDC dc(this);
    OnPrepareDC(&dc);
    dc.LPtoDP(ellipseRect);
    circle.CreateEllipticRgnIndirect(ellipseRect);
    if (circle.PtInRegion(point)) {
        // capturing mouse ensures subsequent LButtonUp message
        SetCapture();
        m_bCaptured = TRUE;
        dc.DPtoLP(&point);
        m_mousePos = point;
        // new mouse cursor is active while mouse is captured
        ::SetCursor(::LoadCursor(NULL, IDC_CROSS));
    }
}
```

```
void CEx05cView::OnLButtonUp(UINT nFlags, CPoint point)
{
    if (m_bCaptured) {
        ReleaseCapture();
        m_bCaptured = FALSE;
    }
}

void CEx05cView::OnMouseMove(UINT nFlags, CPoint point)
{
    CSize  offset;
    CPoint mousePos;
    CRect  ellipseRect, newRect, invalidRect, clientRect, tempRect;

    CClientDC dc(this);
    OnPrepareDC(&dc);
    GetClientRect(clientRect);
    if (m_bCaptured) {
        ellipseRect = m_ellipseRect;
        mousePos = m_mousePos;
        dc.LPtoDP(ellipseRect);
        dc.LPtoDP(&mousePos);
        offset = point - mousePos;
        newRect = ellipseRect + (CPoint(0, 0) + offset);
        tempRect.UnionRect(ellipseRect, newRect);
        invalidRect.IntersectRect(tempRect, clientRect);
        InvalidateRect(invalidRect, TRUE);
        dc.DPtoLP(&point);
        dc.DPtoLP(newRect);
        m_mousePos = point;
        m_ellipseRect = newRect;
    }
}
```

6. **Edit the *CEx05cView* constructor and *OnDraw* function.** AppWizard generated these skeleton functions. Find them in EX05CVW.CPP and code them as follows:

```
CEx05cView::CEx05cView() : m_ellipseRect(0, 0, 100, -100)
{
    m_bCaptured = FALSE;
}

void CEx05cView::OnDraw(CDC* pDC)
{
    pDC->SelectStockObject(GRAY_BRUSH);
    pDC->Ellipse(m_ellipseRect);
}
```

7. **Build and run the EX05C program.** In the Visual Workbench, choose Build from the Project menu, and then choose Execute. The program allows a circle to be dragged with the mouse, and it allows the window to be scrolled.

The EX05C Program Elements

Following is a discussion of the major elements in the EX05C program.

The *CScrollView OnPrepareDC* member function

The *CView* class has a virtual *OnPrepareDC* function that does nothing. The *CScrollView* class implements the function for the purpose of setting up the view's mapping mode, scale factor, and origin, based on the parameters you passed to *SetScrollSizes* in *OnCreate*. The application framework calls *OnPrepareDC* for you prior to calling *OnDraw*, so you don't need to worry about it. You must call *OnPrepareDC* yourself in any other message handler function that uses the view's device context, such as *OnLButtonDown* and *OnMouseMove*.

The *OnMouseMove* coordinate transformation code

As you can see, this function contains quite a few translation statements. The logic can be summarized by the following steps:

1. Convert the previous ellipse rectangle and mouse point (stored in data members) from logical to device coordinates.

2. Update the mouse point and the ellipse rectangle.

3. Generate an invalid rectangle.

4. Convert the ellipse rectangle and mouse point to logical coordinates.

The *CScrollView SetScaleToFitSize* Mode

The *CScrollView* class has a stretch-to-fit mode that displays the entire scrollable area in the view window. The Windows *MM_ANISOTROPIC* mapping mode comes into play, with one restriction: Positive *y* values always increase in the down direction, as in *MM_TEXT* mode.

To use the stretch-to-fit mode, make the following call in your view's *OnCreate* function in place of the call to *SetScrollSizes*:

```
SetScaleToFitSize(totalSize);
```

The example in Chapter 23 makes this call in *OnCreate*, and it also makes it in response to a Shrink To Fit menu item. Thus, the display can toggle between scrolling mode and shrink-to-fit mode.

6

The Modal Dialog

Almost every program for Windows uses a dialog window to interact with the user. The dialog might be a simple OK message box, or it might be a complex data entry form. Calling this powerful element a dialog "box" is an injustice. As you'll see, the dialog is truly a window that receives messages, that can be moved and closed, and that can even accept drawing instructions in its client area.

The two kinds of dialogs are "modal" and "modeless." This chapter explores the commonest type, the modal dialog. You'll be working with a single dialog example that includes most typical dialog "controls" plus a few not-so-typical ones. Chapter 7 introduces the modeless dialog and the special-purpose COMMDLG modal dialogs for opening files, selecting fonts, and so forth.

Modal vs. Modeless Dialogs

The *CDialog* base class supports both modal and modeless dialogs. With a modal dialog, such as the Open File dialog, the user cannot work elsewhere in the application until the dialog is closed. With a modeless dialog, the user can work in another window in the application while the dialog remains on the screen. The Visual Workbench Find dialog is a good example of a modeless dialog; you can edit your program during a global search (once the search is started).

Your choice of a modal or a modeless dialog depends on the application. Modal dialogs are much easier to program, which might influence your decision.

> **FYI:** *The Microsoft Foundation Class Library version 1.0 supported two dialog classes:* CDialog *for modeless dialogs and* CModalDialog *for modal dialogs. The Microsoft Foundation Class Library version 2.0* CDialog *class accommodates both modal and modeless dialogs, but* CModalDialog *still exists as a macro for compatibility. Do not use the* CModalDialog *class in Microsoft Foundation Class Library version 2.0 programs.*

System Modal Dialogs

All modal dialogs restrict the user from working elsewhere in the application that opens the dialog. With an ordinary modal dialog, however, the user can switch to another program. One type of modal dialog, the system modal dialog, absolutely restricts the user to the dialog. The user must close the dialog before continuing with any other Windows task.

Resources and Controls

So now you know a dialog is a window. What makes the dialog different from the *CView* windows you've seen already? For one thing, a dialog window is almost always tied to a Windows resource that identifies the dialog's elements and specifies their layout. Because you can use App Studio to create and edit a dialog resource, you can quickly and efficiently produce dialogs in a visual manner.

A dialog consists of a number of elements called controls. Dialog controls include edit controls (aka text boxes), buttons, list boxes, combo boxes, and static text (aka labels). Windows manages these controls through special grouping and tabbing logic, and that relieves you of a major programming burden. The dialog controls can be referenced either by a *CWnd* pointer (because they themselves are really windows) or by an index number (with an associated *#define* constant) assigned in the resource. Controls can send messages to their dialog in response to user actions such as typing text or clicking a button.

The class library and ClassWizard work together to enhance the dialog logic that Windows provides. With ClassWizard, you can associate dialog class data members with dialog controls, and you can specify editing parameters such as maximum text length and numeric high and low limits. ClassWizard generates calls to the class library data exchange and data validation functions that move information back and forth between the screen and the data members.

Programming a Modal Dialog

Modal dialogs are the most frequently used dialogs. A user action (a menu choice, for example) brings up a dialog on the screen, the user enters data in the dialog, and then the user closes the dialog. Here's a summary of the steps to add a modal dialog to an existing project:

1. Use App Studio to create a dialog resource that contains various controls. App Studio updates the project's resource script (RC) file to include your new dialog resource, and the RESOURCE.H file is updated to include corresponding *#define* constants.

2. Use ClassWizard to create a dialog class that is derived from *CDialog* and attached to the resource created in step 1. ClassWizard adds the associated code and header file to the Visual Workbench project.

3. Use ClassWizard to add data members, exchange functions, and validation functions to the dialog class.

4. Use ClassWizard to add message handlers for the dialog's buttons and special controls.

5. Write the code for special control initialization (in *OnInitDialog*) and for the message handlers. Be sure the *CDialog* virtual member function *OnOK* is called when the user closes the dialog (unless the user cancels the dialog). (Note: *OnOK* is called by default.)

6. Write the code in your view class to activate the dialog. This code consists of a call to your dialog class's constructor followed by a call to the *DoModal* dialog class member function. *DoModal* returns only when the user exits the dialog window.

Now we'll proceed with a real example, one step at a time.

The Dialog That Ate Cincinnati—The EX06A Example

Let's not mess around with wimpy little dialogs. We'll build a monster dialog that contains almost every kind of control. The job will be easy because App Studio is there to help us. The finished product is shown in Figure 6-1.

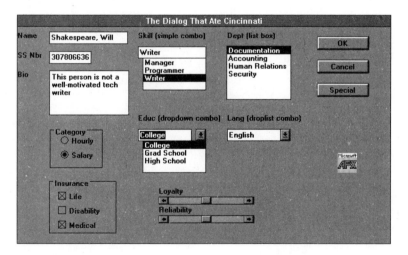

Figure 6-1.
The finished dialog in action.

As you can see, the dialog supports a human resources application. These kinds of business programs are fairly boring, so the challenge is to produce something that could not have been done with 80-column punched cards. The program is brightened a little by the use of scroll bar controls for "loyalty" and "reliability." Here is a classic example of direct action and visual representation of data! Visual Basic controls could add more interest, but they aren't covered until Chapter 8.

Here are the steps for building the dialog resource:

1. **Run AppWizard to generate a project called EX06A.** Choose AppWizard from Visual Workbench's Project menu. The options and the default class names are shown here:

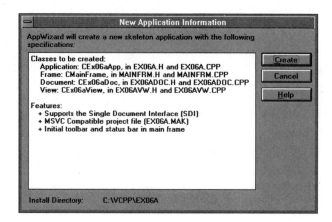

As usual, AppWizard sets the new project to be the Visual Workbench current project.

2. **From the Visual Workbench, open the file EX06A.RC.** Choose App Studio from Visual Workbench's Tools menu. This starts App Studio with the EX06A resource file that AppWizard generated.

3. **Create a new dialog with ID *IDD_DIALOG1*.** Click the New button in the EX06A.RC (MFC Resource Script) window. The New Resource dialog appears. Click on Dialog, and then click on OK. App Studio creates a new dialog resource, as shown here:

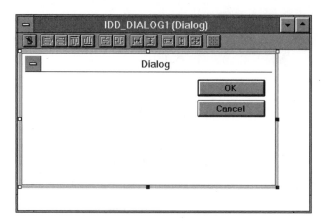

App Studio assigns the resource ID *IDD_DIALOG1* to the new dialog. Change the resource ID to *IDR_DIALOG1*. Notice that App Studio inserts OK and Cancel buttons for the new dialog.

4. **Size the dialog and assign a caption.** When you double-click on the new dialog, or if you choose Show Properties from App Studio's Window menu, the Dialog Properties dialog appears. Type the caption for the new dialog as shown in the following screen. The state of the pushpin button determines whether the Dialog Properties dialog stays on top of other windows. (When the pushpin is "pushed," the dialog stays on top of other windows.) Click the Snap To Grid button to reveal the grid and to help align controls.

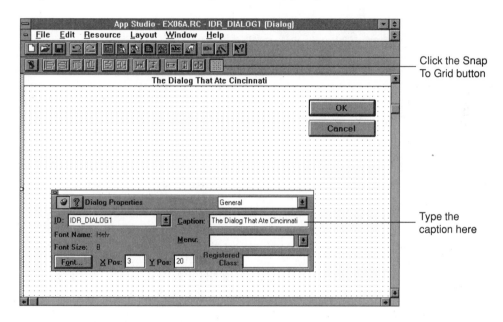

5. **Set the dialog style.** Choose Styles from the drop-down list box at the top right of the Dialog Properties dialog, and then set the style properties as shown here:

99

6. **Add the dialog's controls.** Use the control palette to add each control. Drag controls from the control palette to the new dialog with the mouse, and then position and size the controls, as shown in Figure 6-1 on page 97. (You don't have to be precise when positioning the controls.) Here are the control palette's controls:

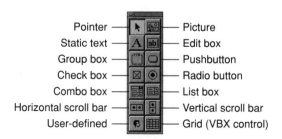

Pointer	Picture
Static text	Edit box
Group box	Pushbutton
Check box	Radio button
Combo box	List box
Horizontal scroll bar	Vertical scroll bar
User-defined	Grid (VBX control)

Note: *App Studio displays the position and size of each control in the status bar. The position units are special "dialog units," or DLUs, <u>not</u> device units. A horizontal DLU is the average width of the dialog font divided by 4. A vertical DLU is the average height of the font divided by 8. The dialog font is normally 8-point MS Sans Serif.*

Here's a brief description of the dialog's controls.

□ **The static text control for the Name field.** A static text control simply paints characters on the screen. No user interaction occurs at runtime. You can type the text after you position the bounding rectangle, and you can resize the rectangle as needed. This is the only static text control you'll see listed in text, but you should also create the other static text controls as shown in Figure 6-1. Follow the same procedure for the other static text controls in the dialog. All static text controls have the same ID, but that doesn't matter because the program doesn't need to access any of them.

□ **The Name edit control.** An edit control is the primary means of entering text in a dialog. Change this control's ID from *IDC_EDIT1* to *IDC_NAME*. Accept the defaults for the rest of the properties. Notice that

Aligning Controls

To align two or more controls, select the controls by clicking on the first control and Shift-clicking on the other controls you want aligned. Next choose one of the alignment commands (Left, Right, Top, or Bottom) from the Align Controls pop-up menu on the Layout menu.

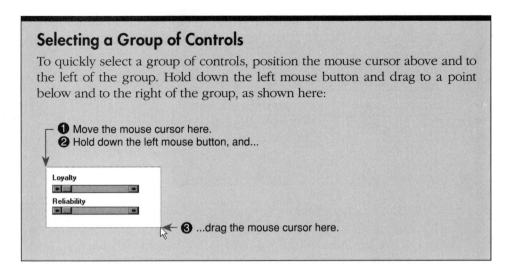

Selecting a Group of Controls

To quickly select a group of controls, position the mouse cursor above and to the left of the group. Hold down the left mouse button and drag to a point below and to the right of the group, as shown here:

the default sets Auto HScroll, which means that the text scrolls horizontally when the box is filled.

☐ **The SSN (social security number) edit control.** As far as App Studio is concerned, this control is exactly the same as the Name edit control. Simply change its ID to *IDC_SSN*. Later you will use ClassWizard to make this a numeric field.

☐ **The Biography edit control.** This is a multiline edit control. Change its ID to *IDC_BIO*, and then set its properties as shown here:

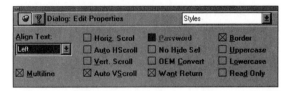

☐ **The Category group box.** This control serves only to group two radio buttons visually. Type in the caption *Category*. The default ID is sufficient.

☐ **The Hourly and Salary radio buttons.** Position these radio buttons inside the Category group box. Set the Hourly button's ID to *IDC_CAT*, and set the other properties as shown at the top of the next page:

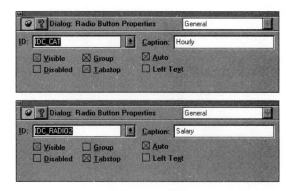

Be sure that both buttons have the Auto property set (the default) and that only the Hourly button has the Group property set. When these properties are set correctly, Windows ensures that only one of the two buttons can be selected at a time. The Category group box has no effect on the buttons' operation.

☐ **The Insurance group box.** This control holds three check boxes. Type in the caption *Insurance.*

☐ **The Life, Disability, and Medical check boxes.** Place these controls inside the Insurance group box. Accept the default properties, but change the IDs to *IDC_LIFE, IDC_DIS,* and *IDC_MED.* Unlike radio buttons, check boxes are independent; the user can set any combination.

   Note: *You must also set the Group property for the control that follows the radio button group, in this case the Life check box.*

☐ **The Skill combo box.** This is the first of three types of combo boxes. Change the ID to *IDC_SKILL;* otherwise, accept all the defaults. Add three skills (terminating each line with Ctrl-Enter) in the Enter List Choices box, as shown here:

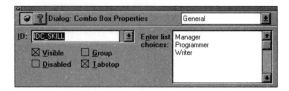

This is a combo box of type Simple. The user can type anything in the top edit control, use the mouse to select an item from the attached list box, or use the Up or Down direction key to select an item from the attached list box.

□ **The Education combo box.** Change the ID to *IDC_EDUC*, and then set the Type option to Dropdown. Add three education levels in the Enter List Choices box, as shown in Figure 6-1 on page 97. With this combo box, the user can type anything in the edit box, click on the arrow and then select an item from the drop-down list box, or use the Up or Down direction key to select an item from the attached list box.

Note: *To set the size for the drop-down portion of a combo box, first click on the box's arrow, and then pull down from the bottom center of the rectangle.*

□ **The Department list box.** Change the ID to *IDC_DEPT*; otherwise, accept all the defaults. In this list box, the user can select only a single item by using the mouse, by using the Up or Down direction key, or by typing the first character of a selection.

□ **The Language combo box.** Change the ID to *IDC_LANG*, and then set the Type option to Drop List. Add three languages (English, French, and Spanish) to the Enter List Choices box. With this combo box, the user can select only from the attached list box. To select, the user can click on the arrow and then choose an entry from the drop-down list, or the user can type the first letter of the selection and then refine the selection with the Up or Down direction key.

□ **The Loyalty and Reliability scroll bars.** Do not confuse scroll bar controls with a window's built-in scroll bars as seen in scrolling views. A scroll bar control behaves in the same manner as do other controls and can be resized at design time. Position and size the horizontal scroll bar controls as shown in Figure 6-1, and then assign the IDs *IDC_LOYAL* and *IDC_RELY*.

□ **The OK, Cancel, and Special pushbuttons.** Type the button captions *OK*, *Cancel*, and *Special*, and then assign the *IDC_SPECIAL* ID to the Special button. Later you'll learn about special meanings that are associated with the default *IDOK* and *IDCANCEL* IDs.

□ **Any icon. (The AFX icon is shown as an example.)** You can display any icon in a dialog, as long as the resource script defines the icon. We'll use the program's AFX icon, identified as *IDR_MAINFRAME*. Set the Type option to Icon, and set the icon to *IDR_MAINFRAME*. Leave the ID as *IDC_STATIC*.

7. **Check the dialog's tabbing order.** Choose Set Tab Order from the App Studio Layout menu. Use the mouse to set the tabbing order, as shown at the top of the next page:

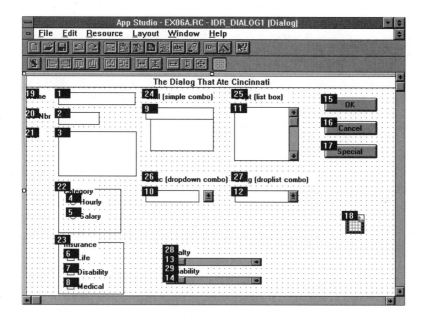

Click on each control in the order shown and then press Enter.

8. **Save the resource file on disk.** Choose Save from the File menu or click the Save button on the toolbar to save EX06A.RC. Keep App Studio running, and keep the newly built dialog on the screen.

ClassWizard and the Dialog Class

You have now built a dialog resource, but you can't use it without a corresponding dialog class. (The section titled "Understanding the EX06A Application" later in this chapter explains the relationship between the dialog window and the underlying classes.) The ClassWizard DLL works in conjunction with App Studio to create that class as follows:

1. **Choose ClassWizard from the App Studio Resource menu.** Be sure that you still have the newly built dialog, *IDR_DIALOG1*, selected in App Studio and that \VCPP\EX06A\EX06A is the current Visual Workbench project.

2. **Add the *CEx06aDialog* class.** Fill in the Add Class dialog, as shown here:

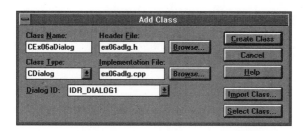

Be sure to enter the information exactly as shown; some of this information is case-sensitive.

Because your newly built dialog was selected in App Studio, ClassWizard knew enough to choose *CDialog* as the base class for *CEx06aDialog* and to make *IDR_DIALOG1* the corresponding resource. Click the Create Class button.

3. **Add the *CEx06aDialog* variables.** After ClassWizard creates the *CEx06a-Dialog* class, the ClassWizard dialog appears. Click the Edit Variables button, and the Edit Member Variables dialog appears, as shown here:

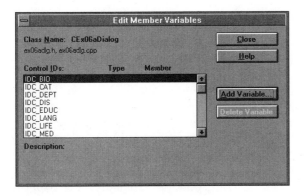

You need to associate data members with each of the dialog's controls. To associate a data member with one of the dialog's controls, click on a control ID and then click the Add Variable button. The Add Member Variable dialog appears, as shown here:

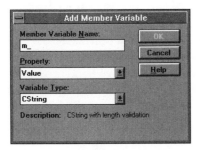

Type in the member variable name and choose the variable type according to the following table. Be sure to type the member variable name exactly as shown; the case of each letter is important. Click OK to return to the Edit Member Variables dialog. Repeat this process for each of the listed controls.

Control ID	Data Member	Type
IDC_BIO	m_bio	CString
IDC_CAT	m_nCat	int
IDC_DEPT	m_dept	CString
IDC_DIS	m_bInsDis	BOOL
IDC_EDUC	m_educ	CString
IDC_LANG	m_lang	CString
IDC_LIFE	m_bInsLife	BOOL
IDC_MED	m_bInsMed	BOOL
IDC_NAME	m_name	CString
IDC_SKILL	m_skill	CString
IDC_SSN	m_lSsn	long

As you select controls in the Edit Member Variables dialog, various edit boxes appear at the bottom of the dialog. If you select a *CString* variable, you can set its maximum number of characters; if you select a numeric variable, you can set its high and low limits. Set the minimum value for *IDC_SSN* to *0* and the maximum value to *999999999*.

Most relationships between control types and variable types are obvious. The way in which radio buttons correspond to variables is not so intuitive, however. The *CDialog* class associates an integer variable with each radio button group, with the first button corresponding to value 0, the second to 1, and so forth. Click the Close button in the Edit Member Variables dialog when you're finished.

4. **Add the message-handling function for the Special button.** *CEx06aDialog* doesn't need many message-handling functions because the *CDialog* base class, with the help of Windows, does most of the dialog management. When you specify the *IDOK* ID for the OK button (ClassWizard's default), for example, the virtual *CDialog* function *OnOK* gets called when the user clicks the button. For other buttons, however, you need message handlers.

The ClassWizard dialog should contain an entry for *IDC_SPECIAL* in the Object IDs list box. Click on this entry, and double-click on the BN_CLICKED message that appears in the Messages list box. ClassWizard invents a member function name, *OnClickedSpecial*, and opens the Add Member Function dialog, as shown here:

You could type your own function name here, but this time accept the default and click OK. Next click the Edit Code button in the ClassWizard dialog. This opens the file EX06ADLG.CPP in Visual Workbench and moves to the *OnClickedSpecial* function. Insert a *TRACE* statement in the *OnClickedSpecial* function by typing in the screened code, which replaces the existing code.

```
void CEx06aDialog::OnClickedSpecial()
{
    TRACE("CEx06aDialog::OnClickedSpecial\n");
}
```

5. Use ClassWizard to add an *OnInitDialog* message-handling function. As you'll see in a moment, ClassWizard generates code that initializes a dialog's controls. This DDX (Dialog Data Exchange) code won't initialize the list box choices, however, so you must override the *CDialog OnInitDialog* function. Although *OnInitDialog* is a virtual member function, ClassWizard can generate the prototype if you map the WM_INITDIALOG message in the derived dialog class. To do so, choose ClassWizard from Visual Workbench's Browse menu. Click on *CEx06aDialog* in the Object IDs list box, and then double-click on the WM_INITDIALOG message in the Messages list box. Click the Edit Code button in the ClassWizard dialog to edit the *OnInitDialog* function. Type in the screened code, which replaces the existing code:

```
BOOL CEx06aDialog::OnInitDialog()
{
    CListBox* pLB = (CListBox*) GetDlgItem(IDC_DEPT);
    pLB->InsertString(-1, "Documentation");
    pLB->InsertString(-1, "Accounting");
    pLB->InsertString(-1, "Human Relations");
    pLB->InsertString(-1, "Security");

    return CDialog::OnInitDialog(); // call after initialization
    // initialize any VB controls after base class OnInitDialog call
}
```

You could use the same initialization technique for the combo boxes if you wanted, in place of the initialization in the resource.

Connecting the Dialog to the View

Now we've got the resource and the code for a dialog, but it's not connected to the view. In most applications, you would probably use a menu choice to activate a dialog, but we haven't studied menus yet. Here we'll use the familiar mouse click message WM_LBUTTONDOWN to start the dialog. The steps are as follows:

1. In ClassWizard, select the *CEx06aView* class. At this point, be sure that \VCPP\EX06A\EX06A is the current Visual Workbench project.

2. **Use ClassWizard to add the *OnLButtonDown* member function.** You've done this in the examples in earlier chapters. Simply select the CEx06aView class name, click on the CEx06aView object ID, and then double-click on WM_LBUTTONDOWN.

3. **Add code to the virtual *OnDraw* function in file EX06AVW.CPP.** To prompt the user to press the left mouse button, code the *CEx06aView OnDraw* function. (The skeleton was generated by AppWizard.) The following screened code (which you type in) replaces the existing code:

```
void CEx06aView::OnDraw(CDC* pDC)
{
    pDC->TextOut(0, 0, "Press the left mouse button here.");
}
```

4. **Write the code for *OnLButtonDown* in file EX06AVW.CPP.** Most of the code consists of *TRACE* statements to print the dialog data members after the user exits the dialog. The *CEx06aDialog* constructor call and the *DoModal* call are the critical statements, however:

```
void CEx06aView::OnLButtonDown(UINT nFlags, CPoint point)
{
    CEx06aDialog dlg;

    dlg.m_name     = "Shakespeare, Will";
    dlg.m_lSsn     = 307806636;
    dlg.m_nCat     = 1;   // 0 = hourly, 1 = salary
    dlg.m_bio      = "This person is not a well-motivated tech writer";
    dlg.m_bInsLife = TRUE;
    dlg.m_bInsDis  = FALSE;
    dlg.m_bInsMed  = TRUE;
    dlg.m_dept     = "Documentation";
    dlg.m_skill    = "Writer";
    dlg.m_lang     = "English";
    dlg.m_educ     = "College";
//  dlg.m_nLoyal   = dlg.m_nRely = 50;
    int ret = dlg.DoModal();
    TRACE("DoModal return = %d\n", ret);
    TRACE("name = %s, ssn = %ld, nCat = %d\n",
        (const char* ) dlg.m_name, dlg.m_lSsn, dlg.m_nCat);
    TRACE("dept = %s, skill = %s, lang = %s, educ = %s\n",
        (const char* ) dlg.m_dept, (const char* ) dlg.m_skill,
        (const char* ) dlg.m_lang, (const char* ) dlg.m_educ);
    TRACE("life = %d, dis = %d, med = %d, bio = %s\n",
        dlg.m_bInsLife, dlg.m_bInsDis, dlg.m_bInsMed,
        (const char* ) dlg.m_bio);
//  TRACE(" loyalty = %d, reliability = %d\n",
//      dlg.m_nLoyal, dlg.m_nRely);
}
```

Note: *The statements that are "commented out" will be used later in this chapter.*

5. **To EX06AVW.CPP, add the dialog class include statement.** The *OnLButton-Down* function above depends on the declaration of class *CEx06aDialog*. You must insert the include statement

```
#include "ex06adlg.h"
```

at the top of the *CEx06aView* class source code file (CEX06AVW.CPP), after the statement

```
#include "ex06avw.h"
```

6. **Build and test the application.** If you have done everything right, you should be able to build and run the EX06A application through Visual Workbench. Try entering data in each control, and then click the OK button and observe the *TRACE* results. Notice that the scroll bar controls don't do much yet, but we'll attend to them later. Notice what happens when you press Enter while entering text data in a control: The dialog closes immediately.

Understanding the EX06A Application

When your program calls *DoModal*, control is returned to your program only when the user closes the dialog. If you understand that, you understand modal dialogs. When you get to modeless dialogs, you'll begin to appreciate the programming simplicity of modal dialogs. A lot happens "out of sight" as a result of that *DoModal* call, however. Here's a "what calls what" summary:

CDialog::DoModal

    CEx06aDialog::OnInitDialog

        ...additional initialization...

        CDialog::OnInitDialog

            CWnd::UpdateData(FALSE)

                CEx06aDialog::DoDataExchange

    user enters data...

    user clicks the OK button

CEx06aDialog::OnOK

    ...additional validation...

    CDialog::OnOK

        CWnd::UpdateData(TRUE)

            CEx06aDialog::DoDataExchange

        CDialog::EndDialog(IDOK)

OnInitDialog and *DoDataExchange* are virtual functions overridden in the *CEx06a-Dialog* class. Windows calls *OnInitDialog* as part of the dialog initialization process, and that results in a call to *DoDataExchange*, a function that was generated by ClassWizard. Here is a listing of that function:

```
void CEx06aDialog::DoDataExchange(CDataExchange* pDX)
{
    CDialog::DoDataExchange(pDX)
    //{{AFX_DATA_MAP(CEx06aDialog)
    DDX_Text(pDX, IDC_BIO, m_bio);
    DDX_Radio(pDX, IDC_CAT, m_nCat);
    DDX_LBString(pDX, IDC_DEPT, m_dept);
    DDX_Check(pDX, IDC_DIS, m_bInsDis);
    DDX_CBString(pDX, IDC_EDUC, m_educ);
    DDX_CBString(pDX, IDC_LANG, m_lang);
    DDX_Check(pDX, IDC_LIFE, m_bInsLife);
    DDX_Check(pDX, IDC_MED, m_bInsMed);
    DDX_Text(pDX, IDC_NAME, m_name);
    DDX_CBString(pDX, IDC_SKILL, m_skill);
    DDX_Text(pDX, IDC_SSN, m_lSsn);
    //}}AFX_DATA_MAP
}
```

DoDataExchange and the *DDX_* (exchange) and *DDV_* (validation) functions are "bi-directional." If *UpdateData* is called with a *FALSE* parameter, the functions transfer data from the data members to the dialog controls. If the parameter is *TRUE*, the functions transfer data from the dialog controls to the data members. *DDX_Text* is overloaded to accommodate a variety of data types.

The *EndDialog* function is critical to the dialog exit procedure. *DoModal* returns the parameter passed to *EndDialog*. *IDOK* accepts the dialog's data, and *IDCANCEL* cancels the dialog.

> **Tip:** *You can write your own "custom" DDX functions and wire them into App Studio. This feature is useful if you're using a unique data type throughout your application. See Technical Note 26 in the* MFCNOTES.HLP *Help file.*

Enhancing the Dialog Program

The EX06A program required little coding for a lot of functionality. Now we'll make a new version of this program that uses some hand-coding to add extra features. We'll eliminate EX06A's rude habit of dumping the user in response to the Enter key, and we'll hook up the scroll bar controls.

Taking Control of the *OnOK* Exit

In the original EX06A program, the *CDialog OnOK* virtual function handled the OK button, which triggered data exchange and the exit from the dialog. The Enter key happens to have the same effect, and that might or might not be what you want.

If the user presses Enter in the Name edit control, for example, he or she is immediately bounced out of the dialog.

What's going on here? When the user presses Enter, Windows looks to see which pushbutton has the "input focus" as indicated by a dotted rectangle. If no button has the focus, Windows looks for the "default pushbutton" that the program or the resource specifies. (The default pushbutton has a thicker border.) If the dialog has no default button, the *OnOK* function is called, even if the dialog does not contain an OK button.

You can disable the Enter key simply by writing a do-nothing *CEx06aDialog OnOK* function and adding the exit code to a new function that responds to the OK button. Here are the steps:

1. Use App Studio to change the OK button ID. Open the resource file EX06A.RC, select dialog *IDR_DIALOG1*, and then select the OK button. Change its ID from *IDOK* to *IDC_OK*, and uncheck its Default Button property.

2. Use ClassWizard to create a member function called *OnClickedOk*. This *CEx06aDialog* class member function is keyed to the BN_CLICKED message from control *IDC_OK*.

For Windows SDK Programmers

Dialog controls send WM_COMMAND "notification messages" to their parent dialogs. For a single button click, for example, *wParam* is the button ID, and *lParam* contains both the button handle and the BN_CLICKED notification code. Most *WndProc* programs process these notification messages with a nested switch statement. Microsoft Foundation Class Library version 2.0 "flattens out" the message processing logic by "promoting" control notification messages to the same level as other Windows messages.

ClassWizard generates notification message map entries similar to this:

```
ON_BN_CLICKED(IDC_DELETE, OnDeleteButtonClicked)
ON_BN_DOUBLECLICKED(IDC_DELETE, OnDeleteButtonDblClicked)
```

Button events are special because they generate "command messages" if your dialog class doesn't have notification handlers like the ones above. As Chapter 13 explains, the application framework routes these command messages, and they are ultimately processed by ON_COMMAND message-handling entries mapped like this:

```
ON_COMMAND(IDC_DELETE, OnDelete)
```

In this case, the *OnDelete* function is unable to distinguish between a single click and a double click, but that's no problem because few Windows-based programs utilize double clicks for buttons.

---

3. **Write the body of the *OnClickedOk* function.** This function calls the base class *OnOK* function, as did the original *CEx06aDialog OnOK* function. Here is the code:

```
void CEx06aDialog::OnClickedOk()
{
    TRACE("CEx06aDialog::OnClickedOk\n");
    CDialog::OnOK();
}
```

4. **Create a dummy *OnOK* function.** Add the following prototype to EX06ADLG.H:

```
void CEX06aDialog::OnOK();
```

Now add the following code in EX06ADLG.CPP:

```
void CEX06aDialog::OnOK()
{
    // dummy OnOK function
    TRACE("CEX06aDialog::OnOK\n");
}
```

Pressing Enter while entering text data in one of the dialog's controls now calls this function.

5. **Build and test the application.** Try the Enter key now. Nothing should happen, but the OK button should work as before.

OnCancel Processing

Just as the Enter key triggers a call to *OnOK*, the Escape key triggers a call to *OnCancel*, which results in an exit from the dialog with a *DoModal* return code of *IDCANCEL*. EX06A does no special processing for *IDCANCEL*; therefore, the Esc key (and the system menu Close command) closes the dialog. You can circumvent this process by substituting a dummy *OnCancel* function, following the same procedure you used for the OK button.

Hooking Up the Scroll Bar Controls

The App Studio dialog editor allows you to put scroll bar controls in your dialog, but ClassWizard doesn't provide any direct support for these controls. You will now add the code that makes the Loyalty and Reliability scroll bars work.

Scroll bar controls have position and range values that can be read and written. If you set the range to (0, 100), for example, and you call the *CScrollBar* member function *SetScrollPos* with parameter 50, the scroll box is positioned at the center of the bar. The scroll bars send the WM_HSCROLL and WM_VSCROLL messages to the dialog when the user drags the scroll box or clicks on the arrows. The dialog's message handlers must decode these messages and position the scroll box accordingly.

One tricky thing about scroll bar controls is that all horizontal bars send the same message, WM_HSCROLL, and all vertical bars send the WM_VSCROLL message. Because this monster dialog contains two horizontal scroll bars, the one and only WM_HSCROLL message handler must figure out which scroll bar sent the scroll message.

Also, scroll bars have no data exchange functions. You must code your own data exchange in the *OnInitDialog* and *OnOK* (or rather *OnClickedOK*) functions.

Here are the steps for adding the scroll bar logic to EX06A:

1. **Add the class data members *m_nLoyal* and *m_nRely*.** Add the following code to the class declaration in EX06ADLG.H, placing the statements <u>outside</u> the *AFX_DATA* brackets:

```
public:
    int m_nLoyal;
    int m_nRely;
```

These data members are made public so that they are consistent with the ClassWizard-generated public data members. Also add *enum* statements for the minimum and maximum scroll range:

```
enum { nMin = 0 };
enum { nMax = 100 };
```

2. **Change the *OnInitDialog* function to add data exchange logic.** The *OnInit-Dialog* function must set the positions of the scroll boxes according to percentage values stored in the *CEx06aDialog* data members. A value of 100 means "Set the scroll box to the extreme right"; a value of 0 means "Set the scroll box to the extreme left."

Add the following code to the *CEx06aDialog* member function *OnInit-Dialog* in the file EX06ADLG.CPP:

```
CScrollBar* pSB = (CScrollBar*) GetDlgItem(IDC_LOYAL);
pSB->SetScrollRange(nMin, nMax);
pSB->SetScrollPos(m_nLoyal);

pSB = (CScrollBar*) GetDlgItem(IDC_RELY);
pSB->SetScrollRange(nMin, nMax);
pSB->SetScrollPos(m_nRely);
```

3. **Change the *OnClickedOK* function to add data exchange logic.** Here is the new *OnClickedOK* function (in EX06ADLG.CPP) that "reads" the scroll box positions and sets the values of *m_nLoyal* and *m_nRely*:

```
void CEx06aDialog::OnClickedOK()
{
    CScrollBar* pSB;

    TRACE("CEx06aDialog::OnClickedOK\n");
    pSB = (CScrollBar*) GetDlgItem(IDC_LOYAL);
    m_nLoyal = pSB->GetScrollPos();

    pSB = (CScrollBar*) GetDlgItem(IDC_RELY);
    m_nRely = pSB->GetScrollPos();

    CDialog::OnOK(); // does data exchange
}
```

4. **Use ClassWizard to add a scroll bar message handler to *CEx06aDialog*.**
Choose the WM_HSCROLL message, and then add the member function
OnHScroll. Enter the following code:

```
void CEx06aDialog::OnHScroll(UINT nSBCode, UINT nPos,
                            CScrollBar* pScrollBar)
{
    int nTemp1, nTemp2;

    nTemp1 = pScrollBar->GetScrollPos();
    switch(nSBCode) {
    case SB_THUMBPOSITION:
        pScrollBar->GetScrollRange(&nMin, &nMax);
        pScrollBar->SetScrollPos(nPos);
        break;
    case SB_LINEUP: // left arrow button
        pScrollBar->GetScrollRange(&nMin, &nMax);
        nTemp2 = (nMax - nMin) / 10;
        if ((nTemp1 - nTemp2) > nMin) {
           nTemp1 -= nTemp2;
        }
        else {
           nTemp1 = nMin;
        }
        pScrollBar->SetScrollPos(nTemp1);
        break;
    case SB_LINEDOWN: // right arrow button
        pScrollBar->GetScrollRange(&nMin, &nMax);
        nTemp2 = (nMax - nMin) / 10;
        if ((nTemp1 + nTemp2) < nMax) {
           nTemp1 += nTemp2;
        }
        else {
           nTemp1 = nMax;
        }
        pScrollBar->SetScrollPos(nTemp1);
    }
}
```

114

5. **In EX06AVW.CPP, add initialization code to *OnLButtonDown*.** To test the data exchange logic, you'll want to set the values of *m_nLoyal* and *m_nRely*. In *OnLButtonDown*, remove the comment characters in front of the lines that relate to *m_nLoyal* and *m_nRely*.

6. **Build and test the application.** Build and run EX06A again. Do the scroll bars work this time? The scroll boxes should "stick" after you drag them with the mouse, and they should move when you click the scroll bars' arrows. (Notice that we haven't added logic for when the user clicks on the scroll bar itself.)

Identifying Controls: *CWnd* Pointers and Control IDs

When you lay out a dialog resource in App Studio, you identify controls by IDs such as *IDC_SSN*. In your program code, however, you often need access to a control's underlying window object. The class library provides the *CWnd GetDlgItem* function for converting an ID to a *CWnd* pointer. You've seen this already in the *OnInitDialog* and *OnSpecialOK* member functions of class *CEx06aDialog*. The application framework "manufactured" this returned *CWnd* pointer because there never was a constructor call for the control objects. This pointer is temporary and should not be stored for later use.

> **Tip:** *If you need to convert a* CWnd *pointer to a control ID, use the class library* GetDlgCtrlID *member function of class* CWnd.

Painting Inside the Dialog Window

You can paint directly in the client area of the dialog window, but you'll avoid overwriting dialog elements if you paint only inside a control window. If you want to display only text, use App Studio to create a blank static control with a unique ID, and then call the *CWnd SetDlgItemText* function in a dialog member function such as *OnInitDialog* to place text in the control.

Displaying graphics is more complicated. You must use ClassWizard to add an *OnPaint* member function to the dialog; this function converts the static control's ID to a *CWnd* pointer and gets its device context. The trick is to draw inside the control window while preventing Windows from overwriting your work later. The *Invalidate/UpdateWindow* sequence achieves this. Here is an *OnPaint* function that paints a small black square in a static control:

```
void CMyDialog::OnPaint()
{
    CPaintDC dc(this);                          // keeps Windows happy
    CWnd* pWnd = GetDlgItem(IDC_STATIC1);       // IDC_STATIC1 specified
                                                //  in App Studio
    CDC* pControlDC = pWnd->GetDC();
```

(continued)

115

```
        pWnd->Invalidate();
        pWnd->UpdateWindow();
        pControlDC->SelectStockObject(BLACK_BRUSH);
        pControlDC->Rectangle(0, 0, 10, 10);      // black square bullet
        pWnd->ReleaseDC(pControlDC);
    }
```

As with all windows, the dialog's *OnPaint* function is called only if some part of the dialog is invalidated. You can force the *OnPaint* call from another dialog member function with the following statement:

```
    Invalidate;
```

Using Other Control Features

You've seen how to "extend" one control class, *CScrollBar*, with code in the *OnInitDialog* member function and the dialog's exit function. You can extend the other controls in similar fashion. Look in the *Class Library Reference* at the control classes, particularly *CListBox* and *CComboBox*. Each has a number of features that ClassWizard does not directly support. List boxes and some combo boxes, for example, can support multiple selections. If you want to use these features, don't use ClassWizard to add data members, but define your own data members and add your own exchange code in *OnInitDialog* and *OnClickedOK*.

7

The Modeless Dialog and the COMMDLG Dialog Classes

In Chapter 6, you saw the ordinary modal dialog and most of the controls for Microsoft Windows. Now you'll move on to the modeless dialog and the Windows COMMDLG classes. Modeless dialogs, as you'll remember, allow the user to work elsewhere in the application while the dialog is active. The COMMDLG classes are the C++ programming interface to the group of Windows utility dialogs that include File Open, Printer Setup, Color Selection, and so forth, which are supported by the dynamic link library COMMDLG.DLL.

In this chapter's first example, you'll build a simple modeless dialog that is controlled from a view. In the second example, you'll derive a class from the COMMDLG *CFileDialog* class, which allows file deletion.

Modeless Dialogs

In Microsoft Foundation Class Library version 2, modal and modeless dialogs share the same base class, *CDialog*, and they both use a dialog resource that you can build with App Studio. If you're using a modeless dialog with a view, you'll need some specialized programming techniques.

Creating Modeless Dialogs

You've already learned that you display a modal dialog window by calling the *DoModal* function and that the window ceases to exist as soon as *DoModal* returns. You can construct a modal dialog object on the stack knowing that the Windows dialog has been destroyed by the time the C++ dialog object goes out of scope. Modeless dialogs are more complicated. You start by constructing a dialog object, but then to create the dialog window you call the *CDialog Create* member function instead of *DoModal.* Control returns immediately with the dialog still on the screen. Now you must worry about exactly when to construct the dialog object, when to create the dialog window, when to destroy the dialog, and when to process user-entered data.

User-Defined Messages

Suppose you want the modeless dialog window destroyed when the user clicks the dialog's OK button. This presents a problem. How does the view know that the user has clicked the OK button? The dialog could call a view class member function directly but that would "marry" the dialog to a particular view class. A better solution is for the dialog to send the view a user-defined message as the result of a call to the OK button message-handling function. When the view gets the message, it can destroy the dialog window (but not the object). This sets the stage for the creation of a new dialog.

You have two options for sending Windows messages. You can use the *CWind SendMessage* function or the *PostMessage* function. The former causes an immediate call to the message-handling function, and the latter posts a message in the Windows message queue. With the *PostMessage* option, there's a slight delay, so it's reasonable to expect that the dialog is completely gone by the time the view gets the message.

Dialog Ownership

Now suppose you've accepted the dialog default pop-up style, which means the dialog isn't confined to the view's client area. As far as Windows is concerned, the dialog's "owner" is the application's main frame window (introduced in Chapter 12), not the view. You need to know the dialog's view to send the view a message. Therefore, your dialog class must track its own view through a data member that the constructor sets.

A Modeless Dialog Example—EX07A

We could convert the Chapter 6 monster dialog to a modeless dialog, but starting from scratch with a simpler dialog is easier. Example EX07A uses a dialog with one edit control, an OK button, and a Cancel button. As in the Chapter 6 example, pressing the left mouse button while the mouse cursor is inside the view window brings up the dialog, but now we have the option of destroying it in response to another event—pressing the right mouse button when the mouse cursor is inside the view window. We'll allow only one dialog at a time, so we must be sure that a second left button press doesn't bring up a duplicate dialog.

To summarize the steps ahead, the EX07A view class has a single associated dialog object that is constructed on the heap when the view is constructed. The dialog window is created and destroyed in response to user actions, but the dialog object is not destroyed until the application terminates.

Here are the steps to create the EX07A example:

1. **Run AppWizard to produce \VCPP\EX07A\EX07A.** Choose AppWizard from Visual Workbench's Project menu. The options and the default class names are shown here:

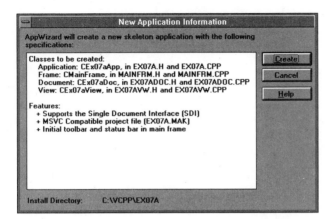

2. **Use App Studio to create a new dialog.** Choose App Studio from Visual Workbench's Tools menu. When App Studio starts up, click the New button and then choose Dialog. App Studio assigns the ID *IDD_DIALOG1* to the new dialog. Change the dialog caption to *Modeless Dialog*. Accept the default OK and Cancel buttons with IDs *IDOK* and *IDCANCEL*, and then add a static text control and an edit control with the default ID *IDC_EDIT1*. Change the static text control's caption to *Edit 1*. This is the completed dialog:

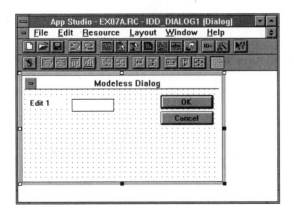

3. **Use ClassWizard to create the *CEx07aDialog* class.** Choose ClassWizard from the App Studio Resource menu. Fill in the Add Class dialog as shown on the next page, and then click the Create Class button.

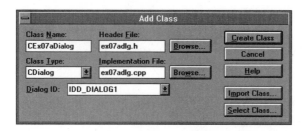

Add the message-handling functions shown below. To add a message-handling function, click on an object ID, click on a message, and click the Add Function button. The Add Member Function dialog box appears. Type the function name and click the OK button.

Object ID	Message	Member Function Name
IDCANCEL	BN_CLICKED	*OnCancel*
IDOK	BN_CLICKED	*OnOK*

4. **Add a variable to the *CEx07aDialog*.** While in ClassWizard, click the Edit Variables button to open the Edit Member Variables dialog, and then click the Add Variable button to add the *CString* variable *m_edit1* to the *IDC_EDIT1* control.

5. **Edit EX07ADLG.H to add a view pointer and function prototypes.** Type in the following screened code in the *CEx07aDialog* class declaration:

```
public:
    CView* m_pView;
```

Also, add the function prototypes as follows:

```
public:
    CEx07aDialog(CView* pView);
    BOOL Create();
```

Note: *Using the* CView *class rather than the* CEx07aView *class allows the dialog class to be used with any view class.*

6. **Add the modeless constructor in file EX07ADLG.CPP.** You could modify the existing *CEx07aDialog* constructor, but if you add a separate one, the dialog class can serve for both modal and modeless dialogs.

```
CEx07aDialog::CEx07aDialog(CView* pView) // modeless constructor
    : CDialog()
{
    m_pView = pView;
}
```

You should also add the following line to the AppWizard-generated modal constructor:

```
m_pView = NULL;
```

The C++ compiler is clever enough to distinguish between the modeless constructor *CEx07aDialog(CView*)* and the modal constructor *CEx07aDialog(CWnd*)*. If the compiler sees an argument of class *CView* or a derived *CView* class, it generates a call to the modeless constructor. If it sees an argument of class *CWnd* or another derived *CWnd* class, it generates a call to the modal constructor.

7. **Add the *Create* function in EX07ADLG.CPP.** This derived dialog class *Create* function calls the base class function with the dialog resource ID as a parameter.

```
BOOL CEx07aDialog::Create()
{
    return CDialog::Create(CEx07aDialog::IDD);
}
```

8. **Edit the *OnOK* and *OnCancel* functions in EX07ADLG.CPP.** These virtual functions generated by ClassWizard are called in response to dialog button clicks.

```
void CEx07aDialog::OnOK()        // not really a message handler
{
    CDialog::OnOK();
    if (m_pView != NULL) {
      m_pView->SendMessage(ID_GOODBYE, IDOK);
    }
}

void CEx07aDialog::OnCancel()    // not really a message handler
{
    CDialog::OnCancel();
    if (m_pView != NULL) {
      m_pView->SendMessage(ID_GOODBYE, IDCANCEL);
    }
}
```

If the dialog is being used as a modeless dialog, it sends the user-defined message ID_GOODBYE to the view. We'll worry about handling it later.

9. **Edit RESOURCE.H to define the *ID_GOODBYE* message ID.** Add the following line of code:

```
#define ID_GOODBYE      WM_USER + 5
```

The Windows constant *WM_USER* is the first message ID available for user-defined messages. The application framework uses a few of these messages, so we'll skip over the first five messages.

Note: *App Studio doesn't understand constants based on other constants. When App Studio reads RESOURCE.H, it ignores* ID_GOODBYE, *and thus you won't see it in the list of symbols. App Studio does rewrite the* ID_GOOD-BYE *definition back to RESOURCE.H on exit, however, so it's not lost.*

10. **Modify the *CEx07aView* constructor and destructor in EX07AVW.CPP.** The *CEx07aView* class has a data member *m_pDlg* that points to the view's *CEx07aDialog* object. The view constructor constructs the dialog object on the heap, and the view destructor deletes it.

```
CEx07aView::CEx07aView()
{
    m_pDlg = new CEx07aDialog(this);
}

CEx07aView::~CEx07aView()
{
    delete m_pDlg; // destroys window if not already destroyed
}
```

11. **Add code to the virtual *OnDraw* function in file EX07AVW.CPP.** The *CEx07aView OnDraw* function (skeleton generated by AppWizard) should be coded as follows in order to prompt the user to press the mouse button:

```
void CEx07aView::OnDraw(CDC* pDC)
{
    pDC->TextOut(0, 0, "Press the left mouse button here.");
}
```

12. **Use ClassWizard to add *CEx07aView* mouse message handlers.** Add handlers for the WM_LBUTTONDOWN and WM_RBUTTONDOWN messages. Now edit the code in file EX07AVW.CPP as follows:

```
void CEx07aView::OnLButtonDown(UINT nFlags, CPoint point)
{
    // creates the dialog if not created already
    if (m_pDlg->GetSafeHwnd() == 0) {
        m_pDlg->Create(); // displays the dialog window
    }
}

void CEx07aView::OnRButtonDown(UINT nFlags, CPoint point)
{
    m_pDlg->DestroyWindow();
    // no problem if window was already destroyed
}
```

For almost all window types except main frame windows, the *DestroyWindow* function does not destroy the C++ object. We want this behavior because we'll take care of the dialog object's destruction in the view destructor.

13. **Add the dialog header include statement to file EX07AVW.CPP.** While you're in EX07AVW.CPP, add the following dialog header include statement after the view header include statement.

```
#include "ex07avw.h"
#include "ex07adlg.h"
```

14. **Add your own message code for the ID_GOODBYE message.** Because ClassWizard does not support user-defined messages, you must write the code yourself. This task makes you appreciate the work ClassWizard does for the other messages.

   □ In EX07AVW.CPP, add the following line after the *BEGIN_MESSAGE_MAP* statement but outside the *AFX_MSG_MAP* brackets:

```
ON_MESSAGE(ID_GOODBYE, OnGoodbye)
```

   □ In EX07AVW.CPP, add the message handler function itself:

```
LONG CEx07aView::OnGoodbye(UINT wParam, LONG lParam)
{
    // message received in response to modeless dialog OK
    // and Cancel buttons
    TRACE("CEx07aView::OnGoodbye %x, %lx\n", wParam, lParam);
    TRACE("Dialog edit1 contents = %s\n", (const char*) m_pDlg->m_edit1);
    m_pDlg->DestroyWindow();
    return 0L;
}
```

   □ In EX07AVW.H, add the function prototype:

```
LONG OnGoodbye(UINT wParam, LONG lParam);
```

With the Windows SDK, the *wParam* and *lParam* parameters are the usual means of passing message data. In a mouse button down message, for example, the mouse *x*- and *y*-coordinates are packed into the *lParam* value. With the class library, message data is passed in more meaningful parameters. The mouse position is passed as a *CPoint* object. User-defined messages must use *wParam* and *lParam*, so you can use these two variables however you want. In this example, we've put the button ID in *wParam*.

15. **Edit the EX07AVW.H header file.** You need a data member to hold the dialog pointer:

```
private:
    CEx07aDialog* m_pDlg;
```

If you add the forward declaration

```
class CEx07aDialog;
```

at the beginning of EX07AVW.H, you won't have to include EX07ADLG.H in every module that includes EX07AVW.H.

16. **Build and test the application.** Build and run EX07A. Try pressing the mouse's left mouse button and then its right button. Also enter some data and click the dialog's OK button. Does the view's *TRACE* statement correctly list the edit control's contents?

   Note: *If you use the EX07A view and dialog classes in an MDI application, each MDI child window can have one modeless dialog. When the user closes an MDI child, the child's modeless dialog is destroyed because the view's destructor calls the dialog destructor, which, in turn, destroys the dialog window.*

The *CFormView* Class—A Modeless Dialog Alternative

If you need an application based on a single modeless dialog, the *CFormView* class will save you a lot of work. You'll have to wait until Chapter 15, however, because the *CFormView* class is most useful when coupled with the *CDocument* class, and we haven't progressed that far in our exploration of the application framework.

COMMDLG Dialogs

Windows provides a group of standard user interface dialogs, and these are supported by the class library classes. You are probably familiar with all or most of these dialogs because so many Windows-based applications, including Visual C++, already use them. Here's a list of the COMMDLG classes:

Class	Purpose
CFileDialog	Allows the user to open a new file or an existing file
CFontDialog	Allows the user to select a font from a list of available fonts
CColorDialog	Allows the user to select or create a color
CPrintDialog	Allows the user to set up the printer and print a document
CFindReplaceDialog	Allows the user to substitute one string for another

The resources for these dialogs are buried inside the COMMDLG.DLL dynamic link library in the \WINDOWS\SYSTEM directory. You can access these resources through App Studio, but you shouldn't try to update them directly. You can use the clipboard to copy the dialogs to your own resource script if you want to.

Using the *CFileDialog* Class Directly

Using the *CFileDialog* class to open a file is easy. Here is some code that opens a file that the user has selected through the dialog:

```
CFileDialog dlg(TRUE, "bmp", "*.bmp");
if (dlg.DoModal() == IDOK){
  CFile file;
  VERIFY(file.Open(dlg.GetPathName(), CFile::modeRead)));
}
```

The first constructor parameter (*TRUE*) specifies that this object is a "File Open" dialog instead of a "File Save" dialog, and "bmp" is the default file extension. The *CFileDialog GetPathName* function returns a *CString* object that contains the full path name of the selected file.

Adding Dialog Controls at Runtime

You can use the App Studio resource editor to create dialog controls at build time. If you need to add a dialog control at runtime, here are the programming steps:

1. Add an embedded control window data member to your dialog class. The class library control window classes include *CButton, CEdit, CListBox*, and *CCombo-Box*. An embedded control window is constructed and destroyed along with the dialog.

2. Use the App Studio symbol editor to add an ID constant for the control.

3. Override the *CDialog* function *OnInitDialog* to call the embedded control window's *Create* member function. This call displays the new control in the dialog.

4. In your derived dialog class, manually add the necessary message handlers for your new control.

Deriving from the COMMDLG Classes

Most of the time you can use the COMMDLG classes directly. If you derive your own COMMDLG classes, however, you can add functionality without duplicating code. You have to be careful, though, because quite a lot happens inside the Windows code before class member functions such as *OnOK* are called. Sometimes you must innovate to get the features you want.

A *CFileDialog* Example—EX07B

In this example, you will derive a class *CEx07bDialog* that adds a working Delete button to the standard file dialog. It also changes the dialog's caption and changes the OK button's caption to Open. The example illustrates how you can create dialog controls "on the fly" without a corresponding resource entry. The new file dialog is activated as in the previous examples—by pressing the left mouse button when the mouse cursor is in the view window. Because you should be gaining skill with Visual C++, the following steps won't be as detailed as those for the earlier examples. Figure 7-1 shows what the dialog looks like.

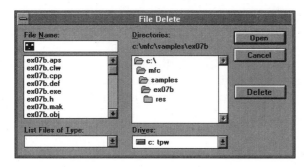

Figure 7-1.
The File Delete dialog in action.

Follow these steps to build the EX07B application:

1. **Run AppWizard to produce \VCPP\EX07B\EX07B.** Choose AppWizard from Visual Workbench's Project menu. The options and the default class names are shown here:

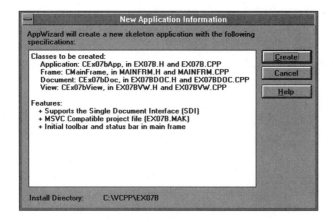

2. **Use ClassWizard to create the *CEX07bDialog* class.** ClassWizard won't let you specify *CFileDialog* as a base class; so you'll have to choose *CDialog*. Fill in the Add Class dialog, as shown at the top of the next page:

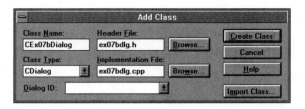

Be sure to leave the Dialog ID edit control empty in the Add Class dialog. When you click the Create Class button, ClassWizard displays the following dialog:

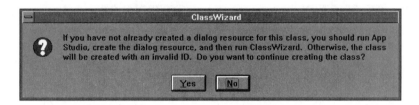

This is OK. Click the Yes button to continue.

ClassWizard produces the files EX07BDLG.H and EX07BDLG.CPP and adds them to the project.

3. Edit the file EX07BDLG.H. Change the line

```
class CEx07bDialog : public CDialog
```

to

```
class CEx07BDialog : public CFileDialog
```

to change the *CEx07BDialog* base class.

In the *CEx07BDialog* class declaration, replace the following lines

```
// Dialog Data
    //{{AFX_DATA(CEx07bDialog)
    enum { IDD = _UNKNOWN_RESOURCE_ID_ };
        // NOTE: the ClassWizard will add data members here
    //}}AFX_DATA
```

with the following data member declarations:

```
public:
    CButton m_deleteButton;
    BOOL    m_bDeleteFlag;
```

And, finally, add the following function prototypes:

```
virtual BOOL OnInitDialog();
afx_msg void OnDeleteButton();
```

4. **Use App Studio to add a define constant for the Delete button.** Choose Symbols from the Edit menu, and then click the New button in the Symbol Browser dialog. In the New Symbols dialog, add the constant *IDC_DELETE*. (You can accept the default value.)

5. **Replace *CDialog* with *CFileDialog* in EX07BDLG.CPP.** Choose Replace from the Visual Workbench Edit menu and replace this name globally.

6. **Replace the *CEx07bDialog* constructor in EX07BDLG.CPP.** The constructor for the *CFileDialog* class takes a long string of optional parameters. We set the first parameter, *bOpenFileDialog*, to *TRUE* (for the File Open dialog) because we want to select an existing file. The third parameter, *lpszFileName*, is the initial filename. If you set it to "*.*", you will see a list of all files in the current directory. The body of the constructor sets the dialog caption by accessing an internal structure called *m_ofn*.

```
CEx07bDialog::CEx07bDialog(CWnd* pParent /*=NULL*/)
    : CFileDialog(TRUE, NULL, "*.*")
{
    m_ofn.lpstrTitle = "File Delete"; // dialog caption
}
```

7. **Add the *OnInitDialog* function in file EX07BDLG.CPP.** This member function calls the *CButton Create* member function to create the new Delete button window and insert it in the dialog. The *SetDlgItemText* function changes the title of the existing OK button.

```
BOOL CEx07bDialog::OnInitDialog()
{
    m_bDeleteFlag = FALSE;
    CRect rect(365, 100, 452, 124); // button location in dialog window
    m_deleteButton.Create("Delete",
                          WS_CHILD | WS_VISIBLE | BS_PUSHBUTTON,
                          rect, this, IDC_DELETE);
    SetDlgItemText(IDOK, "Open"); // change OK button's caption to Open
    return CFileDialog::OnInitDialog();
}
```

8. **Add the Delete button message handler in file EX07BDLG.CPP.** The Windows COMMDLG code does important processing before calling the dialog class's *OnOK* function. Therefore, the dialog must simulate clicking the OK button by sending itself an IDOK button-click message. Calling *EndDialog* or the base class *OnOK* doesn't work. The data member *m_bDeleteFlag* tells the view that the Delete button was clicked rather than the Open button.

```
void CEx07bDialog::OnDeleteButton()
{
    m_bDeleteFlag = TRUE;
    SendMessage(WM_COMMAND, IDOK, BN_CLICKED);
}
```

ClassWizard supports only control handlers that are defined in the dialog resource. This means you'll have to manually insert the following entry in the EX07BDLG.CPP message map.

```
BEGIN_MESSAGE_MAP(CEx07bDialog, CFileDialog)
    //{{AFX_MSG_MAP(CEx07bDialog)
        // NOTE: the ClassWizard will add message map macros here
    ON_BN_CLICKED(IDC_DELETE, OnDeleteButton)
    //}}AFX_MSG_MAP
END_MESSAGE_MAP()
```

You've already put the function prototype in the header file.

9. **Add code to the virtual *OnDraw* function in file EX07BVW.CPP.** The *CEx07bView OnDraw* function (the skeleton was generated by AppWizard) should be coded as follows to prompt the user to press the mouse button:

```
void CEx07bView::OnDraw(CDC* pDC)
{
    pDC->TextOut(0, 0, "Press the left mouse button here.");
}
```

10. **Add the *OnLButtonDown* message handler to the *CEx07bView* class.** Use ClassWizard to create the message handler for WM_LBUTTONDOWN, and then edit the code as follows:

```
void CEx07bView::OnLButtonDown(UINT nFlags, CPoint point)
{
    CEx07bDialog dlg;
    char         text[200];

    dlg.DoModal();
    CString filename = dlg.GetPathName(); // CFileDialog function
    sprintf(text, "Are you sure you want to delete %s?",
            (const char*) filename);
    if (dlg.m_deleteFlag) {
      if (AfxMessageBox(text, MB_YESNO) == IDYES) {
        CFile::Remove(filename);
      }
    }
    else {
      TRACE("Open file %s\n", (const char*) filename);
    }
}
```

129

Using the global *AfxMessageBox* function is a convenient way to pop up a simple dialog that displays some text and that queries the user for a *Yes/No* answer. The *Class Library Reference* describes all the message box variations and options.

Of course, you'll need the statement

```
#include "ex07bdlg.h"
```

after the line

```
#include "ex07bdlg.h"
```

11. **Build and test the application.** Build and run EX07B. Pressing the left mouse button should bring up the Delete dialog, and you should be able to use it to navigate through the disk directory and to delete files.

8

Visual Basic Controls

Microsoft Visual Basic, introduced in 1991, has proven to be a very popular and successful application development system for Microsoft Windows. Part of its success is attributable to its open-ended nature. You can extend the Basic language by adding Visual Basic "controls"—special dynamic link libraries (DDLs), written in C, that are available from Microsoft and from third-party software developers. You can now use these same Visual Basic controls with Visual C++, and App Studio fully supports them. The Professional Edition of Microsoft Visual Basic 3.0 includes a Control Development Kit (CDK) that allows you to write your own custom controls.

In this chapter, you'll learn why Visual Basic controls are different from standard Windows controls and custom Windows controls, and you'll learn how to integrate these controls into a Microsoft Foundation Class Library version 2 program. An example, built with the Visual Basic GRID control included with Visual C++, illustrates the use of control properties, methods, and events. The end result is a crude but workable spreadsheet program.

> **Note:** *See Technical Note 27 in the MFCNOTES.HLP Help file for detailed documentation on each standard VBX event, each standard VBX property, and specific properties and events for the Visual Basic GRID control.*

Standard Controls for Windows and Ordinary Custom Controls

You've already seen the standard Windows controls as represented by the classes *CEdit*, *CButton*, *CScrollBar*, and so forth. These controls are built into Windows, and the class library fully supports them. You can also use ordinary custom controls (written in C and usually implemented as DLLs) with the class library. With App Studio you can size and position ordinary custom controls in a dialog, but at design time you can't see what the controls look like.

Consider any control a "smart window" that's usually (but not always) embedded in a dialog. Many controls accept input, but all controls provide some sort of visual output. Controls can support extensive interaction with the user without the involvement of your application. The Windows *CEdit* control, for example, processes cursor movements and backspace keystrokes, and it supports wordwrap—all by itself. The more work a control does, the less programming you have to do.

C++ Classes and Visual Basic Controls

C++ is a totally flexible object-oriented programming language, but a C++ program's features must be specified at compile time. Visual Basic limits your flexibility, but it allows interactive program development. Visual Basic controls are the closest thing Visual Basic has to classes. These controls are stand-alone modules that interact, both at design time and at runtime, with the Visual Basic environment. With Visual C++, you can use both compiled C++ classes and Visual Basic controls. Comparing the behavior of these two diverse programming elements is useful.

Methods vs. Member Functions

If you write your own C++ class, it can have a member function called *DanceAroundTheTable* if you want it to. Of course, the other classes in your application must know, at compile time, specifically what *DanceAroundTheTable* does and what its parameters are. Classes for Windows controls use hard-coded notification messages and member functions. Some member functions, such as the *CEdit GetLineCount* function, apply to only one control class, but others, such as *CWnd GetDlgItemText*, apply to all controls.

Visual Basic controls have "methods" that are similar to class member functions. These are limited to a predefined set that includes *AddItem*, *RemoveItem*, *Move*, and *Refresh* (among others). Not all Visual Basic controls respond to all the methods. The *Move* method, though, works with all controls.

Properties vs. Data Members

At first the limited set of Visual Basic control methods seems restrictive. Fortunately, Visual Basic controls have "properties" in addition to methods. You could say that Visual Basic properties correspond to C++ data members. Each Visual Basic control can define its own set of properties, which can include strings, long integers, or floating-point numbers. You could create a Visual Basic control with a string property called "DanceAroundTheTable" that could be set to "waltz" or "foxtrot." Most Visual Basic controls recognize a standard set of properties such as BackColor and FontName. The control will list its collection of properties when interrogated.

Properties are limited to three data types, but using a property instead of a fixed data type offers a significant advantage in Visual Basic—namely, that the runtime system requires no advance knowledge of a control's properties when it executes the application program. Other programs besides the Visual Basic runtime can take advantage of this runtime property access. App Studio, for example, can present a list of a control's properties, and it allows you to set initial values.

Some Visual Basic controls support array properties. A graph control, for example, might have an array of numeric points that can be individually set and retrieved.

Visual Basic Control Events vs. Windows Control Notifications

Standard controls send notification messages to a dialog in response to events. A pushbutton sends a BN_CLICKED message, for example. ClassWizard helps you define a dialog class member function to handle the message. Visual Basic controls work in exactly the same way. Most Visual Basic controls send standard messages (called events) such as VBN_CLICK and VBN_KEYDOWN. Some Visual Basic controls send unique messages such as VBN_ROWCOLCHANGE. When you run ClassWizard from inside App Studio (with a dialog selected), Class Wizard knows which Visual Basic control you're using, and it presents a list of the events for the selected control.

Visual Basic Event Registration

Your program must call the global class library function *AfxRegisterVBEvent* for each Visual Basic control event that needs handling. When ClassWizard creates a dialog that uses an event-oriented Visual Basic control, it generates the *AfxRegisterVBEvent* call for you in your program's main module (MYAPP.CPP). If your control uses the GRID control's ROWCOLCHANGE event, the generated code looks like this:

```
//{{AFX_VBX_REGISTER_MAP()
    UINT NEAR VBN_ROWCOLCHANGE = AfxRegisterVBEvent("ROWCOLCHANGE");
//}}AFX_VBX_REGISTER_MAP
```

A corresponding *extern* statement is in the main header file (MYAPP.H) and is included by the programs that use the Visual Basic control:

```
//{{AFX_VBX_REGISTER()
    extern UINT NEAR VBN_ROWCOLCHANGE;
//}}AFX_VBX_REGISTER
```

For every dialog class that uses the Visual Basic control, ClassWizard generates a message map entry such as this:

```
ON_VBXEVENT(VBN_ROWCOLCHANGE, IDC_GRID1, OnRowcolchangeGrid1)
```

The *CVBControl* Class

You've seen that the class library provides classes for the standard Windows controls. As you've probably guessed, it also provides a class for Visual Basic controls. This class, *CVBControl*, is derived from *CWnd* and thus has the characteristics of a window, the same as *CEdit*, *CButton*, and so forth. The *CVBControl* class serves all Visual Basic controls.

In a dialog class member function, you can get a temporary pointer to a *CVBControl* object with a statement such as this:

```
CVBControl* pVBC = GetDlgItem(IDC_GRID1); // IDC_GRID1 defined
                                          //  in RESOURCE.H
```

A better option, though, is to let ClassWizard define a Visual Basic control pointer variable that is initialized in the dialog's *DoDataExchange* member function. The application framework cleans up the *CVBControl* objects when the dialog closes, so don't try to delete a *CVBControl* object unless you have constructed it yourself.

As the *Class Library Reference* shows, the *CVBControl* class contains all the member functions you'll need to access Visual Basic controls. The *Move, Refresh, GetItem,* and *RemoveItem* functions activate a control's methods, and there are functions for setting and getting the different kinds of properties based on data type. You use the *CVBControl Create* member function when you need a Visual Basic control outside a dialog.

The EX08A Example

One Visual Basic control included with Visual C++ is the GRID control, which was originally distributed with the Visual Basic CDK. The EX08A program uses the GRID control to create a simple spreadsheet. Remember that this is only an example, so don't erase Microsoft Excel from your hard disk. Figure 8-1 shows the EX08A program containing data.

	A	B	C	D	E	F	G
1	2.00	3.00	4.00	5.00	6.00	7.00	8.00
2	3.00	4.00	5.00	6.00	7.00	8.00	9.00
3	4.00	5.00	6.00	7.00	8.00	9.00	10.00
4	5.00	6.00	7.00	8.00	9.00	10.00	11.00
5	6.00	7.00	8.00	9.00	10.00	11.00	12.00
6	7.00	8.00	9.00	10.00	11.00	12.00	13.00
7	8.00	9.00	10.00	11.00	12.00	13.00	14.00
8	9.00	10.00	11.00	12.00	13.00	14.00	15.00
9	10.00	11.00	12.00	13.00	14.00	15.00	16.00
10	11.00	12.00	13.00	14.00	15.00	16.00	17.00
11	65.00	75.00	85.00	95.00	105.00	115.00	125.00

OK | Cancel | Add Row | Delete Row | 2.00 | Update Value

Figure 8-1.
The EX08A window.

The EX08A spreadsheet consists of 12 rows and 8 columns. The top row and the left column are used for labels, and the bottom row is used for column sums that the program updates. When the user selects a cell with the mouse, the cell's value is copied to the dialog's edit control. The user can then edit the value, which is copied back into the grid when the user presses Enter.

The Visual Basic GRID Control

The Visual Basic GRID control consists of a rectangular array of addressable cells. The host program sets the initial number of rows and columns, and it stores data in and retrieves data from the individual cells. At runtime, the user can use the mouse (but not the direction keys) to select an individual cell or a range of cells. The GRID control is more an "output control" than an "input control" because the user cannot type directly into the cells. As you'll see in the example, however, you can make it reasonably easy for the user to enter and edit cell data.

> **Note:** *The Visual C++ VBCHART example application, located in the \MSVC\MFC\SAMPLES\VBCHART subdirectory, demonstrates the GRID control's ability to be customized. Because of some clever tricks, such as moving an edit window, the program's grid behaves the same as a real spreadsheet. Be sure to build and run VBCHART to see what is possible with some creative programming.*

The GRID control supports most standard Visual Basic control properties, events, and methods, and it has a number of unique properties and events. The ones you'll use in EX08A are listed here:

Name	Description
Property	
CellSelected (numeric)	True (−1) if a cell is selected; False (0) otherwise
Col (numeric)	Current column
ColAlignment (numeric, indexed)	Non-fixed cells/row labels (0 = left aligned, 1 = right aligned, 2 = centered)
*Cols (numeric)	Total number of columns
ColWidth (numeric, indexed)	Column width in "logical twips"
FixedAlignment (numeric, indexed)	Fixed cells/row labels (0 = left aligned, 1 = right aligned, 2 = centered)
Row (numeric)	Current row
RowHeight (numeric, indexed)	Row height in "logical twips"
*Rows (numeric)	Total number of rows
Text (string)	The text in the selected cell, defined by Col and Row
Event	
SelChange	Notifies the program when the user uses the mouse to select a new cell
Method	
AddItem	Inserts a row
RemoveItem	Deletes a row

* These properties can be set in App Studio; others can be set and read only at runtime.

Building the EX08A Example Program

Before you begin to build the EX08A program, be sure that the files GRID.VBX and VB.LIC are present in the \WINDOWS\SYSTEM subdirectory. Now follow these steps to build the program:

1. **Run AppWizard to produce \VCPP\EX08A\EX08A.** Choose AppWizard from Visual Workbench's Project menu. The options and the default class names are shown here:

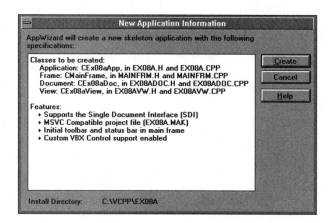

Be sure to check the Custom VBX Controls option.

2. **Add a WM_LBUTTONDOWN message handler to *CEx08aView* in EX08A-VW.CPP.** Use ClassWizard to add the *OnLButtonDown* function, and then edit the function. The following screened code (which you type in) replaces the existing code:

```
void CEx08aView::OnLButtonDown(UINT nFlags, CPoint point)
{
    int         i, j;
    CEx08aDialog dlg;              // constructs the dialog

    for (i = 1; i < 8; i++) {   // fills the data array with test data
      for (j = 1; j < 11; j++) {
        dlg.m_dArray[i][j] = i + j;
      }
    }

    dlg.DoModal();                // starts the dialog

    for (j = 1; j < 11; j++) { // prints the modified array
      for (i = 1; i < 8; i++) {
        TRACE("%8.2f ", dlg.m_dArray[i][j]);
      }
      TRACE("\n");
    }
}
```

This function brings up the modal dialog when the user presses the left mouse button when the mouse cursor is in the view window. It also initializes and prints the data array.

3. **Edit the *OnDraw* function in EX08AVW.CPP.** The following screened code replaces the existing code:

```
void CEx08aView::OnDraw(CDC*pDC)
{
    pDC->TextOut(0,0,"Press the left mouse button here.");
}
```

While you're in EX08AVW.CPP, add the following include statement near the top of the file:

```
#include "ex08adlg.h"
```

4. **Install the GRID control in App Studio.** Start App Studio by choosing App Studio from Visual Workbench's Tools menu. Choose Install Controls from the App Studio File menu, and specify \WINDOWS\SYSTEM\GRID.VBX. A Grid button will appear in the control palette when you edit the dialog.

5. **Use App Studio to create the dialog *IDD_DIALOG1*.** Use the dialog pictured in Figure 8-1 on page 134 as a model. Click on Dialog in the Type list, and then click the New button. The New Resource dialog appears. Click on Dialog in the Resource Type list, and then click the OK button. A new window appears, showing the *IDD_DIALOG1* dialog, and the control palette also appears, containing the Grid button as shown here:

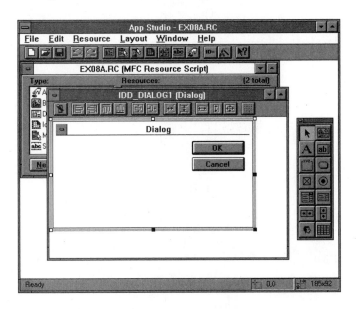

Draw a large GRID control on the *IDD_DIALOG1* dialog. Double-click on the *IDD_DIALOG1* dialog to open the Properties window. Set the GRID control's Rows property to *12* and the Cols property to *8*. Notice that there are many GRID properties you can't set at design time, including the column width, row height, and initial cell text. The GRID control ID defaults to *IDC_GRID1*.

Add buttons to the dialog, and then assign button and edit control IDs as follows:

Control	ID	Caption
OK button	*IDOK* (the default)	OK (the default)
Cancel button	*IDCANCEL* (the default)	Cancel (the default)
Add Row button	*IDC_ADDROW*	Add Row
Delete Row button	*IDC_DELETEROW*	Delete Row
Edit window	*IDC_VALUE*	
Update Value button	*IDC_UPDATEVALUE* (default button)	Update Value

6. **Use ClassWizard to create the *CEx08aDialog* class.** Choose ClassWizard from the App Studio Resource menu. Fill in the Add Class dialog, as shown here:

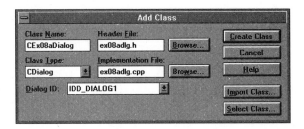

Click the Create Class button. The ClassWizard dialog appears, as shown here:

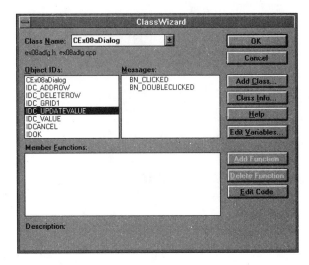

Add message-handling functions as shown in the following table. To add a message-handling function, click on an object ID, click on a message, and then click the Add Function button. The Add Member Function dialog appears. Type the function name, and click the OK button.

Object ID	Message	Function Name
CEx08aDialog	WM_INITDIALOG	OnInitDialog
IDC_ADDROW	BN_CLICKED	OnClickedAddrow
IDC_DELETEROW	BN_CLICKED	OnClickedDeleterow
IDC_GRID1	VBN_SELCHANGE	OnSelchangeGrid1
IDC_UPDATEVALUE	BN_CLICKED	OnClickedUpdatevalue
IDCANCEL	BN_CLICKED	OnCancel
IDOK	BN_CLICKED	OnOK

Now click the Edit Variables button and add the following two dialog data members:

Control ID	Member Variable Name	Property	Variable Type
IDC_VALUE	m_cellValue	Value	CString
IDC_GRID1	m_pVBGrid	Control	CVBControl*

Save changes and exit App Studio when you're done.

7. **Add an array data member in EX08ADLG.H.** The *m_dArray* data member is a two-dimensional array of doubles that correspond to the values in the Grid control. Put the array inside the *CEx08aDialog* declaration but outside the *AFX_DATA* brackets.

```
// Dialog Data
double m_dArray[8][12];
//{{AFX_DATA(CEx08aDialog)
enum { IDD = IDD_DIALOG1 };
CVBControl*  m_pVBGrid;
CString      m_cellValue;
//}}AFX_DATA
```

8. **Add a member function prototype in EX08ADLG.H.** Add the function prototype as shown:

```
// Implementation
private:
    void ComputeSums();
```

9. **Code the *OnInitDialog* function in EX08ADLG.CPP.** Visual Basic controls use a measurement system called "logical twips." If you want to convert between pixels and logical twips, you can't rely on the *CDC* functions *DPtoLP* and *LPtoDP*; rather, you must do the conversions yourself using values returned by the *CDC GetDeviceCaps* function.

The first part of the *OnInitDialog* function sets the column widths to ⅛ of the control's client-area width, and it sets the row height to ¹⁄₁₂ of the total control height. The client-area width in logical twips is computed according to the following formula:

client logical twips = client pixels × 1440 / logical pixels per inch

The *CWnd GetClientRect* function retrieves a rectangle whose width is the width of the client rectangle in device coordinates (pixels).

Now look at the first *for* loop. This code cycles through all 8 columns and sets the column width and column heading, using the *CVBControl Set-NumProperty* and *SetStrProperty* member functions. ColWidth is an indexed property, which means you must use the index parameter to set the element's value. Text is not indexed but depends on both the Col and Row properties having been set to point to a particular cell.

The second *for* loop sets the row heights and row labels. It also sets the indexed FixedAlignment and ColAlignment properties of all the fixed cells (top row, left column) to centered alignment and the ColAlignment property of the other cells to right alignment.

The nested *for* loops near the end of the function set a grid cell's text to the value in the corresponding *m_dArray* data member. The double values must be converted to strings before they can be used to set the cells' Text property. The following screened code replaces the existing code:

```
BOOL CEx08aDialog::OnInitDialog()
{
    CRect rect;
    char  temp[20];
    int   i, j;
    long  lColWidth, lRowHeight;

    VERIFY(CDialog::OnInitDialog());
    VERIFY(m_pVBGrid->GetNumProperty("Cols") == 8L); // set in App Studio
    VERIFY(m_pVBGrid->GetNumProperty("Rows") == 12L);
    CClientDC dc(this);
    m_pVBGrid->GetClientRect(rect); // device coordinates
    lColWidth  = m_pVBGrid->GetNumProperty("ColWidth", 0);
    lRowHeight = m_pVBGrid->GetNumProperty("RowHeight", 0);
    lColWidth  = (1440L * (long) rect.right) /
                 (8L * (long) dc.GetDeviceCaps(LOGPIXELSX)) - 20L;
    lRowHeight = (1440L * (long) rect.bottom) /
                 (12L * (long) dc.GetDeviceCaps(LOGPIXELSY)) - 20L;

    m_pVBGrid->SetNumProperty("Row", 0);
    for (i = 0; i < 8; i++) {
```

```
m_pVBGrid->SetNumProperty("ColWidth", lColWidth, i);
if (i) { // column headings
    m_pVBGrid->SetNumProperty("Col", i);
    m_pVBGrid->SetStrProperty("Text", CString('A' + i - 1));
}
}

m_pVBGrid->SetNumProperty("Col", 0);
for (j = 0; j < 12; j++) {
    m_pVBGrid->SetNumProperty("RowHeight", lRowHeight, j);
    m_pVBGrid->SetNumProperty("FixedAlignment", 2, j); // centered
    m_pVBGrid->SetNumProperty("ColAlignment", 1, j);   // right
    if (j) { // row headings
        m_pVBGrid->SetNumProperty("Row", j);
        sprintf(temp, "%d", j);
        m_pVBGrid->SetStrProperty("Text", temp);
    }
}
// sets the spreadsheet values from m_dArray
for (i = 1; i < 8; i++) {
    m_pVBGrid->SetNumProperty("Col", i);
    for (j = 1; j < 11; j++) {
        m_pVBGrid->SetNumProperty("Row", j);
        sprintf(temp, "%8.2f", m_dArray[i][j]);
        m_pVBGrid->SetStrProperty("Text", temp);
    }
}
ComputeSums();
// be sure there's a selected cell
m_pVBGrid->SetNumProperty("Col", 1L);
m_pVBGrid->SetNumProperty("Row", 1L);
m_cellValue = m_pVBGrid->GetStrProperty("Text");
UpdateData(FALSE); // calls DoDataExchange to update edit control
return TRUE;
}
```

10. **Code the *OnOK* function in EX08ADLG.CPP.** This function retrieves the grid
    cell values and stores them in the *m_dArray* data member. The following
    screened code replaces the existing code:

```
void CEx08aDialog::OnOK()
{
    int i, j;

    for (i = 1; i < 8; i++) {
        m_pVBGrid->SetNumProperty("Col", i);
        for (j = 1; j < 11; j++) {
            m_pVBGrid->SetNumProperty("Row", j);
            m_dArray[i][j] = atof(m_pVBGrid->GetStrProperty("Text"));
        }
    }
    CDialog::OnOK();
}
```

141

11. **Code the *OnClickedAddrow* and *OnClickedDeleterow* functions in EX08A-DLG.CPP.** To add or delete a row, a cell must be currently selected. Notice the use of the *AddItem* and *RemoveItem* method functions. The following screened code replaces the existing code:

```
void CEx08aDialog::OnClickedAddrow()
{
    if (m_pVBGrid->GetNumProperty("CellSelected") == 0) {
        AfxMessageBox("No cell selected");
        return;
    }
    LONG i = m_pVBGrid->GetNumProperty("Row");
    m_pVBGrid->AddItem("new row", i);
    ComputeSums();
}

void CEx08aDialog::OnClickedDeleterow()
{
    if (m_pVBGrid->GetNumProperty("CellSelected") == 0) {
        AfxMessageBox("No cell selected");
        return;
    }
    LONG i = m_pVBGrid->GetNumProperty("Row");
    m_pVBGrid->RemoveItem(i);
    ComputeSums();
}
```

12. **Code the *OnClickedUpdatevalue* function in EX08ADLG.CPP.** This function is activated by the Update Value button, which is the dialog's default button. Its main duty is to transfer the edit control value to the selected grid cell. It also computes the sum of each column and stores the results in row 11. The program takes advantage of the fact that pressing Enter sends the same message as clicking the default button. When the user enters a value in the one-and-only edit control, he or she can press Enter to make *OnClickedUpdatevalue* process the value. The following screened code replaces the existing code:

```
void CEx08aDialog::OnClickedUpdatevalue()
{
    char    temp[30];
    double value;
    LONG    lRow, lCol;

    if (m_pVBGrid->GetNumProperty("CellSelected") == 0) {
        AfxMessageBox("No cell selected");
        return;
    }
    UpdateData(TRUE);
    value = atof(m_cellValue);
    sprintf(temp, "%8.2f", value);

    // saves current cell selection
    lCol = m_pVBGrid->GetNumProperty("Col");
    lRow = m_pVBGrid->GetNumProperty("Row");
```

```
m_pVBGrid->SetStrProperty("Text", temp); // copies new value
                                         //   to selected cell
ComputeSums();

// restores current cell selection
m_pVBGrid->SetNumProperty("Col", lCol);
m_pVBGrid->SetNumProperty("Row", lRow);
}
```

13. **Code the *OnSelchangeGrid1* function in EX08ADLG.CPP.** This function handles the GRID control's SelChange event. It copies the selected cell's value to the edit control so that the user can update it. The *m_pVBGrid* pointer must be tested for a NULL value because the first SelChange event occurs before the pointer is initialized. The following screened code replaces the existing code:

```
void CEx08aDialog::OnSelchangeGrid1(UINT, int, CWnd*, LPVOID)
{
    if (m_pVBGrid) {
        m_cellValue = m_pVBGrid->GetStrProperty("Text");
        UpdateData(FALSE); // calls DoDataExchange to update edit control
        GotoDlgCtrl(GetDlgItem(IDC_VALUE)); // position to edit control
    }
}
```

14. **Code the private *ComputeSums* function in EX08ADLG.CPP.** Type in the following screened code:

```
void CEx08aDialog::ComputeSums()
{
    int     i, j, nRows;
    double sum;
    char    temp[30];

    // add up each column and put the sum in bottom row
    // row count could have been changed by add row/delete row
    nRows = (int) m_pVBGrid->GetNumProperty("Rows");
    for (i = 1; i < 8; i++) {
        m_pVBGrid->SetNumProperty("Col", i);
        sum = 0.0;
        for (j = 1; j < nRows - 1; j++) {
            m_pVBGrid->SetNumProperty("Row", j);
            sum += atof(m_pVBGrid->GetStrProperty("Text"));
        }
        sprintf(temp, "%8.2f", sum);
        m_pVBGrid->SetNumProperty("Row", nRows - 1);
        m_pVBGrid->SetStrProperty("Text", temp);
    }
}
```

15. **Build and run the EX08A program.** In Visual Workbench, choose Build from the Project menu, and then choose Execute. The resulting output looks like that shown in Figure 8-1 on page 134. Try updating values, and then try deleting and adding rows. Check that the sums in the bottom row are correct.

> **Note:** *If you don't see all the numbers in the grid, you need to make the grid larger in App Studio.*

Using Other Visual Basic Controls

The GRID control is not the best example of a Visual Basic control, but it is a good learning tool. Many sophisticated Visual Basic controls are available from third-party software firms. Until the Visual C++ installed base grows, the documentation for these controls will be oriented only to Visual Basic. You will have to "translate" the Visual Basic calling sequences to C++, but this shouldn't be too difficult if you have studied the EX08A example. A few Visual Basic methods, such as *Drag* and *SetFocus*, aren't directly supported by the class library.

Chapter 11 uses another Visual Basic control, CNTR.VBX. This control is available on the companion disk included with this book.

Visual Basic Picture Properties

Some Visual Basic controls, GRID included, support picture properties. Technical Note 27 in the MFCNOTES.HLP Help file explains how the class library supports these Visual Basic picture properties.

Advantages and Disadvantages of Writing and Using Visual Basic Controls

If a developer writes a Visual Basic control, that control can be sold to both Visual Basic and Visual C++ programmers. That in itself should be reason enough to write a Visual Basic control instead of an ordinary custom control. Also, App Studio directly supports Visual Basic controls. Once a Visual Basic control is installed in App Studio, a corresponding button appears in the control palette, the control is visible in a dialog, and the design-time properties can be set.

On the negative side, Visual Basic controls are less efficient than ordinary DLLs because of the need to communicate via properties instead of directly by function calls. You can improve efficiency if you use property index numbers instead of property name strings. The *CVBControl* member function *GetPropIndex* returns a property's index value, which you can use subsequently for getting and setting properties.

Also, Visual Basic controls aren't very compatible with the class library document-view architecture. A GRID control, for example, stores all its spreadsheet data inside itself. This makes it difficult to support multiple views of spreadsheet data.

For the time being, if you write your own Visual Basic controls, you'll have to use C, and that means you won't get the benefit of the class library classes. Of course, you must write ordinary custom control DLLs in C too.

9

Windows Memory Management— Just Say "New"

If you've read about memory management in other books on Microsoft Windows, you'll wonder whether I'm talking about the same Windows operating system here. Yes, indeed I am, but I'm talking about "post real mode" Windows—versions 3.1 and later. The old Intel 8088 microprocessor chips, as found in the original IBM PC, are no longer supported. As the 8088 chip fades from view, so does real mode with its 1-MB memory limitation and lack of hardware memory management. In its place is 16-bit protected mode with a much larger address space and two levels of hardware memory management.

Many of the ugly things the older books about Windows discuss—memory handles, locking, burgermasters, thunks, and so forth—are no longer relevant. Some nasties remain, particularly segments, but even segments are due to disappear when we move to 32-bit Windows.

You were able to get started with Visual C++ programming without knowing anything about Windows memory management. If you've followed the examples up to this point, you've used the C++ *new* operator when you wanted heap memory, and your applications have worked fine. As you write larger and more sophisticated Windows programs, you'll still use *new*, but you'll need to know what Windows does behind the scenes to make some basic decisions. Should you use the medium or large memory model? What's the difference between far and near declarations? Must your program periodically reorganize its heap memory?

This chapter starts with an advance look at 32-bit programming for Windows and suggests a strategy for migration to this up-and-coming environment. Not left out, however, is the here-and-now 16-bit protected mode environment. You'll learn about segments, the near heap, the far heap, and near vs. far function calls. You'll also learn how to make your large-model application run in "multiple instance" mode.

A Memory Model Review

If you've been writing C programs for Intel microprocessors, you're no doubt familiar with the four standard "memory models." The following table shows the relationships between memory models and address lengths:

	16-Bit Data Addresses	32-Bit Data Addresses
16-Bit Code Addresses	Small	Compact
32-Bit Code Addresses	Medium	Large

You'll learn more about the composition of these address fields later.

We're very close to the age of 32-bit Windows, with its flat 32-bit address space. Indeed, Microsoft Foundation Class Library version 2.0 was designed with 32-bit Windows in mind, and it has already been tested with the Windows NT operating system. Most class library applications you write now should be portable to Windows NT with a simple recompilation and relink—that is, unless you make your code too dependent on the current 16-bit memory architecture.

How do you eliminate 16-bit dependencies? For a start, you can use the large memory model for all your applications. This might sound like heresy because other books have warned you specifically to avoid the large model for Windows-based programs. There were some good reasons not to use the large model in the old real mode, but the real mode wicked witch is dead. The 16-bit large memory model generally uses 32-bit addresses for both programs and data, and this closely matches what you'll find in the 32-bit versions of Windows.

Yes, your large-model compiled program will be a bit larger than the medium-model equivalent, and execution will be a little slower, but you will save development time because you won't have to worry about the distinction between 16-bit "near" and 32-bit "far" pointers. If you apply the development time savings to profiling and otherwise optimizing your application, you'll come out ahead, plus you'll have a program that is easily portable to the 32-bit environment.

16-Bit Windows

Now it's back to reality. Users will have Windows version 3.1 for a while, and you'll have to produce 16-bit applications to run on that operating system. So you're stuck learning about segments, near heap memory management, and the various 16-bit memory models.

The Intel Segment Architecture

The Intel 80286, 80386, and 80486 families of microprocessor chips support the 16-bit protected mode. The segment is the basic memory allocation unit, and it can have a maximum size of 64 KB. All memory addresses are composed of a 16-bit segment address (also known as a "selector") and a 16-bit offset within the segment. The microprocessors listed above all support a hardware memory management scheme that uses a descriptor table in memory. Each entry in the table maps a 13-bit descriptor table index, contained in the selector, to a physical memory address range. Windows can shuffle segments in physical memory if it updates the base address in the descriptor table accordingly. If necessary, you can specify that particular segments be fixed in physical memory.

The size of segments can change too. If your program is using a 20-KB segment, for example, and it needs that segment "expanded" to 40 KB, the operating system allocates a new 40-KB segment, copies the contents from the original 20-KB segment, and then frees the original 20-KB segment for subsequent use by other programs. Because the selector does not change (only the base address in the descriptor table changes), your program can continue to use the data in the bottom 20 KB of the new segment as though the data had never moved. Figure 9-1 is a simplified illustration of the descriptor table in action.

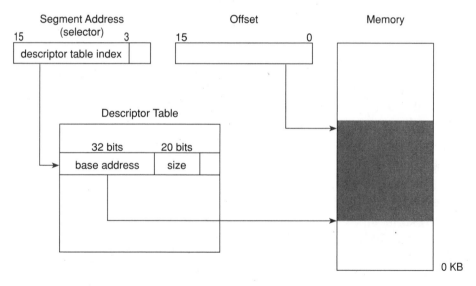

Figure 9-1.
Protected mode addressing for the 80386 microprocessor.

Segments store code or data. Code segments are considered "read-only" because their contents don't change during program execution. Data segments are usually "read/write" because a running program changes memory variables. The Windows memory manager takes an active role in writing and reading segments to and from disk during program execution. If memory is full, the Windows memory manager can discard a code segment that hasn't been used in a while. Windows reloads a discarded code segment when a program needs it. (Discarding an infrequently used code segment is not usually necessary in 386 enhanced mode because of Windows' virtual memory manager.)

The DGROUP Segment and Multi-Instance Programs

All Windows and MS-DOS programs use one special segment: the "default data segment," known as the DGROUP segment. This segment contains the stack together with some (or all) of the application's static data plus data in the local heap (explained later). When a program is running, the data segment (DS) and stack segment (SS) registers are loaded with the DGROUP segment address, in such a manner that subsequent memory reference instructions access data in the DGROUP segment.

> **Note:** *You specify the maximum stack size in the program's Memory Image category of the Linker Options dialog. AppWizard uses a default value of 10,240.*

Under certain conditions, a Windows program can run in multi-instance mode. This means you can start several instances of a program, but only one copy of the program's code will be loaded into memory. Windows Notepad is a good example of a multi-instance program. Each instance of the program has its own DGROUP segment, assigned at startup. For a program to run in multi-instance mode, all its data (with some exceptions) must fit into one segment. This restriction is necessary because the DS register, loaded once for each instance, can address only one segment at a time.

Windows can move a DGROUP segment to another location in physical memory because it is accessed through the descriptor table the same way as any other segment.

Memory Models—One Code Segment or Many?

In the "small" and "compact" memory models, all the application's code must fit into one code segment. Simple Windows SDK programs can be compiled for the small or compact models because most of their functionality is contained in the Windows kernel and DLLs. Class library programs are generally too large for the small model because many class library functions must be statically linked. With the medium and large models, the code is split into several code segments. Therefore, you'll see most Windows programs use these large-code models.

With the medium and large models, the default compiler behavior is to make one code segment for each C or C++ source module. This is fine for applications that typically have three or four source modules. If you used the same strategy for libraries, however, you might have too many code segments. (This would be very rare—the descriptor table can contain up to 8192 8-byte entries.) The compiler directive *#pragma code_seg* enables you to combine the code from multiple source modules into a single code segment. The __*based* keyword or the compiler directive *#pragma alloc_text* allows you to split a C source module's code into several segments.

If you need a Windows application to run on a computer with limited memory, you can "swap-tune" the program by matching functions with code segments according to the program's execution pattern. The Module Definition File (DEF) defines the attributes of the segments. You can, for example, select which segments are initially loaded into memory when the application starts. (See the *Command-Line Utilities User's Guide* for more information.)

> **Note:** *Generally, you cannot mix modules compiled for different memory models. If you compile a module for the medium model, for example, you cannot link it with another module compiled for the small or large model.*

Near Function Calls

By default, in the medium and large memory models, function calls use 32-bit addresses (selector plus offset). This rule applies even to calls within a single segment. If you know that a particular function won't be called from outside its segment, you can declare it near and thus make the compiler generate a shorter, faster, 16-bit calling sequence. Near declarations are handy for private class member functions. If you follow the convention of placing all a class's member functions in one source file, you know that a private function can't be called from outside that module (unless the class or function is declared a *friend*). Here's an example:

```
class CMyView : public CView
{
// constructor, macros, etc. not shown
private:
    void NEAR NearTest();
    void FarTest();
public:
    virtual void OnDraw(CDC* pDC);
};

void CMyView::OnDraw(CDC* pDC)
{
    NearTest();
    FarTest();
}

void NEAR CMyView::NearTest()
{
    int i = 0; // force compiler to generate some code
}
```

(continued)

149

```
void CMyView::FarTest()
{
    int i = 0; // force compiler to generate some code
}
```

It's interesting to look at the generated code for the calls to *NearTest* and *FarTest*. Here is what you get with the medium model:

```
        NearTest();
2737:0271 56                PUSH    SI
2737:0272 E8E700            CALL    CEx12View::NearTest (035C)
        FarTest();
2737:0275 56                PUSH    SI
2737:0276 9A7E033727        CALL    CEx12View::FarTest (2737:037E)
```

You saved 2 bytes by using a near function—big deal.

Here is the equivalent large-model code:

```
        NearTest();
252F:02B7 FF7608            PUSH    WORD PTR [BP+08]
252F:02BA FF7606            PUSH    WORD PTR [This]
252F:02BD E81601            CALL    CEx12View::NearTest (03D6)
        FarTest();
252F:02C0 FF7608            PUSH    WORD PTR [BP+08]
252F:02C3 FF7606            PUSH    WORD PTR [This]
252F:02C6 9AF4032F25        CALL    CEx12View::FarTest (252F:03F4)
```

As you can see, the large model has even more code, and you still save 2 bytes by using a near function.

Memory Models—One Data Segment or Many?

You might think that the small and medium models imply one data segment and that the large and compact models imply several data segments. The rules are more complex than that. A medium-model application, for example, might use several data segments, and a large-model application might use only one data segment. What's going on?

Here is a summary of the data access rules by memory model:

■ *Small and medium models*

□ The default pointer size is 16 bits.

□ The stack, all static variables, and the local heap are in the DGROUP segment.

□ The C++ *new* operator allocates memory from the Windows local heap.

- **Large and compact models**

  □ The default pointer size is 32 bits.

  □ The stack is in the DGROUP segment.

  □ Static variables, excluding non-near C++ objects, are in the DGROUP segment when possible.

  □ DGROUP static variables are accessed via 16-bit addresses where possible.

  □ Large static items are located in their own data segments.

  □ C++ non-near static objects are located in a data segment associated with their code module.

  □ The C++ *new* operator allocates memory from the Windows global heap.

But what do these rules mean to the average programmer? First of all, the medium memory model doesn't give you much data space. You're limited to 64 KB total, and all of that isn't usable. (Some of this memory is used by the stack, uninitialized global and static near data, and compiler-generated near data.) If you want, you can do "mixed-model" programming, which involves declaring far (32-bit) pointers to data in other data segments and using the Windows global memory allocation functions instead of *new*. Maybe the large model isn't such a bad idea after all!

If you're using the large model, you can make your program run multi-instance if you ensure that it has only one data segment. The project's map file (MAP) specifies how many data segments are in your program. To ensure one data segment, don't declare large amounts of static data (either large individual objects or numerous small ones), and be sure that all global C++ objects (particularly your *CWinApp* object) are declared near.

> **Note:** *With the large model, you can force a module's static data to reside in a particular data segment by using the* #pragma data_seg *statement. Be careful when referencing* extern *static data that is not in the DGROUP segment. You must declare the variables* far, *or you must check the Assume* 'extern' *and Uninitialized Data* 'far' *check box in the Memory Model category of the Compiler Options dialog (/Gx- switch).*

Now that you're beginning to understand the difference between near (16-bit offset only) and far (segment address plus offset) addressing, it's time to look at some more compiler-generated code. Assume that *i* is a static integer variable. With the medium model (and, most of the time, with the large model), static variables are stored in the DGROUP segment, and you get the following machine instruction:

```
    i = 0;
247F:02CB C7067E140000   MOV     WORD PTR [?I@@3HE (147E)],0000
```

Now, with the large model and the variable *i* in a different data segment, you get two instructions instead of one:

```
    i = 0;
252F:02CB 8E060C10        MOV        ES,[100C]
252F:02CF 26C70636140000 MOV        WORD PTR ES:[?I@@3HE (1436)],0000
```

The extra MOV instruction loads the extended data segment (ES) register with the segment selector value that is stored in a temporary variable (100C) in the DGROUP segment. Notice the addition of 5 bytes of code. These bytes do add up in a large application. In 32-bit Windows, however, the code will be simpler and shorter.

The Local Heap

If you use the small or medium memory model, the C++ *new* operator is mapped to the compiler's _nmalloc (that is, near *malloc*) function, which in turn is mapped directly to the Windows *LocalAlloc* function. What does this mean? It means that you're using the "local heap" that is entirely contained in your application's DGROUP segment. The initial size of the heap is specified in the module definition file.

When you get memory from the local heap, the underlying DGROUP segment can move and change size, but the allocated memory blocks have fixed offsets within the segment. This means that local heap memory can become fragmented. In the old days, Windows programmers would call *LocalAlloc* themselves and then carefully lock and unlock the returned "memory handles" to allow Windows to shuffle the individual blocks within the heap. There's still some benefit to doing this, but the technique excludes use of the *new* operator. Most fragmentation problems disappear when you switch to the large model and the Windows global heap.

The Global Heap

With the large and compact memory models, the C++ *new* operator is mapped to the compiler's _fmalloc function. In Microsoft C version 6.0, _fmalloc called the Windows *GlobalAlloc* function directly, and *GlobalAlloc* allocated a brand-new movable segment on the "global heap" each time it was called. Because the number of descriptor table entries is limited (4096 segment selectors with 80286 computers and 8192 selectors with 80386- and 80486-based computers), you couldn't afford to use _fmalloc every time you needed a little bit of memory.

With Microsoft C/C++ version 7.0 and with Visual C++, the _fmalloc function works differently (as does the *new* operator). The _fmalloc function now does "sub-segment allocation," which means that it can satisfy many memory requests by allocating a single large segment. The Windows *GlobalAlloc* function is called only when necessary to get a new segment. The amount of memory actually allocated is rounded up to the nearest 4-KB boundary. If a segment needs to grow, it is reallocated with the Windows *GlobalReAlloc* function, also to the nearest 4-KB boundary.

Note: *The 4-KB minimum allocation and reallocation sizes are subject to change. You can set internal Windows variables, and future versions of Windows might change the default values.*

Global heap segments are completely movable and resizable through their descriptor table selectors, but the memory offsets within the segments are fixed. This means that you can still have fragmentation within a segment.

There's another problem too. Suppose your program allocates five memory blocks in three segments and then frees blocks 2, 3, and 5, as shown in Figure 9-2.

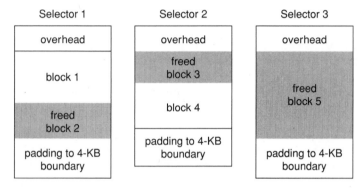

Figure 9-2.
Memory allocation with freed blocks.

All freed memory is available to your program, but the third segment is not returned to Windows, even though your program is not using it. You can avoid this condition if your program frequently calls the _heapmin function. Figure 9-3 shows the effects of _heapmin on the three segments above.

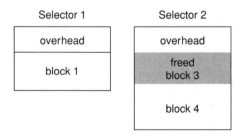

Figure 9-3.
The third segment (Selector 3, shown in Figure 9-2) has been returned to Windows.

Now the second segment has been reallocated, and the third segment has been returned to Windows with the *GlobalFree* function. The padding bytes have been removed too.

Location of the Program's vtable

The "vtable" is the data structure that dispatches calls to C++ virtual functions. In all class library applications, whatever the memory model, the vtable is stored in a code segment. You never have to worry about the vtable using up valuable space in your DGROUP segment.

Direct Use of Windows Memory Allocation Functions

In many Windows applications, you can get away with not directly using any Windows memory allocation functions. (Just say "new.") In a few cases, however, you need them. If you're using the Windows clipboard or dynamic data exchange (DDE), you need sharable memory. You can call *GlobalAlloc* directly with the flag parameter set to *GMEM_DDESHARE*, but then you're stuck using one of those obsolete Windows memory handles. Try using *GlobalAllocPtr* instead. This macro, defined in WINDOWSX.H, allocates memory, locks the handle, and returns a pointer to the locked memory block. The companion *GlobalFreePtr* macro unlocks and frees the memory identified by a pointer. See Chapter 23 for a global memory usage example.

Suppose you've been asked to write a Windows-based program to control the neighborhood nuclear plant. You absolutely can't afford to have the program crash as a result of memory fragmentation. In this case, you might be forced to write your own memory manager, based on *GlobalAllocPtr* and *GlobalFreePtr*. This memory manager might allocate memory in fixed-size chunks, or it might periodically perform garbage collection to compact the heap. The *_fheapwalk* function is helpful if you want to know what memory your program has allocated on the global heap.

The 80386/80486 Virtual Memory Manager

Now that you think you have memory management all figured out, I'm going to throw a whole new memory management system at you. This 386 enhanced mode virtual memory allocation system works separately and <u>on top of</u> the segment scheme you've seen already. Once physical memory fills up, memory pages, each 4 KB in size, are swapped to and from disk. The net result is a linear memory address space that can be as large as 64 megabytes (MB). Usually, the address space is much smaller. It's limited by the size of the Windows swap file (386SPART.PAR, SPART.PAR, or WIN386.SWP), which depends on the amount of physical memory and the space available on the hard disk. Figure 9-4 illustrates 386 enhanced mode memory management.

This virtual memory manager pretty much defeats the Windows segment management capability. Because Windows thinks it has, say, 20 MB of RAM, it won't have to discard or even move its segments until the 20 MB are used up. The virtual memory manager is in control, swapping (but not discarding) 4-KB blocks. This puts a different spin on swap-tuning. The new goal is to combine related code and data in 4-KB chunks. This, incidentally, is the same strategy that you'll need for 32-bit Windows.

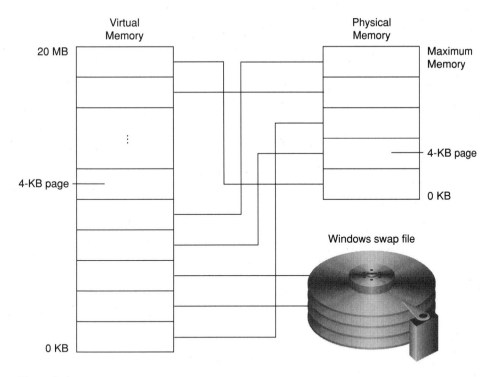

Figure 9-4.
386 enhanced mode memory management.

Detecting Memory Leaks

Memory fragmentation can affect program performance, but memory "leaks" frequently cause programs to crash. A memory leak occurs when your program fails to free an allocated memory block. If you consistently use the *new* operator for allocating heap memory, you can benefit from the application framework's diagnostic memory manager. When you use the Debug build option, *new* is overloaded to write signature bytes for the blocks it allocates. Thus you can request a "snapshot" of the heap at any time. This dump identifies all C++ objects and non-object blocks.

Chapter 15 explains the memory dump process, which requires a knowledge of the *CObject* and *CDumpContext* classes. You'll see that the application framework automatically dumps all allocated memory blocks that have not been freed when the program terminates. Remember that you must allocate memory with *new* to take advantage of this application framework diagnostic feature; if you use *GlobalAlloc*, you can rely on the Windows Debug Kernel to tell you about unfreed allocation units.

10

Bitmaps

Without graphics images, Windows-based applications would be pretty dull. Some applications depend on images for their usefulness, but any application can be spruced up with the addition of decorative clip art from a variety of sources. Windows bitmaps are arrays of bits mapped to display pixels. That might sound simple, but you have to learn a lot about bitmaps before you can use them to create professional Windows-based applications.

This chapter starts with the simplest bitmap program—one that loads and displays a bitmap from a resource. The second example shows you how to use bitmaps for smooth movement of items on the screen. You'll have to wait until Chapter 23, however, to see the real power of bitmaps. There you'll save bitmaps on disk and print them out, and you'll also transfer them to other applications by means of the clipboard.

GDI Bitmaps and Device-Independent Bitmaps (DIBs)

The two kinds of Windows bitmaps are GDI bitmaps and DIBs. GDI bitmap objects are represented by the Microsoft Foundation Class Library version 2.0 *CBitmap* class. The bitmap object has an associated Windows data structure, maintained inside the Windows GDI module, that is device-dependent. Your program can get a copy of the bitmap data, but the bit arrangement depends on the display hardware. GDI bitmaps can be freely transferred among programs on a single computer, but because of the device dependency, transferring them by disk or modem doesn't make sense.

The DIB is an alternative bitmap format that solves the interchangeability problem. Any computer running Windows can process DIBs, which are usually stored in BMP disk files. The wallpaper that forms your background is read from a BMP file when you start Windows. The primary storage format for Windows Paintbrush is the BMP file, and App Studio uses BMP files for toolbar buttons and other images. When a BMP file is read from disk, it's often translated into a GDI bitmap, but programs can work directly from the DIB format if necessary.

Using GDI Bitmaps

A GDI bitmap is simply another GDI object, such as a pen or a font. You must somehow create a bitmap, and then you must select it into a device context. When you're done with the object, you must deselect it and delete it. You know the drill.

There's a catch, though, because the "bitmap" of the display or printer device is effectively the display surface or the printed page itself. Therefore, you can't select a bitmap into a display device context or a printer device context. You have to create a special memory device context for your bitmaps, using the *CreateCompatibleDC* function. You must then use the *CDC* member function *StretchBlt* or *BitBlt* to copy the bits from the memory device context to the "real" device context. These "bit-blitting" functions are generally called in your view class's *OnDraw* function. Of course, you mustn't forget to clean up the memory display context when you're done.

Color Bitmaps and Monochrome Bitmaps

Now might be a good time to reread the "Windows Color Mapping" section in Chapter 5. As you'll see here, Windows deals with color bitmaps a little differently from the way it deals with brush colors.

Most color bitmaps are 16-color. A standard VGA board has 4 contiguous "color planes," with 1 corresponding bit from each plane combining to represent a pixel. The 4-bit color values are set when the bitmap is created. With a standard VGA board, you don't have control of the colors that are displayed. The GDI allows dithered bitmap colors if a color's pixel pattern is simple enough.

With monochrome bitmaps, you have more flexibility. A monochrome bitmap has only one plane. Each pixel is represented by a single bit that is either on or off. The *CDC SetTextColor* function sets the "on" display color, and *SetBkColor* sets the "off" color. You can specify both of these colors with the Windows *RGB* macro.

Loading a GDI Bitmap from a Resource

The easiest way to use a bitmap is to load it from a resource. If you open a resource script with App Studio, you'll find a list of bitmap resources. If you select any bitmap and examine its properties, you'll see a filename. Here's an example entry in an RC file, when viewed by a text editor:

```
IDB_LEAVES              BITMAP  DISCARDABLE     "RES\\LEAVES.BMP"
```

IDB_LEAVES is the resource ID, and the file is LEAVES.BMP in the project's RES subdirectory. (LEAVES is one of the Windows 3.1 wallpaper bitmaps, normally located in the WINDOWS directory.) The resource compiler reads the DIB from disk and stores it in the RES file. The resource-binding process copies the DIB into the program's EXE file. The LEAVES bitmap must be in device-independent format because the EXE can be run with any display board that Windows supports.

The *CDC LoadBitmap* function converts a resource-based DIB to a GDI bitmap. Below is the simplest possible self-contained *OnDraw* function that displays the LEAVES bitmap.

```
CMyView::OnDraw(CDC* pDC)
{
    CDC* pDisplayMemDC = new CDC;
    CBitmap* pBitmap = new CBitmap;
    pBitmap->LoadBitmap(IDB_LEAVES);
    pDisplayMemDC->CreateCompatibleDC(pDC);
    CBitmap* pOldBitmap = (CBitmap*)
                        pDisplayMemDC->SelectObject(pBitmap);
    pDC->BitBlt(100, 100, 200, 150, pDisplayMemDC, 0, 0, SRCCOPY);
    delete pDisplayMemDC->SelectObject(pOldBitmap); // deletes pBitmap
    delete pDisplayMemDC;
}
```

The *BitBlt* function copies the LEAVES pixels from the memory display context to the display (or printer) device context. The LEAVES bitmap is 200 pixels by 150 pixels, and, on the display, it occupies a rectangle 200 logical units by 150 logical units, offset 100 units down and to the right of the upper left corner of the window's client area.

The Effect of the Display Mapping Mode

If the display mapping mode in the LEAVES example is *MM_TEXT*, each bitmap pixel maps to a display pixel, and the bitmap looks nice. If the mapping mode is *MM_LOENGLISH*, the bitmap size is 2.0 inches by 1.5 inches, or 192 pixels by 144 pixels on a VGA screen, and the GDI must do some bit-crunching to make the bitmap fit. Consequently, the bitmap won't look as good with the *MM_LOENGLISH* mapping mode.

Stretching the Bits

What if we want LEAVES to occupy a rectangle exactly 200 pixels by 150 pixels, even though the mapping mode is not *MM_TEXT*? The *StretchBlt* function is the answer. If we replace the *BitBlt* call with the following three statements, LEAVES is displayed cleanly, whatever the mapping mode.

```
CRect rect(0, 0, 320, 240);
pDC->DPtoLP(&rect);
pDC->StretchBlt(0, 0, rect.Width(), rect.Height(),
                pDisplayMemDC, 0, 0, 200, 150, SRCCOPY);
```

With either *BitBlt* or *StretchBlt*, the display update is slow if the GDI has to actually stretch or compress bits. If the GDI determines, as in the case above, that no conversion is necessary, the update is fast.

The EX10A Program

The EX10A example displays a resource-based bitmap in a scrolling view with mapping mode set to *MM_LOENGLISH*. The program uses the *StretchBlt* logic described above, except that the memory device context and the bitmap are created in the view's *OnCreate* member function and last for the life of the program. Also, the program reads the bitmap size through a call to the *CGdiObject* member function *GetObject*, so it's not using hard-coded values as in the examples above.

Here are the steps for building the example:

1. **Run AppWizard to produce \VCPP\EX10A\EX10A.** Choose AppWizard from Visual Workbench's Project menu. The options and the default class names are shown here:

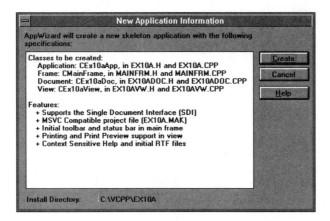

Be sure to select the Context Sensitive Help option in the Options dialog and accept the Printing and Print Preview default.

2. **Change the *CEx10aView* base class from *CView* to *CScrollView*.** Edit EX10AVW.H and EX10AVW.CPP; make the appropriate global replacements.

3. **Use ClassWizard to add a view message handler for WM_CREATE.** Choose the *CEx10aView* class, and then let ClassWizard add the *OnCreate* member function.

4. **Add the following data members to class *CEx10aView*.** Edit the file EX10AVW.H. The memory device context lasts for the life of the view. The integers are the source (bitmap) and destination (display) dimensions.

```
private:
    CDC*    m_pDisplayMemDC;
    HBITMAP m_hOldDisplayBitmap;
    int     m_nSWidth, m_nSHeight, m_nDWidth, m_nDHeight;
```

5. Edit the following member functions in class *CEx10aView*. Edit the file
EX10AVW.CPP. The *OnCreate* function sets up the memory display context
and the bitmap; the *OnDraw* function has only to call *BitBlt*. When *OnCreate*
sets the bitmap destination dimensions, it multiplies the pixel values by 4 to
make a giant-size bitmap. *OnCreate* must save the old bitmap handle in the
data member *m_hOldDisplayBitmap* so that the destructor can restore it later.
You've already seen this technique used for fonts.

```
int CEx10aView::OnCreate(LPCREATESTRUCT lpCreateStruct)
{
    if (CScrollView::OnCreate(lpCreateStruct) == -1)
        return -1;

    BITMAP bm; // Windows BITMAP data structure (see Win 3.1 help)
    CSize totalSize(800, 1050); // 8" x 10.5"
    CSize lineSize = CSize(totalSize.cx / 100, totalSize.cy / 100);
    SetScrollSizes(MM_LOENGLISH, totalSize, totalSize, lineSize);

    CClientDC dc(this);
    OnPrepareDC(&dc);  // necessary
    m_pDisplayMemDC = new CDC;
    CBitmap* pBitmap = new CBitmap;
    pBitmap->LoadBitmap(IDB_APPEXIT);
    m_pDisplayMemDC->CreateCompatibleDC(&dc);
    CBitmap* pOldBitmap = (CBitmap*)
                        (m_pDisplayMemDC->SelectObject(pBitmap));
    m_hOldDisplayBitmap = (HBITMAP) pOldBitmap->GetSafeHandle();

    pBitmap->GetObject(sizeof(bm), &bm);
    m_nSWidth = bm.bmWidth;
    m_nSHeight = bm.bmHeight;
    CRect rect(0, 0, m_nSWidth, m_nSHeight); // size of the bitmap
    dc.DPtoLP(&rect);
    m_nDWidth = rect.Width() * 4;
    m_nDHeight = rect.Height() * 4; // display bitmap dimensions

    return 0;
}

void CEx10aView::OnDraw(CDC* pDC)
{
    pDC->StretchBlt(100, -100, m_nDWidth, m_nDHeight,
                    m_pDisplayMemDC, 0, 0, m_nSWidth,
                    m_nSHeight, SRCCOPY);
}

CEx10aView::~CEx10aView()
{
    // clean up the memory display context and the bitmap
    delete m_pDisplayMemDC->SelectObject(CBitmap::FromHandle
                                (m_hOldDisplayBitmap));
    delete m_pDisplayMemDC;
}
```

6. **In App Studio, import the *IDB_APPEXIT* bitmap.** Choose App Studio from Visual Workbench's Tools menu, and then choose Import from App Studio's Resource menu. Select the file \VCPP\EX10A\HLP\APPEXIT.BMP. AppWizard generated this file when you asked for context-sensitive help. Now App Studio will copy it into the project's RES subdirectory. Assign the ID *IDB_APPEXIT* and save the changes.

7. **Build and test the EX10A application.** Your screen should look like this:

The bitmap "bits" are now exactly 4 pixels by 4 pixels.

8. **Try the Print Preview function.** The bitmap prints to scale because the application framework applies the *MM_LOENGLISH* mapping mode to the printer device context just as it does to the display device context.

Using Bitmaps to Improve the Screen Display

You've seen an example program that displayed a bitmap that originated outside the program. Now you'll see an example program that generates its own bitmap to support smooth motion on the screen. The principle is simple: You draw on a memory device context with a bitmap selected, and then you "zap" the bitmap onto the screen.

The EX10B Program

In the EX05C example, the user can drag a circle with the mouse. As the circle moved, the display flickered because the circle was erased and redrawn on every mouse move message. EX10B uses a GDI bitmap to correct the problem. The EX05C custom code for mouse message processing carries over almost intact; most of the new code is in the *OnPaint* and *OnCreate* functions.

In summary, the EX10B *OnCreate* function creates a memory device context and a bitmap that are compatible with the display. The *OnPaint* function prepares the memory device context for drawing, passes *OnDraw* a handle to the memory device context, and copies the resulting bitmap from the memory device context to the display.

Here are the steps to build EX10B from scratch:

1. Run AppWizard to produce \VCPP\EX10B\EX10B. Choose AppWizard from Visual Workbench's Project menu. The options and the default class names are shown here:

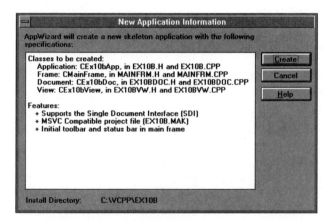

2. Change the *CEx10bView* base class from *CView* to *CScrollView*. The example would work with the ordinary view base class, but it's more general if you use the scroll view. As in EX10A, you must globally replace *CView* with *CScrollView* in EX10BVW.H and EX10BVW.CPP.

3. Use ClassWizard to add *CEx10bView* message handlers. Add message handlers for the following messages:

☐ WM_CREATE

☐ WM_LBUTTONDOWN

☐ WM_LBUTTONUP

☐ WM_MOUSEMOVE

☐ WM_PAINT

4. Edit the EX10BVW.H header file. Add the private data members shown at the top of the following page to the *CEx10bView* class:

```
private:
    CRect    m_ellipseRect;
    CPoint   m_mousePos;
    BOOL     m_bCaptured;
    CDC*     m_pMemDC;
    CBitmap* m_pBitmap;
```

5. **Code the *CEx10bView* constructor and destructor in EX10BVW.CPP.** You need a memory device context object and a bitmap GDI object. These are constructed in the view's constructor and destroyed in the view's destructor.

```
CEx10bView::CEx10bView() : m_ellipseRect(0, 0, 100, -100) // constructor
{
    m_bCaptured = FALSE;
    m_pMemDC    = new CDC;
    m_pBitmap   = new CBitmap;
}

CEx10bView::~CEx10bView()          // destructor
{
    delete m_pBitmap;              // already deselected
    delete m_pMemDC;
}
```

6. **Add code for the *OnCreate* function in EX10BVW.CPP.** The C++ memory device context and bitmap objects are already constructed. This function creates the corresponding Windows objects. Both the device context and the bitmap are compatible with the display context *dc*, but you must explicitly set the memory display context's mapping mode to match the display context. You could create the bitmap in the *OnPaint* function, but the program runs faster if you create it once here.

```
int CEx10bView::OnCreate(LPCREATESTRUCT lpCreateStruct)
{
    if (CScrollView::OnCreate(lpCreateStruct) == -1)
        return -1;

    // sets the scrolling parameters as in EX05C
    CSize totalSize = CSize(800 * 2, 800 * 2);
    CSize pageSize  = CSize(totalSize.cx / 2, totalSize.cy / 2);
    CSize lineSize  = CSize(totalSize.cx / 100, totalSize.cy / 100);
    SetScrollSizes(MM_LOENGLISH, totalSize, pageSize, lineSize);

    // creates the memory device context and the bitmap
    CClientDC dc(this);
    OnPrepareDC(&dc);
    CRect rectMax(0, 0, totalSize.cx, -totalSize.cy);
    dc.LPtoDP(rectMax);
```

```
m_pMemDC->CreateCompatibleDC(&dc);
// makes the bitmap the same size as the display window
m_pBitmap->CreateCompatibleBitmap(&dc, rectMax.right,
                                        rectMax.bottom);
m_pMemDC->SetMapMode(MM_LOENGLISH);

    return 0;
}
```

7. Add code for the *OnPaint* function in EX10BVW.CPP. Normally, it isn't necessary to override *OnPaint* to reduce screen flicker through the use of a memory display context. The *CView* version of *OnPaint* contains the following code:

```
CPaintDC dc(this);
OnPrepareDC(&dc);
OnDraw(&dc);
```

In this example, you will be overriding *OnPaint* to reduce screen flicker through the use of a memory display context. *OnDraw* is passed this memory display context for the display, and it is passed the printer device context for printing. Thus *OnDraw* can perform tasks common to the display and the printer. You don't need to use the bitmap with the printer because the printer has no speed constraint.

The overridden *OnPaint* must perform three steps to prepare the memory device context for drawing. Here are the three steps, in order:

☐ Select the bitmap into the memory device context.

☐ Transfer the invalid rectangle (as calculated by *OnMouseMove*) from the display context to the memory device context. There is no *SetClipRect* function, but the *CDC IntersectClipRect* function, when called after the *CDC SelectClipRgn* function (with a *NULL* parameter), has the same effect. If you don't set the clipping rectangle to the minimum size, the program runs slower.

☐ Initialize the bitmap to the current window background color. The *CDC PatBlt* function fills the specified rectangle with a pattern. In this case, the pattern is the brush pattern for the current window background. That brush must first be constructed and selected into the memory device context.

After the memory device context is prepared, *OnPaint* can call *OnDraw* with a memory device context parameter. Afterward, the *CDC BitBlt* function copies the updated rectangle from the memory device context to the display device context.

```
void CEx10bView::OnPaint()
{
    CRect updateRect;

    CPaintDC dc(this);
    OnPrepareDC(&dc);
    dc.GetClipBox(&updateRect);
    CBitmap* pOldBitmap = (CBitmap*) (m_pMemDC->SelectObject(m_pBitmap));

    m_pMemDC->SelectClipRgn(NULL);
    m_pMemDC->IntersectClipRect(&updateRect);
    CBrush backgroundBrush((COLORREF) ::GetSysColor(COLOR_WINDOW));
    CBrush* pOldBrush = m_pMemDC->SelectObject(&backgroundBrush);
    m_pMemDC->PatBlt(updateRect.left, updateRect.top,
                     updateRect.Width(), updateRect.Height(), PATCOPY);
    OnDraw(m_pMemDC);
    dc.BitBlt(updateRect.left, updateRect.top,
              updateRect.Width(), updateRect.Height(), m_pMemDC,
              updateRect.left, updateRect.top, SRCCOPY);
    m_pMemDC->SelectObject(pOldBitmap);
    m_pMemDC->SelectObject(pOldBrush);
}
```

8. **Code the *OnDraw* function in EX10BVW.CPP.** This *CEx10bView* member function is similar to the EX05C *OnDraw* function except that it draws a stationary black square in addition to the moving circle. In EX10B, *OnDraw* is passed a pointer to a memory device context by the *OnPaint* function. For printing, *OnDraw* is passed a pointer to the printer device context.

```
void CEx10bView::OnDraw(CDC* pDC)
{
    pDC->SelectStockObject(BLACK_BRUSH);
    pDC->Rectangle(100, -100, 200, -200);
    pDC->SelectStockObject(GRAY_BRUSH);
    pDC->Ellipse(m_ellipseRect);
}
```

9. **Copy mouse message-handling code from EX05CVW.CPP.** Copy the following functions from EX05CVW.CPP to EX10BVW.CPP. Be sure to change the class names of these functions from *CEx05cView* to *CEx10bView*.

   ☐ *OnLButtonDown*

   ☐ *OnLButtonUp*

   ☐ *OnMouseMove*

10. **Change one line in the *OnMouseMove* function in EX10BVW.CPP.** Change
the line

```
InvalidateRect(invalidRect, TRUE);
```

to

```
InvalidateRect(invalidRect, FALSE);
```

If the second *CWnd InvalidateRect* parameter is *TRUE*, Windows erases the
background before repainting the invalid rectangle. That's what you needed in
EX05C, but the background erasure is what causes the flicker. Because the entire invalid rectangle is being copied from the bitmap, you no longer need to
erase the background. The *FALSE* parameter prevents this erasure.

11. **Build and run the application.** Here is the EX10B program output:

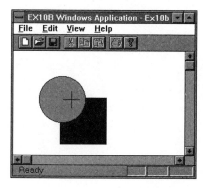

Is the circle's movement smoother now?

Other Uses for GDI Bitmaps

GDI bitmaps are often used in animation. At the start of a program, you might create
a series of bitmaps that correspond to states of an animated object. Logic in the
OnPaint function would then select the appropriate bitmap into the memory display
context, and then *OnPaint* would use the *BitBlt* function to copy from the memory
device context to a specific rectangular region in the display context. If the moving
object is not itself rectangular, you must use some of the more esoteric *BitBlt* "raster
operation codes" (ROPs) to merge the moving object with the rest of the display
image. You might even need a separate "mask" bitmap. The *BitBlt SRCCOPY* ROP
parameter in EX10B causes the source bitmap to be copied directly to the
destination bitmap. See the *Class Library Reference* for information about other
raster operation codes.

11

Bitmap Buttons, the Timer, and On-Idle Processing

This chapter presents a few useful Microsoft Foundation Class Library programming techniques that don't depend on the document–view architecture. First you'll build a dialog that contains graphical bitmap buttons, and then you'll exercise the Windows timer. Last you'll see two places to attach "on-idle" code. (On-idle code can be used to perform background tasks while no messages are being processed.) The on-idle example introduces the application framework's main frame class, thus making this chapter a lead-in to Part 3 of this book.

Bitmap Buttons

The class library's *CBitmapButton* class allows you to easily create buttons that are labeled with graphics instead of text. You <u>don't</u> have to call *BitBlt* or *StretchBlt*. This chapter's first example shows you how to add bitmap buttons to a dialog.

The EX11A Program

In this example, you'll build a dialog with three bitmap buttons. These buttons use Copy, Cut, and Paste bitmaps "stolen" from the help system. So that you'll know the buttons are working, the program displays appropriate text in a static text control and sets a dialog data member when you click the buttons.

Follow these steps closely to construct the example:

1. **Run AppWizard to produce \VCPP\EX11A\EX11A.** Choose AppWizard from Visual Workbench's Project menu. The options and the default class names are shown at the top of the next page:

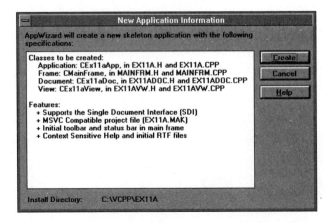

Be sure to specify the Context Sensitive Help option to create the bitmap files that the example needs.

2. **Start App Studio, and then import the button bitmaps.** Choose Import from App Studio's Resource menu to import and name the following bitmap files. You'll be importing each resource <u>twice</u>, once for the button's up (U) state and again for the button's down (D) state.

File	First Resource ID	Second Resource ID
HLP\EDITCOPY.BMP	"COPYU"	"COPYD"
HLP\EDITCUT.BMP	"CUTU"	"CUTD"
HLP\EDITPAST.BMP	"PASTEU"	"PASTED"

Be sure to use quotation marks in the ID field of the Bitmap Properties dialog to ensure that the resources are identified by strings instead of constants. The IDs will thus not appear in the RESOURCE.H file.

3. **Invert the colors for the "down" bitmaps.** Select the COPYD bitmap, and then choose Invert Colors from the App Studio Image menu. Repeat for the CUTD and PASTED bitmaps. At runtime, when a bitmap button changes from the up state to the down state, the U (noninverted) bitmap is replaced with the D (inverted) bitmap, which changes the button's colors. The screen at the top of the next page shows the COPYD bitmap in App Studio.

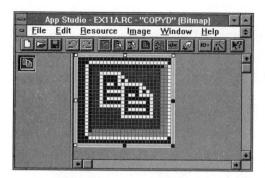

4. Use App Studio to produce the dialog *IDD_BITMAP*. Create the dialog shown here:

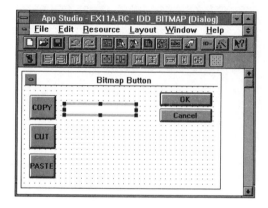

Notice the highlighted static text control in the dialog.

The three bitmap buttons are defined as follows:

Button ID	Caption
IDC_EDIT_COPY	COPY
IDC_EDIT_CUT	CUT
IDC_EDIT_PASTE	PASTE

(Note: Be sure to use uppercase for the captions.)

Check the Owner Draw check box in the Push Button Properties dialog for each bitmap button.

The button captions correspond to the bitmap resource names. When the application framework draws the button COPY, it looks for bitmap resources named COPYD and COPYU.

Change the static text control's ID to *IDC_MESSAGE*.

5. **Use ClassWizard to generate the *CEx11aDialog* class.** If you run Class-Wizard from inside App Studio, you won't have to specify the dialog ID. Fill in the Add Class dialog as shown here:

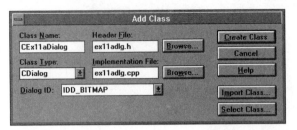

After the class is generated, define the following message handlers:

Object ID	Message	Member Function Name
CEx11aDialog	WM_INITDIALOG	*OnInitDialog*
IDC_EDIT_COPY	BN_CLICKED	*OnClickedEditCopy*
IDC_EDIT_CUT	BN_CLICKED	*OnClickedEditCut*
IDC_EDIT_PASTE	BN_CLICKED	*OnClickedEditPaste*

Don't bother to define any dialog class data members with ClassWizard.

6. **Add data members to the *CEx11aDialog* class.** In the EX11ADLG.H file, add the following *friend* statement and private data members in the *CEx11aDialog* class declaration:

```
friend class CEx11aView;
private:
    CBitmapButton m_editCopy;
    CBitmapButton m_editCut;
    CBitmapButton m_editPaste;
    int m_nButton; // 1=copy, 2=cut, 3=paste, 0=none
```

7. **Edit the EX11ADLG.CPP file.** The *CBitmapButton AutoLoad* function initializes a button by loading the bitmap and sizing the button to fit the bitmap. Call it in the dialog's *OnInitDialog* function.

```
BOOL CEx11aDialog::OnInitDialog()
{
    VERIFY(m_editPaste.AutoLoad(IDC_EDIT_PASTE, this));
    VERIFY(m_editCut.AutoLoad(IDC_EDIT_CUT, this));
    VERIFY(m_editCopy.AutoLoad(IDC_EDIT_COPY, this));
    return CDialog::OnInitDialog();
}
```

The following button message handlers set the text in the dialog's static control, and they set the value of *m_nButton*, which is available to the view class:

```
void CEx11aDialog::OnClickedEditCopy()
{
    SetDlgItemText(IDC_MESSAGE, "Copy");
    m_nButton = 1;
}

void CEx11aDialog::OnClickedEditCut()
{
    SetDlgItemText(IDC_MESSAGE, "Cut");
    m_nButton = 2;
}

void CEx11aDialog::OnClickedEditPaste()
{
    SetDlgItemText(IDC_MESSAGE, "Paste");
    m_nButton = 3;
}
```

Typically, you use these functions to set dialog data members that would be returned to the view.

8. Edit the *CEx11aView* class in EX11AVW.CPP to accommodate the dialog.
With ClassWizard, add a message handler for the WM_LBUTTONDOWN message for the view, and then edit the code as follows:

```
void CEx11aView::OnLButtonDown(UINT nFlags, CPoint point)
{
    CEx11aDialog dlg;

    if (dlg.DoModal() == IDOK) {
        TRACE("Result = %d\n", dlg.m_nButton);
    }
}
```

Pressing the left mouse button while the mouse cursor is inside the view window activates the dialog.

Add the following *#include* statement to EX11AVW.CPP:

```
#include "ex11adlg.h"
```

While you are in EX11AVW.CPP, edit the *OnDraw* function to display a message:

```
void CEx11bView::OnDraw(CDC* pDC)
{
    pDC->TextOut(0, 0, "Press the left mouse button here.");
}
```

9. Build and test the program. When you press the left mouse button while the mouse cursor is inside the view window, you should see the EX11A dialog at the top of the next page:

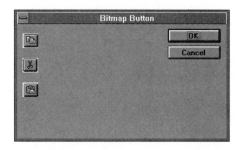

A message appears when you click on a bitmap button. The bitmap buttons are smaller than the rectangles you specified in App Studio. (See the dialog shown in step 4, above.) They shrank because the application framework maps the bitmap bits to pixels in the dialog.

Going Further with Bitmap Buttons

Bitmap buttons can assume "focused" and "disabled" states in addition to the "up" and "down" states you've already seen. If the button has a bitmap resource name that ends in *F*, then that bitmap appears when the button has the input focus. If the resource name ends in *X*, then that bitmap appears when the button is disabled (through a call to the *CWnd EnableWindow* function, for example). See the *Class Library Reference* for more details on the *CBitmapButton* class.

Using a Timer and Yielding Control

You can program a Windows timer to send your program messages at regular intervals independent of microprocessor speed. You can use timers to control animation speed, to trigger alarms, to implement pseudo multitasking, or, as illustrated by the following example, to provide a visual status indication during a long compute process.

Timers

Timers are easy to use. You simply call the *CWnd* function *SetTimer* with an interval parameter, and then you provide, with the help of ClassWizard, a message handler function for the WM_TIMER message. If you set the timer interval to, say, 200 milliseconds, WM_TIMER messages will be generated at that interval until you call the *CWnd* function *KillTimer* or until the timer's window is destroyed.

Simultaneous Timers

Windows version 3.1 allows a total of 32 simultaneous timers. In a real application, you must be prepared for the possibility that all timers are in use, as indicated by a *0* return code from *SetTimer*.

A simple timer-based animation program is trivial. The view's *OnCreate* function starts the timer, and the timer message handler updates position variables and invalidates a rectangle. The *OnDraw* function paints the image according to the position variables. The EX11B sample program later in this chapter is a little more interesting because you'll be using the timer to interrupt a long compute process. While you experiment with the timer, you'll learn more about Windows message processing, and you'll gain some insights for building your own multitasking applications.

Yielding Control

The 16-bit Windows model is definitely not a preemptive multitasking operating system. If your program enters a long compute loop, it takes complete control of the computer unless it is nice enough to yield control. So why yield control? Maybe the user needs to click a Cancel button to terminate the process, or maybe the user would like the ability to switch to another application. In case you haven't guessed, the timer won't work unless your program yields control.

How do you yield control? To understand the answer, you must delve a little deeper into the Windows message-handling process. You've already seen the tail end of the process—your message-handling member functions are called in response to messages such as BN_CLICKED (actually a WM_COMMAND message). Windows provides access to these messages, directly from the message queue, at an early stage in their development. If you put the following code almost anywhere in a Windows program, you can see the raw messages as they come in.

```
MSG Message; // Windows message structure
while (1) {  // infinite loop
    if (::PeekMessage(&Message, NULL, 0, 0, PM_REMOVE)) {
      TRACE("message = %x, wParam = %x, lParam = %lx\n",
            Message.message, Message.wParam, Message.lParam);
      ::TranslateMessage(&Message);
      ::DispatchMessage(&Message);
    }
}
```

If you look for WM_COMMAND or WM_CHAR messages after the *PeekMessage* call, you'll never see any because they don't come into existence until after the call to *TranslateMessage*. This translation function converts WM_KEYDOWN messages to WM_CHAR messages, and, if the user clicks a dialog button, the resulting WM_LBUTTONDOWN message is converted to the appropriate WM_COMMAND message. You'll never see a WM_PAINT message either because these messages bypass the message queue.

The application framework, while in control, gets the raw messages from the queue and calls *TranslateMessage* and *DispatchMessage*. If your program takes control, it must do the dispatch work to keep the messages flowing. All you need to do, every once in a while, is make the calls to *PeekMessage*, *TranslateMessage*, and *DispatchMessage*.

The EX11B Program

Suppose your application has a process that takes several minutes. If you let your program take control of the computer during that interval, even if it displays an hourglass cursor, the user is likely to get frustrated and reboot the machine. It's customary to provide a visual "percent complete" indicator to relieve the user's anxiety. In EX11B, we'll use a scroll bar control as an indicator, and we'll use a timer to update the thumbtrack every 100 milliseconds. (Of course, a real application would never use a scroll bar for this purpose, but it serves as a useful example.) We'll tie the compute process to this EX11B modal dialog:

Here are the steps for building the EX11B application:

1. **Run AppWizard to produce \VCPP\EX11B\EX11B.** Choose AppWizard from Visual Workbench's Project menu. The options and the default class names are shown here:

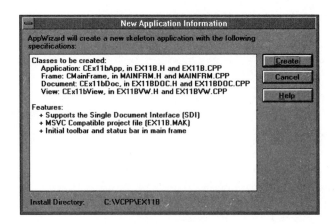

2. **Add a WM_LBUTTONDOWN message handler to *CEx11bView* in EX11B-VW.CPP.** First edit the virtual *OnDraw* function to display a message:

```
void CEx11bView::OnDraw(CDC* pDC)
{
    pDC->TextOut(0, 0, "Press the left mouse button here.");
}
```

Then use ClassWizard to add the *OnLButtonDown* function, and add the following code:

```
void CEx11bView::OnLButtonDown(UINT nFlags, CPoint point)
{
    CEx11bDialog dlg;

    dlg.DoModal();
}
```

This code brings up the modal dialog whenever the user presses the left mouse button while the mouse cursor is in the view window.

While you're in EX11BVW.CPP, add the following #*include* statement:

```
#include "ex11bdlg.h"
```

3. **Use App Studio to create the dialog *IDD_DIALOG1*.** Use the dialog shown in step 1, above, as a model. Keep the default control IDs for the scroll bar and Cancel button, but use *IDC_START* for the Start button. Save the resource script when you're finished.

4. **Use ClassWizard to create the *CEx11bDialog* class.** Choose ClassWizard from the App Studio Resource menu. Fill in the Add Class dialog as shown here:

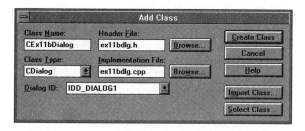

After the class is generated, add message-handling functions for *IDC_START*, *IDCANCEL*, and WM_TIMER. (Add BN_CLICKED message handlers for *IDC_START* and *IDCANCEL*. Accept the default names *OnClickedStart* and *OnCancel*.)

5. **Add the following data members in EX11BDLG.H:**

```
private:
    long m_lCount;
    static const long m_lMaxCount;
```

The *m_lCount* data member of class *CEx11bDialog* is incremented during the compute process. It serves as a percent complete measurement when divided by the static variable *m_lMaxCount*.

6. **Add a static variable to EX11BDLG.CPP.** The static data member *m_lMax-Count* was declared in the class header, but it must be defined in the EX11BDLG.CPP file.

```
const long NEAR CEx11bDialog::m_lMaxCount = 500L;
```

7. **Add initialization code to the *CEx11bDialog* constructor in EX11BLG.CPP.** Add the following line to the constructor to ensure that the Cancel button works if the compute process was not started.

```
m_lCount = 0L;
```

8. **Code the *OnClickedStart* function in EX11BDLG.CPP.** This code is executed when the user clicks the Start button.

```
void CEx11bDialog::OnClickedStart()
{
    MSG Message;
    int nTemp;

    SetTimer(1, 100, NULL); // 1/10 second
    GetDlgItem(IDC_START)->EnableWindow(FALSE);
    for (m_lCount = 0L; m_lCount < m_lMaxCount; m_lCount++) {
        for (nTemp = 0; nTemp < 30000; nTemp++) {} // simulate computation
            if (::PeekMessage(&Message, NULL, 0, 0, PM_REMOVE)) {
                ::TranslateMessage(&Message);
                ::DispatchMessage(&Message);
            }
    }
    KillTimer(1);
    CDialog::OnOK();
}
```

The main *for* loop is controlled by the value of *m_lCount*. Each time through the loop, *PeekMessage* allows other messages, including WM_TIMER, to be processed. The *EnableWindow(FALSE)* call disables the Start button during the computation. If we didn't take this precaution, the *OnClickedStart* function could be reentered.

9. **Code the *OnTimer* function in EX11BDLG.CPP.** When the timer fires, the scroll bar's scroll box is set according to the value of *m_lCount*.

```
void CEx11bDialog::OnTimer(UINT nIDEvent)
{
    CScrollBar* pBar = (CScrollBar*) GetDlgItem(IDC_SCROLLBAR1);
    pBar->SetScrollRange(0, (int) m_lMaxCount);
    pBar->SetScrollPos((int) m_lCount);
}
```

10. **Update the *OnCancel* function in EX11BDLG.CPP.** When the user clicks the Cancel button during computation, we don't destroy the dialog, but we set *m_lCount* to its maximum value, which causes *OnClickedStart* to exit the dialog. If the computation hasn't started, it's OK to exit directly.

```
void CEx11bDialog::OnCancel()
{
    TRACE("entering CEx11bDialog::OnCancel\n");
    if (m_lCount == 0L) { // prior to Start button
        CDialog::OnCancel();
    }
    else { // computation in progress
        m_lCount = m_lMaxCount; // force exit from OnClickedStart
    }
}
```

11. **Build and run the application.** Press the left mouse button while the mouse cursor is inside the view window to bring up the dialog. Try the Start button, and then try Cancel. The scroll bar's scroll box should move during the computation.

On-Idle Processing

When it doesn't have anything else to do, the application framework calls an on-idle function that is, by default, a dummy function. If you have a long computation that can be conveniently broken into chunks or if you must regularly update an element on the screen, you should consider hooking into this on-idle function. Remember that any on-idle function should complete its work and return to Windows as soon as possible; otherwise, the performance of other applications will suffer.

The application framework's standard on-idle function is *CWinApp::OnIdle*. You can override this function in your derived application class if you need to do special processing. *OnIdle* doesn't get called, however, when the menu system or a modal dialog is active. If you need to do on-idle processing for modal dialogs and menus, you'll have to add a message handler function for the WM_ENTERIDLE message, but you must add it to the <u>frame</u> class rather than to the view class. That's because pop-up dialogs are always "owned" by the application's main frame window, not by the view window.

The EX11C Program

This example uses CNTR, a cute little Visual Basic control that acts like an automobile odometer. CNTR.VBX is not included with Visual C++, but a copy of it is on the companion disk. After you install the companion disk, you'll find a copy of the file CNTR.VBX in your \VCPP\EX11C subdirectory. Copy this file to your

\WINDOWS\SYSTEM subdirectory. The CNTR control appears twice in the EX11C example—once in the view window and once in a dialog. Here is EX11C in action:

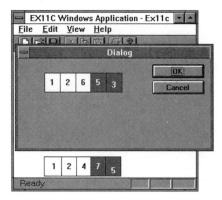

When the program starts, the view's counter runs. When the dialog comes up (in response to a mouse click), the dialog's counter starts and the view's counter stops.

Here are the steps for building the EX11C application:

1. **Run AppWizard to produce \VCPP\EX11C\EX11C.** Choose AppWizard from Visual Workbench's Project menu. The options and the default class names are shown here:

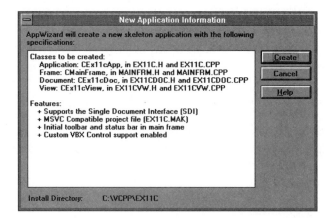

Be sure to select the Custom VBX Controls option.

2. **Add a data member and function prototype to *CEx11cApp*.** The derived application class is declared in the file EX11C.H. For the view's CNTR control, we need an object of class *CVBControl*. The application class is the best place for the control because the application class's *OnIdle* function must be able to access the control. It's easy for the view object to find the application object

when it's time to create the CNTR control window. Because the control object is embedded, we don't have to worry about its destruction.

```
public:
    CVBControl m_cntr;
```

We're going to override the *CWinApp OnIdle* function; so we'll need a function prototype in the application's class.

```
virtual BOOL OnIdle(LONG lCount);
```

3. **Add the *CEx11cApp OnIdle* function in *EX11C.CPP*.** The application framework calls this overridden *OnIdle* function whenever the application's modal dialog and menu are not active. Each time it's called, the function increments the value of the CNTR control, which is a child of the view window.

```
BOOL CEx11cApp::OnIdle(LONG lCount)
{
    CWinApp::OnIdle(lCount);
    float val = m_cntr.GetFloatProperty("value");
    val += (float) .001;
    m_cntr.SetFloatProperty("value", val);
    return TRUE;
}
```

4. **Use ClassWizard to add message handlers in *CEx11cView*.** In EX11CVW.H, add message handlers for WM_CREATE and WM_LBUTTONDOWN.

5. **Code the *CEx11cView OnCreate* message-handling function.** In EX11C-VW.CPP, find the ClassWizard-generated skeleton and add code as shown:

```
int CEx11cView::OnCreate(LPCREATESTRUCT lpCreateStruct)
{
    if (CView::OnCreate(lpCreateStruct) == -1)
        return -1;

    CVBControl* pCntr = &((CEx11cApp*) AfxGetApp())->m_cntr;
    pCntr->Create("CNTR.VBX;Counter;", WS_VISIBLE | WS_CHILD | WS_BORDER,
                  CRect(50, 175, 180, 208), this, 1);
    pCntr->SetNumProperty("DigitsLeft", 3);
    pCntr->SetNumProperty("DigitsRight", 2);
    pCntr->SetFloatProperty("Value", 123.45);

    return 0;
}
```

This function actually creates the CNTR control window for the *CVBControl* object that's embedded in the application object.

6. **Code the *CEx11cView OnLButtonDown* message-handling function.** First, in EX11CVW.CPP, edit the virtual *OnDraw* function to display a message:

```
void CEx11cView::OnDraw(CDC* pDC)
{
    pDC->TextOut(0, 0, "Press the left mouse button here.");
}
```

Then find the ClassWizard-generated skeleton and add code as shown:

```
void CEx11cView::OnLButtonDown(UINT nFlags, CPoint point)
{
    CEx11cDialog dlg;

    dlg.DoModal();
}
```

This function activates the dialog that will contain the other CNTR control.

While you're in EX11CVW.CPP, add the following *#include* statement:

```
#include "ex11cdlg.h"
```

7. **Use App Studio to create a dialog.** Use the dialog shown on page 180 as a model. Accept the default ID *IDD_DIALOG1*. Be sure you first install the Visual Basic control CNTR.VBX. (Choose Install Controls from the App Studio File menu to do so.) Position the CNTR control, and then double-click on it to bring up its Counter Properties dialog. Set its DigitsRight property to *2*. Save the changes when you're finished.

8. **Use ClassWizard to create the *CEx11cDialog* class.** Choose ClassWizard from the App Studio Resource menu.

Fill in the Add Class dialog, as shown here:

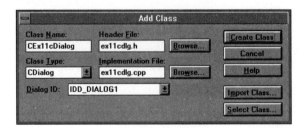

You don't need any message handlers, but you must add data members for the dialog's CNTR control. Click the Edit Variables button, and then add the variables at the top of the next page for the *IDC_COUNTER1* control:

Variable	Property	Type	Description
m_fCntrValue	Value	*float*	Control's floating-point value
m_pVBCntr	Control	*CVBControl*∗	CNTR control pointer

9. **Use ClassWizard to add a WM_ENTERIDLE message handler to *CMain-Frame* in MAINFRM.CPP.** The frame class *OnEnterIdle* function is called when <u>any</u> menu or modal dialog is active. In this example, it updates the dialog's CNTR control. Both the *CEx11cDialog* dialog and the system menu can trigger a call to *OnEnterIdle*. Because there are two dialogs in this program (*IDD_ABOUTBOX* and *IDD_DIALOG1*), the program must be sure that this *OnEnterIdle* call is associated with the dialog that contains the counter. Only the *IDD_DIALOG1* dialog has a control with ID *IDC_COUNTER1*.

```
void CMainFrame::OnEnterIdle(UINT nWhy, CWnd* pWho)
{
    CVBControl* pVBc = ((CVBControl*) pWho)->GetDlgItem(IDC_COUNTER1);
    if (pVBc != NULL) {
      float val = pVBc->GetFloatProperty("value");
      val += (float) .001;
      pVBc->SetFloatProperty("Value", val);
    }
}
```

While you're in MAINFRAM.CPP, add the following *#include* statement:

```
#include "ex11cdlg.h"
```

10. **Build and test the application.** As pictured in the screen on page 180, the lower view CNTR should come up and run when the program starts. When you click inside the view window, the dialog's CNTR dialog should appear and the counter should run. Dismiss the dialog, and then close the main window.

> **FYI:** *Try starting a second instance of the application. This is really interesting. The dialog's counter blocks the view's counter in its own instance, but Windows permits counters to run simultaneously in the other views.*

THE DOCUMENT–VIEW ARCHITECTURE

12

Menus and Keyboard Accelerators

In all the examples to this point, mouse clicks have triggered most program activity. Even though menu selections might have been more appropriate, we've used mouse clicks because mouse click messages are handled simply and directly within the Microsoft Foundation Class Library version 2.0 view window. If you want program activity to be triggered when the user chooses a command from a menu, you must first become familiar with the other application framework elements.

This chapter concentrates on menus and the "command routing architecture." Along the way, it introduces frames and documents, explaining the relationships between these new application framework elements and the already-familiar view element. You'll use App Studio to lay out a menu visually, and you'll use ClassWizard to link document and view member functions to menu items. You'll learn how to use special update command user interface member functions to check and disable menu items, and you'll see how to use keyboard accelerators as menu shortcut keys.

At the end of the chapter is an example that shows you how to create dynamic menus whose content is determined at runtime. Here you'll bypass App Studio and instead use the low-level menu elements together with the extended command message handlers. In case you're tired of the circles used in earlier examples, this chapter introduces the *CEditView* class, which behaves in the same way as does a simple text editor.

The Main Frame Window and Document Classes

Up to now, you've been using a view window as if it were the application's only window. In an SDI application, the view window sits inside another window—the application's main frame window. It's the main frame window that has the title bar and the menu bar. Various child windows, including the view window, the toolbar window, and the status bar window, occupy the main frame window's client area. (See Figure 12-1.) The application framework controls the interaction between the frame and the view by routing messages from the frame to the view.

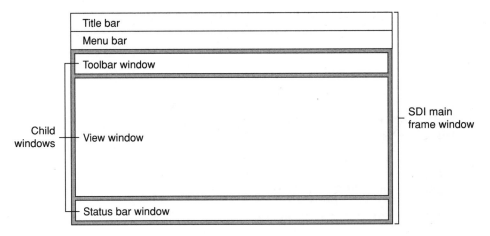

Figure 12-1.
The child windows within an SDI main frame window.

Look again at the files generated by AppWizard. The MAINFRM.H and MAIN-FRM.CPP files contain the code for the application's main frame window class, derived from the class *CFrameWnd*. Other files, with names such as EX12ADOC.CPP and EX12ADOC.H, contain code for the application's document class, which is derived from *CDocument*. Starting with this chapter, you'll be modifying those frame and document files a lot.

Windows Menus

A Windows menu is the familiar application element that consists of a top-level horizontal list of items with associated pop-up menus that appear when the user selects a top-level item. Most of the time, you define a default menu resource for a frame window that loads when the window is created. You can also define a menu resource independently of a frame window. In that case, your program must call the functions necessary to load and activate the menu.

A menu resource completely defines the initial appearance of a menu. Menu items can be grayed or have check marks, and bars can separate groups of menu items. Multiple levels of pop-up menus are possible. If a first-level menu item is associated with a subsidiary popup, the menu item carries a right-pointing arrowhead symbol, as shown in Figure 12-2, next to the Pattern menu item.

App Studio includes an easy-to-use menu resource editing tool. With this tool, you edit menus in a wysiwyg environment. Each menu item has a properties dialog that defines all the characteristics of that item. The resulting resource definition is stored in the application's resource script (RC) file. Each menu item is associated with an ID, such as *ID_FILE_OPEN*, that is defined in the RESOURCE.H file.

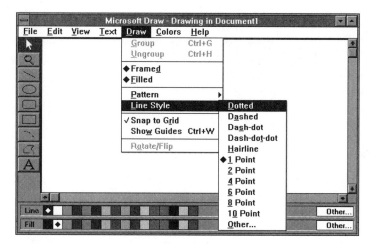

Figure 12-2.
Multilevel pop-up menus (from Microsoft Draw).

Version 2.0 of the Microsoft Foundation Class Library extends the functionality of the standard menus for Windows. Each menu item can have a prompt string that appears in the frame's status bar when the item is highlighted. These prompts are really Windows string resource elements linked to the menu item by a common ID. From the point of view of App Studio, they appear to be part of the menu item definition.

Keyboard Accelerators

You have probably noticed that one letter is underlined in most menu items. In Visual Workbench (and most other applications), pressing Alt-F followed by S activates the File Save menu item. This is the standard Windows method of using the keyboard to choose from menus. If you looked at the application's menu resource script (or the App Studio properties dialog), you would see ampersands (&) in front of the characters that are underlined in the application's menu items.

Windows offers an alternative way of linking keystrokes to a menu item. The keyboard accelerator resource consists of a table of key combinations with associated command IDs. The Edit Copy menu item, for example (with command ID *ID_EDIT_COPY*), might be linked to the Ctrl-C key combination through a keyboard accelerator entry. A keyboard accelerator entry does not have to be associated with a menu item. If there were no Edit Copy menu item, the Ctrl-C key combination would still activate the *ID_EDIT_COPY* command.

> **Note:** *If a keyboard accelerator is associated with a menu item, then the accelerator key is disabled when the menu item is disabled.*

Command Processing

As Chapter 2 pointed out, the application framework provides a sophisticated routing system for command messages. These messages originate from menu selections, keyboard accelerators, and toolbar and dialog button clicks. Also, command messages can be sent by calls to the *CWnd SendMessage* function. Each message is identified by a *#define* constant that is often assigned by App Studio. The application framework has its own set of internal command message IDs, such as ID_FILE_PRINT and ID_FILE_OPEN. Your project's RESOURCE.H file contains IDs that are unique to your application.

Most command messages originate in the application's frame window, and, without the application framework in the picture, that's where you would put the message handlers. With command routing, however, you can handle the message almost anywhere. When the application framework sees a frame window command message, it starts looking for message handlers in one of the sequences listed below:

SDI Application	MDI Application
View	View
Document	Document
SDI main frame	MDI child frame
Application	MDI main frame
	Application

Most applications have a particular command handler in only one class, but suppose your one-view application has an identical handler in both the view and the document classes. Because the view is higher in the command route, only the view's command handler function will be called.

What does it take to install a command handler function? The requirements are similar to those of the window message handlers you've already seen. You need the function itself, a corresponding message map entry, and the function prototype. Suppose you have a menu item called Zoom (with *IDM_ZOOM* as the associated ID) that you want your view class to handle. First you add the following code to your view implementation file:

```
BEGIN_MESSAGE_MAP(CMyView, CView)
    ON_COMMAND(IDM_ZOOM, OnZoom)
END_MESSAGE_MAP()

void CMyView::OnZoom()
{
    // command message processing code
}
```

Now add the following function prototype to the *CMyView* class header file:

```
afx_msg void OnZoom();
```

Of course, ClassWizard automates the process of inserting command message handlers the same way that it facilitates the insertion of window message handlers. You'll learn how in the next example.

Command Message Handling in Derived Classes

The command routing system is one dimension of command message handling. The class hierarchy is a second dimension. If you look at the source code for the class library classes, you'll see lots of ON_COMMAND message map entries. When you derive a class from one of these base classes—*CView*, for example—the derived class inherits all the *CView* message map functions, including the command message functions. To override one of the base class message map functions, you must add both a function and a message map entry to your derived class.

Update Command User Interface (UI) Messages

You often need to change the appearance of a menu item to match the internal state of your application. If you have a Clear All item in your application's Edit menu, for example, you might want to disable that item if there's nothing to clear. You've undoubtedly seen such grayed menu items in Windows-based applications. You've probably seen check marks next to menu items too.

With SDK programming for Windows, it's difficult to keep menu items synchronized with the application's state. Every piece of code that changes the internal state must contain statements to update the menu. The class library takes a different approach by sending a special update command UI message whenever a pop-up menu is first displayed. That message is generally routed to the same object that was the target of the menu item. The message handler function's argument is a *CCmdUI* object, which contains a pointer to the corresponding menu item. The handler function can then use this pointer to modify the menu item's appearance. Update command UI messages apply only to items in pop-up menus, not to top-level menu items that are permanently displayed. You couldn't use an update command UI message to disable the File menu item, for example.

The update command UI coding requirements are similar to those for commands. You need the function itself, a special message map entry, and, of course, the prototype. The associated ID, *IDM_ZOOM* in this case, is the same constant used for the command. Here is an example of the necessary additions to the view class code file:

```
BEGIN_MESSAGE_MAP(CMyView, CView)
    ON_UPDATE_COMMAND_UI(IDM_ZOOM, OnUpdateZoom)
END_MESSAGE_MAP()
```

(continued)

```
void CMyView::OnUpdateZoom(CCmdUI* pCmdUI)
{
    pCmdUI->SetCheck(m_bZoomed); // m_bZoomed is a class data member
}
```

Here is the function prototype that you must add to the class header:

```
afx_msg void OnUpdateZoom(CCmdUI* pCmdUI);
```

Needless to say, ClassWizard automates the process of inserting update command UI messages.

Commands That Originate in Dialogs

Suppose you have a pop-up dialog with buttons, and you want a particular button to send a command message. Command IDs must be in the range 0x8000–0xDFFF, the same ID range that App Studio uses for your menu items. If you assign a dialog button an ID in this range, the button will generate a routable command. The application framework first routes this command to the main frame window because the frame window owns all pop-up dialogs. Then the command routing proceeds normally; if your view has a handler for the button's command, that's where it will be handled. It's not so easy to use update command UI handlers for dialog buttons. See the code in the example program \MSVC\MFC\SRC\BARCORE.CPP for some hints.

To ensure that the ID is in the range 0x8000–0xDFFF, you must use the App Studio symbol editor to enter the ID prior to assigning it to a button.

The Application Framework's Built-In Menu Items

You don't have to start each frame menu from scratch because the class library defines some useful menu items for you, along with all the command handler functions, as shown in Figure 12-3.

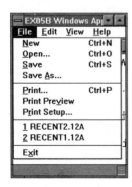

Figure 12-3.   *(continued)*
The standard SDI frame menus.

Figure 12-3. *continued*

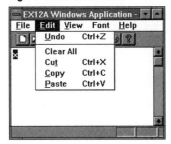

The menu items and command message handlers you get depend on the options you choose in AppWizard. If you don't select printing, for example, you don't get the Print and Print Preview menu items. Because printing is optional, the message map entries are not defined in the *CView* class but are generated in your derived view class. That's why entries such as

```
ON_COMMAND(ID_FILE_PRINT, CView::OnFilePrint)
ON_COMMAND(ID_FILE_PRINT_PREVIEW, CView::OnFilePrintPreview)
```

are defined in your *CMyView* class instead of in the *CView* class.

Enabling/Disabling of Menu Items

The application framework can disable a menu item if it does not find a command message handler in the current command route. This feature saves you the trouble of writing *ON_UPDATE_COMMAND_UI* message handlers. You can disable the feature if you set the *CFrameWnd* data member *m_bAutoMenuEnable* to *FALSE* (the default).

Suppose you have two views for one document, but only the first view class has a message handler for the *IDM_ZOOM* command. The frame menu's Zoom item will be enabled only when the first view is active. For another example, consider the application framework–supplied Edit Cut, Copy, and Paste menu items. These will be disabled if you have not provided message handlers in your derived view or document classes.

The *CEditView* Class

This chapter focuses on command messages, but the *CEditView* class plays a prominent role. This class, itself derived from *CView*, serves as the base class for an application's custom view class. An object of a class derived from *CEditView* is like a *CView* object because it can process command messages. It's also like a *CEdit* object because it permits text editing and formatting. A *CEditView* object is really an ordinary view object whose client area is occupied entirely by an edit control child window. The class member functions make the two related windows act as one object—an ideal tool when you need text input.

As is an edit control, the *CEditView* object's text is contained deep within the *CEdit* part of the object. To access that text (and otherwise interact with the window), you must use specific *CEditView* functions together with functions inherited from *CWnd* and (indirectly) from *CEdit*. The *CEditView* class does not employ C++ multiple inheritance but rather provides the *GetEditCtrl* member function for access to the *CEdit* member functions.

Don't try to build a full-featured word processor with *CEditView*. The class has many limitations that are imposed by the underlying Windows edit control. You cannot mix fonts within the window, for example, and you are limited to a text buffer size of 42 KB (64 KB with the 32-bit versions of Windows). *CEditView* does implement the clipboard Cut, Copy, and Paste commands, however. These are connected to the standard application framework Edit menu items.

> **Note:** *If you need to intercept control notification messages from the* CEditView *internal edit control, manually set up message map entries such as the following:*

```
ON_EN_CHANGE(AFX_IDW_PANE_FIRST, OnEditChange)
```

> *The constant* AFX_IDW_PANE_FIRST *identifies the view's edit control.*

The EX12A Example

This example illustrates the routing of menu and keyboard accelerator commands to both documents and views. The application's view class is derived from *CEditView*. View-directed menu commands, originating from a Font menu, alter the view's font, and a document-directed Clear All menu item erases the document's contents. The Font menu contains items for System and Fixed fonts with the capability for displaying a check mark next to the selected font. The Clear All item, located on the

Edit menu, is grayed when the document is empty. Figure 12-4 shows the EX12A program in use.

Figure 12-4.
The EX12A program in use.

If we exploited the document–view architecture fully, we would keep the edit view's text inside the document, but that's a little too advanced for this chapter. Instead, we'll define a "phony" document *CString* data member called *m_text* that won't be reflected in the view. The initial value of *m_text* is "Hello," and choosing Clear All from the Edit menu sets it to empty. At least you'll start to get the idea about the separation of the document and the view.

The EX12A example exercises the App Studio wysiwyg menu editor and keyboard accelerator editor together with the ClassWizard. You'll need to do very little C++ coding. Simply follow these steps:

1. Run AppWizard to generate \VCPP\EX12A\EX12A. Choose AppWizard from Visual Workbench's Project menu. The options and the default class names are shown here:

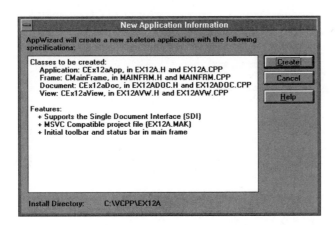

2. **Change the *CEx12aView* base class to *CEditView.*** Use the global replace feature of the Visual Workbench editor to change all *CView* references to *CEditView* in the files EX12AVW.CPP and EX12AVW.H.

   Note: *If you had specified Printing and Print Preview as an AppWizard option, your derived view class would contain* OnPreparePrinting, OnBeginPrinting, *and* OnEndPrinting *virtual function overrides, as described in Chapter 18. However, the* CEditView *class contains its own* OnPreparePrinting, OnBeginPrinting, *and* OnEndPrinting *functions, which you don't want to override. In this case, therefore, you must remove the functions that AppWizard generates. If you use ClassWizard to generate a* CEditView-*derived class, no* OnPrint *override functions are generated.*

3. **Use App Studio to edit the application's main menu.** Choose App Studio from Visual Workbench's Tools menu. Edit the *IDR_MAINFRAME* menu resource to add a Clear All item to the Edit menu so that it looks like this:

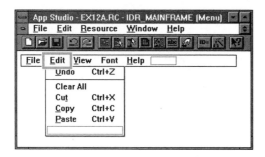

Note: *The App Studio menu resource editor is intuitive, but you might need some help the first time you insert an item in the middle of a menu. Each menu has a blank item at the bottom. Use the mouse to drag the blank item to the insertion position to define a new item. A new blank item will appear at the bottom when you're finished.*

Now add a Font menu, and then define the underlying System and Fixed items as shown here:

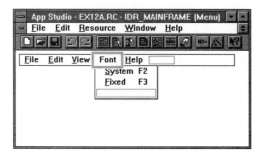

Use the following command IDs for your new menu items:

Menu	Item	Command ID
Edit	Clear All	*ID_EDIT_CLEAR_ALL*
Font	&System\tF2	*IDM_FONT_SYSTEM*
Font	&Fixed\tF3	*IDM_FONT_FIXED*

(Note: \t is a tab character—but type \t, don't press the Tab key.)

The class library has defined the first choice, *ID_EDIT_CLEAR_ALL*.

When you add the menu items, type appropriate prompt strings in the Menu Item Properties dialog. These prompts will appear in the status window when the menu item is highlighted.

4. Use App Studio to add keyboard accelerators. Open the *IDR_MAIN-FRAME* accelerator table, and then add the following items:

Accelerator ID	Key
IDM_FONT_SYSTEM	*VK_F2*
IDM_FONT_FIXED	*VK_F3*

Be sure to turn off the Ctrl, Alt, and Shift modifiers. The App Studio accelerator Properties dialog is shown below:

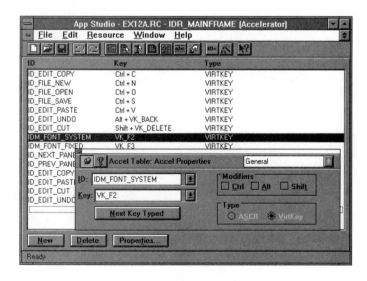

Save the resource file on disk when you are finished.

5. **Use ClassWizard to add the view class command and update command UI message handlers.** Select the *CEx12aView* class, and then add the following member functions:

Object ID	Message	Member Function Name
IDM_FONT_FIXED	COMMAND	*OnFontFixed*
IDM_FONT_FIXED	UPDATE_COMMAND_UI	*OnUpdateFontFixed*
IDM_FONT_SYSTEM	COMMAND	*OnFontSystem*
IDM_FONT_SYSTEM	UPDATE_COMMAND_UI	*OnUpdateFontSystem*

6. **Use ClassWizard to add the document class command and update command UI message handlers.** Select the *CEx12aDoc* class, and then add the following member functions:

Object ID	Message	Member Function
ID_EDIT_CLEAR_ALL	COMMAND	*OnEditClearAll*
ID_EDIT_CLEAR_ALL	UPDATE_COMMAND_UI	*OnUpdateEditClearAll*

7. **Add a data member in file EX12ADOC.H.** Add the following code in the *CEx12aDoc* class definition.

```
private:
    CString m_text; // representation of edit text
```

8. **Add a data member and a function prototype in file EX12AVW.H.** Add the following code in the *CEx12aView* class definition:

```
private:
    int m_nFont; // ID of currently selected stock font
```

Add the following function prototype:

```
virtual BOOL PreCreateWindow(CREATESTRUCT& cs);
```

9. **Edit the document class member functions in EX12ADOC.CPP.** Remember that we're faking the document view interaction in this example. The constructor sets the initial value of *m_text* for only one reason—so that the Edit Clear All menu item is initially enabled.

```
CEx12aDoc::CEx12aDoc() : m_text("Hello")
{
}
```

The Edit Clear All message handler sets *m_text* to empty. You get only one chance to clear the document—once it's cleared, it stays cleared, and the menu item becomes gray (disabled).

A pop-up message box indicates that the function was called.

```
void CEx12aDoc::OnEditClearAll()
{
    AfxMessageBox("Document cleared");
    m_text = "";
}
```

If *m_text* is empty, the Edit Clear All menu item is disabled.

```
void CEx12aDoc::OnUpdateEditClearAll(CCmdUI* pCmdUI)
{
    pCmdUI->Enable(!m_text.IsEmpty());
}
```

10. **Edit the view class member functions in EX12AVW.CPP.** The constructor initializes the font data member so that the font menu check marks match the initial font.

```
CEx12aView::CEx12aView()
{
    m_nFont = SYSTEM_FONT;
}
```

The following two functions are called in direct response to the IDM_-FONT_SYSTEM and IDM_FONT_FIXED menu command messages. They set the *m_nFont* data member to support the update command UI functions.

```
void CEx12aView::OnFontSystem()
{
    CFont font;

    font.CreateStockObject(SYSTEM_FONT);
    SetFont(&font);
    m_nFont = SYSTEM_FONT;
}

void CEx12aView::OnFontFixed()
{
    CFont font;

    font.CreateStockObject(SYSTEM_FIXED_FONT);
    SetFont(&font);
    m_nFont = SYSTEM_FIXED_FONT;
}
```

The following two functions are called when the user chooses an item from the Font menu. The System and Fixed items are checkmarked according to the contents of the *m_nFont* data member.

```
void CEx12aView::OnUpdateFontSystem(CCmdUI* pCmdUI)
{
    pCmdUI->SetCheck(m_nFont == SYSTEM_FONT);
}

void CEx12aView::OnUpdateFontFixed(CCmdUI* pCmdUI)
{
    pCmdUI->SetCheck(m_nFont == SYSTEM_FIXED_FONT);
}
```

If we didn't override the *CWnd* virtual *PreCreateWindow* function, the edit view would have a horizontal scroll bar and would not support wordwrap. This *CEx12aView* function, called by the application framework, sets the style parameter appropriately.

```
BOOL CEx12aView::PreCreateWindow(CREATESTRUCT& cs)
{
    cs.style = AFX_WS_DEFAULT_VIEW | WS_VSCROLL |
               ES_AUTOVSCROLL | ES_MULTILINE | ES_NOHIDESEL;
    return CEditView::PreCreateWindow(cs);
}
```

11. **Build and test the EX12A application.** When the application starts, the Clear All item in the Edit menu should be enabled, and the System menu item in the Font menu should be checkmarked. Type some text, and then change the font. Try pressing the F2 and F3 keys. Next, choose Clear All from the Edit menu. The text won't be cleared, but you should get the pop-up message box, and the Clear All item should be disabled.

The *CMenu* Class

Up to this point, the application framework and App Studio have shielded you from the menu class, *CMenu*. A *CMenu* object can represent each Windows menu, including the top-level menu items and associated popups. Most of the time, the menu's resource is directly attached to a frame window when the window's *Create* function is called, and a *CMenu* object is never explicitly constructed. The *CWnd* member function *GetMenu* returns a temporary *CMenu* pointer. Once you have this pointer, you can freely access and update the menu object.

Suppose you want to switch menus sometime after the application starts. *IDR_-MAINFRAME* always identifies the initial menu in the resource script. If you want a second menu, you use App Studio to create a menu resource with your own ID. Then, in your program you construct a *CMenu* object, use the *CMenu LoadMenu* function to load the menu from the resource, and call the *CWnd SetMenu* function to attach the new menu to the frame window.

You can use a resource to define a menu, and then your program can modify the menu items at runtime. If necessary, however, you can build the whole menu at runtime, without benefit of a resource. In either case, you can use *CMenu* member functions such as *ModifyMenu*, *InsertMenu*, and *DeleteMenu*. Each of these functions operates on an individual menu item identified by ID or by a relative position index.

A menu object is actually composed of a nested structure of submenus. You can use the *GetSubMenu* member function to get a *CMenu* pointer to a pop-up menu contained in the main *CMenu* object. Inserting a new pop-up menu is more difficult because you must use a Windows menu handle (HMENU) instead of a *CMenu* pointer. The *CMenu GetMenuString* function returns the menu item string based on a zero-based index or a command ID. If you use the command ID option, the menu is searched, together with any submenus.

It's possible to use graphics inside menus, and there is a special "free-floating" type of pop-up menu. See the *Class Library Reference* for details on these seldom-used menu features.

Extended Command Processing

In addition to the *ON_COMMAND* message map macro you've seen already, the class library provides an extended variation, *ON_COMMAND_EX*. The extended command message map macro provides two features that are not supplied by the regular command message—a command ID function parameter, and the ability to reject a command at runtime, sending it to the next object in the command route. If the extended command handler returns *TRUE*, the command goes no further; if it returns *FALSE*, the application framework looks for another command handler.

The command ID parameter is useful, as you'll see in EX12B, when you want one function to handle several related command messages. The rejection feature is used in the Help system (introduced in Chapter 20). If a view can't handle a Help request, for example, the request can be passed to the document or the application. You might invent some of your own uses for this feature.

ClassWizard can't help you with extended command handlers, so you'll have to do the coding yourself, outside the *AFX_MSG_MAP* brackets. Assume *IDM_ZOOM_1* and *IDM_ZOOM_2* are related command IDs defined in RESOURCE.H. Here's the class code you'll need to process both messages with one function, *OnZoom*:

```
BEGIN_MESSAGE_MAP(CMyView, CView)
    ON_COMMAND_EX(IDM_ZOOM_1, OnZoom)
    ON_COMMAND_EX(IDM_ZOOM_2, OnZoom)
END_MESSAGE_MAP()

BOOL CMyView::OnZoom(UINT nID)
{
    if (nID == IDM_ZOOM_1) {
        // code specific to first zoom command
    }
```

(continued)

```
    else {
        // code specific to second zoom command
    }
    // code common to both commands
    return TRUE; // command goes no further
}
```

Here's the function prototype:

```
afx_msg BOOL OnZoom(UINT nID);
```

The EX12B Example

This example uses the *CEditView* class, but with a twist. A new top-level menu item allows the user to change the size of the edit window's font. We could hard-code the size choices in the menu resource, but instead we dynamically create the Size popup with eight font sizes, and then we use extended command macros to route the eight distinct command messages to one member function. Figure 12-5 shows the EX12B program in use.

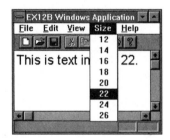

Figure 12-5.
The EX12B program in use.

> **Note:** *If you're serious about font and size selection, you'll probably use the COMMDLG class CFontDialog. EX12B illustrates the use of menu commands, which is not an ideal font selection technique.*

Because menus are always associated with an application's frame window, we must build the font popup in the *CMainFrame* class. We depend on the application framework's command routing to send the resulting command messages to the *CEx12bView* class. We won't attempt to use the extended command's rejection mechanism, though.

Follow these steps to build the EX12B example:

1. **Run AppWizard to generate \VCPP\EX12B\EX12B.** Choose AppWizard from Visual Workbench's Project menu. The options and the default class names are shown here:

202

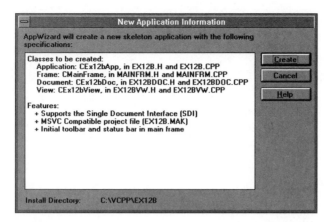

2. **Change the *CEx12bView* base class to *CEditView*.** Use the global replace feature of Visual Workbench to change all *CView* references to *CEditView* in the files EX12BVW.CPP and EX12BVW.H.

3. **Use App Studio to edit the application's main menu.** Choose App Studio from Visual Workbench's Tools menu. Edit the *IDR_MAINFRAME* menu resource to create a menu that looks like this:

You need the dummy Base menu item in the Size menu to force Size to be a pop-up menu rather than an ordinary top-level menu item. This menu item will be replaced at runtime. Use *IDM_SIZE_BASE* for the dummy menu item ID.

Note: *This application requires eight sequential command IDs, starting with* IDM_SIZE_BASE. *If you add menu items, they might overlap the range of size commands. Be sure that App Studio doesn't assign command IDs inside the range* IDM_SIZE_BASE *through* IDM_SIZE_BASE +7.

4. **Add code to the *OnCreate* function in MAINFRM.CPP.** When the application's frame window is created, the *CMainFrame OnCreate* function alters the associated menu, specified in the *IDR_MAINFRAME* resource. The function first locates the Size pop-up submenu, and then it deletes the Base menu item

that was defined in the resource. Finally it adds eight font size entries and creates the initial font. Because the *CEditView* class uses the *MM_TEXT* mapping mode, the font sizes are arbitrary and are not related to points.

```
int CMainFrame::OnCreate(LPCREATESTRUCT lpCreateStruct)
{
    char temp[10];
    int i, j;

    if (CFrameWnd::OnCreate(lpCreateStruct) == -1)
        return -1;

    if (!m_wndToolBar.Create(this) ||
        !m_wndToolBar.LoadBitmap(IDR_MAINFRAME) ||
        !m_wndToolBar.SetButtons(buttons,
          sizeof(buttons)/sizeof(UINT)))
    {
        TRACE("Failed to create toolbar\n");
        return -1;      // fail to create
    }

    if (!m_wndStatusBar.Create(this) ||
        !m_wndStatusBar.SetIndicators(indicators,
          sizeof(indicators)/sizeof(UINT)))
    {
        TRACE("Failed to create status bar\n");
        return -1;      // fail to create
    }

    CMenu* pMenu = GetMenu();
    CMenu* pSubMenu = pMenu->GetSubMenu(3); // Size pop-up menu
    // clear out the existing popup  (assume single item)
    pSubMenu->DeleteMenu(0, MF_BYPOSITION);
    for (i = 0; i < 8; i++) {
        j = 12 + i * 2; // size 12, 14, 16, 18, 20, 22, 24, 26
        pSubMenu->AppendMenu(MF_ENABLED | MF_STRING,
                             (UINT) IDM_SIZE_BASE + i,
                             itoa(j, temp, 10));
    }

    return 0;
}
```

5. **Use ClassWizard to add a *CEx12bView* class message handler.** Add a message handler for WM_CREATE.

6. **Edit the EX12BVW.H header.** You must add the *CEx12bView* function prototype for *OnCommandSize* because ClassWizard doesn't do it for you.

```
afx_msg BOOL OnCommandSize(UINT nID);
```

You also need a font data member in class *CEx12bView*.

```
private:
    CFont* m_pFont;
```

7. **Add the extended command message map entries in EX12BVW.CPP.** Add the following entries after the *BEGIN_MESSAGE_MAP* statement but outside the *AFX_MSG_MAP* brackets:

```
ON_COMMAND_EX(IDM_SIZE_BASE, OnCommandSize)
ON_COMMAND_EX(IDM_SIZE_BASE + 1, OnCommandSize)
ON_COMMAND_EX(IDM_SIZE_BASE + 2, OnCommandSize)
ON_COMMAND_EX(IDM_SIZE_BASE + 3, OnCommandSize)
ON_COMMAND_EX(IDM_SIZE_BASE + 4, OnCommandSize)
ON_COMMAND_EX(IDM_SIZE_BASE + 5, OnCommandSize)
ON_COMMAND_EX(IDM_SIZE_BASE + 6, OnCommandSize)
ON_COMMAND_EX(IDM_SIZE_BASE + 7, OnCommandSize)
```

8. **Edit the *OnCreate* member function in EX12BVW.CPP.** The *OnCreate* function creates the edit view's initial TrueType font:

```
int CEx12bView::OnCreate(LPCREATESTRUCT lpCreateStruct)
{
    if (CEditView::OnCreate(lpCreateStruct) != 0) {
        return -1;
    }

    VERIFY(m_pFont->CreateFont(-12, 0, 0, 0,400, FALSE, FALSE, 0,
                            ANSI_CHARSET, OUT_DEFAULT_PRECIS,
                            CLIP_DEFAULT_PRECIS, DEFAULT_QUALITY,
                            DEFAULT_PITCH | FF_SWISS, "Arial"));
    SetFont(m_pFont);
    return 0;
}
```

9. **Add the *OnCommandSize* member function to EX12BVW.CPP.** This single function is called for all size command messages. The *nID* parameter corresponds to the command ID and thus ranges between *IDM_SIZE_BASE* and *IDM_SIZE_BASE + 7*. Simple arithmetic converts *nID* to a reasonable font size, and then a Windows font object is created. This font must be available when the view's *OnDraw* function paints the text, so the C++ font object can't be defined on the stack. The class data member *m_pFont* holds a pointer to the heap-based *CFont* object.

The temporary *CFont* object font exists only for housekeeping purposes. As pointed out in Chapter 5, font GDI objects must be deleted eventually, and they can't be deleted as long as they're selected. If the *SYSTEM_FONT* stock object is selected, the prior font is released.

```
BOOL CEx12bView::OnCommandSize(UINT nID)
{
    int   nFontSize;
    CFont font;

    font.CreateStockObject(SYSTEM_FONT);
    SetFont(&font); // deselects any prior special font
    m_pFont->DeleteObject(); // deletes the deselected font

    nFontSize = 12 + (nID - (UINT) IDM_SIZE_BASE) * 2;
    VERIFY(m_pFont->CreateFont(-nFontSize, 0, 0, 0, 400, FALSE, FALSE, 0,
                               ANSI_CHARSET, OUT_DEFAULT_PRECIS,
                               CLIP_DEFAULT_PRECIS, DEFAULT_QUALITY,
                               DEFAULT_PITCH ¦ FF_SWISS, "Arial"));
    SetFont(m_pFont);
    return TRUE;
}
```

10. **Edit other view constructor and destructor in EX12BVW.CPP.** The *CEx12b-View* constructor allocates memory for the font object.

```
CEx12bView::CEx12bView()
{
    m_pFont = new CFont;
}
```

Because the *CEditView* class deselects the font, you don't have to. You do have to destroy the font object, however. The destructor takes care of deleting the attached GDI font.

```
CEx12bView::~CEx12bView()
{
    delete m_pFont;
}
```

11. **Build and test the EX12B application.** Test the compiled application by typing in the window and then selecting a font size from the menu. Does the text change size? Are there any unpleasant "undeleted font" messages in the Debug window?

13

Toolbars and Status Bars

All the Visual C++ examples up to this point have included toolbars and status bars. AppWizard generated the code that initialized these application framework elements as long as you accepted the AppWizard default option Initial Toolbar. The default toolbar provides graphics equivalents for many of the standard application framework menu selections, and the default status bar displays menu prompts together with the keyboard state indicators CAP, NUM, and SCRL.

This chapter shows you how to customize the toolbar and status bar for your application. You'll be able to add your own toolbar graphical buttons and control their appearance. You'll also learn how to disable the status bar's normal display of menu prompts and keyboard indicators. This allows your application to take over the status bar for its own use.

Control Bars and the Application Framework

The toolbar is an object of class *CToolBar*, and the status bar is an object of class *CStatusBar*. Both these classes are derived from class *CControlBar*, which is itself derived from *CWnd*. The *CControlBar* class supports control bar windows that are positioned inside frame windows. These control bar windows resize and reposition themselves as the parent frame moves and changes size. The application framework takes care of the construction, window creation, and destruction of the control bar objects. AppWizard generates control bar code for its derived frame class located in the files MAINFRM.CPP and MAINFRM.H.

In a typical SDI application, a *CToolBar* object occupies the top portion of the *CMainFrame* client area, and a *CStatusBar* object occupies the bottom portion. The view occupies the remaining (middle) part of the frame.

Assuming that AppWizard has generated the control bar code for your application, the user can enable and disable the toolbar and the status bar individually by choosing commands in the application's View menu. When a control bar is disabled, it disappears, and the view size is recalculated. Apart from the common behavior just described, toolbar and status bar objects operate independently of each other and have rather different characteristics.

The Toolbar

A toolbar object is a window consisting of a number of horizontally arranged graphical buttons that might be clustered in groups. The programming interface determines the grouping. The graphic images for the buttons are stored in a single bitmap that is attached to the application's resource file. When the buttons are clicked, they send command messages, as do menus and keyboard accelerators. Update command UI message handlers are used to update the buttons' states, which, in turn, are used by the application framework to modify the buttons' graphical images.

The Toolbar Bitmap

Each button in a toolbar appears to have its own bitmap, but actually there is a single bitmap for the entire toolbar. The toolbar bitmap has a tile, 15 pixels high and 16 pixels wide, for each button. The application framework supplies the button borders, and it modifies those borders, together with the button's bitmap tile color, to reflect the current button state. Figure 13-1 shows the relationship between the toolbar bitmap and a typical toolbar. (The last image in each toolbar is for a context-sensitive Help button, which has not been discussed yet.)

Figure 13-1.
A toolbar bitmap and an actual toolbar.

The toolbar bitmap is stored in the file TOOLBAR.BMP in the application's RES subdirectory. It's identified in the RC file as *IDR_MAINFRAME*. You can use App Studio to edit the toolbar bitmap.

Button States

Each button can assume the following states:

State	Meaning
0	Normal, unpressed state (up)
TBBS_PRESSED	Currently selected (pressed) with the mouse
TBBS_CHECKED	In the checked (down) state
TBBS_DISABLED	Unavailable for use
TBBS_INDETERMINATE	Enabled, but neither up nor down
TBBS_CHECKED ¦ TBBS_DISABLED	In the checked state, but unavailable for use

A button can behave in either of two ways. It can be a pushbutton, which is down only when currently selected by the mouse, or it can be a check box button, which can be toggled up and down with mouse clicks. All buttons in the standard application framework toolbar are pushbuttons.

The Toolbar and Command Messages

When the user clicks a toolbar button with the mouse, a command message is generated. This message is routed like the menu command messages you saw in Chapter 12. Most of the time, a toolbar button matches a menu choice. In the standard application framework toolbar, for example, the disk button is equivalent to the File Save menu choice because both generate the ID_FILE_SAVE message. The object receiving the command message doesn't need to know whether the message was produced by a click in the toolbar or by a choice from the menu.

A toolbar button doesn't have to mirror a menu item. If you don't provide the equivalent menu item, however, you are advised to define a keyboard accelerator for the button so that the user can activate the command with the keyboard or with a Windows keyboard macro product. If your application has toolbar buttons without corresponding menu items, ClassWizard can't define command and update command UI message handlers. You'll have to add the functions, message map entries, and prototypes yourself.

The static *buttons* array, defined in the application's main frame class, associates commands with buttons. Here's the code, found in MAINFRM.CPP, that AppWizard normally generates:

```
static UINT BASED_CODE buttons[] =
{
    // same order as in the bitmap 'toolbar.bmp'
    ID_FILE_NEW,
    ID_FILE_OPEN,
    ID_FILE_SAVE,
        ID_SEPARATOR,
```

(continued)

```
    ID_EDIT_CUT,
    ID_EDIT_COPY,
    ID_EDIT_PASTE,
        ID_SEPARATOR,
    ID_FILE_PRINT,
    ID_APP_ABOUT,
    ID_CONTEXT_HELP,
};
```

The *ID_SEPARATOR* constants serve to group the buttons by inserting corresponding spaces in the toolbar. If the number of toolbar bitmap panes exceeds the number of *buttons* array elements (excluding separators), the extra buttons are not displayed.

Toolbar Update Command UI Messages

You remember from Chapter 12 that update command UI message handlers were used to disable or check menu items. These same message handlers apply to toolbar buttons. If your update command UI message handler calls the *CCmdUI Enable* member function with a *FALSE* parameter, the corresponding button is set to the disabled (grayed) state and no longer responds to mouse clicks.

With menu items, the *CCmdUI SetCheck* member function displays a check mark next to the menu item. For the toolbar, the *SetCheck* function implements check box buttons. If the update command UI message handler calls *SetCheck* with a parameter value of 1, the button is toggled to the down (checked) state; if the parameter is 0, the button is toggled up (unchecked).

> ***Note:*** *If the* SetCheck *parameter value is 2, the button is set to the "indeterminate" state. This state looks like the disabled state, but the button is still active and its color is a bit brighter. Microsoft Word for Windows uses the up, down, and indeterminate states for its boldface toolbar button. If the user has selected some text that contains only boldface characters, the boldface button is down. If no selected characters are boldface, the button is up; but if the selected characters are mixed, the button is indeterminate.*

The update command UI message handlers for menu items are called only when the items' drop-down menu is painted. The toolbar is displayed all the time, so when are its update command UI message handlers called? They're called during the application's idle processing, so the buttons can be updated continuously. If the same handler covers a menu item and a toolbar button, it is called both during idle processing and when the drop-down menu is displayed.

> ***Note:*** *Even though a toolbar button is disabled, keyboard accelerators can still send the associated command messages. Your command handlers, therefore, must be able to ignore these accelerator keys and other spurious commands. In other words, you can't count on the command UI message handler totally disabling the command.*

Locating the Main Frame Window

The toolbar and status bar objects you'll be working with are attached to the application's main frame window, not to the view window. How does your view find its main frame window? In an SDI application, you can use the *CWnd GetParentFrame* function. Unfortunately, this function won't work in an MDI application because the view's parent frame is the MDI child frame, not the MDI frame window.

If you want your view class to work in both SDI and MDI applications, you must find the main frame window through the application object. The *AfxGetApp* global function returns a pointer to the application object, and you can use that pointer to get the *CWinApp* data member *m_pMainWnd*. In an MDI application, AppWizard generates code that sets *m_pMainWnd*, but in an SDI application, the framework sets *m_pMainWnd* during the view creation process. Once *m_pMainWnd* is set, you can use it in a view class to get the frame's toolbar with a statement such as this:

```
CToolBar* pToolBar = (CToolBar*)
        AfxGetApp()->m_pMainWnd->GetDescendantWindow(AFX_IDW_TOOLBAR);
```

You can use the same logic to locate menu objects, status bar objects, and dialog objects.

> **Note:** In an SDI application, the value of m_pMainWnd *is not set when the* view's OnCreate *message handler is called. If you need to access the main frame window in your* OnCreate *function, you must use the* GetParent-Frame *function.*

The EX13A Toolbar Example

In this example, you will replace the standard application framework Edit Cut, Copy, and Paste toolbar buttons with three special-purpose buttons that control drawing in the view window. You will also construct a Draw menu with three corresponding menu items as follows:

Menu Item	Function
Circle	Draws a circle in the view window
Square	Draws a square in the view window
Pattern	Toggles a diagonal line fill pattern for new squares and circles

The menu and toolbar choices force the user to alternate between drawing circles and squares. After the user draws a circle, the Circle menu item and toolbar button are disabled; after the user draws a square, the Square menu item and toolbar button are disabled.

In the application's Draw menu, the Pattern menu item gets a check mark when pattern fill is active. In the toolbar, the corresponding button is a check box button that is down when pattern fill is active and up when it is not active.

Figure 13-2 shows the application in action. The user has drawn a circle with pattern fill. Note the states of the three drawing buttons.

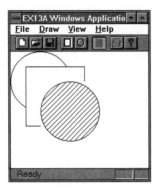

Figure 13-2.
The EX13A program in action.

The EX13A example introduces the App Studio bitmap editor. You'll need to do very little C++ coding. Simply follow these steps:

1. **Run AppWizard to generate \VCPP\EX13A\EX13A.** Choose AppWizard from Visual Workbench's Project menu. The options and the default class names are shown here:

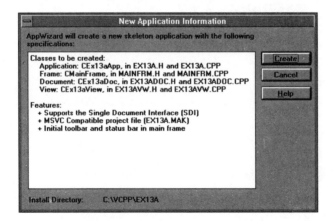

212

2. Use App Studio to edit the application's main menu. Choose App Studio from Visual Workbench's Tools menu. Edit the *IDR_MAINFRAME* menu resource to make a menu that looks like this (you'll need to remove the Edit menu):

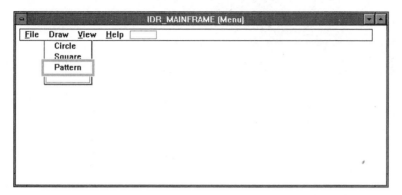

Use the following command IDs for your new menu items:

Menu	Menu Item	Command ID
Draw	Circle	*IDM_DRAW_CIRCLE*
Draw	Square	*IDM_DRAW_SQUARE*
Draw	Pattern	*IDM_DRAW_PATTERN*

When you're in the Menu Item Properties dialog, add some appropriate prompt strings.

3. Use App Studio to edit the application's toolbar. Edit the *IDR_MAIN-FRAME* bitmap resource to create a bitmap that looks like this:

You'll be erasing the Edit Cut, Copy, and Paste tiles (fourth, fifth, and sixth from the left) and replacing them with new patterns. Here's a close-up of the three new tiles:

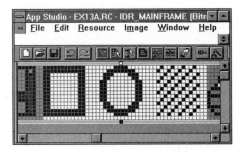

The trick here is to turn on App Studio's tile grid. Choose Grid Settings from the Image menu, and then check the Tile Grid check box and accept the 16-pixel width and 15-pixel height default values. The resulting grid lines separate the individual button images. Remember that you're working with a general-purpose bitmap editor with the tile grid added as a special feature for toolbar buttons.

Use the rectangle and ellipse tools from the bitmap editor's palette. Experiment with different line widths. You can change the magnification by selecting the magnifying glass icon in the Graphics Palette. (To open the Graphics Palette, press F2 or choose Show Graphics Palette from the Window menu.) Save the resource file when you're done.

4. **Edit the MAINFRM.CPP file.** Replace the original *buttons* array with the following:

```
static UINT BASED_CODE buttons[] =
{
    // same order as in the bitmap 'toolbar.bmp'
    ID_FILE_NEW,
    ID_FILE_OPEN,
    ID_FILE_SAVE,
        ID_SEPARATOR,
    IDM_DRAW_SQUARE,
    IDM_DRAW_CIRCLE,
        ID_SEPARATOR,
    IDM_DRAW_PATTERN,
        ID_SEPARATOR,
    ID_FILE_PRINT,
    ID_APP_ABOUT,
};
```

5. **Use ClassWizard to add *CEx13aView* view class message handlers.** Add message handlers for the following command and update command UI messages, and accept the default function names:

Object ID	Message	Member Function Name
IDM_DRAW_CIRCLE	COMMAND	OnDrawCircle
IDM_DRAW_CIRCLE	UPDATE_COMMAND_UI	OnUpdateDrawCircle
IDM_DRAW_PATTERN	COMMAND	OnDrawPattern
IDM_DRAW_PATTERN	UPDATE_COMMAND_UI	OnUpdateDrawPattern
IDM_DRAW_SQUARE	COMMAND	OnDrawSquare
IDM_DRAW_SQUARE	UPDATE_COMMAND_UI	OnUpdateDrawSquare

6. **Edit the EX13AVW.H file.** Add the following data members to the *CEx13a-View* class header.

```
private:
    CRect m_rect;
    BOOL  m_bCircle;
    BOOL  m_bPattern;
```

7. **Edit the EX13AVW.CPP file.** The *CEx13aView* constructor simply initializes the class data members.

```
CEx13aView::CEx13aView() : m_rect(0, 0, 100, 100)
{
    m_bCircle = TRUE;
    m_bPattern = FALSE;
}
```

The *OnDraw* function draws an ellipse or a rectangle, depending on the value of the *m_bCircle* flag. The brush is plain white or a diagonal pattern, depending on the value of *m_bPattern*.

```
void CEx13aView::OnDraw(CDC* pDC)
{
    CBrush brush(HS_BDIAGONAL, 0L); // brush with diagonal pattern

    if (m_bPattern) {
        pDC->SelectObject(&brush);
    }
    else {
        pDC->SelectStockObject(WHITE_BRUSH);
    }
    if (m_bCircle) {
        pDC->Ellipse(m_rect);
    }
    else {
        pDC->Rectangle(m_rect);
    }
    pDC->SelectStockObject(WHITE_BRUSH); // deselects brush if selected
}
```

The *OnDrawCircle* function handles the command message ON_DRAW_-CIRCLE, and the *OnDrawSquare* function handles the command message ON_DRAW_SQUARE. These two functions move the drawing rectangle down and to the right, and then they invalidate the rectangle, causing the *OnDraw* function to redraw it. The effect of this invalidation strategy is a diagonal cascading of alternating squares and circles.

```
void CEx13aView::OnDrawCircle()
{
    m_bCircle = TRUE;
    m_rect += CPoint(25, 25);
    InvalidateRect(m_rect);
}

void CEx13aView::OnDrawSquare()
{
    m_bCircle = FALSE;
    m_rect += CPoint(25, 25);
    InvalidateRect(m_rect);
}
```

The following two update command UI functions alternately enable and disable the Circle and Square buttons and corresponding menu items. Only one item can be enabled at a time.

```
void CEx13aView::OnUpdateDrawCircle(CCmdUI* pCmdUI)
{
    pCmdUI->Enable(!m_bCircle);
}

void CEx13aView::OnUpdateDrawSquare(CCmdUI* pCmdUI)
{
    pCmdUI->Enable(m_bCircle);
}
```

The *OnDrawPattern* function toggles the state of the *m_bPattern* flag. It also accesses the toolbar object to dump a list of the button characteristics.

```
void CEx13aView::OnDrawPattern()
{
    UINT id, style;
    int nCount, i, image;

    m_bPattern = m_bPattern ^ 1;
    // the following code lists the attributes of all toolbar buttons
    // GetParentFrame works in SDI applications only
    CToolBar* pTool = (CToolBar*)
        GetParentFrame()->GetDescendantWindow(AFX_IDW_TOOLBAR);
    TRACE("Toolbar entries:\n");
```

```
    nCount = pTool->GetCount();
    for (i = 0; i < nCount; i++) {
        pTool->GetButtonInfo(i, id, style, image);
        TRACE(" index = %d, command ID = %lx, button style = %lx\n",
        i, (long) id, (long) style);
    }
}
```

The *OnUpdateDrawPattern* function updates the Pattern button and menu item according to the state of the *m_bPattern* flag. The toolbar button appears to move in and out, and the menu item check mark appears and disappears.

```
void CEx13aView::OnUpdateDrawPattern(CCmdUI* pCmdUI)
{
    pCmdUI->SetCheck(m_bPattern);
}
```

8. Build and test the EX13A application. Notice the behavior of the toolbar buttons. Try the corresponding menu items, and notice that they too are enabled, disabled, and checked as the application's state changes.

The Status Bar

The status bar window neither accepts user input nor generates command messages. Its job is simply to display text in panes under program control. The status bar supports two types of text panes—a message line pane and a status indicator pane. To use the status bar for application-specific data, you must first disable the standard status bar that displays the menu prompt and keyboard status.

The Status Bar Definition

The static *indicators* array that AppWizard generates in the MAINFRM.CPP file defines the application's status bar. The constant *ID_SEPARATOR* identifies a message line pane; the other constants are string resource IDs that identify indicator panes. Here is the *indicators* array for the standard framework status bar:

```
static UINT BASED_CODE indicators[] =
{
    ID_SEPARATOR,           // status line indicator
    ID_INDICATOR_CAPS,
    ID_INDICATOR_NUM,
    ID_INDICATOR_SCRL,
};
```

The *CStatusBar SetIndicators* member function, called in the application's derived frame class, configures the status bar according to the contents of the *indicators* array.

The Message Line

A message line pane displays a string that the program supplies dynamically. To set the value of the message line, you must first get access to the status bar object, and then you must call the *CStatusBar SetPaneText* member function with a zero-based index parameter. Pane 0 is the leftmost pane, 1 is the next pane to the right, and so forth. The following code fragment is part of a view class member function. Because the view window is a sibling of the status bar window, it's necessary to access the parent frame window through the application object. The *CWnd GetDescendant-Window* function retrieves a pointer to the status bar that is identified by the constant *ID_MY_STATUS_BAR*.

```
CStatusBar* pStatus =
    (CStatusBar*) AfxGetApp()->m_pMainWnd->GetDescendantWindow(ID_MY_STATUS_BAR);
pStatus->SetPaneText(0, "message line for first pane);
```

Normally, the length of a message line pane is exactly one-fourth the width of the display. If, however, the message line is the first (index 0) pane, it is a stretchy pane without a beveled border. Its minimum length is one-fourth the display width, and it expands if room is available in the status bar.

The Status Indicator

A status indicator pane is linked to a single resource-supplied string that is displayed or hidden by logic in an associated update command UI message handler function. Indicators are identified by a string resource ID, and that same ID is used to route update command UI messages. The Caps Lock indicator is handled in the frame class by the following message map entry and handler function. The *Enable* function turns on the indicator if the Caps Lock mode is set.

```
ON_UPDATE_COMMAND_UI(ID_INDICATOR_CAPS, OnUpdateKeyCapsLock)

void CMainFrame::OnUpdateKeyCapsLock(CCmdUI* pCmdUI)
{
    pCmdUI->Enable(::GetKeyState(VK_CAPITAL) & 1);
}
```

The status bar update command UI functions are called during idle processing so that the status bar is updated continuously.

The length of a status indicator pane is the exact length of the corresponding resource string.

Taking Control of the Status Bar

In the standard application framework implementation, the status bar has the child window ID *AFX_IDW_STATUS_BAR*. The application framework looks for this ID when it wants to display a menu prompt. The update command UI handlers for the keyboard state indicators, embedded in the frame window base class, are linked to the string IDs *ID_INDICATOR_CAPS*, *ID_INDICATOR_NUM*, and *ID_INDICATOR_SCRL*. To take control of the status bar, you must use a different child window ID, and you must use different indicator ID constants.

The status bar window ID is assigned in the *CStatusBar Create* function called by the derived frame class *OnCreate* member function. That function is contained in the MAINFRM.CPP file that AppWizard generates. The window ID is the third *Create* parameter, and it defaults to *AFX_IDW_STATUS_BAR*.

To assign your own ID, you must replace this call:

```
m_wndStatusBar.Create(this);
```

with this call:

```
m_wndStatusBar.Create(this, WS_CHILD | WS_VISIBLE | CBRS_BOTTOM,
                      ID_MY_STATUS_BAR);
```

You must also, of course, define the *ID_MY_STATUS_BAR* constant in the RESOURCE.H file (using App Studio).

We forgot one thing. The standard application framework's View menu allows the user to turn the status bar on and off. That logic is pegged to the *AFX_IDW_-STATUS_BAR* window ID, so you'll have to change the menu logic too. In your derived frame class, you must write message map entries and handlers for the *ID_VIEW_STATUS_BAR* command and update command UI messages. *ID_VIEW_STATUS_BAR* is the ID of the Status Bar menu item. The derived class handlers override the standard handlers in the *CFrameWnd* base class. See the EX13B example for code details.

The EX13B Status Bar Example

The EX13B example replaces the standard application framework status bar with a new status bar with the following text panes:

Pane Index	String ID	Type	Description
0	*ID_SEPARATOR* (0)	Message line	*x* cursor coordinate
1	*ID_SEPARATOR* (0)	Message line	*y* cursor coordinate
2	*ID_INDICATOR_SHIFT*	Status indicator	Keyboard Shift key status
3	*ID_INDICATOR_CTRL*	Status indicator	Keyboard Ctrl key status
4	*ID_INDICATOR_ALT*	Status indicator	Keyboard Alt key status

The resulting status bar is shown in Figure 13-3 on the next page.

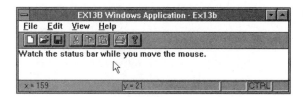

Figure 13-3.
The status bar of the EX13B example.

The leftmost pane stretches past its normal ¼-screen length as the displayed frame window expands to fill more than ¾-screen width.

Follow these steps to produce the EX13B example:

1. **Run AppWizard to generate \VCPP\EX13B\EX13B.** Choose AppWizard from Visual Workbench's Project menu. The options and the default class names are shown here:

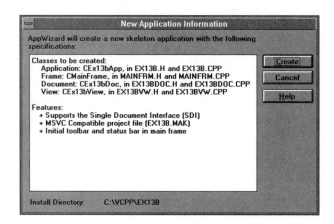

2. **Use App Studio to edit the application's string table resource.** Select any string table segment, and then add the following three strings:

String ID	String Caption
ID_INDICATOR_SHIFT	SHIFT
ID_INDICATOR_CTRL	CTRL
ID_INDICATOR_ALT	ALT

This process adds the three IDs to the symbol table stored in the project's RESOURCE.H file.

3. Use App Studio to edit the application's symbols. Click the symbol toolbar button or choose Symbols from the Edit menu. Add the new status bar identifier, *ID_MY_STATUS_BAR*, and accept the default value.

4. Use ClassWizard to add View menu command handlers in class *CMainFrame*. Add the following command message handlers:

Object ID	Message	Member Function Name
ID_VIEW_STATUS_BAR	COMMAND	*OnViewStatusBar*
ID_VIEW_STATUS_BAR	UPDATE_COMMAND_UI	*OnUpdateViewStatusBar*

5. Add the following function prototypes to MAINFRM.H. You must add these *CMainFrame* message handler prototypes manually because ClassWizard doesn't recognize the associated command message IDs.

```
afx_msg void OnUpdateKeyShift(CCmdUI* pCmdUI);
afx_msg void OnUpdateKeyCtrl(CCmdUI* pCmdUI);
afx_msg void OnUpdateKeyAlt(CCmdUI* pCmdUI);
```

Add the message handler statements inside the *AFX_MSG* brackets so that ClassWizard will let you access and edit the code later.

6. Edit the MAINFRM.CPP file. Replace the original *indicators* array with the following:

```
static UINT BASED_CODE indicators[] =
{
    ID_SEPARATOR,  // first message line pane
    ID_SEPARATOR,  // second message line pane
    ID_INDICATOR_SHIFT,
    ID_INDICATOR_CTRL,
    ID_INDICATOR_ALT,
};
```

Next, edit the *OnCreate* member function as shown here:

```
int CMainFrame::OnCreate(LPCREATESTRUCT lpCreateStruct)
{
    if (CFrameWnd::OnCreate(lpCreateStruct) == -1)
        return -1;

    if (!m_wndToolBar.Create(this) ||
        !m_wndToolBar.LoadBitmap(IDR_MAINFRAME) ||
        !m_wndToolBar.SetButtons(buttons,
          sizeof(buttons)/sizeof(UINT)))
    {
```

(continued)

221

```
        TRACE("Failed to create toolbar\n");
        return -1;      // fail to create
    }

    if (!m_wndStatusBar.Create(this,
        WS_CHILD | WS_VISIBLE | CBRS_BOTTOM, ID_STATUS_BAR) ||
        !m_wndStatusBar.SetIndicators(indicators,
        sizeof(indicators)/sizeof(UINT)))
    {
        TRACE("Failed to create status bar\n");
        return -1;      // fail to create
    }

    return 0;
}
```

The modified call to *Create* uses our own status bar ID, *ID_MY_STATUS_BAR*, instead of *AFX_IDW_STATUS_BAR* (the application framework's status bar object).

Now add the following message map entries for class *CMainFrame*. Again, ClassWizard can't add these for you because it doesn't recognize the string table IDs and the constant *ID_VIEW_STATUS_BAR* as object IDs.

```
ON_UPDATE_COMMAND_UI(ID_INDICATOR_SHIFT, OnUpdateKeyShift)
ON_UPDATE_COMMAND_UI(ID_INDICATOR_CTRL, OnUpdateKeyCtrl)
ON_UPDATE_COMMAND_UI(ID_INDICATOR_ALT, OnUpdateKeyAlt)
```

Next, add the following *CMainFrame* member functions that update the three status indicators:

```
void CMainFrame::OnUpdateKeyShift(CCmdUI* pCmdUI)
{
    pCmdUI->Enable(::GetKeyState(VK_SHIFT) < 0);
}

void CMainFrame::OnUpdateKeyCtrl(CCmdUI* pCmdUI)
{
    pCmdUI->Enable(::GetKeyState(VK_CONTROL) < 0);
}

void CMainFrame::OnUpdateKeyAlt(CCmdUI* pCmdUI)
{
    pCmdUI->Enable(::GetKeyState(VK_MENU) < 0);
}
```

Finally, edit the following View menu functions that ClassWizard originally generated in MAINFRAME.CPP:

```
void CMainFrame::OnViewStatusBar()
{
    CWnd* pBar;

    if (pBar = GetDescendantWindow(ID_MY_STATUS_BAR)) {
      // toggle visible state
      pBar->ShowWindow((pBar->GetStyle() & WS_VISIBLE) == 0);
      RecalcLayout();
    }
}

void CMainFrame::OnUpdateViewStatusBar(CCmdUI* pCmdUI)
{
    CWnd* pBar;

    if (pBar = GetDescendantWindow(ID_MY_STATUS_BAR)) {
      pCmdUI->SetCheck((pBar->GetStyle() & WS_VISIBLE) != 0);
    }
}
```

These functions ensure that the View menu Status Bar command is properly linked to the new status bar.

7. **Use ClassWizard to add a *CEx13bView* class message handler for WM_MOUSEMOVE.** The mouse move message handler updates the status bar with the current mouse cursor position.

8. **Edit the *OnDraw* function in EX13BVW.CPP.** The *OnDraw* function displays a message in the view window.

```
void CEx13bView::OnDraw(CDC* pDC)
{
    pDC->TextOut(0, 0, "Watch the status bar while you move the mouse.");
}
```

9. **Edit the *OnMouseMove* function in EX13BVW.CPP.** This function gets a pointer to the status bar object and then calls the *SetPaneText* function to update the first and second message line panes.

```
void CEx13bView::OnMouseMove(UINT nFlags, CPoint point)
{
    char text[100];

    CStatusBar* pStatus = (CStatusBar*)
        AfxGetApp()->m_pMainWnd->GetDescendantWindow(ID_MY_STATUS_BAR);
    if (pStatus) {
      wsprintf(text, "x = %d", point.x);
      pStatus->SetPaneText(0, text); // first pane
      wsprintf(text, "y = %d", point.y);
      pStatus->SetPaneText(1, text); // second pane
    }
}
```

10. Build and test the EX13B application. Move the mouse, and observe that the left two status bar panes accurately reflect the mouse cursor's position. Also, press Shift and Ctrl. Do the status bar indicators operate correctly? Does Alt toggle the ALT status indicator? Remember that, in Windows, Alt doesn't work like Ctrl and Shift. You don't have to hold Alt down to Alt-Shift another key. Can you toggle the status bar on and off from the View menu?

Note: *If you want the first (0th) status bar pane to have a beveled border like the other panes, include the following line in the* CMainFrame OnCreate *function, after the call to the status bar* Create *function:*

```
m_wndStatusBar .SetPaneInfo(0, 0, SBPS_STRETCH, 0);
```

14

A Reusable Base Class

A promise of C++ is its ability to produce "software Lego blocks" that can be taken "off the shelf" and fitted easily into an application. The Microsoft Foundation Class Library version 2.0 classes are a good example of reusable software. This chapter shows you how to build your own reusable base class that builds on what the class library already provides.

In the process of building the reusable class, you'll learn a few more things about Windows and the class library. In particular, you'll see how the application framework allows access to the Windows "initialization" (INI) file, you'll learn more about the mechanics of the *CFrameWnd* class, and you'll get more exposure to static class variables and the *CString* class.

Why Reusable Base Classes Are Difficult to Write

In a normal application, you write software components that solve particular problems. It's usually a simple matter of meeting the project specification. With reusable base classes, however, you must anticipate future programming needs, both your own and those of others. You have to write a class that's general and complete yet efficient and easy to use.

This chapter's example showed me the difficulty in building reusable software. I started out with the intention of writing a frame class that would "remember" its window size and position. When I got into the job, I discovered that existing Windows-based programs such as Notepad remember whether they have been iconized or whether they have been maximized to full screen. Then there was the oddball case of a window that was both iconized and maximized. After that, I had to worry about the toolbar and the status bar, plus the class had to work in a dynamic link library (DLL). In short, it was surprisingly difficult to write a frame class that would do everything that a programmer might expect.

In a production programming environment, reusable base classes might fall out of the normal software development cycle. A class written for one project might be extracted and further generalized for another project. There's always the temptation, though, to cut and paste existing classes without asking, What can I factor out into a base class? If you're in the software business for the long term, it's really beneficial to start building your library of truly reusable components.

The *CPersistentFrame* Class

In this chapter, you'll be making a class called *CPersistentFrame* that is derived from the *CFrameWnd* class. This *CPersistentFrame* class supports a persistent SDI (Single Document Interface) frame window that remembers the following characteristics:

- Window size

- Window position

- Maximized status

- Iconized status

- Toolbar enablement

- Status bar enablement

When you terminate an application that's built with the *CPersistentFrame* class, the above information is saved on disk in the application's private INI file. When the application starts again, it reads the INI file and restores the frame to its state at the previous exit.

You can use the persistent view class in any SDI application, including the examples in this book. All you have to do is substitute *CPersistentFrame* for *CFrameWnd* in your application's derived frame class files.

The *CFrameWnd* Class and the *ActivateFrame* Member Function

Why choose *CFrameWnd* as the base class for a persistent window? Why not have a persistent view instead? In a class library SDI application, the main frame window is always the parent of the view window. This frame window is created first, and then the control bars and the view are created as child windows. The application framework ensures that the child windows shrink and expand appropriately as the user changes the size of the frame window. It wouldn't make sense to change the view size after the frame was created.

The key to controlling the frame's size is the *CFrameWnd ActivateFrame* member function. The application framework calls this virtual function during the SDI main frame creation process (and in response to the File New and File Open menu items). Its job is to call the *CWnd ShowWindow* function with the parameter *nCmdShow*. *ShowWindow* makes the frame window visible, along with its menu, view window, and control bars. The *nCmdShow* parameter determines whether the window is maximized or iconized or both.

If you override *ActivateFrame* in your derived frame class, you can change the value of *nCmdShow* before passing it to the *CFrameWnd ActivateFrame* function. Also, you can call the *CWnd SetWindowPlacement* function that sets the size and position of the frame window, and you can set the visible status of the control bars. Because all changes are made before the frame window becomes visible, there is no annoying flash on the screen.

You must be careful not to reset the frame window's position and size after every File New or File Open command. A first-time flag data member ensures that your *CPersistentFrame ActivateFrame* function operates only when the application starts.

The Windows INI File

If you've used Windows-based applications before, you've probably seen INI files. The WIN.INI and SYSTEM.INI files, located in the WINDOWS directory, hold important profile information. Older Windows-based applications stored their private profile data in WIN.INI, but current applications store their own INI files in the WINDOWS directory. An application generally reads its INI file on startup and writes it back on exit.

The class library application framework uses an INI file to store a list of most recently used files. The INI file is usually named after the application. The Windows Clock program's INI file is called CLOCK.INI, for example. In a class library program, the INI file is managed by member functions in the *CWinApp* application class. These functions are available for your use. Before you study the functions, however, you should know something about the structure of the INI file.

A Windows INI file is divided into sections, each identified by a heading name in square brackets. Each section consists of a series of entry names with associated string or numeric values. Both heading names and entry names are case-independent. Here's a listing of a hypothetical INI file:

```
[Text formatting]
Font=Helvetica Narrow
Points=12
Tabs=5
[Numeric formatting]
MaxDigits=16.2
Radix=10
```

Heading names are "Text formatting" and "Numeric formatting." Entry names are "Font," "Points," "Tabs," "MaxDigits," and "Radix."

By default, the application framework reads and writes the INI file for you. The class library provides four *CWinApp* member functions for accessing INI file entries:

- *GetProfileInt*

- *WriteProfileInt*

- *GetProfileString*

- *WriteProfileString*

These functions treat INI file entries as either *CString* objects or unsigned integers. If you need floating-point values as entries, you must use the string functions and do the conversion yourself. All the functions take a heading name and an entry name as parameters. Now the INI file is starting to look like a mini hierarchical database.

To use the INI file entry access functions, you need a pointer to the application object. The global function *AfxGetApp* does the job. With the previous sample INI file, you can change the Font and Points entries with the following code:

```
AfxGetApp()->WriteProfileString("Text formatting", "Font", "Times Roman");
AfxGetApp()->WriteProfileInt("Text formatting", "Points", 10);
```

For Windows SDK Programmers

Windows provides three functions for INI file entries— *WritePrivateProfile-String*, *GetPrivateProfileString*, and *GetPrivateProfileInt*. Each of these requires the INI filename as a parameter. For strings, the parameters are long pointers to conventional zero-terminated character arrays. The class library INI file entry access functions wrap these Windows functions and thus eliminate the need to assemble the INI filename.

Using the *CString* Class

The class library *CString* class is a significant de facto extension to the C++ language. As the *Class Library Reference* points out, the *CString* class has many useful operators and member functions, but perhaps its most important feature is its dynamic memory allocation. You never have to worry about the size of a *CString* object. The following statements represent typical uses of *CString* objects:

```
CString firstName("Elvis");
CString lastName("Presley");
CString truth = firstName + " " + lastName; // concatenation
truth += " is alive";
ASSERT(truth == "Elvis Presley is alive");
ASSERT(truth.Left(5) == firstName);
ASSERT(truth[2] == 'v'); // subscript operator
```

In a perfect world, C++ programs would always use all *CString* objects and never use ordinary zero-terminated character arrays. Unfortunately, many runtime library functions still use character arrays, so programs must always mix and match their string representations. Fortunately, the *CString* class provides a *const char* ()* *operator that converts a CString* object to a character pointer. Many of the class library functions have *const char* parameters. Take the global *AfxMessageBox* function, for example. Here is one of its prototypes:

```
int AFXAPI AfxMessageBox(LPCSTR lpszText, UINT nType = MB_OK,
                         UINT nIDHelp = 0);
```

(Note: LPCSTR is <u>not</u> a pointer to a *CString* object but rather is a replacement for *const char FAR*.)

You can call *AfxMessageBox* this way:

```
char szMessageText[] = "Unknown error";
AfxMessageBox(szMessageText);
```

Or you can call it this way:

```
CString messageText("Unknown error");
AfxMessageBox(messageText);
```

Now, suppose you want to use the *wsprintf* function to generate a formatted string. You can easily use a character array such as this:

```
int nError = 23;
char szMessageText[50];
wsprintf(szMessageText, "Error number %d", nError);
AfxMessageBox(szMessageText);
```

It would be inappropriate to use a *CString* object here because it would be awkward to convert the output from *wsprintf* to a *CString* object. What if you really want a

Differences Between *sprintf* and *wsprintf*

Both *sprintf* and *wsprintf* work with Windows, and both require *CString* input parameters to be cast to character pointers. Some differences exist between the two functions, however. The *wsprintf* function does not support floating-point formatting and thus does not require linking of the floating-point library functions. The *sprintf* function, on the other hand, is less fussy about the casting of character pointer input parameters; you can, for example, write

```
char text[50];
CString string("test");
sprintf(text, "%s\n", (const char*) string);
```

But with *wsprintf* you need a stricter cast with medium model:

```
wsprintf(text, "%s\n", (LPCSTR) string);
```

CString? How do you use *wsprintf* to format to a *CString* object? You can't use a *CString* object as the first parameter because the compiler expects a *char**, not the *const char** that the *CString* class provides.

To use a *CString* object as a function <u>output</u> parameter, you must use the *CString* *GetBuffer* and *ReleaseBuffer* functions. The *GetBuffer* function locks down a *CString* object and fixes its size. The *ReleaseBuffer* function makes the *CString* object dynamic again. Here is some code that allows *wsprintf* to send its output to a *CString* object.

```
CString fontFamily("Helvetica");
CString fontModifier("Narrow");
CString font;
wsprintf(font.GetBuffer(20), "%s %s", (LPCSTR) fontFamily,
        (LPCSTR) fontModifier);
font.ReleaseBuffer();
ASSERT(font.MakeUpper() == "HELVETICA NARROW");
```

The *GetBuffer* parameter value of *20* was chosen because the font string is not expected to exceed 20 characters (not counting the null terminator). The *ReleaseBuffer* call is not absolutely necessary here because we're not calling any *CString* member functions for the *font* object.

The *const char** operator takes care of converting a *CString* to a constant character pointer (except for special functions such as *sprintf*), but what about conversion in the other direction? It so happens that the *CString* class has a constructor that converts a constant character pointer to a *CString* object, and it has a set of overloaded operators for these pointers. That's why statements such as this work:

```
truth += " is alive";
```

The special constructor works with functions that take a *CString* reference parameter, such as *CDC::TextOut*. In the following statement, a *CString* object is created on the calling program's stack, and then its address is passed to *TextOut*.

```
pDC->TextOut("Hello world");
```

The Position of a Maximized Window

As a Windows user, you know that you can maximize a window from the system menu or by clicking a button at the top right corner of the window. You can return a maximized window to its original size in a similar fashion. It's obvious that a maximized window remembers its original size and position.

The *CWnd* function *GetWindowRect* retrieves the screen coordinates of a window. If a window is maximized, *GetWindowRect* returns the coordinates of the screen rather than the window's unmaximized coordinates. If a persistent frame class is to work for maximized windows, it has to know the window's unmaximized coordinates. The *CWnd GetWindowPlacement* function retrieves the window's unmaximized coordinates together with some flags that indicate whether the window is currently iconized, maximized, or both.

Static Data Members

If your application uses constants that are associated with a particular class, it makes sense to declare these constants as static data members. This strategy avoids name conflicts, and it makes your programs more modular. Appendix A shows you how to declare and define static data members, but it avoids the issue of memory models. The static data members in the class library are all declared NEAR. In the small and medium models, this designation has no effect, but in the large and compact models, the statics are placed in the DGROUP segment for efficiency and to facilitate multi-instance applications. You should follow this convention in your own classes unless you know that you have a full DGROUP.

> **Note:** *Chapter 26 will discuss the implications of using static data members in a DLL. For now, avoid using initialized* CString *static data members in any class that you might place in an extension DLL.*

The Default Window Rectangle

You're used to defining rectangles with device or logical coordinates. A *CRect* object constructed with the statement

```
CRect rect(CW_USEDEFAULT, CW_USEDEFAULT, 0, 0);
```

has a special meaning. When Windows creates a new window with this special rectangle, it positions the window in a cascade pattern with the top left corner below and to the right of the window most recently created. The right and bottom edges of the window are always within the display's boundaries.

The application framework's global constant *rectDefault* contains the special rectangle in the previous example. The *CPersistentView* class declares its own *rectDefault* default window rectangle with a fixed size and position as a static data member, thus hiding the global *rectDefault* from the class member functions.

The EX14A Example

The EX14A program illustrates the use of a persistent frame window class, *CPersistentFrame*. Figure 14-1 on the following page shows the contents of the files PERSIST.H and PERSIST.CPP, which are included in the EX14A project. In the example, you'll insert the new frame class into an AppWizard-generated SDI application. EX14A is a "do-nothing" application, but you can easily insert the persistent frame class into any of your own SDI "do-something" applications.

PERSIST.H

```
class CPersistentFrame : public CFrameWnd
{ // remembers where it was on the desktop
    DECLARE_DYNAMIC(CPersistentFrame)
private:
    static const CRect NEAR rectDefault;
    CString m_profileHeading, m_profileRect, m_profileIcon;
    CString m_profileMax, m_profileTool, m_profileStatus;
    BOOL    m_bFirstTime;
protected: // create from serialization only
    CPersistentFrame();
    ~CPersistentFrame();
    virtual void ActivateFrame(int nCmdShow = -1);
    //{{AFX_MSG(CPersistentFrame)
    afx_msg void OnDestroy();
    //}}AFX_MSG
    DECLARE_MESSAGE_MAP()
};
```

PERSIST.CPP

```
#include "stdafx.h"
#include "persist.h"

#ifdef _DEBUG
#undef THIS_FILE
static char BASED_CODE THIS_FILE[] = __FILE__;
#endif
/////////////////////////////////////////////////////////////////////////////
// CPersistentFrame

const CRect NEAR CPersistentFrame::rectDefault(10, 10, 500, 400);
// static

IMPLEMENT_DYNAMIC(CPersistentFrame, CFrameWnd)

BEGIN_MESSAGE_MAP(CPersistentFrame, CFrameWnd)
    //{{AFX_MSG_MAP(CPersistentFrame)
    ON_WM_DESTROY()
    //}}AFX_MSG_MAP
END_MESSAGE_MAP()
```

Figure 14-1. *(continued)*
The CPersistentView *class listing.*

Figure 14-1. *continued*

```
/////////////////////////////////////////////////////////////////
CPersistentFrame::CPersistentFrame() :
    m_profileHeading("Window size"), m_profileRect("Rect"),
    m_profileIcon("icon"), m_profileMax("max"),
    m_profileTool("tool"), m_profileStatus("status")
{
    m_bFirstTime = TRUE;

}


/////////////////////////////////////////////////////////////////
CPersistentFrame::~CPersistentFrame()
{
}


/////////////////////////////////////////////////////////////////
void CPersistentFrame::OnDestroy()
{
    CString text, temp;
    CWnd*   pBar;
    BOOL    bIconic, bMaximized;

    WINDOWPLACEMENT wndpl;
    wndpl.length = sizeof(WINDOWPLACEMENT);
    // gets current window position and iconized/maximized status
    BOOL bRet = GetWindowPlacement(&wndpl);
    if (wndpl.showCmd == SW_SHOWNORMAL) {
      bIconic = FALSE;
      bMaximized = FALSE;
    }
    else if (wndpl.showCmd == SW_SHOWMAXIMIZED) {
      bIconic = FALSE;
      bMaximized = TRUE;
    }
    else if (wndpl.showCmd == SW_SHOWMINIMIZED) {
      bIconic = TRUE;
      if (wndpl.flags) {
        bMaximized = TRUE;
      }
      else {
        bMaximized = FALSE;
      }
    }
    wsprintf(text.GetBuffer(20), "%04d %04d %04d %04d",
        wndpl.rcNormalPosition.left, wndpl.rcNormalPosition.top,
        wndpl.rcNormalPosition.right, wndpl.rcNormalPosition.bottom);
```

(continued)

Figure 14-1. *continued*

```
    text.ReleaseBuffer();
    AfxGetApp()->WriteProfileString(m_profileHeading,
                                    m_profileRect, text);
    AfxGetApp()->WriteProfileInt(m_profileHeading,
                                 m_profileIcon, bIconic);
    AfxGetApp()->WriteProfileInt(m_profileHeading,
                                 m_profileMax, bMaximized);
    if (pBar = GetDescendantWindow(AFX_IDW_TOOLBAR)) {
        AfxGetApp()->WriteProfileInt(m_profileHeading, m_profileTool,
            (pBar->GetStyle() & WS_VISIBLE) != 0L);
    }
    if (pBar = GetDescendantWindow(AFX_IDW_STATUS_BAR)) {
        AfxGetApp()->WriteProfileInt(m_profileHeading,
            m_profileStatus, (pBar->GetStyle() & WS_VISIBLE) != 0L);
    }
    CFrameWnd::OnDestroy();
}

/////////////////////////////////////////////////////////////////////
void CPersistentFrame::ActivateFrame(int nCmdShow)
{
    CWnd*           pBar;
    CString         text;
    BOOL            bIconic, bMaximized, bTool, bStatus;
    UINT            flags;
    WINDOWPLACEMENT wndpl;
    CRect           rect;

    if (m_bFirstTime) {
      m_bFirstTime = FALSE;
      text = AfxGetApp()->GetProfileString(m_profileHeading,
                                           m_profileRect);
      if (!text.IsEmpty()) {
        // can't use sscanf in a DLL
        rect.left = atoi((const char*) text);
        rect.top = atoi((const char*) text + 5);
        rect.right = atoi((const char*) text + 10);
        rect.bottom = atoi((const char*) text + 15);
      }
      else {
        rect = rectDefault;
      }

      bIconic = AfxGetApp()->GetProfileInt(m_profileHeading,
                                           m_profileIcon, 0);
      bMaximized = AfxGetApp()->GetProfileInt(m_profileHeading,
                                              m_profileMax, 0);
```

(continued)

Figure 14-1. *continued*

```
      if (bIconic) {
        nCmdShow = SW_SHOWMINNOACTIVE;
        if (bMaximized) {
          flags = WPF_RESTORETOMAXIMIZED;
        }
      }
      else {
        if (bMaximized) {
          nCmdShow = SW_SHOWMAXIMIZED;
          flags = WPF_RESTORETOMAXIMIZED;
        }
        else {
          nCmdShow = SW_NORMAL;
          flags = 0;
        }
      }
      wndpl.length = sizeof(WINDOWPLACEMENT);
      wndpl.showCmd = nCmdShow;
      wndpl.flags = flags;
      wndpl.ptMinPosition = CPoint(0, 0);
      wndpl.ptMaxPosition = CPoint(-::GetSystemMetrics(SM_CXBORDER),
                                   -::GetSystemMetrics(SM_CYBORDER));
      wndpl.rcNormalPosition = rect;

      bTool = AfxGetApp()->GetProfileInt(m_profileHeading,
                                         m_profileTool, 1);
      if (pBar = GetDescendantWindow(AFX_IDW_TOOLBAR)) {
          pBar->ShowWindow(bTool);
      }
      bStatus = AfxGetApp()->GetProfileInt(m_profileHeading,
                                           m_profileStatus, 1);
      if (pBar = GetDescendantWindow(AFX_IDW_STATUS_BAR)) {
          pBar->ShowWindow(bStatus);
      }
      // sets window's position and iconized/maximized status
      BOOL bRet = SetWindowPlacement(&wndpl);
    }
    CFrameWnd::ActivateFrame(nCmdShow);
}
```

Here are the steps for building the EX14A example program:

1. **Run AppWizard to generate \VCPP\EX14A\EX14A.** Choose AppWizard from Visual Workbench's Project menu. The options and the default class names are shown on the following page:

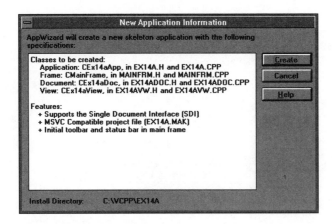

2. **Modify MAINFRM.H.** You must change the base class of *CMainFrame*. To do this, simply change the line

```
class CMainFrame : public CFrameWnd
```

to

```
class CMainFrame : public CPersistentFrame
```

3. **Modify MAINFRM.CPP.** Globally replace all occurrences of *CFrameWnd* with *CPersistentFrame*. Also, add the line

```
#include "persist.h"
```

immediately <u>before</u> the line

```
#include "mainfrm.h"
```

4. **Modify EX14A.CPP.** Add the line

```
#include "persist.h"
```

immediately <u>before</u> the line

```
#include "mainfrm.h"
```

> ***Note:*** *As an alternative to modifying EX14A.CPP, you can insert*
> ```
> #include "persist.h"
> ```
> *at the top of the MAINFRAME.H file. If you do this, you won't need to add the #include statements in MAINFRAME.CPP and EX14A.CPP.*

5. **Add the file PERSIST.CPP to the project.** Use Visual Workbench's Project Edit dialog to add the file PERSIST.CPP.

6. **Use ClassWizard to import the new *CPersistentFrame* class.** Choose ClassWizard from Visual Workbench's Browse menu, and then add the class *CPersistentFrame* with the base class *CFrameWnd*. Fill in the Import Class dialog as shown here:

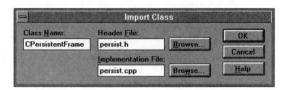

   Be sure that the class header file is PERSIST.H and that the implementation file is PERSIST.CPP.

7. **Build and test the EX14A application.** Size and move the application's frame window, and then close the application. When you restart the application, does its window open at the same location where it was closed? Experiment with maximizing and iconizing, and then change the status of the control bars. Does the persistent frame remember its settings? Examine the file EX14A.INI in the WINDOWS directory. Does it look similar to this?

```
[Window size]
rect=0480 0005 0598 0378
icon=0
max=0
tool=1
status=1
```

Persistent Frames in MDI Applications

You won't get to MDI applications until Chapter 17, but if you're using this book as a reference, you might want to apply the persistent frame technique MDI applications.

The *CPersistentFrame* class, as presented in this chapter, won't work in an MDI application because the MDI main frame window's *ShowWindow* function is called, not by a virtual *ActivateFrame* function, but by the application class's *InitInstance* member function. If you need to control the characteristics of an MDI main frame window, add the necessary code to *InitInstance*.

The *ActivateFrame* function is called, however, for *CMDIChildWnd* objects. This means your MDI application could remember the sizes and positions of its child windows. You could store the information in the INI file, but you would have to accommodate multiple windows. You would have to modify the *CPersistentFrame* class for this purpose.

15

Separating the Document from Its View

Now you're finally going to see the interaction between documents and views. Chapter 12 gave you a preview of this interaction when it showed the routing of command messages to both view objects and document objects. In this chapter, you'll see how the document maintains the application's data and how the view presents the data to the user. You'll also learn how the document and view objects talk to each other while the application executes.

The two examples in this chapter both use the *CFormView* class as the base class for their views. The first example is as simple as possible, with the document holding only one simple object of class *CStudent*, which represents a single student record. The view shows the student's name and grade and allows editing. With the *CStudent* class, you'll get some practice writing classes to represent real-world entities. You'll also get to use the Microsoft Foundation Class Library version 2.0 diagnostic dump functions.

The second example goes further by introducing collection classes, the *CObList* class in particular. Now the document holds a collection of student records, and the view allows the sequencing, insertion, and deletion of individual records. The frame class gets involved too because it contains the toolbar that generates command messages for the view.

Document–View Interaction Functions

You already know that the document object holds the data and that the view object displays the data and allows editing. An SDI application has a document class derived from *CDocument*, and it has one or more view classes, each ultimately derived from *CView*. A complex handshaking process takes place among the document, the view, and the rest of the application framework. To understand this process, you need to know about four important member functions in the document and view classes. Two are virtual functions that you often override in your derived classes; two are nonvirtual base class functions that you call in your derived classes. Let's look at these functions one at a time.

The *CView GetDocument* Function

A view object has only one associated document object. The *GetDocument* function allows an application to navigate from a view to its document. Suppose a view object gets a message that the user has entered new data into an edit control. The view must tell the document object to update its internal data accordingly. The *GetDocument* function provides the document pointer that can be used to access document class member functions or public data members.

The *CDocument GetNextView* function navigates from the document to the view, but, because a document can have more than one view, it's necessary to call this member function once for each view, inside a loop. The *GetDocument* function is used more frequently than *GetNextView*.

When AppWizard generates a derived *CView* class, it creates a special "type-safe" version of the *GetDocument* function that returns not a *CDocument* pointer but a pointer to your derived class. This function is an inline function and looks something like this:

```
CMyDoc* GetDocument()
{
    return (CMyDoc*) m_pDocument;
}
```

When the compiler sees a call to *GetDocument* in your view class code, it uses the derived class version instead of the *CDocument* version, so you do not have to cast the returned pointer to your derived document class. Because the *CView GetDocument* function is <u>not</u> a virtual function, a statement such as

```
pView->GetDocument(); // pView is declared CView*
```

calls the base class *GetDocument* function and thus returns a pointer to a *CDocument* object.

The *CDocument UpdateAllViews* Function

If the document data changes for any reason, all views must be notified so that they can update their representations of that data. If *UpdateAllViews* is called from a member function of a derived document class, its first parameter, *pSender*, is *NULL*. If *UpdateAllViews* is called from a member function of a derived view class, set the *pSender* parameter to the current view like this:

```
GetDocument()->UpdateAllViews(this);
```

The non-null parameter prevents the application framework from notifying the current view. The assumption is that the current view has already updated itself.

The function has optional "hint" parameters that can be used to give the view specific and application-dependent information about which parts of the view to update. This is an advanced use of the function.

How exactly does a view get notified when *UpdateAllViews* gets called? Take a look at the next function, *OnUpdate*.

The *CView OnUpdate* Function

This is a virtual function that the application framework calls in response to your application's call to the *CDocument UpdateAllViews* function. You can, of course, call it directly within your derived *CView* class. Typically, your derived view class's *OnUpdate* function accesses the document, gets the document's data, and then updates the view's data members or controls to reflect the changes. Alternatively, *OnUpdate* can invalidate a portion of the view, causing the view's *OnDraw* function to use document data to draw in the window. The *OnUpdate* function might look something like this:

```
void CMyView::OnUpdate(CViewCView* pSender, LPARAM lHint, CObject* pHint)
{
    CMyDocument* pMyDoc = GetDocument();
    CString lastName = pMyDoc->GetLastName();
    m_pNameStatic->SetWindowText(lastName); // m_pNameStatic is
                                            // a CMyView data member
}
```

The hint information is passed through directly from the call to *UpdateAllViews*. The default *OnUpdate* implementation invalidates the entire window rectangle. In your overridden version, you can choose to define a smaller invalid rectangle as specified by the hint information.

If the *CDocument* function *UpdateAllViews* is called with the *pSender* parameter pointing to a specific view object, *OnUpdate* is called for all the document's views <u>except</u> the specified view.

The *CView OnInitialUpdate* Function

This virtual *CView* function is called when the application starts, when the user chooses New from the File menu, and when the user chooses Open from the File menu. The *CView* base class version of *OnInitialUpdate* does nothing but call *OnUpdate*. If you override *OnIntialUpdate* in your derived view class, be sure it calls the base class's *OnIntialUpdate* function or the derived class's *OnUpdate* function.

You can use your derived class's *OnInitialUpdate* function to initialize your view object. When the application starts, the application framework calls *OnInitial-Update* immediately after *OnCreate* (if you have mapped *OnCreate* in your view class). *OnCreate* is called only once, but *OnInitialUpdate* can be called many times.

The Simplest Document–View Application

Suppose that you don't need multiple views of your document but you plan to take advantage of the application framework's file support. In this case, you can forget about the *UpdateAllViews* and *OnUpdate* functions. Simply follow these steps when you develop the application:

1. In your derived document class header file (generated by AppWizard), declare your document's data members. These data members are the primary data storage for your application. You can make these data members public, or you can declare the derived view class a *friend* of the document class.

2. In your derived view class, override the *OnInitialUpdate* virtual member function. The application framework calls this function when the document data has been initialized or read from disk. (Chapter 16 discusses disk file I/O.) *OnInitialUpdate* should update the view to reflect the current document data.

3. In your derived view class, let your window message and command message handlers update the document data members directly, using *GetDocument* to access the document object.

Here's the sequence of events for this simplified document–view environment:

Application starts	*CMyDocument* object constructed
	CMyView object constructed
	View window created
	CMyView::OnCreate called (if mapped)
	CMyView::OnInitialUpdate called
	View object initialized
	View window displayed
User edits data	*CMyView* functions update *CMyDocument* data members
User exits application	*CMyView* object destroyed
	CMyDocument object destroyed

The *CFormView* Class

The *CFormView* class is a useful view class that has many of the characteristics of a modeless dialog window. Like a class derived from *CDialog*, a derived *CFormView* class is associated with a dialog resource that defines the frame characteristics and enumerates the controls. The *CFormView* class supports the same dialog data exchange and validation (DDX and DDV) functions that you saw in the *CDialog* examples in Chapter 7.

> **Warning:** *When you use App Studio to make a dialog for a form view, you <u>must</u> specify the following items in the Dialog Properties dialog:*
>
> Style = Child
>
> Border = None
>
> Visible = unchecked

A *CFormView* object receives notification messages directly from its controls, and it receives command messages from the application framework. This application framework command-processing ability clearly separates *CFormView* from *CDialog*, and it makes controlling the view from the frame's main menu or toolbar easy.

The *CFormView* class is derived from *CView* (actually, from *CScrollView*) and not from *CDialog*. You can't, therefore, assume that *CDialog* member functions are supported. *CFormView* does <u>not</u> have virtual *OnInitDialog*, *OnOK*, and *OnCancel* functions. *CFormView* does not call *UpdateData* and the DDX functions. You have to call these functions yourself at the appropriate times, usually in response to control notification messages or command messages.

Even though the *CFormView* class is not derived from the *CDialog* class, it is built around the Windows dialog. For this reason, you can use many of the *CDialog* class member functions such as *GotoDlgCtrl* and *NextDlgCtrl*. All you have to do is cast your *CFormView* pointer to a *CDialog* pointer. The following statement, extracted from a member function of a class derived from *CFormView*, sets the focus to a specified control. *GetDlgItem* is a *CWnd* function and is thus inherited by the derived *CFormView* class.

```
((CDialog*) this)->GotoDlgCtrl(GetDlgItem(IDC_NAME));
```

You can use ClassWizard to generate the code for a derived *CFormView* class, but it takes some extra effort to make the form view the application's main view; AppWizard doesn't let you choose your view's base class. Once the derived *CFormView* class is generated, though, you can easily add control notification message handlers, command message handlers, and update command UI handlers. (The example steps beginning on page 248 show you what to do.) You can also define data members and validation criteria.

Note: *If you want ClassWizard to add menu command message handlers to a* CFormView *derived class, you must run ClassWizard from inside App Studio after selecting the appropriate menu.*

The *CObject* Class

If you study the class library hierarchy, you'll notice that the *CObject* class is at the top. All other classes, except *CString* and trivial classes such as *CRect* and *CPoint*, are derived from the *CObject* "root" class. When a class is derived from *CObject*, it inherits a number of important characteristics. The many benefits of *CObject* derivation will become clear as you read the chapters that follow.

In this chapter, you'll see how *CObject* derivation allows objects to participate in the diagnostic dumping scheme and to be elements in the collection classes.

Diagnostic Dumping

The class library gives you some useful tools for diagnostic dumping. You enable these tools when you use the Debug project build option. When you use the Release build option, diagnostic dumping is disabled, and the diagnostic code is not linked to your program.

The *TRACE* Macro

You've seen the *TRACE* macro used throughout the preceding examples in this book. *TRACE* statements are active whenever the constant *_DEBUG* is defined (when you use the Debug project build option and when the *afxTraceEnabled* variable is set to *TRUE*). *TRACE* statements work like C language *printf* statements, but they're completely disabled in the Release version of the program. The output from *TRACE* statements goes to the AUX output device, the debugger's output window, or, more commonly, to the Debug Window (DBWIN.EXE). Here's a typical *TRACE* statement:

```
int nCount = 9;
CString desc("total");
TRACE("Count = %d, Description = %s\n", nCount, (const char*) desc);
```

> **Note:** *You must use the* (const char*) *cast for* CString *objects in a* TRACE *statement. Be careful to match all* TRACE *format strings to variables because the compiler's type checking is turned off in this situation. If the formats are mismatched, the* TRACE *statement will give you incorrect results and thus hinder your debugging efforts.*

The *afxDump* Object

An alternative to the *TRACE* statement is more compatible with the C++ language. The class library *afxDump* object accepts program variables with a syntax similar to that of *cout*, the C++ output stream. You don't need complex formatting strings; instead, overloaded operators control the output format. (Overloaded operators are explained in Appendix A.) The *afxDump* output goes to the same destination as *TRACE* output, but the *afxDump* object is defined only in the Debug version of the class library. Here is a typical stream-oriented diagnostic statement that produces the same output as the *TRACE* statement above:

```
int nCount = 9;
CString desc("total");
#ifdef _DEBUG
    afxDump << "Count = " << nCount << ", Description = " << desc << "\n";
#endif
```

Although both *afxDump* and *cout* use the same insertion operator (<<), they don't share any code. The *cout* object is part of the Visual C++ iostream library, and *afxDump* is part of the class library. Don't assume that any of the *cout* formatting capability is available through *afxDump*.

Classes that aren't derived from *CObject*, such as *CString*, *CTime*, and *CRect*, contain their own overloaded insertion operators for *CDumpContext* objects. The *CDumpContext* class, of which *afxDump* is an instance, includes the overloaded insertion operators for the native C++ data types (*int, double, char*,* and so on). The *CDumpContext* class also contains insertion operators for *CObject* references and pointers, and that's where things get interesting.

The Dump Context and the *CObject* Class

If the *CDumpContext* insertion operator accepts *CObject* pointers and references, it must also accept pointers and references to derived classes. Consider a trivial class, *CEvent*, that is derived from *CObject*:

```
class CEvent : public CObject
{
public:
    int m_nTime;
};
```

What happens when the following statement executes?

```
#ifdef _DEBUG
    afxDump << event; // event is an object of class CEvent
#endif
```

The virtual *CObject Dump* function gets called. If you haven't overridden *Dump* for *CEvent*, you don't get much except for the address of the object. If you have overridden *Dump*, however, you can get the internal state of your object. Here's a *CEvent Dump* function:

```
#ifdef _DEBUG
void CEvent::Dump(CDumpContext& dc) const
{
    CObject::Dump(dc); // always call the base class function
    dc << "\ntime = " << m_nTime << "\n";
}
#endif
```

The base class (*CObject*) *Dump* function prints a line like this:

```
a CObject at $4498
```

If you have called the *DECLARE_DYNAMIC* macro in your *CEvent* class definition and the *IMPLEMENT_DYNAMIC* macro in your *CEvent* declaration, you will see the name of the class in your dump, like this:

```
a CEvent at $4498
```

even if your dump statement looks like this:

```
#ifdef _DEBUG
    afxDump << (CObject*) pEvent;
#endif
```

The two macros work together to include the class library runtime class code in your derived *CObject* class. With this code in place, your program can determine an object's class name at runtime (for the dump, for example), and it can obtain class hierarchy information.

> **Note:** *The macro pairs (DECLARE_SERIAL, IMPLEMENT_SERIAL) and (DECLARE_DYNCREATE, IMPLEMENT_DYNCREATE) provide the same runtime class features as those provided by the (DECLARE_DYNAMIC, IMPLEMENT_DYNAMIC) pair.*

Automatic Dump of Undeleted Objects

With the Debug build mode set, the application framework dumps all objects that are undeleted when your program exits. This dump is a useful diagnostic aid, but if you want it to be really useful, you must be sure to delete <u>all</u> your objects, even the ones that would normally disappear after the exit. This object cleanup is good programming discipline.

The EX15A Example

This first of this chapter's two examples shows simple document-view interaction. The *CEx15aDoc* document class, derived from *CDocument*, allows for a single embedded *CStudent* object. The *CStudent* class represents a student record that is composed of a *CString* name and a long integer grade. The *CEx15aView* view class is derived from *CFormView*. It is a visual representation of a student record that has edit controls for the name and grade. The default Enter pushbutton updates the document with data from the edit controls. Figure 15-1 shows the EX15A window.

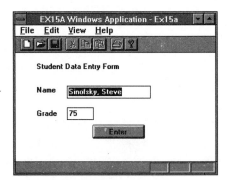

Figure 15-1.
The EX15A program in action.

Figure 15-2 shows the code for the *CStudent* class. Most of the class's features serve EX15A, but a few items carry forward to EX15B and the programs discussed in Chapter 16. For now, take note of the two data members, the default constructor, the operators, and the *Dump* function declaration. The *DECLARE_SERIAL* statement ensures that the class name is available for the diagnostic dump.

STUDENT.H

```cpp
class CStudent : public CObject
{
    DECLARE_SERIAL(CStudent)
public:
    CString m_name;
    LONG    m_lGrade;

    CStudent() {
        m_lGrade = 0;
    }

    CStudent(const char* szName, int lGrade) : m_name(szName) {
        m_lGrade = lGrade;
    }

    CStudent(const CStudent& s) : m_name(s.m_name) {
        m_lGrade = s.m_lGrade;
    }

    const CStudent& operator =(const CStudent& s){
        m_name   = s.m_name;
        m_lGrade = s.m_lGrade;
        return *this;
    }

    BOOL operator ==(const CStudent& s) const
    {
        if ((m_name == s.m_name) && (m_lGrade == s.m_lGrade)) {
            return TRUE;
        }
        else {
            return FALSE;
        }
    }

    BOOL operator !=(const CStudent& s) const
    {
        // Let's make use of the operator we just defined
        return !(*this == s);
    }

#ifdef _DEBUG
    void Dump(CDumpContext& dc) const;
#endif
};
```

Figure 15-2.   *(continued)*

The CStudent *class listing.*

Figure 15-2. *continued*

```
STUDENT.CPP
#include "stdafx.h"
#include "student.h"

IMPLEMENT_SERIAL(CStudent, CObject, 0)

#ifdef _DEBUG
void CStudent::Dump(CDumpContext& dc) const
{
    CObject::Dump(dc);
    dc << "\nm_name = " << m_name << "\nm_1Grade = " << m_1Grade;
}
#endif
```

(Note: The grade data member is declared to be of type *LONG* instead of type *int* to enable the same *CStudent* class to be used for disk input and output in the following chapters.)

Follow these steps to build the EX15A example:

1. **Run AppWizard to generate \VCPP\EX15A\EX15A.** Choose AppWizard from Visual Workbench's Project menu. The options and the default class names are shown here:

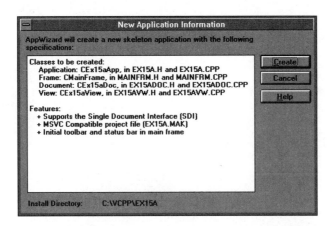

2. **Use App Studio to replace the *IDR_MAINFRAME* Edit menu items.** Delete the current Edit menu items and replace them with a Clear All item, as shown here:

Use the constant *ID_EDIT_CLEAR_ALL*, which is already defined in the application framework.

3. **Use App Studio to create the *IDD_STUDENT* dialog.** Create a new dialog with ID *IDD_STUDENT*, as shown here:

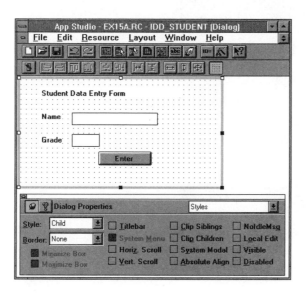

Be sure you set the Style properties <u>exactly</u> as shown in the Dialog Properties dialog.

Use the following IDs for the controls:

Control	ID
Name edit control	*IDC_NAME*
Grade edit control	*IDC_GRADE*
Enter pushbutton	*IDC_ENTER*

4. **Erase the files EX15AVW.H and EX15AVW.CPP.** AppWizard does not let you choose your view's base class. The files EX15AVW.H and EX15AVW.CPP reflect the base class *CView*, but you want *CFormView* as a base class. You will be using ClassWizard to create new files for your *CEx15aView* class, but first you must delete the old files. (The File Manager is useful for deleting files.)

5. **Use ClassWizard to create a new *CEx15aView* class.** Choose ClassWizard from App Studio's Resource menu, and then click the Cancel button in the Add Class dialog. The ClassWizard dialog appears. Choose the *CEx15aView* class

from the Class Name drop-down list. ClassWizard warns you that the files for the class are missing. Click OK. The Repair Class dialog appears as shown here:

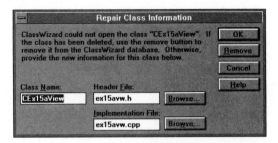

Click the Remove button. ClassWizard removes the class and returns to the ClassWizard dialog. Now click the Add Class button, and fill in the Add Class dialog as shown here:

Click the Create Class button. ClassWizard creates the *CEx15aView* class and returns to the ClassWizard dialog. Click OK to close the dialog.

6. **Use ClassWizard to add message handlers for *CEx15aView*.** Open the IDR_MAINFRAME menu (or bring its window to the front if you left it open). Choose ClassWizard from App Studio's Resource menu. A dialog asks you to select a class name to be associated with the menu, as shown here:

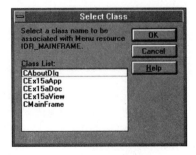

Click on *CEx15aView*, and click the OK button. The ClassWizard dialog appears. Add message handlers for the the following messages:

Object ID	Message	Member Function Name
IDC_ENTER	BN_CLICKED	*OnClickedEnter*
ID_EDIT_CLEAR_ALL	COMMAND	*OnEditClearAll*
ID_EDIT_CLEAR_ALL	UPDATE_COMMAND_UI	*OnUpdateEditClearAll*

Accept the default member function names.

7. **Use ClassWizard to add variables for *CEx15aView*.** Click the Edit Variables button in the ClassWizard dialog, and then add the following variables:

Control ID	Member Variable Name	Property Type	Variable Type
IDC_GRADE	*m_lGrade*	*Value*	*long*
IDC_NAME	*m_name*	*Value*	*CString*

For *m_lGrade*, enter a minimum value of *0* and a maximum value of *100*. Note that ClassWizard generates the code necessary to validate data entered by the user.

8. **Add member function prototypes to EX15AVW.H.** ClassWizard has written a complete header file for class *CEx15aView*, but you must add two function prototypes:

```
protected:
    virtual void OnInitialUpdate();
private:
    void UpdateEntry();
```

9. **Edit EX15AVW.CPP.** Because the view class uses the *CStudent* class, you must include its declaration. Also, ClassWizard did not know about the relationship between the *CEx15aView* class and the *CEx15aDoc* class when it created the view class files. You must add the following statements

```
#include "student.h"
#include "ex15adoc.h"
```

immediately <u>before</u> the statement

```
#include "ex15avw.h"
```

You must enter the following two functions from scratch because ClassWizard did not generate skeleton code for them. The application framework calls the *OnInitialUpdate* function when the application starts. The *UpdateEntry* function is a private member function that transfers data from the document to the *CEx15aView* data members and then to the dialog edit controls. It also sets the focus to the Name edit control.

(Note: ClassWizard did not generate a *GetDocument* member function for *CEx15aView* because it didn't know the associated document's class name. To use the base class version of *GetDocument*, you must cast the returned value to a *CEx15aDoc* pointer.)

```
void CEx15aView::OnInitialUpdate()
{   // called on startup, on File New, and on File Open
    TRACE("Entering CEx15aView::OnInitialUpdate\n");
    UpdateEntry();
}

void CEx15aView::UpdateEntry()
{   // called from OnInitialUpdate and OnEditClearAll
    CEx15aDoc* pDoc = (CEx15aDoc*) GetDocument(); // cast required
    m_lGrade = pDoc->m_student.m_lGrade;
    m_name = pDoc->m_student.m_name;
    UpdateData(FALSE); // calls DDX
    ((CDialog*) this)->GotoDlgCtrl(GetDlgItem(IDC_NAME));
}
```

The *OnClickedEnter* function replaces the *OnOK* function you'd expect to see in a dialog class. The function transfers data from the edit controls to the view's data members and then to the document.

```
void CEx15aView::OnClickedEnter
{
    TRACE("Entering CEx15aView::OnClickedEnter\n")
    CEx15aDoc* pDoc = (CEx15aDoc*) GetDocument();
    UpdateData(TRUE);
    pDoc->m_student.m_lGrade = m_lGrade;
    pDoc->m_student.m_name = m_name;
}
```

In a complex multiview application, the Edit Clear All command would be routed directly to the document. In this simple example, it's routed to the view. The update command UI message handler disables the menu item if the document's student object is blank already.

```
void CEx15aView::OnEditClearAll()
{
    CStudent student;  // default constructor makes 'blank' object
    ((CEx15aDoc*) GetDocument())->m_student = student;
    UpdateEntry();
}
```

```
void CEx15aView::OnUpdateEditClearAll(CCmdUI* pCmdUI)
{
    CStudent student;
    pCmdUI->Enable(((CEx15aDoc*) GetDocument())->m_student != student);
}
```

10. **Edit the EX15ADOC.H file.** The *CEx15aDoc* class provides for an embedded *CStudent* object. The *CStudent* default constructor is called when the document object is constructed, and the *CStudent* destructor is called when the document object is destroyed.

```
public:
    CStudent m_student;
```

11. **Edit the EX15ADOC.CPP file.** Because the document class incorporates the *CStudent* class, you must include its declaration. Add the statement

```
#include "student.h"
```

immediately <u>before</u> the statement

```
#include "ex15adoc.h"
```

Let's use the *CEx15aDoc* constructor to set some initial values for the student object.

```
CEx15aDoc::CEx15aDoc()
{
    TRACE("Document object constructed\n");
    m_student.m_name = "Sinofsky, Steve";
    m_student.m_lGrade = 75L;
}
```

We can't tell whether the EX15A program worked properly unless we dump the document when the program exits. We'll use the destructor to call the document's *Dump* function, which calls the *CStudent Dump* function.

```
CEx15aDoc::~CEx15aDoc()
{
    TRACE("Document object destroyed\n");
#ifdef _DEBUG
    Dump(afxDump);
#endif
}

void CEx15aDoc::Dump(CDumpContext& dc) const
{
    CDocument::Dump(dc);
    dc << "\n" << m_student << "\n";
}
```

12. **Edit the EX15A.CPP file.** Add the statement

```
#include "student.h"
```

immediately <u>before</u> the statement

```
#include "ex15adoc.h"
```

13. **Edit the EX15A project to add STUDENT.CPP.** You must tell Visual Workbench that you are adding the *CStudent* code to the project. When you add the STUDENT.CPP source code file, Visual Workbench will analyze the other project files and establish the STUDENT.H dependencies.

14. **Build and test the EX15A application.** Type a name and a grade, and then click the Enter button. Now exit the application. Does the debug window show messages similar to the following?

```
a CEx15aDoc at $4472
m_strTitle = Ex15a
m_strPathName =
m_bModified = 0
m_pDocTemplate = $438E
a CStudent at $4498
m_name = Sinofsky, Steve
m_lGrade = 75
```

Note: *You must compile the application with the Debug project build option to see these messages.*

A More Advanced Document–View Interaction

If you're laying the groundwork for a multiview application, the document–view interaction must be more complex than the simple interaction in example EX15A. The fundamental problem is this: The user edits in view #1, so view #2 (and any other views) must be updated to reflect the changes. Now you need the *UpdateAllViews* and *OnUpdate* functions because the document is going to act as the clearinghouse for all view updates. The development steps are as follows:

1. In your derived document class header file (generated by AppWizard), declare your document's data members. If you want, you can make these data members private, and you can define member functions to access them or declare the view class as a *friend* of the document class.

2. In your derived view class, override the *OnUpdate* virtual member function. The application framework calls this function whenever the document data has changed for any reason. *OnUpdate* should update the view to reflect the current document data.

3. Evaluate all your command messages. Determine whether each is document-specific or view-specific. (A good example of a document-specific command is

the Clear All command on the Edit menu.) Now map the commands to the appropriate classes.

4. In your derived view class, allow the appropriate command message handlers to update the document data. Be sure that these message handlers call the *CDocument UpdateAllViews* function before they exit. Use the *CView Get-Document* member function to access the view's document.

5. In your derived document class, allow the appropriate command message handlers to update the document data. Be sure that these message handlers call the *CDocument UpdateAllViews* function before they exit.

Here is the sequence of events for the complex document–view interaction:

Application starts	*CMyDocument* object constructed
	CMyView object constructed
	Other view objects constructed
	View windows created
	CMyView::OnCreate called (if mapped)
	CView::OnInitialUpdate called
	Calls *CMyView::OnUpdate*
	Initializes the view
User executes view command	*CMyView* functions update *CMyDocument* data members
	Calls *CDocument::UpdateAllViews*
	Other views' *OnUpdate* function called
User executes document command	*CMyDocument* functions update data members
	Calls *CDocument::UpdateAllViews*
	CMyView::OnUpdate called
	Other views' *OnUpdate* called
User exits application	View objects destroyed
	CMyDocument object destroyed

The *CDocument DeleteContents* Function

At some point, you'll need a function to delete the contents of your document. You could write your own private member function, but it happens that the application framework defines a virtual *DeleteContents* function for the *CDocument* class. The application framework calls your overridden *DeleteContents* function when the document is closed and, as you'll see in the next chapter, at other times as well.

The *CObList* Collection Class

Once you get to know the collection classes, you'll wonder how you ever got along without them. The *CObList* class is a useful representative of the collection class family. If you're familiar with this class, it's easy to learn the other list classes, the array classes, and the map classes.

You might think that collections are something new, but the C programming language has always supported one kind of collection—the array. C arrays must be fixed in size, and they do not support insertion of elements. Many C programmers have written function libraries for other collections, including linked lists, dynamic arrays, and indexed dictionaries. For implementing collections, the C++ class is an obvious and better alternative than a C function library. A list object, for example, neatly encapsulates the list's internal data structures.

The *CObList* class supports ordered lists of pointers to objects of classes derived from *CObject*. Why is the *CObject* class involved at all? Suppose there weren't a *CObject* root class, and you needed a general-purpose list class for storing pointers to objects. How would you declare the return values and parameters of your list class member functions? You could use *void* pointers, but that would require a lot of casting. The *CObject* class solves the problem. If you derive all your collectable object classes from *CObject*, you can store their pointers in a list of *CObject* pointers. You can even mix and match pointers to objects of different derived classes.

Instead of a collection of *CObject* pointers, why not define a collection for a specific derived class such as *CMyObject*? A collection of *CMyObject* pointers would be type-safe because it would accept pointers only to those objects and require no casting whatsoever. Indeed, you could derive your own *CMyObList* class from *CObList*, or you could use the Microsoft Foundation Class Library collection template tool (TEMPLDEF) documented in Technical Note 4 in the MFCNOTES.HLP Help file. Both alternatives are probably more trouble than they're worth. Besides, the template tool is more useful for generating collection classes for native types such as floats and doubles.

The *CObList* class and the other collection classes provide special benefits when you do diagnostic dumping and serialization. You'll see the dump context in this chapter, but you must wait until Chapter 16 to see serialization.

Using the *CObList* Class for a First-In, First-Out (FIFO) List

One of the easiest ways to use a *CObList* object is to add new elements to the tail, or bottom, of the list, and to remove elements from the head, or top, of the list. The first element added to the list will always be the first element removed from the head of the list. Suppose you're working with element objects of class *CEvent*, which is your own custom class derived from *CObject*. Here's an MS-DOS program that puts five elements into a list and then retrieves them in the same sequence:

```
#include <afx.h>
#include <afxcoll.h>

class CEvent : public CObject
{
private:
    int m_nTime;
public:
    CEvent(int nTime) { m_nTime = nTime; } // constructor
                                           // stores integer time value
    void PrintTime() { TRACE("time = %d\n", m_nTime); }
};
```

```
int main()
{
    CEvent* pEvent;
    CObList eventList; // event list constructed on the stack
    int     i;

    // inserts event objects in sequence {0, 1, 2, 3, 4}
    for (i = 0; i < 5; i++) {
      pEvent = new CEvent(i);
      eventList.AddTail(pEvent); // no cast necessary for pEvent
    }

    // retrieves and removes event objects in sequence {0, 1, 2, 3, 4}
    while (!eventList.IsEmpty()) {
      pEvent = (CEvent*) eventList.RemoveHead(); // cast required for
                                                 //   return value
      pEvent->PrintTime();
      delete pEvent;
    }

    return 0;
}
```

Here's what's going on in the program. First a *CObList* object, *eventList*, is constructed. Then the *CObList AddTail* member function inserts pointers to newly constructed *CEvent* objects. No casting is necessary for *pEvent* because *AddTail* takes a *CObject* pointer parameter, and *pEvent* is a pointer to a derived class.

Next the *CEvent* object pointers are removed from the list of the objects deleted. A cast is necessary for the returned value of *RemoveHead* because *RemoveHead* returns a *CObject* pointer that is <u>higher</u> in the class hierarchy than *CEvent*.

When you remove an object pointer from a collection, the object is not automatically deleted. The *delete* statement is necessary for deleting the *CEvent* objects.

> **Note:** *If you have the Visual C++ Professional Edition, you can create MS-DOS projects, which might be helpful for experimenting with the collection classes. The MS-DOS libraries for the class library are not pre-built, however. To build the debug medium-model version, first change to the \MSVC\MFC\SRC directory, be sure that your LIB and INCLUDE environment variables are set correctly, and then call the make processor as follows:*
>
> ```
> NMAKE MODEL=M TARGET=R DEBUG=1
> ```

CObList Iteration—The *POSITION* Variable

Suppose you want to iterate through the elements in a list. The *CObList* class provides a *GetNext* member function that returns a pointer to the "next" list element, but using it is a little tricky. *GetNext* takes a parameter of type *POSITION*, which is simply a long integer. The *POSITION* variable is an internal representation of the retrieved element's position in the list. Because the *POSITION* parameter is declared as a reference (&), the function can change its value.

GetNext does the following:

1. Returns a pointer to the "current" object in the list, identified by the incoming value of the *POSITION* parameter.

2. Increments the value of the *POSITION* parameter to the next list element.

Here's what a *GetNext* loop looks like, assuming that you're using the list generated in the previous example:

```
POSITION pos = eventList.GetHeadPosition();
while (pos != NULL) {
  pEvent = (CEvent*) GetNext(pos);
  pEvent->PrintTime();
}
```

Now, suppose you have an interactive Windows program that uses toolbar buttons to sequence forward and backward through the list, one element at a time. You can't use *GetNext* to retrieve the entry because *GetNext* always <u>increments</u> the *POSITION* variable, and you don't know in advance whether the user is going to want the next element or the previous element. Here's a sample view class command message handler function that gets the next list entry. In the *CMyView* class, *m_eventList* is an embedded *CObList* object, and the *m_position* data member is a *POSITION* variable that holds the current list position.

```
CMyView::OnCommandNext()
{
    POSITION pos;
    CEvent*  pEvent;

    m_eventList.GetNext(pos = m_position);
    if (pos != NULL) { // pos is NULL at end of list
      pEvent = m_eventList.GetAt(pos);
      pEvent->PrintTime();
      m_position = pos;
    }
    else {
      AfxMessageBox("End of list");
    }
}
```

Now *GetNext* is called first to increment the list position, and the *CObList GetAt* member function is called to retrieve the entry. The *m_position* variable is updated only when we're sure we're not at the tail of the list.

The Dump Context and Collections

The *Dump* function for *CObList* and the other collection classes has a useful property. If you call *Dump* for a collection object, you can get a display of each object in the collection. If the element objects employ the *DECLARE_DYNAMIC* and *IMPLEMENT_DYNAMIC* macros, the dump will show the class name for each object.

The default behavior of the collection *Dump* functions is to display only class names and addresses of element objects. If you want the collection *Dump* functions to call the *Dump* function for each element object, you must, somewhere at the start of your program, make the following call:

```
#ifdef _DEBUG
    afxDump.SetDepth(1);
#endif
```

Now the statement

```
#ifdef _DEBUG
    afxDump << eventList;
#endif
```

produces output such as this:

```
a CObList with 4 elements

    a CEvent at $4CD6
time = 0
    a CEvent at $5632
time = 1
    a CEvent at $568E
time = 2
    a CEvent at $56EA
time = 3
```

The EX15B Example

This second *SDI* example improves on EX15A in the following ways:

- Instead of a single embedded *CStudent* object, the document now contains a list of *CStudent* objects.

- Toolbar buttons allow the user to sequence through the list.

- The application is structured to allow the addition of extra views. The Edit Clear All command is now routed to the document object, so the document's *UpdateAllViews* function and view's *OnUpdate* function are brought into play.

- The student-specific view code is isolated so that the *CEx15bView* class can later be transformed into a base class that contains only general-purpose code. Derived classes can override selected functions to accommodate lists of application-specific objects.

The EX15B window, shown in Figure 15-3 on the following page, looks a little different from the EX15A window (shown in Figure 15-1). The toolbar buttons are enabled only when appropriate. The Next (arrow-down graphic) button, for example, is disabled when we're positioned at the bottom of the list.

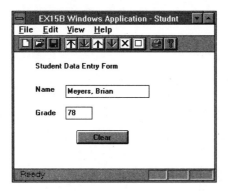

Figure 15-3.
The EX15B program in action.

The toolbar buttons function as follows:

Button	Function
⤒	Retrieves the first student record
⤓	Retrieves the last student record
↑	Retrieves the previous student record
↓	Retrieves the next student record
✕	Deletes the current student record
▢	Inserts a new student record

The Clear button in the view window clears the contents of the Name and Grade edit controls. The Clear All command on the Edit menu deletes all the student records in the list and clears the view's edit controls.

This example deviates from the step-by-step format in the previous examples. Because there's now more code, we'll simply list selected code and the resource requirements. In the listing figures, shaded code indicates that the user entered additional code or entered other changes to the output from AppWizard and ClassWizard. The frequent use of *TRACE* statements lets you follow the program's execution in the debugging window.

Here's a list of the files and classes in the EX15B example:

Header File	Source Code File	Classes	Description
EX15B.H	EX15B.CPP	*CEx15bApp*	Application class (from AppWizard)
		CAboutDlg	About dialog
MAINFRM.H	MAINFRM.CPP	*CMainFrame*	SDI main frame
STUDOC.H	STUDOC.CPP	*CStudentDoc*	Student document
STUVIEW.H	STUVIEW.CPP	*CStudentView*	Student form view (derived from *CFormView*)
STUDENT.H	STUDENT.CPP	*CStudent*	Student record (from EX15A)
STDAFX.H	STDAFX.CPP		Includes the standard precompiled headers

CEx15bApp

EX15B.CPP is standard AppWizard output except for the following line:

```
#include "student.h"
```

included immediately <u>before</u> the statement

```
#include "studoc.h"
```

CMainFrame

The code for the *CMainFrame* class in *MAINFRM.CPP* is the standard output from AppWizard except for the toolbar button array:

```
static UINT BASED_CODE buttons[] =
{
    // same order as in the bitmap 'toolbar.bmp'
    ID_FILE_NEW,
    ID_FILE_OPEN,
    ID_FILE_SAVE,
        ID_SEPARATOR,
    ID_POS_HOME,
    ID_POS_END,
    ID_POS_PREV,
    ID_POS_NEXT,
    ID_POS_DEL,
    ID_POS_INS,
        ID_SEPARATOR,
    ID_FILE_PRINT,
    ID_APP_ABOUT,
};
```

CStudentDoc

AppWizard originally generated the *CStudentDoc* class. Figure 15-4 shows the code used in the EX15B example.

```
STUDOC.H
// studoc.h : interface of the CStudentDoc class

class CStudentDoc : public CDocument
{
    DECLARE_DYNCREATE(CStudentDoc)
private:
    CObList m_studentList;
protected: // create from serialization only
    CStudentDoc();

// Attributes
public:
    CObList* GetList() {
        return &m_studentList;
    }

// Operations
public:

// Implementation
public:
    virtual ~CStudentDoc();
    virtual void Serialize(CArchive& ar); // overridden for document i/o
#ifdef _DEBUG
virtual void AssertValid() const;
    virtual void Dump(CDumpContext& dc) const;
#endif
protected:
    virtual BOOL OnNewDocument();
    virtual void DeleteContents();
// Generated message map functions
protected:
    //{{AFX_MSG(CStudentDoc)
    afx_msg void OnEditClearAll();
    afx_msg void OnUpdateEditClearAll(CCmdUI* pCmdUI);
    //}}AFX_MSG
    DECLARE_MESSAGE_MAP()
};

/////////////////////////////////////////////////////////////////////
```

Figure 15-4. *(continued)*

The CStudentDoc *class listing.*

Figure 15-4. *continued*

```
STUDOC.CPP
// studoc.cpp : implementation of the CStudentDoc class

#include "stdafx.h"
#include "resource.h"

#include "student.h"
#include "studoc.h"

#ifdef _DEBUG
#undef THIS_FILE
static char BASED_CODE THIS_FILE[] = __FILE__;
#endif

/////////////////////////////////////////////////////////////////////
// CStudentDoc

//IMPLEMENT_SERIAL(CStudentDoc, CDocument, 0)
IMPLEMENT_DYNCREATE(CStudentDoc, CDocument)

BEGIN_MESSAGE_MAP(CStudentDoc, CDocument)
    //{{AFX_MSG_MAP(CStudentDoc)
    ON_COMMAND(ID_EDIT_CLEAR_ALL, OnEditClearAll)
    ON_UPDATE_COMMAND_UI(ID_EDIT_CLEAR_ALL, OnUpdateEditClearAll)
    //}}AFX_MSG_MAP
END_MESSAGE_MAP()

/////////////////////////////////////////////////////////////////////
// CStudentDoc construction/destruction

CStudentDoc::CStudentDoc()
{
#ifdef _DEBUG
    afxDump.SetDepth(1); // dumps list elements
#endif
}

CStudentDoc::~CStudentDoc()
{
}

/////////////////////////////////////////////////////////////////////
BOOL CStudentDoc::OnNewDocument()
{
    TRACE("Entering CStudentDoc::OnNewDocument\n");
    if (!CDocument::OnNewDocument())
      return FALSE;
    return TRUE;
}
```

(continued)

Figure 15-4. *continued*

```
/////////////////////////////////////////////////////////////////
// CStudentDoc serialization

void CStudentDoc::Serialize(CArchive& ar)
{
    if (ar.IsStoring()) {
      // any other document variables to archive
    }
    else {
      // any other document variables from archive
    }
}

/////////////////////////////////////////////////////////////////
void CStudentDoc::DeleteContents()
{
#ifdef _DEBUG
    Dump(afxDump);
#endif
    while (m_studentList.GetHeadPosition()) {
      delete m_studentList.RemoveHead();
    }
}

/////////////////////////////////////////////////////////////////
// CStudentDoc diagnostics

#ifdef _DEBUG
void CStudentDoc::AssertValid() const
{
    CDocument::AssertValid();
}

void CStudentDoc::Dump(CDumpContext& dc) const
{
    CDocument::Dump(dc);
    dc << "\n" << m_studentList << "\n";
}

#endif //_DEBUG

/////////////////////////////////////////////////////////////////
// CStudentDoc commands


void CStudentDoc::OnEditClearAll()
{
    DeleteContents();
    UpdateAllViews(NULL);
}
```

(continued)

Figure 15-4. *continued*

```
///////////////////////////////////////////////////////////////////////
void CStudentDoc::OnUpdateEditClearAll(CCmdUI* pCmdUI)
{
    pCmdUI->Enable(!m_studentList.IsEmpty());
}
```

ClassWizard and *CStudentDoc*

The Edit Clear All command is handled in the document class. The following message handlers were added through ClassWizard:

Object ID	Message	Member Function Name
ID_EDIT_CLEAR_ALL	COMMAND	*OnEditClearAll*
ID_EDIT_CLEAR_ALL	ON_UPDATE_COMMAND_UI	*OnUpdateEditClearAll*

Data Members

The document class provides for an embedded *CObList* object, *m_studentList*, that holds pointers to *CStudent* objects. The list object is constructed when the *CStudentDoc* object is constructed, and it is destroyed at program exit.

Constructor and Destructor

The document constructor sets the depth of the dump context so that a dump of the list causes a dump of the individual list elements.

GetList

The inline *GetList* function helps isolate the view from the document. The document class must be specific to the type of object in the list, in this case objects of the class *CStudent*. A view base class, however, can use a member function to get a pointer to the list without knowing the name of the list object.

DeleteContents

The *DeleteContents* function is a virtual override function that is called by other document functions and by the application framework. Its job is to remove all student object pointers from the document's list and to delete those student objects. An important point to remember here is that *SDI* document objects are reused after they are closed. *DeleteContents* also dumps the student list.

Dump

AppWizard generates the *Dump* function skeleton inside the usual *#ifdef _DEBUG-/#endif* brackets. Because the *afxDump* depth was set to *1* in the document constructor, all the *CStudent* objects contained in the list are dumped.

CStudentView

Figure 15-5 shows the code for the *CStudentView* class. This code will be carried over into the next two chapters.

```
STUVIEW.H
// stuview.h : interface of the CStudentView class

class CStudentView : public CFormView
{
    DECLARE_DYNCREATE(CStudentView)
protected: // create from serialization only
    CStudentView();
// Form data
public:
    //{{AFX_DATA(CStudentView)
    enum { IDD = IDD_STUDENT };
    CString m_name;
    long    m_lGrade;
    //}}AFX_DATA

// Attributes
public:
    CStudentDoc* GetDocument()
    {
        ASSERT(m_pDocument->IsKindOf(RUNTIME_CLASS(CStudentDoc)));
        return (CStudentDoc*) m_pDocument;
    }

// Operations
public:

// Implementation
protected:
    POSITION m_position; // current position in document list
    CObList* m_pList;    // copied from document
public:
    virtual ~CStudentView();
    virtual void DoDataExchange(CDataExchange* pDX);   // DDX/DDV
                                                       // support
    virtual void OnDraw(CDC* pDC);  // overridden to draw this view
```

Figure 15-5. *(continued)*

The CStudentView *class listing.*

Figure 15-5. *continued*

```
#ifdef _DEBUG
    virtual void AssertValid() const;
    virtual void Dump(CDumpContext& dc) const;
#endif

    // Printing support
protected:
    virtual void OnInitialUpdate();
    virtual void OnUpdate(CView* pSender, LPARAM lHint, CObject* pHint);

// Generated message map functions
protected:
    //{{AFX_MSG(CStudentView)
    afx_msg void OnCommandHome();
    afx_msg void OnUpdateCommandHome(CCmdUI* pCmdUI);
    afx_msg void OnCommandEnd();
    afx_msg void OnUpdateCommandEnd(CCmdUI* pCmdUI);
    afx_msg void OnCommandPrev();
    afx_msg void OnUpdateCommandPrev(CCmdUI* pCmdUI);
    afx_msg void OnCommandNext();
    afx_msg void OnUpdateCommandNext(CCmdUI* pCmdUI);
    afx_msg void OnCommandDel();
    afx_msg void OnUpdateCommandDel(CCmdUI* pCmdUI);
    afx_msg void OnCommandIns();
    afx_msg void OnClickedClear();
    //}}AFX_MSG
protected:
    virtual void GetEntry(POSITION position);
    virtual void InsertEntry(POSITION position);
    virtual void ClearEntry();

    DECLARE_MESSAGE_MAP()
};

/////////////////////////////////////////////////////////////////
```

STUVIEW.CPP

```
// stuvw.cpp : implementation of the CStudentView class

#include "stdafx.h"
#include "resource.h"

#include "student.h"
#include "studoc.h"
#include "stuview.h"
```

(continued)

Figure 15-5. *continued*

```
#ifdef _DEBUG
#undef THIS_FILE
static char BASED_CODE THIS_FILE[] = __FILE__;
#endif

/////////////////////////////////////////////////////////////
// CStudentView

IMPLEMENT_DYNCREATE(CStudentView, CFormView)

BEGIN_MESSAGE_MAP(CStudentView, CFormView)
    //{{AFX_MSG_MAP(CStudentView)
    ON_COMMAND(ID_POS_HOME, OnCommandHome)
    ON_UPDATE_COMMAND_UI(ID_POS_HOME, OnUpdateCommandHome)
    ON_COMMAND(ID_POS_END, OnCommandEnd)
    ON_UPDATE_COMMAND_UI(ID_POS_END, OnUpdateCommandEnd)
    ON_COMMAND(ID_POS_PREV, OnCommandPrev)
    ON_UPDATE_COMMAND_UI(ID_POS_PREV, OnUpdateCommandPrev)
    ON_COMMAND(ID_POS_NEXT, OnCommandNext)
    ON_UPDATE_COMMAND_UI(ID_POS_NEXT, OnUpdateCommandNext)
    ON_COMMAND(ID_POS_DEL, OnCommandDel)
    ON_UPDATE_COMMAND_UI(ID_POS_DEL, OnUpdateCommandDel)
    ON_COMMAND(ID_POS_INS, OnCommandIns)
    ON_BN_CLICKED(IDC_CLEAR, OnClickedClear)
    //}}AFX_MSG_MAP
    // Standard printing commands
END_MESSAGE_MAP()

/////////////////////////////////////////////////////////////
// CStudentView construction/destruction

CStudentView::CStudentView()
    : CFormView(CStudentView::IDD)
{
    TRACE("Entering CStudentView constructor\n");
    //{{AFX_DATA_INIT(CStudentView)
    m_lGrade = 0;
    //}}AFX_DATA_INIT
    m_position = NULL;
}

CStudentView::~CStudentView()
{
}

/////////////////////////////////////////////////////////////
void CStudentView::OnInitialUpdate()
{
    // called on startup, on file new, and on file open
    TRACE("Entering CStudentView::OnInitialUpdate\n");
```

(continued)

Figure 15-5. *continued*

```
    OnUpdate(this, NULL, NULL);
}

////////////////////////////////////////////////////////////////
void CStudentView::OnUpdate(CView* pSender, LPARAM lHint, CObject* pHint)
{
    // called by OnInitialUpdate and by UpdateAllViews
    TRACE("Entering CStudentView::OnUpdate\n");
    m_pList = GetDocument()->GetList();
    m_position = m_pList->GetHeadPosition();
    GetEntry(m_position); // initial data for view
}

////////////////////////////////////////////////////////////////
void CStudentView::OnDraw(CDC* pDC)
{
    CStudentDoc* pDoc = GetDocument();

    // TODO: add draw code here
}

////////////////////////////////////////////////////////////////
// CStudentView diagnostics

#ifdef _DEBUG
void CStudentView::AssertValid() const
{
    CFormView::AssertValid();
}

void CStudentView::Dump(CDumpContext& dc) const
{
    CFormView::Dump(dc);
}

#endif //_DEBUG

////////////////////////////////////////////////////////////////
// CStudentView commands

void CStudentView::DoDataExchange(CDataExchange* pDX)
{
    TRACE("Entering CStudentView::DoDataExchange\n");
    CFormView::DoDataExchange(pDX);
    //{{AFX_DATA_MAP(CStudentView)
    DDX_Text(pDX, IDC_NAME, m_name);
    DDV_MaxChars(pDX, m_name, 20);
    DDX_Text(pDX, IDC_GRADE, m_lGrade);
    DDV_MinMaxLong(pDX, m_lGrade, 0, 100);
    //}}AFX_DATA_MAP
}
```

(continued)

Figure 15-5. *continued*

```
///////////////////////////////////////////////////////////
void CStudentView::OnCommandHome()
{
    // need to deal with the list empty condition
    TRACE("Entering CStudentView::OnCommandHome\n");
    if (!m_pList->IsEmpty()) {
      m_position = m_pList->GetHeadPosition();
      GetEntry(m_position);
    }
}

///////////////////////////////////////////////////////////
void CStudentView::OnCommandNext()
{
    POSITION pos;

    TRACE("Entering CStudentView::OnCommandNext\n");
    if ((pos = m_position) != NULL) {
      m_pList->GetNext(pos);
      if (pos) {
        GetEntry(pos);
        m_position = pos;
      }
    }
}

///////////////////////////////////////////////////////////
void CStudentView::OnCommandEnd()
{
    TRACE("Entering CStudentView::OnCommandEnd\n");
    if (!m_pList->IsEmpty()) {
      m_position = m_pList->GetTailPosition();
      GetEntry(m_position);
    }
}

///////////////////////////////////////////////////////////
void CStudentView::OnCommandPrev()
{
    POSITION pos;

    TRACE("Entering CStudentView::OnCommandPrev\n");
    if ((pos = m_position) != NULL) {
      m_pList->GetPrev(pos);
      if (pos) {
        GetEntry(pos);
        m_position = pos;
      }
    }
}
```

(continued)

Figure 15-5. *continued*

```
/////////////////////////////////////////////////////////////////
void CStudentView::OnCommandDel()
{
    // deletes current entry and positions to next one or head
    POSITION pos;

    TRACE("Entering CStudentView::OnCommandDel\n");
    if ((pos = m_position) != NULL) {
      m_pList->GetNext(pos);
      if (pos == NULL) {
        pos = m_pList->GetHeadPosition();
        TRACE("GetHeadPos = %ld\n", pos);
        if (pos == m_position) {
          pos = NULL;
        }
      }
      GetEntry(pos);
      CObject* ps = m_pList->GetAt(m_position);
      m_pList->RemoveAt(m_position);
      delete ps;
      m_position = pos;
      GetDocument()->SetModifiedFlag();
      GetDocument()->UpdateAllViews(this);
    }
}

/////////////////////////////////////////////////////////////////
void CStudentView::OnCommandIns()
{
    TRACE("Entering CStudentView::OnCommandIns\n");
    InsertEntry(m_position);
    GetDocument()->SetModifiedFlag();
    GetDocument()->UpdateAllViews(this);
}

/////////////////////////////////////////////////////////////////
void CStudentView::OnUpdateCommandHome(CCmdUI* pCmdUI)
{
    // called during IDLE processing
    POSITION pos;

    // enables button if list not empty and not at home already
    pos = m_pList->GetHeadPosition();
    pCmdUI->Enable((m_position != NULL) && (pos != m_position));
}

/////////////////////////////////////////////////////////////////
void CStudentView::OnUpdateCommandEnd(CCmdUI* pCmdUI)
{
    // called during IDLE processing
    POSITION pos;
```

(continued)

Figure 15-5. *continued*

```
    // enables button if list not empty and not at end already
    pos = m_pList->GetTailPosition();
    pCmdUI->Enable((m_position != NULL) && (pos != m_position));
}

///////////////////////////////////////////////////////////////
void CStudentView::OnUpdateCommandPrev(CCmdUI* pCmdUI)
{
    // called during IDLE processing
    POSITION pos;

    // enables button if list not empty and prev item(s) exist
    if ((pos = m_position) != NULL) {
      m_pList->GetPrev(pos);
    }
    pCmdUI->Enable((m_position != NULL) && (pos != NULL));
}

///////////////////////////////////////////////////////////////
void CStudentView::OnUpdateCommandNext(CCmdUI* pCmdUI)
{
    // called during IDLE processing
    POSITION pos;

    // enables button if list not empty and following item(s) exist
    if ((pos = m_position) != NULL) {
      m_pList->GetNext(pos);
    }
    pCmdUI->Enable((m_position != NULL) && (pos != NULL));
}

///////////////////////////////////////////////////////////////
void CStudentView::OnUpdateCommandDel(CCmdUI* pCmdUI)
{
    // called during IDLE processing
    pCmdUI->Enable(m_position != NULL);
}

///////////////////////////////////////////////////////////////
void CStudentView::OnClickedClear()
{
    TRACE("Entering CStudentView::OnClickedClear\n");
    ClearEntry();
}

///////////////////////////////////////////////////////////////
// protected virtual functions

void CStudentView::GetEntry(POSITION position)
{
```

(continued)

Figure 15-5. *continued*

```
    if (position) {
      CStudent* pStudent = (CStudent*) m_pList->GetAt(position);
      m_name = pStudent->m_name;
      m_lGrade = pStudent->m_lGrade;
    }
    else {
      ClearEntry();
    }
    UpdateData(FALSE);
}


//////////////////////////////////////////////////////////////////
void CStudentView::InsertEntry(POSITION position)
{
    if (UpdateData(TRUE)) {
      // UpdateData returns FALSE if it detects a user error
      CStudent* pStudent = new CStudent;
      pStudent->m_name = m_name;
      pStudent->m_lGrade = m_lGrade;
      m_position = m_pList->InsertAfter(m_position, pStudent);
    }
}


//////////////////////////////////////////////////////////////////
void CStudentView::ClearEntry()
{
    m_name = "";
    m_lGrade = 0;
    UpdateData(FALSE);
    ((CDialog*) this)->GotoDlgCtrl(GetDlgItem(IDC_NAME));
}
```

ClassWizard and *CStudentView*

ClassWizard was used to map the *CStudentView* Clear pushbutton notification message as follows:

Object ID	Message	Member Function Name
IDC_CLEAR	BN_CLICKED	*OnClickedClear*

Because *CStudentView* is derived from *CFormView*, ClassWizard supports the definition of dialog data members. The variables on the next page were added with the Edit Variables button:

Control ID	Member Variable Name	Property Type	Variable Type
IDC_GRADE	m_lGrade	Value	long
IDC_NAME	m_name	Value	CString

Set the minimum value of the *m_lGrade* data member to *0* and its maximum value to *100.*

Because the toolbar buttons aren't duplicated by menu items, ClassWizard won't help you with the message handlers. You must add the command and update command UI function prototypes manually.

Data Members

The *m_position* data member is a kind of cursor for the document's collection. It points to the *CStudent* object that is currently displayed. The *m_pList* variable provides a quick way to get at the student list in the document.

OnInitialUpdate

The virtual *OnInitialUpdate* function is called when you start the application. It sets the view's *m_pList* data member for subsequent access to the document's list object.

OnUpdate

The virtual *OnUpdate* function is called both by *OnInitialUpdate* and by the *CDocument UpdateAllViews* function. It resets the list position to the head of the list, and it displays the head entry. In this example, the *UpdateAllViews* function is called only in response to the Edit Clear All command. In a multiview application, you might need a different strategy for setting the *CStudentView m_position* variable in response to document updates from another view.

Toolbar Button Command Message Handlers

These functions are called in response to toolbar button clicks:

OnCommandHome
OnCommandEnd
OnCommandPrev
OnCommandNext
OnCommandDel
OnCommandIns

Each function has built-in error checking.

Toolbar Button Update Command UI Message Handlers

These functions are called during idle processing to update the state of the toolbar buttons:

OnUpdateCommandHome

OnUpdateCommandEnd

OnUpdateCommandPrev

OnUpdateCommandNext

OnUpdateCommandDel

For example, this button,

which retrieves the first student record, is disabled when the list is empty and when the *m_position* variable is already set to the head of the list. Because a delay sometimes occurs in calling the update command UI functions, the command message handlers must check for error conditions.

Protected Virtual Functions

These three functions are protected virtual functions that deal specifically with *CStudent* objects:

GetEntry

InsertEntry

ClearEntry

Move these to a derived class if you want to isolate the general-purpose list-handling features in a base class.

Resource Requirements

The file EX15B.RC defines the application's resources as follows:

Symbols

Because the toolbar buttons aren't duplicated by menu items, you must add the command symbols manually. If you click the App Studio ID= toolbar button, you'll see the following symbols (among others):

Symbol	Value
ID_POS_DEL	0x8005
ID_POS_END	0x8002

(continued)

275

continued

Symbol	Value
ID_POS_HOME	0x8001
ID_POS_INS	0x8006
ID_POS_NEXT	0x8004
ID_POS_PREV	0x8003

Edit Menu

On the Edit menu, the clipboard menu items are replaced by the Clear All menu item. See step 2 on page 248 for an illustration of the Edit menu.

The *IDD_STUDENT* Dialog

The *IDD_STUDENT* dialog, shown here, is similar to the EX15A dialog shown in Figure 15-1 except that the Enter pushbutton has been replaced by the Clear pushbutton:

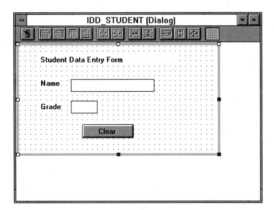

The following IDs identify the controls:

Control	ID
Name edit control	*IDC_NAME*
Grade edit control	*IDC_GRADE*
Clear pushbutton	*IDC_CLEAR*

The controls' styles are the same as for the *EX15A* program.

Toolbar

Here's the *IDR_MAINFRAME* bitmap resource:

The bitmap was created by erasing the Edit Cut, Copy, and Paste tiles (fourth, fifth, and sixth from the left) and replacing them with six new patterns. The Flip Vertical command (on the Image menu) was used to duplicate some of the tiles.

Testing the EX15B Application

Fill in the student name and grade fields, and then click this button

to insert the entry into the list. Repeat this action several more times, using the Clear pushbutton to erase the data from the previous entry. When you exit the application, the debug output should look similar to this:

```
a CStudentDoc at $48EE
m_strTitle = Ex15b
m_strPathName =
m_bModified = 0
m_pDocTemplate = $46AE
a CObList with 4 elements

    a CStudent at $4DC2
m_name = Fisher, Lon
m_lGrade = 67
    a CStudent at $50FA
m_name = Meyers, Brian
m_lGrade = 80
    a CStudent at $5152
m_name = Seghers, John
m_lGrade = 92
    a CStudent at $51AA
m_name = Anderson, Bob
m_lGrade = 87
```

Two Exercises for the Reader

You might have noticed the absence of a modify toolbar button. Without such a button, you can't modify an existing student record. Can you add the necessary toolbar button and message handlers? The most difficult task might be designing a graphic for the button's tile.

Recall that the *CStudentView* class is almost ready to be a general-purpose base class. Try separating the *CStudent*-specific virtual functions into a derived class. After that, make another derived class that uses a new element class other than *CStudent*.

16

Reading and Writing Documents—Single Document Interface

As you've probably noticed, every AppWizard-generated program has a File menu that contains the familiar New, Open, Save, and Save As commands. In this chapter, you'll learn how to make your application respond to read and write documents.

Here we'll stick with the Single Document Interface (SDI) application because it's familiar territory. Chapter 17 introduces the Multiple Document Interface (MDI) application, which is more flexible in its handling of documents and files. In both chapters, you'll get a heavy but necessary dose of application framework theory; you'll learn a lot about the various helper classes that have been concealed up to this point. The going will be rough, but, believe me, you really have to know the details to get the most out of the application framework.

This chapter's example, EX16A, is an SDI application based on EX15B from the previous chapter. It uses the student list document with a *CFormView*-derived view class minus some of the frills such as the Edit Clear All command. Now the student list can be written to and read from disk through a process called serialization. Chapter 17 shows you how to use the same view and document classes to make an MDI application, and it shows how to retrofit an SDI application with the drag-and-drop file capability that is normally reserved for MDI applications.

Serialization—What Is It?

The term "serialization" might be new to you, but it's already seen some use in the world of object-oriented programming. The idea is that objects can be persistent, which means they can be saved on disk when a program exits and restored when the program is restarted. The process of saving and restoring objects is called serialization. In the Microsoft Foundation Class Library, designated classes have a member function named *Serialize*. When the application framework calls *Serialize* for a particular object—for example, an object of class *CStudent*—the data for the student is either saved on disk or read from disk.

In the class library, serialization is not a substitute for a database management system. All the objects associated with a document are <u>sequentially</u> read from or written to a single disk file. It's not possible to access individual objects at random disk file addresses. If you need database capability in your application, consider using the Microsoft Open Database Connectivity (ODBC) software. Chapter 24 shows you how to use ODBC with the class library application framework.

Disk Files and Archives

How do know whether *Serialize* should read or write data? How is *Serialize* connected to a disk file? With the class library, disk files are represented by objects of class *CFile*. A *CFile* object encapsulates the file handle that you get through the C runtime function *_open*. This is <u>not</u> the buffered *FILE* pointer that you'd get with a call to *fopen*; rather, it's a handle to a binary file. This file handle is used by the application framework for *_read*, *_write*, and *_lseek* calls.

If your application does no direct disk I/O but instead relies on the serialization process, you can avoid direct use of *CFile* objects. Between the *Serialize* function and the *CFile* object is an archive object (of class *CArchive*), as shown in Figure 16-1.

The *CArchive* object buffers data for the *CFile* object, and it maintains an internal flag that indicates whether the archive is storing (writing to disk) or loading (reading from disk). Only one active archive is associated with a file at any one time. The

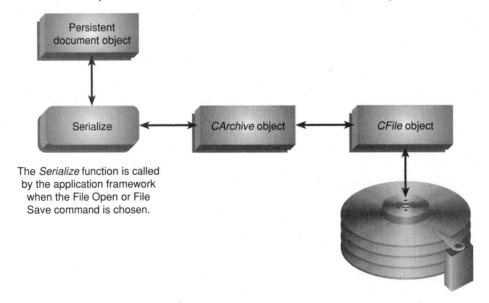

Figure 16-1.
The serialization process.

application framework takes care of constructing the *CFile* and *CArchive* objects, opening the disk file for the *CFile* object, and associating the archive object with the file. All you have to do, in your *Serialize* function, is load data from or store data in the archive object. The application framework calls the document's *Serialize* function during the File Open and File Save processes.

Making a Class Serializable

A serializable class must be derived directly or indirectly from *CObject*. In addition, the class declaration must contain the *DECLARE_SERIAL* macro call, and the class implementation file must contain the *IMPLEMENT_SERIAL* macro call. (See the *Class Library Reference* for a description of these macros.) The *CStudent* class, which you'll be using in this chapter's examples, already uses these macros.

Writing a *Serialize* Function

In Chapter 15, you saw a *CStudent* class, derived from *CObject*, with these data members:

```
public:
    CString m_name;
    LONG    m_lGrade;
```

Now your job is to write a *Serialize* member function for *CStudent*. Because *Serialize* is a virtual member function of class *CObject*, you must be sure that the return value and parameter types match the *CObject* declaration. Here's the *Serialize* function for the *CStudent* class:

```
void CStudent::Serialize(CArchive& ar)
{
    if (ar.IsStoring())
        ar << m_name << m_lGrade;
    else
        ar >> m_name >> m_lGrade;
}
```

Serialization functions generally call the *Serialize* function of their base class. If *CStudent* were derived from *CPerson*, for example, the first line of the *Serialize* function would be

```
CPerson::Serialize(ar);
```

The *Serialize* functions for *CObject* and *CDocument* don't do anything useful, so there's no need to call them.

Notice that *ar* is a *CArchive* reference parameter that identifies the application's archive object. The *CArchive IsStoring* member function tells us whether the archive is currently being used for storing or loading. The *CArchive* class has overloaded insertion operators (<<) and extraction operators (>>) for many of the

C++ built-in types. Class library classes that are not derived from *CObject*, such as *CString* and *CRect*, have their own overloaded insertion and extraction operators for *CArchive*.

Loading from an Archive—Embedded Objects vs. Pointers

Now, suppose your *CStudent* object has other objects embedded in it, and these objects are not instances of standard classes such as *CString*, *CTime*, and *CRect*. Let's add a new data member to the *CStudent* class:

```
public:
    CTranscript m_transcript;
```

Making Persistent Object Data Portable

A design goal for Microsoft Foundation Class Library version 2.0 was to make persistent object data portable between 16-bit Windows systems and 32-bit Windows systems (for example, Microsoft Windows NT). For this reason, *CArchive* does not have overloaded insertion operators and extraction operators for word-width-dependent types such as *int*. *CArchive* does support the following types, however:

Type	Description
BYTE	8 bits unsigned
WORD	16 bits unsigned
LONG	32 bits signed
DWORD	32 bits unsigned
float	32 bits
double	64 bits, IEEE standard

If you need to use word-width-dependent types, cast them to one of the supported types, as shown here:

```
void CStudent::Serialize(CArchive& ar)
{
    WORD w;

    if (ar.IsStoring()) {
      ar << (WORD) m_nMyInt;
    }
    else {
      ar >> w;
      m_nMyInt = (int) w;
    }
}
```

Assume that *CTranscript* is a custom class, derived from *CObject*, with its own *Serialize* member function. The *CStudent Serialize* function now becomes

```
void CStudent::Serialize(CArchive& ar)
{
    if (ar.IsStoring())
        ar << m_name << m_lGrade;
    else
        ar >> m_name >> m_lGrade;
    m_transcript.Serialize(ar);
}
```

Before the *CStudent Serialize* function can be called to load a student record from the archive, a *CStudent* object must be constructed somewhere. The embedded *CTranscript* object *m_transcript* is constructed along with the *CStudent* object before the call to the *CTranscript Serialize* function. When the *CTranscript Serialize* function does get called, it can load the archived transcript data into the embedded *m_transcript* object.

Suppose that, instead of an embedded object, your *CStudent* object contained a *CTranscript* <u>pointer</u> data member such as this:

```
public:
    CTranscript* m_pTranscript;
```

You could write your *Serialize* function as shown below, but as you can see, you must construct a new *CTranscript* object yourself:

```
void CStudent::Serialize(CArchive& ar)
{
    if (ar.IsStoring())
        ar << m_name << m_lGrade;
    else {
        m_pTranscript = new CTranscript;
        ar >> m_name >> m_lGrade;
    }
    m_pTranscript->Serialize(ar);
}
```

Because the *CArchive* insertion and extraction operators are overloaded for *CObject* pointers, you could write *Serialize* this way instead:

```
void CStudent::Serialize(CArchive& ar)
{
    if (ar.IsStoring())
        ar << m_name << m_lGrade << m_pTranscript;
    else
        ar >> m_name >> m_lGrade >> m_pTranscript;
}
```

In the second case, the *CObject* runtime class capability ensures that the *CTranscript Serialize* function is called instead of the do-nothing *CObject Serialize* function. When a *CStudent* object is loaded from the archive, the *CArchive* extraction operator constructs a new *CTranscript* object on the heap and then stores its pointer in the *CStudent* object (in the *m_pTranscript* data member). To avoid a memory leak, you must be sure that *m_pTranscript* doesn't already contain a pointer to a *CTranscript* object. If the *CStudent* object was just constructed and thus was not previously loaded from the archive, the transcript pointer will be null.

The insertion and extraction operators do <u>not</u> work with embedded objects of classes derived from *CObject*.

```
ar >> m_name >> m_lGrade >> &m_transcript; // don't try this
```

Serializing Collections

Because all collection classes are derived from the *CObject* class and the collection class declarations contain the *DECLARE_SERIAL* macro call, you can conveniently serialize collections with a call to the collection class's *Serialize* member function. If you call *Serialize* for a *CObList* collection of *CStudent* objects, for example, the *Serialize* function for each *CStudent* object will be called in turn. You should, however, know some specific things about loading collections from an archive:

- If a collection contains pointers to objects of mixed classes (all derived from *CObject*), the individual class names in essence are stored in the archive so that the objects can be properly constructed with the appropriate class constructor.

- If a container object, such as a document, contains an <u>embedded</u> collection, loaded data is appended to the existing collection. You might need to empty the collection before loading from the archive. This is usually done in a *Delete-Contents* function, which is called by the application framework.

- If a container object contains a pointer to a collection, a new collection object is constructed when the extraction operator loads data from the archive. A pointer to the new collection is stored in the container object's pointer data member. You might need to destroy the old collection object (after emptying it) before loading from the archive.

- When a collection of *CObject* pointers is loaded from an archive, the following processing steps take place for each object in the collection:

  □ The object's class is identified.

  □ Heap storage is allocated for the object.

  □ The object's data is loaded into the newly allocated storage.

  □ A pointer to the new object is stored in the collection.

The EX16A example shows serialization of an embedded *CObList* collection.

The *Serialize* Function and the Application Framework

OK, so you know how to write serialize functions, and you know that these function calls can be nested. But do you know when the first *Serialize* function gets called to start the serialization process? With the application framework, everything is keyed to the document (the object of a class derived from *CDocument*). When you choose Save or Open from the File menu, the application framework creates a *CArchive* object (and underlying *CFile* object) and then calls your document class's *Serialize* function, passing a reference to the *CArchive* object. Your derived document class *Serialize* function then serializes each of its nontemporary data members.

> **Note:** *If you take a look at any AppWizard-generated document class, you'll notice that the class includes the* DECLARE_DYNCREATE *and* IMPLEMENT_DYNCREATE *macros instead of the* DECLARE_SERIAL *and* IMPLEMENT_SERIAL *macros. The* SERIAL *macros are not needed because document objects are never used in conjunction with the* CArchive *extraction operator or included in collections; the application framework calls the document's* Serialize *member function directly. You should include the* DECLARE_SERIAL *and* IMPLEMENT_SERIAL *macros in all other serializable classes.*

The SDI Application

You've seen many SDI applications that have one document class and one view class. We'll stick to a single view class in this chapter, but we'll explore the interrelationships among the application object, the main frame window, the document, the view, the document template object, and the associated string and menu resources.

The Windows Application Object

For each of your applications, AppWizard has been quietly generating a class derived from *CWinApp*. It has also been generating a statement such as this:

```
CMyApp theApp;
```

What you're seeing here is the mechanism that starts a class library application. The class *CMyApp* is derived from the class *CWinApp*, and *theApp* is a globally declared instance of the class. This global object is called the Windows application object. Here's a summary of the startup steps in a Microsoft Windows class library application:

1. Windows loads your program into memory.

2. The global object *theApp* is constructed. (All globally declared objects are constructed immediately when the program is loaded.)

3. Windows calls the global function *WinMain*, which is part of the class library. (*WinMain* is equivalent to the non-Windows *main* function—each is a main program entry point.)

4. *WinMain* searches for the one and only instance of a class derived from *CWinApp*.

5. *WinMain* calls the *InitInstance* member function for *theApp*, which is over-ridden in your derived application class.

6. Your overridden *InitInstance* function starts the process of loading a document and displaying the main frame and view windows.

7. *WinMain* calls the *Run* member function for *theApp*, which starts the processes of dispatching window messages and command messages.

You can override another important *CWinApp* member function. The *ExitInstance* function is called when the application terminates, after all its windows are closed.

> **Note:** *Under certain conditions, Windows allows multiple instances of programs to run. Code is shared, but read/write data is not shared. The* InitInstance *function is called each time a program instance starts up. Another* CWinApp *function,* InitApplication, *is called when the <u>first</u> instance starts up. You can override* InitApplication *in your derived application class, but there's seldom a reason to do so.*

The Document Template Class

If you look at the *InitInstance* function that AppWizard generates for your derived application class, you'll see the following statement featured prominently:

```
AddDocTemplate(new CSingleDocTemplate(IDR_MAINFRAME,
            RUNTIME_CLASS(CMyDoc),
            RUNTIME_CLASS(CMainFrame),      // main SDI frame window
            RUNTIME_CLASS(CMyView)));
```

Unless you start doing fancy things with splitter windows and multiple views, this is the only time you'll actually see a document template object. In this case it's an object of the class *CSingleDocTemplate*, which is derived from *CDocTemplate*. The *CSingleDocTemplate* class applies only to SDI applications because SDI applications are limited to one document object. *AddDocTemplate* is a member function of class *CWinApp*.

The *AddDocTemplate* call, together with the document template constructor call, establishes the relationships among <u>classes</u>—the application class, the document class, the view window class, and the main frame window class. The application object exists, of course, before template construction, but the document, view, and frame objects are <u>not</u> constructed at this time. The application framework later dynamically constructs these objects when they are needed.

This dynamic construction is a sophisticated use of the C++ language. Through the use of the *DECLARE_DYNCREATE* and *IMPLEMENT_DYNCREATE* macros in the class declaration and implementation, the class library is able to construct objects of specified classes dynamically. If this dynamic construction capability weren't present, more relationships among your application's classes would have to be hard-coded. Your derived application class, for example, would need code for constructing document, view, and frame objects of your specific derived classes. This would compromise the object-oriented nature of your program.

With the template system, all that's required in your application class is use of the *RUNTIME_CLASS* macro, which converts a class name to a special pointer that the class library runtime mechanism can process. Notice that the target class's declaration must be included for this macro to work.

Figure 16-2 illustrates the relationships among the various classes, and Figure 16-3 on the following page illustrates the object relationships. The application can have more than one template (and associated class groups), but when the SDI program is running there can be only one document object and only one main frame window object.

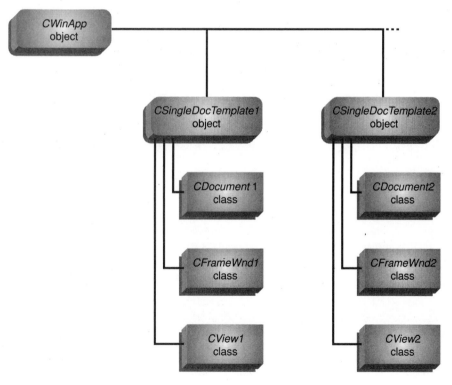

Figure 16-2.
Class relationships.

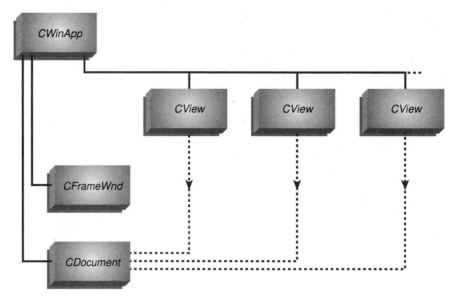

Figure 16-3.
Object relationships.

The Document Template Resource

The first *AddDocTemplate* parameter is *IDR_MAINFRAME*, the identifier for a string table resource. Here is the corresponding string that AppWizard might generate in the application's RC file:

```
IDR_MAINFRAME
    "MYAPP Windows Application\n"      // application window caption
    "MYAPP\n"                          // root for default document name
    "MYAPP Document\n"                 // document type name
    "MYAPP Files (*.xyz)\n"            // document type description & filter
    ".xyz"                             // extension for documents of this type
```

(Note: The resource compiler won't accept the string concatenations as shown above. If you examine the EX16A.RC file, you'll see the substrings combined in one large string.)

IDR_MAINFRAME specifies one string that is separated into substrings by \n. The substrings show up in various places when the application executes. The string *xyz* is the default document file extension specified to AppWizard.

The *IDR_MAINFRAME* ID, in addition to specifying the application's strings, identifies the application's icon, toolbar bitmap, and menus. AppWizard generates these resources, and App Studio maintains them.

So now you've seen how the *AddDocTemplate* call ties all the application elements together. Be aware, though, that no windows have been created yet, and therefore nothing appears on the screen.

Multiple Document Types

An SDI application supports only one document object, but it can support multiple document types. You simply make a separate *AddDocTemplate* call for each document class, and when the user starts the program or chooses New from the File menu, the application framework prompts the user to choose a document type from a list box. You'll probably want a separate document template resource string and menus for each document type. The serialization process identifies the document type from the filename extension.

Multiple Views of an SDI Document

Providing multiple views of an SDI document is a little more complicated. You could simply provide a menu item that allows the user to choose a view, or you could allow multiple views in a splitter window. Chapter 19 shows you how to use a splitter window.

Creating an Empty Document— The *CWinApp OnFileNew* Function

After your application class's *InitInstance* function calls *AddDocTemplate*, it calls *OnFileNew*, another important *CWinApp* member function. *OnFileNew*, through a call to another *CWinApp* function, *OpenDocumentFile*, sorts through the web of interconnected class names and does the following:

1. Constructs the document object but does not attempt to read data from disk.

2. Constructs the main frame object (of class *CMainFrame*); also creates the main frame window but does not show it. The main frame window includes the *IDR_MAINFRAME* menu, the toolbar, and the status bar.

3. Constructs the view object; also creates the view window but doesn't show it.

4. Establishes connections among the document, main frame, and view <u>objects</u>. Do not confuse these object connections with the <u>class</u> connections established by the call to *AddDocTemplate*.

5. Calls the virtual *OnNewDocument* member function for the document object, which calls the virtual *DeleteContents* function.

6. Calls the virtual *OnInitialUpdate* member function for the view object.

7. Calls the virtual *ActivateFrame* for the frame object to show the main frame window together with the menus, view window, and control bars.

Note: *Some functions listed above are not called directly by* OpenDocumentFile *but are called indirectly through the application framework.*

In an SDI application, the document, main frame, and view objects are created only once, and they last for the life of the program. The *CWinApp OnFileNew* function is called by *InitInstance*. It's also called in response to the File New menu item. In this case, *OnFileNew* must behave a little differently. It can't construct the document, frame, and view objects because they're already constructed. Instead, it reuses the existing document object and performs the last three of the steps listed above. Note that *OnFileNew* always calls *DeleteContents* to empty the document.

The Document Class's *OnNewDocument* Function

You've seen the view class *OnInitialUpdate* member function in Chapter 15, but the document class *OnNewDocument* member function is new. If an SDI application didn't reuse the same document object, you wouldn't need *OnNewDocument* because you could perform all document initialization in your document class constructor. Now you must override *OnNewDocument* to initialize your document object each time the user chooses File New or File Open. AppWizard helps you by providing a skeleton function in the derived document class it generates.

Connecting File Open to Your Serialization Code—*OnFileOpen*

When AppWizard generates an application, it maps the File Open menu item to the *CWinApp OnFileOpen* member function, which, through a call to the *CWinApp* function *OpenDocumentFile*, does the following:

1. Calls the virtual *OnOpenDocument* member function for the already existing document object. This function prompts the user to select a file and then opens the file, constructs a *CArchive* object set for loading, and calls *DeleteContents*.

2. Calls the document's *Serialize* function, which loads data from the archive.

3. Calls the view's *OnInitialUpdate* function.

Note: *Some of the functions listed above are not called directly by* OpenDocumentFile *but are called indirectly through the application framework.*

The Most Recently Used (MRU) file list is a handy alternative to the File Open menu item. The application framework tracks the four most recently used files and displays their names on the File menu. These filenames are stored in the application's INI file between program executions.

The Document Class's *DeleteContents* Function

When you load an existing SDI document object from a disk file, you must somehow erase the existing contents of the document object. The best way to do this is to override the *CDocument DeleteContents* virtual function in your derived document class. The overridden function, as you've seen in Chapter 15, does whatever is necessary to clean up your document class's data members. In response to both the File New and the File Open menu items, the *CDocument OnFileNew* and *OnFileOpen* functions both call the *DeleteContents* function, which means *Delete-Contents* is called immediately after the document object is first constructed. It's called again when you close a document.

If you want your document classes to work in SDI applications, plan on emptying the document's contents in the *DeleteContents* member function rather than in the destructor. Use the destructor only to clean up items that last for the life of the object.

Connecting File Save and File Save As to Your Serialization Code

When AppWizard generates an application, it maps the File Save menu item to the *OnFileSave* member function of the *CDocument* class. *OnFileSave* calls the *CDocument* function *OnSaveDocument*, which in turn calls your document's *Serialize* function with an archive object set for storing. The File Save As menu item is handled in a similar manner; it is mapped to the *CDocument* function *OnFileSaveAs*, which calls *OnSaveDocument*. Here the application framework does all the file management necessary to save a document on disk.

> **Note:** *Yes, it's true that the File New and File Open menu choices are mapped to <u>application</u> class member functions, but File Save and File Save As are mapped to <u>document</u> class member functions. File New is mapped to* OnFileNew. *The SDI version of* InitInstance *calls* OnFileNew *also. No document object exists when the application framework calls* InitInstance, *so* OnFileNew *can't possibly be a member function of* CDocument. *When a document is saved, however, a document object certainly exists.*

The Document's *IsModified* Flag

Many document-oriented applications for Windows track the user's modification of a document. If the user tries to close a document or exit the program, a message box asks whether the user wants to save the document. The class library application framework directly supports this behavior with the *CDocument* data member *m_bModified*. This Boolean variable is *TRUE* if the document has been modified; otherwise, it is *FALSE*.

The protected *m_bModified* flag is accessed through the *CDocument* member functions *SetModifiedFlag* and *IsModified*. A document object's flag is set to *FALSE* when the document is created or read from disk and when it is saved on disk. You, the programmer, must use the *SetModifiedFlag* function to set the flag to *TRUE* when the document data changes.

In Visual Workbench, the toolbar disk button, which corresponds to the File Save menu item, is disabled whenever the currently selected document has not been modified. In the EX16A example, you'll see how a one-line update command UI function can use *IsModified* to control the state of the disk button and the corresponding menu item.

> **Note:** *In one respect, Microsoft Foundation Class Library version 2.0 SDI applications behave a little differently from other Windows SDI applications such as Notepad and Paintbrush. Here's a typical sequence of events:*
>
> *1. The user creates a document and saves it on disk under the name, say, TEST.DAT.*
>
> *2. The user modifies the document.*
>
> *3. The user chooses File Open and then specifies TEST.DAT.*
>
> *When the user chooses File Open, both Notepad and Paintbrush ask whether the user wants to save the changes made to the document (in step 2, above). If the user says no, the program rereads TEST.DAT from disk. A Microsoft Foundation Class Library version 2.0 application, on the other hand, assumes the changes are permanent and does not reread the file.*

EX16A—An SDI Example with Serialization

This example is similar to example EX15B. The student dialog and bitmaps are the same, and the view class is the same. Serialization has been added, together with an update command UI function for File Save. The header and implementation files for the view and document classes will be reused in example EX17A in the next chapter.

All the new code (code that is different from EX15B) is listed, with additions and changes to the AppWizard-generated code and ClassWizard code shaded.

Here is a list of the files and classes in the EX16A example:

Header File	Source Code File	Class	Description
EX16A.H	EX16A.CPP	*CEx16aApp*	Application class (from AppWizard)
		CAboutDlg	About dialog
MAINFRM.H	MAINFRM.CPP	*CMainFrame*	SDI main frame
STUDOC.H	STUDOC.CPP	*CStudentDoc*	Student document
STUVIEW.H	STUVIEW.CPP	*CStudentView*	Student form view (from EX15B)
STUDENT.H	STUDENT.CPP	*CStudent*	Student record
STDAFX.H	STDAFX.CPP		Precompiled headers

CStudent

The EX16A STUDENT.H file is based on the file in the EX15A project (shown in Figure 15-2 on page 247) and contains a prototype added for the *Serialize* function, as shown in Figure 16-4. The *CStudent* implementation file, STUDENT.CPP, now has the *Serialize* member function added, as shown in Figure 16-4.

STUDENT.H

```
// student.h
class CStudent : public CObject
{
    DECLARE_SERIAL(CStudent)
public:
    CString m_name;
    LONG    m_lGrade;
    CStudent() {
        m_lGrade = 0;
    }
    CStudent(const char* szName, int lGrade) : m_name(szName) {
        m_lGrade = lGrade;
    }

    CStudent(const CStudent& s) : m_name(s.m_name) {
        m_lGrade = s.m_lGrade;
    }

    const CStudent& operator =(const CStudent& s)
    {
        m_name   = s.m_name;
        m_lGrade = s.m_lGrade;
        return *this;
    }

    BOOL operator ==(const CStudent& s) const
    {
        if ((m_name == s.m_name) && (m_lGrade == s.m_lGrade)) {
          return TRUE;
        }
        else {
          return FALSE;
        }
    }
```

Figure 16-4. (continued)
The STUDENT.H and STUDENT.CPP listings.

Figure 16-4. *continued*

```
    BOOL operator !=(const CStudent& s) const
    {
        // let's make use of the operator we just defined
        return !(*this == s);
    }

    virtual void Serialize(CArchive& ar);
#ifdef _DEBUG
    void Dump(CDumpContext& dc) const;
#endif
};
```

STUDENT.CPP
```
#include "stdafx.h"
#include "student.h"

IMPLEMENT_SERIAL(CStudent, CObject, 0)

void CStudent::Serialize(CArchive& ar)
{
    TRACE("Entering CStudent::Serialize\n");
    if (ar.IsStoring()) {
        ar << m_name << m_lGrade;
    }
    else {
        ar >> m_name >> m_lGrade;
    }
}

#ifdef _DEBUG
    void CStudent::Dump(CDumpContext& dc) const {
        CObject::Dump(dc);
        dc << "\nm_name = " << m_name << "\nm_lGrade = " << m_lGrade;
    }
#endif
```

CEx16aApp

Look carefully at the AppWizard-generated application class, shown in Figure 16-5, because it illustrates much of what we talked about earlier in this chapter. Your input to AppWizard determines how the application class opens documents. If you specify a file extension in the Classes dialog for the document class, you get the following code:

```
// simple command line parsing
if (m_lpCmdLine[0] == '\0')
{
    // create a new (empty) document
    OnFileNew();
}
else
{
    // open an existing document
    OpenDocumentFile(m_lpCmdLine);
}
```

In this case, the application accepts a document name on the command line. You can start the program from File Manager, and you can specify a file when setting up a Program Manager icon.

If you leave the file extension blank (the default case), you get this code:

```
// create a new (empty) document
OnFileNew();

if (m_lpCmdLine[0] != '\0')
{
    // TODO: add command line processing here
}
```

Now the application won't accept a filename command-line argument.

EX16A.H
```
#ifndef __AFXWIN_H__
    #error include 'stdafx.h' before including this file for PCH
#endif

#include "resource.h"        // main symbols


/////////////////////////////////////////////////////////////////////
// CEx16aApp:
// See ex16a.cpp for the implementation of this class
//

class CEx16aApp : public CWinApp
{
public:
    CEx16aApp();

// Overrides
    virtual BOOL InitInstance();
```

Figure 16-5. (continued)
The CEx16aApp class listing.

Figure 16-5. *continued*

```
// Implementation

    //{{AFX_MSG(CEx16aApp)
    afx_msg void OnAppAbout();
        // NOTE - the ClassWizard will add and remove member functions here.
        //    DO NOT EDIT what you see in these blocks of generated code !
    //}}AFX_MSG
    DECLARE_MESSAGE_MAP()
};
```

```
EX16A.CPP
#include "stdafx.h"
#include "ex16a.h"

#include "mainfrm.h"
#include "studoc.h"
#include "stuview.h"

#ifdef _DEBUG
#undef THIS_FILE
static char BASED_CODE THIS_FILE[] = __FILE__;
#endif

/////////////////////////////////////////////////////////////////////////
// CEx16aApp

BEGIN_MESSAGE_MAP(CEx16aApp, CWinApp)
    //{{AFX_MSG_MAP(CEx16aApp)
    ON_COMMAND(ID_APP_ABOUT, OnAppAbout)
        // NOTE - the ClassWizard will add and remove mapping macros here.
        //    DO NOT EDIT what you see in these blocks of generated code !
    //}}AFX_MSG_MAP
    // Standard file based document commands
    ON_COMMAND(ID_FILE_NEW, CWinApp::OnFileNew)
    ON_COMMAND(ID_FILE_OPEN, CWinApp::OnFileOpen)
END_MESSAGE_MAP()

/////////////////////////////////////////////////////////////////////////
// CEx16aApp construction

CEx16aApp::CEx16aApp()
{
    // TODO: add construction code here,
    // Place all significant initialization in InitInstance
}
```

(continued)

Figure 16-5. *continued*

```
///////////////////////////////////////////////////////////////////////
// The one and only CEx16aApp object

CEx16aApp NEAR theApp;

///////////////////////////////////////////////////////////////////////
// CEx16aApp initialization

BOOL CEx16aApp::InitInstance()
{
    // Standard initialization
    // If you are not using these features and wish to reduce the size
    //  of your final executable, you should remove from the following
    //  the specific initialization routines you do not need.

    SetDialogBkColor();           // set dialog background color to gray
    LoadStdProfileSettings();     // Load standard INI file options
                                  //  (including MRU)

    // Register the application's document templates.  Document templates
    //  serve as the connection between documents, frame windows and views.

    AddDocTemplate(new CSingleDocTemplate(IDR_MAINFRAME,
            RUNTIME_CLASS(CStudentDoc),
            RUNTIME_CLASS(CMainFrame),      // main SDI frame window
            RUNTIME_CLASS(CStudentView)));

    // simple command line parsing
    if (m_lpCmdLine[0] == '\0')
    {
        // create a new (empty) document
        OnFileNew();
    }
    else
    {
        // open an existing document
        OpenDocumentFile(m_lpCmdLine);
    }

    return TRUE;
}
///////////////////////////////////////////////////////////////////////
// CAboutDlg dialog used for App About

class CAboutDlg : public CDialog
{
public:
    CAboutDlg() : CDialog(CAboutDlg::IDD)
```

(continued)

Figure 16-5. *continued*

```
        {
            //{{AFX_DATA_INIT(CAboutDlg)
            //}}AFX_DATA_INIT
        }

// Dialog Data
    //{{AFX_DATA(CAboutDlg)
        enum { IDD = IDD_ABOUTBOX };
    //}}AFX_DATA

// Implementation
protected:
    virtual void DoDataExchange(CDataExchange* pDX);    // DDX/DDV support
    //{{AFX_MSG(CAboutDlg)
        // No message handlers
    //}}AFX_MSG
    DECLARE_MESSAGE_MAP()
};

void CAboutDlg::DoDataExchange(CDataExchange* pDX)
{
    CDialog::DoDataExchange(pDX);
    //{{AFX_DATA_MAP(CAboutDlg)
    //}}AFX_DATA_MAP
}

BEGIN_MESSAGE_MAP(CAboutDlg, CDialog)
    //{{AFX_MSG_MAP(CAboutDlg)
        // No message handlers
    //}}AFX_MSG_MAP
END_MESSAGE_MAP()

// App command to run the dialog
void CEx16aApp::OnAppAbout()
{
    CAboutDlg aboutDlg;
    aboutDlg.DoModal();
}
```

CFrameWnd

The main frame window class code, shown in Figure 16-6, is almost unchanged from the code that AppWizard generated. The toolbar button constants are added, and the overridden *ActivateFrame* function exists solely for trace purposes.

MAINFRAME.H

```
class CMainFrame : public CFrameWnd
{
protected: // create from serialization only
    CMainFrame();
    DECLARE_DYNCREATE(CMainFrame)

// Attributes
public:

// Operations
public:

// Implementation
public:
    virtual ~CMainFrame();
    virtual void ActivateFrame(int nCmdhow = -1);

protected:      // control bar embedded members
    CStatusBar      m_wndStatusBar;
    CToolBar        m_wndToolBar;

// Generated message map functions
protected:
    //{{AFX_MSG(CMainFrame)
    afx_msg int OnCreate(LPCREATESTRUCT lpCreateStruct);
        // NOTE - the ClassWizard will add and remove member functions here.
        //    DO NOT EDIT what you see in these blocks of generated code !
    //}}AFX_MSG
    DECLARE_MESSAGE_MAP()
};
```

MAINFRAME.CPP

```
#include "stdafx.h"
#include "ex16a.h"

#include "mainfrm.h"

#ifdef _DEBUG
#undef THIS_FILE
static char BASED_CODE THIS_FILE[] = __FILE__;
#endif
```

Figure 16-6.   *(continued)*
The CMainFrame *class listing.*

Figure 16-6. *continued*

```
/////////////////////////////////////////////////////////////////////
// CMainFrame

IMPLEMENT_DYNCREATE(CMainFrame, CFrameWnd)

BEGIN_MESSAGE_MAP(CMainFrame, CFrameWnd)
    //{{AFX_MSG_MAP(CMainFrame)
        // NOTE - the ClassWizard will add and remove mapping macros here.
        //    DO NOT EDIT what you see in these blocks of generated code !
    ON_WM_CREATE()
    //}}AFX_MSG_MAP
END_MESSAGE_MAP()


/////////////////////////////////////////////////////////////////////
// arrays of IDs used to initialize control bars

// toolbar buttons - IDs are command buttons
static UINT BASED_CODE buttons[] =
{
    // same order as in the bitmap 'toolbar.bmp'
    ID_FILE_NEW,
    ID_FILE_OPEN,
    ID_FILE_SAVE,
        ID_SEPARATOR,
    ID_POS_HOME,
    ID_POS_END,
    ID_POS_PREV,
    ID_POS_NEXT,
    ID_POS_DEL,
    ID_POS_INS,
        ID_SEPARATOR,
    ID_FILE_PRINT,
    ID_APP_ABOUT,
};

static UINT BASED_CODE indicators[] =
{
    ID_SEPARATOR,           // status line indicator
    ID_INDICATOR_CAPS,
    ID_INDICATOR_NUM,
    ID_INDICATOR_SCRL,
};


/////////////////////////////////////////////////////////////////////
// CMainFrame construction/destruction

CMainFrame::CMainFrame()
{
    // TODO: add member initialization code here
}
```

(continued)

Figure 16-6. *continued*

```
CMainFrame::~CMainFrame()
{
}

void CMainFrame::ActivateFrame(int nCmdShow)
{
    // overridden here only for tracing
    TRACE("Entering CMainFrame::ActivateFrame\n");
    CFrameWnd::ActivateFrame(nCmdShow);
}

int CMainFrame::OnCreate(LPCREATESTRUCT lpCreateStruct)
{
    if (CFrameWnd::OnCreate(lpCreateStruct) == -1)
        return -1;

    if (!m_wndToolBar.Create(this) ||
        !m_wndToolBar.LoadBitmap(IDR_MAINFRAME) ||
        !m_wndToolBar.SetButtons(buttons,
          sizeof(buttons)/sizeof(UINT)))
    {
        TRACE("Failed to create toolbar\n");
        return -1;        // fail to create
    }

    if (!m_wndStatusBar.Create(this) ||
        !m_wndStatusBar.SetIndicators(indicators,
          sizeof(indicators)/sizeof(UINT)))
    {
        TRACE("Failed to create status bar\n");
        return -1;        // fail to create
    }

    return 0;
}
```

CStudentDoc

The *CStudentDoc* class is the same as the *CStudentDoc* class from the previous chapter (shown in Figure 15-4 on page 262) except for three functions: *Serialize*, *OnOpenDocument*, and *OnUpdateFileSave*.

Serialize

One line has been added to the AppWizard-generated function to serialize the document's student list.

```
/////////////////////////////////////////////////////////////////////////
// CStudentDoc serialization

void CStudentDoc::Serialize(CArchive& ar)
{
    if (ar.IsStoring())
    {
        // TODO: add storing code here for other data members
    }
    else
    {
        // TODO: add loading code here for other data members
    }
    m_studentList.Serialize(ar);
}
```

OnOpenDocument

This virtual function is overridden only for the purpose of displaying a *TRACE* message.

```
BOOL CStudentDoc::OnOpenDocument(const char* pszPathName)
{
    TRACE("Entering CStudentDoc::OnOpenDocument\n");
    if (!CDocument::OnOpenDocument(pszPathName))
        return FALSE;
    return TRUE;
}
```

OnUpdateFileSave

This is a message map function that grays the File Save toolbar button when the document is in the unmodified state. The view controls this state by calling the document's *SetModifiedFlag* function.

```
void CStudentDoc::OnUpdateFileSave(CCmdUI* pCmdUI)
{
    // disable disk toolbar button if file is not modified
    pCmdUI->Enable(IsModified());
}
```

CStudentView

The code for the *CStudentView* class comes from the previous chapter. Figure 15-5 on page 266 shows the code.

AppWizard and EX16A

If you were using AppWizard to start the EX16A project, you would specify document type name *Student* and file extension *16a* in the Classes dialog as shown in Figure 16-7.

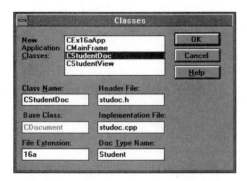

Figure 16-7.
The EX16A AppWizard Classes dialog.

This ensures that the document template resource string contains the correct default extension.

Testing the EX16A Application

Build the program, and then test it by typing some data and saving it on disk with the filename *TEST.16A*. (You don't need to type the *.16A*.) Now the window should look similar to Figure 16-8.

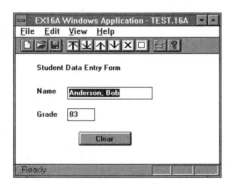

Figure 16-8.
The EX16A window.

Exit the program, and then restart it and open the file you saved. Did the names come back? Take a look at the Debug Messages window and observe the sequence of function calls. Is the following sequence produced when you start the application?

```
Entering CStudentDoc constructor
Entering CMainFrame constructor
Entering CStudentView constructor
Entering CStudentDoc::OnNewDocument
Entering CStudentDoc::DeleteContents
Entering CStudentView::OnInitialUpdate
Entering CStudentView::OnUpdate
Entering CMainFrame::ActivateFrame
```

File Manager Document Association

Start the Windows File Manager, and then open the directory \VCPP\EX16A. Widen the file search to include Other Files, and then select the file TEST.16A. Choose Associate from the File menu. Fill in the dialog as shown in Figure 16-9.

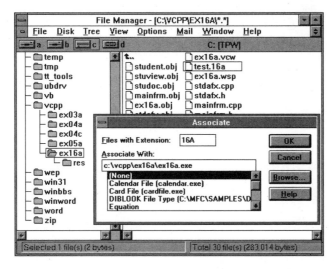

Figure 16-9.
File Manager window with File Manager Associate dialog.

Now narrow the File Manager's search to Documents. Only files with the 16A suffix will be shown, denoted by this document symbol:

Double-click TEST.16A. Does the EX16A program start up? If you look in WIN.INI, you'll see the line

```
16A=c:\vcpp\ex16a\ex16a.exe ^.16A
```

File Manager also inserts a new (redundant) entry in the Windows Registration Database; you'll learn more about that in the next chapter.

17

Reading and Writing Documents—MDI

This chapter introduces the Microsoft Foundation Class Library version 2.0 Multiple Document Interface (MDI) application and explains how it reads and writes its document files. The MDI application is really the preferred class library program style. AppWizard endows only MDI applications with capabilities such as File Manager drag and drop, and most of the sample programs that come with Microsoft Visual C++ are MDI applications.

Here you'll learn the similarities and differences between Single Document Interface (SDI) and MDI applications, and you'll see how the MDI application handles files dragged and dropped from Windows File Manager. You'll also learn how, with little effort, you can retrofit SDI applications with this drag-and-drop capability. Be sure you thoroughly understand the SDI application, as described in Chapter 16, before you attack the MDI application.

The MDI Application

Before you look at the class library code for MDI applications, you should be familiar with the operation of Windows MDI programs. Take a close look at the Visual C++ Visual Workbench now. It's an MDI application whose "multiple documents" are program source code files. Visual Workbench is not the most typical MDI application, though, because it collects its documents into projects. It's better to examine Microsoft Word for Windows or, better yet, to examine a real class library MDI application—the kind that AppWizard generates.

A Typical MDI Application, Class Library Style

This chapter's first example, EX17A, is an MDI version of EX16A. Look back at Figure 16-8 on page 303 to see an illustration of the SDI version after the user has selected a file. Now look at the MDI equivalent in Figure 17-1 on the next page.

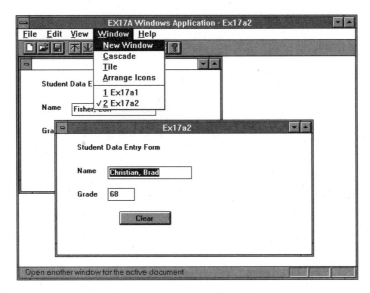

Figure 17-1.
The EX17A application with two files open and the Window menu shown.

The user has two separate document files open, each in a separate MDI child window, but only one child window is active—the lower window that lies on top of the other child window. The application has only one menu and one toolbar, and all commands are routed to the active child window. The main window's title bar reflects the name of the active child window's document file.

For Windows SDK Programmers

Starting with version 3.0, Windows has directly supported MDI applications. The Microsoft Foundation Class Library version 2.0 builds on this Windows support to make an MDI environment that parallels the SDI environment. In an SDK MDI application, a main application frame window contains the menu and a single client window. The client window manages various child windows that correspond to documents. The MDI client window has its own preregistered window class (not to be confused with a C++ class) with a procedure that handles special messages such as WM_MDICASCADE and WM_MDITILE. An MDI child window procedure is pretty much the same as the window procedure for an SDI main window.

In the class library, the *CMDIFrameWnd* class encapsulates the functions of both the main frame window and the MDI client window. This class has message handlers for all the Windows MDI messages and thus can manage its child windows, which are represented by objects of class *CMDIChildWnd*.

The child window's minimize box allows the user to reduce the child window to an icon in the main window. The application's Window menu (shown in Figure 17-1) lets the user control the presentation through the following items:

Menu Item	Action
New Window	Opens an additional child window for the selected document
Cascade	Arranges the existing windows in an overlapped pattern
Tile	Arranges the existing windows in a nonoverlapped, tiled pattern
Arrange Icons	Arranges iconized windows in the frame window
(document names)	Selects the corresponding child window and brings it to the top

If the user saves and closes both child windows (and opens the File menu), the application looks like Figure 17-2.

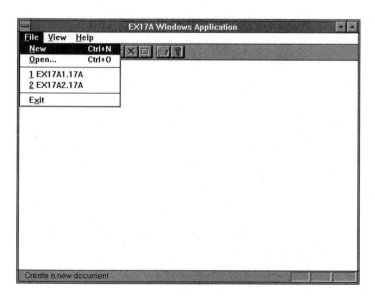

Figure 17-2.
EX17A with no child windows.

The menu is different: Most toolbar buttons are disabled, and the window caption does not show a filename. About the only thing the user can do is start a new document or open an existing document from disk.

Figure 17-3 on the next page shows the application when it first starts up and a new document is created. The single child window has been maximized.

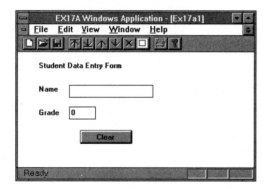

Figure 17-3.
EX17A with initial child window.

The single, empty child window has the default document name Ex17a1. This name is based on the Doc Type Name you selected in the AppWizard Classes dialog, Ex17a. The first new file is Ex17a1, the second is Ex17a2, and so forth. The user normally chooses a different name when saving the document.

Class library MDI applications, like many commercial MDI applications, start up with a new, empty document. (Visual Workbench is an exception.) If you want your application to start up with a blank frame, you can remove the *OnFileNew* call in the application class file as shown in example EX17A.

The MDI Application Object

You're probably wondering how an MDI application works and what code makes it different from an SDI application. Actually, the startup sequences are pretty much the same. An application object, of a class derived from class *CWinApp*, has an overridden *InitInstance* member function. This *InitInstance* function is somewhat different from the SDI *InitInstance*, starting with the call to *AddDocTemplate*.

The MDI Document Template Class

The MDI template construction call in *InitInstance* looks like this:

```
AddDocTemplate(new CMultiDocTemplate(IDR_MYDOCTYPE,
        RUNTIME_CLASS(CMyDoc),
        RUNTIME_CLASS(CMDIChildWnd),    // standard MDI child frame
        RUNTIME_CLASS(CMyView)));
```

Like the *CSingleDocTemplate* class you saw in Chapter 16, the *CMultiDocTemplate* class allows an application to use multiple document types, but, unlike the *CSingleDocTemplate* class, it allows the simultaneous existence of more than one document object. This is the essence of the MDI application.

The single *AddDocTemplate* call shown above permits the MDI application to support multiple child windows, each connected to a document object and a view object. It's possible to have several child windows (and corresponding view objects) connected to the same document object. In this chapter we'll start with only one view class and one document class. You'll see multiple view classes and multiple document classes in Chapter 19.

The MDI Frame Window and Child Window

The SDI examples had only one frame window class and only one frame window object. For SDI applications, AppWizard generated a class called *CMainFrame*, which was derived from the class *CFrameWnd*. An MDI application has two frame window base classes and many frame objects, as shown in the table below. The MDI frame–view window relationship is shown in Figure 17-4.

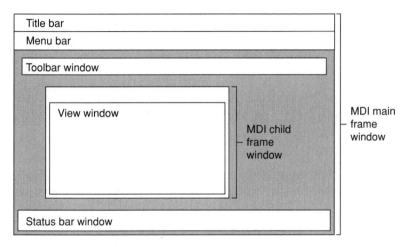

Figure 17-4.
The MDI frame–view window relationship.

Base Class	AppWizard-Generated Class	Number of Objects	Menu and Control Bars	Contains a View	Object Constructed
CMDIFrameWnd	*CMainFrame*	1 only	Yes	No	In application class's *InitInstance* function
CMDIChildWnd	No derivation	1 per child window	No	Yes	By application framework when a new child window is opened

In an SDI application, the *CMainFrame* object framed the application <u>and</u> contained the view object. In an MDI application, the two roles are separated. Now the *CMainFrame* object is constructed in *InitInstance*, and the *CMDIChildWnd* object contains the view. AppWizard generates code as shown here:

```
CMainFrame* pMainFrame = new CMainFrame;
if (!pMainFrame->LoadFrame(IDR_MAINFRAME))
    return FALSE;
pMainFrame->ShowWindow(m_nCmdShow);
pMainFrame->UpdateWindow();
m_pMainWnd = pMainFrame;
```

The application framework can create the *CMDIChildWnd* objects dynamically because the *CMDIChildWnd* class is passed to the *CMultiDocTemplate* constructor.

(Note: The MDI *InitInstance* function sets the *CWinApp* data member *m_p-MainWnd* to point to the application's main frame window. This means you can access *m_pMainWnd* through the global *AfxGetApp* function any time you need to get your application's main frame window.)

The Main Frame and Document Template Resources

An MDI application has two separate string and menu resources, identified by the constants *IDR_MAINFRAME* and *IDR_MYDOCTYPE*. The first resource set goes with the empty main frame window; the second set goes with the occupied main frame window. Here are the two string resources with substrings broken out:

```
IDR_MAINFRAME
    "MYAPP Windows Application"          // application window caption

IDR_MYDOCTYPE
    "\nn                                // application window caption
    "MYAPP\n"                           // root for default document name
    "MYAPP Document\n"                  // document type name
    "MYAPP Files (*.16b)\n"             // document type description and filter
    ".16b\n"                            // extension for documents of this type
    "MYAPPFileType\n"                   // registration database document ID
    "MYAPP File Type"                   // registration database document
                                        //  description
```

(Note: The resource compiler won't accept the string concatenations as shown above. If you examine the EX16A.RC file, you'll see the substrings combined in one large string.)

The application window caption comes from the *IDR_MAINFRAME* string. When a document is open, the document filename is appended. The last two substrings in the *IDR_MYDOCTYPE* string are there to support drag and drop.

Creating an Empty Document— The *CWinApp OnFileNew* Function

The MDI *InitInstance* function calls *OnFileNew*, as did the SDI *InitInstance* function. This time, however, the main frame window has already been created. *OnFileNew*, through a call to the *CWinApp* function *OpenDocumentFile*, now does the following:

1. Constructs a document object but does not attempt to read data from disk.

2. Constructs a child frame window object (of class *CMDIChildWnd*). Also creates the child frame window but does not show it. In the main frame window, the *IDR_MAINFRAME* menu is replaced by the *IDR_MYDOCTYPE* menu.

3. Constructs a view object. Also creates the view window but does not show it.

4. Establishes connections among the document, the main frame, and view objects. Do not confuse these object connections with the class associations established by the call to *AddDocTemplate*.

5. Calls the virtual *OnNewDocument* member function for the document object.

6. Calls the virtual *OnInitialUpdate* member function for the view object.

7. Calls the virtual *ActivateFrame* for the child frame object to show the frame window and view window.

(Note: Some functions listed above are not called directly by *OpenDocumentFile* but are called indirectly through the application framework.)

The *OnFileNew* function is also called in response to the File New menu command. In an MDI application, *OnFileNew* performs the exact same steps as it does when called from *InitInstance*.

Creating an Additional View for an Existing Document

If you choose New Window from the Window menu, the application framework opens a new child window that's linked to the currently selected document. The associated *CMDIFrameWnd* function, *OnWindowNew*, does the following:

1. Constructs a child frame object (of class *CMDIChildWnd*). Also creates the child frame window but does not show it.

2. Constructs a view object. Also creates the view window but does not show it.

3. Establishes connections between the new view object and the existing document and main frame objects.

4. Calls the virtual *OnInitialUpdate* member function for the view object.

5. Calls the virtual *ActivateFrame* for the child frame object to show the frame window and the view window.

Loading and Storing Documents

In MDI applications, documents are loaded and stored the same way as in SDI applications, but with two important differences: A new document object is constructed each time a document file is loaded from disk, and the document object is destroyed when the child window is closed. Don't worry about clearing a document's contents before loading—but you should override the *CDocument DeleteContents* function anyway to make the class portable to the SDI environment.

Drag and Drop—Programs and Documents

In the IBM PC world, users are accustomed to starting up a program and then selecting a disk file (sometimes called a document) that contains data the program understands. All MS-DOS programs worked this way, and Windows improved things by allowing the user to double-click on a program icon instead of typing a program name. Meanwhile the Apple Macintosh users were double-clicking on a document icon, and the Macintosh operating system figured out which program to run.

Windows version 3.1 also allows users to double-click on a document icon to run programs. But how does Windows know which program to run when a user double-clicks a document icon? In Chapter 16, you used File Manager to manually associate a file type with a program. This association process placed a line in the [Extensions] section of WIN.INI that linked a three-character file extension with the program name. When File Manager started the program, it put the selected filename in the command line, and the program opened the file on startup.

Now we'll take this process to a new level. No longer will we (or the user) need to manually associate a document type with a program. After the user executes the program the first time as part of the installation process, he or she will be able to drag a file from File Manager and drop it into a running application's main window. The user can still double-click on a document icon in File Manager, but the program launch process is quite different.

Program Registration

Windows maintains a database of program information in a file called REG.DAT. This registration database supports both OLE and File Manager drag and drop. As far as drag and drop is concerned, each database entry contains program parameters, including the program identifier, the file type description, and the command line. A Windows utility program, REGEDIT, allows editing of the registration database. Figure 17-5 shows a typical REGEDIT window for a class library MDI program.

You and your user don't have to mess with REGEDIT because Windows provides a function to register a program, and the application framework wraps this function with a *CWinApp* member function. The following line in your derived application class *InitInstance* function does the job:

```
RegisterShellFileTypes();
```

The first time your MDI program is run (from Visual Workbench or from Program Manager), the registration database is updated to include the program's identifier and command line parameters, and the WIN.INI file is updated to associate the file extension with the program identifier. You might notice a slight delay while the files are updated.

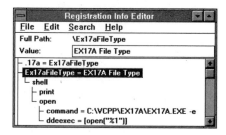

Figure 17-5.
The REGEDIT window.

> **Note:** *REGEDIT was run with the /v switch.*

Enabling Drag and Drop

If you want your already-running program to open files dragged from File Manager, you must call the *CWnd* function *DragAcceptFiles* for the application's main frame window. The application object's public data member *m_pMainWnd* points to the *CMDIFrameWnd* object. The following line in *InitInstance* enables drag and drop:

```
m_pMainWnd->DragAcceptFiles();
```

Enabling Embedded Launch

In the SDI example EX16A, File Manager started an associated program by including the document filename in the program's command line. File Manager can also start a program through an embedded launch procedure, and that's what AppWizard sets up for MDI applications. An embedded launch is a two-step process. First, the program is executed with the *-e* parameter as specified in the registration database. After it's running, the program gets a message via Windows' Dynamic Data Exchange (DDE) that tells it to load a file.

The following call to a *CWinApp* member function is included in *InitInstance*:

```
EnableShellOpen();
```

This function does the setup necessary for the program to accept DDE messages.

Program Startup Parameters

When a class library MDI program is run from Program Manager, there is usually no command line parameter. When it's run from File Manager (an embedded launch), the registration database ensures that the program is run with the *-e* parameter. Here's the code in the derived application class *InitInstance* function that processes the command line:

```
if (m_lpCmdLine[0] == '\0')
{
    // create a new (empty) document
    OnFileNew();
}
else if ((m_lpCmdLine[0] == '-' || m_lpCmdLine[0] == '/') &&
         (m_lpCmdLine[1] == 'e' || m_lpCmdLine[1] == 'E'))
{
    // program launched embedded - wait for DDE or OLE open
}
else
{
    // open an existing document
    OpenDocumentFile(m_lpCmdLine);
}
```

If there's no command line argument, the program creates a new, empty child window. If the command line contains something that looks like a filename, the program creates a new child window and loads that file. In an embedded launch, the program waits for a DDE message.

Responding to DDE Messages

The base classes take care of the DDE messages that result from drag and drop and File Manager embedded launch (with the *-e* command line parameter). In drag and drop, the application framework calls the *CWinApp* function *OpenDocumentFile* with the filename as a parameter. In an embedded launch, the application framework calls two *CWinApp* functions: *OnDDECommand* and *OpenDocumentFile*. You normally don't need to override these functions in your derived application class. Let the application framework do the work.

The EX17A Example

This example is the MDI version of EX16A from the previous chapter. It uses exactly the same document and view class code and the same resources (except for the program name). The application code and main frame class code are different, however. All the new code is listed here, including the code that AppWizard generates.

Here's a list of the files and classes in the EX17A example:

Header File	Source Code File	Class	Description
EX17A.H	EX17A.CPP	*CEx17aApp*	Application class (from AppWizard)
		CAboutDlg	About dialog
MAINFRM.H	MAINFRM.CPP	*CMainFrame*	MDI main frame
STUDOC.H	STUDOC.CPP	*CStudentDoc*	Student document (from EX16A)
STUVIEW.H	STUVIEW.CPP	*CStudentView*	Student form view (from EX15B)
STUDENT.H	STUDENT.CPP	*CStudent*	Student record (from EX16A)
STDAFX.H	STDAFX.CPP		Precompiled headers

CEx17aApp

Two functions, *OpenDocumentFile* and *OnDDECommand*, are overridden only for the purpose of inserting *TRACE* statements. Also, the *OnFileNew* call in *InitInstance* has been commented out to prevent the creation of an empty document window on startup. Figure 17-6 shows the source code.

EX17A.H

```
#ifndef __AFXWIN_H__
    #error include 'stdafx.h' before including this file for PCH
#endif

#include "resource.h"        // main symbols

/////////////////////////////////////////////////////////////////////////
// CEx17aApp:
// See ex17a.cpp for the implementation of this class
//

class CEx17aApp : public CWinApp
{
public:
    CEx17aApp();

// Overrides
    virtual BOOL InitInstance();
    // open named file
    virtual CDocument* OpenDocumentFile(LPCSTR lpszFileName);
    virtual BOOL OnDDECommand(char* pszCommand);
```

Figure 17-6.
The CEx17aApp source listing.

(continued)

Figure 17-6. *continued*

```
// Implementation

    //{{AFX_MSG(CEx17aApp)
    afx_msg void OnAppAbout();
        // NOTE - the ClassWizard will add and remove member functions here.
        //    DO NOT EDIT what you see in these blocks of generated code !
    //}}AFX_MSG
    DECLARE_MESSAGE_MAP()
};
```

EX17A.CPP
```
#include "stdafx.h"
#include "ex17a.h"

#include "mainfrm.h"
#include "student.h"
#include "studoc.h"
#include "stuview.h"

#ifdef _DEBUG
#undef THIS_FILE
static char BASED_CODE THIS_FILE[] = __FILE__;
#endif

/////////////////////////////////////////////////////////////////////
// CEx17aApp

BEGIN_MESSAGE_MAP(CEx17aApp, CWinApp)
    //{{AFX_MSG_MAP(CEx17aApp)
    ON_COMMAND(ID_APP_ABOUT, OnAppAbout)
        // NOTE - the ClassWizard will add and remove mapping macros here.
        //    DO NOT EDIT what you see in these blocks of generated code !
    //}}AFX_MSG_MAP
    // Standard file based document commands
    ON_COMMAND(ID_FILE_NEW, CWinApp::OnFileNew)
    ON_COMMAND(ID_FILE_OPEN, CWinApp::OnFileOpen)
END_MESSAGE_MAP()

/////////////////////////////////////////////////////////////////////
// CEx17aApp construction

CEx17aApp::CEx17aApp()
{
    // TODO: add construction code here
    // Place all significant initialization in InitInstance
}
```

(continued)

Figure 17-6. *continued*

```
/////////////////////////////////////////////////////////////////////
// The one and only CEx17aApp object

CEx17aApp NEAR theApp;

/////////////////////////////////////////////////////////////////////
// CEx17aApp initialization

BOOL CEx17aApp::InitInstance()
{
    // Standard initialization
    // If you are not using these features and wish to reduce the size
    //  of your final executable, you should remove from the following
    //  the specific initialization routines you do not need.

    SetDialogBkColor();          // set dialog background color to gray
    LoadStdProfileSettings();    // Load standard INI file options
                                 //  (including MRU)

    // Register the application's document templates.  Document templates
    //  serve as the connection between documents,
    //  frame windows and views.

    AddDocTemplate(new CMultiDocTemplate(IDR_EX17ATYPE,
            RUNTIME_CLASS(CStudentDoc),
            RUNTIME_CLASS(CMDIChildWnd),        // standard MDI
                                                // child frame
            RUNTIME_CLASS(CStudentView)));

    // create main MDI Frame window
    CMainFrame* pMainFrame = new CMainFrame;
    if (!pMainFrame->LoadFrame(IDR_MAINFRAME))
        return FALSE;
    pMainFrame->ShowWindow(m_nCmdShow);
    pMainFrame->UpdateWindow();
    m_pMainWnd = pMainFrame;

    // enable file manager drag/drop and DDE Execute open
    m_pMainWnd->DragAcceptFiles();
    EnableShellOpen();
    RegisterShellFileTypes();

    // simple command line parsing
    if (m_lpCmdLine[0] == '\0')
    {
        // create a new (empty) document
//      OnFileNew();
    }
```

(continued)

Figure 17-6. *continued*

```
    else if ((m_lpCmdLine[0] == '-' || m_lpCmdLine[0] == '/') &&
        (m_lpCmdLine[1] == 'e' || m_lpCmdLine[1] == 'E'))
    {
        // program launched embedded - wait for DDE or OLE open
    }
    else
    {
        // open an existing document
        OpenDocumentFile(m_lpCmdLine);
    }

    return TRUE;
}

/////////////////////////////////////////////////////////////////////
CDocument* CEx17aApp::OpenDocumentFile(LPCSTR lpszFileName)
{
    TRACE("Entering CEx17aApp::OpenDocumentFile - %s\n", lpszFileName);
    return CWinApp::OpenDocumentFile(lpszFileName);
}

/////////////////////////////////////////////////////////////////////
BOOL CEx17aApp::OnDDECommand(char* pszCommand)
{
    TRACE("Entering CEx17aApp::OnDDECommand - %s\n", pszCommand);
    return CWinApp::OnDDECommand(pszCommand);
}

/////////////////////////////////////////////////////////////////////
// CAboutDlg dialog used for App About

class CAboutDlg : public CDialog
{
public:
    CAboutDlg();

// Dialog Data
    //{{AFX_DATA(CAboutDlg)
    enum { IDD = IDD_ABOUTBOX };
    //}}AFX_DATA

// Implementation
protected:
    virtual void DoDataExchange(CDataExchange* pDX); // DDX/DDV support
    //{{AFX_MSG(CAboutDlg)
        // No message handlers
    //}}AFX_MSG
    DECLARE_MESSAGE_MAP()
};
```

(continued)

Figure 17-6. *continued*

```
CAboutDlg::CAboutDlg() : CDialog(CAboutDlg::IDD)
{
    //{{AFX_DATA_INIT(CAboutDlg)
    //}}AFX_DATA_INIT
}

void CAboutDlg::DoDataExchange(CDataExchange* pDX)
{
    CDialog::DoDataExchange(pDX);
    //{{AFX_DATA_MAP(CAboutDlg)
    //}}AFX_DATA_MAP
}

BEGIN_MESSAGE_MAP(CAboutDlg, CDialog)
    //{{AFX_MSG_MAP(CAboutDlg)
        // No message handlers
    //}}AFX_MSG_MAP
END_MESSAGE_MAP()

// App command to run the dialog
void CEx17aApp::OnAppAbout()
{
    CAboutDlg aboutDlg;
    aboutDlg.DoModal();
}


/////////////////////////////////////////////////////////////////
// CEx17aApp commands
```

CMainFrame

This main frame class, listed in Figure 17-7, is almost identical to the SDI version, except that it is derived from *CMDIFrameWnd* instead of from *CFrameWnd*. The same toolbar definitions are included.

MAINFRM.H
```
class CMainFrame : public CMDIFrameWnd
{
    DECLARE_DYNAMIC(CMainFrame)
public:
    CMainFrame();

// Attributes
public:
```

Figure 17-7.   *(continued)*
The CMainFrame *class listing.*

Figure 17-7. *continued*

```
// Operations
public:

// Implementation
public:
    virtual ~CMainFrame();

protected:    // control bar embedded members
    CStatusBar    m_wndStatusBar;
    CToolBar      m_wndToolBar;

// Generated message map functions
protected:
    //{{AFX_MSG(CMainFrame)
    afx_msg int OnCreate(LPCREATESTRUCT lpCreateStruct);
        // NOTE - the ClassWizard will add and remove member functions here.
        //    DO NOT EDIT what you see in these blocks of generated code !
    //}}AFX_MSG
    DECLARE_MESSAGE_MAP()
};
```

MAINFRM.CPP (the class implementation file)

```
#include "stdafx.h"
#include "ex17a.h"

#include "mainfrm.h"

#ifdef _DEBUG
#undef THIS_FILE
static char BASED_CODE THIS_FILE[] = __FILE__;
#endif


/////////////////////////////////////////////////////////////////////////
// CMainFrame

IMPLEMENT_DYNAMIC(CMainFrame, CMDIFrameWnd)

BEGIN_MESSAGE_MAP(CMainFrame, CMDIFrameWnd)
    //{{AFX_MSG_MAP(CMainFrame)
        // NOTE - the ClassWizard will add and remove mapping macros here.
        //    DO NOT EDIT what you see in these blocks of generated code !
    ON_WM_CREATE()
    //}}AFX_MSG_MAP
END_MESSAGE_MAP()
```

(continued)

Figure 17-7. *continued*

```
///////////////////////////////////////////////////////////////////
// arrays of IDs used to initialize control bars

// toolbar buttons - IDs are command buttons
static UINT BASED_CODE buttons[] =
{
    // same order as in the bitmap 'toolbar.bmp'
    ID_FILE_NEW,
    ID_FILE_OPEN,
    ID_FILE_SAVE,
        ID_SEPARATOR,
    ID_POS_HOME,
    ID_POS_END,
    ID_POS_PREV,
    ID_POS_NEXT,
    ID_POS_DEL,
    ID_POS_INS,
        ID_SEPARATOR,
    ID_FILE_PRINT,
    ID_APP_ABOUT,
};

static UINT BASED_CODE indicators[] =
{
    ID_SEPARATOR,               // status line indicator
    ID_INDICATOR_CAPS,
    ID_INDICATOR_NUM,
    ID_INDICATOR_SCRL,
};

///////////////////////////////////////////////////////////////////
// CMainFrame construction/destruction

CMainFrame::CMainFrame()
{
    // TODO: add member initialization code here
}

CMainFrame::~CMainFrame()
{
}

int CMainFrame::OnCreate(LPCREATESTRUCT lpCreateStruct)
{
    if (CMDIFrameWnd::OnCreate(lpCreateStruct) == -1)
        return -1;

    if (!m_wndToolBar.Create(this) ||
        !m_wndToolBar.LoadBitmap(IDR_MAINFRAME) ||
```

(continued)

Figure 17-7. *continued*

```
        !m_wndToolBar.SetButtons(buttons,
          sizeof(buttons)/sizeof(UINT)))
    {
        TRACE("Failed to create toolbar\n");
        return -1;         // fail to create
    }

    if (!m_wndStatusBar.Create(this) ||
        !m_wndStatusBar.SetIndicators(indicators,
          sizeof(indicators)/sizeof(UINT)))
    {
        TRACE("Failed to create status bar\n");
        return -1;         // fail to create
    }

    return 0;
}

/////////////////////////////////////////////////////////////////
// CMainFrame diagnostics

#ifdef _DEBUG
void CMainFrame::AssertValid() const
{
    CMDIFrameWnd::AssertValid();
}

void CMainFrame::Dump(CDumpContext& dc) const
{
    CMDIFrameWnd::Dump(dc);
}

#endif //_DEBUG

/////////////////////////////////////////////////////////////////
// CMainFrame message handlers
```

Testing the EX17A Application

Do the build, run the program from Visual Workbench, and then make several documents. Try saving the documents on disk, closing them, and reloading them. Now exit the program and start File Manager. The files you created should show up with File Manager document icons. Double-click on a document icon and see whether the EX17A program starts up. Now, with both File Manager and EX17A on the screen, drag a document from File Manager to EX17A. Was the file opened?

Note: *If File Manager is already running when you first start EX17A, it won't recognize the changes made to the registration database. You must exit File Manager and restart or drag a file into the EX17A main frame window for File Manager to recognize the changes made to the registration database.*

The EX17B Example

In this example, you'll retrofit the embedded launch and drag-and-drop capabilities into an SDI application. You need to modify only the application class and the main frame class. The resulting program does nothing, but you can apply the same changes to any SDI program, including EX16A. We'll go back to the old step-by-step method because so little code is new.

1. Run AppWizard to generate \VCPP\EX17B\EX17B. Choose AppWizard from Visual Workbench's Project menu. The options and default class names are shown here:

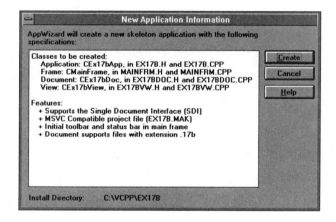

Be sure you turn off the Multiple Document Interface check box. For the document class, specify a file extension of *17b.*

2. Edit the derived application class *InitInstance* function in EX17B.CPP. After updating the registration database and enabling an embedded launch, this function calls *OnFileNew* when it detects an embedded launch. This call constructs, creates, and shows all the necessary windows. The application framework *CWinApp* functions *OnDDECommand* and *OpenDocumentFile* can then handle the DDE messages.

```
BOOL CEx17bApp::InitInstance()
{
    // Standard initialization
    // If you are not using these features and wish to reduce the size
    // of your final executable, you should remove from the following
    // the specific initialization routines you do not need.

    SetDialogBkColor();         // set dialog background color to BTNFACE
    LoadStdProfileSettings();    // load standard INI file options
                                 //  (including MRU)

    // Register the application's document templates.  Document templates
    //  serve as the connection between documents,
    //  frame windows and views.

    AddDocTemplate(new CSingleDocTemplate(IDR_MAINFRAME,
            RUNTIME_CLASS(CEx17bDoc),
            RUNTIME_CLASS(CMainFrame),     // main SDI frame window
            RUNTIME_CLASS(CEx17bView)));

    EnableShellOpen();
    RegisterShellFileTypes();

// create a new (empty) document
    if (m_lpCmdLine[0] == '\0')
    {
        // create a new (empty) document
        TRACE("create a new empty document\n");
        OnFileNew();
    }
    else if ((m_lpCmdLine[0] == '-' || m_lpCmdLine[0] == '/') &&
            (m_lpCmdLine[1] == 'e' || m_lpCmdLine[1] == 'E'))
    {
        TRACE("program launched embedded\n");
        OnFileNew();
        // program launched embedded - wait for DDE or OLE open
    }
    else
    {
        TRACE("open an existing document - %s\n", m_lpCmdLine);
        // open an existing document
        OpenDocumentFile(m_lpCmdLine);
    }

    return TRUE;
}
```

3. **Use App Studio to edit the IDR_MAINFRAME string resource.** Choose String Table, and then select the IDR_MAINFRAME string. Add the following text to the end of the AppWizard-generated string:

```
\nEX17BFileType\nEx17B File Type
```

The resulting string should look like this:

```
EX17B Windows Application\nEx17b\nEX17B Document\nEX17B Files
(*.17b)\n.17b\nEX17BFileType\nEx17B File Type
```

4. Edit the main frame window *OnCreate* function in MAINFRM.CPP. Add the following line at the end of the *CMainFrame OnCreate* function, immediately before the return statement:

```
DragAcceptFiles();
```

When the frame window is created, the drag-and-drop capability is activated.

5. Build and test the resulting application. It's not interesting to test a do-nothing application, but you can create zero-length files and load them later. Run the program first from Visual Workbench to update the registration database. Save a file, exit the program, and then run File Manager. The newly saved file should show up in File Manager as a document icon, and you should be able to execute EX17B by double-clicking on the document icon. Drag and drop should work too.

18

Printing and Print Preview

If you're depending on the Windows SDK alone, printing is one of the tougher programming jobs you'll have. If you don't believe me, just skim through the 60-page chapter ("Using the Printer") in Charles Petzold's *Programming Windows*. Other books about Microsoft Windows ignore the subject completely. The Microsoft Foundation Class Library application framework goes a long way toward making printing easy. As a bonus, it adds a print preview capability that behaves like the print preview functions in commercial Windows-based programs such as Microsoft Word for Windows and Microsoft Excel.

In this chapter, you'll learn how to use the class library Print and Print Preview functions. In the process, you'll get a feeling for what's involved in Windows printing and how it's different from MS-DOS printing. First you'll do some wysiwyg printing, in which the printer output matches the screen display (except for the scale factor). This option requires careful use of Windows' mapping modes. Later you'll print a paginated data processing style report that doesn't reflect the screen display at all. In that example, you will learn how to structure your document so that the program can print any specified range of pages on demand.

Windows Printing

In the old days, programmers had to worry about configuring their applications for dozens of printers. Now Windows makes life easy because it provides all the printer drivers you'll ever need. It also supplies a consistent user interface for printing.

Standard Printer Dialogs

When the user chooses Print from the File menu of an application for Windows, the standard Print dialog appears, as shown in Figure 18-1 on the next page.

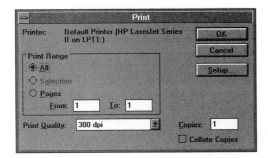

Figure 18-1.
The standard Print dialog.

If the user clicks the Setup button, the standard Print Setup dialog appears, as shown in Figure 18-2.

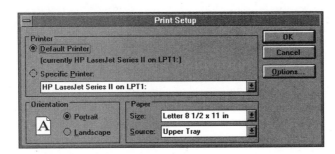

Figure 18-2.
The standard Print Setup dialog.

During the printing process, the application displays a standard status dialog, as shown in Figure 18-3.

Figure 18-3.
The standard printer status dialog.

Interactive Print Page Selection

If you've worked in the data processing field, you're used to batch-mode printing. A program reads a record and then formats and prints selected information as a line in a report. Every time, say, 50 lines have been printed, the program ejects the paper and prints a new page heading. The programmer assumes that the whole report will be printed at one time and makes no allowance for interactively printing selected pages.

As Figure 18-1 shows, page numbers are important in Windows-based printing. A program must respond to a user's page selection by calculating which information to print and then printing the selected pages. If you're aware of this page selection requirement, you can design your application's data structures accordingly.

Remember the student list from Chapter 16? What if there were 1000 students and the user wanted page 5 of a student report? If you assumed that each student record required one print line and that a page held 50 lines, page 5 would include records 201 through 250. With the *CObList* class, you're stuck iterating through the first 200 list elements before you can start printing. Maybe the list isn't the ideal data structure. How about an array instead? With the *CObArray* class, you can directly access the 201st student record.

Not every application has elements that map to a fixed number of print lines. Suppose the student record contained a multiline text biography field? Because you don't know how many biography lines each record has, you'd have to search through the whole file to determine the page breaks. If your program remembered those page breaks as it calculated them, its efficiency would increase.

Display Pages vs. Printed Pages

In many cases, you'll want a printed page to correspond to a display page. As you learned in Chapter 5, you cannot guarantee that objects will be printed exactly as they are displayed. With TrueType fonts, however, and some extra margin room, you can get pretty close. If you're working with full-size paper and you want the corresponding display to be readable, you'll certainly want a display window that's larger than the screen. Thus, the *CScrollView* class is ideal for your printable views.

Sometimes, however, you might not care about display pages. Perhaps your view holds its data in a list box, or maybe you don't need to display the data at all. In these cases, your program can contain stand-alone print logic that simply extracts data from the document and sends it to the printer. Of course, the program must properly respond to a user's page range request. If you query the printer to find out the paper size and portrait/landscape configuration, you can adjust the pagination accordingly.

Print Preview

The Microsoft Foundation Class Library version 2.0 Print Preview feature shows you on screen the <u>exact</u> page breaks and line breaks you'll get when you print your document on the selected printer. The fonts might look a little funny, especially in the smaller sizes, but it's not a problem. Look now at the print preview windows that appear on pages 336 and 337.

Print Preview is a class library feature, not a Windows feature. Don't underestimate how much effort went into programming Print Preview. The Print Preview program examines each character individually, determining its position based on the printer's device context. After selecting an approximating font, the program displays the character in the print preview window at the proper location.

Programming for the Printer

The application framework does most of the work for printing and print preview. To use the printer effectively, you must understand the sequence of function calls and know which functions to override.

The Printer Device Context and the *CView OnDraw* Function

When your program prints on the printer, it uses a device context object of class *CDC*. Don't worry about where the object comes from; the application framework constructs it and passes it as a parameter to your view's *OnDraw* function. If your application uses the printer to duplicate the display, the *OnDraw* function can do double duty. If you're displaying, *OnPaint* calls *OnDraw*, and the device context is the display context. If you're printing, *OnDraw* is called by another *CView* function, *OnPrint*, with a printer device context. The *OnPrint* function is called once to print an entire page.

In print preview mode, the *CDC* object is linked to another device context object of class *CPreviewDC*, but that linkage is transparent. Your *OnPrint* and *OnDraw* functions work the same regardless of whether you're printing or previewing.

The *CView OnPrint* Function

You know that *OnPrint* calls *OnDraw*, and that *OnDraw* can use both a display device context and a printer device context. The mapping mode should be set before *OnPrint* is called. You can override *OnPrint* to print items that you don't need on the display, such as a title page, headers, and footers. The *OnPrint* parameters are

- A pointer to the device context

- A pointer to a print information structure (*CPrintInfo*) that includes page dimensions, the current page number, and the maximum page number

In your overridden *OnPrint* function, you can elect not to call *OnDraw* at all to support print logic that is totally independent of the display logic. If you need distinct mapping modes for the display and the printer, you can call the *CDC SetMapMode* function to override the display mapping mode that was set earlier in *OnPrepareDC*.

The application framework calls the *OnPrint* function once for each page to be printed, with the current page number in the *CPrintInfo* structure. You're about to find out how the application framework determines the page number.

Preparing the Device Context— The *CView OnPrepareDC* Function

If you need a display mapping mode other than *MM_TEXT* (and you usually do), that mode is generally set in the view's *OnPrepareDC* function. You override this function yourself if your view class is derived directly from *CView*, but it's already overridden if your view is derived from *CScrollView*. The *OnPrepareDC* function is called in *OnPaint* immediately before the call to *OnDraw*. If you're printing, the same *OnPrepareDC* function is called, this time immediately before the application framework calls *OnPrint*. Thus, the mapping mode is set before both the painting of the view and the printing of a page.

If you do not know in advance how many pages your print job requires, your overridden *OnPrepareDC* function can detect the end of the document and reset the *m_bContinuePrinting* flag in the *CPrintInfo* structure. (A pointer to this structure is passed to *OnPrepareDC* as an argument.) When this flag is *FALSE*, the *OnPrint* function won't be called, and control will pass to the end of the print loop.

> *Tip:* *If your view class is derived from the* CScrollView *class and your* OnPrepareDC *function sets the* m_bContinuePrinting *flag, the base class* OnPrepareDC *function must be called <u>before</u> the flag is set.*

The Start and End of a Print Job

When a print job starts, the application framework calls two *CView* functions, *OnPreparePrinting* and *OnBeginPrinting*. The first function, *OnPreparePrinting*, is called before the display of the Print dialog. You must override this function to enable printing and print preview. (AppWizard generates the *OnPreparePrinting*, *OnBeginPrinting*, and *OnEndPrinting* functions for you if you select the Printing And Print Preview option.) If you know the minimum and maximum page numbers, call *SetMinPages* and *SetMaxPages* in *OnPreparePrinting*. The numbers you pass to these functions will appear in the Print dialog for the user to override.

The second function, *OnBeginPrinting*, is called after the Print dialog exits. Override this function to create Graphics Device Interface (GDI) objects, such as fonts, that you need for the entire print job. A program runs faster if you create a font once instead of creating it repetitively for each page.

The *CView* function *OnEndPrinting* is called at the end of the print job, after the last page has been printed. Override this function to get rid of GDI objects created in *OnBeginPrinting*.

Here's a summary of the important overridable *CView* print loop functions:

OnPreparePrinting	Sets minimum and maximum page numbers
OnBeginPrinting	Creates GDI objects
OnPrepareDC (for each page)	Sets mapping mode and optionally detects end of print job
OnPrint (for each page)	Does print-specific output and then calls *OnDraw*
OnEndPrinting	Deletes GDI objects

Example EX18A—A wysiwyg Print Program

This example displays and prints a single page of text stored in a document. The printed image is supposed to match the displayed image. In the first iteration, the program uses the *MM_TWIPS* mapping mode for both the printer and the display. Because the application uses a 10-point font, the text is too small to read on the display. The second iteration changes the display's mapping mode to *MM_HI-ENGLISH*, making the display text legible.

Here are the steps for building the example:

1. **Run AppWizard to produce \VCPP\EX18A\EX18A.** Choose AppWizard from Visual Workbench's Project menu. The options and the default class names are shown here:

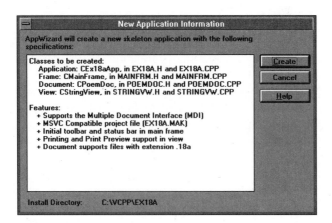

Be sure to accept the Printing And Print Preview default option. Name the document and view classes exactly as specified. You will be using them again in later chapters. Remember that we're accepting the MDI option this time.

2. **Change the *CStringView* base class from *CView* to *CScrollView*.** Globally replace *CView* with *CScrollView* in STRINGVW.H and STRINGVW.CPP.

3. **Add a WM_CREATE message handler for *CStringView*.** Use ClassWizard to add the skeleton function *OnCreate*.

4. **Edit the POEMDOC.H header file.** The document data is stored in a string array. You need not set a maximum dimension in the declaration because the array is dynamic. Add the following lines to the *CPoemDoc* class declaration:

```
public:
    CStringArray m_stringArray;
```

Also add a prototype for the virtual *DeleteContents* function:

```
virtual void DeleteContents();
```

5. **Edit three *CPoemDoc* member functions in file POEMDOC.CPP.** We'll initialize the poem document in the overridden *OnNewDocument* function. *Delete-Contents* is called in *CDocument::OnNewDocument*, so we're sure the poem won't be deleted. (The poem, by the way, is an excerpt from the twentieth poem in Lawrence Ferlinghetti's book *A Coney Island of the Mind*.) Type 10 lines of your choice. It could be another poem or maybe your favorite Windows function description.

```
BOOL CPoemDoc::OnNewDocument()
{
    if (!CDocument::OnNewDocument())
        return FALSE;

    m_stringArray.SetSize(10);
    m_stringArray[0] = "The pennycandystore beyond the El";
    m_stringArray[1] = "is where I first";
    m_stringArray[2] = "                    fell in love";
    m_stringArray[3] = "                        with unreality";
    m_stringArray[4] = "Jellybeans glowed in the semi-gloom";
    m_stringArray[5] = "of that september afternoon";
    m_stringArray[6] = "A cat upon the counter moved among";
    m_stringArray[7] = "                    the licorice sticks";
    m_stringArray[8] = "                    and tootsie rolls";
    m_stringArray[9] = "            and Oh Boy Gum";

    return TRUE;
}
```

(Note: The *CStringArray* class supports dynamic arrays, but here we're using the *m_stringArray* object as though it were a static array of 10 elements. You'll see arrays used more dynamically in examples EX21A and EX26B.)

The application framework calls the document's virtual *DeleteContents* function when it closes the document; this action deletes the strings in the array. A *CStringArray* contains actual objects, and a *CObArray* contains pointers to objects. This distinction is important when it is time to delete the array elements. Here the *RemoveAll* function actually deletes the string objects.

```
void CPoemDoc::DeleteContents()
{
    // called before OnNewDocument and when document is closed
    m_stringArray.RemoveAll();
}
```

Serialization isn't important in this example, but the following function illustrates how easy it is to serialize strings. The application framework calls the *DeleteContents* function before loading from the archive, so you don't have to worry about emptying the array.

```
void CPoemDoc::Serialize(CArchive& ar)
{
    m_stringArray.Serialize(ar);
}
```

6. **Edit the *OnCreate* function in STRINGVW.CPP.** You must override the *OnCreate* function for all classes derived from *CScrollView*. This function's job is to set the logical window size and the mapping mode.

```
int CStringView::OnCreate(LPCREATESTRUCT lpCreateStruct)
{
    if (CScrollView::OnCreate(lpCreateStruct) == -1)
        return -1;

    CSize totalSize = CSize(11520, 15120);       // 8" x 10.5"
    CSize pageSize = CSize(totalSize.cx / 2,
                           totalSize.cy / 2);    // for page scroll
    CSize lineSize = CSize(totalSize.cx / 100,
                           totalSize.cy / 100);  // line scroll
    SetScrollSizes(MM_TWIPS, totalSize, pageSize,
                   lineSize);                    // CScrollView function

    return 0;
}
```

7. **Edit the *OnDraw* function in STRINGVW.CPP.** The *OnDraw* function of class *CStringView* draws on both the display and the printer. In addition to displaying the poem text lines in 10-point roman font, it draws a border around the printable area together with a crude ruler along the top and left margins. The function assumes an HP LaserJet printer that has a printable area of 8 inches by 10.5 inches offset from the upper left corner of the paper. Also assumed is the *MM_TWIPS* mapping mode, in which 1 inch = 1440 units.

Note: *A more general function could call the Windows GetDeviceCaps function to retrieve the actual dimensions of the printable area, and then it could adjust the printed output accordingly.*

```
void CStringView::OnDraw(CDC* pDC)
{
    int       i, j, nHeight;
    char      temp[10];
    CFont     font;
    TEXTMETRIC tm;

    CPoemDoc* pDoc = GetDocument();
    // draw a border 8 x 10.5
    pDC->MoveTo(CPoint(0, 0));
    pDC->LineTo(CPoint(11505, 0));
    pDC->LineTo(CPoint(11505, -15105));
    pDC->LineTo(CPoint(0, -15105));
    pDC->LineTo(CPoint(0, 0));
    // draw horizontal and vertical rulers
    for (i = 0; i <= 8; i++) {
       wsprintf(temp, "%02d", i);
       pDC->TextOut(i * 1440, 0, temp);
    }
    for (i = 0; i <= 10; i++) {
       wsprintf(temp, "%02d", i);
       pDC->TextOut(0, -i * 1440, temp);
    }

    // print the poem 0.5 inch down and over
    // use 10-point roman font
    font.CreateFont(-200, 0, 0, 0, 400, FALSE, FALSE, 0, ANSI_CHARSET,
                    OUT_DEFAULT_PRECIS, CLIP_DEFAULT_PRECIS,
                    DEFAULT_QUALITY, DEFAULT_PITCH | FF_ROMAN,
                    "Times New Roman");
    CFont* pOldFont = (CFont*) pDC->SelectObject(&font);
    pDC->GetTextMetrics(&tm);
    nHeight = tm.tmHeight + tm.tmExternalLeading;
    TRACE("font height = %d, internal leading = %d\n",
          nHeight, tm.tmInternalLeading);
    j = pDoc->m_stringArray.GetSize();
    TRACE("array size = %d\n", j);
    for (i = 0; i < j; i++) {
       pDC->TextOut(720, -i * nHeight - 720, pDoc->m_stringArray[i]);
    }
    pDC->SelectObject(pOldFont);
}
```

8. **Edit the *OnPreparePrinting* function in STRINGVW.CPP.** This function sets the maximum number of pages in the print job. This example has only one page. It's absolutely necessary to call the base class *DoPreparePrinting* function in your overridden *OnPreparePrinting* function.

```
BOOL CStringView::OnPreparePrinting(CPrintInfo* pInfo)
{
    pInfo->SetMaxPage(1);
    return DoPreparePrinting(pInfo);
}
```

9. **Build and test the application.** When you start the EX18A application, your MDI child window should look like this:

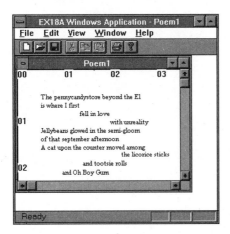

The window text is too small, isn't it? Go ahead and choose Print Preview from the File menu, and then use the magnifying glass to zoom in on the text at the upper left corner. The window should look like this:

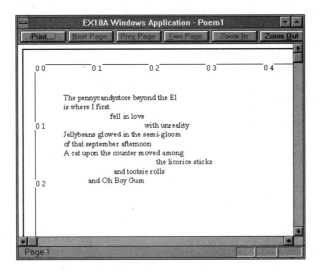

10. **Edit the STRINGVW.H header file.** Now we're going to override the *CString-View OnPrint* function to set a different mapping mode for the printer. Here's the prototype:

```
virtual void OnPrint(CDC* pDC, CPrintInfo* pInfo);
```

11. **Change the mapping mode in *OnCreate* in STRINGVW.CPP.** Previously, both the display and the printer used the *MM_TWIPS* mapping mode. Now we are going to change the view's mapping mode to *MM_HIENGLISH* to enlarge the text. Change the *SetScrollSizes* line in *CStringView OnCreate* as follows:

```
SetScrollSizes(MM_HIENGLISH, totalSize, pageSize, lineSize);
```

   Note: *We can't use the logical twips mapping mode in a* CScrollView *view. With the* MM_HIENGLISH *mode, the text comes out a little larger than we'd like, but it's better than having the text appear too small.*

12. **Insert the *OnPrint* function in STRINGVW.CPP.** The display's mapping mode is *MM_HIENGLISH*, but we still need *MM_TWIPS* for the printer. If we override *OnPrint*, we can set the printer's mapping mode before calling *OnDraw*:

```
void CStringView::OnPrint(CDC* pDC, CPrintInfo* pInfo)
{
    pDC->SetMapMode(MM_TWIPS);
    OnDraw(pDC);
}
```

13. **Build and test the application.** This time the text should be bigger—by a factor of 1.44, to be exact. Here's what the child window should look like now:

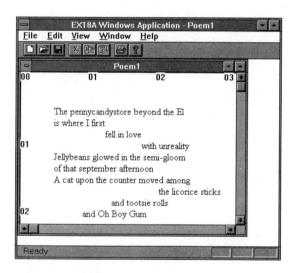

Example EX18B—A Multipage Print Program

In this example, the document contains an array of 50 *CRect* objects that define circles. The circles are randomly positioned in a 6-by-6-inch area and have random diameters of as much as 0.5 inch. The circles, when drawn on the display, look like two-dimensional simulations of soap bubbles. Instead of drawing the circles on the printer, the application prints the corresponding *CRect* coordinates in numeric form, 12 to a page with headers and footers.

1. **Run AppWizard to produce \VCPP\EX18B\EX18B.** Choose AppWizard from Visual Workbench's Project menu. The options and the default class names are shown here:

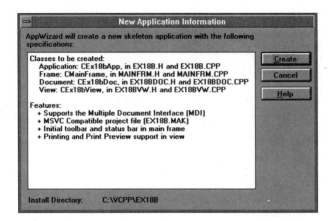

2. **Edit the EX18BDOC.H header file.** In the EX18A example, the document data consisted of strings stored in a *CStringArray* collection. Here we need an array of bounding rectangles for the circles. Because the *CRect* class is not derived from *CObject*, we can't use the *CObArray* class. We could use the TEMPLDEF program to generate a special array class for rectangles, but it's easier to use a normal fixed-size array, *m_ellipseArray*. That means, of course, that the document must contain a member variable, *m_nEllipseQty*, that tracks the array size. We'll also need a static member variable that specifies the number of printed lines (or records) per page. Here's the code that you'll need to add to the *CEx18bDoc* header file:

```
public:
    CRect  m_ellipseArray[50];
    int    m_nEllipseQty;
    static const int NEAR nLinesPerPage;
```

3. **Edit the EX18BDOC.CPP implementation file.** The document constructor initializes the ellipse array with some random values. This saves the trouble of writing serialization code. The static member variable, *nLinesPerPage*, needs to be initialized in the class implementation file.

```
CEx18bDoc::CEx18bDoc()
{
    int n1, n2, n3;
    // make 50 random circles
    srand((unsigned) time(NULL));
    m_nEllipseQty = 50;
```

```
for (int i = 0; i < m_nEllipseQty; i++) {
    n1 = (long) rand() * 600L / RAND_MAX;
    n2 = (long) rand() * 600L / RAND_MAX;
    n3 = (long) rand() * 50L / RAND_MAX;
    m_ellipseArray[i] = CRect(n1, -n2, n1 + n3, -(n2 + n3));
}
}
```

```
const int NEAR CEx18bDoc::nLinesPerPage = 12;
```

4. **Edit the EX18BVW.H header file.** The *m_nPage* data member holds the document's current page number for printing. The public function prototypes are for overrides of application framework functions, and the private function prototypes are for the header and footer subroutines.

```
public:
    UINT m_nPage;
public:
    virtual void OnPrint(CDC* pDC, CPrintInfo* pInfo);
protected:
    virtual void OnPrepareDC(CDC* pDC, CPrintInfo* pInfo = NULL);
private:
    void PrintPageHeader(CDC* pDC);
    void PrintPageFooter(CDC* pDC);
```

5. **Edit the *OnDraw* function in EX18BVW.CPP.** The overridden *OnDraw* function simply draws the bubbles in the view window:

```
void CEx18bView::OnDraw(CDC* pDC)
{
    int i, j;

    CEx18bDoc* pDoc = GetDocument();
    j = pDoc->m_nEllipseQty;
    for (i = 0; i < j; i++) {
        pDC->Ellipse(pDoc->m_ellipseArray[i]);
    }
}
```

6. **Insert the *OnPrepareDC* function in EX18BVW.CPP.** The view class is not a scrolling view, so the mapping mode must be set in this function.

```
void CEx18bView::OnPrepareDC(CDC* pDC, CPrintInfo* pInfo)
{
    pDC->SetMapMode(MM_LOENGLISH);
}
```

7. **Insert the *OnPrint* function in EX18BVW.CPP.** The *CView* default *OnPrint* function calls *OnDraw*. In this example, we want the printed output to be entirely different from the displayed output, so the *OnPrint* function must take care of the print output without calling *OnDraw*. *OnPrint* first sets the mapping mode to *MM_TWIPS* and then creates a fixed-pitch font. After printing

the numeric contents of 12 *m_ellipseArray* elements, it deselects the font. You could have created the font once in *OnBeginPrinting*, but you wouldn't have noticed the increase in efficiency.

```
void CEx18bView::OnPrint(CDC* pDC, CPrintInfo* pInfo)
{
    int i,      nStart, nEnd, nHeight;
    char        temp[133];
    CPoint      point(720, -1440);
    CFont       font;
    TEXTMETRIC tm;

    pDC->SetMapMode(MM_TWIPS);
    CEx18bDoc* pDoc = GetDocument();
    m_nPage = pInfo->m_nCurPage; // for PrintPageFooter's benefit
    nStart = (m_nPage - 1) * CEx18bDoc::nLinesPerPage;
    nEnd = nStart + CEx18bDoc::nLinesPerPage;
    // 14-point fixed-pitch font
    font.CreateFont(-280, 0, 0, 0, 400, FALSE, FALSE,
                    0, ANSI_CHARSET, OUT_DEFAULT_PRECIS,
                    CLIP_DEFAULT_PRECIS, DEFAULT_QUALITY,
                    DEFAULT_PITCH | FF_MODERN, "Courier New"); // TrueType
    CFont* pOldFont = (CFont*) (pDC->SelectObject(&font));
    PrintPageHeader(pDC);
    pDC->GetTextMetrics(&tm);
    nHeight = tm.tmHeight + tm.tmExternalLeading;
    for (i = nStart; i < nEnd; i++) {
      if (i >= pDoc->m_nEllipseQty)
        break;
      wsprintf(temp, "%6d %6d %6d %6d %6d", i + 1,
               pDoc->m_ellipseArray[i].left,
               pDoc->m_ellipseArray[i].top,
               pDoc->m_ellipseArray[i].right,
               pDoc->m_ellipseArray[i].bottom);
      point.y -= nHeight;
      pDC->TextOut(point.x, point.y, temp);
    }
    PrintPageFooter(pDC);
    pDC->SelectObject(pOldFont);
}
```

8. **Edit the *OnPreparePrinting* function in EX18BVW.CPP.** The *OnPreparePrinting* function computes the number of pages in the document and then communicates that value to the application framework through the *SetMaxPage* function.

```
BOOL CEx18bView::OnPreparePrinting(CPrintInfo* pInfo)
{
    CEx18bDoc* pDoc = GetDocument();
    pInfo->SetMaxPage(pDoc->m_nEllipseQty / CEx18bDoc::nLinesPerPage + 1);
    return DoPreparePrinting(pInfo);
}
```

9. **Insert the page header and footer functions in EX18BVW.CPP.** These private functions, called from *OnPrint*, print the page headers and the page footers. The page footer includes the page number, stored by *OnPrint* in the view class data member *m_nPage*. The *CDC GetTextExtent* function right-justifies the page number.

```
void CEx18bView::PrintPageHeader(CDC* pDC)
{
    char temp[133];

    CPoint point(0, 0);
    pDC->TextOut(point.x, point.y, "Bubble Report");
    point += CSize(720, -720);
    wsprintf(temp, "%6.6s %6.6s %6.6s %6.6s %6.6s",
            (LPCSTR) "Index", (LPCSTR) "Left", (LPCSTR) "Top",
            (LPCSTR) "Right", (LPCSTR) "Bottom");
    pDC->TextOut(point.x, point.y, temp);
}

void CEx18bView::PrintPageFooter(CDC* pDC)
{
    char temp[133];

    CPoint point(0, -14400); // 10" down
    CEx18bDoc* pDoc = GetDocument();
    wsprintf(temp, "Document %s",(LPCSTR) pDoc->GetTitle());
    pDC->TextOut(point.x, point.y, temp);
    wsprintf(temp, "Page %d", m_nPage);
    CSize size = pDC->GetTextExtent(temp, strlen(temp));
    point.x += 11520 - size.cx;
    pDC->TextOut(point.x, point.y, temp); // right-justified
}
```

10. **Build and test the application.** For one set of random numbers, the bubble child window looks like this:

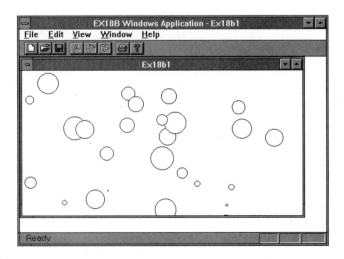

In Print Preview, the first page of the output should look like this:

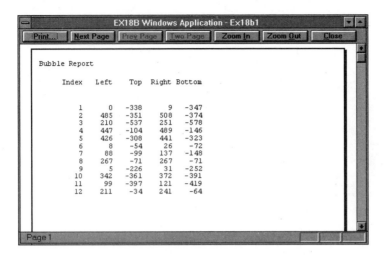

Exercises for the Reader

Pretend that the function *OnPreparePrinting* can't compute the number of pages to be printed. Instead, modify *OnPrepareDC* to reset the *m_bContinuePrinting* flag (in the *CPrintInfo* structure) when there are no more elements to print.

The printing examples in this chapter have assumed a standard 8-inch-by-10.5-inch printable area. The actual printable area depends on the installed printer driver, however. Some printers, such as the Hewlett-Packard LaserJet, can be switched between portrait and landscape mode. Try modifying the print examples to use the actual printable area dimensions stored in the *m_rectDraw* data member of the *CPrintInfo* structure. The rectangle is in logical coordinates as specified by *OnPrepareDC*, so you might have to do some mapping mode conversion.

19

Splitter Windows and Multiple Views

Up to now, you've seen only one view attached to a document. If you've used a Windows-based word processor, you know that it's convenient to have two windows open simultaneously on various parts of a document. Both windows might contain a normal view, or one window might contain a page layout view and another might contain an outline view.

The application framework has several ways to present multiple views—the splitter window and multiple MDI child windows. You'll learn about both presentation options here, and you'll see that in each it's easy to make multiple view objects of the same view class (the normal view). It's slightly more difficult, though, to use two or more view classes in the same application (say, the outline view and the page layout view).

This chapter emphasizes the selection and presentation of multiple views. The examples depend on a document with data initialized in the *OnNewDocument* function. Look back to Chapter 15 for a review of document–view communication, and look ahead to Chapter 21 for a multiview example that exercises the full suite of application framework features.

The Splitter Window

A splitter window appears as a special type of frame window that holds several views in panes. The application can split the window on creation, or the user can split the window by choosing a menu command or by dragging a splitter box in the splitter window's scroll bar. After the window is split, the user can move the "sashes," or boundaries, with the mouse to adjust the relative sizes of the panes. Splitter windows can be used in both SDI and MDI applications. You can see illustrations of splitter windows in the sections ahead, on pages 346 and 349.

The splitter window is represented by the class *CSplitterWnd*. As far as Windows is concerned, a *CSplitterWnd* object is an actual window that fully occupies the frame window (*CFrameWnd* or *CMDIChildWnd*) client area. The view windows occupy the splitter window pane areas. The splitter window does not take part in the command dispatch mechanism. The active view window (in the splitter pane) is logically connected directly to its frame window.

Multiple View Options

When you combine multiview presentation methods with application models, you get a number of permutations. Here are some of them:

- **SDI application with splitter window, single view class**—This chapter's first example, EX19A, covers this case. Each splitter window pane can be scrolled to a different part of the document. The programmer determines the maximum number of horizontal and vertical panes; the user makes the split at runtime.

- **SDI application with splitter window, multiple view classes**—The EX19B example illustrates this case. The programmer determines the number of panes and the sequence of views; the user can change the pane size at runtime.

- **MDI application with no splitter windows, single view class**—This is the standard MDI application you've seen already. The New Window menu item lets the user open a new child window for a document that's open already.

- **MDI application with no splitter windows, multiple view classes**—A small change to the standard MDI application allows the use of multiple views. As example EX19C shows, all that's necessary is replacing the New Window menu item with menu items and functions for each of the available view classes.

- **MDI application with splitter child windows**—This case is covered thoroughly in the *Class Library User's Guide*. The SCRIBBLE example illustrates the splitting of an MDI child window.

Dynamic and Static Splitter Windows

A dynamic splitter window allows the user to split the window at any time either by choosing a menu item or by dragging a splitter box located on the scroll bar. The panes in a dynamic splitter window generally use the same view class. The top left pane is initialized to a particular view when the splitter is created. In a dynamic splitter window, scroll bars are shared among the views. In a window with a single horizontal split, for example, the bottom scroll bar controls both views.

The panes of a static splitter window are defined when the window is first created, and they cannot be changed. The user can move the sashes but cannot unsplit or resplit the window. Static splitter windows can accommodate multiple view classes, with the configuration set at creation time. In a static splitter window, each pane has separate scroll bars.

EX19A—A Single View Class SDI Dynamic Splitter Example

In this example, the user can dynamically split the view into four panes. A four-way split produces four separate view objects, all managed by a single view class. We'll use the document and the view code from EX18A. The application class is standard AppWizard issue, but the main frame window class code has been modified.

CMainFrame

The application's main frame window class needs a splitter window data member and a prototype for an overridden *OnCreateClient* function. The following code has been added to the AppWizard-generated *CMainFrame* class declaration in MAINFRM.H:

```
protected:
    CSplitterWnd m_wndSplitter;
protected:
    virtual BOOL OnCreateClient(LPCREATESTRUCT lpcs,
                                CCreateContext* pContext);
```

The application framework calls the *CFrameWnd OnCreateClient* virtual member function when the frame object is created. The base class version creates a single view window as specified by the document template. The overridden *OnCreate-Client* version here (in MAINFRM.CPP) creates a splitter window instead, and the splitter window creates the first view.

```
BOOL CMainFrame::OnCreateClient(LPCREATESTRUCT lpcs,
                                CCreateContext* pContext)
{
    return m_wndSplitter.Create(this, 2, 2, CSize(1, 1), pContext);
}
```

The *CSplitterWnd Create* member function makes a dynamic splitter window. The *CSplitterWnd* object knows the view class because its name is embedded in the *CCreateContext* structure that's passed as a parameter to *Create*.

The second and third *Create* parameters (*2, 2*) specify that the window can be split into a maximum of two rows and two columns. The *CSize* parameter specifies the minimum pane size.

Resource Requirements

EX19A has an added Window main menu item and a pop-up menu with a Split item, as shown in Figure 19-1 on the next page. The menu command ID is *ID_ WINDOW_- SPLIT*. The application framework recognizes this constant; its handler initiates the window-splitting action.

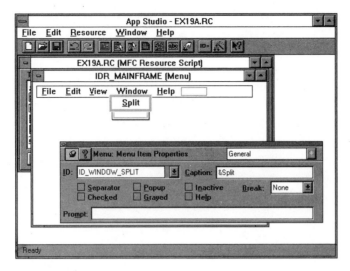

Figure 19-1.
The EX19A Window menu.

Testing the EX19A Application

When the application starts, you can split the window by choosing Split from the Window menu or by dragging the splitter boxes at the left and top of the scroll bars. Figure 19-2 shows a typical single view window with a four-way split.

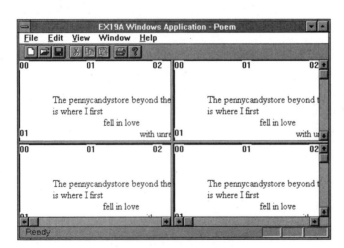

Figure 19-2.
A single view window with a four-way split.

Multiple views share the scroll bars.

EX19B—A Double View Class
SDI Static Splitter Example

In EX19B, we'll extend EX19A by defining a second view class and allowing a static splitter window to show the two views. (The H and CPP files are cloned from the original view class.) This time the splitter window works a little differently. Instead of starting off as a single pane, the splitter is initialized with two panes. The user can move the sash with the splitter box on the right scroll bar or with the Window Split menu item.

CHexView

The *CHexView* class is essentially the same as *CStringView* except for the *OnDraw* member function:

```
void CHexView::OnDraw(CDC* pDC)
{
    // hex dump of document strings
    int        i, j, k, l, nHeight;
    long       n;
    char       temp[10];
    CString    outputLine;
    TEXTMETRIC tm;
    CFont      font;

    CPoemDoc* pDoc = GetDocument();
    font.CreateFont(-160, 80, 0, 0, 400, FALSE, FALSE, 0, ANSI_CHARSET,
                    OUT_DEFAULT_PRECIS, CLIP_DEFAULT_PRECIS, DEFAULT_QUALITY,
                    DEFAULT_PITCH | FF_SWISS, "Arial");
    CFont* pOldFont = (CFont*) pDC->SelectObject(&font);
    pDC->GetTextMetrics(&tm);
    nHeight = tm.tmHeight + tm.tmExternalLeading;

    j = pDoc->m_stringArray.GetSize();
    for (i = 0; i < j; i++) {
        wsprintf(temp, "%02x   ", i);
        outputLine = temp;
        l = pDoc->m_stringArray[i].GetLength();
        for (k = 0; k < l; k++) {
            n = pDoc->m_stringArray[i][k] & 0x00ff;
            wsprintf(temp, "%02lx ", n);
            outputLine += temp;
        }
        pDC->TextOut(720, -i * nHeight - 720, outputLine);
    }
    pDC->SelectObject(pOldFont);
}
```

This function displays a hexadecimal dump of all strings in the document's *m_stringArray* collection. Notice the use of the subscript operator to access individual characters in a *CString* object.

CMainFrame

As in the previous example, the application's main frame window class needs a splitter window data member and a prototype for an overridden *OnCreateClient* function. The following code has been added to the AppWizard-generated *CMainFrame* class declaration file MAINFRM.H:

```
protected:
    CSplitterWnd m_wndSplitter;
protected:
    virtual BOOL OnCreateClient(LPCREATESTRUCT lpcs,
                                CCreateContext* pContext);
```

The implementation file, MAINFRM.CPP, needs both view class headers (and the prerequisite document header):

```
#include "poemdoc.h"
#include "stringvw.h"
#include "hexvw.h"
```

The overridden *OnCreateClient* function creates the splitter window as it did in EX19A, but this time it calls the *CSplitterWnd CreateStatic* function, which is tailored for multiple view classes. The following calls to *CSplitterWnd CreateView* attach the two view classes. As the second two *CreateStatic* parameters (*2, 1*) dictate, this splitter window contains only two panes, with an initial horizontal split 100 device units from the top of the window. The top pane is the string view; the bottom pane is the hex dump view. The user can change the splitter sash position but cannot change the view configuration.

```
BOOL CMainFrame::OnCreateClient(LPCREATESTRUCT lpcs,
                                CCreateContext* pContext)
{
    BOOL rtn = m_wndSplitter.CreateStatic(this, 2, 1);
    rtn |= m_wndSplitter.CreateView(0, 0, RUNTIME_CLASS(CStringView),
                                    CSize(100, 100), pContext);
    rtn |= m_wndSplitter.CreateView(1, 0, RUNTIME_CLASS(CHexView),
                                    CSize(100, 100), pContext);
    return rtn;
}
```

Testing the EX19B Application

When you start the EX19B application, the window should look like the one at the top of the next page:

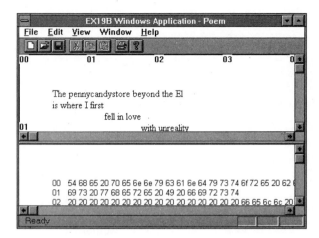

Notice the separate horizontal scroll bars for the two views.

EX19C—A Multiple View Class MDI Example

The final example, EX19C, uses the previous document and view classes to create a multiple view class MDI application without a splitter window. The logic is different from the logic in the other multiple view class application, EX19B. This time the action takes place in the application class rather than in the main frame class. As you study EX19C, you'll gain some more insight into the use of *CDocTemplate* objects.

This example was generated with the AppWizard Context Sensitive Help option. In Chapter 20, you'll be activating the context-sensitive help capability.

CEx19cApp

In the application class header file, EX19C.H, the following data members and function prototype have been added:

```
public:
    CMultiDocTemplate* m_pTemplate1;
    CMultiDocTemplate* m_pTemplate2;
    int ExitInstance();
```

The implementation file, EX19C.CPP, contains the following *#include* statements:

```
#include "poemdoc.h"
#include "stringvw.h"
#include "hexvw.h"
```

The *CEx19cApp InitInstance* member function has the following code inserted immediately after the *AddDocTemplate* function call:

```
m_pTemplate1 = new CMultiDocTemplate(IDR_POEMTYPE,
        RUNTIME_CLASS(CPoemDoc),
        RUNTIME_CLASS(CMDIChildWnd),
        RUNTIME_CLASS(CStringView));

m_pTemplate2 = new CMultiDocTemplate(IDR_POEMTYPE,
        RUNTIME_CLASS(CPoemDoc),
        RUNTIME_CLASS(CMDIChildWnd),
        RUNTIME_CLASS(CHexView));
```

The *AddDocTemplate* call generated by AppWizard established the primary document/frame/view combination for the application that is effective when the program starts. The two template objects above are secondary templates that can be activated in response to menu items.

Now all you need is an *ExitInstance* member function that cleans up the secondary templates:

```
int CEx19cApp::ExitInstance()
{
    delete m_pTemplate1;
    delete m_pTemplate2;
    return CWinApp::ExitInstance(); // saves profile settings
}
```

CMainFrame

The main frame class implementation file, MAINFRM.CPP, has both view class headers (and the prerequisite document header) included:

```
#include "poemdoc.h"
#include "stringvw.h"
#include "hexvw.h"
```

The base frame window class, *CMDIChildWnd*, has an *OnWindowNew* function that is normally connected to the standard Window New menu item. The following two command-handling functions are clones of *OnWindowNew*, adapted for the two view-specific templates that are defined in *InitInstance*. They create new child windows based on the specified view class.

```
void CMainFrame::OnWindowNew1() // ordinary text view
{
    CMDIChildWnd* pActiveChild = MDIGetActive();
    CDocument* pDocument;
    if (pActiveChild == NULL ||
        (pDocument = pActiveChild->GetActiveDocument()) == NULL)
    {
```

```
        TRACE0("Warning: No active document for WindowNew command\n");
        AfxMessageBox(AFX_IDP_COMMAND_FAILURE);
        return;          // command failed
    }

    // otherwise we have a new frame !
    CDocTemplate* pTemplate = ((CEx19cApp*) AfxGetApp())->m_pTemplate1;
    ASSERT_VALID(pTemplate);
    CFrameWnd* pFrame = pTemplate->CreateNewFrame(pDocument,
                                                  pActiveChild);
    if (pFrame == NULL)
    {
        TRACE0("Warning: failed to create new frame\n");
        AfxMessageBox(AFX_IDP_COMMAND_FAILURE);
        return;          // command failed
    }

    pTemplate->InitialUpdateFrame(pFrame, pDocument);
}

void CMainFrame::OnWindowNew2() // hex dump view
{
    CMDIChildWnd* pActiveChild = MDIGetActive();
    CDocument* pDocument;
    if (pActiveChild == NULL ||
        (pDocument = pActiveChild->GetActiveDocument()) == NULL)
    {
        TRACE0("Warning: No active document for WindowNew command\n");
        AfxMessageBox(AFX_IDP_COMMAND_FAILURE);
        return;          // command failed
    }

    // otherwise we have a new frame !
    CDocTemplate* pTemplate = ((CEx19cApp*) AfxGetApp())->m_pTemplate2;
    ASSERT_VALID(pTemplate);
    CFrameWnd* pFrame = pTemplate->CreateNewFrame(pDocument,
                                                  pActiveChild);
    if (pFrame == NULL)
    {
        TRACE0("Warning: failed to create new frame\n");
        AfxMessageBox(AFX_IDP_COMMAND_FAILURE);
        return;          // command failed
    }

    pTemplate->InitialUpdateFrame(pFrame, pDocument);
}
```

The function cloning above is a useful class library programming technique. You first find a base class function that does almost what you want, and then you copy it from the \MSVC\MFC\SRC subdirectory into your derived class, changing it as required. The only danger is that subsequent versions of the class library will implement the original function differently.

Resource Requirements

The following two items have been added to the Window menu identified by *IDR_POEMTYPE*:

Menu Item	Command ID	Function
New &String Window	*ID_WINDOW_NEW1*	*OnWindowNew1* (replaces New Window item)
New &Hex Window	*ID_WINDOW_NEW2*	*OnWindowNew2*

ClassWizard was used to add the command-handling functions to the *CMainFrame* class.

Testing the EX19C Application

When you start the EX19C application, a text view child window appears. Choose New Hex Window from the Window menu. The application should look like this:

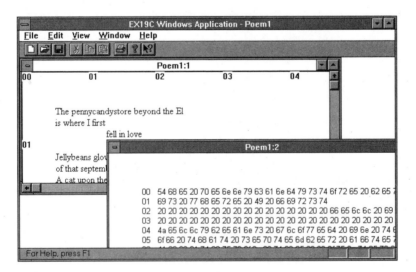

20

Context-Sensitive Help

Most commercial Windows-based programs, including Visual Workbench, take advantage of the powerful WINHELP help engine that's included with Windows. The Microsoft Foundation Class Library version 2.0 application framework allows you to use this same help engine for context-sensitive help in your own applications. This chapter first shows you how to construct and process a simple stand-alone help file that has a table of contents and allows the user to jump between topics. Next, you'll see how your class library program activates WINHELP with help context IDs that are derived from window and command IDs that are keyed to an AppWizard-generated help file. Finally, you'll learn how to modify the class library help message-handling system to customize the help capability.

> **Note:** *This chapter relies on the Microsoft Help Compiler, which is available only with the Professional Edition of Visual C++.*

The Windows WINHELP Program

If you've used commercial Windows-based applications, you've probably marveled at their sophisticated help screens with graphics, hyperlinks, and popups. At some software firms, including Microsoft, help authoring has been elevated to a profession in its own right. This section can't turn you into a help expert, but it can get you started by showing you how to prepare a simple no-frills help file.

Rich Text Format (RTF)

The Windows SDK documentation shows you how to format help files with an ASCII file format called Rich Text Format (RTF). We'll be using Rich Text Format too, but we'll be working in wysiwyg mode, thereby avoiding the direct use of awkward ASCII codes. You write with the same fonts, sizes, and styles that your user sees on the help screens. You'll definitely need a word processor that handles RTF. I've used Microsoft Word for Windows for this book, but many other word processors accommodate the RTF format.

(Note: Several commercial Windows help tools are available, including RoboHELP from Blue Sky Software and The Windows Help Magician from Software Interphase. These products are easier to use than an ordinary word processor and can thus reduce the effort needed to produce help files. Some of these products are templates for Word for Windows; others are stand-alone programs.)

Writing a Simple Help File

We're going to write a simple help file with a table of contents and three topics. This help file is designed to be run directly from WINHELP, started from the Windows Program Manager. No C++ programming is involved. Here are the steps:

1. Create a \VCPP\EX20A subdirectory.

2. Write the main help text file. Use Microsoft Word for Windows (or another RTF-compatible word processor) to type text as shown here:

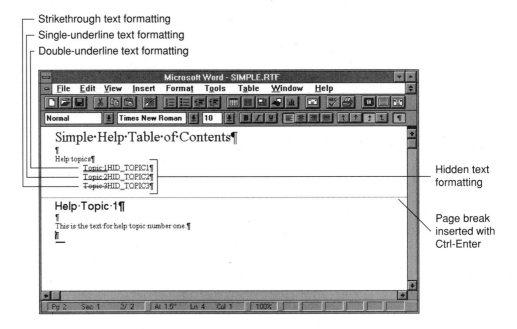

Be sure to apply the double-underline and hidden formats correctly and to insert the page break at the right place.

3. Insert footnotes for the Table of Contents screen. The Table of Contents screen is the first topic screen in this help system. Turn on the word processor's footnote view, and then insert the following footnotes at the beginning of the topic title, using the specified custom footnote marks:

Footnote Mark	Text	Description
#	HID_CONTENTS	Help context ID
$	SIMPLE Help Contents	Topic title

When you're finished with this step, the document should look like this:

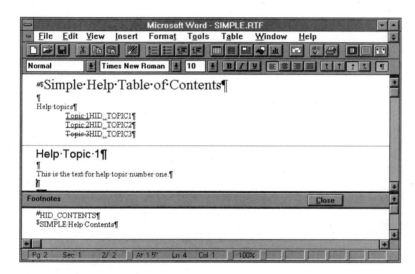

4. **Insert footnotes for the Topic 1 screen.** The Topic 1 screen is the second topic screen in the help system. Insert the following footnotes, using the specified custom footnote marks:

Footnote Mark	Text	Description
#	HID_TOPIC1	Help context ID
$	SIMPLE Help Topic 1	Topic title
K	SIMPLE Topics	Keyword text

5. **Clone the Topic 1 screen.** Copy the entire Topic 1 section of the document, including the page break, to the clipboard, and then paste two copies of the text into the document. The footnotes are copied along with the text. In the first copy, change all occurrences of *1* to *2*. In the second copy, change all occurrences of *1* to *3*. Don't forget to change the footnotes. With Word for Windows, it's a little difficult to see which footnote goes with which topic, so be careful. When you're finished with this step, the document text should look like that shown at the top of the next page:

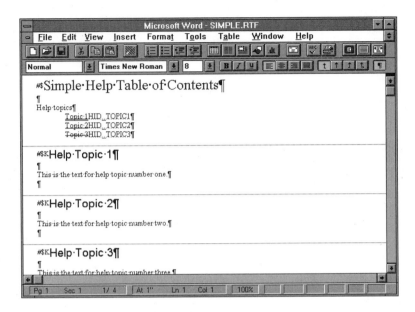

The footnotes should look like this:

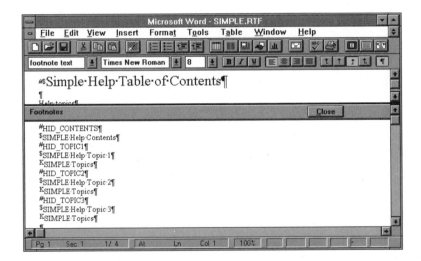

6. **Save the document.** Save the document as \VCPP\EX20A\SIMPLE.RTF. Specify Rich Text Format as the file type.

7. **Write a help project file.** Using your word processor, create a file named \VCPP\EX20A\SIMPLE.HPJ, as follows:

```
[OPTIONS]
CONTENTS=HID_CONTENTS
TITLE=SIMPLE Application Help
```

```
COMPRESS=true
WARNING=2

[FILES]
simple.rtf
```

This file specifies the context ID of the Table of Contents screen and the name of the RTF file that contains the help text. Be sure to save the file in text (ASCII) format.

8. **Build the help file.** At the MS-DOS command prompt, type the following MS-DOS commands:

```
cd \vcpp\ex20a
hc31 simple.hpj
```

This step runs the Windows Help Compiler with the project file SIMPLE.HPJ. The output is the help file SIMPLE.HLP. This example assumes that the \MSVC\BIN subdirectory is in your computer's search path. Use the MSVCVARS.BAT batch file in \MSV\BIN to set your computer's search path.

9. **Run WINHELP with the new help file.** From the Windows Program Manager, run WINHELP and then open the file \VCPP\EX20A\SIMPLE.HLP. The Table of Contents screen should look like this:

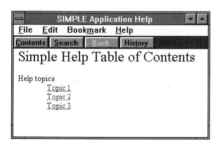

Now move the mouse cursor to Topic 1, and notice that the mouse cursor changes from an arrow to a pointing hand. When you press the left mouse button, the Topic 1 screen should appear as shown here:

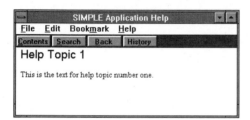

The *HID_TOPIC1* text in the Table of Contents screen links to the corresponding context ID (the # footnote) in the topic page. This link is known as a "jump."

The link to Topic 2 is coded as a pop-up jump. When you click on Topic 2, here's what you see:

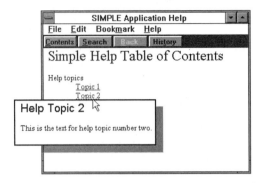

10. **Try the WINHELP Contents pushbutton.** Clicking this button should take you to the Table of Contents screen, as shown in step 9. WINHELP knows the ID of the Table of Contents screen because you specified it in the HPJ file.

11. **Try the WINHELP Search pushbutton.** When you click the Search button, WINHELP opens Help's Search dialog, which displays the Help file's list of keywords. In SIMPLE.HLP, all topics (excluding the table of contents) have the same keyword (the K footnotes), SIMPLE Topics. When you double-click on this keyword, you see all associated topic titles (the $ footnotes), as shown here:

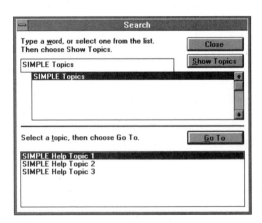

What you have here is a two-level search hierarchy. The user can type the first few letters of the keyword and then select a topic from a list box. The more carefully you select your keywords and topic titles, the more effective your help system will be.

The Application Framework and WINHELP

You've seen WINHELP running as a stand-alone program. The application framework and WINHELP cooperate to give you context-sensitive help. Here's a summary of how this works:

1. You select the Context Sensitive Help option when you run AppWizard.

2. AppWizard generates Contents and Search items on your application's Help menu, and it creates one or more generic RTF files together with an HPJ file and a batch file that runs the Help Compiler.

3. AppWizard inserts a keyboard accelerator for the F1 key, and it maps the F1 key and the Help menu items to *CWinApp* member functions.

4. When your program runs, it calls WINHELP when the user presses F1 or chooses an item from the Help menu, passing a context ID that determines which help topic is displayed.

You now need to understand how WINHELP is called from another application and how your application generates context IDs for WINHELP.

Calling WINHELP

The *CWinApp* member function *WinHelp* activates WINHELP from within your application. If you look up *WinHelp* in the *Class Library Reference,* you'll see a long list of actions that the optional second parameter controls. Ignore the second parameter and pretend that *WinHelp* has only one unsigned long integer parameter, *dwData*. This parameter corresponds to a help topic. Suppose that the SIMPLE help file is available and that your program contains the statement

```
AfxGetApp()->WinHelp(HID_TOPIC1);
```

When the statement is executed, in response to the F1 key or some other event, the Topic 1 Help screen comes up, as it would if the user had clicked on Topic 1 in the Help Table of Contents screen.

"Wait a minute," you say. "How does WINHELP know what help file to use?" The name of the help file matches the application name. If the executable program name is SIMPLE.EXE, the help file is named SIMPLE.HLP.

> **Note:** *You can force WinHelp to use a different Help file by setting the CWinApp data member m_pszHelpFilePath.*

"And how does WINHELP match the program constant *HID_TOPIC1* to the help file's context ID?" you ask. The Help project file must contain a MAP section that maps context IDs to numbers. If your application's RESOURCE.H file defines *HID_TOPIC1* as 101, the SIMPLE.HPJ MAP section looks like this:

```
[MAP]
HID_TOPIC1        101
```

The program's *#define* constant name doesn't have to match the help context ID; only the numbers must match. Making the names correspond, however, is good practice.

Using Search Strings

For a text-based application, you might need help based on a keyword rather than a numeric context ID. In that case, use the WinHelp *HELP_KEY* or *HELP_PARTIALKEY* option as follows:

```
CString string("find this string");
AfxGetApp()->WinHelp((DWORD) (LPCSTR) string, HELP_KEY);
```

The double cast for *string* is necessary because the first *WinHelp* parameter is multi-purpose; its meaning depends on the value of the second parameter.

Help Context Aliases

The ALIAS section of the HPJ file allows you to equate one context ID to another. Suppose your HPJ file contained the following statements:

```
[ALIAS]
HID_TOPIC1 = HID_GETTING_STARTED

[MAP]
HID_TOPIC1        101
```

Your *RTF* files could use *HID_TOPIC1* and *HID_GETTING_STARTED* interchangeably. Both would be mapped to the help context 101 as generated by your application.

Determining the Help Context

You now have enough information to add a simple context-sensitive help system to the class library program. You define F1 (the standard class library Help key) as a keyboard accelerator, and then you write a command handler that maps the program's help context to a *WinHelp* parameter. You could invent your own method for mapping the program state to a context ID, but why not take advantage of the system that's already built into the application framework?

The application framework determines the help context based on the ID of the active program element. These identified program elements include menu commands, frame windows, dialog windows, message boxes, and control bars. A menu item might be identified as *ID_EDIT_CLEAR_ALL*, for example, and the main frame window usually has the identifier *IDR_MAINFRAME*. You might expect these identifiers to map directly to help contexts. *IDR_MAINFRAME*, for example, would map to a help context of the same name. But what if a frame ID and a command ID had the same numeric value? Obviously, you need a way to prevent these overlaps.

The application framework solves the overlap problem by defining a new set of help *#define* constants that are derived from program element IDs. These help constants are the sum of the element ID and a base value as follows:

Program Element	Element ID Prefix	Help Context ID Prefix	Base (Hexadecimal)
Menu item	*ID_*	*HID_*	10000
Frame or dialog	*IDR_, IDD_*	*HIDR_, HIDD_*	20000
Error message box	*IDP_*	*HIDP_*	30000
Nonclient areas	Other	*H....*	40000
Control bar	*IDW_*	*HIDW_*	50000

HID_EDIT_CLEAR_ALL (0x1E121) corresponds to *ID_EDIT_CLEAR_ALL* (0xE121), and *HIDR_MAINFRAME* (0x20002) corresponds to *IDR_MAINFRAME* (2).

Menu Access to Help

If you've checked the AppWizard Context Sensitive Help option, your application will have an Index item on its Help menu. This item brings up the Help Table of Contents screen, and the user can navigate the help file through jumps and searches.

F1 Help

Two separate context-sensitive help access methods are built into a class library application and are available if you've checked the AppWizard Context Sensitive Help option. The first is standard F1 help. The user presses F1; the program makes its best guess about the help context and then calls WINHELP. In this mode, it is possible to determine the menu item currently selected with the keyboard or the currently selected window (frame, view, dialog, or message box).

Shift-F1 Help

This second context-sensitive help mode is more powerful than the F1 mode. With Shift-F1 help, the program can identify the following help contexts:

■ A menu item selected with the mouse cursor

■ A toolbar button

■ A frame window

■ A view window

■ A specific graphics element within a view window

■ The status bar

■ Various nonclient elements such as the system menu control

The user activates Shift-F1 help by pressing Shift-F1 or by clicking the Context Help toolbar button shown here:

In either case, the mouse cursor changes to

On the next mouse click, the help topic appears, with the position of the mouse cursor determining the context.

Shift-F1 help doesn't work with modal dialogs or message boxes.

Message Box Help—The *AfxMessageBox* Function

The global function *AfxMessageBox* displays application framework error messages. This function is similar to the *CWnd MessageBox* member function except that it has a prompt ID as a parameter. The application framework maps this prompt ID to a help context ID and then calls WINHELP when the user presses F1. You can use *AfxMessageBox* for your own messages if you use prompt IDs that begin with *IDP_*. In your RTF file, use help contexts that begin with *HIDP_*.

There are two versions of *AfxMessageBox*. In the first version, the prompt string is specified by a pointer to a character-array parameter. In the second version, the prompt ID parameter specifies a string resource. If you use the second version, your executable program will be more efficient. Both *AfxMessageBox* versions take a style parameter that makes the message box display an exclamation point, a question mark, or another graphics symbol.

Generic Help

When context-sensitive help is enabled, AppWizard assembles a series of default help topics that are associated with standard class library program elements. Following are some of the standard topics:

- Menu and toolbar commands (File, Edit, and so forth)

- Nonclient window elements (maximize box, caption bar, and so forth)

- Status bar

- Error message boxes

These topics are contained in the files AFXCORE.RTF and AFXPRINT.RTF, which are contained, along with associated bitmap files, in the application's HLP subdirectory. Your job is to customize the generic help files.

Note: *AppWizard generates AFXPRINT.RTF only if you specify the Printing And Print Preview option.*

A Help Example—No Programming Required

If you followed the instructions for EX19C in Chapter 19, you selected the AppWizard Context Sensitive Help option. We'll now return to that example and explore the application framework's built-in help capability. You'll see how easy it is to link help topics to menu command IDs and frame window resource IDs. You edit RTF files, not CPP files.

Here are the steps for customizing the help for EX19C:

1. **From the EX19C project directory, run MAKEHELP.** At the MS-DOS prompt, type the following commands:

```
CD \VCPP\EX19C
MAKEHELP
```

The MAKEHELP batch file builds the application's ready-to-use HLP file from components located mostly in the project's HLP subdirectory. Be sure the \MSVC\BIN subdirectory is in your computer's search path. The project should also be on the same hard drive as Visual C++. (Some of the commands in the MAKEHELP batch file assume this.)

2. **Test the generic help file.** Run the EX19C application. Try the following experiments:

☐ Move the mouse cursor into the application's main frame window, and then press F1. You should see the generic Application Help screen as shown:

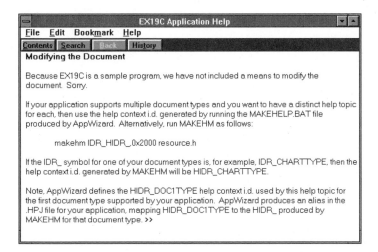

363

☐ Close the Help dialog and then press Alt-F, F1. This should bring up the Help topic for the File New command.

☐ Close the Help dialog, click the Context Help toolbar button (shown on page 362), and then choose Save from the File menu. Do you get the appropriate Help topic?

☐ Click the Context Help toolbar button again, and then select the frame window's title bar. You should get an explanation of a Windows title bar.

☐ Choose New from the EX19C File menu. Select the Poem document frame, and then press F1. You should see a generic Application Help screen with the title Modifying The Document.

3. **Change the application title.** The file AFXCORE.RTF, in the \VCPP\EX19C-\HLP directory, contains the string *<<YourApp>>* throughout. Replace it globally with *EX19C*.

4. **Change the Modifying The Document help screen.** The AFXCORE.RTF file in the \VCPP\EX19C\HLP subdirectory contains text for the generic Application Help screen. Search for Modifying The Document, and then change the text to something appropriate for the application. This topic has the help context ID *HIDR_DOC1TYPE*. The EX19C.HPJ file provides the alias *HIDR_POEMTYPE*.

5. **Add a topic for the Window New String Window menu item.** The New String Window menu item was added to EX19C and thus didn't have associated help text. Add a topic to AFXCORE.RTF, as shown here:

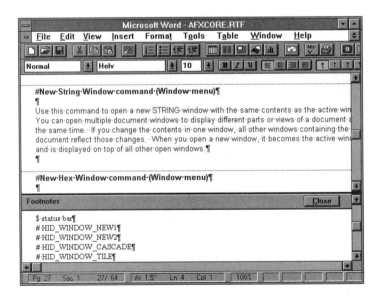

Notice the # footnote that links the topic to the context ID *HID_WIN-DOW_NEW1* as defined in HLP\EX19C.HM. The program's command ID for the New String Window menu item is, of course, *ID_WINDOW_NEW1*.

6. Rebuild the help file and test the application. Run the MAKEHELP batch file again, and then rerun the EX19C program. Try the two new help links.

The MAKEHELP Process

The process of building the application's HLP file is complex. Part of the complexity results from the Help Compiler's nonacceptance of statements such as

```
HID_MAINFRAME = ID_MAINFRAME + 0x20000
```

Because of this nonacceptance, a special preprocessing program, MAKEHM.EXE, must read the RESOURCE.H file to produce a help map file that defines the help context values. Here's a diagram of the entire MAKEHELP process:

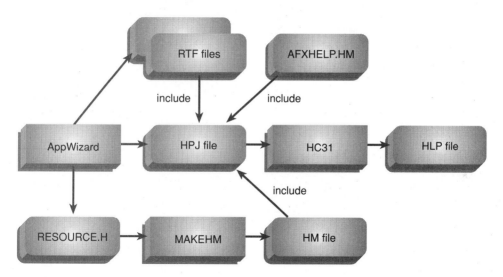

AppWizard generates the application's Help project file (HPJ). Its FILES section brings in the RTF files, and its MAP section contains *#include* statements for both the generic and the application-specific help map (HM) files. The Help Compiler, HC31, processes the project file to produce the help file that WINHELP reads.

Help Command Processing

You've seen the components of a help file, and you've seen the effects of F1 and Shift-F1. You know how the application element IDs are linked to help context IDs. What you haven't seen is the application framework's internal processing of the help requests. Why should you be concerned? Suppose you want to provide help on a specific view window instead of a frame window. What if you need help topics linked to specific graphics items in a view window? These and other needs can be met only by overriding the Help command processing functions.

Help command processing is different because it depends on whether the help request was an F1 request or a Shift-F1 request. The processing of each help request will be described separately.

F1 Processing

The F1 key is normally handled by a keyboard accelerator entry that AppWizard inserts in the RC file. The accelerator associates the F1 key with an *ID_HELP* command that is mapped to the *CWinApp* member function *OnHelp*.

> **Note:** *In an active modal dialog or menu selection in progress, the F1 key is processed by a Windows hook that causes the same* OnHelp *function to be called.*

The *CWinApp OnHelp* function sends a WM_COMMANDHELP message to the outermost frame window. In an SDI application, that message is handled by the main frame base class function, *CFrameWnd OnCommandHelp*, which calls WINHELP with help context *HIDR_MAINFAME*. The main frame window is the top-level window, and that is the starting point for daisy-chained WM_COMMANDHELP message processing. If you need to show help for a view window or another child window, you must map WM_COMMANDHELP in your derived frame class. Your *OnCommandHelp* function should then send the WM_COMMANDHELP message down the line to the active view window. When the view window gets the message, it calls WINHELP with an appropriate help context ID.

In an MDI application, the WM_COMMANDHELP message is mapped in both the *CMDIFrameWnd* class and the *CMDIChildWnd* class. If there are no MDI children, the frame window sets the context to *HIDR_MAINFRAME*; if there are one or more children, the frame window sends the message to the active child window, which sets the help context for the document. If you need Help for views, you must derive a class from *CMDIChildWnd* and then map the *OnCommandHelp* function in that derived class. This function then sends the WM_COMMANDHELP message down to the view.

Remember that F1 WM_COMMANDHELP processing is always in top-down order. The application first sends the message to the top-level window, which has the option of delegating the message to a child window. This routing is different from the normal command routing.

Shift-F1 Processing

When the user presses Shift-F1 or clicks the Context Help toolbar button, a mapped menu command message is sent to the *CWinApp* function *OnContextHelp*. When the user clicks the mouse again after positioning the mouse cursor, a WM_HELP-HITTEST message is sent to the innermost window, where the mouse click is detected. If the message is not mapped in that window's class, the next outer window gets a chance at it.

In an SDI application, WM_HELPHITTEST is mapped to the *CFrameWnd* class member function *OnHelpHitTest*, which sets the help context to *HIDR_MAIN-FRAME*. In an MDI application, the message is mapped to both the *CMDIChildWnd* and the *CMDIFrameWnd* classes. If the mouse cursor is in the child window, the document help context is set; otherwise, the context is set to *HIDR_MAINFRAME*.

If you want a view-specific help context, simply map WM_HELPHITTEST in your view class and don't pass the message on to the frame. The *lParam* parameter of *OnHelpHitTest* contains the mouse coordinates in device units, relative to the upper left corner of the window's client area. The y value is in the high-order half; the x value is in the low-order half. You can use these coordinates to set the help context specifically for an item in the view.

Remember that Shift-F1 processing is always in bottom-up order. The message is first sent to the lowest-level window. If that window doesn't map the message, it's sent to the parent window.

A Help Command Processing Example, EX20B

This example, EX20B, is based on example EX19C from Chapter 19. It's a two-view MDI application with view-specific help added. The purpose of the added code is as follows:

- A new derived MDI child frame window class delegates the F1 help response to the active view object, and each of the two view classes has the necessary *OnCommandHelp* message handler.

- Each view class has an *OnHelpHitTest* message handler to process Shift-F1 help requests.

Header Requirements

The compiler recognizes help-specific identifiers only if the following *#include* statement is present:

```
#include <afxpriv.h>
```

In EX20B, the statement is in the STDAFX.H file.

CEx20bApp

You need a special MDI child frame window class, *CMDIHelpWnd*, to accommodate the new Help processing. This class is specified in the application class *Add-DocTemplate* calls. Replace the EX19C.CPP line

```
RUNTIME_CLASS(CMDIChildWnd)
```

with

```
RUNTIME_CLASS(CMDIHelpWnd)
```

CMDIHelpWnd

The new class declaration is added to the MAINFRM.H header file as follows:

```
class CMDIHelpWnd : public CMDIChildWnd
{
    DECLARE_DYNCREATE(CMDIHelpWnd)
protected:
    //{{AFX_MSG(CMainFrame)
    afx_msg LRESULT OnCommandHelp(WPARAM wParam, LPARAM lParam);
    //}}AFX_MSG
    DECLARE_MESSAGE_MAP()
};
```

Here is the *CMDIHelpWnd* implementation code, inserted in MAINFRM.CPP.

```
IMPLEMENT_DYNCREATE(CMDIHelpWnd, CMDIChildWnd)

BEGIN_MESSAGE_MAP(CMDIHelpWnd, CMDIChildWnd)
    //{{AFX_MSG_MAP(CMDIHelpWnd)
    ON_MESSAGE(WM_COMMANDHELP, OnCommandHelp)
    //}}AFX_MSG_MAP
END_MESSAGE_MAP()

LRESULT CMDIHelpWnd::OnCommandHelp(WPARAM wParam, LPARAM lParam)
{
    if (lParam == 0) {
        if (m_nIDTracking > 0xe001) {
            // frame's own menu (system menu)
            lParam = HID_BASE_COMMAND + m_nIDTracking;
        }
        else {
            CView* pView = GetActiveView();
            if (pView) {
                // delegate the Help command to the view
                return pView->SendMessage(WM_COMMANDHELP, wParam, 0L);
            }
            else {
                lParam = HID_BASE_RESOURCE + IDR_MAINFRAME;
            }
        }
    }
    if (lParam != 0) {
        AfxGetApp()->WinHelp(lParam);
```

```
        return TRUE;
    }
    return FALSE;
}
```

The *OnCommandHelp* function first tests the *m_nIDTracking* data member to see whether the user was asking for help on a menu item. If no menu was open, the function tries to pass the WM_COMMANDHELP command message on to the active view. If no view is available, the function brings up the Help topic for the MDI client window. The document-specific topic isn't needed here because a document MDI child window can't exist without a view.

CStringView

The modified string view in STRINGVW.H needs message map function prototypes for both F1 help and Shift-F1 help:

```
afx_msg LRESULT OnCommandHelp(WPARAM wParam, LPARAM lParam);
afx_msg LRESULT OnHelpHitTest(WPARAM wParam, LPARAM lParam);
```

Here are the message map entries in STRINGVW.CPP:

```
ON_MESSAGE(WM_COMMANDHELP, OnCommandHelp)
ON_MESSAGE(WM_HELPHITTEST, OnHelpHitTest)
```

The *OnCommandHelp* message-handling member function in STRINGVW.CPP processes F1 help requests. It responds to the message sent from the MDI child frame and displays the help topic for the string view window.

```
LRESULT CStringView::OnCommandHelp(WPARAM wParam, LPARAM lParam)
{
    if (lParam == 0) {
        lParam = HID_BASE_RESOURCE + IDR_STRINGVIEW;
    }
    // context already determined above--we don't modify it
    AfxGetApp()->WinHelp(lParam);
    return TRUE;
}
```

Finally, the *OnHelpHitTest* member function handles Shift-F1 help.

```
LRESULT CStringView::OnHelpHitTest(WPARAM wParam, LPARAM lParam)
{
    return HID_BASE_RESOURCE + IDR_STRINGVIEW;
}
```

In a more complex application, you might want *OnHelpHitTest* to set the help context based on the mouse cursor position.

CHexView

The *CHexView* class processes help requests the same way the *CStringView* class does. Here is the necessary header code in HEXVW.H:

```
afx_msg LRESULT OnCommandHelp(WPARAM wParam, LPARAM lParam);
afx_msg LRESULT OnHelpHitTest(WPARAM wParam, LPARAM lParam);
```

Here are the message map entries in HEXVW.CPP:

```
ON_MESSAGE(WM_COMMANDHELP, OnCommandHelp)
ON_MESSAGE(WM_HELPHITTEST, OnHelpHitTest)
```

And here is the implementation code in HEXVW.CPP:

```
LRESULT CHexView::OnCommandHelp(WPARAM wParam, LPARAM lParam)
{
    if(lParam == 0) {
        lParam = HID_BASE_RESOURCE + IDR_HEXVIEW;
    }
    // context already determined above--we don't modify it
    AfxGetApp()->WinHelp(lParam);
    return TRUE;
}

LRESULT CHexView::OnHelpHitTest(WPARAM wParam, LPARAM lParam)
{
    return HID_BASE_RESOURCE + IDR_HEXVIEW;
}
```

Resource Requirements

Two new symbols were added to the resource file. Here are their values and corresponding help context IDs:

Symbol	Value	Help Context	Value
IDR_STRINGVIEW	101	*HIDR_STRINGVIEW*	0x20065
IDR_HEXVIEW	102	*HIDR_HEXVIEW*	0x20066

Help File Requirements

Two topics were added to the AFXCORE.RTF file with the help context IDs *HIDR_STRINGVIEW* and *HIDR_HEXVIEW* as shown here:

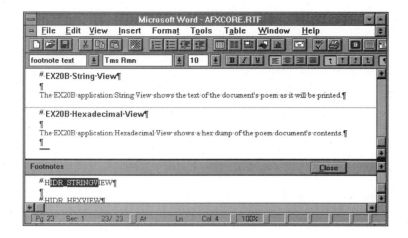

The generated EX20B.HM file, in the project's HLP subdirectory, should look like this:

```
// MAKEHELP.BAT generated Help Map file.  Used by EX20B.HPJ.

// Commands (ID_* and IDM_*)
HID_WINDOW_NEW1                          0x18000
HID_WINDOW_NEW2                          0x18001

// Prompts (IDP_*)

// Resources (IDR_*)
HIDR_MAINFRAME                           0x20002
HIDR_POEMTYPE                            0x20003
HIDR_STRINGVIEW                          0x20065
HIDR_HEXVIEW                             0x20066

// Dialogs (IDD_*)
HIDD_ABOUTBOX                            0x20064

// Frame Controls (IDW_*)
```

Build and Test the Application

Bring up a string child window and a hexadecimal child window. Test the action of F1 help and Shift-F1 help.

21

A Practical Windows-Based Application

The examples in the preceding chapters have illustrated specific Microsoft Foundation Class Library version 2.0 features. This chapter is different. It shows a complete two-view-class MDI application that combines most of the elements you've seen already, including

- Mouse capture and tracking

- Bit-block transfers

- A scrolling view

- Document-view interaction

- Dynamic array usage

- Serialization

- wysiwyg printing

- Non-wysiwyg printing with pagination

- Menu command processing

- Dialog data exchange

- Context-sensitive help linked to the view

In addition, the application illustrates the use of the list box as a central view element, and it shows the use of a document item class that streamlines the interface between view and document.

This chapter's presentation is a little different too. You won't see step-by-step instructions but rather selected code plus a summary of the resource requirements. The entire source is, of course, included on the companion disk. The class and file names are application-oriented and thus are not based on the chapter number.

The example is a materials planning application, named MATPLAN, that takes advantage of Windows' graphical user interface—the user can directly manipulate data with the mouse. I hope that the MATPLAN application will give you ideas for your own applications.

The MATPLAN Application

Have you ever planned a home project, a doghouse for example, that required plywood pieces cut from 4-foot-by-8-foot sheets? Or has your boss ever asked you to design a jet fighter that needed skin sections cut from sheets of titanium? The MATPLAN application addresses both these common, everyday problems.

Typically, the project design dictates the dimensions of the pieces of material. The challenge is to cut the pieces with a minimum amount of waste. MATPLAN uses a document that consists of an array of "piece" objects. The lengths, widths, and descriptions of the pieces are maintained through the list view; the user types the data for each piece in a dialog. The pieces are arranged through the graphical plan view; the user moves the pieces with the mouse on a grid that shows the material sheet boundaries.

Look at Figure 21-1 to get an idea of how MATPLAN works. Both the list view (in the top child window) and the plan view (in the bottom child window) are updated as the document's data changes.

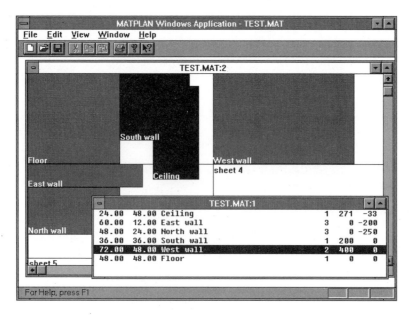

Figure 21-1.
The MATPLAN application in action, with two views active.

When the user double-clicks on a line in the list view, a dialog appears, as shown in Figure 21-2.

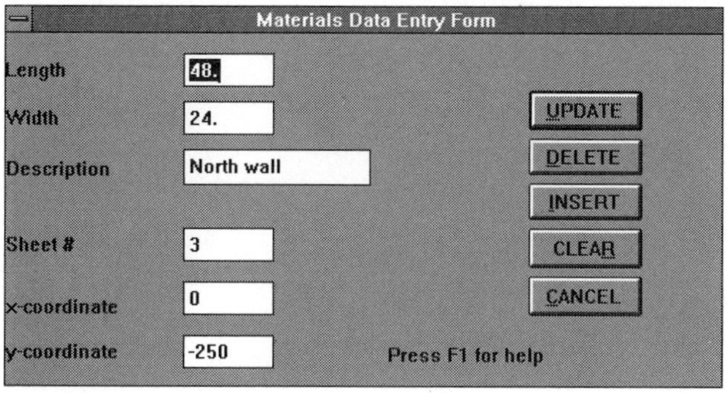

Figure 21-2.
The MATPLAN dialog.

The dialog's edit controls correspond to the columns in the list view. The *x* and *y* values represent the plan grid coordinates of the piece's top left corner. As the user moves the pieces in the plan view, the list view is updated to reflect the new coordinates. As the user changes the dimensions and descriptions in the list view, the plan view is updated accordingly. Of course, the computer could figure out how to lay out the pieces by itself, but that wouldn't be any fun. MATPLAN does offer some help to the user during the layout process. Overlapping pieces are displayed in black, and if the user double-clicks on a piece, it drops into place (like a piece in the TETRIS game).

MATPLAN fully supports the printer and Print Preview from both views. In the plan view, the entire grid of eight sheets is printed on one page. In the list view, list entries are printed report-style, three lines per page. (The lines-per-page is small to more easily illustrate paginated printing.)

The Anatomy of the MATPLAN Application

The MATPLAN application structure should start making sense quickly because of your work with this book's earlier examples. That's the idea behind programming with a standard application framework. First you identify the document and view and document classes, and then you analyze the other classes and find out how they interrelate.

Let's start with a list of the files and classes at the top of the next page:

Header File	Source Code File	Classes	Description
MATPLAN.H	MATPLAN.CPP	*CMatplanApp* *CAboutDlg*	Application class About dialog
MAINFRM.H	MAINFRM.CPP	*CMainFrame* *CMDISpecialChildWnd*	MDI main frame MDI child frame
MATDOC.H	MATDOC.CPP	*CMatplanDoc*	MATPLAN document
LISTVIEW.H	LISTVIEW.CPP	*CListView*	List view
PLANVIEW.H	PLANVIEW.CPP	*CPlanView*	Plan view
MATDLG.H	MATDLG.CPP	*CMatplanDialog*	Data entry dialog
MATPIECE.H	MATPIECE.CPP	*CPiece*	Document item
STDAFX.H	STDAFX.CPP		Standard class library include files
RESOURCE.H			Constants from App Studio

Now we'll discuss each class separately, and we'll look at some of the important member functions.

CMatplanApp

This class is the standard AppWizard-generated application class derived from *CWinApp*. Only its *InitInstance* and *ExitInstance* functions are unique.

InitInstance

As in the EX19C example, the *InitInstance* member function constructs two secondary document template objects, one for the list view and the other for the plan view, as shown below:

```
m_pTemplate1 = new CMultiDocTemplate(IDR_MATTYPE,
    RUNTIME_CLASS(CMatplanDoc),
    RUNTIME_CLASS(CMDISpecialChildWnd),
    RUNTIME_CLASS(CListView));

m_pTemplate2 = new CMultiDocTemplate(IDR_MATTYPE,
    RUNTIME_CLASS(CMatplanDoc),
    RUNTIME_CLASS(CMDISpecialChildWnd),
    RUNTIME_CLASS(CPlanView));
```

ExitInstance

This function destroys the templates constructed in *InitInstance*.

CMainFrame

As in EX19C, this class, derived from *CMDIFrameWnd*, has command message handlers for the New List Window and New Plan Window menu items.

OnWindowNew1

This function opens a new MDI child frame window and associated list view, based on the document that is currently active. It is associated with the New List Window item on the Window menu and with the *ID_WINDOW_NEW1* constant.

OnWindowNew2

This function opens a new MDI child frame window and associated plan view, based on the document that is currently active. It is associated with the New Plan Window item on the Window menu and with the *ID_WINDOW_NEW2* constant.

CMDISpecialChildWnd

This class, derived from *CMDIChildWnd*, exists only to support view-related, context-sensitive F1 help.

OnCommandHelp

This function handles the WM_COMMANDHELP message that the MDI main frame sends. It delegates the F1 help request to the active view.

CMatplanDoc

This is the materials planning document class. It contains a dynamic array of *CPiece* object pointers, *m_pieceArray*, and is a friend to both view classes. This friendship allows the view class member functions to access the private piece array.

The piece array contains the primary copy of the application's data. The plan view accesses the *CPiece* objects directly, and the list view copies all the information contained in the array to and from its list box.

Constructor

The *CMatplanDoc* constructor illustrates the initialization of a dynamic array. The *CObArray SetSize* member function sets the initial array size to 0, but it sets the grow factor to 20. That means that the *new* operator is called only after the addition of every twentieth element to improve performance. The array elements are added in the *CListView* class with the *CObArray SetAtGrow* member function.

```
CMatplanDoc::CMatplanDoc()
{
    m_pieceArray.SetSize(0, 20); // allocate mem 20 elements at a time
}
```

Serialize

The document class's *Serialize* function simply serializes *m_pieceArray*, which, in turn, serializes each *CPiece* object.

DeleteContents

A *CObArray* collection contains pointers to objects, not the objects themselves. This overridden virtual function not only removes the object pointers from the collection but also deletes the objects.

```
void CMatplanDoc::DeleteContents()
{
    for (int i = m_pieceArray.GetUpperBound(); i >= 0; i--) {
        delete m_pieceArray.GetAt(i);
    }
    m_pieceArray::RemoveAll();
}
```

OnEditClearAll

In addition to emptying the array, the *OnEditClearAll* function marks the document as modified and updates all views.

```
void CMatplanDoc::OnEditClearAll()
{   // gets rid of the old piece array in the document
    DeleteContents();
    SetModifiedFlag();
    UpdateAllViews(NULL);
}
```

OnUpdateEditClearAll

The Edit Clear All menu item should be grayed when the document's array is empty.

```
void CMatplanDoc::OnUpdateEditClearAll(CCmdUI* pCmdUI)
{
    pCmdUI->Enable(m_pieceArray.GetUpperBound() != -1);
}
```

OnUpdateFileSave

This update command UI function tests the modified flag and enables the toolbar disk (File Save) button accordingly.

CPiece

A MATPLAN document is composed of an array of *CPiece* objects. These pieces, known as document items, can draw and print themselves. This capability seems to violate the separation of view from document, but it's an accepted programming technique.

The *CPiece* class has data members for length, width, description, and position on the material grid. The length and width are maintained in physical coordinates—double-precision floating-point variables representing inches—and that's what the user edits in the dialog. Those physical coordinate values are converted to logical coordinates (1 logical unit = 0.01 inch) within the *CPiece* member functions, and subsequently they're converted to device coordinates.

Draw

The *CPiece Draw* function is called from the plan view *OnDraw* function for each piece in the array. The object's data members convey sufficient information to draw a rectangle representing the piece. If the *m_bOverlap* flag indicates that the piece overlaps another piece, the rectangle's fill color is black. *Draw* is designed to work with both the display and the printer.

```
void CPiece::Draw(CDC* pDC, int yChar)
{
    CRect rect;
    GetRect(rect);

    pDC->SelectStockObject(BLACK_PEN);
    if (m_bOverlap) {
        pDC->SelectStockObject(BLACK_BRUSH);
    }
    else {
        pDC->SelectStockObject(GRAY_BRUSH);
    }
    pDC->Rectangle(rect);
    int hdcSave = pDC->SaveDC();
    pDC->SetTextColor((COLORREF) 0x00FFFFFF); // white
    pDC->SetBkMode(TRANSPARENT);
    pDC->IntersectClipRect(rect);   // restricts text to piece rectangle
    pDC->TextOut(rect.left, rect.bottom + yChar + 2, m_desc);
    pDC->RestoreDC(hdcSave);
}
```

The piece description is printed in white, and that works fine on the display and with PostScript printers. Standard HP LaserJet printers can't print fonts white-on-black, however.

PrintLine

The list view *OnDraw* function calls the *CPiece PrintLine* function for each piece in the array. *PrintLine* is designed for printing only.

```
void CPiece::PrintLine(CDC* pDC, CPoint point)
{
    char temp[100];

    pDC->SetTextColor((COLORREF) 0x00000000); // black
    sprintf(temp, "%6.2f %6.2f %-30.30s%5ld%5ld%5ld",
            m_length, m_width, (const char*) m_desc, m_sheet, m_x, m_y);
    pDC->TextOut(point.x, point.y, temp);
}
```

MATPLAN uses a fixed-pitch font, and that allows use of the *sprintf* function. If you wanted a proportional font, you would have to compute the starting positions for each field.

Serialize

The *Serialize* function does disk I/O for all the *CPiece* data members except the flags *m_bNewList* and *m_bOverlap*.

```
void CPiece::Serialize(CArchive& ar)
{
    if (ar.IsStoring()) {
        ar << m_length << m_width << m_desc << m_sheet << m_x << m_y;
    }
    else {
        ar >> m_length >> m_width >> m_desc >> m_sheet >> m_x >> m_y;
    }
}
```

InsertInList, ExtractFromList

A *CPiece* object is represented by an entry in the *CListView* list box. These two functions transfer the piece object's data members to and from a specified (by index) list box entry, which consists of a single formatted string.

```
void CPiece::InsertInList(CListBox* pListBox, int index)
{   // copies data from this CPiece object into a list box entry
    char temp[100];

    sprintf(temp, "%6.2f %6.2f %-30.30s%5ld%5ld%5ld",
            m_length, m_width, (const char*) m_desc, m_sheet, m_x, m_y);
    pListBox->InsertString(index, temp);
}

void CPiece::ExtractFromList(CListBox* pListBox, int index)
{   // copies data from a list box entry into a CPiece object
    char temp1[100], temp2[100];

    // sscanf won't work here because the description
    //   can contain embedded spaces
    pListBox->GetText(index, temp1);
    strncpy(temp2, temp1, 6); temp2[6] = '\0';
    m_length = atof(temp2);
    strncpy(temp2, temp1+7, 6); temp2[6] = '\0';
    m_width= atof(temp2);
    strncpy(temp2, temp1+14, 30); temp2[30] = '\0';
    m_desc = temp2;
    strncpy(temp2, temp1+44, 5); temp2[5] = '\0';
    m_sheet = atol(temp2);
    strncpy(temp2, temp1+49, 5); temp2[5] = '\0';
    m_x = atol(temp2);
    strncpy(temp2, temp1+54, 5); temp2[5] = '\0';
    m_y = atol(temp2);
}
```

Note: *In MATPLAN, all the document's data must be copied to or from the list box every time the document is updated. For large documents, performance suffers, and the document–view architecture is compromised. In Chapters 24 and 26, you'll see the* CRowView *class, which displays rows consisting of separate fields. This class eliminates the need for* strncpy *gymnastics, and it better supports the document–view architecture. With* CRowView, *the only rows copied are the rows actually being displayed.*

CMatplanDialog

This modal dialog class, based on the dialog resource *IDD_FORM*, is the data entry form for material pieces. It works differently from the standard ClassWizard-generated dialog because it doesn't have individual data members for its edit controls. Instead, it has a single *CPiece* object pointer as a data member. The list view object owns the actual *CPiece* object.

Constructor

The *CMatplanDialog* constructor initializes the *m_pPiece* data member.

```
CMatplanDialog::CMatplanDialog(CWnd* pParentWnd, CPiece* pPiece)
        : CModalDialog(CMatplanDialog::IDD, pParentWnd)
{
    m_pPiece = pPiece; // this replaces ClassWizard's initialization
}
```

DoDataExchange

ClassWizard did not generate this *DoDataExchange* virtual function. It was hand-coded with references to *CPiece* data members. The Description field, for example, is referenced by the expression *m_pPiece->m_desc*. The first part is the *CMatplanDialog* data member that points to the view's *CPiece* object; the second part is the *CPiece* data member that holds the description string.

The *DoDataExchange* function also adjusts the default pushbutton. If the user is modifying an existing piece, the default button is the Update button; otherwise, it is the Insert button. Because we're taking control of the default pushbutton, overriding the virtual *OnOK* function is unnecessary. The function simply doesn't get called.

```
void CMatplanDialog::DoDataExchange(CDataExchange* pDX)
{
    // no data map here because we're using a CPiece object
    CDialog::DoDataExchange(pDX);
    DDX_Text(pDX, IDC_LENGTH, m_pPiece->m_length);
    DDV_MinMaxDouble(pDX, m_pPiece->m_length, 0.0, 96.0);
    DDX_Text(pDX, IDC_WIDTH, m_pPiece->m_width);
    DDV_MinMaxDouble(pDX, m_pPiece->m_width, 0.0, 96.0);
    DDX_Text(pDX, IDC_DESC, m_pPiece->m_desc);
```

(continued)

```
DDX_Text(pDX, IDC_SHEET, m_pPiece->m_sheet);
DDV_MinMaxLong(pDX, m_pPiece->m_sheet, 0, 8);
DDX_Text(pDX, IDC_X, m_pPiece->m_x);
DDV_MinMaxLong(pDX, m_pPiece->m_x, 0, 800);
DDX_Text(pDX, IDC_Y, m_pPiece->m_y);
DDV_MinMaxLong(pDX, m_pPiece->m_y, -800, 0);

if (m_pPiece->m_bNewList) {
    SetDefID(IDC_INSERT);
}
else {
    SetDefID(IDC_UPDATE);
}
}
```

OnCancel

The virtual *OnCancel* function, called in response to the Esc key, is overridden to make the dialog return the *MDB_CANCEL* code.

```
void CMatplanDialog::OnCancel()
{   // Esc key pressed
    EndDialog(IDC_CANCEL); // simulate CANCEL button
}
```

OnClickedCancel, OnClickedClear, OnClickedDelete, OnClickedInsert, OnClickedUpdate

These command message handler functions are called in response to associated pushbuttons. Their main function is to pass the button's ID code to the *CDialog EndDialog* function, which establishes the return value from *DoModal*. Here is the *OnClickedInsert* function, which triggers a call to *DoDataExchange*.

```
void CMatplanDialog::OnClickedInsert()
{
    if (!UpdateData(TRUE))
        return; // returns on error
    EndDialog(IDC_INSERT);
}
```

The *OnClickedClear* function clears *CPiece* data members and sets the Insert button as the default.

```
void CMatplanDialog::OnClickedClear()
{
    m_pPiece->m_length = m_pPiece->m_width = 0.0;
    m_pPiece->m_desc = "";
    m_pPiece->m_sheet = m_pPiece->m_x = m_pPiece->m_y = 0;
    UpdateData(FALSE);
    SetDefID(IDC_INSERT); // insert is the next logical operation
    GotoDlgCtrl(GetDlgItem(IDC_LENGTH));
}
```

OnClose

This message handler override is necessary only to prevent the default *OnOK* function being called when the user closes the dialog from the system menu. This *OnClose* function displays a message box through which the user confirms that he or she wants to exit the dialog. If the user chooses OK, the *MDB_CANCEL* code is returned from *DoModal*.

```
void CMatplanDialog::OnClose()
{
    if (AfxMessageBox("Exit Dialog? (F1 for help)", MB_OKCANCEL,
                      IDP_EXIT_DLG) == IDOK)
    {
        EndDialog(IDC_CANCEL);
    }
}
```

The *IDP_EXIT_DLG* symbol maps to a help context.

CListView

This is the MATPLAN list view class. A *CListView* object contains a pointer to a single *CListBox* object that occupies the entire view client area. It also contains pointers to a dialog object and to a *CPiece* object. Both the list box and the dialog pointer data members specify heap-allocated objects that belong to the view object. The *CPiece* pointer, however, specifies the current piece, which is associated with the selected item in the view's list box.

OnPrepareDC

The *OnPrepareDC* function sets the view's map mode and selects the font for printing.

```
void CListView::OnPrepareDC(CDC* pDC, CPrintInfo* pInfo)
{
    pDC->SetMapMode(MM_LOENGLISH);
    pDC->SelectObject(m_pPrintFont); // need to do it every page
}
```

OnDraw

This view's *OnDraw* function is not called for the display; it's called only for printing. It gets the document's piece array, and then it calls the *CPiece PrintLine* member function for each piece that appears on the current page.

```
void CListView::OnDraw(CDC* pDC)
{   // called for Print/Print Preview ONLY, not for display
    CPoint  point(0, 0);
    CPiece* pPiece;
    int     nLineMin, nLineMax; // zero-based line numbers
```

(continued)

383

```
    CMatplanDoc* pDoc = GetDocument();
    nLineMin = (m_nPage - 1) * CMatplanDoc::m_nLinesPerPage;
    nLineMax = nLineMin + CMatplanDoc::m_nLinesPerPage - 1;
    if (nLineMax > pDoc->m_pieceArray.GetUpperBound()) {
        nLineMax = pDoc->m_pieceArray.GetUpperBound();
    }
    point += m_drawOffset;
    point.y -= m_yChar * 2; // space for col head & blank line
    for (int i = nLineMin; i <= nLineMax; i++) {
        pPiece = (CPiece*) (pDoc->m_pieceArray.GetAt(i));
        point.y -= m_yChar;
        pPiece->PrintLine(pDC, point);
    }
}
```

OnPrint

The application framework calls *OnPrint* for each printed page. The function prints the page header and then calls the *OnDraw* function. It also sets the value of the *m_nPage* data member so that the page footer function can access the current page.

```
void CListView::OnPrint(CDC* pDC, CPrintInfo* pInfo)
{
    // application framework calls OnPrepareDC prior to OnPrint
    PrintPageHeader(pDC);
    m_nPage = pInfo->m_nCurPage; // for OnDraw's and
                                 //   PrintPageFooter's benefit
    OnDraw(pDC);
    PrintPageFooter(pDC);
}
```

OnUpdate

This important virtual member function copies all the information in the document's *CPiece* array to the view's list box. It is called on File New, on File Open after the document has been read from disk, and when the document's *UpdateAllViews* function is called from some other view. *OnUpdate* is called by the application framework on File New, on File Open after the document has been read from disk, and when the document's *UpdateAllViews* function is called from some other view. If the piece array is empty, the *StartNewList* member function is called.

```
void CListView::OnUpdate(CView* pSender, LPARAM lHint, CObject* pHint)
{   // refreshes list box from array in document
    // when application starts, this function is called
    //  before the window is shown
    CPiece* pPiece;

    m_pListBox->ResetContent(); // empty the list box
    CMatplanDoc* pDoc = GetDocument();
    int nCount = pDoc->m_pieceArray.GetUpperBound();
    if (nCount == -1) {
        StartNewList();
    }
```

```
    else {
        // copy all data from the document's piece array
        //   to the view's list box
        for (int i = 0; i <= nCount; i++) {
            pPiece = (CPiece*) pDoc->m_pieceArray.GetAt(i);
            pPiece->InsertInList(m_pListBox, -1); // AddString
        }
    }
}
```

OnPreparePrinting

The *OnPreparePrinting* function is called immediately before the application framework's print dialog appears, and it sets the maximum page number based on the *CPiece* array size and the number of entries per page.

OnBeginPrinting, OnEndPrinting

A special fixed-pitch font is created in *OnBeginPrinting* and deleted in *OnEndPrinting*. This font exists for the duration of the print process.

OnCreate

The view's list box is created in this message handler. The list box uses a fixed-pitch font because that's an easy way to line up the columns.

```
int CListView::OnCreate(LPCREATESTRUCT lpcs)
{
    CRect rect;
    CFont font;

    // makes a list box the exact size of the window
    GetClientRect(&rect);
    rect.InflateRect(GetSystemMetrics(SM_CXBORDER),
                     GetSystemMetrics(SM_CYBORDER));
    m_pListBox->Create(WS_CHILD | WS_HSCROLL | WS_VSCROLL | WS_VISIBLE |
                       LBS_NOTIFY | LBS_NOINTEGRALHEIGHT,
                       rect, this, IDR_LISTBOX);
    // creates and attaches a fixed font to the list box

    font.CreateStockObject(SYSTEM_FIXED_FONT);
    m_pListBox->SetFont(&font);
    return CView::OnCreate(lpcs);
}
```

OnPaint

The base class *OnPaint* message handler calls *OnDraw*. We don't want to call *OnDraw* here, so we override *OnPaint*. The function must construct a *CPaintDC* object to validate the rectangle that contains the list box, thus assuring proper repainting of the list box.

```
void CListView::OnPaint()
{
    CPaintDC dc(this); // this statement is necessary to generate
                       //   the BeginPaint and EndPaint calls to
                       //   validate the rectangle
}
```

OnSize

This message handler ensures that the list box is resized every time the view window is resized.

```
void CListView::OnSize(UINT nType, int cx, int cy)
{
    CRect rect;

    if (m_pListBox) {
        GetClientRect(&rect);
        rect.InflateRect(GetSystemMetrics(SM_CXBORDER),
                         GetSystemMetrics(SM_CYBORDER));
        m_pListBox->MoveWindow(rect);
    }
}
```

OnListBoxDblClk

When the user double-clicks on a list box entry, a dialog pops up, allowing the user to edit the length, width, and description for the selected piece. The user can also delete the piece or insert a new piece. If the list box is empty, the user obviously can't select an entry; so the user must close the view and use File New to create a new view.

```
void CListView::OnListBoxDblClk()
{   // called only if the list box is not empty
    int i = m_pListBox->GetCurSel();
    m_pPiece->ExtractFromList(m_pListBox, i);
    m_pPiece->m_bNewList = FALSE;
    m_pDialog = new CMatplanDialog(this, m_pPiece);
    int rtn = m_pDialog->DoModal();
    switch(rtn) {
    case IDC_UPDATE:
        m_pListBox->DeleteString(i);
        m_pPiece->InsertInList(m_pListBox, i);
        m_pListBox->SetCurSel(i);
        UpdatePlanDocument();
        break;
    case IDC_DELETE:
        m_pListBox->DeleteString(i);
        m_pListBox->SetCurSel(i);
        UpdatePlanDocument();
        break;
```

```
case IDC_INSERT:
    m_pPiece->InsertInList(m_pListBox, i);
    m_pListBox->SetCurSel(i);
    UpdatePlanDocument();
    break;
case IDC_CANCEL: // same as IDCANCEL
    break;
case IDOK:
    break;
default:
    ASSERT(0);
    break;
}
    delete m_pDialog;
}
```

OnCommandHelp, OnHelpHitTest

These two functions process the WM_COMMANDHELP and WM_HELPHITTEST messages, thus implementing context-sensitive help for the list view.

StartNewList

This private member function really doesn't create a new list—that's done in *OnCreate. StartNewList*, called when the document *CPiece* array is empty, brings up an empty dialog and invites the user to insert a new entry in the list box, which, up to this point, is empty.

UpdatePlanDocument

This private member function copies the entire contents of the list box to the document's *CPiece* array. It is called when the user changes an entry through the dialog.

```
void CListView::UpdatePlanDocument()
{   // transfers all data from view (list box) to document
    CPiece* pPiece;
    int     i;

    CMatplanDoc* pDoc = GetDocument();

    // gets rid of the old piece list in the document
    for (i = pDoc->m_pieceArray.GetUpperBound(); i >= 0; i--) {
        pPiece = (CPiece*) pDoc->m_pieceArray.GetAt(i);
        delete pDoc->m_pieceArray.GetAt(i);
        pDoc->m_pieceArray.RemoveAt(i);
    }
    // copies all strings from view's list box to document's piece list
    int listLen = m_pListBox->GetCount();
    for (i = 0; i < listLen; i++) {
```

(continued)

387

```
        pPiece = new CPiece;
        pPiece->ExtractFromList(m_pListBox, i);
        pDoc->m_pieceArray.SetAtGrow(i, pPiece);
    }
    pDoc->SetModifiedFlag();
    pDoc->UpdateAllViews(this); // except ourselves
}
```

CPlanView

This is the MATPLAN <u>plan</u> view class. It shows a visual representation of each piece as a rectangle. The user can position the pieces with the mouse, but the size of the pieces is controlled from the list view. As does the list view, the plan view has a pointer to the current piece. The plan view's list pointer refers to an element in the document's *CPiece* array.

OnDraw

The application framework calls this function both from *OnPaint* (for the display) and from *OnPrint* (for the printer). The mapping mode is the same for both destinations. For the display, *OnDraw* is passed a memory display context, but for the printer, *OnDraw* is passed a printer device context.

OnDraw calls the *Draw* member function for each piece in the document's array. The array order determines the drawing sequence so that the last piece in the list is always on top.

```
void CPlanView::OnDraw(CDC* pDC)
{
    CPiece* pPiece;
    DrawBackground(pDC);

    CMatplanDoc* pDoc = GetDocument();
    // draw all the pieces that are in the update region
    int nCount = pDoc-> m_pieceArray.GetUpperBound();
    for (int i = 0; i <= nCount; i++) {
        pPiece = (CPiece*) pDoc->m_pieceArray.GetAt(i);
        pPiece->Draw(pDC, m_yChar);
    }
}
```

OnPreparePrinting

The material grid fits on one printed page, so *OnPreparePrinting* sets the maximum page number to 1.

OnUpdate

The virtual *OnUpdate* function calls *ShowOverlap* to recalculate overlapping rectangles, and then it invalidates the client rectangle. This forces *OnDraw* to refresh the screen from the current document. *OnUpdate* is called by the application framework on File New, on File Open after the document has been read from disk, and when the document's *UpdateAllViews* function is called from some other view. The repaint process has not been optimized because the draw time of rectangles is not a concern. The draw time is more critical for complex shapes such as ellipses.

```
void CPlanView::OnUpdate(CView* pSender, LPARAM lHint, CObject* pHint)
{
    ShowOverlap();
    Invalidate(TRUE); // forces total redraw
}
```

OnCreate

The *OnCreate* message handler initializes the scroll view and creates a memory device context and bitmap to support the *BitBlt* calls when a piece rectangle is moved with the mouse. The bitmap and device context are deleted in the view's destructor.

```
int CPlanView::OnCreate(LPCREATESTRUCT lpcs)
{
    TEXTMETRIC tm;

    CSize totalSize = CSize(800, 800);
    CSize lineSize = CSize(totalSize.cx / 100, totalSize.cy / 100);
    SetScrollSizes(MM_LOENGLISH, totalSize, totalSize, lineSize);

    CClientDC dc(this);
    dc.GetTextMetrics(&tm);
    m_xChar = tm.tmAveCharWidth;
    m_yChar = tm.tmHeight + tm.tmExternalLeading;

    OnPrepareDC(&dc);
    CRect rectMax(CPoint(0, 0), totalSize);
    dc.LPtoDP(rectMax);

    m_pMemDC->CreateCompatibleDC(&dc);
    CBitmap* pBitmap = new CBitmap;
    pBitmap->CreateCompatibleBitmap(&dc, rectMax.right,
                                    -rectMax.bottom);
    CBitmap* pOldBitmap = (CBitmap*) (m_pMemDC->SelectObject(pBitmap));
// this temp returned pointer doesn't remain valid past IDLE processing
//  therefore we must save the handle instead
    m_hOldBitmap = (HBITMAP) pOldBitmap->m_hObject;
    m_pMemDC->SetMapMode(MM_LOENGLISH);

    return CScrollView::OnCreate(lpcs);
}
```

OnPaint

The *OnPaint* message handler is overridden in this view to permit use of the memory device context and bitmap. *OnPaint* clears the bitmap, calls *OnDraw*, and then uses the *BitBlt* function to copy the piece rectangle from the memory device context to the display. This process ensures smooth movement of the rectangle.

```
void CPlanView::OnPaint()
{
    CRect updateRect;

    CPaintDC dc(this);
    OnPrepareDC(&dc);
    dc.GetClipBox(updateRect); // updateRect is already
                               //   in logical coordinates
    m_pMemDC->SelectClipRgn(NULL);
    m_pMemDC->IntersectClipRect(updateRect);
    m_pMemDC->PatBlt(updateRect.left, updateRect.top,
                     updateRect.Width(), updateRect.Height(),
                     WHITENESS);
    OnDraw(m_pMemDC);
    dc.BitBlt(updateRect.left, updateRect.top,
              updateRect.Width(), updateRect.Height(), m_pMemDC,
              updateRect.left, updateRect.top, SRCCOPY);
}
```

OnLButtonDown

When the user clicks on a piece rectangle, the mouse is captured, and piece movement can begin. The *OnLButtonDown* function sets the view's *m_pPiece* data member to point to the selected piece object.

```
void CPlanView::OnLButtonDown(UINT nFlags, CPoint point)
{
    CRect    rect;
    CPiece*  pPiece;

    m_pPiece = NULL; // no piece selected
    CClientDC dc(this);
    OnPrepareDC(&dc);
    CMatplanDoc* pDoc = GetDocument();
    for (int i = pDoc->m_pieceArray.GetUpperBound(); i >= 0; i--) {
        pPiece = (CPiece*) pDoc->m_pieceArray.GetAt(i);
        pPiece->GetRect(rect);
        dc.LPtoDP(&rect);
        // PtInRect works only for device coordinates
        if (rect.PtInRect(point)) {
            SetCapture();
            m_bCaptured = TRUE;
            m_pPiece = pPiece;
            dc.DPtoLP(&point);
            m_mousePoint = point;
            ::SetCursor(::LoadCursor(NULL, IDC_CROSS));
            break;
        }
    }
}
```

OnMouseMove

As the mouse moves, this function updates the *xy*-coordinates for the current piece, which is stored in the document's *CPiece* array. If the user moves the piece outside the view, the view is scrolled accordingly. This scrolling continues as long as the mouse is in motion. The *OnMouseMove* function invalidates the union of the previous rectangle and the new rectangle.

```
void CPlanView::OnMouseMove(UINT nFlags, CPoint point)
{
    CSize offset;
    CRect clientRect, priorRect, newRect, invalidRect;

    if (m_bCaptured) {
        // let's work in device coords for scrolling
        CPoint scrollPos = GetDeviceScrollPosition();
        // scrolls in response to mouse movement outside client area
        GetClientRect(&clientRect);
        if (point.y > clientRect.bottom) {
            scrollPos.y += point.y - clientRect.bottom;
            SafeScrollTo(scrollPos);
        }
        if (point.y < 0) {
            scrollPos.y += point.y;
            SafeScrollTo(scrollPos);
        }
        if (point.x > clientRect.right) {
            scrollPos.x += point.x - clientRect.right;
            SafeScrollTo(scrollPos);
        }
        if (point.x < 0) {
            scrollPos.x += point.x;
            SafeScrollTo(scrollPos);
        }

        CClientDC dc(this);
        OnPrepareDC(&dc);
        dc.DPtoLP(&point);
        offset = point - m_mousePoint;
        m_mousePoint = point;
        m_pPiece->GetRect(priorRect);
        dc.LPtoDP(&priorRect);
        m_pPiece->m_x += offset.cx;
        m_pPiece->m_y += offset.cy;
        m_pPiece->GetRect(newRect);
        dc.LPtoDP(&newRect);
        invalidRect.UnionRect(priorRect, newRect);
#ifdef _WIN32
        invalidRect.InflateRect(1, 1);
#endif
        InvalidateRect(&invalidRect, FALSE);
    }
}
```

OnLButtonUp

When the mouse button is released, mouse capture is turned off, and the *OnL-ButtonUp* message handler calls *UpdateAllViews* to update the list view with the new piece position. If the user has moved any part of the piece rectangle outside the grid boundaries, the piece is brought back into the grid.

```
void CPlanView::OnLButtonUp(UINT nFlags, CPoint point)
{
    CMatplanDoc* pDoc = GetDocument();
    if (m_bCaptured) {
        // if piece is outside view, move it back in now
        long length = (LONG) (m_pPiece->m_length / .24);
        long width = (LONG) (m_pPiece->m_width / .24);
        if ((m_pPiece->m_x <= 0)) {
            m_pPiece->m_x = 0;
        }
        if (m_pPiece->m_x + length > m_totalLog.cx) {
            m_pPiece->m_x = m_totalLog.cx - length;
        }
        if ((m_pPiece->m_y >= 0)) {
            m_pPiece->m_y = 0;
        }
        if (m_pPiece->m_y - width < -m_totalLog.cx) {
            m_pPiece->m_y = -m_totalLog.cy + width;
        }
        ReleaseCapture();
        m_bCaptured = FALSE;
        ShowOverlap();
        pDoc->SetModifiedFlag();
        pDoc->UpdateAllViews(this); // except this
    }
}
```

OnLButtonDblClk

This is the so-called TETRIS function. When the user double-clicks on a piece, the piece drops into place in the upper left corner of the sheet. If the upper left corner is occupied, the selected piece drops into the closest available position.

OnKeyDown

This message handler implements view scrolling from the keyboard.

OnCommandHelp, OnHelpHitTest

These two functions process the WM_COMMANDHELP and WM_HELPHITTEST messages, thus implementing context-sensitive help for the plan view. The *OnHelpHitTest lParam* parameter contains the cursor position in device coordinates.

```
LRESULT CPlanView::OnHelpHitTest(WPARAM wParam, LPARAM lParam)
{
    TRACE("Mouse position = (%d, %d)\n",
        (int) HIWORD(lParam), (int) LOWORD(lParam));
    return HID_BASE_RESOURCE + IDR_PLANVIEW;
}
```

ShowOverlap

The *ShowOverlap* private member function computes which piece rectangles overlap other piece rectangles. The function sets the *m_bOverlap* flag for overlapping pieces.

SafeScrollTo

The *CScrollView* class establishes a logical size for the view window. The scroll bar control handlers are programmed to restrict scrolling to this area. No such restriction exists for the *CScrollView ScrollToDevicePosition* function, however. The *SafeScrollTo* private member function wraps the *ScrollToDevicePosition* function in such a way that scrolling is limited to the logical window area.

```
void CPlanView::SafeScrollTo(CPoint posDev)
{   // executes scroll only if viewport is within window bounds
    CRect clientRect;

    GetClientRect(&clientRect);
    clientRect += posDev;
    if (clientRect.top < 0) {
        posDev.y = 0;
    }
    if (clientRect.bottom > m_totalDev.cy) {
        posDev.y = m_totalDev.cy;
    }
    if (clientRect.left < 0) {
        posDev.x = 0;
    }
    if (clientRect.right > m_totalDev.cx) {
        posDev.x = m_totalDev.cx;
    }
    ScrollToDevicePosition(posDev);
}
```

The MATPLAN Resource File

App Studio was used to enhance the application's resource file, which was originally generated by AppWizard.

The *IDD_FORM* Dialog

The most important element in MATPLAN.RC is the form dialog resource *IDD_FORM*. You've seen the form image in Figure 21-2 on page 375. Here are the dialog controls as input to App Studio:

Text	Text Control ID	Data Member
Width	IDC_WIDTH	m_pPiece->m_width
Length	IDC_LENGTH	m_pPiece->m_length
Description	IDC_DESC	m_pPiece->m_desc
Sheet #	IDC_SHEET	m_pPiece->m_sheet
x-coordinate	IDC_X	m_pPiece->m_x
y-coordinate	IDC_Y	m_pPiece->m_y

Button Caption	Button ID	CMatplanDialog Member Function
&CANCEL	IDC_CANCEL	OnClickedCancel
CLEA&R	IDC_CLEAR	OnClickedClear
&DELETE	IDC_DELETE	OnClickedDelete
&INSERT	IDC_INSERT	OnClickedInsert
&UPDATE	IDC_UPDATE	OnClickedUpdate

The *IDR_MATTYPE* Menu

The following table shows the new MATPLAN menu items:

Menu	Menu Item	Command ID
Edit	Clear All	ID_EDIT_CLEAR_ALL
Window	New List Window	ID_WINDOW_NEW1
	New Plan Window	ID_WINDOW_NEW2

Symbols

Here are the new symbols for MATPLAN:

Symbol	Description
IDP_EXIT_DLG	Dialog exit error prompt ID for help
IDR_LISTBOX	Identifier for list box child window
IDR_LISTVIEW	List view window ID for help
IDR_PLANVIEW	Plan view window ID for help

Header Files

The file STDAFX.H contains the following *#include* statements:

```
#include <afxwin.h>        // MFC core and standard components
#include <afxext.h>        // CPrintInfo
#include <afxpriv.h>       // help
```

Building and Testing the MATPLAN Application

After you build MATPLAN from the Visual Workbench, be sure to run MAKEHELP to create the Help file.

When you run MATPLAN, you must choose New from the File menu to start a new plan document. The Materials Data Entry Form dialog pops up to let you insert the first piece. After that, double-click on the list box to insert more pieces, and then, from the Window menu, choose New Plan Window. Move the pieces with the mouse, and double-click on a rectangle to test the autopositioning feature. Next, try Print Preview and Print for both views. Also check Help for the views, the dialog, and the dialog exit message box.

ADVANCED TOPICS

22

Microsoft Foundation Class Library Version 2.0 Programs Without Documents or Views

The document–view architecture is useful for many applications, but sometimes a simpler program structure is sufficient. This chapter illustrates three applications—a Single Document Interface (SDI) program, a dialog-based program, and a Multiple Document Interface (MDI) program. None of these programs use document, view, or document–template classes, but they use command routing and some other Microsoft Foundation Class Library features. When you build the examples, you don't use AppWizard, but you do use App Studio and ClassWizard. The source code for these applications is also on the companion disk.

The greatest benefit from avoiding documents and view is reduced code size. A normal do-nothing SDI application is about 66 KB (without debugging information), but a stripped-down version is only about 36 KB. If you don't need the document–view features such as serialization, print support, and control bars, why include them in your program? If you don't care about saving 30 KB, you can still learn more about Windows and the application framework by studying this chapter's examples.

The following three examples don't have a lot in common, but they all do use an application object of a class derived from *CWinApp*. The examples start to diverge in the application class's *InitInstance* function.

> **Warning:** *There's a bug in the class library that can cause serious memory leaks, particularly when an application draws directly inside a frame window. See article Q98867 in the MS Developer Knowledgebase (GO MSDK) on CompuServe for information on fixing this bug.*

The EX22A Example—An SDI Application

This SDI "Hello, world!" example builds on the code you saw way back in Chapter 2. The application has only one window, an object of a class derived from *CFrameWnd*. All drawing occurs inside the frame window, and all messages are handled there. Besides the frame and application classes, here are the application's necessary elements:

- **A main menu.** You can have a Windows-based application without a menu; you don't even need a resource script. But EX22A has both. The application framework routes menu commands to message handlers in the frame class.

- **An icon.** An icon is necessary if the program is to be activated from Windows Program Manager. It's also useful when the application's main frame window is minimized. The icon is stored in the resource, along with the menu.

- **Window Close message command handler.** Many applications need to do special processing when their main window is closed. If you were using documents, you could override the *CDocument SaveModified* function, as illustrated in Chapter 24. Here, to take control of the Close process, you must write message handlers to process "close" messages sent as a result of user actions and by Windows itself when it shuts down.

- **Precompiled headers.** Precompiled headers offer such a compile speed advantage that you can't afford not to use them. This demands two extra files in the project, but they are short and simple.

Except for the precompiled header files, STDAFX.H and STDAFX.CPP, all this example's code is combined into two files, EX22A.H and EX22A.CPP. The only other file is the resource script, EX22A.RC. The *AFX_MSG* brackets allow you to use ClassWizard to add message handlers. The listings for the EX22A header and implementation files are shown in Figure 22-1.

```
EX22A.H
// application class
#include "resource.h"
class CEx22aApp : public CWinApp
{
public:
    virtual BOOL InitInstance();
};

// frame window class
class CMainFrame : public CFrameWnd
{
public:
```

Figure 22-1. *(continued)*
The EX22A header and implementation file listings.

Figure 22-1. *continued*

```
    CMainFrame();
protected:
    //{{AFX_MSG(CMainFrame)
    afx_msg void OnPaint();
    afx_msg void OnClose();
    afx_msg BOOL OnQueryEndSession();
    afx_msg void OnFile();
    afx_msg void OnHlp();
    //}}AFX_MSG
    DECLARE_MESSAGE_MAP()
};
```

EX22A.CPP

```
#include "stdafx.h"
#include "ex22a.h"

CEx22aApp NEAR theApp; // the one and only CEx22aApp object

BOOL CEx22aApp::InitInstance()
{
    m_pMainWnd = new CMainFrame();
    ASSERT(m_pMainWnd != NULL); // error checking only
    m_pMainWnd->ShowWindow(m_nCmdShow);
    m_pMainWnd->UpdateWindow();
    return TRUE;
}


///////////////////////////////////////////////////////////////////////
BEGIN_MESSAGE_MAP(CMainFrame, CFrameWnd)
    //{{AFX_MSG_MAP(CMainFrame)
    ON_WM_PAINT()
    ON_WM_CLOSE()
    ON_WM_QUERYENDSESSION()
    ON_COMMAND(ID_FILE, OnFile)
    ON_COMMAND(ID_HLP, OnHlp)
    //}}AFX_MSG_MAP
END_MESSAGE_MAP()


///////////////////////////////////////////////////////////////////////
CMainFrame::CMainFrame()
{
    Create(NULL, "EX22A Application",
           WS_OVERLAPPEDWINDOW, rectDefault, NULL,
           MAKEINTRESOURCE(IDR_MAINFRAME));
}
```

(continued)

Figure 22-1. *continued*

```
///////////////////////////////////////////////////////////////////////
void CMainFrame::OnPaint()
{
    CPaintDC dc(this);
    dc.TextOut(0, 0, "Hello, world!");
}

///////////////////////////////////////////////////////////////////////
void CMainFrame::OnClose()
{
    if (AfxMessageBox("OK to close window?", MB_YESNO) == IDYES) {
        CFrameWnd::OnClose();
    }
}

///////////////////////////////////////////////////////////////////////
BOOL CMainFrame::OnQueryEndSession()
{
    // received when user quits Windows
    SendMessage(WM_CLOSE);
    return TRUE;
}

// menu command handlers
///////////////////////////////////////////////////////////////////////
void CMainFrame::OnFile()
{
    TRACE("Entering CMainFrame::OnFile\n");
}

///////////////////////////////////////////////////////////////////////
void CMainFrame::OnHlp()
{
    TRACE("Entering CMainFrame::OnHlp\n");
}
```

STDAFX.H
```
#include <afxwin.h>
```

STDAFX.CPP
```
#include "stdafx.h"
```

CEx22aApp

This is the standard Microsoft Foundation Class Library application class. All class library applications depend on the existence of a global object of a class derived from *CWinApp*.

InitInstance

This function is modeled on the *InitInstance* function you see in a typical full-scale MDI application. It simply creates a main frame window and shows it.

CMainFrame

This is the main frame window class, derived from *CFrameWnd*. It is the only window class in the application, and there is only one *CMainFrame* object.

Constructor

The *CMainFrame* constructor calls the *CFrameWnd Create* function to create the window. The first parameter specifies the default application framework–defined window registration class (not to be confused with a C++ class) that attaches an icon resource with ID = 2. The last parameter specifies the menu resource.

> **Note:** *Placing the window* Create *call in a window class constructor is a shortcut. Everything works fine unless you derive another class from* CMainFrame. *In that case, the base class* OnCreate *function gets called instead of the derived class* OnCreate *function. You would be more nearly correct to use two-phase construction here. The* Create *call would reside in its own base class or derived class member function, separate from the constructor.*

OnPaint

If you've been using view classes, you're accustomed to using the virtual *OnDraw* function for painting in the window. Without the view class in the picture, you must use *OnPaint*.

OnClose

The *OnClose* function is called when the user closes the window. It's mapped here to allow the application to perform shutdown processing. In this application, a message box appears to confirm that you want to close the window.

OnQueryEndSession

When Windows itself shuts down, it sends the WM_QUERYENDSESSION message to all applications. If you had thought that the WM_CLOSE message is automatically sent in this case, you'd be wrong. Here the *OnQueryEndSession* function sends the WM_CLOSE message, which is handled by the *CMainFrame OnClose* member function.

OnFile, OnHlp

These two dummy functions are linked to the application's menu. This lets you observe that command routing is operational.

Resource Requirements

The application framework expects the application's icon resource to have an ID of 2. Use the *IDR_MAINFRAME* identifier to be consistent with other programs, but be sure that it's set to 2 in RESOURCE.H. You can use *IDR_MAINFRAME* for the menu also.

It doesn't matter what's on the menu, but the message handlers expect the identifiers *ID_FILE* and *ID_HLP*.

The EX22B Example—A Dialog-Based Application

When a resizable main frame window is unnecessary, a dialog can be sufficient for an application's user interface. The dialog window appears straightaway when the user starts the application. Obviously, there's no way to iconize the program, but as long as the dialog is not system modal, the user can freely switch to other applications.

In this example, the dialog functions as a simple calculator, as shown in Figure 22-2. ClassWizard takes charge of defining the class data members and generating the dialog data exchange (DDX) function calls. The application's resource script, EX22B.RC, defines an icon as well as the dialog.

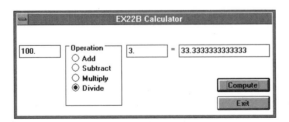

Figure 22-2.
The EX22B Calculator dialog.

The listings for the EX22B header and implementation files are shown in Figure 22-3. The precompiled header files, STDAFX.H and STDAFX.CPP, are the same as in the previous example.

EX22B.H

```
#include "resource.h"
class CEx22bDialog : public CDialog
{
public:
    CEx22bDialog();

// Dialog Data
    //{{AFX_DATA(CEx22bDialog)
    enum { IDD = IDD_EX22BDLG };
    double    m_d1;
    double    m_d2;
    double    m_d3;
    int       m_nOpr;
    //}}AFX_DATA

// Implementation
protected:
    virtual void DoDataExchange(CDataExchange* pDX); // DDX/DDV support
    //{{AFX_MSG(CEx22bDialog)
    afx_msg void OnClickedCompute();
    //}}AFX_MSG
    DECLARE_MESSAGE_MAP()
};

class CEx22bApp : public CWinApp
{
private:
    CEx22bDialog m_dialog;
public:
    BOOL InitInstance();
};
```

EX22B.CPP

```
#include "stdafx.h"
#include "ex22b.h"

CEx22bApp NEAR theApp;

BOOL CEx22bApp::InitInstance()
{
    m_dialog.DoModal(); // returns when Exit button clicked
    return FALSE;
}
```

Figure 22-3. *(continued)*
The EX22B header and implementation file listings.

405

Figure 22-3. *continued*

```
/////////////////////////////////////////////////////////////////////
BEGIN_MESSAGE_MAP(CEx22bDialog, CDialog)
    //{{AFX_MSG_MAP(CEx22bDialog)
    ON_BN_CLICKED(ID_COMPUTE, OnClickedCompute)
    //}}AFX_MSG_MAP
END_MESSAGE_MAP()

/////////////////////////////////////////////////////////////////////
CEx22bDialog::CEx22bDialog() : CDialog(CEx22bDialog::IDD)
{
    //{{AFX_DATA_INIT(CEx22bDialog)
    m_d1 = 0;
    m_d2 = 0;
    m_d3 = 0;
    m_nOpr = 0; // changed from default -1
    //}}AFX_DATA_INIT
}

/////////////////////////////////////////////////////////////////////
void CEx22bDialog::DoDataExchange(CDataExchange* pDX)
{
    CDialog::DoDataExchange(pDX);
    //{{AFX_DATA_MAP(CEx22bDialog)
    DDX_Text(pDX, IDC_EDIT1, m_d1);
    DDX_Text(pDX, IDC_EDIT2, m_d2);
    DDX_Text(pDX, IDC_EDIT3, m_d3);
    DDX_Radio(pDX, IDC_RADIO1, m_nOpr);
    //}}AFX_DATA_MAP
}

/////////////////////////////////////////////////////////////////////
void CEx22bDialog::OnClickedCompute()
{
    UpdateData(TRUE);
    switch (m_nOpr) {
    case 0:  // add
        m_d3 = m_d1 + m_d2;
        break;
    case 1:  // subtract
        m_d3 = m_d1 - m_d2;
        break;
    case 2:  // multiply
        m_d3 = m_d1 * m_d2;
        break;
    case 3:  // divide
        if (m_d2 != 0.0) {
            m_d3 = m_d1 / m_d2;
        }
```

(continued)

Figure 22-3. *continued*

```
        else {
            AfxMessageBox("Divide by zero");
            m_d3 = 0.0;
        }
        break;
    default:
        TRACE("default m_nOpr = %d\n", m_nOpr);
    }
    UpdateData(FALSE);
}
```

CEx22bApp

The EX22B application class is unique. Because there is no main window, there is no need for the *Run* function to translate and dispatch messages. All commands are handled within the application framework and the dialog.

Data Members

The variable *m_dialog* holds a dialog object of class *CEx22bDialog*. Because the object is embedded, the dialog is constructed and destroyed along with the application object.

InitInstance

The *CEx22bApp InitInstance* function calls *DoModal* for *m_dialog*. After the user exits the dialog (through the *CDialog OnCancel* function), *InitInstance* returns 0, thereby signaling the application framework to terminate the application immediately. The *CWinApp Run* and *ExitInstance* functions are never called.

CEx22bDialog

This a standard dialog class derived from *CDialog*. The *AFX_MSG* brackets permit ClassWizard to operate on the code.

Data Members

ClassWizard helps you define data members for each dialog control. The edit controls have *double* values attached (*m_d1, m_d2, m_d3*), and the radio button group has an integer (*m_nOpr*) that takes on the value 0, 1, or 2.

Constructor

The constructor is tied to the dialog resource ID, *IDD_EX22BDLG*.

DoDataExchange

This function calls the DDX functions that ClassWizard assigned.

OnClickedCompute

This notification message handler is activated by the dialog's Compute button and by the Enter key (because Compute is the default button).

Resource Requirements

The application's resource script, EX22B.RC, contains the dialog resource, identified as *IDD_EX22BDLG*, and a reference to the icon, *IDR_MAINFRAME* (set to 2). The dialog controls are listed in the following table, in their tabbing order:

Description	Type	ID	Tab Stop	Group
First Input	Edit control	*IDC_EDIT1*	X	
Add	Radio button	*IDC_RADIO1*	X	X
Subtract	Radio button	*IDC_RADIO2*	X	
Multiply	Radio button	*IDC_RADIO3*	X	
Divide	Radio button	*IDC_RADIO4*	X	
Second Input	Edit control	*IDC_EDIT2*	X	X
Result	Edit control (no input)	*IDC_EDIT3*		
Compute	Default pushbutton	*ID_COMPUTE*		
Exit	Pushbutton	*IDOK*		

The Second Input edit control needs the Group property set to terminate the preceding radio button group.

The EX22C Example—An MDI Application

This bare-bones MDI example isn't as simple as the SDI example, EX22A. Remember, from Chapter 17, that an MDI application consists of a main frame window and one or more child windows. Also, a single MDI client window is attached to the main frame window, but the application framework keeps that window hidden. If you use EX22C as a prototype, you'll be doing most of your programming in classes derived from *CMDIChildWnd*. Child window objects can receive and process messages as did the frame window object in example EX22A.

The EX22C MDI program doesn't have all the features of a full-blown document–view MDI application, but it does have these basic elements:

■ **A main menu.** A full-blown MDI application has two (or more) menus. EX22C has only one menu, and that menu is attached to the main frame window. The MDI Window submenu (with the Cascade, Tile, and child selection items) is part of this main menu structure, but the items (along with the File Close item) are disabled when no child windows are present.

■ **An icon.** Every Windows-based program needs an icon. The EX22C resource script defines one for this application.

■ **Initial child window.** Many MDI applications open an empty child window on startup. EX22C is no exception. If you use EX22C as a prototype for your own MDI application, you can easily disable this feature.

■ **Window Close message command handler.** MDI window close logic is more complex than SDI window close logic because of the many windows involved. Child windows can be closed individually or as a result of the main frame window's closure. In the EX22C program, the main frame window sends WM_CLOSE messages to all child windows, and the child window message handlers can process these messages. The Window menu even has a Close All item, a feature not present in a standard document–view MDI application.

■ **Precompiled headers.** As in the previous examples, EX22C uses precompiled headers to speed compilation.

The listings for the EX22C header and implementation files are shown in Figure 22-4.

EX22C.H

```
#include "resource.h"

class CEx22cApp : public CWinApp
{
public:
    virtual BOOL InitInstance();
};

// MDI frame window class
class CMainFrame : public CMDIFrameWnd
{
public:
    CMainFrame();
protected:
    //{{AFX_MSG(CMainFrame)
    afx_msg void OnFileNew();
    afx_msg void OnWindowCloseAll();
    afx_msg void OnUpdateWindowCloseAll(CCmdUI* pCmdUI);
    afx_msg void OnClose();
    afx_msg BOOL OnQueryEndSession();
```

Figure 22-4.
The EX22C header and implementation file listings.

(continued)

Figure 22-4. *continued*

```
    //}}AFX_MSG
    DECLARE_MESSAGE_MAP()
protected:
    BOOL CloseAllChildWindows();
};

// MDI child frame window class
class CChildFrame : public CMDIChildWnd
{
public:
    static int NEAR nChild;
    CChildFrame(BOOL bMaximized = FALSE);
protected:
    //{{AFX_MSG(CChildFrame)
    afx_msg void OnPaint();
    afx_msg void OnFileClose();
    afx_msg void OnClose();
    //}}AFX_MSG
    DECLARE_MESSAGE_MAP()
};
```

EX22C.CPP

```
#include "stdafx.h"
#include "ex22c.h"

CEx22cApp NEAR theApp; // the one and only CEx22cApp object

BOOL CEx22cApp::InitInstance()
{
    m_pMainWnd = new CMainFrame();
    m_pMainWnd->ShowWindow(m_nCmdShow);
    m_pMainWnd->UpdateWindow();
    new CChildFrame();
    return TRUE;
}


/////////////////////////////////////////////////////////////////////////
BEGIN_MESSAGE_MAP(CMainFrame, CMDIFrameWnd)
    //{{AFX_MSG_MAP(CMainFrame)
    ON_WM_CLOSE()
    ON_WM_QUERYENDSESSION()
    ON_COMMAND(ID_FILE_NEW, OnFileNew)
    ON_COMMAND(ID_WINDOW_CLOSE_ALL, OnWindowCloseAll)
```

(continued)

Figure 22-4. *continued*

```
    ON_UPDATE_COMMAND_UI(ID_WINDOW_CLOSE_ALL, OnUpdateWindowCloseAll)
    //}}AFX_MSG_MAP
END_MESSAGE_MAP()

//////////////////////////////////////////////////////////////////////
CMainFrame::CMainFrame()
{
    Create(NULL, "EX22C Application",
           WS_OVERLAPPEDWINDOW,
           rectDefault, NULL,
           MAKEINTRESOURCE(IDR_MAINFRAME));
}

//////////////////////////////////////////////////////////////////////
void CMainFrame::OnClose()
{
    if (CloseAllChildWindows()) {
        CMDIFrameWnd::OnClose();
    }
}

//////////////////////////////////////////////////////////////////////
BOOL CMainFrame::OnQueryEndSession()
{
    return CloseAllChildWindows();
}

//////////////////////////////////////////////////////////////////////
void CMainFrame::OnFileNew()
{
    BOOL bMaximized = FALSE;
    // creates a new child window, maximized if active child is maximized
    CChildFrame* pActiveChild = (CChildFrame*) MDIGetActive(&bMaximized);
    new CChildFrame(bMaximized);
}

//////////////////////////////////////////////////////////////////////
void CMainFrame::OnWindowCloseAll()
{
    CloseAllChildWindows();
}

//////////////////////////////////////////////////////////////////////
void CMainFrame::OnUpdateWindowCloseAll(CCmdUI* pCmdUI)
{
    pCmdUI->Enable(MDIGetActive() != NULL);
}
```

(continued)

Figure 22-4. *continued*

```
///////////////////////////////////////////////////////////////////////
BOOL CMainFrame::CloseAllChildWindows()
{
    // returns TRUE if all child windows permit closure
    CChildFrame* pChild;
    CChildFrame* pPrevChild = NULL;
    while ((pChild = (CChildFrame*) MDIGetActive()) != NULL) {
        if (pChild == pPrevChild)
            return FALSE; // closure not permitted
        pPrevChild = pChild;
        pChild->SendMessage(WM_CLOSE);
    }
    return TRUE;
}


///////////////////////////////////////////////////////////////////////
BEGIN_MESSAGE_MAP(CChildFrame, CMDIChildWnd)
    //{{AFX_MSG_MAP(CChildFrame)
    ON_WM_PAINT()
    ON_WM_CLOSE()
    ON_COMMAND(ID_FILE_CLOSE, OnFileClose)
    //}}AFX_MSG_MAP
END_MESSAGE_MAP()

int NEAR CChildFrame::nChild = 1; // static

///////////////////////////////////////////////////////////////////////
CChildFrame::CChildFrame(BOOL bMaximized /*= FALSE*/)
{
    char szTitle[30];
    wsprintf(szTitle, "EX22C Child Window %d", nChild++);
    CMainFrame* pFrameWnd = (CMainFrame*) AfxGetApp()->m_pMainWnd;
    Create(NULL, szTitle,
            WS_CHILD | WS_VISIBLE | WS_OVERLAPPEDWINDOW |
            (bMaximized ? WS_MAXIMIZE : 0),
            rectDefault, pFrameWnd);
}


///////////////////////////////////////////////////////////////////////
void CChildFrame::OnPaint()
{
    CPaintDC dc(this);
    dc.TextOut(0, 0, "Hello, world!");
}


///////////////////////////////////////////////////////////////////////
void CChildFrame::OnClose()
```

(continued)

Figure 22-4. *continued*

```
{
    if (AfxMessageBox("OK to close window?", MB_YESNO) == IDYES) {
        CMDIChildWnd::OnClose();
    }
}

////////////////////////////////////////////////////////////////////////////
void CChildFrame::OnFileClose()
{
    SendMessage(WM_CLOSE);
}
```

CEx22cApp

This is the standard application class again, derived from *CWinApp*.

InitInstance

In this MDI example, *InitInstance* performs one of the same functions that it performs in a document–view MDI application. It constructs an object of class *CMainFrame* and then shows the window. It also constructs the initial child window.

CMainFrame

You can use this class directly in your own minimalist MDI applications, or you can rename it and use it as a base class.

Constructor

The *CMainFrame* constructor creates the main frame window object. The note on page 403 about the EX22A two-phase constructor applies here also.

OnClose

The *CMainFrame OnClose* function is called only when the user closes the main frame window from the system menu or with Alt-F4. Its purpose is to send WM_CLOSE messages to all the child windows. If this function weren't mapped, the child windows would be summarily destroyed without the opportunity to process the close message.

OnQueryEndSession

When Windows itself is shutting down, it sends the WM_QUERYENDSESSION message to the main windows of all applications. If any application returns 0, Windows does not shut down. The message handler here does the same thing as *OnClose*.

OnFileNew

The File New menu item, through the *OnFileNew* message handler, causes construction of a new child window. If the current active child is maximized, the new child is maximized.

OnWindowCloseAll

The application's Window menu has a Close All item that is mapped to this function. The *OnWindowCloseAll* function sends a WM_CLOSE message to all child windows.

OnUpdateWindowCloseAll

The Window menu Close All item is enabled only when there is at least one child window.

CloseAllChildWindows

This is a protected member function that sends the WM_CLOSE message to the child windows. In a loop, the function sends the close message to the current active child window. If the active child refuses to be closed (the window stays active), the looping terminates, and the function returns failure status (*FALSE*).

CChildFrame

This class is derived from *CMDIChildWnd*. Add your own message handlers and *OnPaint* code to customize this class.

Data Members

The *CChildFrame* class has a static data member *nChild* that is incremented each time a new child window is created. This number is used in the child window titles.

Constructor

The *CChildFrame* constructor creates the child window object. If the optional *bMaximized* parameter is *TRUE*, the child window occupies the entire main frame client area. The window title includes a sequential window number from the

---

For Windows SDK Programmers

If you look at the *Create* function call in the constructor, you might think that the child frame is being created directly. Actually, the *CMDIChildWnd Create* function loads a structure and then sends a WM_MDICREATE message to the MDI client window (owned by the main frame window). The client window then creates the child window.

static *nChild* data member. The note on page 403 about the EX22A two-phase constructor applies here also.

OnPaint

As in EX22A, you must use *OnPaint* for painting in the window.

OnClose

This message handler is called in response to the WM_CLOSE message, sent by the main frame window or by the user's closing of a child window. This *OnClose* function displays a message box that asks the user for permission to close the window.

OnFileClose

This function is called when the user chooses Close from the File menu. It sends the WM_CLOSE message so that the *OnClose* member function can veto the window closing. The File Close menu item is disabled if there are no child windows.

Destroying *CMDIChildWnd* objects

You might have noticed that child frame window objects are constructed with the *new* operator and not explicitly destroyed. These window objects are destroyed by the application framework in the *CWnd* virtual function *PostNCDestroy* (which is overridden in *CFrameWnd*) when the window itself is destroyed as a result of user action. Technical Note 17 in the MFCNOTES.HLP Help file tells you which window objects are destroyed.

Resource Requirements

The EX22C program needs an icon resource with ID *IDR_MAINFRAME* set to 2. The EX22C Window menu, shown in Figure 22-5, uses the same ID.

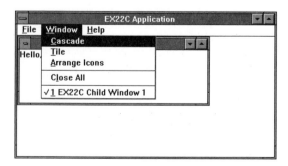

Figure 22-5.
The EX22C Window menu.

For Windows to insert the child window list at the bottom of the Window menu, the Window menu <u>must</u> be second from the right on the main menu.

Here are the command IDs for the menu items:

Menu Items	Command ID
File New	ID_FILE_NEW
File Close	ID_FILE_CLOSE
File Exit	ID_APP_EXIT
Window Cascade	ID_WINDOW_CASCADE
Window Tile	ID_WINDOW_TILE_HORZ
Window Arrange Icons	ID_WINDOW_ARRANGE
Window Close All	ID_WINDOW_CLOSE_ALL
Help	ID_HELP

23

Storing Bitmaps in a Document—DIBs and the Clipboard

In Chapter 10, you studied GDI bitmaps, and you saw how easy it was to load a device-independent bitmap (DIB) from a resource. Direct disk accessing of DIBs is more difficult, but this chapter presents a class, called *CDib*, that simplifies DIB processing. The EX23A example program, built around the *CDib* class, illustrates serialization of DIBs, direct file I/O, and transferring of GDI bitmaps through the Windows clipboard.

The Windows DIB Format

If you want to save bitmaps in a document file (or database) that other computers can read, you must use a device-independent format. The Windows DIB format is a good candidate because the Windows API directly supports it. Many applications, including Windows Paintbrush, process disk files in DIB format (BMP files). The standard DIB format supports monochrome, 16-color, and 256-color bitmaps, and it also supports 24-bit color bitmaps.

The DIB format has compression options for 16-color and 256-color bitmaps, and this compression can save substantial amounts of disk space and RAM. An uncompressed 16-color VGA screen dump bitmap, for example, requires 154 KB, but a compressed version might be as small as 30 KB.

A DIB is different from a GDI bitmap in that you have direct access to the DIB's data. As a matter of fact, you must allocate memory for the DIBs you create. In a DIB data structure, each pixel is represented by 1, 4, 8, or 24 adjacent bits. The bits are packed into bytes, which are organized by row and then by column as shown in Figure 23-1. Rows are padded to 4-byte boundaries, and a header provides the necessary access information. For the DIB header layout, look up the *BITMAPINFOHEADER* structure in the *Microsoft Windows 3.1 Programmer's*

Reference. Figure 23-1 shows the layout of a 16-color DIB that is 10 pixels wide by 7 pixels high. Notice that the DIB requires 56 bytes of storage, plus the header.

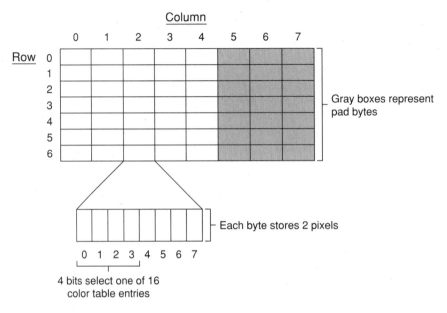

Figure 23-1.
The organization of a 16-color DIB.

DIBs, Colors, and Palettes

Refer to Chapter 5 for a description of the default color mapping for the common types of display boards in Windows systems. Be sure you're familiar with the standard pure colors that the VGA and 256-color display drivers support.

Because we are talking about a device-independent format, the DIB color information must be device-independent. A DIB contains its own color table. A 16-color DIB, for example, contains sixteen 24-bit absolute red-green-blue color values. Windows doesn't use dithered colors in bitmaps; it uses the closest matching pure color. Monochrome DIBs (with 1 bit per pixel) contain values for both the foreground and background colors.

When Windows displays a monochrome or a 16-color DIB (or converts it to a GDI bitmap) with a standard VGA display board, it chooses standard pure colors that most closely match the specified colors. You have no control over this process. Color palettes have no effect with a standard VGA display board.

With a 256-color display board, however, you have more flexibility. If you don't use color palettes (the default), Windows maps a DIB's colors to the driver's 20 standard colors. If you do use color palettes, Windows maps the DIB's colors as best it can to the colors that the display board supports; 20 palette colors are always reserved for the standard colors, but 236 palette colors can be changed to accommodate the bitmap.

Color palette programming is quite complex because you have to consider the interactions both among applications and among sibling MDI child windows. The 256-color display board can display only 256 colors at any time, as specified by the system palette. Suppose, for example, that a window gets the input focus and replaces the system palette's dark green entry with neon pink. Suppose a second window is showing a forest scene bitmap. Because you don't want neon pink trees, even in an inactive window, you must remap the inactive window's colors to enable Windows to choose another shade of green for the trees.

Inactive window programs can respond to the Windows message WM_PALETTE-CHANGED, which is sent to all windows when the system palette is changed. When a program gets the input focus, it receives a WM_QUERYNEWPALETTE message if the system palette has been changed. In both cases, the program realizes its own color palette into the system palette. See the DIBLOOK program in the \MSVC\MFC\SAMPLES subdirectory for an example of the use of DIBs with color palettes. Remember that color palette programming applies only to color-intensive programs running on 256-color display boards.

A 24-bit DIB doesn't need a color table because the pixel groups specify colors directly. If you display a 24-bit DIB with a 24-bit display board, you don't need a color palette. If you display a 24-bit DIB with a 256-color display board, you can define your own 256-color palette that contains appropriate color values. Windows then matches the DIB's colors with the closest matching palette colors. If you don't define a palette, the DIB will be displayed with the 20 standard colors.

Passing Images via the Clipboard

As a Windows user, you're probably aware that the clipboard is a useful tool for transferring information among Windows-based programs. The clipboard can accommodate both text and image data, but the clipboard writer program and the clipboard reader program must agree on a format. The clipboard writer often provides data in several formats, and the reader chooses one that it understands. It's possible to transfer DIBs via the clipboard, but few programs use the DIB format. Many Windows programs use the GDI bitmap format, however, so that's the format we'll use in the EX23A example.

Bitmap Clipboard Rules

When you use the clipboard, first be aware that all applications must share one clipboard. Then be prepared to follow some strict rules when transferring GDI bitmaps via the clipboard.

■ The clipboard must be open before you can transfer information. Call the *CWnd OpenClipboard* member function. If it returns *TRUE*, you have exclusive access to the clipboard; otherwise, you know that another program is using it.

■ If you are going to place information on the clipboard, you must first empty the clipboard with the Windows API function *EmptyClipboard*.

419

- The Windows API function *SetClipboardData* accepts a GDI bitmap <u>handle</u> (*HBITMAP*). The designated bitmap <u>cannot</u> be selected into a device context when you call *SetClipboardData*. You cannot use the bitmap again after you send it to the clipboard. This means that you'll have to copy the bitmap if your *OnDraw* function needs to display it.

- The clipboard deletes *HBITMAP* entities that have been sent to it. If you've used a *CBitmap* object, you can't delete that object until you've called the *CGdiObject* member function *Detach*. The *Detach* function separates the GDI bitmap handle from the C++ object so that the destructor doesn't delete the bitmap. *Detach* returns the bitmap handle.

- The Windows API function *GetClipboardData* returns a GDI bitmap handle (*HBITMAP*). The *CGdiObject FromHandle* static function converts the handle to a temporary *CBitmap* object pointer. You don't have to worry about deleting this object or detaching the handle from it. You cannot, however, leave the bitmap selected into a device context. If you want to display the bitmap, you must copy it.

- When you're finished with the clipboard, you must use the Windows *CloseClipboard* function.

  Note: *Be careful with dialogs and message boxes that you create while the clipboard is open. If you don't make these dialogs system modal, the user could try to access the busy clipboard from another program.*

DIBs in Microsoft Foundation Class Library Documents

Microsoft Foundation Class Library application data is stored in *CDocument* objects and transferred to and from document files. If your application needs to save and retrieve images, those images must be stored in the document in device-independent format. In this chapter's example, EX23A, the document maintains an image in Windows DIB format.

The *CDib* Class

The Microsoft Foundation Class Library has no *CDib* class, so we'll write our own. This class works fairly well, but it's designed as a teaching tool rather than as a piece of commercial software. You might want to add more error checking plus other features such as palette support and OS/2 Presentation Manager DIB file support. The *CDib* class is designed to be used directly. There are no virtual functions to implement in derived classes.

A *CDib* object represents a single device-independent bitmap. The image bits, together with all necessary decoding information, are contained within the object. There is no copy constructor or assignment operator because DIBs are often big, and it doesn't make much sense to copy them within a program. Also, there are no public data members.

A document can contain a single *CDib* object, or multiple *CDib* objects can exist in a document structure, such as a list or an array. Thus, DIBs can be serialized along with the rest of the document data.

Figure 23-2 shows the *CDib* class declaration:

```
CDIB.H
class CDib : public CObject
{
    DECLARE_SERIAL(CDib)
private:
    char huge* m_lpBuf;    // DIB data buffer
    DWORD      m_dwLength; // total buffer length, including file header
    int        m_nBits;    // number of color bits per pixel
    // pointers for internal use
    LPBITMAPFILEHEADER m_lpBMFH;
    LPBITMAPINFOHEADER m_lpBMIH;
    LPBITMAPINFO       m_lpBMI;
    LPSTR              m_lpData;
public:
    CDib();
    CDib(CDC* pDC, int nBt = 0, BOOL bCompr = TRUE);
    // nBt = 0 means use default bits/pixel
    ~CDib();
    virtual void Serialize(CArchive &ar);
    BOOL Read(CFile* pFile);
    BOOL Write(CFile* pFile);
    CBitmap* MakeBitmap(CDC* pDC, CSize& bmSize);
    BOOL Display(CDC*, CPoint origin);
    BOOL Stretch(CDC*, CPoint origin, CSize size);
    int GetColorBits();
    DWORD GetLength();
    void SetMonoColors(DWORD dwForeground, DWORD dwBackground);
    BOOL GetMonoColors(DWORD& dwForeground, DWORD& dwBackground);
private:
    BOOL AllocateMemory(BOOL bRealloc = FALSE);
};
```

Figure 23-2.
The CDib *class declaration.*

Here's a rundown of the *CDib* member functions. (The implementation code is shown in Figure 23-3 beginning on page 427.)

- **Default Constructor**—You'll use the default constructor when you're loading a DIB from an archive or from a file. It creates an empty DIB object.

- **Bitmap Constructor**—Despite the absence of a *CBitmap* parameter, this second constructor makes a DIB from a GDI bitmap. The bitmap must have been previously selected into a memory device context.

Parameter	Description
pDC	A pointer to the memory device context into which the GDI bitmap is selected.
nBt	The number of color bits for the DIB; *0* means use the value from the GDI bitmap.
bCompr	*TRUE* for a compressed DIB (the default); *FALSE* for an uncompressed DIB.

- **Destructor**—The *CDib* destructor frees all allocated DIB memory.

- *Serialize*—See the *Class Library Reference* for a description of the *CObject* virtual *Serialize* function.

- *Read*—This function reads a BMP file into the *CDib* object. The file must have been successfully opened.

Parameter	Description
pFile	A pointer to a *CFile* object. The corresponding disk file contains the DIB.
Return value	*TRUE* if successful.

- *Write*—This function writes a BMP file from the *CDib* object. The file must have been successfully opened or created.

Parameter	Description
pFile	A pointer to a *CFile* object. The DIB will be written to the corresponding disk file.
Return value	*TRUE* if successful.

- *MakeBitmap*—This function creates a GDI bitmap from the contents of the *CDib* object. The bitmap is then selected into the memory device context that is passed as a parameter. The bitmap size and number of color bits are set according to the DIB characteristics.

Parameter	Description
pDC	A pointer to the memory device context into which the GDI bitmap will be selected.
bmSize	A reference to a *CSize* object that holds the GDI bitmap size. The *MakeBitmap* function sets the value of this parameter.
Return value	A pointer to the previously selected GDI bitmap.

422

■ **Display**—This function sends this *CDib* object to the display (or printer) without creating an intermediate GDI bitmap. The function does no scaling under any circumstances.

Parameter	Description
pDC	A pointer to the display or printer device context that will receive the DIB image.
origin	A *CPoint* object that holds the logical coordinates at which the DIB will be displayed.
Return value	*TRUE* if successful.

■ **Stretch**—This function outputs this *CDib* object to the display (or printer) without creating an intermediate GDI bitmap. The bitmap will be stretched as necessary to fit the specified rectangle.

Parameter	Description
pDC	A pointer to the display or printer device context that will receive the DIB image.
origin	A *CPoint* object that holds the logical coordinates at which the DIB will be displayed.
size	A *CSize* object that represents the display rectangle's width and height in logical units.
Return value	*TRUE* if successful.

■ **GetColorBits**—This function returns the number of color bits per pixel for this *CDib* object. If the DIB is empty, *0* is returned.

■ **GetLength**—This function returns the total number of bytes in the *CDib* data buffer. This is the length of a corresponding BMP file. If the DIB is empty, *0* is returned.

■ **SetMonoColors, GetMonoColors**—Monochrome DIBs contain the values for the bitmap's foreground and background colors. Because this information is not part of the GDI bitmap structure, we need functions to set and retrieve the two color values. *GetMonoColors* returns *TRUE* if the DIB is a monochrome bitmap.

DIB Access Functions

The *CDib* class uses four important Windows DIB access functions. None of these functions are class library functions, so you'll need to refer to the Windows SDK documentation (or the online help) for details. Here's a summary:

- **SetDIBitsToDevice**—The *CDib Display* member function uses this function. It displays a DIB directly on the display or printer. No scaling occurs; one bitmap bit corresponds to one display pixel or one printer dot. This scaling restriction limits the function's usefulness. The function doesn't work like *BitBlt* because *BitBlt* uses logical coordinates.

- **StretchDIBits**—The *CDib Stretch* member function uses this function. It displays a DIB directly on the display or printer in a manner similar to that of *StretchBlt*.

- **GetDIBits**—The *CDib* bitmap constructor uses this function. It constructs a DIB from a GDI bitmap, using memory that you allocate. You have some control over the format of the DIB because you can specify the number of color bits per pixel and the compression. If you are using compression, you have to call *GetDIBits* twice, once to calculate the memory needed and again to generate the DIB data.

- **CreateDIBitmap**—Contrary to its name, this function creates a GDI bitmap from a DIB. The *CDib MakeBitmap* member function uses it. Before you call *CreateDIBitmap*, you must have a memory device context with a selected prototype bitmap that has the same characteristics as the bitmap you want *CreateDIBitmap* to create. If you want a 16-color bitmap, for example, you must first construct a 16-color prototype bitmap. If you don't first select a bitmap into the memory device context, *CreateDIBitmap* provides a monochrome bitmap.

A strange thing happens when *CreateDIBitmap* processes a monochrome DIB. The function switches the image bits depending on the DIB's two color values. In the *CDib* class, we circumvent this behavior and preserve the original DIB bit values.

The EX23A Example

The EX23A example program uses a serializable document to hold a single *CDib* object. The one and only view class allows the display of the DIB in a scrolling view with a shrink-to-fit option. The view also supports the Printing and Print Preview features. The Edit menu has items for cutting, copying, and pasting bitmaps (in GDI format) to and from the clipboard. It also has Copy To and Paste From items for writing and reading BMP files. EX23A fully exploits the new *CDib* class.

As was the MATPLAN example in Chapter 21, this example is presented with code highlights and resource requirements. Here is a table of the files and classes:

Header File	Source Code File	Class	Description
EX23A.H	EX23A.CPP	CEx23aApp	Main application—from AppWizard
MAINFRM.H	MAINFRM.CPP	CMainFrame	SDI main frame—from AppWizard
EX23ADOC.H	EX23ADOC.CPP	CEx23aDoc	EX23A document
EX23AVW.H	EX23AVW.CPP	CEx23aView	Scrolling view class
BITSDLG.H	BITSDLG.CPP	CBitsDialog	Dialog for color bits and compression
CDIB.H	CDIB.CPP	CDib	DIB class
STDAFX.H	STDAFX.CPP		Precompiled headers

The application and main frame class consist of standard code generated by AppWizard, so they are not listed or described. The other classes are described together with their member functions.

CEx23aDoc

This document class contains a single <u>pointer</u> to a *CDib* object. Why not use an embedded object? Consider the problem of replacing the document's DIB with a new DIB just read from the clipboard or disk. With an embedded *CDib* object, the class would need an assignment operator, or the serialization code would have to delete old data. With the *CDib* pointer, we simply delete the old object and construct a new one.

Constructor, Destructor

The *CEx23aDoc* constructor constructs the initial *CDib* object on the heap, and the destructor destroys it.

DeleteContents

This overridden application framework virtual function deletes the document's current *CDib* object and constructs a new, empty one. This function is crucial in SDI applications because it's called every time the user opens a new document or loads a document from disk.

```
void CEx23aDoc::DeleteContents()
{
    delete m_pDib;
    m_pDib = new CDib;
}
```

Serialize

This overridden application framework virtual function calls the *Serialize* function for the document's *CDib* object.

OnEditClearAll

This message handler responds to the Edit Clear All menu item.

```
void CEx23aDoc::OnEditClearAll()
{
    DeleteContents();
    UpdateAllViews(NULL);
    SetModifiedFlag();
}
```

CBitsDialog

The *CBitsDialog* class is generated entirely by ClassWizard. It's based on the dialog resource discussed in the EX23A resource file section.

CDib

You've already seen the *CDib* class declaration and member function descriptions. Figure 23-3 lists the *CDib* implementation code. Below are a couple of important observations about the class.

Memory Allocation

Memory is allocated and freed with the WINDOWSX.H macros *GlobalAllocPtr*, *GlobalReAllocPtr*, and *GlobalFreePtr*. These functions are suitable for the large memory blocks that bitmaps often require. Memory is allocated in the private member function *AllocateMemory*.

Serialization of Large Bitmaps

Because so many bitmaps are larger than 64 KB, the *CDib* class must use *huge* pointers to manage data. The *CFile* class has the *ReadHuge* and *WriteHuge* member functions for reading and writing large data blocks, but there are no equivalent *CArchive* member functions. It's easy enough to get the archive's associated file object so that you can use the *CFile* functions for huge pointers. You must call the *CArchive Flush* function before reading or writing, however, to synchronize the archive's buffer. Here are the two key statements from the loading section of the *CDib Serialize* function:

```
ar.Flush();
ar.GetFile()->ReadHuge(m_lpBuf, m_dwLength);
```

The *CDib Write* function, shown below, is the first place where we've had to use the class library exception-handling mechanism. The *TRY* and *CATCH* macros work together to process errors where there is no error return value. These macros will be replaced when the C++ compiler officially supports exception handling.

```
BOOL CDib::Write(CFile* pFile)
{
    TRY {
        pFile->WriteHuge(m_lpBuf, m_dwLength);
    }
    CATCH (CException, e) {
        AfxMessageBox("Write error--possible disk full condition");
        return FALSE;
    }
    END_CATCH
    return TRUE;
}
```

```
CDIB.CPP
#include "stdafx.h"
#include "resource.h"
#include "cdib.h"
#include <windowsx.h>  // for GlobalAllocPtr

IMPLEMENT_SERIAL(CDib, CObject, 0)

/////////////////////////////////////////////////////////////////////
CDib::CDib()
{
    m_dwLength = 0L;
    m_nBits    = 0;
    m_lpBuf    = NULL;
}


/////////////////////////////////////////////////////////////////////
CDib::CDib(CDC* pDC, int nBt, BOOL bCompr)
// pDC is memory DC ptr
// nBt is color bits per pixel (default = 0)
// bCompr is compression (default = TRUE)
{
// constructs a DIB from the contents of a bitmap
    BITMAP bm;
    int    nPaletteSize;

    CBitmap* pEmptyBitmap = new CBitmap;
    pEmptyBitmap->CreateCompatibleBitmap(pDC, 0, 0);
    CBitmap* pBitmap = (CBitmap*) (pDC->SelectObject(pEmptyBitmap));
    pBitmap->GetObject(sizeof(bm), &bm);
    if ((nBt == 1) || (nBt == 4) || (nBt == 8) || (nBt == 24)) {
        m_nBits = nBt;
```

Figure 23-3. *(continued)*
The CDib *implementation code listing.*

427

Figure 23-3. *continued*

```
    }
    else {    // nBt = 0
        m_nBits = bm.bmPlanes * bm.bmBitsPixel; // color bits per pixel
    }
    if (m_nBits == 1) {
        nPaletteSize = 2;
    }
    else {
        if (m_nBits == 4) {
            nPaletteSize = 16;
        }
        else {
            if (m_nBits == 8) {
                nPaletteSize = 256;
            }
            else {
                nPaletteSize = 0; // no palette for 24-bit display
            }
        }
    }
    // fills out row to 4-byte boundary
    DWORD dwBytes = ((DWORD) bm.bmWidth * m_nBits) / 32;
    if (((DWORD) bm.bmWidth * m_nBits) % 32) {
        dwBytes ++;
    }
    dwBytes *= 4;

    m_dwLength = sizeof(BITMAPFILEHEADER) + sizeof(BITMAPINFOHEADER) +
                 sizeof(RGBQUAD) * nPaletteSize;
    if (!AllocateMemory()) return;

    m_lpBMIH->biSize = sizeof(BITMAPINFOHEADER);
    m_lpBMIH->biWidth = bm.bmWidth;
    m_lpBMIH->biHeight = bm.bmHeight;
    m_lpBMIH->biPlanes = 1;
    m_lpBMIH->biBitCount = m_nBits; // 1, 4, 8, or 24
    if (bCompr && (m_nBits == 4)) {
        m_lpBMIH->biCompression = BI_RLE4;
    }
    else {
        if (bCompr && (m_nBits == 8)) {
            m_lpBMIH->biCompression = BI_RLE8;
        }
        else {
            m_lpBMIH->biCompression = BI_RGB;
        }
    }
    m_lpBMIH->biSizeImage = 0;
    m_lpBMIH->biXPelsPerMeter = 0;
```

(continued)

Figure 23-3. *continued*

```
    m_lpBMIH->biYPelsPerMeter = 0;
    m_lpBMIH->biClrUsed = 0;
    m_lpBMIH->biClrImportant = 0;

    // calls GetDIBits with null data pointer to get size of DIB
    ::GetDIBits(pDC->GetSafeHdc(), (HBITMAP) pBitmap->GetSafeHandle(),
             0, (WORD) bm.bmHeight, NULL, m_lpBMI, DIB_RGB_COLORS);

    if (m_lpBMIH->biSizeImage == 0) {
        m_dwLength += dwBytes * bm.bmHeight;
        m_lpBMIH->biCompression = BI_RGB;
        // escape route for device drivers that don't do compression
        TRACE("Can't do compression\n");
    }
    else {
        m_dwLength += m_lpBMIH->biSizeImage;
    }
    if (!AllocateMemory(TRUE)) {
        return;
    }
    m_lpData = (LPSTR) m_lpBMIH + sizeof(BITMAPINFOHEADER) +
             sizeof(RGBQUAD) * nPaletteSize;
    m_lpBMFH->bfType = 0x4d42; // 'BM'
    m_lpBMFH->bfSize = m_dwLength;
    m_lpBMFH->bfReserved1 = 0;
    m_lpBMFH->bfReserved2 = 0;
    m_lpBMFH->bfOffBits = (char huge*) m_lpData - m_lpBuf;

    // second GetDIBits call to make DIB
    if (!::GetDIBits(pDC->GetSafeHdc(), (HBITMAP)
        pBitmap->GetSafeHandle(), 0, (WORD) bm.bmHeight, m_lpData,
        m_lpBMI, DIB_RGB_COLORS)) {
        m_dwLength = 0L;
    }
    delete pDC->SelectObject(pBitmap); // delete pEmptyBitmap
}

/////////////////////////////////////////////////////////////////////
CDib::~CDib()
{
    if (m_lpBuf) {
        GlobalFreePtr(m_lpBuf);  // free the DIB memory
    }
}

/////////////////////////////////////////////////////////////////////
void CDib::Serialize(CArchive& ar)
{
    WORD wBM;
```

(continued)

Figure 23-3. *continued*

```
    CObject::Serialize(ar);
    if (ar.IsStoring()) {
    // 'BA' distinct from 'BM' so we don't read BMP files by mistake
        ar << (WORD) 0x4142 << m_dwLength;  // 'BA' for bitmap archive
        ar.Flush();
        ar.GetFile()->WriteHuge(m_lpBuf, m_dwLength);
    }
    else {
        ASSERT(m_dwLength == 0L); // DIB must be empty
        ar >> wBM >> m_dwLength;
        if (m_dwLength > 0L) {
            if (wBM == (WORD) 0x4142) {
                if (!AllocateMemory()) {
                    return;
                }
                ar.Flush();
                ar.GetFile()->ReadHuge(m_lpBuf, m_dwLength);
                m_lpData = (LPSTR) m_lpBMFH + m_lpBMFH->bfOffBits;
                m_nBits = m_lpBMIH->biBitCount;
            }
            else {
                AfxMessageBox("Invalid DIB archive");
                m_dwLength = 0L;
                m_nBits = 0;
            }
        }
    }
}


//////////////////////////////////////////////////////////////////
BOOL CDib::Read(CFile* pFile)
{
    // file assumed to be open
    ASSERT(m_dwLength == 0L); // DIB must be empty
    m_dwLength = pFile->GetLength();
    if (!AllocateMemory()) {
        return FALSE;
    }
    DWORD dwCount = pFile->ReadHuge(m_lpBuf, m_dwLength);
    if (dwCount != m_dwLength) {
        AfxMessageBox("Read error");
        return FALSE;
    }
    if (m_lpBMFH->bfType != 0x4d42) {
        AfxMessageBox("Invalid bitmap file");
        return FALSE;
    }
```

(continued)

Figure 23-3. *continued*

```
    ASSERT((m_lpBMIH->biBitCount == 1) || (m_lpBMIH->biBitCount == 4) ||
           (m_lpBMIH->biBitCount == 8) || (m_lpBMIH->biBitCount == 24));
    m_lpData = (LPSTR) m_lpBMFH + m_lpBMFH->bfOffBits;
    m_nBits = m_lpBMIH->biBitCount;
    return TRUE;
}

/////////////////////////////////////////////////////////////////////
BOOL CDib::Write(CFile* pFile)
{
    TRY {
        pFile->WriteHuge(m_lpBuf, m_dwLength);
    }
    CATCH (CException, e) {
        AfxMessageBox("Write error--possible disk full condition");
        return FALSE;
    }
    END_CATCH
    return TRUE;
}

/////////////////////////////////////////////////////////////////////
CBitmap* CDib::MakeBitmap(CDC* pDC, CSize& bmSize)
{
    // replaces the DC's existing bitmap with a new one from the DIB
    // returns the old one
    BITMAP bm;
    DWORD  dwFore, dwBack;
    // checks to see whether DIB buffer is properly loaded
    if (m_dwLength == 0L) {
        bmSize.cx = bmSize.cy = 0;
        return NULL;
    }

    // this code conditions the bitmap for mono or color
    int nPlanes = pDC->GetDeviceCaps(PLANES);
    int nBitsPixel = pDC->GetDeviceCaps(BITSPIXEL);
    CBitmap* pConfigBitmap = new CBitmap;
    char bits[100];
    if (m_lpBMIH->biBitCount == 1) {
        pConfigBitmap->CreateBitmap(1, 1, 1, 1, bits);
    }
    else {
        pConfigBitmap->CreateBitmap(1, 1, nPlanes, nBitsPixel, bits);
    }
    CBitmap* pOriginalBitmap =
        (CBitmap*) pDC->SelectObject(pConfigBitmap);
```

(continued)

Figure 23-3. *continued*

```
// CreateDIBitmap "switches bits" for mono bitmaps, depending on colors,
//   so we'll fool it
    if (GetMonoColors(dwFore, dwBack)) {
        SetMonoColors(0L, 0xFFFFFFFL);
    }

#ifdef _WIN32
    HBITMAP hBitmap = ::CreateDIBitmap(pDC->GetSafeHdc(), m_lpBMIH,
            CBM_INIT, (CONST BYTE*) (m_lpBuf + m_lpBMFH->bfOffBits),
            m_lpBMI, DIB_RGB_COLORS);
#else
    HBITMAP hBitmap = ::CreateDIBitmap(pDC->GetSafeHdc(), m_lpBMIH,
            CBM_INIT, (LPSTR) (m_lpBuf + m_lpBMFH->bfOffBits),
            m_lpBMI, DIB_RGB_COLORS);
#endif
    if (hBitmap == NULL) {
        TRACE("null bitmap\n");
        delete pDC->SelectObject(pOriginalBitmap); // del. config bitmap
        return NULL; // untested error logic
    }

    SetMonoColors(dwFore, dwBack);

    // Can't use CBitmap::FromHandle here because we need to
    //   delete the object later
    CBitmap* pBitmap = new CBitmap;
    pBitmap->Attach(hBitmap);
    pBitmap->GetObject(sizeof(bm), &bm);
    bmSize.cx = bm.bmWidth;
    bmSize.cy = bm.bmHeight;
    delete pDC->SelectObject(pBitmap); // delete configuration bitmap
    return pOriginalBitmap;
}

/////////////////////////////////////////////////////////////////////
BOOL CDib::Display(CDC* pDC, CPoint origin)
{
    // direct to device--bypass the GDI bitmap
    if (!m_lpBuf) {
        return FALSE; // nothing to display
    }
    if (!::SetDIBitsToDevice(pDC->GetSafeHdc(), origin.x, origin.y,
        (WORD) m_lpBMIH->biWidth, (WORD) m_lpBMIH->biHeight, 0, 0, 0,
        (WORD) m_lpBMIH->biHeight, m_lpData, m_lpBMI,
        DIB_RGB_COLORS)) {
        return FALSE;
    }
    return TRUE;
}
```

(continued)

Figure 23-3. *continued*

```
///////////////////////////////////////////////////////////////////////
BOOL CDib::Stretch(CDC* pDC, CPoint origin, CSize size)
{
    // direct to device--bypass the GDI bitmap
    if (!m_lpBuf) {
        return FALSE; // nothing to display
    }
    if (!::StretchDIBits(pDC->GetSafeHdc(), origin.x, origin.y,
        size.cx, size.cy, 0, 0, (WORD) m_lpBMIH->biWidth,
        (WORD) m_lpBMIH->biHeight, m_lpData, m_lpBMI,
        DIB_RGB_COLORS, SRCCOPY)) {
        return FALSE;
    }
    return TRUE;
}


///////////////////////////////////////////////////////////////////////
int CDib::GetColorBits()
{
    return m_nBits;
}


///////////////////////////////////////////////////////////////////////
DWORD CDib::GetLength()
{
    return m_dwLength;
}


///////////////////////////////////////////////////////////////////////
void CDib::SetMonoColors(DWORD dwForeground, DWORD dwBackground)
{
    if (m_nBits != 1) {
        return;
    }
    unsigned long far* pPalette = (unsigned long far*)
                    ((LPSTR) m_lpBMIH + sizeof(BITMAPINFOHEADER));
    *pPalette = dwForeground;
    *(++pPalette) = dwBackground;
    return;
}


///////////////////////////////////////////////////////////////////////
BOOL CDib::GetMonoColors(DWORD& dwForeground, DWORD& dwBackground)
{
    if (m_nBits != 1) {
        return FALSE;
    }
    unsigned long far* pPalette = (unsigned long far*)
                    ((LPSTR) m_lpBMIH + sizeof(BITMAPINFOHEADER));
```

(continued)

Figure 23-3. *continued*

```
        dwForeground = *pPalette;
        dwBackground = *(++pPalette);
        return TRUE;
    }


    ////////////////////////////////////////////////////////////////
    BOOL CDib::AllocateMemory(BOOL bRealloc) // bRealloc default = FALSE
    {
        if (bRealloc) {
            m_lpBuf = (char huge*) GlobalReAllocPtr(m_lpBuf,
                                                    m_dwLength, GHND);
        }
        else {
            m_lpBuf = (char huge*) GlobalAllocPtr(GHND, m_dwLength);
        }
        if (!m_lpBuf) {
            AfxMessageBox("Unable to allocate DIB memory");
            m_dwLength = 0L;
            m_nBits = 0;
            return FALSE;
        }
        m_lpBMFH = (LPBITMAPFILEHEADER) m_lpBuf;
        m_lpBMIH = (LPBITMAPINFOHEADER) (m_lpBuf + sizeof(BITMAPFILEHEADER));
        m_lpBMI = (LPBITMAPINFO) m_lpBMIH;
        return TRUE;
    }
```

CEx23aView

This class, derived from *CScrollView*, does most of the application's work. All the Edit menu items are routed to *CEx23aView* except for Edit Clear All. The view's most important data member, *m_pDisplayMemDC*, is a pointer to the memory device context that's used throughout the application. Other data members hold the size of the view and the view's GDI bitmap. The *m_bShrinkToFit* member, controlled from the View menu, indicates whether the bitmap occupies the whole view.

The *CEx23aView* class uses the MM_TEXT mapping mode so that it can take advantage of the *CScrollView* shrink-to-fit feature. When the shrink-to-fit mode is active, the entire view is visible in the window; otherwise, the view scrolls normally.

Constructor, Destructor

The *CEx23aView* constructor and destructor take care of routine housekeeping. The destructor ensures that the view's memory display context and last bitmap are deleted.

```
CEx23aView::CEx23aView() : m_totalSize(800, 1050) // 8" x 10.5" when printed
{
    m_pDisplayMemDC = new CDC;  // DC lasts for the life of the view
    m_bShrinkToFit = FALSE;
}

CEx23aView::~CEx23aView()
{
    delete m_pDisplayMemDC->SelectObject
        (CBitmap::FromHandle(m_hOldDisplayBitmap));
    delete m_pDisplayMemDC;
}
```

OnCreate

As in any view class derived from *CScrollView*, the *OnCreate* message handler must set the scroll sizes. The *OnCreate* function also sets the shrink-to-fit mode flag, and it sets up the memory device context for later use. The display mapping mode is MM_TEXT, but the print mapping mode is a modified MM_LOENGLISH.

```
int CEx23aView::OnCreate(LPCREATESTRUCT lpCreateStruct)
{
    if (CScrollView::OnCreate(lpCreateStruct)) {
        return -1;
    }
    if (m_bShrinkToFit) {
        SetScaleToFitSize(m_totalSize);
    }
    else {
        SetScrollSizes(MM_TEXT, m_totalSize);
    }
    // 'prime the pump' with an empty bitmap
    CClientDC dc(this);
    m_pDisplayMemDC->CreateCompatibleDC(&dc);
    CBitmap* pEmptyBitmap = new CBitmap;
    pEmptyBitmap->CreateCompatibleBitmap(&dc, 0, 0);
    CBitmap* pOldBitmap =
        (CBitmap*) m_pDisplayMemDC->SelectObject(pEmptyBitmap);
    // so we'll have an old bitmap to switch to at the end
    m_hOldDisplayBitmap = (HBITMAP) pOldBitmap->GetSafeHandle();
    return 0;
}
```

OnDraw

This function is actually four functions in one. The *DRAW_ALT* preprocessor constant determines which alternative drawing code is compiled. Here's a list of the alternatives with their key bitmap display function calls:

- **Alternative 1—*StretchBlt*:** Even though the application's bitmap is stored in the document as a DIB, the view keeps a GDI bitmap in memory, selected into the *m_pDisplayMemDC* memory display context. Every time a DIB is read from disk, this bitmap is refreshed. It's more efficient to draw from a GDI bitmap than directly from a DIB because the color conversion is done once when the DIB is read. In the *StretchBlt* display alternative, the bitmap occupies the entire view—800 by 1050 logical units.

```
pDC->StretchBlt(0, 0, m_totalSize.cx, m_totalSize.cy,
            m_pDisplayMemDC, 0, 0, m_bmSize.cx,
            m_bmSize.cy, SRCCOPY);
```

The *StretchBlt* call above works in both scroll mode and shrink-to-fit mode. In shrink-to-fit mode, the bitmap size exactly matches the window size. Scroll mode can slow *StretchBlt* because we're mapping bits to a much larger area than the window. A second version of the code chops down the bitmap size to match the window rectangle.

```
pDC->StretchBlt(clientRect.left, clientRect.top,
            clientRect.Width(), clientRect.Height(),
            m_pDisplayMemDC,
            (int) ((long) m_bmSize.cx * (long) clientRect.left /
                (long) m_totalSize.cx),
            (int) ((long) m_bmSize.cy * (long) clientRect.top /
                (long) m_totalSize.cy),
            (int) ((long) m_bmSize.cx * (long) clientRect.Width() /
                (long) m_totalSize.cx),
            (int) ((long) m_bmSize.cy * (long) clientRect.Height() /
                (long) m_totalSize.cy), SRCCOPY);
```

- **Alternative 2—*BitBlt*:** With this alternative, the bitmap bits are mapped directly to pixels, but only in scroll mode. If the bitmap size is 400 by 525 pixels, for example, the bitmap occupies the top left quadrant of the view. In the view's shrink-to-fit mode, the bitmap pixels are mapped to logical units in such a way that the 800-by-1050-unit document occupies the entire window. Display update is faster in scroll mode than it is in shrink-to-fit mode.

```
pDC->BitBlt(0, 0, m_bmSize.cx, m_bmSize.cy,
            m_pDisplayMemDC, 0, 0, SRCCOPY);
```

- **Alternative 3—*CDib Stretch*:** This alternative produces the same result as Alternative 1. This time the bitmap is rendered directly from the DIB.

```
GetDocument()->m_pDib->Stretch(pDC, CPoint(0, 0), m_totalSize);
```

- **Alternative 4—*CDib Display*:** This alternative does not produce the same result as Alternative 2. The bitmap pixels are always mapped one to one to the display (or printer).

```
GetDocument()->m_pDib->Display(pDC, CPoint(0, 0));
```

436

OnEditCopy

This command message handler is called in response to the Edit Copy menu item. Its job is to send a GDI bitmap to the clipboard, but remember that a bitmap can't be sent if it's selected into a device context. We need a bitmap selected, though, to create it and to display it. The *OnEditPaste* function solves the problem with two GDI bitmaps. First the function calls the *CDib MakeBitmap* function to create a new bitmap from the document's DIB. *MakeBitmap* then selects the new bitmap into the memory device context and returns the previously selected bitmap, which contains the same bit pattern. The deselected bitmap is passed to the clipboard.

```
void CEx23aView::OnEditCopy()
{
    CBitmap* pBitmap =
        GetDocument()->m_pDib->MakeBitmap(m_pDisplayMemDC, m_bmSize);
    if (pBitmap) {
        VERIFY(OpenClipboard());
        VERIFY(::EmptyClipboard());
        VERIFY(::SetClipboardData(CF_BITMAP, pBitmap->Detach()));
        VERIFY(::CloseClipboard());
        delete pBitmap;
    }
}
```

OnEditCopyTo

This function copies the document's *CDib* object to a device-independent bitmap disk file, usually with a BMP extension. It's called in response to the Edit Copy To menu item. This function does not involve GDI bitmaps or the memory display contents. It merely writes out the data in the document's *CDib* object.

OnEditCut

The *OnEditCut* message handler, called in response to the Edit Cut menu item, first calls *OnEditCopy* and then clears the document. When the document is cleared, its *CDib* object is reset and the view's *OnUpdate* function is called. The *OnUpdate* function loads the view's GDI bitmap from an empty DIB and thus clears the view window.

OnEditPaste

This command message handler is called in response to the Edit Paste menu item. It gets a GDI bitmap from the clipboard and then converts it to a DIB for storage in the document. It also updates the view's memory device context so that *OnDraw* displays the new bitmap. The *OnEditPaste* function uses a dialog of class *CBitsDialog* to query the user for some DIB specifications. The user can decide whether the DIB will use 1, 4, 8, or 24 bits per pixel and whether the DIB will be stored in compressed format.

First the clipboard GDI bitmap is selected into the view's memory device context, and then a *CDib* object is constructed from the GDI bitmap, replacing the existing *CDib* object. The new DIB is used to construct a second, identical, GDI bitmap, which is selected into the device context, thereby deselecting the clipboard's bitmap. The corresponding C++ bitmap object doesn't have to be deleted because it's a temporary object.

The *OnEditPaste* function displays, through the Windows debug window, the available clipboard formats. If a particular application doesn't copy GDI bitmaps to the clipboard, at least you'll know which formats it does copy.

OnEditPasteFrom

This command message handler is called in response to the Edit Paste From menu item. It reads a device-independent bitmap file, usually a file with a BMP extension, into the document's *CDib* object. In the process, the file is converted to a GDI bitmap for the *OnDraw* function.

A new, empty *CDib* object is constructed to replace the existing object, and then the *CDib Read* function reads data from an open file. The *MakeBitmap* function creates the GDI bitmap that is selected into the memory device context. The previously selected bitmap is deleted.

OnPrint

The *OnPrint* function prepares the printer device context for the *OnDraw* function. What we have here is a custom mapping mode that's really "upside-down MM_LO-ENGLISH." There are 100 logical units per inch, but, unlike in the real MM_-LOENGLISH mode, *y* values increase from top to bottom. We can't simply use MM_LOENGLISH because that mapping mode is incompatible with the view's shrink-to-fit capability.

```
void CEx23aView::OnPrint(CDC* pDC, CPrintInfo* pInfo)
{
    int nHsize = (int) (pDC->GetDeviceCaps(HORZSIZE) * 1000L / 254L);
    int nVsize = (int) (pDC->GetDeviceCaps(VERTSIZE) * 1000L / 254L);
    pDC->SetMapMode(MM_ANISOTROPIC);
    pDC->SetWindowExt(nHsize, nVsize);
    pDC->SetViewportExt(pDC->GetDeviceCaps(HORZRES),
                        pDC->GetDeviceCaps(VERTRES));
    OnDraw(pDC);
}
```

OnUpdate

The application framework calls the view's *OnUpdate* function when the document changes. This overridden function makes a new GDI bitmap from the document's *CDib* object.

```
void CEx23aView::OnUpdate(CView* pSender, LPARAM lHint, CObject* pHint)
{
    delete GetDocument()->m_pDib->MakeBitmap(m_pDisplayMemDC, m_bmSize);
    if (!m_bShrinkToFit) {
        ScrollToPosition(CPoint(0, 0));
    }
    Invalidate();
}
```

The Update Command UI Functions

The *OnUpdateEditPaste* and *OnUpdateEditCopy* functions enable the Edit menu items and corresponding toolbar buttons according to the status of the clipboard and the document.

The EX23A Resource File

The EX23A.RC resource script was generated by AppWizard and enhanced with App Studio. There are a new dialog and some extra menu items:

The *IDD_BITS* Dialog Resource

The *IDD_BITS* dialog is arranged as shown in Figure 23-4.

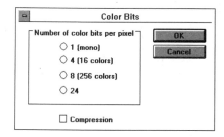

Figure 23-4.
The EX23A Color Bits dialog layout from App Studio.

This dialog appears when you paste a bitmap from the clipboard into the application. Notice the default OK and Cancel buttons. Add the radio buttons and the check box with data members as shown in the table below:

Button Caption	Type	Group	Symbol	Data Member
1 (mono)	Radio	Yes	IDC_BITS1	m_nBits
4 (16 colors)	Radio	No	IDC_BITS4	
8 (256 colors)	Radio	No	IDD_BITS	
24	Radio	No	IDC_BITS24	
Compression	Check box	Yes	IDC_COMPRESSION	m_bCompression

The *IDR_MAINFRAME* Menu Resource

You must add the items in the following table to the standard menu. Use ClassWizard to define the functions.

Menu	Menu Item	Command ID	Function	Update UI Function
Edit	Clear All	*ID_EDIT_CLEAR_ALL*	*OnEditClearAll*	
	Cut	*ID_EDIT_CUT*	*OnEditCut*	*OnUpdateEditCut*
	Copy	*ID_EDIT_COPY*	*OnEditCopy*	*OnUpdateEditCopy*
	Copy To	*ID_EDIT_COPY_TO*	*OnEditCopyTo*	*OnUpdateEditCopyTo*
	Paste	*ID_EDIT_PASTE*	*OnEditPaste*	*OnUpdateEditPaste*
	Paste From	*ID_EDIT_PASTE_FROM*	*OnEditPasteFrom*	
View	Shrink To Fit	*ID_VIEW_SHRINK*	*OnViewShrink*	*OnUpdateViewShrink*

Testing the EX23A Application

Try building EX23A with all four drawing alternatives (as determined by the value of *DRAW_ALT* in EX23AVW.CPP). Try scroll mode and shrink-to-fit mode with all alternatives. Remember that File Save is different from Edit Copy To. The former creates a class library archive file with the DIB extension, and the latter creates a standard BMP file. The two formats are not compatible. Figure 23-5 shows the EX23A display with drawing Alternative 2 in scroll mode.

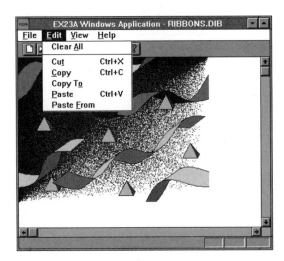

Figure 23-5.
The EX23A display.

Bitmap Manipulation

Every bitmap you've seen so far has originated in another program. You can build and modify bitmaps in your own programs if you want. You've already seen how the *CBitmap* member function *CreateCompatibleBitmap* can create a blank bitmap of a specified size. The *CBitmap* member functions *GetBitmapBits* and *SetBitmapBits* allow you to copy bytes from and to a GDI bitmap. If you use these functions, you must carefully account for the bitmap's number of planes, bits per pixel, and byte alignment. These parameters are hardware-dependent, but they are readily available from the *BITMAP* structure returned by the *CGdiObject GetObject* member function.

Bitmap access might be easier if you use the hardware-independent DIB format. You have direct access to the bits, and the format is fixed. Be careful, though, that the DIBs you work with are not compressed.

24

Database Management with Microsoft ODBC

Many business applications require fast access to individual records in a large database. Up to now, most database programming for microcomputers has been centered on the dBASE/Xbase language. The Microsoft Open Database Connectivity (ODBC) software standard provides a way for Microsoft Foundation Class Library programmers to create powerful database applications for Windows. Programmers get the advantages of both object-oriented programming and the SQL (Structured Query Language) database access language. They can even access dBASE files.

Visual C++ does not contain the ODBC tools necessary to create database applications. The ODBC Software Development Kit, which includes the ODBC *Programmer's Reference,* is available from Microsoft.

This chapter's example application shows how ODBC and SQL fit into the database world. You'll see a functional class library/ODBC application that's useful as a database query tool. The example also introduces the class library dialog bar, and it shows you how to take control of an application's shutdown sequence. Included is a useful row–view base class that manages the scrolling display of row-oriented data items.

Database Management vs. Serialization

The serialization process, introduced in Chapters 16 and 17, ties a document object to a disk file. All the document's data must be read into memory when the document is opened, and all the data must be written back to disk when an updated document is closed. Obviously, you can't serialize a document that's bigger than available virtual memory. Even if the document is small enough to fit in memory, you might not need to read and write all the data every time the program runs.

You could, of course, program your own random disk file access, thus inventing your own database management system (DBMS), but you probably have enough other work to do. Besides, using a real DBMS gives you many advantages, including these:

- **Use of standard file formats**—Many people think of dBASE/Xbase DBF files when they think of database formats. This is only one database file format, but it's a popular one. A lot of data is distributed in DBF files, and many programs can read and write in this format.

- **Indexed file access**—If you need quick access to records by key (a customer name, for example), you need indexed file access. You could always write your own B-tree file access routines, but that's a tedious job that's been done already. All DBMSs contain efficient indexed access routines.

- **Data integrity safeguards**—Many professional DBMS products have procedures for protecting their data. One example is transaction processing. A transaction encompasses a series of related changes. If the entire transaction can't be processed, it is rolled back so that the database reverts to its original state before the transaction.

- **Multiuser access control**—If your application doesn't need multiuser access now, it might in the future. Most DBMSs provide record locking to prevent interference among simultaneous users. Some multiuser DBMSs use the client-server model, which means that most processing is handled on a single database server computer; the workstations handle the user interface. Other multiuser DBMSs handle database processing on the workstations, and they control each workstation's access to shared files.

SQL

You could not have worked in the software field without at least hearing about SQL, a standard database access language with its own grammar. In the SQL world, a database is a collection of tables that consist of rows and columns. Many DBMS products support SQL, and many programmers know SQL. The SQL standard is continually evolving, but SQL grammar varies among products. SQL extensions, such as binary large object (blob) capability, allow storage of pictures, sound, and complex data structures.

The ODBC Standard

The Microsoft Open Database Connectivity standard defines not only the rules of SQL grammar but also the C-language programming interface to an SQL database. It's now possible for a single compiled C or C++ program to access any DBMS that has an ODBC driver. The ODBC Software Development Kit includes a driver for DBF files, and there are already drivers for Microsoft SQL Server and Microsoft Access. Established database companies, including Oracle, Informix, Progress, Ingress, and Gupta, are rapidly finishing ODBC drivers for their own DBMSs. Another company, Raima, is developing a new database server around the ODBC standard.

If you develop a program with the dBASE/Xbase driver, you can run the same program with another database driver. No recompilation is necessary—the program simply loads a different DLL.

The ODBC Architecture

ODBC has a unique DLL-based architecture that makes the system fully modular. A small top-level DLL, ODBC.DLL, defines the application programming interface. ODBC.DLL calls database-specific DLLs, known as drivers, during program execution. With the help of the ODBC.INI file, ODBC.DLL tracks which database-specific DLLs are available and thus allows a single program to access data in several DBMSs simultaneously. A program could, for example, keep some local tables in DBF format and use other tables controlled by a database server. Figure 24-1 shows the ODBC DLL hierarchy.

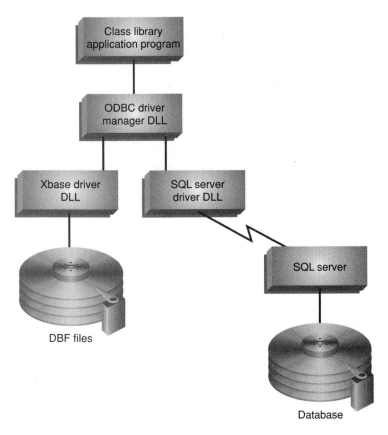

Figure 24-1.
Typical ODBC architecture.

ODBC Environments, Connections, and Statements

When you write a C or C++ program with ODBC database access, you must know about three important ODBC elements: the environment, the connection, and the statement. All three are accessed through handles. First you need an environment, which establishes the link between your program and the ODBC system. An application usually has only one environment handle.

Next you need one or more connections. The connection references a specific driver and data source combination. You might have several connections to subdirectories containing DBF files, and you might have connections to several SQL servers on the same network. A specific ODBC connection can be hard-wired in a program, or the user can be allowed to choose from a list of available drivers and data sources. ODBC.DLL has a built-in Windows dialog that lists the connections that are defined in the INI file.

Once you have a connection, you need an SQL statement to execute. The statement might be a query such as

```
select au_fname, au_lname, city from authors where state = 'UT'
```

or it could be an update statement such as

```
update authors set phone = '801 232-5780' where au_id = '357-86-4343'
```

Because query statements need a program loop to process the results, your program might need several statements active at the same time. ODBC allows multiple active statement handles per connection.

The ODBC API

The focus of the ODBC version 1.0 application programming interface is integration of SQL with C or C++. The ODBC documentation and help files list 54 C functions. This chapter's example uses only 13 functions. They're summarized alphabetically here so that you can get a feel for the ODBC API.

SQLAllocConnect(*henv, phdbc*)

henv   handle for a previously allocated environment

phdbc   pointer to a new connection handle

This function performs allocation for a database connection. This is the first connection function to be called after the environment is allocated.

SQLAllocEnv(*phenv*)

phenv   pointer to a new environment handle

This function performs allocation for the ODBC environment. This is generally the first ODBC statement called.

SQLAllocStmt(*hdbc, phstmt*)

hdbc	handle for a previously allocated database connection
phstmt	pointer to a new statement handle

This function performs allocation for an SQL statement.

SQLBindCol(*hstmt, icol, fCType, rgbValue, cbValueMax, pcbValue*)

hstmt	statement handle
icol	column number
fCType	C data type (*SQL_C_CHAR*, *SQL_C_SHORT*, *SQL_C_DOUBLE*, and so forth)
rgbValue	pointer to data storage
cbValueMax	maximum length of output data
pcbValue	pointer to the number of bytes returned

After an SQL query statement is executed, *SQLBindCol* is called once for each column. Its purpose is to bind the column to a C variable so that data can be returned to that variable (and appropriately converted) when the query rows are processed.

SQLDescribeCol(*hstmt, icol, szColName, cbColNameMax, pcbColName, pfSqlType, pcbColDef, pibScale, pfNullable*)

hstmt	statement handle
icol	column number
szColName	column name
cbColNameMax	maximum length for name
pcbColName	pointer to actual length of returned column name
pfSqlType	pointer to column data type (*SQL_BIGINT*, *SQL_BINARY*, *SQL_BIT*, and so forth)
pcbColDef	pointer to precision of column on data source
pibScale	pointer to scale of column on data source
pfNullable	pointer to an integer that indicates whether column allows NULL values

After an SQL query statement is executed, *SQLDescribeCol* is called once for each column. Its purpose is to retrieve the name of the column for use in report headings.

SQLDisconnect(*hdbc*)

hdbc	connection handle

This function terminates an ODBC connection.

SQLDriverConnect(*hdbc, hwnd, szConnStrIn, cbConnStrIn, szConnStrOut, cbConnStrOutMax, pcbConnStrOut, fDriverCompletion*)

hdbc	handle to previously allocated connection
hwnd	window handle for dialog
szConnStrIn	pointer to connection specification string (input)
cbConnStrIn	length of input connection string (*SQL_NTS* = null-terminated)
szConnStrOut	pointer to connection specification string (output)
cbConnStrOutMax	maximum length of output connection string
pcbConnStrOut	pointer to actual length of returned output connection string
fDriverCompletion	flag that specifies how user interacts with dialog

This function opens a database connection. If the program supplies a formatted input connection string such as

```
DSN=DBF test;DBQ=\odbc\dbftest;FIL=DBASE4
```

SQLDriverConnect can establish the connection without user interaction. If necessary, the user can be prompted for the driver name and data source.

SQLExecDirect(*hstmt, szSqlStr, cbSqlStr*)

hstmt	statement handle
szSqlStr	pointer to SQL string
cbSqlStr	length of SQL string (*SQL_NTS* = null-terminated)

This function is the main SQL statement processing function. If the statement is a query statement, *SQLExecDirect* does all necessary joining, sorting, and summarizing before returning. Your program must then call other ODBC functions to retrieve the row data.

SQLFetch(*hstmt*)

hstmt	statement handle

After an SQL query statement is executed and you have bound the result columns to variables, you call *SQLFetch* for each row in the result set. The function stores data in the variables specified in *SQLBindColumn*.

SQLFreeConnect(*hdbc*)

hdbc	connection handle

This function frees the connection memory allocated by *SQLAllocConnect*. You must call *SQLFreeConnect* after you call *SQLDisconnect*.

SQLFreeEnv(*henv*)

henv   environment handle

This function frees the environment memory allocated by *SQLAllocEnv*. This is generally the last ODBC function call in a program.

SQLFreeStmt(*hstmt, fOption*)

hstmt   statement handle

fOption   flag that governs memory reuse for subsequent statement execution

This function frees the statement memory allocated by *SQLAllocEnv*. Call the *SQLFreeStmt* function when you're finished retrieving column data and rows.

SQLNumResultCols(*hstmt, pccol*)

hstmt   statement handle

pccol   pointer to an integer that will receive number of columns

After an SQL statement is executed, your program must iterate through the columns to get names and to bind storage. The *SQLNumResultCols* function retrieves the number of columns returned by the query.

> **Note:** *The 13 functions listed above are oriented to dynamic database queries—the programmer doesn't know the content of the SQL statements. Other ODBC functions are tailored to static SQL usage—the programmer knows what kind of row data will be returned. In the latter case, SQL statements can be prepared in advance for more efficiency.*

A Database Access Program

Below is pseudocode for a typical ODBC database access program. The program accepts an SQL query statement from the user, and then it retrieves individual column data for each row in the result set.

```
HENV    henv
HDBC    hdbc
HSTMT   hstmt
int     nCols

SQLAllocEnv(&henv)
    SQLAllocConnect(henv, &hdbc)
    SQLDriverConnect(hdbc, ...)
        SQLAllocStmt(hdbc, &hstmt)
            get SQL query text from user
            SQLExecDirect(hstmt, SQLStatement, ...)
            SQLNumResultCols(hstmt, &nCols)
```

(continued)

```
            for each column {
                SQLDescribeCol(hstmt, col, ColName, ...)
                SQLBindCol(hstmt, col, ..., variable, ...)
            }
            for each row {
                SQLFetch(hstmt)
                for each column {
                    process field data from column variable
                }
            }
        SQLFreeStmt(hstmt, ...)
    SQLDisconnect(hdbc)
    SQLFreeConnect(hdbc)
SQLFreeEnv(henv)
```

ODBC, the Class Library, and Object-Oriented Programming

In the SQL database world, data is stored in neat tables. In the world of object-oriented programming, data is stored in complex structures of nested objects. One author has said that storing object-oriented data in an SQL database was like "taking your car apart every night instead of just parking it in your garage." Some applications, such as computer-aided design (CAD), are distinctly incompatible with SQL. Many object-oriented business applications can be SQL-compatible, however, and this allows the use of commercial SQL report generators and SQL-based macro languages.

You'll notice that the ODBC API is C-oriented, not C++-oriented. It would be easy to write a C++ wrapper for ODBC. It would include classes for the environment, the connection, and the statement, and you would use object pointers instead of handles. If an environment object were allocated on the stack, for example, its destructor could free the environment when the object went out of scope.

In the meantime, we'll be using the C API, and the question is, What's the best way of integrating ODBC into the class library application framework? How about a new application base class that incorporates an ODBC environment? What about a document base class that incorporates a connection and a statement? These are possibilities, but in this chapter's example, we'll take the "just do it" approach. We'll embed an environment handle in our derived application class, and we'll embed connection and statement handles in the derived document class. The document class also contains data structures to hold the entire query result set. You could choose a completely different approach for your own applications.

On the wish list would be a *CDatabaseView* class that allows forward and backward scrolling directly from a query result set without intermediate memory storage. Unfortunately, this class must wait for the ODBC level 2 extensions. These extensions include the *SQLExtendedFetch* function, which supports scrollable cursors. Level 2 extensions are not supported by the DBF driver that's included with the ODBC verison 1.0 SDK.

450

The Class Library Dialog Bar

You haven't seen the *CDialogBar* class yet because it didn't make sense to use it in the earlier examples. (A dialog bar is a border region of the frame window that is arranged according to a dialog template resource and that routes commands similar to a toolbar.) It fits well in the ODBC example, however. Look at Figure 24-3 on page 464, which shows the ODBC example in operation. The dialog bar has a multiline edit control for the SQL query text, and it has buttons to execute the query and to view a list of tables. The buttons send standard command messages that can be handled in the view, and they can be disabled by update command UI messages. Most dialog bars live at the top of the frame window, immediately under the toolbar.

It's surprisingly easy to add a dialog bar to an application. You don't even need a new derived class. Here are the steps:

1. Use App Studio to lay out the dialog. Apply the following styles:

   Style = Child
   Border = None
   Visible = unchecked

   You could choose a horizontally oriented bar for the top or bottom of the frame, or you could choose a vertically oriented bar for the left or right. Add any controls you need, including buttons and edit controls.

2. Declare an embedded *CDialogBar* object in your derived main frame class declaration, like this:

   ```
   CDialogBar m_wndMyBar;
   ```

3. Add dialog bar object creation code in your main frame class *OnCreate* member function:

   ```
   if (!m_wndMyBar.Create(this, IDD_MY_BAR, CBRS_TOP, IDD_MY_BAR)) {
       TRACE("Failed to create dialog bar\n");
       return -1;
       }
   ```

   IDD_MY_BAR is the dialog resource ID assigned in App Studio, which is also the dialog bar's control window ID. The *CBRS_TOP* style tells the application framework to place the dialog bar at the top of the frame window.

Application Shutdown

Up to now, you haven't been too concerned about the process of shutting down an application. With ordinary document-oriented class library applications, your calling the *CDocument SetModifiedFlag* function ensured that the application framework would prompt the user to save documents. With ODBC, however, you've got to be careful that you terminate connections and free handles before your program exits.

The application framework provides the means for trapping the user's attempt to exit the application. It's all done at the document level through the virtual *CDocument SaveModified* member function. The application framework calls this function whenever a document is to be closed, even if the closing was triggered by the user's attempt to close the application's main frame window or to shut down Windows. If SaveModified returns 0, the application framework doesn't close the document. In the ODBC example, the derived document class overrides *SaveModified* to check whether the database is still connected. There's one catch, however. *SaveModified* gets called only if the document's *m_bModified* flag is set. You can ensure that the flag is set by calling *SetModifiedFlag* after a new document is created, saved, or read from disk.

A Row–View Class

Database applications are often built around scrolling lists of database records. This chapter's ODBC example is no exception. If you've read other books about Windows, you know that authors spend lots of time on the problem of scrolling lists. This is a tricky programming exercise that must be repeated over and over again. Why not encapsulate a scrolling list in a base class? All the ugly details would be hidden, and you could get on with the business of writing your application.

The *CRowView* class, adapted from the class of the identical name in the \MSVC\MFC\SAMPLES\CHKBOOK directory, does the job. Through its use of virtual callback functions, it serves as a model for other derivable base classes. *CRowView* has some limitations, and it's not up to industrial-strength specifications, but it works well in the ODBC example. See Figure 24-2 for a complete listing.

```
ROWVIEW.H
class CRowView : public CScrollView  // abstract base class
{
DECLARE_DYNAMIC(CRowView)
protected:
// Construction/destruction
    CRowView();
    virtual ~CRowView();
// Attributes
protected:
    int m_nRowWidth;            // width of row in logical units
    int m_nRowHeight;           // height of row in logical units
    int m_nCharWidth;           // avg char width in logical units
    int m_nPrevSelectedRow;     // index of the most recently selected row
    int m_nPrevRowCount;        // most recent row count, before update
    int m_nRowsPerPrintedPage;  // how many rows fit on a printed page
```

Figure 24-2. *(continued)*
The CRowView *listing.*

Figure 24-2. *continued*

```
// Operations-Attributes
protected:
    virtual void UpdateRow(int nInvalidRow); // called by derived class OnUpdate
    virtual void CalculateRowMetrics(CDC* pDC)
            { GetRowWidthHeight(pDC, m_nRowWidth, m_nRowHeight, m_nCharWidth); }
    virtual void UpdateScrollSizes();
    virtual CRect RowToWndRect(CDC* pDC, int nRow);
    virtual int RowToYPos(int nRow);
    virtual void RectLPtoRowRange(const CRect& rectLP, int& nFirstRow,
                                 int& nLastRow, BOOL bIncludePartiallyShownRows);
    virtual int LastViewableRow();

// Overridables
protected:
    virtual void GetRowWidthHeight(CDC* pDC, int& nRowWidth,
                                   int& nRowHeight, int& nCharWidth) = 0;
    virtual int GetActiveRow() = 0;
    virtual int GetRowCount() = 0;
    virtual void OnDrawRow(CDC* pDC, int nRow, int y, BOOL bSelected) = 0;
    virtual void ChangeSelectionNextRow(BOOL bNext) = 0;
    virtual void ChangeSelectionToRow(int nRow) = 0;

// Implementation
protected:
    // standard overrides of MFC classes
    virtual void OnInitialUpdate();
    virtual void OnDraw(CDC* pDC);  // overridden to draw this view
    virtual void OnPrepareDC(CDC* pDC, CPrintInfo* pInfo = NULL);
    virtual BOOL OnPreparePrinting(CPrintInfo* pInfo);
    virtual void OnBeginPrinting(CDC* pDC, CPrintInfo* pInfo);
    virtual void OnPrint(CDC* pDC, CPrintInfo* pInfo);

// Generated message map functions
protected:
    //{{AFX_MSG(CRowView)
    afx_msg void OnKeyDown(UINT nChar, UINT nRepCnt, UINT nFlags);
    afx_msg void OnSize(UINT nType, int cx, int cy);
    afx_msg void OnLButtonDown(UINT nFlags, CPoint point);
    //}}AFX_MSG
    DECLARE_MESSAGE_MAP()
};
```

ROWVIEW.CPP

```
#include "stdafx.h"
#include "resource.h" // for IDS_TOO_MANY_ROWS
```

(continued)

Figure 24-2. *continued*

```
#include "rowview.h"
#include <limits.h> // for INT_MAX

#ifdef _DEBUG
#undef THIS_FILE
static char BASED_CODE THIS_FILE[] = __FILE__;
#endif

IMPLEMENT_DYNAMIC(CRowView, CScrollView)

/////////////////////////////////////////////////////////////////////////////
// CRowView

BEGIN_MESSAGE_MAP(CRowView, CScrollView)
    //{{AFX_MSG_MAP(CRowView)
    ON_WM_KEYDOWN()
    ON_WM_SIZE()
    ON_WM_LBUTTONDOWN()
    //}}AFX_MSG_MAP
    // Standard printing commands
    ON_COMMAND(ID_FILE_PRINT, CView::OnFilePrint)
    ON_COMMAND(ID_FILE_PRINT_PREVIEW, CView::OnFilePrintPreview)
END_MESSAGE_MAP()

/////////////////////////////////////////////////////////////////////////////
// CRowView construction, initialization, and destruction

CRowView::CRowView()
{
    m_nPrevSelectedRow = 0;
}


CRowView::~CRowView()
{
}


/////////////////////////////////////////////////////////////////////////////
// CRowView updating and drawing

void CRowView::OnInitialUpdate()
{
    m_nPrevRowCount = GetRowCount();
    m_nPrevSelectedRow = GetActiveRow();
    OnUpdate(this, 0, NULL);
}


/////////////////////////////////////////////////////////////////////////////
void CRowView::UpdateRow(int nInvalidRow)
{
    int nRowCount = GetRowCount();
```

(continued)

Figure 24-2. *continued*

```
    // If the number of rows has changed, adjust the scrolling range.
    if (nRowCount != m_nPrevRowCount) {
        UpdateScrollSizes();
        m_nPrevRowCount = nRowCount;
    }


    // When the currently selected row changes,
    //   scroll the view so that the newly selected row is visible, and
    //   ask the derived class to repaint the selected and previously
    //   selected rows.

    CClientDC dc(this);
    OnPrepareDC(&dc);


    // Determine the range of the rows that are currently fully visible
    //   in the window.  We want to do discrete scrolling by so that
    //   the next or previous row is always fully visible.

    int    nFirstRow, nLastRow;
    CRect rectClient;

    GetClientRect(&rectClient);
    dc.DPtoLP(&rectClient);
    RectLPtoRowRange(rectClient, nFirstRow, nLastRow, FALSE);


    // If necessary, scroll the window so that the newly selected row is
    //   visible.

    POINT pt = GetDeviceScrollPosition();
    BOOL  bNeedToScroll = TRUE;


    if (nInvalidRow < nFirstRow) {
        // The newly selected row is above those currently visible
        //   in the window.  Scroll so that the newly selected row is at the
        //   very top of the window. The last row in the window might
        //   be only partially visible.
        pt.y = RowToYPos(nInvalidRow);
    }
    else if (nInvalidRow > nLastRow){
        // The newly selected row is below those currently visible
        //   in the window.  Scroll so that the newly selected row is at the
        //   very bottom of the window.  The first row in the window might
        //   be only partially visible.
        pt.y = max(0, RowToYPos(nInvalidRow+1) - rectClient.Height());
    }
    else {
        bNeedToScroll = FALSE;
    }
```

(continued)

Figure 24-2. *continued*

```
    if (bNeedToScroll) {
        ScrollToDevicePosition(pt);
        // Scrolling will cause the newly selected row to be
        //   redrawn in the invalidated area of the window.

        OnPrepareDC(&dc);  // Need to prepare the DC again because
            //  ScrollToDevicePosition() will have changed the viewport
            //  origin.  The DC is used some more below.
    }

    CRect rectInvalid = RowToWndRect(&dc, nInvalidRow);
    InvalidateRect(&rectInvalid);

    // Give the derived class an opportunity to repaint the
    //   previously selected row, perhaps to un-highlight it.

    int nSelectedRow = GetActiveRow();
    if (m_nPrevSelectedRow != nSelectedRow)     {
        CRect rectOldSelection = RowToWndRect(&dc, m_nPrevSelectedRow);
        InvalidateRect(&rectOldSelection);
        m_nPrevSelectedRow = nSelectedRow;
    }
}


//////////////////////////////////////////////////////////////////////////
void CRowView::UpdateScrollSizes()
{
    // UpdateScrollSizes() is called when it is necessary to adjust the
    //   scrolling range or page/line sizes.  There are two occasions
    //   where this is necessary:  (1) when a new row is added--see
    //   UpdateRow()--and (2) when the window size changes--see OnSize().

    CRect rectClient;
    GetClientRect(&rectClient);

    CClientDC dc(this);
    CalculateRowMetrics(&dc);

    // The vert scrolling range is the total display height of all
    //   of the rows.
    CSize sizeTotal(m_nRowWidth, m_nRowHeight *
                (min(GetRowCount(), LastViewableRow())));

    // The vertical per-page scrolling distance is equal to
    //   how many rows can be displayed in the current window, less
    //   one row for paging overlap.
    CSize sizePage(m_nRowWidth / 5, max(m_nRowHeight,
                ((rectClient.bottom / m_nRowHeight) - 1) * m_nRowHeight));
```

(continued)

Figure 24-2. *continued*

```
    // The vertical per-line scrolling distance is equal to the
    //   height of the row.
    CSize sizeLine(m_nRowWidth / 20, m_nRowHeight);

    SetScrollSizes(MM_TEXT, sizeTotal, sizePage, sizeLine);
}

/////////////////////////////////////////////////////////////////////////
void CRowView::OnDraw(CDC* pDC)
{
    if (GetRowCount() == 0) {
        return;
    }
    // The window has been invalidated and needs to be repainted,
    //   or a page needs to be printed (or previewed).
    // First determine the range of rows that need to be displayed or
    //   printed.

    int    nFirstRow, nLastRow;
    CRect rectClip;

    pDC->GetClipBox(&rectClip);      // Get the invalidated region.
    RectLPtoRowRange(rectClip, nFirstRow, nLastRow, TRUE);

    // Draw each row in the invalidated region of the window
    //   or on the printed (previewed) page.

    int nActiveRow = GetActiveRow();
    int nRow, y;
    int nLastViewableRow = LastViewableRow();

    for (nRow = nFirstRow, y = m_nRowHeight * nFirstRow;
        nRow <= nLastRow; nRow++, y += m_nRowHeight) {
        if (nRow >= (nLastViewableRow - 1)) {
            CString strWarning;
            strWarning.LoadString(IDS_TOO_MANY_ROWS);
            pDC->TextOut(0, y, strWarning);
            break;
        }
        // Prepare for highlighting or un-highlighting the row, depending
        //   on whether it is the currently selected row or not.  And
        //   paint the background (behind the text) accordingly.

        CBrush    brushBackground;
        COLORREF  crOldText, crOldBackground;
        if (!pDC->IsPrinting()) {
            if (nRow == nActiveRow)    {
                brushBackground.CreateSolidBrush(::GetSysColor(COLOR_HIGHLIGHT));
```

(continued)

Figure 24-2. *continued*

```
                    crOldBackground = pDC->SetBkColor(::GetSysColor(COLOR_HIGHLIGHT));
                    crOldText = pDC->SetTextColor(::GetSysColor(COLOR_HIGHLIGHTTEXT));
            }
            else {
                    brushBackground.CreateSolidBrush(::GetSysColor(COLOR_WINDOW));
            }

            CRect rectSelection;
            pDC->GetClipBox(&rectSelection);
            rectSelection.top = y;
            rectSelection.bottom = y + m_nRowHeight;
            pDC->FillRect(&rectSelection, &brushBackground);
        }
        OnDrawRow(pDC, nRow, y, nRow == nActiveRow);
        // Restore the DC. (MOVED FROM DERIVED CLASS)
        if (!pDC->IsPrinting() && (nRow == nActiveRow))      {
            pDC->SetBkColor(crOldBackground);
            pDC->SetTextColor(crOldText);
        }
    }
}


//////////////////////////////////////////////////////////////////////////
// Implementation

int CRowView::RowToYPos(int nRow)
{
    return (nRow * m_nRowHeight);
}


//////////////////////////////////////////////////////////////////////////
CRect CRowView::RowToWndRect(CDC* pDC, int nRow)
{
    CRect clientRect;

    GetClientRect(clientRect);
    pDC->DPtoLP(clientRect);
    CRect rect(clientRect.left, nRow * m_nRowHeight,
            clientRect.right, (nRow + 1) * m_nRowHeight);
    pDC->LPtoDP(&rect);
    return rect;
}


//////////////////////////////////////////////////////////////////////////
int CRowView::LastViewableRow()
{
    return (INT_MAX / m_nRowHeight - 1);
}
```

(continued)

Figure 24-2. *continued*

```
///////////////////////////////////////////////////////////////////////
void CRowView::RectLPtoRowRange(const CRect& rect, int& nFirstRow,
                                int& nLastRow,
                                BOOL bIncludePartiallyShownRows)
{
    int nRounding = bIncludePartiallyShownRows ? 0 : (m_nRowHeight - 1);
    nFirstRow = (rect.top + nRounding) / m_nRowHeight;
    nLastRow = min( (rect.bottom - nRounding) / m_nRowHeight,
        GetRowCount() - 1);
}


///////////////////////////////////////////////////////////////////////
void CRowView::OnPrepareDC(CDC* pDC, CPrintInfo* pInfo)
{
    // The size of text that is displayed, printed, or previewed changes
    //   depending on the DC.  We explicitly call OnPrepareDC() to prepare
    //   CClientDC objects used for calculating text positions and to
    //   prepare the text metric member variables of the CRowView object.
    //   The application framework also calls OnPrepareDC() before passing
    //   the DC to OnDraw().

    CScrollView::OnPrepareDC(pDC, pInfo);
    CalculateRowMetrics(pDC);
}


///////////////////////////////////////////////////////////////////////
// Overrides of CView for implementing printing.

BOOL CRowView::OnPreparePrinting(CPrintInfo* pInfo)
{
    return DoPreparePrinting(pInfo);
}


///////////////////////////////////////////////////////////////////////
void CRowView::OnBeginPrinting(CDC* pDC, CPrintInfo* pInfo)
{
    // OnBeginPrinting() is called after the user has committed to
    //   printing by OK'ing the Print dialog, and after the application
    //   framework has created a CDC object for the printer or the preview
    //   view.

    // This is the right opportunity to set up the page range.
    // Given the CDC object, we can determine how many rows will
    //   fit on a page, so we can in turn determine how many printed
    //   pages represent the entire document.

    int nPageHeight = pDC->GetDeviceCaps(VERTRES);
    CalculateRowMetrics(pDC);
    m_nRowsPerPrintedPage = nPageHeight / m_nRowHeight;
```

(continued)

Figure 24-2. *continued*

```
    int nPrintableRowCount = LastViewableRow() + 1;
    if (GetRowCount() < nPrintableRowCount) {
        nPrintableRowCount = GetRowCount();
    }
    pInfo->SetMaxPage((nPrintableRowCount + m_nRowsPerPrintedPage - 1) /
                    m_nRowsPerPrintedPage);
    pInfo->m_nCurPage = 1;     // start previewing at page# 1
}

///////////////////////////////////////////////////////////////////////////
void CRowView::OnPrint(CDC* pDC, CPrintInfo* pInfo)
{
    // Print the rows for the current page.

    int yTopOfPage = (pInfo->m_nCurPage -1) * m_nRowsPerPrintedPage *
                    m_nRowHeight;

    // Orient the viewport so that the first row to be printed
    //   has a viewport coordinate of (0,0).
    pDC->SetViewportOrg(0, -yTopOfPage);

    // Draw as many rows as will fit on the printed page.
    // Clip the printed page so that there is no partially shown
    //   row at the bottom of the page (the same row that will be fully
    //   shown at the top of the next page).

    int nPageWidth = pDC->GetDeviceCaps(HORZRES);

    CRect rectClip = CRect(0, yTopOfPage, nPageWidth, yTopOfPage +
                        m_nRowsPerPrintedPage * m_nRowHeight);
    pDC->IntersectClipRect(&rectClip);
    OnDraw(pDC);
}

///////////////////////////////////////////////////////////////////////////
// CRowView commands

void CRowView::OnSize(UINT nType, int cx, int cy)
{
    UpdateScrollSizes();
    CScrollView::OnSize(nType, cx, cy);
}

///////////////////////////////////////////////////////////////////////////
void CRowView::OnKeyDown(UINT nChar, UINT nRepCnt, UINT nFlags)
{
    CRect clientRect;
```

(continued)

Figure 24-2. *continued*

```
    GetClientRect(clientRect);
    CClientDC dc(this);
    dc.DPtoLP(clientRect);

    switch (nChar)
    {
        case VK_HOME:
            ChangeSelectionToRow(0);
            break;
        case VK_END:
            ChangeSelectionToRow(min(GetRowCount() - 1,
                                 LastViewableRow() - 2));
            break;
        case VK_UP:
            ChangeSelectionNextRow(FALSE);
            break;
        case VK_DOWN:
            ChangeSelectionNextRow(TRUE);
            break;
        case VK_LEFT:
            if (clientRect.Width() < GetTotalSize().cx) {
                OnScroll(SB_HORZ, SB_LINEUP, 0);
            }
            break;
        case VK_RIGHT:
            if (clientRect.Width() < GetTotalSize().cx) {
                OnScroll(SB_HORZ, SB_LINEDOWN, 0);
            }
            break;
        case VK_PRIOR:
            if (clientRect.Height() < GetTotalSize().cy) {
                OnScroll(SB_VERT, SB_PAGEUP, 0);
            }
            break;
        case VK_NEXT:
            if (clientRect.Height() < GetTotalSize().cy) {
                OnScroll(SB_VERT, SB_PAGEDOWN, 0);
            }
            break;
        default:
            CScrollView::OnKeyDown(nChar, nRepCnt, nFlags);
    }
}

////////////////////////////////////////////////////////////////////////////
void CRowView::OnLButtonDown(UINT, CPoint point)
{
    CClientDC dc(this);
    OnPrepareDC(&dc);
```

(continued)

Figure 24-2. *continued*

```
   dc.DPtoLP(&point);

   CRect rect(point, CSize(1,1));
   int   nFirstRow, nLastRow;

   RectLPtoRowRange(rect, nFirstRow, nLastRow, TRUE);
   if (nFirstRow <= (GetRowCount() - 1)) {
       ChangeSelectionToRow(nFirstRow);
   }
}
```

The Scrolling Problem

You've seen the *CScrollView* class used in several of this book's examples. The scroll view's window consists of an area as large as 32,767 units high by 32,767 units wide, only a small part of which is visible on the screen. Suppose you had a list of 2000 database query result rows, each 14 units high. Your view class *OnDraw* function could use the *CDC TextOut* function to paint all 2000 records each time the list was updated. This would work, but it would be terribly slow. As you probably guessed, the trick is to paint only those rows that fall within the invalid rectangle that corresponds to the display screen. This is what *CRowView* does.

Dividing the Work Between Base and Derived Classes

Because the *CRowView* class (itself derived from *CScrollView*) is designed to be a base class, it is as general as possible. *CRowView* relies on its derived class to access and paint the row's data. The EX24A example document class stores its row data in a *CObArray* collection, easily accessible through a subscript, but the CHKBOOK example uses a random-access disk file. The *CRowView* class serves both examples effectively. It supports the concept of a selected row that is highlighted in the view. Through the *CRowView* virtual member functions, the derived class is alerted when the user changes the selected row.

The *CRowView* Pure Virtual Member Functions

Classes derived from *CRowView* <u>must</u> implement the following pure virtual functions:

■ *GetRowWidthHeight* —This function returns the character width and height of the currently selected font, and it returns the width of the row, based on average character widths. As the device context switches between printer and display, the returned font metric values change accordingly.

- **GetActiveRow**—The base class calls this function frequently, so if another view changes the selected row, this view can track it.

- **ChangeSelectionNextRow**, **ChangeSelectionToRow**—These two functions serve to alert the derived class that the user has changed the selected row. The derived class can then update the document (and other views) if necessary.

- **OnDrawRow**—The *OnDrawRow* function is called by the *CRowView* *OnDraw* function to draw a specific row.

Other *CRowView* Functions

Three other *CRowView* functions are available to be called by derived classes and the application framework. These are *UpdateRow*, *UpdateScrollSizes*, and *OnPrint*.

- **UpdateRow**—This public function triggers a view update when the row selection changes. Normally, only the newly selected row and the deselected row are invalidated, and this means that the final invalid rectangle spans both rows. If the number of rows has changed, *UpdateRow* calls *UpdateScrollSizes*.

- **UpdateScrollSizes**—This is a virtual function, so you can override it if necessary. The *CRowView* implementation updates the size of the view, which invalidates the visible portion. *UpdateScrollSizes* is called by *OnSize* and by *OnUpdate* (after the user executes a new query).

- **OnPrint**—The *CRowView* class overrides this function to cleverly adjust the viewport origin and clipping rectangle so that *OnDraw* can paint on the printed page as it does in the visible portion of a window.

The EX24A Example

Now we'll put everything together and build a working program—an MDI application that connects to an ODBC database. The application displays the results of SQL queries in a scrolling view. AppWizard generates the usual MDI application, main frame, document, and view classes, and we change the view class base to *CRowView* and add the ODBC-specific code. Figure 24-3 on the next page shows the EX24A program in operation.

You can learn a lot about this application by looking at the three view windows. The two views on the left are tied to the same document, STOCK.QRY, and the right-hand view is tied to another document, SHARE.QRY. The dialog bar shows the SQL statement that's associated with the active view window.

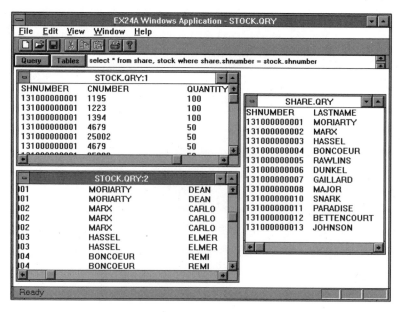

Figure 24-3.
The EX24A program in operation.

The EX24A example is presented with source code listings and resource requirements. Here's a table of the files and classes:

Header File	Source Code File	Class	Description
EX24A.H	EX24A.CPP	*CEx24aApp*	Main application
MAINFRM.H	MAINFRM.CPP	*CMainFrame*	MDI main frame
EX24ADOC.H	EX24ADOC.CPP	*CEx24aDoc*	EX24A document
EX24AVW.H	EX24AVW.CPP	*CEx24aView*	Scrolling database view class
ROWVIEW.H	ROWVIEW.CPP	*CRowView*	Row view base class
STDAFX.H	STDAFX.CPP		Precompiled headers

Now we'll go through the application's classes one at a time, excluding *CRowView*.

CEx24aApp

The application class contains the ODBC environment handle, *m_henv*, which is allocated in *InitInstance* and freed in *ExitInstance*.

CMainFrame

This class is the standard output from AppWizard except for the addition of the dialog bar.

CEx24aDoc

The document class is associated with an ODBC connection and an SQL statement. Only one SQL statement can be associated with a document at any one time. Through the class library serialization process, the document remembers its SQL statement and connection information.

Data Members

The important *CEx24aDoc* data members are as follows:

m_hdbc	ODBC database connection handle
m_hstmt	ODBC statement handle
m_stringArray	An array of string list pointers that represents the results of the most recent query
m_query	The current SQL statement string (stored in the document file)
m_connect	ODBC connect string that specifies the driver and data source (stored in the document file)

Other data members track the lengths of the query result columns, number of columns, row width in characters, and connection status.

OnNewDocument, OnOpenDocument, OnSaveDocument

These overridden *CDocument* functions set the document's modified status to ensure that the application framework calls *SaveModified* when the document is closed.

DeleteContents

The application framework calls this virtual *CDocument* function whenever a document is closed. In this class, it frees the array of string lists. This job includes deleting the strings, deleting the *CStringList* objects, and removing the *CObArray* elements. The embedded *CObArray* object is not deleted, however.

```
void CEx24aDoc::DeleteContents()
{
    CStringList* pList;
    for (int i = 0; i < m_stringArray.GetSize(); i++) {
        pList = (CStringList*) m_stringArray[i];
        pList->RemoveAll();
        delete pList;
    }
    m_stringArray.RemoveAll();
}
```

SaveModified

This virtual function, called by the application framework when the user tries to close a document, checks to see whether the document's database connection is open. If it is, the document is not closed, and the program warns the user with a message box.

Serialize

The document's SQL query and connection string are serialized.

OnFileConnect, OnFileDisconnect

These are menu command message handlers, activated from the File menu. They open and close the database connection. Companion update command UI handlers enable and disable the dialog bar buttons and menu items as appropriate.

```
void CEx24aDoc::OnFileConnect()
{
    UCHAR szConnStrIn[256];
    UCHAR szConnStrOut[256];
    SWORD pcbConnStrOut;

    strcpy((char*) szConnStrIn, m_connect);
    VERIFY(SQLAllocConnect(((CEx24aApp*) AfxGetApp())->m_henv, &m_hdbc)
        == SQL_SUCCESS);

    if (SQLDriverConnect(m_hdbc, AfxGetApp()->m_pMainWnd->GetSafeHwnd(),
            (UCHAR FAR*) szConnStrIn, SQL_NTS, (UCHAR FAR*) szConnStrOut,
            255, &pcbConnStrOut, SQL_DRIVER_PROMPT) != SQL_SUCCESS) {
        AfxMessageBox("SQL connection error");
        return;
    }
    m_bConnected = TRUE;
    m_connect = (const char*) szConnStrOut;
}

void CEx24aDoc::OnFileDisconnect()
{
    SQLDisconnect(m_hdbc);
    SQLFreeConnect(m_hdbc);
    m_bConnected = FALSE;
}
```

CEx24aView

This view class is derived from *CRowView* and implements the necessary pure virtual functions of its base class. The *CEx24aView* class presents a scrolling view of a query result set, subject to the 32,767-by-32,767-logical-unit size limitation of a window.

Data Members

The view uses the variable *m_nSelectedRow* to track the currently selected row.

OnUpdate

This virtual *CView* function is called through the application framework when the document's contents change in response to a new query. If several views are active for a given document, all views reflect the current query, but each can maintain different current rows and scroll positions.

OnDrawRow, GetRowWidthHeight, GetActiveRow, GetRowCount, ChangeSelectionNextRow, ChangeSelectionToRow

These functions are implementations of the *CRowView* class pure virtual functions. They take care of drawing a specified query result row, and they track the current selection. The *OnDrawRow* function shows how the query results are extracted from the document.

```
void CEx24aView::OnDrawRow(CDC* pDC, int nRow, int y, BOOL bSelected)
{
    int         i;
    int         x = 0;
    CStringList* pList;
    POSITION    pos;
    CEx24aDoc* pDoc = GetDocument();
    pList = (CStringList*) pDoc->m_stringArray[nRow];
    pos = pList->GetHeadPosition();
    for(i = 0; i < pDoc->m_nresultcols; i++) {
    pDC->TextOut(x, y, pList->GetNext(pos));
        x += m_nCharWidth * ((int) pDoc->m_collen[i] + 4);
    }
}
```

OnQueryExecute

This command message handler does the real query processing work in the application. It refers to the document for the query statement handle and other parameters, and it stores the query result rows in the document. This function takes care of statement handle allocation and deallocation, so there's no possibility of multiple simultaneous statements for the same document.

```
void CEx24aView::OnQueryExecute()
{
    SWORD       coltype, colnamelen, nullable, scale;
    RETCODE     ret;
```

(continued)

```
UCHAR*        data[MAXCOLS];
UCHAR         colname[32];
SDWORD        outlen[MAXCOLS];
CStringList* pList;
int           i, j, n;

CEx24aDoc* pDoc = GetDocument();
if (!pDoc->m_bConnected) {
    return;   // in case of accelerator activation
}
BeginWaitCursor();
SQLAllocStmt(pDoc->m_hdbc, &(pDoc->m_hstmt));
CDialogBar* pBar = (CDialogBar*)
    AfxGetApp()->m_pMainWnd->GetDlgItem(IDD_QUERY_BAR);
// copies SQL statement from dialog bar to document
pBar->GetDlgItemText(IDC_SQL, pDoc->m_query.GetBuffer(MAX_BUF), MAX_BUF);
ret = SQLExecDirect(pDoc->m_hstmt, (UCHAR FAR*)
                    pDoc->m_query.GetBuffer(MAX_BUF), SQL_NTS);
pDoc->m_query.ReleaseBuffer();
if ((ret != SQL_SUCCESS) && (ret != SQL_SUCCESS_WITH_INFO)) {
    // improve by using SQLError
    AfxMessageBox("SQL error");
}
else {
    SQLNumResultCols(pDoc->m_hstmt, &(pDoc->m_nresultcols));
    if (pDoc->m_nresultcols) {
        pDoc->DeleteContents();
        // retrieves column names and column specifications
        pList = new CStringList;
        pDoc->m_nRowChars = 0;
        pDoc->m_stringArray.SetAtGrow(0, pList);
        for (i = 0; i < pDoc->m_nresultcols; i++) {
            ret = SQLDescribeCol(pDoc->m_hstmt, i + 1, colname,
                (SWORD) sizeof(colname), &colnamelen, &coltype,
                &(pDoc->m_collen[i]), &scale, &nullable);
            pDoc->m_collen[i] = display_size(coltype,
                pDoc->m_collen[i], colnamelen);
            pDoc->m_nRowChars += (int) pDoc->m_collen[i] + 4;
            // col margin=4
            pList->AddTail((const char*) colname);
            data[i] = (UCHAR *) new char[(int) pDoc->m_collen[i]];
            SQLBindCol(pDoc->m_hstmt, i + 1, SQL_C_CHAR, data[i],
                       pDoc->m_collen[i] + 1, &outlen[i]);
        }
        j = 1;
        // iterates through all rows
        for (n = 0; n < MAXROWS; n++) {
            ret = SQLFetch(pDoc->m_hstmt);
            if ((ret == SQL_SUCCESS) || (ret == SQL_SUCCESS_WITH_INFO)) {
                pList = new CStringList;
                pDoc->m_stringArray.SetAtGrow(n + 1, pList);
                // retrieves all columns for the selected row
```

```
        for (i = 0; i < pDoc->m_nresultcols; i++) {
            if (outlen[i] == SQL_NULL_DATA) {
                strcpy((char*) data[i], "NULL");
            }
            else if ((UDWORD) outlen[i] > pDoc->m_collen[i]) {
                strcpy((char*) data[i], "err");
            }
            pList->AddTail((const char*) data[i]);
        }
    }
    else {
        break;
    }
}
// frees allocated column memory
for (i = 0; i < pDoc->m_nresultcols; i++) {
    delete data[i];
}
        }
    }
    SQLFreeStmt(pDoc->m_hstmt, SQL_DROP);
    EndWaitCursor();
    pDoc->UpdateAllViews(NULL); // including this one
}
```

OnSetFocus

Each time the user activates a view, the *OnSetFocus* message handler updates the dialog bar's edit control to reflect the document's current SQL statement.

```
void CEx24aView::OnSetFocus(CWnd* pOldWnd)
{
    // updates dialog bar SQL statement for this view's document
    CEx24aDoc* pDoc = GetDocument();
    CDialogBar* pBar = (CDialogBar*)
        AfxGetApp()->m_pMainWnd->GetDlgItem(IDD_QUERY_BAR);
    pBar->SetDlgItemText(IDC_SQL, pDoc->m_query);
    CRowView::OnSetFocus(pOldWnd);
}
```

OnMouseActivate

A single MDI child window presents a slight problem. When the user clicks in the child window, the focus is not transferred from the dialog bar. You can fix this problem with a *WM_MOUSEACTIVATE* message handler that sets the focus to the current view.

```
int CEx24aView::OnMouseActivate(CWnd* pDesktopWnd, UINT nHitTest, UINT message)
{
    SetFocus();
    return CRowView::OnMouseActivate(pDesktopWnd, nHitTest, message);
}
```

The EX24A Resource File

This application uses a dialog bar, so you'll need a dialog resource for it. Figure 24-3 on page 464 shows the dialog bar. The controls are listed here:

Control	ID
Button	ID_QUERY_EXECUTE
Button	ID_QUERY_TABLES
Edit	IDC_SQL

The dialog resource ID is *IDD_QUERY_BAR*, and the following styles are set:

Style = Child
Border = None
Visible = unchecked

The File menu has two added items:

Menu Item	Command ID
ODBC Connect	ID_FILE_CONNECT
ODBC Disconnect	ID_FILE_DISCONNECT

Running the EX24A Program

To compile and run this program, you must have the ODBC Software Development Kit software properly installed, including the dBASE/Xbase driver, SIMBA.DLL. Be sure that the ODBC Visual Basic demo works correctly. Also, be sure that the ODBC import library, ODBC.LIB, is installed where the linker can find it, and be sure the include files, SQL.H and SQLEXT.H, are installed where the compiler can find them. The DLL files ODBC.DLL and SIMBA.DLL should be located in the \WINDOWS\SYSTEM subdirectory.

This book's companion disk includes two relatable sample database files, SHARE.DBF and STOCK.DBF. These files are in the \VCPP\EX24A subdirectory, along with the example's source code. The EX24A MAK file specifies the large memory model (necessary for storing query results) and the ODBC import library.

After you have built EX24A.EXE, follow these steps:

1. Start the program. You'll find out immediately if the ODBC.DLL file is not available.

2. Choose ODBC Connect from the File menu, and then enter data in the two dialogs as shown at the top of the next page:

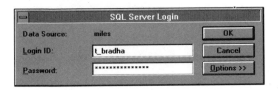

3. Type the following query

```
select * from share, stock where share.shnumber = stock.shnumber
```

and then observe the results.

4. Try to close the application's main window, and observe the message box that says you can't do that.

5. Choose New Window from the Window menu, and observe that you now have two views of the same query results.

6. Try Print Preview and Print.

7. Save the document on disk. The SQL statement and connect information will be saved.

8. Choose ODBC Disconnect from the File menu.

9. Exit the application.

Going Further with EX24A

The EX24A program is a workable SQL query tool, but you could easily improve it in the following ways:

- Add a *CFormView* view class or a modal dialog to give a full-screen picture of the currently selected row. See the Visual C++ CHKBOOK example in the \MSVC\MFC\SAMPLES\CHKBOOK subdirectory or EX21A in Chapter 21 for some ideas.

- Change *CRowView* to eliminate the 32,767-unit size restriction. Your new *CRowView* class would be better derived directly from *CView* rather than from *CScrollView*.

PART 4: ADVANCED TOPICS

- Add clipboard support for the SQL statement and for the result rows.

- Use a font other than the System font. If you switched to a TrueType font, the printed font would be small because of the view's *MM_TEXT* mapping mode. You would need a separate font for the printer, or you would have to convert *CRowView* to another mapping mode.

- Write the Tables command handler. This was left as a stub in the example code. Use the ODBC *SQLTables* function to get a list of the tables stored in the database.

You can buy general-purpose database query programs at the software store. The class library with ODBC is more suited to special-purpose applications with fixed database layouts. Those applications will often need to update the database with the SQL UPDATE statement. In most cases, the user will be completely insulated from SQL statements.

25

Object Linking and Embedding (OLE)

OLE is a set of Microsoft protocols that allow programs in Windows to cooperate with one another. OLE is yet another "building block" option for creating applications. Now you have C++ classes, Visual Basic controls, and OLE items in your toolkit (or, shall we say, arsenal).

This chapter explains the important OLE concepts and shows how Microsoft Foundation Class Library version 2.0 improves on the original C-language OLE API. You'll also see two examples that work with each other and with other OLE applications. The Post-it Note example is a typical OLE miniserver application. The other example is the Chapters 15–17 student record program extended into an OLE client application. Student records can now contain pictures, documents, and even something akin to Post-it Notes.

In previous chapters, you've seen assorted Windows tidbits mixed in with the examples. This chapter is no exception. Here you'll draw an icon in a window, and you'll set the background color of an edit control.

OLE Fundamentals

OLE programming is a complex subject. Plan to spend some time studying the principles before you jump into the examples.

OLE from the User's Point of View

Before you start OLE program development, you should be thoroughly familiar with the operation of existing OLE applications. (After all, the users of your application must know how to run an OLE-aware program.) Several OLE applications—Write, Paintbrush, and Sound Recorder—come bundled with Windows. Many commercial Windows-based applications, including Microsoft Word and Microsoft Excel, use the OLE protocols.

Experiment now with Write. Type a few sentences, and then choose Insert Object from the Edit menu. When you choose Paintbrush Picture from the dialog, the Paintbrush application runs. Exercise your artistic talent in Paintbrush, and then choose Update from the Paintbrush File menu. Your masterpiece should now appear inside the Write document, as shown in Figure 25-1.

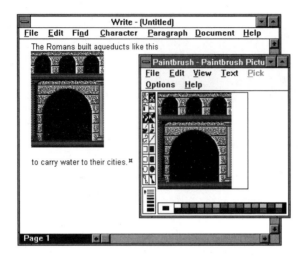

Figure 25-1.
A Paintbrush object inserted in Write.

Now exit Paintbrush and restart it from the Program Manager. Load a file such as MARBLE.BMP, and then use the scissors tool to select a rectangular area. When you choose Copy from the Edit menu, the selected part of the image is copied to the Windows clipboard. Now return to Write and choose Paste from the Edit menu. The selected image should appear in the Write document. Go back to Paintbrush and exit, and then return to Write again. If you double-click on the new image, Paintbrush should start up again. When you save the Write document, the embedded pictures are saved as part of the WRI file.

Keep working with Write and Paintbrush until you understand the interaction. Try the Paste Link item on Write's Edit menu, and then choose Links from Write's Edit menu. The difference between embedded and linked items will become clear as you read this chapter.

> **Note:** *Program menus and the C-oriented OLE documentation both use the term* object *to refer to entities such as Paintbrush pictures. Because we're using the term* object *in the context of C++, we'll use the term* item *to refer to OLE objects.*

Clients vs. Servers

The two kinds of OLE-aware programs are clients and servers. OLE servers produce OLE items; OLE clients can embed OLE items within their documents. Some programs, such as Microsoft Word, can be both a client and a server, but that's a special case. Windows Write is an OLE client, and Paintbrush is an OLE server. A client document can contain one or more server items. The client application manages the document and the server applications, and the server application manages its own items.

An OLE server must support multiple clients. (Several Write documents could simultaneously use the Paintbrush server.) A server such as Microsoft Excel is really two servers in one; it supports both graph and spreadsheet items, and each item type could have multiple clients.

The programming techniques you use depend on whether you are writing client applications or server applications. In this chapter, you'll study each separately.

Full Servers vs. Miniservers

The Paintbrush application is a full server because it can operate both as a stand-alone program and as an OLE server. A miniserver cannot operate on its own (you can't run it from Program Manager), it can't open and save its own document files, and it doesn't generally support the clipboard. The EX25B server, something akin to a Post-it Note, is an example of a miniserver. A full server example is in the \MSVC\-MFC\SAMPLES\HIERSVR subdirectory.

OLE Items vs. C++ Objects

You already know about C++-style object-oriented programming. The C++ class behavior, which the programmer determines, is flexible. A class's member functions can exchange any kind of information through data members, parameters, and return values. If Class A calls a Class B member function, though, the programmer of Class A must know the Class B interface details. A Class B member function could, for example, return the coordinates of a point, but Class A must know, at compile time, the exact format of those coordinates.

OLE items are different from C++ objects because any OLE client can communicate with any OLE server. The client and server communicate at runtime, not at compile or link time. This communication requirement severely restricts the ways in which clients and servers interact. A client can direct a server item to display itself on a device context, it can allow the user to edit the selected item, or it can initiate some other activity such as the playing of a sound.

If the user edits the item, the server application, not the client application, controls the editing. Thus, the client is completely unaware of the server's data storage format. How, you might ask, does the client manage to store the server's data on disk as you saw with Write and Paintbrush? The client processes a stream of bytes in the server's native format that the server sends via the OLE protocols.

If the OLE server is Microsoft Excel, for example, the client application cannot read or write the numbers in the worksheet cells; it can only display, store, and retrieve the worksheet, and it can execute Excel to allow the user to edit the worksheet. There are some workarounds, however. Excel transfers clipboard data in a standard DIF format that allows access to numbers and strings. Because Microsoft has published the Excel file format, a client program could extract numbers, strings, and formulas from the worksheet native format.

Inserting vs. Pasting

In the first Write–Paintbrush exercise, you inserted OLE items into a client document. Choosing Insert Object from the Edit menu and choosing the server name from the dialog loaded the server application, but you were prevented from loading a file from disk (except through Paintbrush's Paste From menu item). Write's Paste menu item is more flexible than the Insert Object menu item because Paste lets you use the server with any data on the clipboard, including disk data. Depending on the server, the Paste menu item lets you select a portion of a graphics image.

Embedded vs. Linked Items

Embedded items are wholly contained inside their client document. A linked item uses data stored in a named disk file. The filename is recorded in the client document, and the file is read and written in response to user actions. Using a linked item gives you several advantages over using an embedded item. Client document size is reduced, and data redundancy is eliminated.

Manual vs. Automatic Links

New OLE links are created in automatic mode by default. Automatic links cause their corresponding items to be updated whenever the client document is loaded. If you choose Edit Links from the client's Edit menu, an OLE Links dialog allows you to view and edit the document's links. (In some client applications, the Edit Links menu item is enabled only if there are active links.) If you change a link from automatic to manual, the client item will no longer be updated automatically. You must click the Update Now button in the Links dialog to update manual links.

OLE Verbs

If you double-click on an embedded Paintbrush item in an OLE client document, Paintbrush comes up and allows you to edit the item. Most OLE servers support only one primary action, expressed by a verb. In the Paintbrush case, the primary (and only) verb is Edit.

Sound Recorder (a multimedia OLE server included with Windows version 3.1) has two verbs, Play and Edit. In a client document, the sound-item icon looks like this:

If you double-click on a sound item and if you have a sound board in your computer, you hear the sound contained in the OLE item. Play is Sound Recorder's primary verb, and Edit is the secondary verb.

After you insert a Sound Recorder item in a client document, click on the item and choose Sound Object from the client's Edit menu. A small pop-up menu appears with the Play and Edit items, as shown in Figure 25-2.

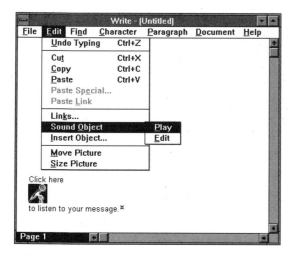

Figure 25-2.
The Write Edit Sound Object pop-up menu.

If you choose Edit, you can edit the item. OLE and the application framework supply this pop-up menu because the server supplies more than one verb.

This chapter's second example, EX25B, is an OLE server with two verbs, Read and Edit. Read displays a yellow Post-it Note on the screen, and Edit allows the user to edit the note's text.

OLE Server Registration

If any OLE client can talk to any OLE server, how does a client know which servers exist and where they are stored on disk? As you might suspect, a central registration database, which is actually a binary file named REG.DAT, is in the WINDOWS sub-directory. This file contains information about all installed OLE servers, including their full program path names, document file extensions, command-line switches, and OLE verbs. The OLE system interrogates this registration database when a client opens a server.

(The registration database is not only for OLE. It contains other information, such as the document-type associations described in Chapter 17. Therefore, REG.DAT can contain entries for Windows-based applications that aren't OLE servers.)

The Windows installation procedure updates the registration database for the OLE servers that are bundled with Windows. Most commercial OLE-aware applications update REG.DAT on initial setup. When you write your own OLE servers, you must plan to update the registration database on the computer where the server is installed.

You have two options for updating REG.DAT to accommodate a new OLE server (referred to simply as "server" from now on). You can write a load script for a Windows utility named REGLOAD, or you can have the server itself update the database. If you choose the latter option, you must be sure that the server program is executed once in stand-alone mode before you run it as a server.

Windows has another utility named REGEDIT, which was introduced in Chapter 17. REGEDIT allows you to edit manually all the information in the registration database, but you must run it with the /v advanced interface option. Figure 25-3 shows the registration entry for Sound Recorder.

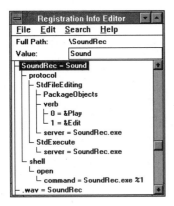

Figure 25-3.
The registration entry for Sound Recorder.

You can see the hierarchical structure of REG.DAT. There are OLE APIs for reading and setting REG.DAT data.

Client–Server Data Exchange Formats

The client application and the server application are separate programs in the Windows operating system, yet they must interact in specific ways. If you use the

Write client together with the Paintbrush server, you must conclude that the client must have access to enough server data to draw a picture in the client's window and to save the picture information on disk in such a way that it can be later retrieved and reedited.

You might think that the two data requirements could be satisfied by the "save on disk" native data format alone. In theory they could, but unless the client understands the server's native format, the server program would have to be present every time the item was repainted. Actually, two distinct formats are used (and stored) by OLE client applications—native format and Windows presentation format.

Consider the native format requirement. If the server is Microsoft Excel, for example, this native data format is exactly the same as the Excel worksheet disk format (XLS format). In effect, a complete Excel XLS file is stored inside the client's document file.

The Windows presentation format, actually a Windows metafile, is a visual rendering of the underlying data. The server draws on a memory-based metafile device context whenever the item's content changes. Thereafter, the client executes the GDI instructions from the metafile every time the item is resized or otherwise repainted. Thus, the client's version of the item can be resized and redrawn without need for the server application to be loaded.

> **Note:** *Windows Paintbrush is an atypical example for server data formats. If Paintbrush items were stored both in native format (device-independent bitmap) and metafile format, you would expect a picture item to be twice as big as the corresponding BMP file. Paintbrush and OLE cooperate to eliminate redundant data storage.*

It's up to the server to determine what to show in the client item viewing area. Paintbrush draws the actual picture, but Sound Recorder displays only a microphone bitmap. Some servers display nothing at all.

Microsoft Foundation Class Library Version 2.0 and OLE

The OLE protocols were originally distributed as two DLLs, OLECLI.DLL and OLESVR.DLL, with only a C-language programming interface (a header file and an import library) plus a help file. C-language OLE programming was difficult; so Microsoft provided a C++ interface to OLE, first in version 1.0 of the Microsoft Foundation Class Library and then in version 2.0. Version 2.0 OLE classes are integrated with the application framework, but the original OLE DLLs are still there underneath.

Figure 25-4 on the next page shows the interrelationship among the OLE classes and the OLE DLLs in the class library.

Notice the callbacks from OLE base classes to OLE derived classes. You've seen callbacks before throughout the class library. The application framework calls the

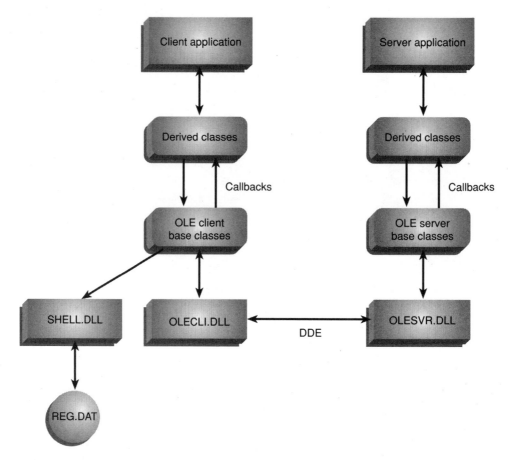

Figure 25-4.
The OLE class–DLL relationships.

application class virtual *InitInstance* function, for example. You are required to override that function in your derived class. With OLE, you must process lots of callbacks in overridden functions.

> ***Note:*** *The illustration in Figure 25-4 assumes that both the client application and the server application are written with Microsoft Foundation Class Library version 2.0. This isn't a requirement. Microsoft Foundation Class Library clients can use C-language servers, and vice versa.*

Also notice the communication between the client application and the server application. The two DLLs use Dynamic Data Exchange (DDE) as a communication protocol, but that protocol is entirely hidden from the programmer. In fact, a different data transfer method could be substituted in some later version of OLE without requiring any changes to existing applications.

As you get into client and server programming, you'll learn about the member functions and the flow of data between programs. Refer to Figure 25-4 to get your bearings.

OLE Version 1.0 vs. OLE Version 2.0

Software is always improving, and so you must cope with frequent new versions of every product. When Visual C++ was released, it contained the classes and DLLs for OLE version 1.0, even though Microsoft had released the version 2.0 DLLs. OLE version 2.0 introduces new features that integrate clients and servers more tightly. An OLE version 2.0 server can, for example, take over the client's main menu so that the user isn't aware that he or she is using a different application.

The C-language API changed a lot between OLE version 1.0 and OLE version 2.0, but the AFX developers have promised that the OLE class library interface won't change much at all. Only a few member functions will be added. Any Microsoft Foundation Class Library version 2.0 application you build with OLE version 1.0 can be easily ported to OLE version 2.0 when the version 2.0 classes are available.

The OLE Client Application

Writing OLE client and server applications are separate jobs, and there are separate classes for each. This section describes the elements of an OLE client application and presents an example.

The OLE Client Classes

You'll need only two OLE base classes in a client application, *COleClientDoc* and *COleClientItem*. You'll derive your document classes from *COleClientDoc*, and you'll derive document item classes from *COleClientItem*. A document is what you expect it to be, but a document item is something new—it's that element in your document that corresponds to an OLE item. An OLE document object contains client item objects. The client item has a pointer back to the document that owns it.

The *COleClientDoc* and *COleClientItem* base classes encapsulate a substantial amount of the OLE client logic. Because so much default functionality is programmed in, you need only override a few selected functions to complete the OLE part of your client application.

When you run AppWizard and select the OLE Client option, you get a document class derived from *COleClientDoc*. You also get some OLE-specific items in your application's document menu resource.

You must write the derived *COleClientItem* class yourself. The constructor, which takes a *COleClientDoc* pointer argument, makes an empty C++ object. The object is connected to the OLE system when you call create functions such as *CreateNewObject* or *CreateFromClipboard*.

The Client Document Structure

The structure of the document class is important in any class library document–view application, OLE applications included. The *COleClientDoc* class contains its own list for *COleClientItem* pointers. Sometimes you can get by with this structure alone, but frequently you'll want to integrate OLE items into your document's application-specific structure. For example, your document could contain a list of employee records, and each of the employee records could have a list of attached OLE items.

You can't interfere with the document base class's private list, but you can keep your own duplicate OLE item pointers in your derived class. When you delete an object of a class derived from *COleClientItem*, the application framework removes the pointer from the base class list.

Client Initiatives

The OLE client application must take the initiative frequently when communicating with a server. Here are some actions the client must take. Some you must program yourself; the application framework takes care of others.

Registering the client document

This registration has nothing to do with the registration database. The client application must inform the OLE DLLs that it is up and running by calling the *COleClientDoc RegisterClientDoc* member function. OLE then updates tables in memory. Normally, the application framework registers the client document in the *COleClientDoc OnOpenDocument* and *OnNewDocument* member functions.

Inserting an embedded item

Most of the time, the user chooses Insert New Object from the client application's Edit menu (generated by AppWizard). This maps to an *OnInsertObject* command message handler in the AppWizard-generated view class. Here's a simplified *On-InsertObject* function:

```
void CMyView::OnInsertObject()
{
    char    szItemName[OLE_MAXNAMESIZE];
    CString strTypeName;

    AfxOleInsertDialog(strTypeName)  // user chooses server from list
    BeginWaitCursor();
    CreateNewUniqueName(szItemName); // helper function generates
                                     //  unique item name

    CMyDoc* pDoc = GetDocument();
    // the m_pSelectedItem data member points to the currently
    //  selected OLE item
    if (m_pSelectedItem) {           // delete any prior item
        delete m_pSelectedItem;
    }
```

```
    m_pSelectedItem = new CMyItem(pDoc);
    VERIFY(m_pSelectedItem->CreateNewObject(strTypeName, szItemName));
    EndWaitCursor();
}
```

Error-checking logic is minimal, and it's assumed that the document contains only one OLE item. The important OLE base class function called is *CreateNewObject*. It launches the server program (if it was not already running) and turns control over to the user.

Pasting an embedded item from the clipboard

The framework ensures that the Paste item on the Edit menu is enabled only when an OLE item is available to paste. You must map the Paste item to a command handler such as *OnEditPaste*. Here's a typical *OnEditPaste* implementation:

```
void CMyView::OnEditPaste()
{
    if (!OpenClipboard())
        return;          // couldn't open the clipboard
    BeginWaitCursor();

    CMyDoc* pDoc = GetDocument();
    if (m_pSelectedItem) {  // delete any prior item
        delete m_pSelectedItem;
    }
    m_pSelectedItem = new CMyItem(pDoc);
    char szName[OLE_MAXNAMESIZE];
    CreateNewUniqueName(szName);
    VERIFY(m_pSelectedItem->CreateFromClipboard(szName));
    CloseClipboard();
}
```

CreateFromClipboard is the significant OLE base class function called here. It copies the server data from the clipboard and thus completes the creation of the *CMyItem* object.

Pasting a linked item from the clipboard

The application framework ensures that the Paste Link item on the Edit menu is enabled only when an OLE item is available to paste. The choice could be enabled, however, when an item that is not linkable is available. You must map the Paste Link item to a command handler such as *OnEditPasteLink*. Here's a typical *OnEdit-PasteLink* implementation:

```
void CMyView::OnEditPasteLink()
{
    if (!OpenClipboard())
        return;          // couldn't open the clipboard
    BeginWaitCursor();
```

(continued)

```
    CMyDoc* pDoc = GetDocument();
    if (m_pSelectedItem) {  // delete any prior item
        delete m_pSelectedItem;
    }
    m_pSelectedItem = new CMyItem(pDoc);
    char szName[OLE_MAXNAMESIZE];
    CreateNewUniqueName(szName);
    if (!m_pSelectedItem->CreateLinkFromClipboard(szName)){
        delete m_pSelectedItem;
        m_pSelectedItem = NULL;
    }
    CloseClipboard();
}
```

The significant OLE base class function called here is *CreateLinkFromClipboard*. It copies the necessary server data from the clipboard and thus completes the creation of the *CMyItem* object. The server data includes the link file information and the presentation metafile.

Copying an item to or cutting an item from the clipboard

If an item is selected (see "Returning the selected OLE item" later in this chapter), the application framework enables the Copy and Cut items on the Edit menu. You must map these items to command handlers, most likely in your view class. Here's a sample *OnEditCopy* function:

```
void CMyView::OnEditCopy()
{
    if (!OpenClipboard())
        return;
    EmptyClipboard();
    // assumes m_pSelectedItem points to valid OLE client item
    m_pSelectedItem->CopyToClipboard();
    CloseClipboard();
}
```

The base class *CopyToClipboard* function does the work here. It selects the necessary clipboard formats for you.

Drawing an item

If the client needs a visual representation of an item, it must play the server item's metafile in the client window. The *COleClientItem Draw* function does the job, and it's often called from the client view's *OnDraw* function. *Draw* takes a device context pointer and a client rectangle as parameters. It's up to the client application to invalidate the proper rectangle.

Activating server verbs

The application framework takes care of everything here. When the user chooses a verb from the menu, the base document class calls the virtual *DoVerb* function for the currently selected item. The single *DoVerb* parameter is 0 for the primary verb, 1 for the secondary verb, and so forth. If the server program isn't loaded when the verb is activated, the OLE system loads it and sends it the necessary data.

Deleting an item

This job's easy. You simply delete the *COleClientItem* object. The virtual destructor takes care of everything. If necessary, the server program is terminated.

Serializing an item

OLE serialization sounds difficult at first. The client must load and store server data without knowing anything about its format. Actually, the application framework makes OLE serialization easy. You write a *Serialize* function for your client document that traverses the document item list to serialize each document; this function ultimately calls the *COleClientItem* base class *Serialize* function. In the case of storing, the client already has the necessary native-format data in memory, so it simply writes the data to disk. In the case of loading, the client reads and keeps the data until the user takes some action, such as activating a verb, that requires the data to be sent to the server.

> **Note:** *Do not assume that because a client document has its own list of client items the base class document class will serialize those items. You control serialization in your derived document class.*

Getting and setting OLE item bounds

If your client application needs to know the size of the OLE item, it can call the *COleClientItem GetBounds* function. Windows Write makes this call to set the size of the OLE item in the document. Other clients, such as the EX25A example program, paint the server's icon in a fixed rectangle, so they don't need to call *GetBounds*.

Sometimes a client needs to tell a server to repaint its data in a rectangle that better serves the client's needs. The *COleClientItem SetBounds* function triggers the *OnSetBounds* callback at the server. All bounds are assumed to be in MM_HI-METRIC logical units.

Cleaning up the document

If you're using the *COleClientDoc* internal item list, the deletion of OLE items is automatic. It's handled in the *COleClientDoc* virtual *DeleteContents* function. If your document structure requires that the document keep its own *COleClientItem* pointers, however, you have to be careful about deleting the OLE item objects. Do not delete these objects in your document destructor. By the time the destructor gets called, the *DeleteContents* function has done its job, and you'll be double-deleting objects. If you need to delete OLE item objects when your document is closed, override *DeleteContents*, and do your deletions before calling the base class *DeleteContents* function. Remember that the *COleClientItem* destructor removes the object pointer from the *COleClientDoc* private collection.

Client Responses

You've seen the client initiatives. Now you'll see how the client responds to OLE callbacks.

Returning the selected OLE item

The OLE system needs to know which *COleClientItem* object is currently selected. You must override the virtual *CView IsSelected* function for this purpose. Here is a sample:

```
BOOL CMyView::IsSelected(const CObject* pDocItem) const
{
    return (m_pSelectedItem == pDocItem);
}
```

Updating the client edit menu items to match the server

The application framework takes care of this chore for you through the global *AfxOleSetEditMenu* function, which uses information stored in REG.DAT. If the server has one verb, the application framework updates the bottom item on the Edit menu with the server's name and primary verb. If the server has multiple verbs, the application framework creates and attaches a submenu.

Processing the *OnChange* callback

This is the most critical client response. When an item is first embedded, through a call to *CreateNewObject*, it is empty; the user hasn't entered any data through the server yet. After working for a while, the user chooses Update from the server's File menu, and the *OnChange* function is called for the selected client item. Simultaneously, the client item's data is updated from the server. Now the embedded item contains data, and the client views can be updated. Here's a simple *OnChange* implementation:

```
void CMyItem::OnChange(OLE_NOTIFICATION wNotification)
{
    CMyDoc* pDoc = GetDocument();
    if (wNotification == OLE_SAVED || wNotification == OLE_CHANGED) {
        pDoc->SetModifiedFlag();
        pDoc->UpdateAllViews(NULL);
    }
}
```

What if the user bails out of the server without choosing Update? Your client application must handle this case. You have to figure out that the user has closed the server (notification code *OLE_CLOSED*) without saving or changing the data, and then you must delete the client item object and do the necessary document and view housekeeping. The EX25A example shows one way of doing this.

The EX25A OLE Client Example

The sample program in the Visual C++ \MSVC\MFC\SAMPLES\OCLIENT sub-directory is an OLE client example that allows OLE items to be positioned and sized in a wysiwyg document. It's rather like Windows Write except that it doesn't support text in the main window. Use OCLIENT as a starting point if you need a special-purpose word-processor-like application because it has logic for placing OLE clients inside movable rectangles.

The EX25A example is different. It's more of a data processing example that builds on the EX15A student record program. Each MDI child window contains a single student record with one attached OLE item, displayed in a fixed location in the view window. The code is designed to accommodate a list of student records (as in EX15B, EX16A, and EX17A). You could even extend the example to allow multiple OLE items per student record.

Figure 25-5 illustrates the EX25A client running with the Microsoft WordArt server (a utility included with Microsoft Word for Windows). The client *CFormView* window

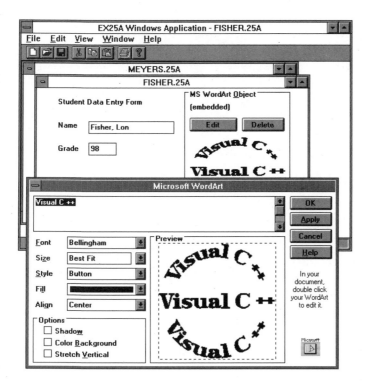

Figure 25-5.
The EX25A client with WordArt server.

shows the server's name, a visual representation of the client's data, and a text field that indicates whether the OLE item is embedded or linked. A primary verb button duplicates the primary verb on the Edit menu. Item insertion and multiple verb selection are handled from the Edit menu.

The EX25A example is presented with code highlights and resource requirements. Here's a table of the files and classes:

Header File	Source Code File	Class	Description
EX25A.H	EX25A.CPP	CEx25aApp	Main application—from AppWizard
MAINFRM.H	MAINFRM.CPP	CMainFrame	MDI main frame—from AppWizard
EX25ADOC.H	EX25ADOC.CPP	CEx25aDoc	EX25A document (derived from COleClientDoc)
EX25AVW.H	EX25AVW.CPP	CEx25aView	Student form view class
EX25AITM.H	EX25AITM.CPP	CEx25aItem	OLE item (derived from COleClientItem)
STUDENT.H	STUDENT.CPP	CStudent	Student record
STDAFX.H	STDAFX.CPP		Precompiled headers

Now we'll go through the application's classes one at a time.

CEx25aApp

This is the standard AppWizard-generated application class, which is derived from *CWinApp*.

CMainFrame

When you select the OLE Client option in AppWizard, the resulting derived frame window class contains a special *OnCommand* message handler that disables the main menu while the application is waiting for the server.

CEx25aDoc

This class is derived from *COleClientDoc*. The class represents the application's document, as it does in a non-OLE application.

The *CEx25aDoc* class has an *m_pStudent* data member that holds a pointer to the document's one and only student record object. A pointer was used instead of an embedded object so that the application could more easily be converted to a list of student records.

OnNewDocument

Because the document's student record object is not embedded, the document class must construct and destroy it. The *CStudent* object is constructed here instead of in the document constructor so that the class can work in the SDI environment from which *DeleteContents* is called multiple times for the same document object.

```
BOOL CEx25aDoc::OnNewDocument()
{
    TRACE("Entering CEx25aDoc::OnNewDocument\n");
    if (!COleClientDoc::OnNewDocument()) {
        return FALSE;
    }
    m_pStudent = new CStudent;
    return TRUE;
}
```

DeleteContents

The base class *OnNewDocument* function calls this virtual function. The overridden version cleans up the derived class document data members before calling the base class *DeleteContents*. It deletes the document's *CStudent* object.

```
void CEx25aDoc::DeleteContents()
{
    if (m_pStudent) {
        delete m_pStudent; // sequence is critical
        m_pStudent = NULL;
    }
    COleClientDoc::DeleteContents();
}
```

Serialize

The *Serialize* function must construct a *CStudent* object on loading. It also caches a pointer (declared in the *CEx25aApp* class) to the current document object so that subsequently constructed and loaded *CEx25aItem* objects receive the document pointers they need.

```
void CEx25aDoc::Serialize(CArchive& ar)
{
    if (!ar.IsStoring()) {
        ((CEx25aApp*) AfxGetApp())->m_pDocSerialize = this;
        m_pStudent = new CStudent;
    }
    m_pStudent->Serialize(ar);
}
```

CStudent

The student record is similar to the student record of Chapters 15 and 16 except that it accommodates a *COleClientItem* pointer, *m_pOleItem*. We could have combined the student data with the OLE item in a single *COleStudentItem* class, but this strategy would have made it impossible to convert to multiple items per student later on.

Destructor

The *CStudent* destructor must delete its OLE item object.

```
CStudent::~CStudent()
{
    TRACE("Entering CStudent destructor\n");
    if (m_pOleItem) {
        delete m_pOleItem;
    }
}
```

Serialize

The *CStudent Serialize* function must take into consideration that some student records don't have attached OLE items. A long integer is 9999 if item data follows; otherwise, it is 0. The OLE item constructor demands a pointer to the item's document. The *CStudent Serialize* function gets this from the *CEx25aApp* data member that the *CEx25aDoc Serialize* function set.

```
void CStudent::Serialize(CArchive& ar)
{
    LONG lItemFollows;
    TRACE("Entering CStudent::Serialize - storing = %d\n",
        ar.IsStoring());
    if (ar.IsStoring())    {
        ar << m_name << m_lGrade;
        if (m_pOleItem) {
            ar << (LONG) 9999;
            m_pOleItem->Serialize(ar);
        }
        else {
            ar << (LONG) 0;
        }
    }
    else {
        ar >> m_name >> m_lGrade >> lItemFollows;
        if (lItemFollows == 9999L) {
            m_pOleItem =
                new CEx25aItem(((CEx25aApp*)
                            AfxGetApp())->m_pDocSerialize);
```

```
        m_pOleItem->Serialize(ar);
    }
  }
}
```

CEx25aItem

This class represents the student record's OLE item. The *m_pStudent* data member is set only while item creation is in progress.

OnChange

This OLE callback is triggered when the user changes, saves, or closes the server item. *OnChange* uses the *CEx25aItem m_pStudent* data member to detect an OLE item close without prior save or change. (You don't want to save the client item if the user closes the server without first asking to save the item.) Either this function sets the document's modified flag and updates the view, or it destroys the *CEx25aItem* object.

```
void CEx25aItem::OnChange(OLE_NOTIFICATION wNotification)
{
    TRACE("Entering CEx25aItem::OnChange, wNotification = %x\n",
        wNotification);
    CEx25aDoc* pDoc = GetDocument();
    if (wNotification == OLE_SAVED || wNotification == OLE_CHANGED) {
        if (m_pStudent) {
            m_pStudent->m_pOleItem = this;
            m_pStudent = NULL;
        }
        pDoc->SetModifiedFlag();
        pDoc->UpdateAllViews(NULL);
    }
    else {
        if (m_pStudent) {
            delete this; // OLE_CLOSED without prior OLE_SAVED
                         //   or OLE_CHANGED
            pDoc->UpdateAllViews(NULL);
        }
    }
}
```

CEx25aView

This class is derived from *CFormView* and behaves the same as a normal form view class. Its dialog resource, *IDD_STUDENT*, contains a static control, *IDC_IMAGE*, on which the OLE item data is drawn.

The data member *m_pSelectedItem* points to the selected OLE item object. Only one OLE item per view is possible in this application, but if you enhanced the program for multiple students, for example, the *m_pSelectedItem* pointer would change as different items were selected. If *m_pSelectedItem* is NULL, no OLE item is selected.

OnDraw

As with all view classes, the application framework calls *OnDraw* when it is necessary to redraw the view's client area. This function calls the OLE *Draw* function to draw the selected item in the static *IDC_IMAGE* window. The preceding *Invalidate* and *UpdateWindow* calls ensure that the static control is not overwritten.

```
void CEx25aView::OnDraw(CDC* pDC)
{
    TRACE("Entering CEx25aView::OnDraw\n");
    // draws the OLE item in the client form view's
    //   static IDC_IMAGE window
    CEx25aDoc* pDoc = GetDocument();
    CRect clientRect;
    CWnd* pStatic = GetDlgItem(IDC_IMAGE);
    pStatic->GetClientRect(&clientRect);
    CClientDC dcStatic(pStatic);
    pStatic->Invalidate();
    pStatic->UpdateWindow();
    if (m_pSelectedItem) {
        m_pSelectedItem->Draw(&dcStatic, clientRect);
    }
}
```

IsSelected

The application framework iterates through all a document's items and calls the virtual *IsSelected* function to determine whether a given item is selected. The item selection process is trivial in this program. The item is selected if its pointer value matches the pointer stored in the *m_pSelectedItem* data member.

```
BOOL CEx25aView::IsSelected(const CObject* pDocItem) const
{
    TRACE("Entering CEx25aView::IsSelected\n");
    return(m_pSelectedItem == pDocItem);
}
```

OnInsertObject

This function is called in response to the Insert New Object item on the Edit menu. A new *CEx25aItem* object is created, and the OLE *CreateNewObject* function is called. If an item existed previously, it is deleted. The new item object is not immediately inserted into the student record. That happens only after the OLE change or save change notification is received at the item level.

```
void CEx25aView::OnInsertObject()
{
    char szItemName[OLE_MAXNAMESIZE];
    CString strTypeName;

    if (!AfxOleInsertDialog(strTypeName)) {
        return;            // no OLE class selected
    }
    BeginWaitCursor();
    CreateNewUniqueName(szItemName);

    CEx25aDoc* pDoc = GetDocument();
    if (m_pSelectedItem) {  // delete any prior item
        delete m_pSelectedItem;
        pDoc->SetModifiedFlag();
        pDoc->m_pStudent->m_pOleItem = m_pSelectedItem = NULL;
    }
    CEx25aItem* pSelectedItem = new CEx25aItem(pDoc);
    if (pSelectedItem->CreateNewObject(strTypeName, szItemName) == NULL) {
        AfxMessageBox("Error loading server--check server installation.");
        delete pSelectedItem;
    }
    else {
        pSelectedItem->m_pStudent = pDoc->m_pStudent;
    }
    EndWaitCursor();
}
```

OnClickedPrimary

The EX25A example provides a primary verb pushbutton in the view window that shows the name of the server's primary verb. (See Figure 25-5 on page 487.) When the user clicks this button, *OnClickedPrimary* is called, which calls *DoVerb* with a 0 parameter. Other OLE client applications use the mouse double click to activate the primary verb.

```
void CEx25aView::OnClickedPrimary()
{
    if (m_pSelectedItem) {
        m_pSelectedItem->DoVerb(0);
    }
}
```

OnEditPaste, OnEditPasteLink, OnEditCopy, OnEditCut

These functions, called in response to Edit menu items, copy OLE items from and to the clipboard, using the *COleClientItem* clipboard functions.

UpdateOleControls

The application framework updates the main frame window's Edit menu with the server name and verbs for the selected OLE item. The *UpdateOleControls* private member function creates a dummy menu, calls *AfxOleSetEditMenu* to update this menu, and then transfers menu text to the form view controls. It's easier to extract the names from the menu than it is to use the native OLE functions. The *UpdateOleControls* function updates the primary verb button as well as the group control title and the static control that shows (*embedded*) or (*linked*).

EX25A Resource Requirements

The EX25A program requires a dialog resource, as shown in Figure 25-5, with the following controls (permanent static text controls omitted):

Control Type	Symbol	Caption	Data Member
Edit	IDC_NAME		m_name
Edit	IDC_GRADE		m_lGrade
Pushbutton	IDC_ENTER	Enter	
Group box	IDC_ITEM_NAME	Item Name	
Static	IDC_STATIC	Student Data Entry Form	
Static	IDC_STATIC	Name	
Static	IDC_STATIC	Grade	
Static	IDC_ITEM_TYPE	Item Type	
Pushbutton	IDC_PRIMARY	Primary Verb	
Pushbutton	IDC_DELETE	Delete	
Static	IDC_IMAGE		

AppWizard generates the necessary OLE Edit menu.

The OLE Server Application

Now for an OLE server application. You won't see example code here like you saw in the client section because server code tends to be more application-specific. Look at the EX25B server example if you want to see code.

The OLE Server Classes

For OLE server applications there are four base classes—*COleServer*, *COleTemplateServer*, *COleServerDoc*, and *COleServerItem*. Server applications generally need classes derived from three of the base classes, as follows:

Miniserver	Full Server
COleServer	COleTemplateServer
COleServerDoc	COleServerDoc
COleServerItem	COleServerItem

The many possible server architecture variations include the following:

■ **SDI server, multi-instance**—This is the most common type of OLE server, and it's the easiest to implement. The SDI server uses one server object and one document object. Each time a client needs a server, a new server instance is launched. Miniservers, which don't support links, have only one item object. Full servers need multiple item objects only when multiple clients are linked to the same disk-based document.

Class Type	# Classes	# Objects (Miniserver)	# Objects (Full Server)
Server	One	One	One
Document	One	One	One
Item	One	One	Multiple

■ **MDI server, single server type, single-instance**—You need an MDI server if DGROUP memory constraints preclude a multi-instance server or if you want a full server to be MDI when it runs in stand-alone mode. Each client actively using the server has one document object. In the miniserver case, there is still one item per document.

Class Type	# Classes	# Objects (Miniserver)	# Objects (Full Server)
Server	One	One	One
Document	One	Multiple	Multiple
Item	One	Multiple	Multiple

■ **MDI server, multiple server types, single-instance**—An example of this type of architecture is Microsoft Excel, which supports both charts and spreadsheets. A miniserver doesn't make sense here because you would simply write two separate miniservers. Each server class has one document class and each server object has one document object. Because full servers support links, a document could have multiple item objects, but each document class could have multiple item classes.

Class Type	# Classes	# Objects (Full Server)
Server	Multiple	Multiple
Document	Multiple	Multiple
Item	Multiple	Multiple

Client–Server OLE Object Relationships

Server OLE items correspond to client OLE items, but server documents and client documents do not correspond. Figure 25-6 shows a typical scenario. A client application has two active embedded OLE items and two active linked OLE items. The linked items are both of the same type and thus use the same server program.

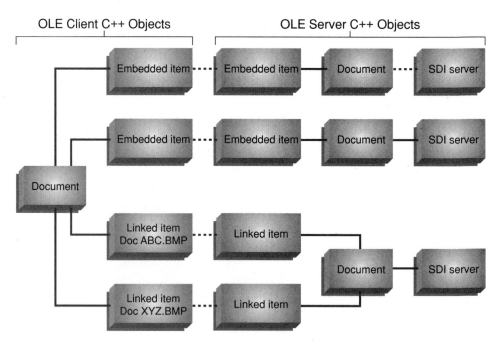

Figure 25-6.
A typical OLE scenario.

Three SDI server instances are loaded. These could be the same program, but they don't have to be.

Launching the Server

Server programs can be launched embedded from a client, or they can be launched as Windows-based applications in stand-alone mode. Full servers need to support both launch methods, but miniservers need support only embedded launching. It's common practice, however, to have miniservers update REG.DAT when they are launched in stand-alone mode. A miniserver should, at the least, display a message box if the user tries to run it in stand-alone mode.

How does a program know whether it's being launched embedded? It checks for the string */Embedding* on the command line. The application class *InitInstance* function is a good place to determine launch status. If the program is being run embedded, *InitInstance* can create the application's main window and the necessary OLE objects.

Server Initiatives

In contrast to the client application, the server application does more responding than initiating. The following server initiatives are important, however.

Updating the registration database
You've seen the REG.DAT registration database file already. If you want your server to make an entry in this database, place the code in the application class *InitInstance* function. The *AfxOleRegisterServerName* function takes care of single-verb servers, but you need to call the Windows function *RegCreateKey* if you want to register extra verbs. Here is some sample code:

```
VERIFY(AfxOleRegisterServerName(SERVER_NAME, SERVER_LOCAL_NAME));
// registers the application's two verbs
VERIFY(::RegCreateKey(HKEY_CLASSES_ROOT,
        "SAMPLE\\protocol\\StdFileEditing",
        &hkProtocol) == ERROR_SUCCESS);
::RegSetValue(hkProtocol, "verb\\0",  REG_SZ, "Read", 4);
::RegSetValue(hkProtocol, "verb\\1",  REG_SZ, "Edit", 4);
::RegCloseKey(hkProtocol);
MessageBox(NULL,
        "Server registered, please run from within host application.",
        AfxGetAppName(), MB_OK);
```

(Note: If you're using the *COleTemplateServer* class in a full server, the application framework calls *AfxOleRegisterServerName* for you.)

Registering the server
Don't confuse this task with updating the registration database. The server must be registered on launch so that the OLE system can track it. Call the *COleServer Register* member function in your application's *InitInstance* function. (Note: If you're using the *COleTemplateServer* class in a full server, the application framework calls *Register* for you.)

Registering the document
You need to register the document only for a full server that supports links. Use the *COleServerDoc RegisterServerDoc* member function. (Note: If you're using the

COleTemplateServer class in a full server, the application framework calls *Register-ServerDoc* for you in the *COleServerDoc OnNewDocument* and *OnOpenDocument* member functions.)

Copying or cutting an item to the clipboard

Only full servers need to do this. You, the programmer, must select items and enable the Copy and Cut items on the Edit menu. When the user chooses one of these menu items, the program calls the *COleServerItem CopyToClipboard* member function.

Notifying the client on save, close, or change

When the user saves (full servers only), closes, or updates a server item, the client must be notified. In your handler for the application framework–supplied File Update menu item, you should call the *COleServerDoc NotifySaved* function for an embedded item. The *NotifyChanged* member functions of *COleServerDoc* and *COleServerItem* are reserved for linked items. The application framework calls the *COleServerDoc NotifyChanged* function for you when the user closes the document.

Setting the bounding rectangle

Some clients, such as Write, need to know the OLE item's bounding rectangle in MM_HIMETRIC coordinates. This bounding rectangle is stored in the *COleServerItem* public data member *m_rectBounds*. If the bounding rectangle doesn't change, set the bounds in the item constructor; otherwise, set the bounds in the view class's *OnDraw* member function.

Shutting down the server

When it's time to exit the server, the *COleServer BeginRevoke* function is called. This causes the OLE system to terminate the server instance. (The OLE system could also terminate the server when launched embedded, with clients no longer using it.)

Server Responses

The user is running the server application from inside the client, so naturally the server needs to respond to many client commands. Here are some of the important server responses, some of which the Microsoft Foundation Class Library OLE base classes handle.

Modifying the server's menu

When a program is being run as an OLE server, its File menu must have an Update item. When the server item is being embedded, the Update item replaces the Save item and the Save Copy As item replaces the Save As item. The application framework replaces these menu items for you.

Processing the server's *OnCreateDoc* callback

The application framework calls the virtual *COleServer OnCreateDoc* when the client program inserts a new embedded item. You must override the *OnCreateDoc* function to return a pointer to a *COleServerDoc* object. For SDI server programs, the derived server object generally contains a single embedded document object that is constructed when the server program starts. For MDI applications, you must construct a new *COleServerDoc* object on each *OnCreateDoc* callback. (Note: If you're using the *COleTemplateServer* class in a full server, the application framework manages the document pointer; therefore, you don't have to override *OnCreateDoc*.)

Processing the server's *OnEditDoc* callback

The application framework calls the virtual *COleServer OnEditDoc* when the client program edits an existing embedded item. You must override the *OnEditDoc* function to return a pointer to a *COleServerDoc* object. For SDI server programs, the derived server object contains a single embedded document object. For MDI applications, you must match the item name to an existing *COleServerDoc* object. (Note: If you're using the *COleTemplateServer* class in a full server, the application framework manages the document pointer; therefore, you don't have to override *OnEditDoc*.)

Processing the server's *OnOpenDoc* callback

The application framework calls the virtual *COleServer OnOpenDoc* when the client program (a full server) opens an existing linked item. You must override the *OnOpenDoc* function to return a pointer to a *COleServerDoc* object and to open the file with the specified name. (Note: If you're using the *COleTemplateServer* class in a full server, the application framework manages the document pointer; therefore, you don't have to override *OnOpenDoc*.)

Processing the server document's *OnGetEmbeddedItem* callback

The application framework calls the *COleServerDoc OnGetEmbeddedItem* function immediately after the *COleServer OnCreateDoc* and *OnEditDoc* functions. You must override *OnGetEmbeddedItem* to return a pointer to a *COleServerItem* object. For embedded items, each *COleServerDoc* object has one *COleServerItem* object.

Processing the server document's *OnGetLinkedItem* callback

Only full servers support linked items. The *COleServerDoc* class implementation of *OnGetLinkedItem* searches its own list of linked items and returns a pointer to the requested item. You need override this function only if you implement your own method of storing and retrieving linked items. The item name is passed to *OnGetLinkedItem* as a parameter.

Serializing an OLE item

The application framework calls the *COleServerItem Serialize* function when it needs to transfer an item's data to or from the client application. You must override *Serialize* for your derived *COleServerItem* class, but for a miniserver you <u>don't</u> need to write *Serialize* functions for either your server class or your server document class.

The OLE system takes care of all the communication. You simply write the item *Serialize* function exactly as you would for a normal application. If your application is a full server, that same *Serialize* function will be used for saving and loading a document to and from disk.

Processing the client's verb activation

When the client application calls *DoVerb* for an OLE client item, the application framework calls the *COleServerItem OnDoVerb* function. The base class *DoVerb* function calls another *COleServerItem* virtual function, *OnShow*, which you should override to activate the server's main window.

For single-verb servers, overriding *OnShow* is sufficient. For multiverb servers, the base class *OnDoVerb* function calls the *OnExtraVerb* virtual function, but the *OnShow* function always gets called. If you don't want *OnShow* to be called for all the server's verbs, you must override *OnDoVerb* also.

Drawing in the client's window

A server doesn't actually draw in the client's window. It makes a metafile, which is sent to the client program. You decide what your server will draw on the metafile (most servers draw at least an icon or a bitmap), and then you override the *COleServerItem OnDraw* function. This virtual function is called in response to a call to the client item's *Draw* function.

The GDI operations in *OnDraw* use the metafile device context that is passed (by pointer) as a parameter. First, *OnDraw* must set the window size with the *CDC SetWindowExt* function. If *OnDraw* doesn't set the metafile device context mapping mode, this window size is mapped to the rectangle specified by the client item's *Draw* function. If the user changes the client rectangle size, the item is rescaled accordingly. If the server view class sets the mapping mode to a fixed mode such as MM_LOENGLISH, the client will be unable to rescale the item.

Be well aware that the *COleServerItem OnDraw* function doesn't do anything in the server's window. To draw in the server's window, you need a view class with an *OnDraw* function, or you must map the WM_PAINT message in the server's main frame window.

The EX25B OLE Server Example

The EX25B example is a two-verb miniserver that implements something akin to yellow Post-it Notes. It's a cheap imitation of the Note-It server that's part of Microsoft Works for Windows. When an EX25B item is embedded in a document, a notepad icon is displayed. When the user activates the primary verb Read (by double-clicking on the notepad icon in Write, for example), the yellow note pops up. Pressing Enter or Esc dismisses it. The Edit verb brings up a resizable edit window.

Figure 25-7 shows EX25B in action with Windows Write. Naturally, the server works with the EX25A client as well.

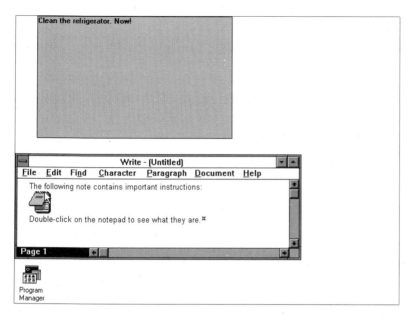

Figure 25-7.
An EX25B yellow note embedded in Write.

The EX25B example is presented with source code listings and resource requirements. Here's a table of the files and classes:

Header File	Source Code File	Class	Description
EX25B.H	EX25B.CPP	*CEx25bApp*	Main application class
		CEx25bServer	OLE server class (derived from *COleServer*)
EX25B.H	MAINWND.CPP	*CMainWnd*	Main frame window
		CReadDialog	Modal dialog for Post-it Note
EX25B.H	EX25BITM.CPP	*CEx25bItem*	OLE item (derived from *COleServerItem*)
		CEx25bDoc	OLE server document (derived from *COleServerDoc*)
STDAFX.H	STDAFX.CPP		Precompiled headers

Now we'll go through the application's classes one at a time. Think of this application as one of those Russian doll sets in which each doll fits inside another. The main window object contains an embedded OLE server object, which contains an OLE server document object, which contains an OLE server item object.

CEx25bApp

The *CEx25bApp* class, derived from *CWinApp*, creates and destroys the application's main frame window, which is used for editing the note text. The *InitInstance* member function doesn't show the window, though. That job is left for the *CEx25bItem OnShow* function.

The *CEx25bApp InitInstance* member function updates the registration database if the application is launched in stand-alone mode.

CMainWnd

This is the application's main frame window class. There is no view class here; all messages are mapped directly in the *CMainWnd* class. The main window has an embedded edit control, identified by the data member *m_wndEdit*. This edit control occupies the entire client area and is used to edit the note text. Another data member, *m_server*, represents the embedded OLE server object.

Constructor

The constructor links the main window to the OLE server. Using *this* in the embedded constructor call is legal, so we've disabled the compiler warning.

```
CMainWnd::CMainWnd() : m_server(this)
{
    Create(NULL, SERVER_LOCAL_NAME, WS_OVERLAPPEDWINDOW,
        CRect(0, 200, 200, 400), NULL,
        MAKEINTRESOURCE(IDR_MAINFRAME));
}
```

OnCreate

This function creates an edit control window that occupies the entire window client area.

OnSize

Each time the main frame window is resized, the edit control must be resized to fit in the new client area.

OnUpdateClient

When the user chooses Update from the File menu, this command handler is called. The function extracts the text from the edit window, stores it in the OLE item, and then notifies the server with the *COleServerDoc NotifySaved* function. The OLE system then transmits the item data to the client, and the client's *OnChange* function is called.

```
void CMainWnd::OnUpdateClient()
{
    TRACE("Entering CMainWnd::OnUpdateClient\n");
    m_server.m_doc.m_item.m_bModified = FALSE;
    m_wndEdit.GetWindowText(m_server.m_doc.m_item.m_noteText);
    TRY {
        m_server.m_doc.NotifySaved();
    }
    CATCH (CException, e) {
        AfxMessageBox("Could not update client");
    }
    END_CATCH
}
```

OnExit

When the user chooses Exit And Return from the File menu, the *OnExit* command handler calls the OLE server's *BeginRevoke* function to terminate the application without giving the user the option to update the client.

```
void CMainWnd::OnExit()
{
    m_server.BeginRevoke();
}
```

OnClose

When the user closes the main frame window, the *OnClose* function gives the user an opportunity to update the client (through *OnUpdateClient*), and then it calls *OnExit*. This user interaction is necessary only if the item's text has been modified since the last update.

OnEditChange

The edit control, *m_wndEdit*, notifies the parent window when the user updates the text. The *OnEditChange* handler sets the OLE server item's modified flag.

```
void CMainWnd::OnEditChange()
{
    m_server.m_doc.m_item.m_bModified = TRUE;
}
```

CEx25bServer

The *CEx25bServer* object is constructed when the main frame window is constructed. An embedded *CEx25bServerDoc* item is constructed at the same time. The *OnCreateDoc* and *OnEditDoc* OLE callback member functions each return a pointer to the *CEx25bServerDoc* item.

CEx25bServerDoc

In the miniserver application, the server document class doesn't have to do much. Its constructor simply constructs the single embedded *CEx25bServerItem* object. The *OnGetEmbeddedItem* callback returns a pointer to the OLE server item object.

CEx25bItem

Most OLE server callbacks are handled at the item level. In a miniserver, each application instance has only one item.

Constructor

Because the EX25B application's visual representation rectangle doesn't change, the *CEx25bItem* constructor can set the base class *m_rectBounds* data member.

```
CEx25bItem::CEx25bItem(CEx25bDoc* pContainerDoc)
    : COleServerItem(pContainerDoc)
{
    m_bModified = FALSE;
    // bounds necessary for clients such as WRITE
    CClientDC dcTmp(NULL);
    dcTmp.SetMapMode(MM_HIMETRIC);
    m_rectBounds.SetRect(0, 0, ::GetSystemMetrics(SM_CXICON),
                         ::GetSystemMetrics(SM_CYICON));
    dcTmp.DPtoLP(&m_rectBounds);        // rectBounds in HIMETRIC
}
```

OnDoVerb

This OLE callback is triggered whenever the client item *DoVerb* function is called. The EX25B primary verb is Read, which doesn't require the main window to be shown. In the Read case, there is no call to *OnShow* but rather a call to the private member function *OnRead*. For the secondary verb, Edit, there's a call to *OnShow*.

```
OLESTATUS CEx25bItem::OnDoVerb(UINT nVerb, BOOL bShow, BOOL bTakeFocus)
{
    if (nVerb == 0) {
        return OnRead();
    }
    return OnShow(bShow);
}
```

OnShow

The *OnShow* virtual function is called by *OnDoVerb* in response to the secondary verb, Edit. It updates the edit control's text and then shows the main window.

```
OLESTATUS CEx25bItem::OnShow(BOOL /* bTakeFocus */)
{
    // window shown here instead of in InitInstance
    CMainWnd* pMainWnd = (CMainWnd*) AfxGetApp()->m_pMainWnd;
    pMainWnd->ShowWindow(SW_SHOW);
    pMainWnd->UpdateWindow();
    pMainWnd->m_wndEdit.SetWindowText(m_noteText);
    pMainWnd->m_wndEdit.SetFocus();
    return OLE_OK;
}
```

OnDraw

This OLE callback sets the window extents and draws the application's notepad icon on the metafile device context that ultimately will be placed in the client window. Note the use of the *LoadIcon* and *DrawIcon* functions. *LoadIcon* returns not an object pointer but an *HICON* handle, but that's what *DrawIcon* needs as a parameter. The class library has no class for icons.

```
BOOL CEx25bItem::OnDraw(CDC* pDC)
{
    ASSERT_VALID(pDC);
    pDC->SetWindowExt(::GetSystemMetrics(SM_CXICON),
                      ::GetSystemMetrics(SM_CYICON));
    pDC->DrawIcon(0, 0, AfxGetApp()->LoadIcon(IDR_MAINFRAME));
    return TRUE;
}
```

OnRead

OnRead is a private member function that implements the server's Read verb. It pops up a system modal dialog of class *CReadDialog* that's dismissed when the user presses Enter or Esc.

```
OLESTATUS CEx25bItem::OnRead()
{
    TRACE("Entering CEx25bItem::OnRead\n");
    CReadDialog dlg(this);
    dlg.DoModal();
    return OLE_OK;
}
```

Serialize

The application framework calls this serialize function when data is to be transferred to or from the client. There's nothing special here. We're simply serializing the note text string.

```
void CEx25bItem::Serialize(CArchive& ar)
{
    if (ar.IsStoring()) {
        ar << m_noteText;
    }
    else {
        ar >> m_noteText;
    }
}
```

CReadDialog

The *CReadDialog* class depends on the *IDD_READDLG* dialog resource. Its purpose is to display the server note's text in response to the Edit verb. The dialog contains only one control, a read-only edit control that is distinct from the main frame window's edit control. The edit control is smart enough to wordwrap the text as it is displayed. We haven't used the DDX functions this time because we don't need bidirectional data transfer. The *m_pItem* data member, set by the constructor, links the dialog to the OLE item.

OnInitDialog

This virtual function copies the text from the server item to the edit control. It also creates a yellow brush to be used for coloring the edit control.

```
BOOL CReadDialog::OnInitDialog()
{
    SetDlgItemText(IDC_EDIT1, m_pItem->m_noteText);
    m_hBrush = ::CreateSolidBrush(RGB(255, 255, 0)); // yellow
    return TRUE;
}
```

OnCtlColor

Setting a dialog control's color is not as simple as you might expect. There is no "*SetDlgItemColor*" function. Instead, each control sends a WM_CTLCOLOR message to the parent dialog immediately before the control is displayed. The dialog's *OnCtlColor* message handler can then set the text background color and provide a background brush for the control's nontext area. The EX25B example has only one control; so testing the control's window handle is not necessary.

```
HBRUSH CReadDialog::OnCtlColor(CDC* pDC, CWnd* pWnd, UINT nCtlColor)
{
    // sets edit control's background color
    TRACE("Entering CReadDialog::OnCtlColor\n");
    if (nCtlColor == CTLCOLOR_EDIT) {
        pDC->SetBkColor(RGB(255, 255, 0)); // yellow
```

```
        return m_hBrush;
    }
    return CDialog::OnCtlColor(pDC, pWnd, nCtlColor);
}
```

OnDestroy

The *OnDestroy* message handler deletes the yellow brush created in *OnInitDialog*.

```
void CReadDialog::OnDestroy()
{
    CDialog::OnDestroy();
    VERIFY(::DeleteObject(m_hBrush));
}
```

EX25B Resource Requirements

App Studio was used to create the server application's resource file as follows:

- **The *IDD_READDLG* dialog resource**—A single edit control completely fills the dialog. The dialog and edit control properties are set as follows:

Dialog Properties	Edit Control Properties
Popup Style	Left-Align Text
Thin Border	Multiline
System Modal	Visible
Absolute Align	Disabled
Visible	

- **The *IDR_MAINFRAME* menu resource**—The server's menu has these items:

Menu Item	Command ID
File Update	*IDM_UPDATE*
File Exit And Return	*IDM_EXIT*
Help About Ex25B	*IDM_ABOUT*

- **The *IDR_MAINFRAME* icon resource**—The server icon is stored in the file EX25B.ICO in the main project subdirectory. It's a copy of the Windows Notepad icon.

26

Dynamic Link Libraries (DLLs)

The dynamic link library (DLL) has always been an important part of Windows-based programming. Now Microsoft Foundation Class Library version 2.0 programmers can take advantage of this powerful programming technique. You'll find that a class library DLL is somewhat different from the normal C-language API DLLs you might have worked with before. This chapter points out the differences and shows you how to build and use a class library DLL. You'll start by using MFC200.DLL, which packages the entire class library. Then you'll extend this ready-made DLL by writing your own custom DLL.

Why Use a DLL?

DLLs are Windows-based program modules that can be loaded and linked at runtime. Many applications can benefit by being split into a series of main programs and DLLs. Suppose you are developing a large integrated accounting system. This job is too big for a single executable program. You might have separate programs, or modules, for Payroll, Accounts Receivable, and so forth, but these programs have a lot of functionality in common. All modules might share the same list management and database access classes, for example. If you put the shared code in one or more DLLs, the individual modules will be smaller on disk and therefore quicker to load. If the user has both the Payroll and Accounts Receivable programs loaded at the same time, only one copy of the DLL code will be in memory, shared by the two client applications.

Another use for DLLs is national language support. If you isolate language-dependent functions and resources into DLLs for, say, the English, French, or Spanish language, the user can choose the proper DLL during the installation process or at runtime. You'll probably think of other uses for DLLs in your own applications.

Conventional DLLs

Even if you haven't written your own Windows DLLs, you've probably used the DLLs that come with Windows or those that other software vendors produce. File dialog and drag-and-drop support, for instance, are in the Windows DLLs COMMDLG.DLL and SHELL.DLG. The EX24A example used ODBC.DLL, which, in turn, loaded another DLL for the selected DBMS. Using a C-language API DLL is no big deal. You simply ensure that your make file includes a reference to the DLL's import library, and you ensure that the DLL file is available on disk at runtime. You call a DLL C function the same way you call a function that's in your own project.

Conventional C-language API DLLs have one important characteristic: They can be used with any C compiler and with other languages and programming environments. A database DLL written in Borland C, for example, can be called from a Microsoft C program, from a Microsoft Visual Basic program, or from a Toolbook script.

You can think of a conventional DLL as an independent program with its own instance handle, its own global memory, its own heap, and its own resources. The DLL shares the client's stack, however. DLLs do not have their own Windows message loops. The DLL is loaded at startup or when needed, and it is unloaded after the last client application terminates. If the conventional DLL allocates memory, that memory is released when the DLL terminates, not when a client terminates. Often a DLL's API will require the client to allocate memory. The client passes a buffer address to the DLL, the DLL operates on the buffer, and then the client frees the memory. With ODBC, for example, the client allocates a buffer for column data, and the DLL writes in the buffer.

There are several DLL linkage options. The import library is the most common option for compiled C programs. The client uses a symbolic name to call a DLL function, and Windows matches calls to DLL function addresses when the DLL is loaded. The functions can be matched symbolically or through ordinal numbers. The ordinal method, in which each DLL function is assigned a unique integer, is more efficient. Interpreted-language Windows environments often use DLLs in a more dynamic manner. They can select and load DLLs at runtime, and they can call DLL functions without prior address resolution.

A DLL can be updated without client recompilation if the existing function prototypes remain exactly the same. If you change a function name, return data type, or parameter data type, you should count on recompiling the client applications.

Visual C++ supports the creation of conventional DLLs written with the class library classes but with a C-language external interface. Technical Note 11 in the MFCNOTES.HLP Help file describes the process of writing what is known as a user DLL (_USRDLL). The sample program in the \MSVC\MFC\SAMPLES\DLLTRACE subdirectory illustrates such a DLL. This chapter focuses on a different kind of DLL—the class library DLL that's compatible with the C++ language.

The Class Library DLL

A class library DLL can accommodate entire C++ classes. You can use these DLL-resident classes the same way you use statically linked classes. You can construct objects of DLL-resident classes, and you can use them as base classes. There are some major differences between conventional DLLs and class library DLLs, however.

Class Library DLL Usage Restricted to Microsoft C++ Compilers

Unlike conventional DLLs, class library DLLs can be used only in Microsoft class library applications. Why the restriction? The Microsoft C++ compiler uses special internal function names that combine the class name, function name, return data type, parameter data types, and public/protected/private access. With the Microsoft C++ compiler, for example, the function

```
CWnd* GetDescendantWindow(int nID) const
```

is assigned the mangled or decorated name

```
?GetDescendantWindow@CWnd@@RFCPEV1@H@Z
```

Other compilers use different name-mangling algorithms, so if a Borland C++ client program contained a *GetDescendantWindow* call, the Borland mangled name wouldn't match the Microsoft mangled name. Maybe in the future there'll be an industrywide name-mangling algorithm.

The Class Library Classes as a DLL

The easiest way to use the class library DLL technology in your application is to use the MFC200 and MFC200D DLLs included with Visual C++. These DLLs contain all the class library functionality, with some minor exceptions such as time formatting. MFC200.DLL is the release version, and MFC200D.DLL is the debugging equivalent. Converting a statically linked class library application to a DLL-based application is easy. You simply change some Visual Workbench options (or change some switches in your make file for NMAKE), as shown later in this chapter.

For Windows SDK Programmers

If you've written a Windows DLL client application in the SDK environment, you're probably used to exporting client callback functions (functions in the client program that are called by Windows and by the DLL). You have undoubtedly used the Windows *MakeProcInstance* function for these exported functions. Forget this stuff. With Microsoft C/C++ versions 7.0 and later (with the /GA switch), these exports are unnecessary.

Windows Prolog/Epilog
⊙ Protected Mode Application Functions

Do you want your class library applications to be DLL-based? Your answer depends on your needs. You should develop your applications first with static linking for easier debugging. If you're distributing a large suite of programs that each use many class library features, using MFC200.DLL will conserve your users' disk space and memory. If, on the other hand, you have a few small programs, using MFC200.DLL might lead to a larger net program size because the class library DLL approach forces you to use the large memory model and because MFC200.DLL contains <u>all</u> the class library classes and functions.

Here are some actual numbers for you. The size of the MFC200.DLL file is 298 KB. The medium-model statically linked MATPLAN.EXE example program from Chapter 21 is about 124 KB, and the large-model equivalent is about 148 KB. With the DLL, the MATPLAN.EXE file's size is 43 KB. It's obviously not worth using the DLL if you're distributing only a single MATPLAN-type application.

Using MFC200D.DLL in an Application

Now it's time to turn on the computer. It's so easy to switch an application from using the static class library to using the dynamic library that we don't need a separate project for it. Simply choose any project from an earlier chapter. The MATPLAN example from Chapter 21 is fine. If you want to double-check on the option settings, look at the EX26B project, which uses MFC200D.DLL plus an extension DLL.

Here are the steps for converting a statically linked project to a dynamically linked one:

1. In Visual Workbench's Project Options dialog, <u>uncheck</u> the Use Microsoft Foundation Classes check box.

2. In the C/C++ Compiler Options dialog, change the following Common To Both build options:

   □ Memory Model: Set "Model" to "Large."

   □ Preprocessor: Add "_AFXDLL" to "Symbols and Macros to Define."

   □ Windows Prolog/Epilog: Check the "Generate for __far Functions" check box.

3. In the Project's Linker Options dialog, add *MFC200* at the <u>head</u> of the Input Library list for the Release Specific build option.

4. In the Project's Linker Options dialog, add *MFC200D* at the <u>head</u> of the Input Library list for the Debug Specific build option.

If you want to reduce the size of your client EXE file, eliminate redundant resources from your resource script. To do so, start App Studio and choose Set Includes from App Studio's File menu. Delete the references to the standard AFX resources from the Compile-Time Directives list box in the Set Includes dialog box that appears, and then click on OK. Remember that the application framework searches the client resources before it searches the MFC200.DLL resources, so you can override standard AFX resources if necessary.

You must select Rebuild All from the Visual Workbench Project menu after you make the changes listed above.

Class Library Extension DLLs

If you want to add new classes to the class library DLL, you should not rebuild MFC200.DLL but rather write your own class library extension DLL that client programs can load along with MFC200.DLL. When you write your extension DLL, you must follow some clearly defined conventions, which are highlighted in this chapter's first example.

> **Warning:** *If you modify MFC200.DLL, you could create problems for other applications that depend on Microsoft's version of the DLL.*

Class Library DLL Memory Usage

In a class library extension DLL, memory is managed by the client application—which means that if you use the *new* operator in the class library DLL (*new* and *delete* are specially overloaded for DLLs), client application memory will be allocated. When the client application terminates, all its allocated memory is released, including memory allocated in DLL functions. Now the DLL is starting to look less like an independent program and more like part of the client application! As in conventional DLLs, the DLL and the client application share the stack. The DLL owns the global variables.

> **Note:** *A statically linked class library application references global variables, defined inside the class library, that identify per-application elements such as the current application object, the current instance handle, and the current resource handle. A class library DLL moves these global variables to a fixed location in the client application's stack segment.*

Required Code for Extension DLLs

Each class library extension DLL you write must contain boilerplate code similar to the following code. The *LibMain* function is the DLL equivalent of *WinMain*, and Windows calls it when the DLL is loaded. The DLL initialization function, named *InitMyDLL* here, is optionally called from your client application. You'll see why later.

```
#include <afxdllx.h>          // prior #include <afxwin.h> assumed

extern AFX_EXTENSION_MODULE NEAR extensionDLL = {NULL, NULL};
```

(continued)

```
extern "C" int CALLBACK LibMain(HINSTANCE hInstance, WORD, WORD, LPSTR)
{
    // do not allocate memory or use TRACE, ASSERT, or MessageBox here
    AfxInitExtensionModule(extensionDLL, hInstance);
    return 1; // OK
}

// following DLL initialization function is called from the client app
extern "C" extern void WINAPI InitMyDLL()
{
    new CDynLinkLibrary(extensionDLL);
}
```

Searching for Resources

Both a DLL and a client application can have their own resources. Suppose a program contains the following code:

```
CString strError;
strError.LoadString(IDS_ERROR1);
```

Where does the application framework search for the string identified by *IDS_ERROR1*—in the class library client application's resources or in the DLL's? The default behavior (assuming that you've written the DLL initialization function discussed in the previous section) is to search for resources in this sequence:

1. Client application resources

2. Your extension DLL resources

3. MFC200 standard AFX resources

> **Note:** *Because MFC200.DLL contains the standard AFX resources, your project's AppWizard-generated RC file need not duplicate them. You can choose Set Includes from App Studio's File menu and then remove the following lines from your resource script file:*
>
> ```
> #include "afxres.rc"
> #include "afxprint.rc"
> ```
>
> *and you can use the Visual Workbench editor to remove many of the string resource definitions (such as the file and edit menu prompts). Because the application framework searches the client resources before it searches the MFC200.DLL resources, you can override standard AFX resources if you need to.*

You can change the default search behavior by forcing a DLL to search its own resources first. The following code switches the application framework's instance handle from the client application to a DLL, accessing the resource, and then it switches the instance handle back to the client application:

```
HINSTANCE hInstResourceClient = AfxGetResourceHandle();
AfxSetResourceHandle(extensionDLL.hModule);    // uses DLL's instance
                                               //  handle
strError.LoadString(IDS_ERROR1);
AfxSetResourceHandle(hInstResourceClient);     // restores client's
                                               //  instance handle
```

Inline Constructors

Do not use inline constructors for DLL-resident classes. Inline constructors complicate the process of exporting class member functions.

Extension DLL Exports

You must specifically "export" selected extension DLL functions and variables. Which ones do you export? That depends on whether you're constructing objects from a DLL-resident class or deriving classes from a DLL-resident class. Here are some rules:

A DLL-resident class used directly

- Export all nonvirtual member functions that your client program calls directly.

- You don't need to export virtual functions that are declared in a base class. (Note: This rule applies to classes that do not have inline constructors. You should not use inline constructors for classes you intend to use in a DLL.)

- If the class has a message map, export the static *messageMap* entry, as shown on the next page.

  Note: The use of the RUNTIME_CLASS macro is restricted. In a client application, you cannot dynamically create objects of DLL-resident classes. This means, for example, that you can't place a view class in a DLL and then use it in your client application's AddDocTemplate call. You can place the AddDocTemplate call in the DLL's initialization function, however, as the example program in the \MSVC\MFC\SAMPLES\DLLHUSK subdirectory illustrates.

A DLL-resident class used for derivation

- Export all public nonvirtual member functions that your client program calls directly.

- Export all nonvirtual member functions that a derived class might want to call.

- Export all virtual member functions (except pure virtual functions).

- If the class has a message map, export the static *messageMap* entry, as shown on the next page.

- Export the *CRuntimeClass* entry, as shown on the next page.

515

You export a DLL function by listing its mangled name, together with an ordinal number, in the EXPORTS section of the DLL's DEF file. If your DLL contained a view class *CMyBaseView* with an overridden *OnDraw* function, for example, you would export the *OnDraw* function with a line such as this:

```
?OnDraw@CMyBaseView1@@VECXPEVCDC@@@Z                    @101 NONAME
```

The function's arbitrary (but unique) ordinal number is 101.

The *CRuntimeClass* entry is exported like this:

```
?classCMyBaseView@CMyBaseView@@2UCRuntimeClass@@A      @114 NONAME
```

and the *messageMap* entry is exported as follows:

```
?messageMap@CMyBaseView@@1UAFX_MSGMAP@@A              @115 NONAME
```

The project's MAP file is the source for these exported mangled names. In Visual Workbench, click on the Miscellaneous category in the Linker Options dialog, and then set Other Options to /MAP:FULL. For each exported function, search the MAP file for the function name, and then extract the mangled name on the previous line. For the runtime class and message map entries, use the lines above, with your own class name substituted for *CMyBaseView*.

> **Note:** *The DLL project switch settings ensure that all far functions have the proper prolog and epilog code for export. Do __not__ use the _export keyword in your DLL source. This option has undesirable side effects in the class library environment. In particular, it precludes the use of space-saving ordinals in the executable program.*

Static Class Data Members

You can define static data members for your DLL classes, but be careful that the definitions don't allocate memory. You can, for example, define a static *CRect* object like this:

```
const CRect NEAR CMyView::rect(10, 10, 500, 400);
```

but you can't define a *CString* object like this:

```
const CString NEAR CMyView::string("test"); // don't do this in a DLL
```

The latter definition causes major problems because the *new* operator is called before the application framework has had a chance to install the correct *new* implementation.

Extension DLL Runtime Class Identification

As mentioned above, the *RUNTIME_CLASS* macro, when used in a client program, doesn't work for a class that is resident in a class library extension DLL. The *GetRuntimeClass* function does work, however, if you have declared the class to be dynamic.

Creating the DLL

Visual Workbench has a specific project type for Windows-based DLLs. When you select this option, the linker produces a DLL file, and the compiler and linker switches are set accordingly. Be sure the DLL file is available to its client applications at runtime. Windows version 3.1 first searches for DLLs in the subdirectories specified in the PATH environment variable, and then it searches the \WINDOWS and \WINDOWS\SYSTEM subdirectories. If you install the necessary extension DLLs in the client project's own subdirectory, you will eliminate the chance of conflict with other DLLs with the same names. If you install the DLLs in the \WINDOWS\SYSTEM subdirectory, all applications can share them.

Creating the Import Library

You must create an import library for your class library extension DLL. Even though Visual Workbench generates an import library, that library does not correspond to your DEF file and is therefore useless. Use the Visual C++ IMPLIB utility from the command line as follows (substituting your application's name for *myapp*):

```
implib myapp.lib myapp.def
```

Once the import library is created, be sure the linker can find it when you are building a client project. Copy the import library to the \MSVC\MFC\LIB subdirectory or choose Options Directory from the Visual Workbench menu to modify the library search path.

Debug and Release DLL Versions

After you have switched from static linking to dynamic linking, you might still need to debug your extension DLLs and client applications. It's good practice to maintain both a debug and a release version of your extension DLLs. By convention, the debug version name ends with a D. You'll need separate DEF files too because the DEF file contains the name of the DLL. Also, you'll want separate import libraries that follow the DLL naming convention.

EX26A—Writing Your Own Class Library Extension DLL

The EX26A example project combines the *CStudent* class (from Chapter 15), the *CPersistentFrame* class (from Chapter 14), and the *CRowView* class (from Chapter 24) into a single dynamic link library, EX26AD.DLL. (EX26A.DLL is the companion release version.) The *CRowView* and *CPersistentFrame* classes are included because they are typical class library base classes. The *CStudent* class is included to demonstrate that the objects of a DLL-resident class can be serialized in a client application.

The EX26A classes have mostly the same source code as their statically linked counterparts, except for some added code that demonstrates resource searching and runtime class access. This chapter's second example, EX26B, is a client application that uses the EX26A DLL.

The EX26A subdirectory actually contains two projects—EX26A.MAK for the release DLL and EX26AD.MAK for the debugging DLL. It also contains two separate DEF files—EX26A.DEF and EX26AD.DEF. The source code is split into the following source code files, which the two projects share:

Header File	Source Code File	Class	Description
STDAFX.H	EX26A.CPP		*LibMain* function and DLL initializer
PERSIST.H	PERSIST.CPP	*CPersistentFrame*	SDI Persistent frame base class
ROWVIEW.H	ROWVIEW.CPP	*CRowView*	Row view base class
STUDENT.H	STUDENT.CPP	*CStudent*	Student record class

A resource file, EX26A.RC, contains the *CRowView IDS_TOO_MANY_ROWS* error message string.

You've seen the *CStudent*, *CPersistentFrame*, and *CRowView* code before. The *CStudent* class was modified to eliminate the inline constructor and to add the following constructor:

```
CStudent::CStudent(const char* szName, long lGrade): m_name(szName)
{
    m_lGrade = lGrade;
}
```

The code in EX26A.CPP is almost identical to the DLL boilerplate code listed previously. For this application, the DLL initializer function is named *InitEx26aDLL*.

The EX26AD.DEF File

Figure 26-1 shows the complete DEF file for the project (debugging version). Only those functions used in the EX26B example are exported. The EX26A.DEF file is identical except for the library name. You can use this file as a prototype for your own extension DLL DEF files.

```
LIBRARY    EX26AD
DESCRIPTION  'ROWVIEW/PERSISTENTVIEW DLL'
EXETYPE WINDOWS
CODE    LOADONCALL MOVEABLE DISCARDABLE
DATA    PRELOAD MOVEABLE SINGLE

SEGMENTS
    _TEXT   PRELOAD MOVEABLE DISCARDABLE
    WEP_TEXT PRELOAD MOVEABLE DISCARDABLE

HEAPSIZE  1024

EXPORTS
    WEP @1 RESIDENTNAME PRIVATE ;; required WEP entry point (uses library WEP)

    ; Explicitly exported initialization routine
    INITEX26ADLL                                        @2 NONAME;

; CRowView
    ; Constructor and Destructor
    ??0CRowView@@JEC@XZ                                 @100 NONAME
    ??1CRowView@@NEC@XZ                                 @101 NONAME
    ; operations/attributes
    ?RowToWndRect@CRowView@@NEC?EVCRect@@PEVCDC@@H@Z     @102 NONAME
    ?LastViewableRow@CRowView@@NECHXZ                   @103 NONAME
    ?RowToYPos@CRowView@@NECHH@Z                        @104 NONAME
    ?RectLPtoRowRange@CRowView@@NECXAFVCRect@@AEH1H@Z   @105 NONAME
    ?UpdateRow@CRowView@@NECXH@Z                        @106 NONAME
    ; Virtual overrides (called by framework)
    ?OnPreparePrinting@CRowView@@NECHPEUCPrintInfo@@@Z  @107 NONAME
    ?OnBeginPrinting@CRowView@@NECXPEVCDC@@PEUCPrintInfo@@@Z  @108 NONAME
    ?OnDraw@CRowView@@NECXPEVCDC@@@Z                    @109 NONAME
    ?OnInitialUpdate@CRowView@@NECXXZ                   @110 NONAME
    ?OnPrepareDC@CRowView@@NECXPEVCDC@@PEUCPrintInfo@@@Z  @111 NONAME
    ?OnPrint@CRowView@@NECXPEVCDC@@PEUCPrintInfo@@@Z    @112 NONAME
    ?UpdateScrollSizes@CRowView@@NECXXZ                 @113 NONAME
    ; runtime class & message map
    ?classCRowView@CRowView@@2UCRuntimeClass@@A         @114 NONAME
    ?messageMap@CRowView@@1UAFX_MSGMAP@@A               @115 NONAME

; CPersistentFrame
    ; Constructor and Destructor
    ??0CPersistentFrame@@JEC@XZ                         @200 NONAME
    ??1CPersistentFrame@@NEC@XZ                         @201 NONAME
    ;
    ?ActivateFrame@CPersistentFrame@@NECXH@Z            @202 NONAME
    ; runtime class & message map
    ?classCPersistentFrame@CPersistentFrame@@2UCRuntimeClass@@A  @203 NONAME
    ?messageMap@CPersistentFrame@@1UAFX_MSGMAP@@A       @204 NONAME
```

Figure 26-1.
The EX26AD.DEF file listing.

(continued)

Figure 26-1. *continued*

```
; CStudent
    ; Constructors
    ??0CStudent@@REC@XZ                                    @300 NONAME
    ??0CStudent@@REC@PFDJ@Z                                @301 NONAME
```

(Note: The *CRowView* member functions *GetRowWidthHeight*, *GetActiveRow*, *Get-RowCount*, *OnDrawRow*, *ChangeSelectionNextRow*, and *ChangeSelectionToRow* don't need to be exported because they are pure virtual functions and therefore must be overridden in derived classes.)

Visual Workbench Options for the EX26AD Project

Following are the Visual Workbench options for the EX26AD class library extension DLL. The instructions assume you are starting a new project. (AppWizard doesn't generate MAK files for DLL projects.)

1. In Visual Workbench's Project Options dialog, set Project Type to "Windows dynamic link library (DLL)."

2. While still in the Project Options dialog, <u>uncheck</u> the Use Microsoft Foundation Classes check box.

3. In the C/C++ Compiler Options dialog, change the following Debug Specific build options for the categories shown:

   □ Memory Model: Set "Model" to "Large."

   □ Preprocessor: Add "_AFXDLL" to "Symbols and Macros to Define."

   □ Windows Prolog/Epilog: Check the "Generate for __far Functions" check box.

   □ Precompiled Headers: Precompile through Header—"STDAFX.H"
                          Precompile with Source—"EX26A.CPP"

4. In the Linker Options dialog, add *MFC200D* at the head of the Input Libraries list for the Debug Specific build option.

Creating the Import Library and Copying the DLL

After you have successfully built the EX26AD project, use the command line

```
implib \msvc\mfc\lib\ex26ad.lib ex26ad.def
```

to create a debug import library that is accessible to the client project link step. You might want to make a batch file for this job. Next, copy the new extension DLL to the \WINDOWS\SYSTEM directory.

EX26B—Using a Class Library Extension DLL

The EX26B project consists of an SDI class library application that uses the EX26AD DLL that you built in the previous section. The EX26B program also relies on MFC200D.DLL, as do all class library DLL client applications. You can use the new DLL with the EX14A, EX15B, and EX24A examples, but it's more fun to build a new program that uses all three EX26A classes. The new program is yet another student list variation.

Here are the source code files involved in the EX26B project:

Header File	Source Code File	Class	Description
EX26B.H	EX26B.CPP	CEx26bApp	Main application class
PERSIST.H		CPersistentFrame	SDI Persistent frame base class
MAINFRM.H	MAINFRM.CPP	CMainFrame	Main frame class (derived from CPersistentFrame)
EX26BDOC.H	EX26BDOC.CPP	CEx26bDoc	Document class
ROWVIEW.H	ROWVIEW.CPP	CRowView	Row view base class
EX26BVW.H	EX26BVW.CPP	CEx26bView	View class (derived from CRowView)
STUDENT.H		CStudent	Student record class
STUDLG.H	STUDLG.CPP	CStudentDialog	Student modal dialog class
STDAFX.H	STDAFX.CPP		Precompiled headers

Following are descriptions of the new classes for EX26B.

CEx26bApp

This class is the standard AppWizard-generated SDI application class, except for the call to the DLL initialization routine at the beginning of *InitInstance*.

EX26B.H

```
extern "C" extern void WINAPI InitEx26aDLL();
```

EX26B.CPP

```
#ifdef _AFXDLL
    InitEx26aDLL(); // necessary for DLL resource access and IsKindOf
#endif
```

CEx26bDoc

The document class contains an embedded object pointer array that is called *m_studentArray*. This array is emptied in the *DeleteContents* member function.

CEx26bView

The *CEx26bView* class is derived from *CRowView* and is similar to the *CEx24bView* class from the ODBC example. The *OnDrawRow* function is perhaps the most interesting overridden pure virtual function.

```
void CEx26bView::OnDrawRow(CDC* pDC, int nRow, int y, BOOL bSelected)
{
    // Gets the data for the specific student
    CStudent* pStudent = (CStudent*)
                    (GetDocument()->m_studentArray[nRow]);

    TEXTMETRIC tm;
    pDC->GetTextMetrics(&tm);
    char grade[10];

    // Displays the student record in 1 line of text
    pDC->TextOut(STUDENT_NAME_COL*tm.tmAveCharWidth, y, pStudent->m_name);
    _itoa((int) (pStudent->m_lGrade), grade, 10);
    pDC->TextOut(STUDENT_GRADE_COL*tm.tmAveCharWidth, y, grade, strlen(grade));
}
```

The *OnLButtonDblClk* message handler brings up the student dialog for the row that has been selected.

```
void CEx26bView::OnLButtonDblClk(UINT, CPoint point)
{
// Brings up a dialog for the selected student record
// First click selected the row, so we don't have to here
    CStudent* pStudent1;
    CStudent* pStudent2;
    int ret;

    CEx26bDoc* pDoc = GetDocument();
    if (GetRowCount()) { // there's at least one student record
        CStudentDialog dlg(IDB_UPDATE);
        pStudent1 = (CStudent*)
                    (pDoc->m_studentArray[m_nSelectedStudent]);
        dlg.m_name = pStudent1->m_name;
        dlg.m_lGrade = pStudent1->m_lGrade;
        ret = dlg.DoModal();
        switch(ret) {
        case IDB_UPDATE:
            pStudent1->m_name = dlg.m_name;
            pStudent1->m_lGrade = dlg.m_lGrade;
            break;
        case IDB_INSERT:
            pStudent2 = new CStudent(dlg.m_name, dlg.m_lGrade);
            pDoc->m_studentArray.InsertAt(m_nSelectedStudent, pStudent2);
            break;
        case IDB_DELETE:
            pDoc->m_studentArray.RemoveAt(m_nSelectedStudent);
            break;
```

```
        case IDB_CANCEL:
            break;
        default:
            ASSERT(0);
            break;
        }
    }
    else {
        CStudentDialog dlg(IDB_INSERT);
        pStudent2 = new CStudent("", 0); // array was empty
        dlg.m_name = pStudent2->m_name;
        dlg.m_lGrade = pStudent2->m_lGrade;
        ret = dlg.DoModal();
        if (ret == IDB_INSERT) {
            pStudent2->m_name = dlg.m_name;
            pStudent2->m_lGrade = dlg.m_lGrade;
            pDoc->m_studentArray.InsertAt(0, pStudent2);
        }
    }
    pDoc->SetModifiedFlag();
    pDoc->UpdateAllViews(NULL);
}
```

CStudentDialog

The code for this class is compatible with ClassWizard. The behavior is similar to that of the *CMatplanDialog* class from Chapter 21. The *DoModal* return value indicates which button the user clicked.

Building and Testing the EX26B Program

Building the EX26B class library DLL extension client application is similar to building an MFC200D.DLL client application: You compile with the large memory model, and you specify MFC200D.DLL and EX26AD.DLL to the linker. Don't forget to uncheck the Use Microsoft Foundation Classes option in the Project Options dialog and to define _AFXDLL. The Input category of the Linker Options dialog is shown in Figure 26-2 on the next page.

If you did everything right when you built the EX26A example, the EX26AD import library and DLL will be available. You should be able to build and run the EX26B client application. The output should look something like that shown in Figure 26-3 on the next page.

If you double-click in an empty frame or on a student record in the row view, an editing dialog pops up as shown. Document file I/O and printing are implemented.

> **Note:** *If you look in the debug window after EX26B exits, you'll notice some messages regarding undeleted GDI objects. These messages result from a DLL-related bug in the Windows Debug Kernel. Ignore them.*

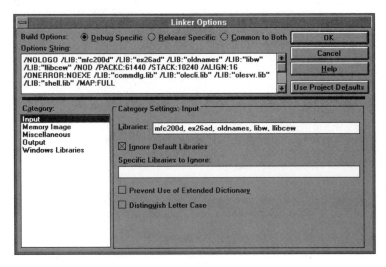

Figure 26-2.
The Linker Options dialog showing libraries.

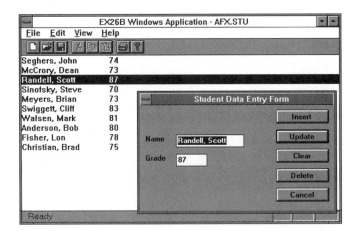

Figure 26-3.
The EX26B screen with student list.

Accessing Resources

The EX26A DLL and the EX26B client each contain diagnostic code that allows you to see how the application framework finds resources. A string resource, *IDS_TOO_MANY_ROWS* (with value 3), is defined in <u>both</u> the DLL resource script and the client resource script. The string values are a little different, however, as shown here:

Resource Script	Value of IDS_TOO_MANY_ROWS
EX26A.RC	EX26A: You have exceeded the storage capacity of the scrolling view
EX26B.RC	EX26B: You have exceeded the storage capacity of the scrolling view

This difference allows you to see which resources were accessed.

The *CRowView* constructor (located in \VCPP\EX26A\ROWVIEW.CPP) contains the following code:

```
CString strRes;
strRes.LoadString(IDS_TOO_MANY_ROWS);
TRACE("resource string = %s\n", (const char*) strRes);

#ifdef _AFXDLL
    HINSTANCE hInstResourceClient = AfxGetResourceHandle();
    AfxSetResourceHandle(extensionDLL.hModule);    // uses client's
                                                   //  instance handle
    strRes.LoadString(IDS_TOO_MANY_ROWS);
    TRACE("resource string = %s\n", (const char*) strRes);
    AfxSetResourceHandle(hInstResourceClient);     // restores client's
                                                   //  instance handle
#endif
```

The first *LoadString* call exercises the class library resource search capability. Because the *InitInstance* function, in the client file EX26B.CPP, contains the following code:

```
#ifdef _AFXDLL
    InitEx26aDLL();
#endif
```

the first *LoadString* call uses the <u>client's</u> resource. If you remove the *InitEx26aDLL* call, *LoadString* fails, returning a null string.

The second *LoadString* call above uses the DLL's resource.

The *CEx26bView* constructor (located in \VCPP\EX26B\EX26BVW.CPP) contains the following code:

```
CString strRes;
strRes.LoadString(IDS_TOO_MANY_ROWS);
TRACE("resource string = %s\n", (const char*) strRes);
```

The *LoadString* call here always uses the client's resource, whether or not the *InitEx26aDLL* call is present.

APPENDIXES

Appendix A

A Personal View of the C++ Language

Have you ever started reading a C++ textbook and given up because there was too much detail and you weren't motivated? If so, then this appendix is for you. It's based on an example that I used when I taught myself C++, but it's flavored by my experience learning the classes of Microsoft Foundation Class Library version 2.0. It's not meant to be comprehensive, and each C++ expert will find something to complain about, but I think it serves well as a C++ crash course.

As you read the appendix, you'll be hit straightaway by the essence of C++—classes and objects—and then you'll learn how to "wire" objects together to build an application. Important details are introduced as you need them, but I recommend that you keep a C++ textbook close at hand. The more you already know about C programming, the better.

An Introduction to Classes and Objects

The class is the language element that C++ programmers use to write modular, maintainable programs. This section teaches you how the class encapsulates code and data. Later sections introduce two other C++ features you might have heard about: inheritance and polymorphism.

Because classes and objects are such important C++ concepts, you must understand them thoroughly before proceeding. Understanding C's *struct* and *typedef* syntax will help you get started.

User-Defined Types in C

A C++ class declaration is an outgrowth of the C structure declaration. In C, the following code declares a structure with the name *xy*, but the compiler allocates no storage:

```
struct xy {
    double x;
    double y;
};
```

After you declare the structure, you can use *xy* instances in your C code this way:

```
struct xy topLeft = { 0.0, 0.0 };
struct xy bottomRight = { 1.0, 1.0 };
printf("topLeft = (%f, %f)\n", topLeft.x, topLeft.y);
printf("bottomRight = (%f, %f)\n", bottomRight.x, bottomRight.y);
```

If you use the C *typedef* syntax, the code becomes a little cleaner:

```
typedef struct xy {
    double x;
    double y;
} XY;
```

The type definition *XY* now substitutes for the more awkward *struct xy*:

```
XY topLeft = { 0.0, 0.0 };
XY bottomRight = { 1.0, 1.0 };
printf("topLeft = (%f, %f)\n", topLeft.x, topLeft.y);
printf("bottomRight = (%f, %f)\n", bottomRight.x, bottomRight.y);
```

Instances of *XY*, such as *topLeft* and *bottomRight*, correspond to C++ objects. Each occupies storage on the stack, and you can get away with writing simple assignment statements such as

```
bottomRight = topLeft;
```

However, the C compiler doesn't understand statements such as

```
bottomRight = topLeft + 1;
```

Moving to C++

Now let's recode the previous example in C++, using real classes and objects. Here's the simplest form of the class declaration:

```
class XY {
public:
    double x;
    double y;
};
```

The *public* keyword allows direct access to x and y, as though x and y were structure members.

Here's the code to make an *XY* object:

```
XY bottomRight; // an uninitialized object
bottomRight.x = 1.0;
bottomRight.y = 1.0;
printf("bottomRight = (%f, %f)\n", bottomRight.x, bottomRight.y);
```

The class elements *x* and *y*, called data members, were individually assigned values because, for most classes, the C++ compiler won't accept a statement like

```
XY bottomRight = { 1.0, 1.0 };
```

> *Note: The compiler does indeed accept the statement above for the simple* XY *class, but it won't accept it after you add the class's constructor, described in the following section.*

Constructors

You've seen how awkward it is to initialize the data members of an *XY* object with assignment statements. As you'll see later, C++ classes, unlike C structures, can contain "member functions" as well as data members. Member functions have full access to all data members of the class. All C++ classes have one or more special member functions, called "constructors," that are called to initialize objects. If you don't specify a constructor function in your class definition, the compiler generates a default constructor with no arguments. This default constructor calls the constructors for any C++ objects that are data members of the class. When the compiler generates a call to the default constructor, the compiler assigns storage for an object of the class but does not initialize values of built-in types. Indeed, in the previous example, the *XY* default constructor is called in the following function:

```
void func()
{
    XY bottomRight;   // XY object bottomRight constructed on the stack
                      // x and y values are uninitialized
}
```

> *Note: Many beginning C++ programmers try to call default constructors by writing code in this way:*
>
> ```
> XY bottomRight(); // don't do this!
> ```
>
> *The compiler interprets the statement as a forward declaration of a function called* bottomRight *that returns an object of type* XY—*clearly not the intended result.*

A reasonable explicit constructor for the *XY* class would take two double-precision arguments. Here is a new *XY* class declaration with this constructor added:

```
class XY {
public:
    double x, y;
    XY(double xarg, double yarg)  { x = xarg; y = yarg; }
};
```

The constructor function name is always the same as the class name, and the constructor always returns nothing. In this example, the constructor is defined "inline," which means that the compiler directly substitutes the two assignment statements wherever the constructor is called. Now the previous example code becomes

```
XY bottomRight(1.0, 1.0);  // object named bottomRight of class XY
printf("bottomRight = (%f, %f)\n", bottomRight.x, bottomRight.y);
```

Yes, defining a function called *XY* is a little weird, but you're calling it by the name *bottomRight*, which is just the way C++ works. It makes sense if you consider that, for the default constructor, the statement

```
XY topLeft;
```

is analogous to

```
double x;
```

Both result in the creation of an entity on the stack—a C++ object of class *XY* or standard type *double*. Now, with the two-argument constructor, the statement

```
XY bottomRight(1.0, 1.0);
```

is a logical extension of

```
XY bottomRight;
```

Because you have written your own constructor, the compiler does not generate a default constructor. The compiler now rejects the statement

```
XY bottomRight;
```

If you write your own default (empty argument list) constructor that sets the data members to *0*, the class declaration, with two constructors, looks like this:

```
class XY {
public:
    double x, y;
    XY() { x = 0.0; y = 0.0; }
    XY(double xarg, double yarg)    {x = xarg; y = yarg;}
};
```

Now two functions are called *XY*, a situation clearly not generally allowed in C. The C++ compiler does permit multiple declarations and, furthermore, can tell from the function call statement which version of *XY()* you want. Thus, both of the following statements are legal in the same program:

```
XY topLeft;
XY bottomRight(1.0, 1.0);
```

Destructors

No discussion of constructors would be complete without a companion discussion of "destructors." A destructor is another special C++ member function; its name is the class name preceded by a tilde (~). Each class has one and only one destructor function, and that function takes no arguments and returns nothing. The destructor is automatically called for any object when that object goes out of scope.

Even though we have no need for an explicit *XY* destructor, we'll write one anyway. This time, neither the constructors nor the destructor will be inline, so we can show off some new C++ notation.

```
class XY {
public:
    double x, y;
    XY();    // default constructor
    XY(double xarg, double yarg);
    ~XY();   // destructor
};

XY::XY()
{
    printf("XY default constructor called\n");
    x = y = 0.0;
}

XY::XY(double xarg, double yarg)
{
    printf("XY explicit constructor called\n");
    x = xarg;
    y = yarg;
}

XY::~XY()
{
    printf("XY destructor called\n");
}
```

Now for an explanation of the new notation: The tilde character preceding the class name identifies the destructor and is part of the function name. The *XY::* prefix, used for both the constructor and the destructor definitions, tells the compiler that a function is a member function of the *XY* class.

If you made the following function call

```
void func() {
    XY bottomRight(1.0, 1.0);
    printf("the x coordinate is: %5.1f\n", bottomRight.x);
}
```

the output would be

```
XY explicit constructor called
the x coordinate is: 1.0
XY destructor called
```

Notice that the destructor is called automatically when the *bottomRight* object goes out of scope at the end of *func*'s execution.

If you don't write a destructor, the compiler generates a default destructor for you. For data members that are C++ objects, the default constructor calls those objects' destructors. When the compiler generates a call to a destructor for an object, the compiler generates code that releases storage occupied by that object.

Other Member Functions

You've seen the constructor and destructor member functions, and you know that they're always present, even if the compiler has to generate them for you. You can also write your own special-purpose class member functions.

Suppose you need member functions that retrieve the x and y values of an *XY* object. Here is the class declaration that includes the inline member functions *Getx* and *Gety*:

```
class XY {
public:
    double x, y;
    XY();
    XY(double xarg, double yarg);
    double Getx() const { return x; }
    double Gety() const { return y; }
};
```

Getx and *Gety* can directly access all data members of their class functions, as can other member functions (including constructors and destructors).

> **Note:** *The* const *modifier used with* Getx *and* Gety *indicates that these functions do not modify class data members. This means that the compiler rejects any statements inside these functions that write to data members.*

In the application code, *assert* is a C/C++ diagnostic macro that tests the given condition:

```
XY bottomRight(1.0, 1.0);
assert(bottomRight.Getx() == 1.0);
```

The notation *bottomRight.Getx()* means "Call the *Getx* member function for the object *bottomRight*." That's all there is to it.

> **Note:** *In Microsoft Foundation Class Library version 2.0 code, you'll see the class library* ASSERT *macro used instead of the C/C++* assert *macro.*

Private vs. Public Class Members

Up to now, the *x* and *y* data members in our *XY* class have been "public" and thus accessible throughout the program, as they are in a C structure. C++ allows a class's data to be hidden. If you designate a data member as "private," it is inaccessible outside the class; only class member functions can get at it.

Now that the *XY* class has member functions that return the coordinate values, we can write a useful program that doesn't require direct access to any data members. Here is the new class declaration:

```
class XY {
private:
    double x, y;
public:
    XY();
    XY(double xarg, double yarg);
    double Getx() const;
    double Gety() const;
};
```

Class members are private by default, so technically we could eliminate the *private* keyword. The program is easier to read, however, if we leave it in.

Now the same application code still works:

```
XY bottomRight(1.0, 1.0);
assert(bottomRight.Getx() == 1.0);
```

But, outside the class, the compiler no longer accepts statements such as

```
bottomRight.x = 1.0;
```

The *x* data member is now private and accessible only through the *Getx* member function. This clearly illustrates C++'s encapsulation feature. Encapsulation is particularly useful in more complex classes, where a need exists for tight control over internal data access.

Member functions can also be private. A private member function isn't callable outside the class, but it is accessible to other member functions of the same class. As with any member function, a private member function can be named anything you want, even something like *sqrt*, because you know it won't conflict with other like-named functions, even global ones.

Helper Functions

Sometimes you need to write new class-related functions without changing the class declaration or writing a derived class. If, for example, you need a function *Show* that displays the values of the *XY* data members, you could write a global function such as this:

```
void Show(XY xy)
{
    printf("x = %f, y = %f\n", xy.Getx(), xy.Gety());
}
```

This technique works only when the existing class member functions provide all the necessary access to the data members (or if the data members are public). An alternative method is the friend function, described later, which does require a change to the *XY* class declaration.

Even though *Show* is global, it won't conflict with other *Show* functions because the compiler matches the calls according to parameter types.

C++ Encapsulation—A Recap

You've just learned about one of the big three C++ features: encapsulation. The data elements in the *XY* class example, *x* and *y*, are encapsulated with a set of useful functions that operate on them. The resulting *XY* class is a modular programming unit that, as you will see, you can use as a building block in an application.

Inheritance and Polymorphism—An Example

You're probably bored with the *XY* class by now, so let's move on to something out of this world. We'll create a two-dimensional simulation of the solar system, adaptable to both video games and StarWars defense projects. This exercise in object-oriented design lets you relate C++ objects to physical entities.

We want a computer program containing objects that represent heavenly bodies (such as planets and moons) and spaceships, that move in the sun's gravitational field. Ultimately we'd like to display the moving planets and spaceships on the screen, but we'll leave that as an exercise for the reader.

The *Orbiter* Base Class and Virtual Functions

An important step in object-oriented design, after initially identifying classes, is arranging the classes into a hierarchy with common functionality factored out to a "base class." In the solar system example, we define a base class *Orbiter* that has functionality common to both planets and spaceships. An orbiter is aware of Kepler's laws and thus knows how to move in the sun's gravitational field.

Here's the first try at an *Orbiter* class declaration:

```
class Orbiter {
private:             // data members
    double m_mass; // 'm_' is the prefix convention for data members
    XY      m_current, m_prior, m_thrust;
public:              // member functions
    Orbiter(XY current, XY prior, double mass); // constructor
    XY GetPosition() const;
    void Fly();
};
```

536

Notice your old friend the *XY* class. Objects of class *XY* represent sun-based position coordinates that are embedded within an *Orbiter* object, as is the standard type *m_mass*.

The *GetPosition* member function returns an object of class *XY* that corresponds to the orbiter's current position. (Later you'll learn how references make this process more efficient.) The *Fly* member function (not shown) applies a formula to the current and prior coordinate values, thus moving the orbiter through space. On the next iteration, the new prior coordinates are set to this iteration's current coordinates.

The *m_thrust* data member is included in the *Orbiter* class, even though planets don't have thrust, because the *Fly* member function needs thrust for its calculations, and we want a single general *Fly* function. For planets, *m_thrust* is always (0, 0).

Before we can "derive" the planet and spaceship classes from *Orbiter*, we must fix a few things. First, if the *Orbiter* data members are all private, they will be totally inaccessible to the derived classes. The C++ *protected* keyword allows a derived class to access base-class data members.

Next we need a member function that displays an orbiter. This *Display* function must be implemented differently for each derived *Orbiter* class because, for example, spaceships look different from planets. The C++ keyword *virtual* in the base-class declaration identifies *Display* as a function of this special category. Here is the new class declaration:

```
class Orbiter {
protected:
    double m_mass;
    XY      m_current, m_prior, m_thrust;
public:
    Orbiter(XY current, XY prior, double mass) {
        m_current = current;
        m_prior = prior;
        m_mass = mass;
    }
    XY GetPosition() const;
    void Fly();
    virtual void Display() const;
};
```

Now, if you have an array of orbiters, including planets, spaceships, and other space junk, you call the *Fly* function to update positions, and you call *Display* to show the objects on the screen. You call the same *Fly* function for each object, but which *Display* function you call depends on the object's class. The use of the virtual *Display* function illustrates the C++ polymorphism feature.

The following example assumes that *orbiterArray* contains pointers to a mixture of objects of classes derived from *Orbiter*:

```
extern Orbiter* orbiterArray[];
for(int i = 0; i < MAX; i++) {
    orbiterArray[i]->Fly();
    orbiterArray[i]->Display();
}
```

This example uses pointers to *Orbiter* objects rather than the objects themselves.
You'll see more object pointer usage later.

Pure Virtual Functions

In the example above, a program could construct objects of class *Orbiter*, but that
doesn't make sense because an orbiter is an abstract concept. You can prevent
construction of *Orbiter* base-class objects by declaring one or more functions as
"pure virtual" with this syntax:

```
virtual void Display() const = 0; // '= 0' means pure virtual
```

Now *Orbiter* is officially an "abstract base class," and the compiler forces all derived
classes (which are used for constructing objects) to provide implementations of the
Display member function.

Derived Classes

We'll be writing two classes derived from *Orbiter*: *Planet* and *Spaceship*. The *Planet*
derived class isn't very interesting. Perhaps all it needs is its own *Display* function
and, of course, a constructor. Here's the declaration:

```
class Planet : public Orbiter {
public:
    Planet(XY current, XY prior, double mass) :
        Orbiter(current, prior, mass) {}
    void Display() const;
};
```

The first line says that the *Planet* class is publicly derived from the *Orbiter* class.
Any derived class inherits all the data members and member functions (except
constructors and destructors) of its base class. For a publicly derived class, inherited
public base-class members are public, and inherited protected base-class members
are protected. All the derived classes in this book are publicly derived.

The colon (:) notation in the *Planet* class constructor declaration means that the
base-class (*Orbiter*) constructor is called first to make the *Orbiter* component of the
Planet object. Any *Planet*-specific code (nothing, in this case) is then executed.
Actually, all the memory for both the base-class and the derived-class data members
is allocated prior to execution of any constructor code.

Note: *If you had not included the* Orbiter *constructor as part of the* Planet *constructor, the compiler would have rejected the statement. Why? The compiler would have tried to use a default* Orbiter *constructor, but, because you had declared only an explicit three-argument* Orbiter *constructor, the compiler would have given up.*

The *Spaceship* class is more complex than the *Planet* class because it has its own data members and a new member function:

```
class Spaceship : public Orbiter {
private:
    double m_fuel;
    XY       m_orientation;
public:
    Spaceship(XY current, XY prior, XY thrust, double mass,
             double fuel, XY orientation) :
        Orbiter(current, prior, mass) {
            m_fuel = fuel;
            m_orientation = orientation;
            m_thrust = thrust; // m_thrust is an Orbiter data member
        }
    void Display() const;
    void FireThrusters();
};
```

Now you must provide constructor code to initialize the spaceship-specific data members.

Virtual Functions Called in Base Classes

You've seen the virtual *Display* function called for elements of an *Orbiter* object array. Virtual functions can be called in a base class as well as from outside the class. Suppose that the *Orbiter Fly* function needs to compute angular momentum and that this computation is specific to the derived class. If the *Orbiter* class contains the following declaration

```
protected:
    virtual XY GetAngularMomemtum() const = 0;
```

then derived classes are obliged to provide override functions.

Embedded Objects

What about the *XY* objects embedded in the *Planet* and *Spaceship* objects? When are they constructed? Here things get complicated, but you must understand the process to prepare yourself for the more complex C++ class interrelationships you'll see in class library programming. Before you go any further, however, you need to know about copy constructors and assignment operators.

Copy Constructors

Like the default constructor, the copy constructor is a class member function that the compiler often generates. Indeed, the compiler frequently generates invisible calls to the copy constructor, sometimes where you least expect them.

The purpose of the copy constructor is to make a new object of the same class from an existing object that is passed as an argument. An inline copy constructor for the *XY* class looks like this:

```
XY(const XY& xy) {
    x = xy.x;
    y = xy.y;
}
```

> **Note:** *The* const *modifier indicates that the function does not modify the values referenced by the* xy *parameter. The absence of* const *would alert you to the possibility that the function might indeed modify the values.*

If you don't define a copy constructor for a class, the compiler generates one for you that simply does a memberwise copy of all the object's data. (The compiler can safely optimize this to a bitwise copy when appropriate.) Because the *XY* class is so simple, the default copy constructor is sufficient. For more complex classes, such as those that require memory allocation or other special processing, the default copy constructor isn't sufficient. It's good practice to write copy constructors for all but the most trivial classes.

The notation *const XY&* that you saw earlier in the *Orbiter* class declaration is a C++ *reference,* and its use is required in copy constructors. The compiler passes the address of the *XY* object as an argument to the *XY* copy constructor rather than passing a copy of the object itself. It's like passing a pointer, but the notation is cleaner. You'll see references again, and you'll learn why they're more than a pointer substitute.

An obvious use for a compiler-generated copy constructor call is in code such as the following example:

```
XY alpha(1.0, 2.0);
XY beta = alpha;
XY gamma(alpha); // same result as preceding statement
```

Here two new *XY* objects, *beta* and *gamma*, are constructed from the existing object *alpha.*

Less obvious is the copy constructor call in the following sequence:

```
void func(XY xy);
XY alpha(2.0, 3.0);
func(alpha);
```

Here the *alpha* object is constructed on the stack using the explicit constructor, and then the copy constructor is called to copy the *alpha* object to the argument list for *func.*

Assignment Operators

The assignment operator is a lot like a copy constructor except that it operates on an existing object rather than creating a new object. The compiler generates default assignment operators, and it generates calls to them. The assignment operator is an example of a C++ overloaded operator, which you'll learn more about later in this appendix. You need to understand the use of of assignment operators now, however.

If you were to write your own inline assignment operator for the *XY* class, it would look like this:

```
const XY& operator=(const XY& xy) { // uses references
    x = xy.x;                        // copies the values
    y = xy.y;
    return *this;
}
```

> *Note:* *The returned* XY *reference permits assignment operators to be "chained," as in the statement*
>
> ```
> xy1 = xy2 = XY(0.0, 0.0);
> ```
>
> *The first* const *modifier indicates that the result of the assignment can be used only where a* const *parameter is specified. If* ClearContents *is declared as a non-*const XY *member function, the compiler rejects this statement:*
>
> ```
> (xy1 = xy2).ClearContents();
> ```
>
> *but the compiler accepts the statement*
>
> ```
> (xy1 = xy2).Getx();
> ```
>
> *because* Getx *is declared a* const *function.* (See also the section titled "Use of the *this* Pointer," later in this appendix.)

The following code illustrates an obvious use of the assignment operator:

```
XY alpha(1.0, 2.0);
XY beta(3.0, 4.0);
beta = alpha;
```

Here the contents of *alpha* are copied to *beta*, overwriting the latter's previous contents.

Here's another example:

```
class Container {
private:
    XY m_point;
public:
    Container(XY point) { m_point = point; }
};
```

When an object of class *Container* is constructed, the *XY* default constructor is called to make an *m_point* object before the body of the *Container* constructor is executed. The assignment statement

```
m_point = point;
```

triggers a call to the *XY* assignment operator.

The compiler-generated default assignment operator does a memberwise copy of all the object's data, and that's sufficient for the *XY* class. Plan to write your own assignment operators for more complex classes.

C++ References—Increasing Efficiency

The following application code constructs our home planet:

```
XY current(100.0, 200.0); // constructs current XY coordinate pair
XY prior(100.1, 200.1);   // constructs prior XY coordinate pair
Planet earth(current, prior, 1.0E+10); // constructs Earth object
```

If you use the following versions of the class declarations that you've already seen

```
class XY {
public:
    double x, y;
    XY() { x = 0.0; y = 0.0; }          // default constructor
    XY(double xarg, double yarg)        // explicit constructor
        { x = xarg; y = yarg; }
    XY(const XY& xy) {                  // copy constructor
        x = xy.x;
        y = xy.y;
    }
    const XY& operator=(const XY& xy) { // assignment operator
        x = xy.x;
        y = xy.y;
        return *this;
    }
};

class Orbiter {
protected:
    double m_mass;
    XY      m_current, m_prior, m_thrust;
```

```
public:
    Orbiter(XY current, XY prior, double mass) {
        m_current = current;
        m_prior = prior;
        m_mass = mass;
    }
    XY GetPosition() const;
    void Fly();
    virtual void Display() = 0;
};

class Planet : public Orbiter {
public:
    Planet(XY current, XY prior, double mass)
        : Orbiter(current, prior, mass) { }
    void Display();
};
```

the following sequence of *XY* constructor calls is necessary to make an object called *earth*:

1. The explicit *XY* constructor creates *current* and *prior* objects on the stack.

2. The *XY* copy constructor copies the *current* and *prior* objects to the *Planet* constructor's argument list.

3. The *XY* copy constructor copies the *current* and *prior* objects from the *Planet* constructor's argument list to the *Orbiter* constructor's argument list.

4. The *XY* default constructor (required) creates *m_current*, *m_prior*, and *m_thrust* data members and initializes them to (0, 0).

5. The *XY* assignment operator copies the *current* and *prior* objects from the *Orbiter* constructor's argument list to the corresponding data members.

Wow! That's a lot of construction! For efficiency's sake, we'll rearrange the *Orbiter* and *Planet* code, particularly that of the constructors:

```
class Orbiter {
protected:
    double m_mass;
    XY      m_current, m_prior, m_thrust;
public:
    Orbiter(XY& current, XY& prior, double mass)
        : m_current(current), m_prior(prior), m_mass(mass) { }
    const XY& GetPosition() const;
    void Fly();
    virtual void Display() = 0;
};

class Planet : public Orbiter {
```

(continued)

```
public:
    // copy constructor and assignment operator not shown
    Planet(XY& current, XY& prior, double mass)
        : Orbiter(current, prior, mass) { }
    void Display();
};
```

You'll notice that the *Orbiter* and *Planet* constructors use *XY* references now. Also, the *Orbiter* constructor is quite different. We've dropped the statements

```
m_current = current;
m_prior = prior;
m_mass = mass;
```

and substituted the clause

```
    : m_current(current), m_prior(prior), m_mass(mass) { }
```

> ***Note:*** *C++ allows the syntax* m_mass(mass) *even though* m_mass *is a data member of a built-in data type (double).*

Now, instead of generating two calls to the *XY* default constructor and two calls to the assignment operator, the compiler simply generates two calls to the *XY* copy constructor ahead of the mass assignment (in the *Orbiter* constructor body). This should give you some insight into the real meaning of the constructor colon syntax: The statements after the colon, including (but not limited to) calls to the base class and contained object constructors, are executed before the constructor body.

To increase efficiency, we'll rewrite the "create Earth" code as follows:

```
Planet earth(XY(100.00, 200.00), XY(100.01, 200.01), 1.0E+10);
```

Here you see another variation of constructor call syntax, one that saves a copy operation. Now the *XY* constructor calls for planet Earth are as follows:

1. Temporary current and prior objects are constructed in the constructor's argument list with the explicit *XY* constructor.

2. The *m_thrust* object is created with the default *XY* constructor, which sets both the *x* and *y* components to *0*.

3. The *m_current* and *m_prior* objects are constructed, with the *XY* copy constructor, from the objects from step 1. Those objects were passed all the way down to the *Orbiter* constructor as references, thereby avoiding extra copy operations.

> ***Note:*** *If you write a C++ function that returns a reference, you could end up making the same mistake that beginning C programmers often make. Here's the classic C example:*

```
double *GetNumber()
{
    double result = (double) (rand() / (double) RAND_MAX;
    return &result; /* don't do this */
}
```

The function returns a pointer to stack memory that will be used for something else after the function returns.
   Here's the C++ equivalent with a reference:

```
double& GetNumber()
{
    double result = (double) (rand() / (double) RAND_MAX;
    return result; // don't do this either
}
```

It's just as wrong as the C example because the compiler is still returning a pointer to a temporary variable. If GetNumber *were a member of some class, it would make sense to return a reference to a class data member because the underlying address is valid as long as the object exists.*

Construction of Embedded Objects—A Summary

You've seen the construction sequence for a *Planet* object. The *Spaceship* class is more interesting because both the *Orbiter* and *Spaceship* classes have their own embedded objects. Here's the construction sequence for a *Spaceship* object:

1. The compiler already knows how much total memory a *Spaceship* object (including all embedded objects) requires, so that amount of memory is allocated.

2. The *m_current, m_prior,* and *m_thrust* embedded objects are constructed.

3. The *Orbiter* constructor function is called.

4. The *m_orientation* embedded object is constructed.

5. The *Spaceship* constructor function is called.

The class design and initial *Spaceship* constructor call determine exactly which constructors (default, explicit, or copy) are called, but the list above is an accurate summary.

Destruction of Embedded Objects

Consider what happens when an object of class *Spaceship* is destroyed. The *Spaceship* class is interesting because it's a derived class with embedded objects defined both in the base class and in the derived class. Here's the sequence of events:

1. The compiler-generated *Spaceship* destructor is called.

2. The *m_orientation* embedded object is destroyed.

3. The compiler-generated *Orbiter* destructor is called.

4. The *m_current*, *m_prior*, and *m_thrust* embedded objects are destroyed.

5. The memory allocated for the *Spaceship* object is freed.

Notice that this destruction sequence is the exact opposite of the construction sequence.

Allocation of Objects on the Heap

So far, all objects have been allocated on the stack, and, except for the virtual *Display* function, the objects have been referenced directly. You'll recall that stack objects are destroyed when they go out of scope. As you do in C with the help of the runtime library, when you program in C++ you allocate objects on the heap so that their memory remains in use until you specifically free it. You keep track of heap objects with pointers.

The C++ *new* and *delete* Operators

The operators *new* and *delete* are roughly equivalent to the C *malloc* and *free* functions. You can use *new* to allocate raw storage this way:

```
char* pCommBuffer = new char[4096];
```

More often, however, you'll use *new* to construct objects on the heap this way:

```
Planet* pEarth = new Planet(XY(100.0, 200.0), XY(100.1, 200.1), 1.0E+10);
```

The variable *pEarth* contains the address of an object of class *Planet* and is thus a pointer. Note that the constructor syntax for heap allocation is different from the syntax for stack allocation.

To get rid of *pEarth*, simply call the *Planet* destructor this way:

```
delete pEarth;
```

All the contained objects are destroyed, as they are when a stack-allocated *Planet* object goes out of scope.

Referring to Objects Through Pointers

You can see that pointers go hand in hand with heap-allocated objects. You could use pointers to stack objects, but then you'd be vulnerable to a common programming error—the use of a pointer to an object that has gone out of scope.

Once you have a pointer to an object, you can call its class member functions using this convenient notation:

```
pEarth->Fly();
```

Pointers are necessary if you want to reference objects polymorphically. For example, you could construct an object of class *Planet*, but you would store its pointer as an *Orbiter* pointer this way:

```
Orbiter* pAny = new Planet(XY(100.0, 200.0), XY(100.1, 200.1), 1.0E+10);
```

Pointer Declarations—A C++ Coding Convention

The following pointer examples illustrate a C++ coding convention that is used both in this book and in the Microsoft Foundation Class Library documentation. In pointer declarations, the asterisk always appears next to the type name rather than next to the variable name; this is different from the usual C convention. For example:

```
char *szLastName; /* C-style pointer declaration */
char* szLastname; // C++/class library-style pointer declaration
```

This convention has two advantages:

- It differentiates between pointer declarations and dereference operators.
  The following statement, at first glance, appears to assign the first characters of the *szLastName* string the value of the *szDefault* pointer:

```
char *szLastName = szDefault;
```

With the C++ notation, however, the statement clearly declares a new pointer and assigns it the value of *szDefault*:

```
char* szLastName = szDefault;
```

- It's compatible with the C++ reference notation.
  References are always indicated by an ampersand (&) following the type name to distinguish them from the "address of" operator. References to pointers, then, are shown this way:

```
XY*& pxy;
```

The disadvantage of the convention shows up in multiple declarations in a single statement. With the familiar C notation, the following statement declares three character pointers:

```
char *a, *b, *c;
```

With the new convention, the following statement declares one pointer and two individual character variables:

```
char* a, b, c;  // perhaps not what you wanted
```

If you consistently use the new convention, you must use separate statements for each declaration, like this:

```
char* a; char* b; char* c;
```

C++ allows this conversion because the *Planet* class is derived from *Orbiter*. You could not convert an *Orbiter* pointer to a *Planet* pointer without a specific (and dangerous) cast operator.

Now you can call *Orbiter* virtual functions this way:

```
pAny->Display();
```

At runtime, the *Display* function of the *Planet* class is called because a compiler-generated structure (called a "vtable") maps *pAny* to the *Planet* class.

Virtual Destructors

Be aware that destructors are not inherited, that the compiler generates a default destructor for each class if you do not explicitly write one, and that a derived-class destructor <u>always</u> calls its base-class destructor. What if you had a pointer to an object of an unknown class derived from *Orbiter* and you wanted to destroy that object? If you called the *Orbiter* default destructor, it would destroy only those object elements specified by the *Orbiter* class itself. Suppose you constructed a *Spaceship* object on the heap, assigned its address to an *Orbiter* pointer, and then deleted the pointer like this:

```
Orbiter* pAny = new Spaceship(current, prior, thrust, mass,
                              fuel, orientation);
delete pAny;
```

The *Spaceship* object's deletion would be incomplete. In particular, the destructor for the *XY* object *m_orientation* would not be called.

How do you solve this problem? You declare a "virtual destructor" for the *Orbiter* class:

```
virtual ~Orbiter() { }
```

You don't need any code or declarations for derived-class destructors unless you're not satisfied with the compiler-generated defaults.

If you repeat the previous example now, the statement

```
delete pAny;
```

calls the proper derived-class destructor, in this case the destructor for class *Spaceship*, which first destroys all elements particular to spaceships, including *m_orientation*, and then calls the *Orbiter* destructor.

Allocation of Global Objects

You've seen stack objects, heap objects, and objects contained in other objects. Global objects are constructed before your main program is called, and they are destroyed after the main program exits. Like global variables, global objects are accessible to all functions in your program.

Suppose you have encapsulated all the Microsoft non-Windows graphics functions (declared in GRAPH.H) in a C++ class called *GraphScreen*. The program skeleton would look like this:

```
class GraphScreen {
private:
    // misc. data members
public:
    GraphScreen();  // constructor that initializes the display for
                    //  graphics
    ~GraphScreen(); // destructor that resets the screen back to
                    //  text mode
    void MoveTo(int x, int y);
    void LineTo(int x, int y);
    // more member functions
};

GraphScreen screen; // a single global screen object

void main() {
    screen.MoveTo(100, 200);
    screen.LineTo(200, 200);  // draws a line from (100, 200) to
                              //  (200, 200)
}
```

Because the *GraphScreen* constructor is called before *main*, it can do any necessary video mode initialization. Because the destructor is called automatically after *main* exits, it can reset the video.

Object Interrelationships—Pointer Data Members

You'll recall that the *Planet* class provided for several embedded *XY* objects. Because an *XY* object is only 16 bytes long, and because these objects aren't shared among *Planet* objects, it's reasonable to make them embedded objects. A benefit of this arrangement is the automatic destruction of all *XY* objects when the *Planet* object is destroyed. A restriction is that the compiler must see the *XY* class declaration before the *Planet* class declaration.

What if you want to establish a relationship between two existing objects? Suppose your universe contains moons, in addition to planets and spaceships, and you want to associate each moon to its planet. Our moon has little effect on the motion of the Earth around the sun, but the Earth profoundly affects the moon's motion. The Earth has only one moon, but other planets have several moons. It makes sense, then, for the *Moon* class to have a *Planet* pointer data member, as shown below:

```
class Planet;

class Moon : public Orbiter {
private:
    Planet* m_pPlanet; // pointer to associated Planet object
public:
    Moon(XY& current, XY& prior, double mass, Planet* pPlanet)
        : Orbiter(current, prior, mass), m_pPlanet(pPlanet) { }
    void Display() const { } // necessary because Display is pure virtual
    Planet* GetPlanet() const { return m_pPlanet; }
    void SetPlanet(const Planet* pPlanet) { m_pPlanet = pPlanet; }
};
```

The *Moon* constructor takes a *Planet* pointer as an argument. The *GetPlanet* and *SetPlanet* member functions allow access to the pointer. Notice that the compiler doesn't have to see the complete *Planet* class declaration prior to the *Moon* declaration. The forward declaration

```
class Planet;
```

is sufficient because the compiler merely has to reserve space for a pointer, and all object pointers are the same size. The size of the *Moon* object itself is of no consequence.

Now, when you construct a *Moon* object, you must include a *Planet* object pointer in the constructor call:

```
Planet* pEarth = new Planet(XY(100.00, 200.00),
                            XY(100.01, 200.01), 1.0E+10);
Moon* pMoon = new Moon(XY(100.10, 200.10),
                       XY(100.11, 200.11), 1.0E+10, pEarth);
```

Please be careful when deleting interrelated objects. If, in this example, you deleted the *earth* object, your program would crash if it continued to use the dependent *Moon* object.

> **Note:** *The addition of moons to the solar system seriously complicates the* Orbiter Fly *function. Now an* Orbiter *object's state is no longer solely dependent on current and prior sun-based coordinates. We must make* Fly *a virtual function with a special version for moons, or we must rewrite* Fly *to process gravitational interactions among all heavenly bodies.*

Use of the *this* Pointer

The C++ language provides a self-reference syntax that allows a program to obtain a pointer to the current object. This pointer, denoted by the keyword *this*, can be used as a function call parameter, and it can be returned by a member function or an overloaded operator. In the following example, a *Planet* class member function connects to a specified *Moon* object:

```
void Planet::ConnectToMoon(Moon* pMoon) {
    pMoon->SetPlanet(this); // this planet object
}
```

References to Pointers

Most C++ textbooks explain references and illustrate pointer usage. Few, however, give good examples of references to pointers, a feature used in some class library classes. You've already seen the separate *Moon* class member functions *SetPlanet* and *GetPlanet*. You can combine these two functions into one easy-to-use function like this:

```
Planet*& Moon::GetPlanet() { return m_pPlanet; }
```

The returned reference to a pointer is, in effect, a double pointer; therefore, you can place *GetPlanet* on either the right or the left of an assignment statement:

```
XY      xy11, xy12, xy21, xy22, xy31, xy32;
double mass1, mass2, mass3;

Planet* pEarth = new Planet(xy11, xy12, mass1);
Planet* pMars = new Planet(xy21, xy22, mass2);
Moon*   pMoon = new Moon(xy31, xy32, mass3, pEarth);
assert(pMoon->GetPlanet() == pEarth); // rvalue
pMoon->GetPlanet() = pMars;           // lvalue
assert(pMoon->GetPlanet() == pMars);  // rvalue
```

If you're confused, consider the more C-like equivalent notation:

```
Planet** Moon::GetPlanet() { return &m_pPlanet; }

*(pMoon-GetPlanet()) = pMars;
```

Does that make it any better?

In the class library classes, the declaration

```
Planet*& Moon::GetPlanet();
```

is often paired with the declaration

```
Planet* Moon::GetPlanet() const;
```

This second overloaded variation allows *GetPlanet* to be used (on the right side of an assignment statement) with *const* pointers to *Planet* objects. The following example shows use of the *const* variation of *GetPlanet*:

```
const Moon* cpMoon = new Moon(xy1, xy2, mass, pEarth);
Planet* pPlanet = cpMoon->GetPlanet();
```

The compiler will not accept the second statement unless the second *GetPlanet* declaration is present. For more information on *const* pointers, refer to a C++ textbook.

Friend Classes and Friend Functions

Sometimes two classes are closely related, and the C++ "friendship" feature can formalize this relationship. Class friendship is similar to human friendship. For example, you are free to declare yourself a friend to the president of the United States, but that doesn't give you the right to show up at the White House for dinner. If, on the other hand, the president declares you a friend, chances are you can drop by any time, as long as you bring a campaign contribution.

Friend Classes

Moving from Washington, D.C., out to space for a minute, it would be handy if *Moon* objects could directly access *Planet* data members, particularly the planet's mass and current position. This is possible only if the *Planet* class is declared a friend to class *Moon* like this:

```
class Planet : public Orbiter {
    friend class Moon;  // no prior declaration required
public:
    // constructors and other member functions
};
```

Now the following code is allowed in all *Moon* class member functions:

```
double Moon::MassProduct() {
    return GetPlanet()->m_mass * m_mass; // planet's mass * moon's mass
}
```

You could restrict friendship to the *MassProduct* member function like this:

```
class Planet : public Orbiter {
    friend double Moon::MassProduct();
public:
    // constructors and other member functions
};
```

Global Friend Functions

Suppose, in a particular application, that the *XY* class represents a vector and that you need the tangent of the vector's angle. You could write an ordinary *tan* member function as follows:

```
double XY::tan() {
    if (y != 0.0) {
        return x / y;
    }
    else {
        return 0.0;
    }
}
```

You could then call *tan* as you would any class member function:

```
XY      vector(1.0, 1.0);
double result = vector.tan();
```

If you want a more familiar calling syntax, however, you can declare *tan* as a global friend function to class *XY* as follows:

```
class XY {
    friend double tan(const XY& xy);
private:
    double x, y;
public:
    // constructors, etc.
};

double tan(const XY& xy) {
    if (xy.y != 0.0) {
        return xy.x / xy.y;
    }
    else {
        return 0.0;
    }
}
```

You now call the new *tan* function like this:

```
XY      vector(1.0, 1.0);
double result = tan(vector);
```

There won't be a conflict with the standard library *tan* functions because the compiler selects the proper function by looking at the parameter types.

Static Class Members

What if you needed a count of all currently active space orbiters? You could define a global variable, but that would compromise encapsulation. C++ provides static data members and static member functions that are associated with a class rather than with any specific object.

Static Data Members

Here's the *Orbiter* class declaration with a static integer data member, *nCount*:

```
class Orbiter {
protected:
    double m_mass;
    XY      m_current, m_prior, m_thrust;
public:
    static int nCount;
    Orbiter(XY& current, XY& prior, double mass);
    const XY& GetPosition() const;
    void Fly();
    virtual void Display() const = 0;
};
```

There will be only one copy of *nCount*, no matter how many orbiter objects there are. The class declaration above declares the class, but it doesn't reserve memory for *nCount*. You must write your own global definition code, to appear only once in the link, similar to the following:

```
int Orbiter::nCount = 0; // initialization is optional
```

Because the variable is declared public, you can use it in your program like this:

```
Orbiter::nCount++;
```

Of course, if you access *nCount* inside an *Orbiter* member function, such as a constructor, you can omit *Orbiter::*.

If you declare a constant static data member like this:

```
static const int nMaxCount;
```

you can still initialize it globally like this:

```
const int Orbiter::nMaxCount = 256;
```

Enumerated Types—A Static Data Member Shortcut

If your class needs a constant static integer, you can use a shortcut that avoids a separate initialization statement. You simply place an *enum* statement in your class declaration like this:

```
enum { nMaxCount = 256 };
```

Static Member Functions

If the static *Orbiter* data member *nCount* were private, you would need a static member function to access it. If you define a public function *Count* that returns a reference to an integer, you can use it on either side of an assignment statement:

```
public:
    static int& Count() { return nCount; }
```

Here's some code that uses the new *Count* function:

```
int nOldCount = Orbiter::Count()++;
int nNewCount = Orbiter::Count();
assert(nNewCount == nOldCount + 1);
```

A more interesting use of static class member functions is the construction of objects. Suppose you need to construct a new orbiting object but you don't know until runtime which derived *Orbiter* class you want. Here's a static construction function that uses a *case* statement to choose the object class:

```
static Orbiter* Orbiter::MakeNew(int selection, XY& current, XY& prior,
                                 double mass, XY& thrust, double fuel,
                                 XY& orientation, Planet* pPlanet)
{
    switch (selection) {
    case 0:
        return new Planet(current, prior, mass);
    case 1:
        return new Spaceship(current, prior, thrust, mass, fuel,
                             orientation);
    case 2:
        return new Moon(current, prior, mass, pPlanet);
    default:
        return NULL;
    }
}
```

Now you can fill up an array of *Orbiter* pointers:

```
Orbiter* pOrbiterArray[MAX]
XY       current, prior, thrust, orientation;
double   mass, fuel;
Planet*  pPlanet;

for (int i = 0; i < MAX; i++) {
    pOrbiterArray[i] = Orbiter::MakeNew(i % 3, current, prior, mass,
                                        thrust, fuel, orientation,
                                        pPlanet);
}
```

Once you stuff the *Planet, Spaceship,* and *Moon* pointers into the *Orbiter* pointer array, how do you ever sort out which is which? Of course, you don't need to know the class if you simply call *Fly* and *Display* and then destroy the objects. If you do need to know the class, C++ doesn't help much. You could, of course, add an *Orbiter* data member and associated access functions that indicate the class. As you'll see later, the class library's runtime class mechanism lets you determine an object's class at runtime.

Overloaded Operators

You might not write many overloaded operators in the early stages of class library programming, but you will certainly use the ones that the class library provides. The more you know about writing overloaded operators, though, the easier it will be to use them.

Overloaded operators are useful because they can make C++ application code easier to write and read, but some programmers get carried away. Use overloaded operators only when their meanings are intuitive and natural. After all, they are nothing but substitutes for member function calls, and sometimes member function calls make more sense.

Member Function Operators

Many overloaded operators are implemented as class member functions. In this appendix's examples, *XY* objects are mostly *xy*-coordinate pairs, and the obvious thing to do with coordinate pairs is to add and subtract them. Here's the code for the add and subtract operators:

```
XY XY::operator +(const XY& xy) const { // add
    return XY(x + xy.x, y + xy.y);
}

XY XY::operator -(const XY& xy) const { // subtract
    return XY(x - xy.x, y - xy.y);
}
```

(The declarations are shown in the section titled "Separating Class Declarations from Code," later in this chapter.)

Notice the use of references. For the *XY* class, with its small-size objects, you could get away without the references, but you've already seen how references make the code more efficient, and you've seen that they're required for assignment operators.

Now you use the + operator like this:

```
XY xy1(1.0, 2.0), xy2(3.0, 4.0);
XY xy3 = xy1 + xy2; // should be (4.0, 6.0)
```

That was easy. What about some more operators? The unary minus is another useful one. Notice that it doesn't have an argument.

```
XY XY::operator -() const { // unary minus
    return XY(-x, -y);
}
```

What about the multiply operator? It doesn't make sense to multiply one coordinate pair by another, but you can multiply a coordinate pair by a scalar. Here's the code for the * and *= operators:

556

```
XY operator *(double mult) { // scalar multiply
    return XY(x * mult, y * mult);
}

const XY& operator *=(const double mult) {
    x *= mult;
    y *= mult;
    return *this;
}
```

And here's the application code:

```
XY xy1(1.0, 2.0);
XY xy2 = xy1 * 3.0; // should be (3.0, 6.0)
xy2 *= 2.0;         // should be (6.0, 12.0)
```

And now for something a little more difficult. In the *Spaceship* class, you might have noticed an *XY* data member called *m_orientation*. This isn't really a coordinate pair but a representation of an angle. (There's a possible case for a derived *XY* class here.) You could, of course, represent an angle by a scalar radian or a degree value, but subsequent math is easier if you store the angle as a cosine/sine pair. We'll now expropriate the C++ right-shift and left-shift operators and make them rotation operators for *XY* objects:

```
XY operator >>(const XY& xy) const { // rotate cos/sin pair plus
    return XY(x * xy.x - y * xy.y, y * xy.x + x * xy.y);
}

XY operator <<(const XY& xy) const { // rotate cos/sin pair minus
    return XY(x * xy.x + y * xy.y, y * xy.x - x * xy.y);
}
```

The formulas are standard trigonometric identities that require no use of the *sin* or *cos* function.

Here are the new rotation operators in use:

```
XY angle1(0.707, 0.707);     // 45 degrees
XY rotation(0.0, 1.0);       // 90 degrees
XY angle2 = angle1 >> rotation; // should be (-0.707, .070), 135 degrees
```

In a video game application I designed, the player controlled the spaceship's master rotation angle from the keyboard. The spaceship outline points were stored in an array of polar coordinates consisting of an *XY* angle and a scalar distance from the center of the ship. For each point, the *XY* value was rotated by the current angle and then multiplied by the scalar value, yielding a new *xy*-coordinate pair for the display.

Conversion Operators

Both C and C++ allow extensive automatic conversion among built-in types. Consider these statements:

557

```
int    radians = 2;
double result = atan(radians);
```

The function *atan* expects a *double* argument, so the compiler converts the integer *radians* to a *double* before passing it to the function.

What about conversions for your own classes? You must write them yourself, of course. Suppose you have a *String* class that contains a character array *m_pch*. The following operator function returns a constant pointer to an object's internal array:

```
String::operator const char*() const
{
    return (const char*) m_pch;
}
```

You can now use a *String* argument anywhere the compiler expects a *const char** argument—for example:

```
String s1("test");     // construct S1 from character array
String s2;
char   c1[20];
int    n = strlen(s1); // OK
strcpy(s2, s1);        // won't compile because first parameter is not const
strcpy(c1, s1);        // OK
```

We purposely didn't declare a (non-*const*) *char** operator because getting data into a *String* object isn't as easy as extracting it.

The class library provides a useful string class called *CString* that has this same overloaded *const char** conversion operator. You'll use this operator quite frequently when you write class library programs.

Helper Operators

The operators you've seen so far are class member functions. Suppose you need a new operator but you don't want to derive a new class. If your class has public data members and member functions sufficient to access the required data, you can write stand-alone helper operators.

Because we "forgot" to write a divide member function operator for the *XY* class, we'll write one now, but the code is a little different from the overloaded multiply operator you've seen already:

```
XY operator / (const XY& xy, const double div) // scalar divide helper
{
    return XY(xy.x / div, yx.y / div);
}
```

Notice that the data members x and y must be public, or if they are not, you must write *XY* member functions that access them.

Helper operators can enhance the arithmetic capabilities of a class. The XY multiply member function operator that you've already seen is called by this expression:

```
XY xy2 = xy1 * 3.0;
```

But it won't work for this expression:

```
XY xy2 = 3.0 * xy1;
```

For the second case, you need a multiply helper operator like this one:

```
XY operator *(const double mult, const XY& xy)  // scalar multiply
{
    return XY(xy.x * mult, xy.y * mult);
}
```

Separating Class Declarations from Code

In the previous examples, class declarations have been mixed with code. The modularity of C++ depends, however, on the separation of the class implementation code from the class declaration. Class "users" need only the declarations; class "authors" write the code and might choose to deliver it in compiled, linkable form only.

Often, as in the case of the class library, all the class declarations are combined into one or several H files, and the code, broken into small, independently linkable modules, is stored in a LIB file. Application programmers include the H file in their C++ source code, and then they link with the corresponding library.

Below is a view of what the solar system header might look like (minus the moon):

```
// SOLAR.H class declaration file

class XY { // all member functions are inline
private:
    double x, y;
public:
    XY();
    XY(double xarg, double yarg);
    XY(const XY& xy);
    const XY& operator =(const XY& xy);
    XY operator +(const XY& xy) const;
    XY operator -(const XY& xy) const;
    XY operator *(const XY& xy) const;
    XY operator /(const XY& xy) const;
    XY operator -() const;
};

class Orbiter {
```

(continued)

```
protected:
    double m_mass;
    XY      m_current, m_prior, m_thrust;
public:
    static int nCount;
    Orbiter(XY& current, XY& prior, double mass); // inline
    const XY& GetPosition() const;
    void Fly();
    virtual void Display() const = 0;
};

class Planet : public Orbiter {
public:
    // copy constructor and assignment operator not shown
    Planet(XY& current, XY& prior, double mass) :
        Orbiter(current, prior, mass) { }
    void Display();
};

class Spaceship : public Orbiter {
private:
    double m_fuel;
    XY      m_orientation;
public:
    // copy constructor and assignment operator not shown
    Spaceship(XY& current, XY& prior, XY& thrust,
            double mass, double fuel, XY& orientation); // inline
    void Display();
    void FireThrusters();
};
// **** all XY class inline functions here ****
```

Some programmers choose to nest *#include* files, but this requires that code not be inadvertently included more than once, and it complicates make file dependencies. Class library programs, by convention, don't generally nest their *#include* files. Your class library CPP files will always show you exactly which header files are included.

Notice that all the inline functions are grouped at the bottom of the header. This isn't necessary for the solar system example, but it makes the declaration more readable, and it allows the inline functions to be moved to a separate *#include* file. Some applications require the separation because inline code might depend on prior declarations.

The non-inline functions—*Orbiter Fly, Orbiter GetPosition, Planet Display, Spaceship Display*, and *Spaceship FireThrusters*—are kept in CPP files. You choose how to split them up. If you put them all in one file, they are all linked even if only one is used (unless you set the compiler's function-level linking option). Often you'll separate member functions by class. A class code file is a good place for static data member definitions.

Appendix B

Message Map Functions in the Microsoft Foundation Class Library

HANDLERS FOR WM_COMMAND MESSAGES

Map Entry	Function Prototype
ON_COMMAND(<id>, <memberFxn>)	afx_msg void memberFxn( );

HANDLERS FOR CHILD WINDOW NOTIFICATION MESSAGES

Map Entry	Function Prototype
Generic Control Notification Codes	
ON_CONTROL(<wNotifyCode>, <id>, <memberFxn>)	afx_msg void memberFxn( );
User Button Notification Codes	
ON_BN_CLICKED(<id>, <memberFxn>)	afx_msg void memberFxn( );
ON_BN_DISABLE(<id>, <memberFxn>)	afx_msg void memberFxn( );
ON_BN_DOUBLECLICKED(<id>, <memberFxn>)	afx_msg void memberFxn( );
ON_BN_HILITE(<id>, <memberFxn>)	afx_msg void memberFxn( );
ON_BN_PAINT(<id>, <memberFxn>)	afx_msg void memberFxn( );
ON_BN_UNHILITE(<id>, <memberFxn>)	afx_msg void memberFxn( );
Combo Box Notification Codes	
ON_CBN_CLOSEUP(<id>, <memberFxn>)	afx_msg void memberFxn( );[†]
ON_CBN_DBLCLK(<id>, <memberFxn>)	afx_msg void memberFxn( );

[†] For Windows 3.1 only.

(continued)

HANDLERS FOR CHILD WINDOW NOTIFICATION MESSAGES *continued*

Map Entry	Function Prototype
Combo Box Notification Codes *continued*	
ON_CBN_DROPDOWN(<id>, <memberFxn>)	afx_msg void memberFxn( );
ON_CBN_EDITCHANGE(<id>, <memberFxn>)	afx_msg void memberFxn( );
ON_CBN_EDITUPDATE(<id>, <memberFxn>)	afx_msg void memberFxn( );
ON_CBN_ERRSPACE(<id>, <memberFxn>)	afx_msg void memberFxn( );
ON_CBN_KILLFOCUS(<id>, <memberFxn>)	afx_msg void memberFxn( );
ON_CBN_SELCHANGE(<id>, <memberFxn>)	afx_msg void memberFxn( );
ON_CBN_SELENDCANCEL(<id>, <memberFxn>)	afx_msg void memberFxn( );[†]
ON_CBN_SELENDOK(<id>, <memberFxn>)	afx_msg void memberFxn( );[†]
ON_CBN_SETFOCUS(<id>, <memberFxn>)	afx_msg void memberFxn( );
Edit Control Notification Codes	
ON_EN_CHANGE(<id>, <memberFxn>)	afx_msg void memberFxn( );
ON_EN_ERRSPACE(<id>, <memberFxn>)	afx_msg void memberFxn( );
ON_EN_HSCROLL(<id>, <memberFxn>)	afx_msg void memberFxn( );
ON_EN_KILLFOCUS(<id>, <memberFxn>)	afx_msg void memberFxn( );
ON_EN_MAXTEXT(<id>, <memberFxn>)	afx_msg void memberFxn( );
ON_EN_SETFOCUS(<id>, <memberFxn>)	afx_msg void memberFxn( );
ON_EN_UPDATE(<id>, <memberFxn>)	afx_msg void memberFxn( );
ON_EN_VSCROLL(<id>, <memberFxn>)	afx_msg void memberFxn( );
List Box Notification Codes	
ON_LBN_DBLCLK(<id>, <memberFxn>)	afx_msg void memberFxn( );
ON_LBN_ERRSPACE(<id>, <memberFxn>)	afx_msg void memberFxn( );
ON_LBN_KILLFOCUS(<id>, <memberFxn>)	afx_msg void memberFxn( );
ON_LBN_SELCHANGE(<id>, <memberFxn>)	afx_msg void memberFxn( );
ON_LBN_SETFOCUS(<id>, <memberFxn>)	afx_msg void memberFxn( );

[†] For Windows 3.1 only.

HANDLERS FOR WINDOWS NOTIFICATION MESSAGES

Map Entry	Function Prototype
ON_WM_ACTIVATE( )	afx_msg void OnActivate(UINT, CWnd*, BOOL);
ON_WM_ACTIVATEAPP( )	afx_msg void OnActivateApp(BOOL, HANDLE);
ON_WM_ASKCBFORMATNAME( )	afx_msg void OnAskCbFormatName(UINT, LPSTR);
ON_WM_CANCELMODE( )	afx_msg void OnCancelMode( );
ON_WM_CHANGECBCHAIN( )	afx_msg void OnChangeCbChain(HWND, HWND);
ON_WM_CHAR( )	afx_msg void OnChar(UINT, UINT, UINT);

(continued)

HANDLERS FOR WINDOWS NOTIFICATION MESSAGES *continued*

Map Entry	Function Prototype
ON_WM_CHARTOITEM( )	afx_msg int OnCharToItem(UINT, CWnd*, UINT);
ON_WM_CHILDACTIVATE( )	afx_msg void OnChildActivate( );
ON_WM_CLOSE( )	afx_msg void OnClose( );
ON_WM_COMPACTING( )	afx_msg void OnCompacting(UINT);
ON_WM_COMPAREITEM( )	afx_msg int OnCompareItem(LPCOMPAREITEMSTRUCT);
ON_WM_CREATE( )	afx_msg int OnCreate(LPCREATESTRUCT);
ON_WM_CTLCOLOR( )	afx_msg HBRUSH OnCtlColor(CDC*, CWnd*, UINT);
ON_WM_DEADCHAR( )	afx_msg void OnDeadChar(UINT, UINT, UINT);
ON_WM_DELETEITEM( )	afx_msg void OnDeleteItem(LPDELETEITEMSTRUCT);
ON_WM_DESTROY( )	afx_msg void OnDestroy( );
ON_WM_DESTROYCLIPBOARD( )	afx_msg void OnDestroyClipboard( );
ON_WM_DEVMODECHANGE( )	afx_msg void OnDevModeChange(LPSTR);
ON_WM_DRAWCLIPBOARD( )	afx_msg void OnDrawClipboard( );
ON_WM_DRAWITEM( )	afx_msg void OnDrawItem(LPDRAWITEMSTRUCT);
ON_WM_DROPFILES()	afx_msg void OnDropFiles(HANDLE);†
ON_WM_ENABLE( )	afx_msg void OnEnable(BOOL);
ON_WM_ENDSESSION( )	afx_msg void OnEndSession(BOOL);
ON_WM_ENTERIDLE( )	afx_msg void OnEnterIdle(UINT, CWnd*);
ON_WM_ERASEBKGND( )	afx_msg BOOL OnEraseBkgnd(CDC*);
ON_WM_FONTCHANGE( )	afx_msg void OnFontChange( );
ON_WM_GETDLGCODE( )	afx_msg UINT OnGetDlgCode( );
ON_WM_GETMINMAXINFO( )	afx_msg void OnGetMinMaxInfo(LPPOINT);
ON_WM_HSCROLL( )	afx_msg void OnHScroll(UINT, UINT, CWnd*);
ON_WM_HSCROLLCLIPBOARD( )	afx_msg void OnHScrollClipboard(CWnd*, UINT, UINT);
ON_WM_ICONERASEBKGND( )	afx_msg void OnIconEraseBkgnd(CDC*);
ON_WM_INITMENU( )	afx_msg void OnInitMenu(CMenu*);
ON_WM_INITMENUPOPUP( )	afx_msg void OnInitMenuPopup(CMenu*, UINT, BOOL);
ON_WM_KEYDOWN( )	afx_msg void OnKeyDown(UINT, UINT, UINT);
ON_WM_KEYUP( )	afx_msg void OnKeyUp(UINT, UINT, UINT);
ON_WM_KILLFOCUS( )	afx_msg void OnKillFocus(CWnd*);
ON_WM_LBUTTONDBLCLK( )	afx_msg void OnLButtonDblClk(UINT, CPoint);
ON_WM_LBUTTONDOWN( )	afx_msg void OnLButtonDown(UINT, CPoint);
ON_WM_LBUTTONUP( )	afx_msg void OnLButtonUp(UINT, CPoint);
ON_WM_MBUTTONDBLCLK( )	afx_msg void OnMButtonDblClk(UINT, CPoint);
ON_WM_MBUTTONDOWN( )	afx_msg void OnMButtonDown(UINT, CPoint);
ON_WM_MBUTTONUP( )	afx_msg void OnMButtonUp(UINT, CPoint);
ON_WM_MDIACTIVATE( )	afx_msg void OnMDIActivate(BOOL, CWnd*, CWnd*);

†For Windows 3.1 only.

(continued)

HANDLERS FOR WINDOWS NOTIFICATION MESSAGES *continued*

Map Entry	Function Prototype
ON_WM_MEASUREITEM( )	afx_msg void OnMeasureItem(LPMEASUREITEMSTRUCT);
ON_WM_MENUCHAR( )	afx_msg LONG OnMenuChar(UINT, UINT, CMenu*);
ON_WM_MENUSELECT( )	afx_msg void OnMenuSelect(UINT, UINT, HMENU);
ON_WM_MOUSEACTIVATE( )	afx_msg int OnMouseActivate(CWnd*, UINT, UINT);
ON_WM_MOUSEMOVE( )	afx_msg void OnMouseMove(UINT, CPoint);
ON_WM_MOVE( )	afx_msg void OnMove(int, int);
ON_WM_NCACTIVATE( )	afx_msg BOOL OnNcActivate(BOOL);
ON_WM_NCCALCSIZE( )	afx_msg void OnNcCalcSize(LPRECT);
ON_WM_NCCREATE( )	afx_msg BOOL OnNcCreate(LPCREATESTRUCT);
ON_WM_NCDESTROY( )	afx_msg void OnNcDestroy( );
ON_WM_NCHITTEST( )	afx_msg UINT OnNcHitTest(CPoint);
ON_WM_NCLBUTTONDBLCLK( )	afx_msg void OnNcLButtonDblClk(UINT, CPoint);
ON_WM_NCLBUTTONDOWN( )	afx_msg void OnNcLButtonDown(UINT, CPoint);
ON_WM_NCLBUTTONUP( )	afx_msg void OnNcLButtonUp(UINT, CPoint);
ON_WM_NCMBUTTONDBLCLK( )	afx_msg void OnNcMButtonDblClk(UINT, CPoint);
ON_WM_NCMBUTTONDOWN( )	afx_msg void OnNcMButtonDown(UINT, CPoint);
ON_WM_NCMBUTTONUP( )	afx_msg void OnNcMButtonUp(UINT, CPoint);
ON_WM_NCMOUSEMOVE( )	afx_msg void OnNcMouseMove(UINT, CPoint);
ON_WM_NCPAINT( )	afx_msg void OnNcPaint();
ON_WM_NCRBUTTONDBLCLK( )	afx_msg void OnNcRButtonDblClk(UINT, CPoint);
ON_WM_NCRBUTTONDOWN( )	afx_msg void OnNcRButtonDown(UINT, CPoint);
ON_WM_NCRBUTTONUP( )	afx_msg void OnNcRButtonUp(UINT, CPoint);
ON_WM_PAINT( )	afx_msg void OnPaint( );
ON_WM_PAINTCLIPBOARD( )	afx_msg void OnPaintClipboard(CWnd*, HANDLE);
ON_WM_PALETTECHANGED( )	afx_msg void OnPaletteChanged(CWnd*);
ON_WM_PALETTEISCHANGING( )	afx_msg void OnPaletteIsChanging(CWnd*);
ON_WM_PARENTNOTIFY( )	afx_msg void OnParentNotify(UINT, LONG);
ON_WM_QUERYDRAGICON( )	afx_msg HCURSOR OnQueryDragIcon( );
ON_WM_QUERYENDSESSION( )	afx_msg BOOL OnQueryEndSession( );
ON_WM_QUERYNEWPALETTE( )	afx_msg BOOL OnQueryNewPalette( );
ON_WM_QUERYOPEN( )	afx_msg BOOL OnQueryOpen( );
ON_WM_RBUTTONDBLCLK( )	afx_msg void OnRButtonDblClk(UINT, CPoint);
ON_WM_RBUTTONDOWN( )	afx_msg void OnRButtonDown(UINT, CPoint);
ON_WM_RBUTTONUP( )	afx_msg void OnRButtonUp(UINT, CPoint);
ON_WM_RENDERALLFORMATS( )	afx_msg void OnRenderAllFormats( );
ON_WM_RENDERFORMAT( )	afx_msg void OnRenderFormat(UINT);
ON_WM_SETCURSOR( )	afx_msg BOOL OnSetCursor(CWnd*, UINT, UINT);
ON_WM_SETFOCUS( )	afx_msg void OnSetFocus(CWnd*);

(continued)

HANDLERS FOR WINDOWS NOTIFICATION MESSAGES *continued*

Map Entry	Function Prototype
ON_WM_SHOWWINDOW( )	afx_msg void OnShowWindow(BOOL, UINT);
ON_WM_SIZE( )	afx_msg void OnSize(UINT, int, int);
ON_WM_SIZECLIPBOARD( )	afx_msg void OnSizeClipboard(CWnd*, HANDLE);
ON_WM_SPOOLERSTATUS( )	afx_msg void OnSpoolerStatus(UINT, UINT);
ON_WM_SYSCHAR( )	afx_msg void OnSysChar(UINT, UINT, UINT);
ON_WM_SYSCOLORCHANGE( )	afx_msg void OnSysColorChange( );
ON_WM_SYSCOMMAND( )	afx_msg void OnSysCommand(UINT, LONG);
ON_WM_SYSDEADCHAR( )	afx_msg void OnSysDeadChar(UINT, UINT, UINT);
ON_WM_SYSKEYDOWN( )	afx_msg void OnSysKeyDown(UINT, UINT, UINT);
ON_WM_SYSKEYUP( )	afx_msg void OnSysKeyUp(UINT, UINT, UINT);
ON_WM_TIMECHANGE( )	afx_msg void OnTimeChange( );
ON_WM_TIMER( )	afx_msg void OnTimer(UINT);
ON_WM_VKEYTOITEM( )	afx_msg int OnVKeyToItem(UINT, CWnd*, UINT);
ON_WM_VSCROLL( )	afx_msg void OnVScroll(UINT, UINT, CWnd*);
ON_WM_VSCROLLCLIPBOARD( )	afx_msg void OnVScrollClipboard(CWnd*, UINT, UINT);
ON_WM_WINDOWPOSCHANGED( )	afx_msg void OnWindowPosChanged(WINDOWPOS FAR*);[†]
ON_WM_WINDOWPOSCHANGING( )	afx_msg void OnWindowPosChanging(WINDOWPOS FAR*);[†]
ON_WM_WININICHANGE( )	afx_msg void OnWinIniChange(LPSTR);

[†] For Windows 3.1 only.

USER-DEFINED MESSAGE CODES

Map Entry	Function Prototype
ON_MESSAGE(<message>, <memberFxn>)	afx_msg LONG memberFxn(UINT, LONG);
ON_REGISTERED_MESSAGE(<nMessageVariable>, <memberFxn>)	afx_msg LONG memberFxn(UINT, LONG);

Appendix C

Microsoft Windows Functions Used in This Book

The Visual C++ printed documentation (and online help) covers all the Microsoft Foundation Class Library classes and functions. The class library wraps a significant number of Windows Software Development Kit (SDK) functions, but at times you must call Windows SDK functions directly. The Windows SDK functions are documented in the Visual C++ online help and in printed manuals that are available separately. This appendix summarizes those Windows SDK functions that are used in this book's examples. This is by no means a complete list of unwrapped Windows functions. Refer to the Windows 3.1 SDK online help for details.

Windows SDK Function	Purpose
CloseClipboard	Closes the Windows clipboard. The *CWnd OpenClipboard* member function opens the clipboard.
CreateDIBitmap	Creates a GDI bitmap from a device-independent bitmap and optionally sets bits in the bitmap.
CreateSolidBrush	Creates a brush that has a specified solid color. Returns an HBRUSH handle.
DeleteObject	Deletes a GDI object from Windows memory. The *CGdiObject DeleteObject* function requires an object pointer, but you'll need this *DeleteObject* function if you have an HGDIOBJ handle instead.
DispatchMessage	Dispatches a Windows message that was retrieved by the *GetMessage* and *PeekMessage* functions.
EmptyClipboard	Empties the Windows clipboard.

(continued)

continued

Windows SDK Function	Purpose
EnumClipboardFormats	Retrieves the currently available clipboard formats. Should be called in a loop.
GetClipboardData	Retrieves a handle to the clipboard data as specified by the format parameter.
GetDIBits	Converts a device-independent bitmap to a GDI bitmap.
GetKeyState	Gets the state of a specified virtual key.
GetSysColor	Gets the color of a specified display element such as the window background or the title bar.
GetSystemMetrics	Retrieves the widths and heights of various Windows display elements such as windows, borders, and fonts. Also indicates whether the current version of Windows is a debugging version and whether a mouse is present.
IsClipboardFormatAvailable	Tests whether the clipboard contains a specified format.
LoadCursor	Loads a specified mouse cursor from a resource or loads a standard Windows mouse cursor. Used with *SetCursor*.
PeekMessage	Retrieves a message from the application's message queue and, except for WM_PAINT messages, removes it from the queue. The function does not wait for a message to become available but returns 0 if the queue is empty. *PeekMessage* is often used with *DispatchMessage* and *TranslateMessage* to yield control during a long compute process.
RegCloseKey	Releases a key in the Windows registration database. When all keys are released, the database is updated.
RegCreateKey	Creates or opens a Windows registration database key.
RegSetValue	Sets the value of an open key to a text string.
SetClipboardData	Transfers data to the clipboard. The clipboard must have been previously opened.
SetCursor	Changes the Windows mouse cursor as specified by the cursor resource created by *LoadCursor*.
SetDIBitsToDevice	Displays a device-independent bitmap without scaling.
StretchDIBits	Displays a device-independent bitmap with scaling.
TranslateMessage	Translates a virtual key code to a character. Used with *PeekMessage* and *DispatchMessage*.

Appendix D

Visual C++, Windows NT Edition

Along with the final release of Windows NT, Microsoft Corporation introduced a Windows NT version of Visual C++, which constitutes a complete set of tools for 32-bit software development. Visual C++, Windows NT Edition, contains its own version of the Microsoft Foundation Class Library, which is largely compatible with the class library included with Visual C++ for Microsoft Windows 3.1. This appendix highlights the similarities and differences between the two class libraries, and it presents some strategies for developing multiplatform C++ applications.

32-Bit Programming

Programs written for Windows NT use a flat 32-bit memory model. All pointers and integers are 32 bits wide. The modifiers *near* and *far* have no meaning, and there are no segments. This makes 32-bit programming easier than 16-bit programming. Here's a list of common type sizes (in bits):

Type	Size in Windows 3.1	Size in 32-Bit Windows
BYTE	8	8
double	64	64
DWORD	32	32
float	32	32
int	16	32
long	32	32
long double	80	64
LONG (lParam)	32	32
short	16	16
SHORT	16	16
UINT (wParam)	16	32
WORD	16	16

The application programming interface used in Windows NT is commonly referred to as the Win32 API. With Win32, all handles (including *HWND*s and *HDC*s) for Windows NT are 32 bits wide, and GDI functions take 32-bit parameters. Some device coordinates are still returned as 16-bit values, however. For example, the WM_LBUTTONDOWN message returns the *x* and *y* cursor coordinates packed in the *lParam* parameter, which is still 32 bits wide.

Many Win32 functions look the same as their Windows 3.1 counterparts. Take the *SetPixel* function, for example:

```
DWORD SetPixel(HDC hDC, int X, int Y, COLORREF crColor);
```

The declaration is the same for both Win32 and Windows 3.1. The widths of the *hDC*, *X*, and *Y* parameters are different, however.

In the area of file input/output, the Win32 API is very different. For example, the old *_lread* and *_lwrite* functions have been replaced by the new functions *ReadFile* and *WriteFile*. There are hundreds of brand-new functions too, supporting features such as threads, multibyte characters, and Bézier curves.

Porting 16-Bit Microsoft Foundation Class Library Applications to Windows NT

Because the Microsoft Foundation Class Library was designed for portability, it's easy to port most applications from Windows 3.1 to Windows NT. Simply recompile and relink. If your application uses the *CFile* class, for example, the class library connects to the new Win32 file functions. The compiler will catch most incompatibilities, which usually involve direct calls to Windows-based functions rather than calls to class library functions. Here's an example of one change that was made in the *CDib* class from the Chapter 23 example EX23A:

```
#ifdef _WIN32
    HBITMAP hBitmap = ::CreateDIBitmap(pDC->GetSafeHdc(), m_lpBMIH,
            CBM_INIT, (CONST BYTE*) (m_lpBuf + m_lpBMFH->bfOffBits),
            m_lpBMI, DIB_RGB_COLORS);
#else
    HBITMAP hBitmap = ::CreateDIBitmap(pDC->GetSafeHdc(), m_lpBMIH,
            CBM_INIT, (LPSTR) (m_lpBuf + m_lpBMFH->bfOffBits),
            m_lpBMI, DIB_RGB_COLORS);
#endif
```

Notice that the fourth *CreateDIBitmap* parameter has changed between Windows NT and Windows 3.1. The preprocessor statements ensure that the code compiles in both environments.

The above change was about the only change I made when I ported the examples in this book. Recompilation under Windows NT did expose a few bugs, however, but those were easy to fix. I couldn't port the examples that use Visual Basic controls or extension DLLs (EX08A, EX11C, EX26A, and EX26B). Why? Because with the Win32 API, the *wParam* message parameter is 32 bits wide, and this means that some messages pack the *lParam* and *wParam* parameters differently. (Also, the 32-bit ODBC library was not available, but the EX24A program compiled with the existing header files.) Because the class library decodes message parameters for you, you're mostly insulated from these changes. If your program handles the WM_COMMAND message directly, for example, you must allow for the packing differences. The files WINDOWSX.H and WINDOWSX.H16 contain "message-cracker macros" that help you write portable code.

> ***Hint:*** *Applications generated by AppWizard under Windows 3.1 often include the file VER.H. The equivalent Windows NT file is WINVER.H. If you copy WINVER.H to VER.H in the \MSVCNT\INCLUDE subdirectory, your ported applications will compile.*

Archive Portability Between Windows 3.1 and Win32

As summarized in Chapter 16, the class library *CArchive* class supports only built-in types that are the same size in both Windows environments. Thus *int* is not supported, but *LONG* is. Most archive files written under Windows 3.1 can be read under Windows NT. Notice that the sizes for *CRect*, *CPoint*, and *CSize* objects are different, so archive files that contain these items are not portable.

Some Class Library Features for Windows 3.1 Not Supported Under Win32

A few class library and tool features for Windows 3.1 are not supported under Win32. These include:

- Visual Basic controls—The Visual Basic control API is inherently a 16-bit API that uses pointers and data structures that are not compatible with Win32. The controls themselves are 16-bit DLLs and thus won't run with 32-bit applications. For the time being, Visual Basic controls are not supported by the class library, AppWizard, or App Studio.

- Extension DLLs—MFC200.DLL has no equivalent in Windows NT, so it isn't possible to write extension DLLs. This problem will be addressed in a future version of the class library.

- Microsoft Windows for Pen Computing classes—You wouldn't expect to use Windows NT for pen computing applications, so the pen classes *CHEdit* and *CBEdit* aren't supported.

- App Studio EXE, RES, and DLL editing capability—In the Windows NT environment, App Studio can edit only RC files.

Enhanced Microsoft Foundation Class Library Features for Win32

On the positive side, the Microsoft Foundation Class Library for Win32 has a few new features:

- *CTime* class improvements—The *CTime* class has been extended to support the system and file times offered by Windows NT.

- Collection memory restrictions removed—Under Windows 3.1, array collection (*CObArray*, *CStringArray*, and so on) size was limited to 64 KB for small and medium memory models, and the number of array elements was limited to 32-KB elements for all models; under Win32, array size is limited only by available memory.

Win32 Features Not Supported by the Microsoft Foundation Class Library

The first version of the class library for Windows NT was designed as a bridge from Windows 3.1 to Windows NT. No new Win32 features (such as multiple threads, communications, and improved graphics) are supported. You can, of course, use the new Win32 features in a program that includes the class library, but you must call the appropriate Win32 functions directly. Because the class library is not thread-safe, you can use the classes only in the main thread of your application.

Windows NT Debugging Considerations

Visual C++, Windows NT Edition, contains a Windows-hosted debugger similar to the one included in Visual C++ for Windows 3.1, as well as a symbolic debugger, NTSD. Both these debuggers can display the output of *TRACE* and *afxDump* statements if you've built your application with the Debug build option. You don't have to set the compiler and linker debugging information options to get trace output from the debugger.

Windows NT has no equivalent of DBWIN, so you must use one of the debuggers to get trace output. Also, the Windows 3.1 Debug Kernel has no equivalent, which means you can't determine which GDI objects are not deleted. Windows NT does release all GDI memory when an application terminates, however. Once you've written a 32-bit class library application, it might be a good idea to port it back to Windows 3.1 to test it with the Debug Kernel.

The Win32s Subsystem

When you buy Visual C++ for Windows NT, you get the Win32s Software Development Kit (SDK), which enables 32-bit applications to run under Windows 3.1. The Win32s SDK is a collection of DLLs plus a device driver that you can ship with your application. You can view Win32s as a mapping layer between the Win32 API and the underlying Windows 3.1 system. Many Windows NT functions are not supported under Win32s—in particular, multiple threads and the advanced Windows NT file system calls. These functions are "stubbed out" to return error codes.

Be aware that Windows NT can run many existing Windows 3.1 binary programs (not Visual C++ for Windows 3.1, however) using its Windows on Win32 (WOW) component. So why bother with Win32s, which requires use of a mapping layer and the distribution of extra DLLs? The answer is that 32-bit programs run faster than 16-bit programs, particularly if they're compute-intensive. Some CAD programs run twice as fast in 32-bit mode, despite the inefficiencies of the mapping layer.

As you would expect, Win32 programs written using the class library run with Win32s. Visual C++, Windows NT Edition, does not run with Win32s, however.

Multiplatform Development Strategy

If you stick to the programming elements contained in the class library, you'll have no trouble supporting applications for Windows 3.1, Windows NT, Win32s, and future versions of Windows, all with one set of source code. Real applications, however, often need features outside the class library, and that's where you run into incompatibilities. Take serial communication, for instance. Suppose you want your application to download information from an online service. Windows 3.1 provides a set of communications functions (supported by the standard communications driver) that depend on the WM_COMMNOTIFY message. Windows NT doesn't use WM_COMMNOTIFY but rather provides a new set of functions, including one called *WaitCommEvent*, that beg for multithread programming. Win32s supports neither communications interface but requires you to implement something called "universal thunks."

How do you deal with platform incompatibilities? First you analyze the market to determine which platforms you need to support. If you determine that you must support several platforms, you begin the design process by isolating the functionality that is common to all platforms. Most of this common functionality can be handled by the class library.

Next you design the platform-dependent components to be as modular as possible. C++ classes can help you with this process. In the hypothetical serial communication example discussed above, Windows 3.1 might dictate that you write a *CComm* class that is derived from *CWnd* (to map the WM_COMMNOTIFY message). For Windows NT, your *CComm* class wouldn't use any class library elements; rather, it would encapsulate a separate communication thread that would handle the download task. The *CComm* class member functions would be identical in both cases, however.

Index

N

O

David Kruglinski

David Kruglinski considers himself a programmer who writes rather than a writer who programs. He wrote his first program at Purdue University in 1966 ("probably a game of some sort"), and he got started with microcomputers in 1976 after a friend fished an 8080 board out of a garbage bin.

After some accidental periods of gainful employment, David wrote four books on subjects ranging from microcomputer database management systems to PC communications. He also started a successful software tools company.

When David isn't frantically trying to keep up with all the latest software developments, he is a consultant and also teaches Microsoft Visual C++ training classes. His Internet address is v-davidk@microsoft.com.

The manuscript for this book was prepared and submitted to Microsoft Press in electronic form. Text files were prepared using Microsoft Word for Windows 2.0.

Principal editorial compositor: Barb Runyan
Principal proofreader/copy editor: Shawn Peck
Principal typographer: Ruth Pettis
Interior text designer: Kim Eggleston
Principal illustrator: Lisa Sandburg
Cover designer: Rebecca Geisler
Cover illustrator: Studio MD
Cover color separator: Color Service
Indexer: Shane-Armstrong Information Systems

Text composition by Microsoft Press in Garamond with display type in Futura Heavy, using the Magna composition system. Composed pages were delivered to the printer as electronic prepress files.

Printed on recycled paper stock.